I0890065

CARIBBEAN POETICS:

TOWARDS AN AESTHETIC OF

WEST INDIAN LITERATURE

ALSO BY SILVIO TORRES-SAILLANT

El Tigueraje Intelectual (Intellectual Thugs). 2nd edition (1st ed. 2002). (Santo Domingo: Editora Mediabyte, 2011).

An Intellectual History of the Caribbean. New Directions on the Americas Series. (New York: Palgrave, 2006).

Diasporic Disquisitions: Dominicanists, Transnationalism, and the Community. Working Papers Series (New York: CUNY Dominican Studies Institute, 2000).

El retorno de las yolas (Santo Domingo: Ediciones Librería La Trinitaria and Editora Manatí, 1999).

Introduction to Dominican Blackness. Working Papers Series (New York: CUNY Dominican Studies Institute, City College of New York, 1999).

The Dominican-Americans [with Ramona Hernández] (Westport, CT: Greenwood Press, 1998).

Caribbean Poetics (New York: Cambridge University Press, 1997)

As Editor:

The Challenges of Higher Education in the Hispanic Caribbean. Ed. Maria J. Canino and Silvio Torres-Saillant (Princeton: Markus Wiener Publishers, 2004).

Desde la orilla: Hacia una nacionalidad sin desalojos. Ed. Silvio Torres-Saillant, Ramona Hernandez and Blas Jiménez (Santo Domingo: Ediciones Librería La Trinitaria and Editora Manati, 2004).

Recovering the US Hispanic Literary Heritage. Vol. IV. Ed. Silvio Torres-Saillant and Jose Aranda (Houston: Arte Público, 2002).

SILVIO TORRES-SAILLANT

CARIBBEAN POETICS: TOWARDS AN AESTHETIC OF WEST INDIAN LITERATURE

PEEPAL TREE

First published in the USA in 1997
by Cambridge University Press
This new and revised edition published in
Great Britain in 2013
Peepal Tree Press Ltd
17 King's Avenue
Leeds LS6 1QS
England

ISBN13: 9781845231071

Supported using public funding by
ARTS COUNCIL
ENGLAND

CONTENTS

To
Aida Torres, my mother,
temple of endurance and the will to survive

To
Oneira, my daughter, and Maxim, my son,
vessels of hope, of future dissidence, of present love

In Memoriam

To
Silvio V. Saillant (1910-1987),
progenitor

To
Tulio A. Saillant (1957-1994),
younger brother, too soon gone

PREFACE TO THE SECOND EDITION

Appearing over fifteen years after the original version, out-of-print for some time now, this second edition of *Caribbean Poetics* comes out thanks to the enthusiasm of the managing editor of Peepal Tree Press, Jeremy Poynting, a literary scholar and passionate reader of Caribbean texts who one day shot an electronic message from Leeds saying that he wanted to reissue the book in order to be able to read it. His show of appreciation challenged me to envision a new life for a book that I thought had already done the job that it came into the world to do, and so I accepted to work on some revisions to justify to myself the audacity of bringing the book once more into existence. Jeremy's critical acumen proved invaluable as I took on the task, and the cordial prodding of marketing director Hannah Bannister gave me the necessary push to try to meet the final deadline. As the book goes out again, yearning to engage another generation of readers in conversation about the place of Caribbean literature in the world, I am grateful to Jeremy and Hannah for urging me to entertain the notion that perhaps the book has not yet outlived its usefulness.

Caribbean Poetics, emerging out of the scholarly project that served as my doctoral dissertation, set out to outline a map of Caribbean writing that would account for its ontological autonomy by placing its production within a given historical experience, a culture area, and a system of significance. I argued that the aesthetic behaviour of the Antillean corpus corresponded to the nature of life in the social setting that produced the works involved and that, as a result, one could identify family ties among the texts of authors writing in different languages across the various societies of the region irrespective of whether or not they may have read one another. To illustrate the cross-lingual and pan-regional valence of the poetics that regulated the corpus under study, I chose to draw the core of my illustrations from the works of one towering figure from each of the three language areas of which at the time I could boast the greatest command: Anglophone Kamau Brathwaite, Francophone René Depestre, and Spanish-speaking Pedro Mir. Mindful of the meagre presence of Caribbean letters in the U.S. academy from which I spoke as a student of comparative literature, I wanted to attempt comprehensive studies of the writers' oeuvres that, in addition to helping me illustrate my conceptual claims, could also serve as general introductions that would disseminate knowledge about the literary accomplishments of these authors. I settled for three male writers because the magnitude of their achievements impressed me very deeply, but in doing so I remained cautious of enthroning masculinist paradigms by deploying a gender-inflected critique whenever the texts under perusal veered toward patriarchal assumptions. In the chapters that provide background and develop the argument for a pan-Caribbean literature with internal coherence, the study also acknowledges the importance of women as key partners with their male counterparts in the production of the overall corpus.

In 1991, when I completed the first draft of the study that would subsequently appear in print as *Caribbean Poetics*, I found the literary production of the Antillean world severely underrepresented, when not simply absent, from general accounts of world literature, and I hoped my work could help address the marginality of artistic writing from the region. I located myself in contradistinction to previous scholars who had spoken about the Caribbean strictly from the knowledge of one language area even when they made cultural claims about the entire Antillean world. I also made the move to interpret the literary production from the region using the tools of explication that the texts themselves made available to the reader, confident that Caribbean literature had produced its own meta-discourse insofar as a poetics is necessarily keyed to a particular literary system. At the time that sort of declaration of critical independence seemed a daring move, one that from the mid-1990s onward became increasingly more daring given the rise of postmodernism and postcolonialism as wholesale paradigms that pervaded the study of the human sciences in the Western academy, resulting in a hermeneutic homogenization that caused young scholars to invoke the same cohort of European and American thinkers and to deploy a shared critical lexicon that made all sound alike even while seeking to speak about separate and distinct societies, human experiences, and cultural productions.

The present edition of *Caribbean Poetics* retains the political and theoretical thrust of the original edition. I have overcome the temptation to alter the emphases, units of analysis, and arrangements of details in the study in order to reflect my own intellectual evolution more than fifteen years later. I thought that the alteration would have resulted in another book. I am persuaded that for it to be authentically regarded as a second edition, the book has to continue to reflect the vision and the zeal of the younger scholar who conceived and executed it. For the same reason, I have made no substantial effort to update the bibliography. Any engagement with the current scholarship, as it has evolved since my study first appeared in print, would lead me into directions that would run the risk of undermining the intention of the original project. Instead, I have tried to account for important trends in the behaviour of Caribbean texts over the last two decades by adding an "Afterword" that undertakes to map those features that I did not tackle in the original edition, though they have become characteristic of the corpus under study.

I have also revised the language that I originally used to name the region by distancing myself throughout from the nomenclature that reduces the region to "islands" of an "archipelago." In 1997 I had not yet set foot on the continental Caribbean. I had not thought carefully about the extent to which the rapport of the African heritage with Amerindian life in Suriname has much to do with the continental expanse of the South American landmass that helped to preserve indigenous populations from extinction during the most violent stages of the colonial transaction. I had not seen the cultural exchange between blacks and Amerindians on the Caribbean coast of Colombia or on the Atlantic littoral of other Central and South American societies. Nor had I stopped to consider the pre-Columbian linguistic and cultural sources that inform much of the mythopoesis in the works of Wilson Harris as linked inextricably to Guyana's continentality. Therefore, it did not occur to me, then, that when one thinks of the Caribbean as "islands," one leaves languages, populations, and large chunks of the human experience of the region out of the story. In this edition I have deleted the words "islands" and "archipelago" from every sentence or clause where I had used them to signify the region as a whole.

Since 1997 I have also become more cognizant of the place of the diaspora as a factor in the Caribbean experience. I have since argued for the need to recognize that apart from the "tellurian geography" of the Antillean region, consisting of islands and continental landmasses, the "cultural or existential geography of the diaspora" plays a role in the configuration of the Caribbean people. But I have also become troubled with the tendency in the recent scholarship to treat the cultural geography of the diaspora and the tellurian geography of the physical region as one seamless space. In 2003 I participated in an ambitious conference at the University of Antwerp on "the Caribbean writer as warrior of the imaginary" in which I witnessed three days of learned exchange that mixed presentations about diaspora authors Caryl Phillips, Jamaica Kincaid, Julia Alvarez, and Edwidge Danticat, along with Wilson Harris, Aimé Césaire, Derek Walcott, and other foundational figures of twentieth-century Caribbean literature in the region, as if they all formed part of the same literary cosmos. I look at a monograph published in 2010 that deals with "contemporary Caribbean literature", and it dismays me to find that the writers included, though connected ancestrally to Haiti, the Dominican Republic, and the Anglophone Caribbean, hail predominantly from the United States, but the scholar has not judged it necessary to explain the absence in her study of writers from the actual Caribbean region. One is almost provoked to the lugubrious view that the scholar expects the adjective "contemporary" to signal the diasporic location of the writers included, thus relegating their counterparts from the region to a generational praeteriteness. The present edition of *Caribbean Poetics* remains as committed as the original version to affirming the distinctness of the literary production of the region, the tellurian geography, even if, as the new "Afterword" concedes, one must necessarily come to terms with the way the region negotiates culturally with its diaspora. The tellurian geography and the diaspora constitute separate geographies of knowledge even while they may at key points intersect. The Barbadian Brathwaite noted this difficult interconnection more than four decades ago when reviewing the novel *The Chosen Place, The Timeless People* (1969) by the Barbadian-descended American fiction writer Paule Marshall. He presciently observed that had Marshall "been a West Indian, she probably would not have written this book. Had she not been an Afro-American of West Indian parentage, she probably would not have written it either."

I would like to reiterate my gratitude to all the individuals – friends, family members, allies, or colleagues – and institutions whose proximity and support contributed to the coming into being of the first edition of *Caribbean Poetics*. When the book came out, it received the warmest salutation from inestimable colleagues Harold A. Waters and Colbert I. Nepaulsingh who reviewed it respectively for *World Literature Today* and *The Latino/a Review of Books* in terms so generous that I can only do my best to make myself deserving in the future through continuous pursuit of scholarly excellence. I acknowledge the openhandedness of Cambridge University Press in facilitating the process of liberating the copyright to the first edition of the book, thus enabling me to find a new home for it at Peepal Tree Press. I also acknowledge Klaus Stierstorfer, editor of *Reading the Caribbean: Approaches to Anglophone Caribbean Literature and Culture* (Heidelberg: Universitätsverlag Winter, 2007) for permission to reproduce the opening chapter (pp. 13-50), which I have used here with some modifications as the "Afterword".

Finally, I am grateful for the collaboration with Professor Nancy Kang of the University of Baltimore whose insightful energy in a book on Dominican-born American poet Rhina P. Espaillat that we are writing together has functioned as a salutary contagion, spreading onto my other work to my great benefit.

Syracuse, New York, January 2013

INTRODUCTION

> My gardens require a gardener's piety
> (Requieren mis jardines piedad de jardinero)
> Alfonsina Storni (1987: 65)

The present study seeks to contribute to the field of comparative poetics by mapping literary activity in the Caribbean area as one differentiated corpus with an internal logic of its own. I shall examine recurring thematic motifs and stylistic choices exhibited by literary works written in different nations and linguistic blocs of the Antillean world to articulate a comprehensive view of the cultural and historical imperatives that govern artistic writing in the region. I intend to demonstrate that Caribbean literary texts, at least since the early twentieth-century, are linked amongst themselves by an aesthetic kinship born of the more or less common experience lived by Caribbean societies. Determined by historical circumstances indigenous to this peculiar part of the world, their aesthetic kinship also distinguishes Caribbean texts from those texts of other literary systems, chiefly the Western literary tradition. I contend that Caribbean literature, though written primarily in European languages, constitutes an autonomous system. The claim may seem daring to those who view language as the infallible carrier of culture and tradition. But we shall see that Caribbean literature has become a mature artistic corpus precisely in the extent to which writers in the region have succeeded in emancipating their works from the hegemonic culture of the West by forging an alternative literary discourse which achieves ontological autonomy even while it may regularly converse with inherited Western models.

I concur with T.S. Eliot's view "of the literature of the world, of the literature of Europe, of the literature of a single country, not as a collection of the writings of individuals, but as 'organic wholes', as systems in relation to which, and only in relation to which, individual works of literary art, and the works of individual literary artists, have their significance" (Eliot 1950: 12-13). Eliot's notion of "organic wholes", understood in a socio-cultural sense, may provide a useful stepping stone for tackling the system of significance to which Caribbean texts correspond. A good many critics have convincingly argued that the nature and texture of artistic products generally obey the command of the socio-cultural context that informs their conception. In this respect the Argentinian theorist Alejandro Losada sought to demonstrate how this dynamic takes place in the specific setting of Latin America and how it gives Latin American literature a separate socio-aesthetic identity from that of European letters (Losada 1983: 8-9). The present work purports to show that the study of Caribbean literature demands a still further specification since its organic whole differs not only in relation to Europe but also to mainland Latin America.

Definitions

Delineating the socio-aesthetic boundaries of Caribbean literary art will lead to the poetics revealed by the works written in the region, that is, to the articulation of the "internal theory of literature" evinced in the texts from the area. In my use of the concept of Caribbean poetics, I have taken into consideration the notion that poetics "proposes to elaborate categories that allow us to grasp simultaneously the unity and variety of literary work" (Ducrot and Todorov 1979: 78-79). Similarly, in delimiting the regional contours of my analysis, I have favoured the view that describes the Caribbean geographically as "the islands from the Bahamas to Trinidad, and the continental enclaves of Belize, Guyana, Suriname, and French Guiana", a description which includes "all those territories with a closely related history, whose patterns of evolution have followed a remarkably parallel trajectory in the modern period" (Knight and Palmer 1989: 3). Using the term "Caribbean" interchangeably with "Antilles" and "West Indies", in addition to "Antillean world", I maintain the hypothesis that any intelligent assessment of the area's literary production requires an understanding of the poetics that governs it. Indeed, one may affirm that approaching Caribbean literature without such an understanding would be equivalent to approaching the works of Dante, Racine, and Milton without a previous knowledge of the system of values inherent in the cultural and intellectual assumptions found in the texts of the Western literary tradition.

Comparative Poetics

In a larger sense, the study of Caribbean poetics offers an opportunity for reflection on the nature of literary theory, that is, "the study of the principles of literature, its categories, criteria, and the like" (Wellek and Warren 1977: 39). Today we generally admit, except for those who hold on to ethnocentric views of the world, that the phenomenon called literature varies in accordance with the particularities of the socio-cultural setting in which it occurs. Thus, it follows that literature's "principles" and the literary theory studying "its principles" must vary accordingly.

It does not take much daring to assert that beauty, in addition to its various other properties, is culture-specific. Aesthetic objects that are the result of human craftsmanship, when viewed as containers of the beautiful, are cultural products.

The universality we ascribe to aesthetic objects often hinges on phenomena unrelated to artistic achievement. Heretical as it may sound, one can assert that T. S. Eliot and Paul Valéry became more "universal" than any poet active at the same time as they in Sri Lanka or Burundi for other than just artistic reasons. All questions of aesthetic merit and poetic genius aside, one cannot deny that the former – not the latter – have enjoyed the benefit of coming from countries with political control over large territorial domains and over various peoples and cultures of the earth. This asymmetry applies, strangely enough, even to societies with older histories of intellectual accomplishment, such as that of India. The works of Eliot and Valéry have, as a result, travelled and gained recognition in a larger portion of the "universe". The texts from nations with a history of imperial expansion automatically possess a greater chance of being "universalized" than those from nations with less influence over the affairs of the world (Torres-Saillant 1989: 84-85).

An awareness of the sociology behind the transmission of literary texts would convince us that, contrary to what a critic speaking from the vantage point of the hegemonic culture might assume, a work of literary art does not carry with it its own user's manual. A reader coming from a culture without contact with the West or with the ideals of Christianity may actually fail to understand the quest for divine grace undertaken by the speaker in Dante's *Divina commedia*. Unable to identify the context of its significance, that hypothetical reader may very well miss the value of the Italian poem. The plausibility of our imaginary reader's aesthetic response becomes real if we recall our own experience in the classroom. Teachers of literature often find that the greater bulk of their effort on the job consists in helping students "see" the greatness of literary texts and recognize their relevancy for our daily lives. Even when Western readers confront Western texts such as Goethe's *Faust* or *The Cantos* of Pound, which few would grudge a space in the canon, communication rarely takes place without the readers' previous training. Readers, that is, need first to avail themselves of the contextual body of knowledge and the aesthetic attitude necessary for appreciation of the texts in question. The same dynamic, only more acutely so, applies to one's interaction with a culturally unfamiliar literary tradition.

In conceiving of literary theory as the study of the principles of literature we must grant that the principles may differ from literature to literature. In this respect, the Cuban critic Roberto Fernández Retamar warns us against what he calls "pseudo-universality", affirming that "literary theory means the theory of a literature" (1984: 40). The truth of Fernández Retamar's affirmation becomes most evident when we attempt to carry literary theory across historical and socio-cultural boundaries. We have good examples of the virtual untransferability of literary theory from as early as the Middle Ages, when Aristotle's *Poetics*, to which Western discourse on literature normally traces its origin, fell into the hands of thinkers from non-Hellenic cultures. One thinks principally of Arab commentators such as Ibn Sina (Avicenna, 980-1037) and Ibn Rushd (Averroes, 1126-1198). The latter authored commentaries on practically all of the Stagirite's works and devoted much of his career to making the Greek thinker's teachings better understood in the Arabic-speaking world. Both Arab thinkers provide excellent illustration of the problem at hand here. For, while they admired Aristotle's conceptualizing about literature, they had no access to the literary texts that served as the philosopher's empirical data. As a result, they had to rely solely on texts drawn from their own literary tradition to illustrate the ideas of the Greek thinker. This led to their unintentional highlighting of clear disparities between the poetic systems of the Greeks and the Arabs.

In commenting on the *Poetics* of Aristotle, Avicenna often lapsed into a comparative tenor. To discuss genres, for instance, he states: "they [the Greeks] had conventions peculiar to them, just as the Arabs have conventions" (1974: 70). The comparison, as this quotation suggests, in most cases invites a contrast. In order to explain a point proposed by the Greek theorist, Avicenna frequently finds himself indicating that the Arabic texts follow a different model. Concerning the subject of *mimesis*, for example, he says that the Greeks, contrary to the Arabs, did not pursue the imitation of persons (Avicenna 1974: 74). Likewise, regarding the functions of literature, he again stresses the distinction: "The Arabs used to compose poetry for two purposes: (i) to affect the soul by presenting a given matter that moves in the direction of an action or an emotion; and (ii) for pleasure alone [whereas] the Greeks intended, by means of speech, to induce or prevent action" (1974: 74).

Perhaps even more aware of the implications of the difference between Greek and Arab literature, Averroes wrote his *Middle Commentary* to explain "those universal rules" in Aristotle's text which permit a general application, taking into consideration that, as he remarks at the outset, "many of its contents are either rules particularly characteristic of their poems and their customs therein or are not found in the speech of the Arabs" (1986: 59). In keeping with the qualification of his opening, much of his discourse throughout the *Commentary* involves contrastive analysis and negative example. We learn, for instance, that Arabic poetry differs from Greek metrically. He says that "mixed meters" were found in the texts of the Greeks, but "they are not found among us," which means by implication that certain kinds of poems in which Aristotle had established a link between meter and sense are either hard to find "in the poems of the Arabs or they are not found in them – since their meters are limited" (Averroes 1986: 65, 113).

The differences revealed by Averroes actually range from the most technical, such as the distinct nature of each of the two languages involved, to the absence among the Arabs of certain genres which Aristotle had deemed important (such as the "four kinds of eulogies" and the representation of past "time periods"), to the lack or predominance of certain stylistic elements (pp. 123, 112). Among these stylistic elements is descriptive vividness, which Aristotle had associated with narrative excellence but which among the Arabs, we are told, existed "only with respect to indecent actions or when the intention is simply congruity in the imitation" (pp. 135, 109). Like Avicenna's, Averroes's *Commentary* gives the impression that the rules of the Greek theorist could not easily fit the non-Hellenic literary products of the Arabs. A reading of the two commentaries, contrary to the intentions of their authors, shows the socio-cultural limitations of literary theory.

We must admit, however, that the socio-cultural disparity between Aristotle's Greece and Arabic antiquity is far easier to recognize than that between the Caribbean and the West. The Caribbean and the West have historically been closely interconnected. The West literally created the Caribbean. Europe, responding to the dynamics of colonial expansion, gave birth to the Caribbean beginning in the late fifteenth-century. But to recognize this interconnection between the two worlds is equivalent to saying that they are not nor can be one and the same. Indeed, they are worlds apart. Both regions, for instance, dealt with slavery and sugar plantations, but certainly not in the same way. People in the hegemonic nations of the West knew about those institutions only through the benefits their countries reaped from them. In the Caribbean those institutions had a direct impact on the daily lives of all inhabitants, blacks, aborigines and whites, and later Indians and Chinese. The West has a history of conquests and a formidable legacy of systematic and successful attempts to "civilize" (i.e., westernize) other peoples of the earth. The inhabitants of the Caribbean, on the other hand, have a history of subjection by outside colonial powers and, with the exception of revolutionary Cuba, their voices have had little resonance in the international arena. We have here two quite different histories indeed.

We have here, consequently, two different peoples since it is in history – not outside of it – that human beings shape the contours of their identity. The imperial nations of the West have produced a hegemonic culture. The dependent and object nations of the Caribbean have produced a marginal culture. The two worlds resemble each other, then, only because at a certain stage of the colonial transaction, the former imposed its ways upon the latter. But we need not overemphasize the resemblance. Underneath the layer of resemblance lies a very deep and awesome contingency. In fact, later in the colonial transaction, when the people of the Caribbean felt the need to articulate their selfhood, they sought to define it by exploiting their substratum of difference. They undertook to establish the validity of their human identity by exalting precisely the features which distinguish them from the West. In this sense, the contemporary Caribbean differs from the West in a way that parallels the socio-cultural disparity between the Arabs and the Greeks.

Theoretical Assumptions

Literary theory, in order to account successfully for the "principles" of Caribbean literature, must be tailored to fit the socio-cultural context that gives rise to its system of significance. Apart from drawing on the value system inherent in Caribbean culture, which will become clear in the chapter that follows, Caribbean literary texts reflect the dynamics of a peculiar history. Historical imperatives play a very serious role in regulating, as it were, the aesthetic endeavours of Caribbean writers. In this respect, Caribbean writers follow the same path normally followed by most non-hegemonic artists. Houston Baker, Jr., who has sought to delineate an African-American poetics in the United States, has made a good case for the decisive intervention of historical imperatives in shaping the development of black American literature. Sustaining that "modernism" could simply not mean for Afro-Americans what it meant for their Anglo-American, British, and Irish counterparts, Baker has argued that while the latter at the turn of the century were "bashing the bourgeoisie", Afro-American "spokespersons were attempting to create one. And far from repudiating the emergent age [they] welcomed a new century as a time when shackles of slavery and impoverishment would fall decisively away" (Baker 1988: 4). A point that follows from Baker's observation is that the literature of Afro-Americans, the literature of a marginal people that for centuries lived in the throes of a most devastating oppression in the United States, cannot be chronicled by means of the same historiographical taxonomy devised for chronicling the literature of the dominant culture.

The monolithic assumptions often contained in periodological demarcations need to be qualified when applied to the achievements of non-dominant social sectors. In this regard, the late historian Joan Kelly argued persuasively that European women during the Renaissance did not have a Renaissance as men did. She claims that, on the contrary, women were adversely affected by many of the social, cultural, and political developments which gave that historical moment its peculiar accent. Kelly's research on the relationship between men and women during that period revealed to her that noblewomen as well as women of the patrician bourgeoisie actually lost some of the prerogatives they had enjoyed during the preceding Medieval era. She put it succinctly thus: "Renaissance ideas on love and manners, more classical than medieval, and almost exclusively a male product, expressed this new subordination of women to the interests of husbands and male-dominated kin groups and served to justify the removal of women from an 'unladylike' position of power and erotic independence" (Kelly 1984: 47).

If gender difference among Europeans themselves can enable a scholar to challenge the unqualified applicability of standard historiographical periods, stretching those classifications across cultures should raise even graver questions. We can, indeed, argue that Caribbean literature has a discrete historical development and that it is unlikely to be effectively chronicled by means of the divisions used to chart the development of other literatures. Born out of peculiar socio-historical conjunctures, Caribbean literature has consequently followed a peculiar progression. Far from paralleling the sequence of *-isms* identified by historians of the Western tradition, its development corresponds, it seems, to a pace dictated by an insistent nation-building effort which characterized the countries of the region for most of the twentieth century. One need only think of Surrealism and its effect on individuals like Aimé Césaire. Contemporaneous with the first great period in the rise of Caribbean letters, Surrealism, was a movement that entailed a distrustful attitude towards language and generally fostered the production of non-linear, fragmented, and telegraphic texts. It was vibrantly in vogue in Paris when the Martinican lived there. Interestingly, though living amidst French Surrealist writers who had proclaimed the negation of language, Césaire wrote his *Cahier d'un retour an pays natal* (1939), a long poem which constitutes an affirmation of language and a celebration of the word. The *Cahier* might seem inconsistent, even paradoxical or anachronistic, in a Surrealist context. But the explanation is simple: Césaire, a Caribbean writer, did not distrust or feel any compulsion to negate the value of language. Caribbean literature simply did not share the intellectual mood attributable to European writers. At the end of the nineteenth century, language in Europe "was felt to be in the throes of a deep crisis," says Terry Eagleton (1983: 139-40). As the critic points out, it became questionable whether one could "write, in an industrial society where discourse had become degraded to a mere instrument of science, commerce, advertising and bureaucracy" (Eagleton 1983: 139-40). On the contrary, at that time Caribbean intellectuals and artists were enthusiastically asserting their right to brandish language as a means to delineate for themselves the contours of their human identity. The Caribbean quest for decolonization in the twentieth century can be construed, as the Barbadian George Lamming has proposed, as a people's continuous and necessary battle for language.

Most of the major Western critical theories in the twentieth century have in their different ways consisted of responses to the same dilemma: the obsessive preoccupation with language brought about by the "deep crisis" spoken of by Eagleton. In that respect one wonders whether contemporary literary theory in the West which results from such compulsions may accord with the literary phenomenon as it has occurred in the Caribbean during the period of this study. We would contend that the intellectual discourse of such prominent contemporary figures as Jacques Derrida, Jacques Lacan, Julia Kristeva, Paul de Man, and Jürgen Habermas has little to say regarding the literary art of the Caribbean. These are Western intellectuals whose theories have derived from their reflection on Western problems. We would seriously hesitate to assign to them universal applicability. By the same token, a discourse that sets out to explain Caribbean literature must bear in mind the socio-cultural specificity and the historical imperatives governing its development.

In keeping with the foregoing assumptions, this study will rely mostly on theoretical texts written by Caribbean writers or Caribbeanists from outside the area. At this stage of its maturity, Caribbean literature has already produced a large corpus of critical discourse by writers from the region. We do not claim that only Caribbean people can adequately talk about this literature, for many a critic from the outside has contributed important studies of the area's literary art. But one ought to keep in mind that the theoretical stance or cultural worldview with which a commentator approaches the region's corpus matters a great deal. Someone, for instance, who understands the colonial transaction as a service to humanity, or one who merely subscribes to a radically Eurocentric view of the world, may lack the intellectual and even moral tools to recognize Caribbean people as worthy producers of aesthetic objects. Understanding another's culture normally presupposes an acceptance of it as an object that is worthy of one's cognition.

Also, a crucial assumption affecting our choice of secondary sources has been the conviction that in the study of literature, as in anything else, what or how we see depends largely on our position in relation to the objects of our perception. The perceivers' interests, biases, values, socio-cultural conditioning, and the like, largely determine their reaction to and aesthetic judgment on a work of literary art. The Kenyan novelist Ngugi Wa Thiong'o would go so far as to place all critical judgment in the context of an ideological struggle. Succinctly, he has said: "A critic who in real life is suspicious of people fighting for liberation will suspect characters who, though only in a novel, are fighting for liberation. A critic who in real life is impatient with all the talk about classes, class struggle, resistance to imperialism, racism, and struggle against racism, of reactionary versus revolutionary violence, will be equally impatient when he or she finds the same themes dominant in a work of art. In criticism as in creative writing, there is an ideological struggle" (Ngugi 1986: 104).

Ngugi's contention of the inseparability of critical judgment and ideological biases should surprise no one. Elaine Showalter's well-known charge that Irving Howe's reading of Hardy's *The Mayor of Casterbridge* tends to construe the text as a "male document" sheds light on precisely the same phenomenon (cited in Culler 1982: 43-44). But we could actually go back to the very beginning, to the *Poetics* of Aristotle, to illustrate how inextricable from ideology aesthetic judgment is. In chapter XV, the section devoted to propriety in the depiction of character, the philosopher states that "goodness" may be present in every class of people, even in a woman or in a slave, "though the woman may be said to be an inferior being, and the slave quite worthless" (Aristotle 1951: 53). But regarding the positive qualities attributable to a female character, he sees a serious limitation: "There is a type of manly valour; but valour in a woman, or unscrupulous cleverness, is inappropriate" (p. 53). One wonders how Aristotle's observation can be expected to match with the female characters one finds in the tragedies which he purports to be describing.

Certainly Aeschylus's Clytemnestra steals our intellectual attention more readily than does Agamemnon. Sophocles' Antigone strikes our moral fibre far more profoundly than does Creon. Nor does Euripides' Hippolytus ever match the psychological depth exhibited by Phaedra. Contrary to Aristotle's reading, most of the complex, courageous, multidimensional, intelligent, profound, and truly memorable characters in the Athenian tragic theatre are indeed women. Whence, then, the apparent misreading? Certainly Aristotle knew the tragic plays better than any other ancient theorist whose work has come down to us. The answer seems to reside in the sociocultural forces that shaped his perception. We have here none other than a politically prominent male reader in a male-centred society. He lived in the Athens where it seemed conceivable for upper-class men to claim, as we gather from Plato's *Symposium*, that true love could not exist in a heterosexual couple because love can only exist between equals. Aristotle knew and seems to have been perfectly comfortable with the unequal place accorded to women in Athenian society. He probably had more at stake in the androcentric social structure than the three tragedians, hence his inability to grasp qualities which Aeschylus, Sophocles, and Euripides made it their business to highlight in their women characters. Thus, when describing the role of female characters in drama, his sociopolitical views concerning the relations between men and women in society hopelessly override his knowledge of the plays. Aristotle's inaccurate rendition of women characters in tragedy serves to illustrate the validity of Ngugi's claim that how we see things outside of a book shapes the way we see them inside of it. It should also serve to support our tenet here that the question of one's position matters greatly when one approaches Caribbean literature.

Conversation with the Canon

While pursuing objectivity in the articulation of the poetics informing Caribbean literature, the present study seeks also to converse with comparative literature as a discipline and with the values that inform canon formation. We seek here to procure a significant space for Caribbean texts in comparative literature fora, which in US universities have traditionally catered to predominantly Eurocentric views of literary art and its development. Hopefully studies such as this may contribute to the recognition of Caribbean literature as an artistic corpus with its own socio-aesthetic identity that can teach us about literary creation as well as any other tradition. Our broader aim, then, is to show that the lesser status commonly assigned to it in Western accounts of "world literature" does not correspond necessarily to matters of artistic merit. It corresponds, rather, to the dynamics inherent in the relationship between hegemonic and non-hegemonic cultures.

Our inquiry may also contribute to "literary theory" in a much larger sense, by suggesting that Western literature, too, may conceivably belong to the realm of ethnic studies. In our society nothing Western ever gets classified as ethnic. But that merely has to do with the centrality the West has occupied in the affairs of the world since the advent of Western colonialism. The centre of power tends to define its ways as human characteristics and those of the other, the peoples who exist at the margins, as ethnic characteristics. In the same way, the artistic texts coming from the dominant sector are baptized "literature" while those coming from the margins are dubbed "ethnic literatures". We start from the conviction that the present state of affairs reflects in the field of literature a legacy of human inequality forged and legitimized by power. We believe this defective arrangement must and will inevitably come to an end, because the global society cannot thrive in a world where we still see one another through the distorted images that an imperial prism generates.

Structural Arrangement

The present work attempts to lay out the intellectual groundwork for articulating a regional theory of literature and to illustrate it empirically by means of a close reading of major figures from three of the Caribbean's linguistic blocs. The study is divided into six chapters. Chapter 1 makes a case for asserting the unity of the Caribbean on socio-historical and cultural grounds. It surveys models of construing the Caribbean since the start of the colonial transaction, from the views that privilege foreign policy interests, to those that stress fragmentation, to those that advocate the search for a native vision of wholeness. Chapter 2 provides the theoretical framework for the definition of Caribbean poetics. Since the notion of Caribbean poetics springs from our view of literature as the artistic manifestation of a given culture, the chapter draws from the findings of literary scholars, artists, and social scientists to define the Caribbean as a culture area and adduces available data to show that the region constitutes a coherent cultural whole. It traces the nineteenth-century ideological precedents to the thesis of regional unity in the ideas of Ramón Emeterio Betances, Eugenio María de Hostos, Gregorio Luperón, and José Martí, thinkers for whom the very survival of the peoples of the Caribbean depended on a recognition of their necessary coming together as one large republic.

Previous attempts to identify a principle of coherence in the literary expression of the region are also noted here to stress the need for the present study. Unlike the authors of earlier works, I base my claim for the literary homogeneity of the Caribbean on a translingual and comparative reading of the texts from the area, which in the past has been done only on a very minor scale. A pioneering work by Coulthard (1962) and a later one by Bajeux (1983) stand out among the very few that have ventured panoptic and translingual accounts of Caribbean literature. However, their stressing blackness as a principle of coherence among writers from throughout the region falls short of accounting for the work of literary artists of different nationalities, diverse colours and races, writing in various languages. Most studies of this kind have tended to circumscribe their focus to one linguistic bloc. Also, by pursuing the articulation of the area's literary unity in a shared historical and cultural experience rather than exclusively in race, our study circumvents the inexorable *cul-de-sac* of ethnic essentialism which mars the validity of many studies of the area's artistic endeavours.

The chapter closes with an illustrative discussion of the pervasive presence of history, religion, and language in the literature of the contemporary Caribbean. I draw examples from the works of many prominent literary artists from the region to show their persistent treatment of those topics. The purpose is to show how in their reworking of the original Western heritage contained in the three concepts, which they recast into a regionally relevant mold, Caribbean writers exhibit the worldview that shapes their autochthonous poetics. History, religion, and language are not the only categories one can draw from in an illustration of Caribbean poetics, but I have found them particularly useful.

Chapter 3 covers the works of the Barbadian poet, literary critic, and historian Kamau Brathwaite, from his first publications in the 1950s to

Barabajan Poems (1994). He has written further significant books since the time covered by the first edition of this work, but none I think materially alters the case I wanted to make. His experiments with typography – his Sycorax Video style – and his recasting of some of his earlier work, such as *Ancestors* (2001) – can be seen as a visual analogy for his emphasis on sound described below. I look at Brathwaite's preoccupation with language. The Barbadian poet, an avowed speaker of the language of Caliban, exemplifies the Caribbean writer's often desperate search for a decolonized language, one that would authentically express the Caribbean worldview. Celebrating what he perceives as Caribbean people's recasting of the old master's *logos* into a regionally relevant speech of liberation, each of Brathwaite's texts constitutes a further exploration of linguistic possibilities. Like many contemporary Caribbean writers, he experiments with local sounds, regional speech patterns, vernacular or dialect or Creole forms – all of which he names under the single term of "nation-language" – as well as rhythmic tonalities which Brathwaite initially draws from jazz, and later from reggae, which highlight the creolised African component of Caribbean culture passed on in traditions of drumming and dance. His search entails the articulation of a native cosmology, a philosophy of history, and a regional aesthetics.

Chapter 4 examines the works of the Haitian poet, novelist, and essayist René Depestre, from his first volume of poems, *Etincelles* (1945), to *Eros dans un train chinois* (1992), his provocative collection of short stories. Read here from the point of view of the concern with the sacred, Depestre's works elaborate the primer of a religious gospel. Necessarily syncretic in nature, his imagery and symbology derive from the fusion of Caribbean religious expressions and the spiritual legacy of the Christian West. His concern with the sacred, objectified in the socio-historical context of the local milieu, largely exemplifies the spiritual imperative which characterizes many literary artists practising in the Caribbean in the twentieth century. From the mid 1980s his work has shown an increasing detachment from the political ideals he had upheld in the first four decades of his career, exhibiting an almost obsessive concern with sexual adventures. Depestre's peculiar handling of women in his work becomes elucidated by comparison with selected works by women writers from the Francophone Caribbean such as Marie Chauvet and Maryse Condé.

Chapter 5 consists of a reading of the works of the Dominican poet, novelist, and historian Pedro Mir, from his first published poems in the early 1940s to his collected poems *Poesías (casi) completas* (1994). Mir's works, the intellectual labour of nearly fifty years, are characterized by a constant concern with historical processes. Establishing appropriate parallels between Mir's works and those of other important Caribbean writers of the same period, I read his texts primarily as an illustration of the

Caribbean writer's emphasis on the explanatory power of past events in the region and the search for a more accurate rendition of the area's history as a means to access the dynamics of present conditions. The parallels with important women authors from the Dominican Republic, from Manuela Aybar to Salomé Ureña to Evangelina Rodríguez to Aída Cartagena Portalatín to Julia Alvarez, creates the space for a dialogue along gender lines for a writer who has held somewhat traditional views of women.

Chapter 6 begins by highlighting the points of contact between the three writers studied. It shows that they exhibit a notable hybridization of form and a handling of language that oscillates between the loftiness of high-sounding oratory and the demotic style of everyday street talk. Sharing a sort of generic amalgamation, the three writers move easily from the novel, to poetry, to short fiction, to the critical essay, the monograph, the historical treatise with equal zeal and often treating the same themes. In each case one finds it difficult to separate the thinker from the artist, as they seem to engage all aspects of their intellectual production in clarifying socio-historical issues, chief among which is their people's sense of cultural identity.

Representative exponents of Caribbean poetics, Brathwaite, Depestre, and Mir devote the bulk of their texts to the exercise of socio-cultural self-definition. Even when Brathwaite's confidence in the imminence of political and cultural revolution was severely dented by the turn to the political right in the Anglophone Caribbean and the upsurge of criminality and drug-related violence, he never lapses into an ontological pessimism. Seeing themselves as carriers of a message of light, these writers share the confidence that literature, the artistic rendition of the word, can significantly contribute to improving the lot of the people of the region. At the same time they demonstrate their internationalist vocation and their strong advocacy for a global humanism, namely the recognition that the good of the people of the Caribbean is not likely to come about without the necessarily equal and peaceful coexistence of all the peoples of the globe.

Marginality and Poetics

The latter half of Chapter 5 contains some generalizations regarding the place of Caribbean poetics in the larger spectrum of world literature. Maintaining that the literary unity of the Caribbean has its roots in the historical dynamics of colonialism, I argue that Caribbean poetics is inescapably connected to *and* disconnected from the Western tradition. Vaunting their marginality in relation to the dominant discourse of the West, with which they are typically linked in a love-hate relationship, Caribbean writers generally opt for the forging of a counter-discourse that constantly questions the norms and assumptions of the hegemonic culture. Witness the corrective impulse displayed by Caribbean writers when they revisit or rewrite some of the texts of the Western corpus, as we can see in their recurring engagement with *The Tempest*. Comprising the set of ideas, intentions, stylistic preferences, and general aesthetic pursuits typically upheld by literary artists coming from a marginal society or culture, the poetics of the marginal results from the immediacy of the historical reality which gives rise to it. Writers from marginal cultures must come to terms with the fact that the categories which modulate their everyday existence such as truth, goodness, normalcy, beauty, humanity, universality, and the like, have generally been dictated by the dominant discourse of the West in the course of the colonial transaction. As a result, any attempt at achieving authenticity will entail a reassessment of those categories, leading, for some, to a disturbingly ambivalent acceptance and, for the majority, to a systematic modification or redefinition of the categories in order to render them more relevant to the socio-historical conditions of the non-hegemonic setting. In general, practitioners of the poetics of the marginal will assume their subversion by upholding a set of tenets that tend to challenge the assumptions apparent in the Western literary canon. In this sense, Caribbean poetics constitutes a discrete, socio-historically specific, localised regional manifestation of the counter-discourse of the culturally marginal. I use this term because even though Brathwaite and Mir seek to put the folk/el pueblo at the centre of their cosmos, outside of poeisis, the unequal relations of power between the imperial society and the neocolony remain.

In short, Caribbean literature ought to be understood as a tradition whose texts contain within them an argument of how they can be read, to paraphrase Henry Louis Gates, Jr. Focusing on African American literature, Gates has advanced the notion that one must "draw on the black tradition itself to define a theory of its nature and function" (Gates 1988: xxiv). Perhaps the articulation of a Caribbean poetics will suggest ways of reading that may be useful in the study of other literatures. Françoise Lionnet, for instance, has used the critical positions of two Caribbean literary artists, Edouard Glissant and Nancy Morejón, in her study of Mauritian, Caribbean, and African-American women writers. Though her study is informed by the autobiographical constructions found in texts by Augustine and Nietzsche, she draws substantially on the aesthetic positions of Glissant and Morejón. She argues that their "aesthetics is potentially emancipatory because it creates a space where the mimetic illusions of Western representational systems are deconstructed. In that space, which is neither *ou-topia* nor *eu-topia*, differences are not sublimated and the ethnocentric self does not establish itself by selectively defining an 'other' to be assimilated and subjugated" (Lionnet 1989: 246).

This study subscribes to the valorization of specificities that Lionnet attributes to Glissant and Morejón while I hope it also sheds some light on the kinship between marginal literatures internationally and transculturally. The study concludes with a reflection on the possibility for a new system of canon formation. It proposes an internationalist view of literature which would allow for the incorporation of texts from different socio-cultural settings and would avoid the aesthetic hierarchization brought about by the dynamics of hegemonic versus non-hegemonic cultures. It proposes a literary world order without a centre which does not have recourse to relations of power as a means to measure the literary achievements of a people. It calls for an end to the predominance of the imperial imagination in literary theory and criticism.

CHAPTER 1
THE UNITY OF CARIBBEAN LITERATURE

> The Caribbean space has lived a life of its own, just as the Caribbean Mediterranean has cyclones of its own.
>
> Michel Devèze (1977: 9)

The unity of Caribbean literature, like the unity of European letters, stems from the socio-historical and cultural unity of the region that produces it. But, unlike European literary scholars, who start from the assumption of a commonality among the multiplicity of texts that make up their field of inquiry, Caribbeanists more often than not are called upon to prove and defend the cohesiveness of their field of endeavour. Too many of our colleagues require demonstration before accepting the multilingual and plurinational corpus of artistic writings produced in the Caribbean region as belonging in a more or less common literary tradition. Due to the region's colonial history, we must face the fact that Caribbean literature for long was not among the "literatures that have a suitable theory or body of criticism arising from typological features of their own works" (García Sierra and Sanz 1993: 1). Perhaps henceforward the proper stance for Caribbeanists should be to proclaim the coherence of the region's literary production *a priori*. Scholars would do well to affirm the cognitive wholeness of Caribbean literature as a theoretical given. They must take Caribbean literature for granted just as one takes Western literary artifacts for granted.

Both the Caribbean and Europe serve as arenas for various political realities, separate religious traumas, different cultural mythologies, diverse languages, and many distinct national histories. Certainly, we can find worlds of cultural, spiritual, and epistemological distance between, say, *La chanson de Roland*, *Beowulf*, and the *Nibelungenlied*, so much so that we might view them as incompatible texts if we did not possess the willing reflexes whereby we can manoeuvre to apprehend them as constituent parts of one large and flexible corpus. What is there in common between Ireland, Italy, and Germany, one might ask? Yet, who would begrudge the likes of William Butler Yeats, Salvatore Quasimodo, and Rainer Maria Rilke the right to sit together at the common table of European literature.

Scholars seldom hesitate to spread the mantle of unity over enormous stretches of space and time in their assumption of a culturally fathomable Western tradition. We feel no need to question the validity of panoramic vistas like that of the German philologist, Ernst Robert Curtius, who unearthed from the Latin Middle Ages the unchallenged coherence of European literature. Curtius, who credited Homer with the rank of "founding hero of European literature", conceived the works of European authors through the centuries as an "intelligible unit" having "an autonomous structure" (Curtius 1953: 14, 16). He posited that European literature "can only be seen as a whole" (p. 15). Arguing for a "comparative perusal" that draws on "the methods and subjects of classical, medieval Latin, and modern philology, Curtius discouraged the exclusive focus on "the modern national literatures" of Europe as an approach that might "cut into pieces" a corpus that can best be studied in its entirety (pp. 14-15).

Similarly, we recall Erich Auerbach, whose far-reaching survey from the Hebrew Scriptures to Homer to contemporary authors swept across vast historical periods and national spaces to arrive at the unifying principle of *mimesis*, wherein he believed he had found a clue to the representation of reality in Western literature (Auerbach 1953). By the same token, we feel hardly any apprehension about accepting the project of Arthur O. Lovejoy, who traced the principle of plenitude from Plato to modern times in order to show the great chain of being that has linked Western minds through the centuries (Lovejoy 1936). Finally, to name one case from recent decades, we have witnessed the advent of Harold Bloom's forceful defence of "the now-threatened Western canon" from the onslaught of feminists, afrocentrists, multiculturalists, New Historicists, Marxists, and deconstructors, all intellectual constituencies that he disparagingly calls "members of the School of Resentment" (Bloom 1994: 20). Bloom articulates his adamant defence as an exploration of twenty-six canonical writers from Dante to Beckett with Shakespeare functioning as a compelling centre of gravity around whom the canon revolves. What is most significant for us is that never once does Bloom exhibit the slightest need to justify the fact that his Western canon includes authors from a multiplicity of languages and countries.

Frankly, one wishes Caribbeanists attained the self-assurance evinced in the pronouncements of Curtius, Auerbach, Lovejoy, and Bloom regarding the ontological coherence of their field of study. They should reject the intellectual burden of having to prove the oneness of Caribbean literature. Instead, they should merely assert it. That having been done, they can then go on to investigate the principles that hold the corpus together as a differentiated entity. There's a welcome confidence in Colbert Nepaulsingh's tone when he says: "The way to read West Indian Literature is not to deal with the individual books but to see them all together"

(Nepaulsingh 1993: 204). His assertion of the literary unity of the Caribbean invokes the region's oneness both in the societal and in the natural order: "The earth is 71% water. The islands are 90% water," he observes, which in his estimation suffices to invalidate "land-based solutions to the region." Both society and nature seem to require talent and institutions tailored to fit the region's peculiar needs: "the islands deserve to have not only the best Comparative Literature Departments in the world, but especially the world's leading oceanographers, wind technologists, solar energy experts, and land conservationists" (p. 206).

Ontological Impurity and the Caribbean

Clearly, the Caribbean, like the West, houses, embraces, and absorbs disparities, contradictions, and incongruities as painfully and efficiently as any other culture area in the world. The region as a culture area and as the *locus* of five hundred years of post-Columbian experience can withstand the application of descriptive metaphors such as Sisyphean or El Doradian with the potentialities and the ensnaring temptations of both. Orlando Patterson's novel *The Children of Sisyphus* (1964) tackles one, and V.S. Naipaul's nonfiction book *The Loss of El Dorado* (1969) addresses the delusions of the other, whilst in *Palace of the Peacock* (1961), Wilson Harris moves the quest from one of material pursuit to an inner-directed search for human community. The futile quest of imperial explorers searching for the city of gold can indeed share room in the Caribbean imaginary with the existential dilemma of a citizen confined to the underworld, fated to look eternally and ceaselessly for meaning in the dry realm of senseless action.

But one soon finds that no metaphor contains as many layers of signification as would be necessary to exhaust the multifaceted human experience of the Caribbean. To represent the region in all its complex amplitude one might think of devising an amalgamated image, a composite metaphor that points to the contemporaneous coexistence of multiple signs. Similarly, questions that ask whether one should speak of two or three Caribbeans instead of one may be nonchalantly disregarded as pointless distractions. Certainly, there are many Caribbeans in the Caribbean just as there are many pieces in a puzzle. But, conceptually, one must argue, despite the discrete shape of the individual pieces, they all enter a sort of structural fit within the larger regional scheme. Indeed, paradoxical as it may sound, the identity of each separate part of a puzzle as well as of each discrete piece of the Caribbean consists as much of its own specific shape as of its integration into the whole.

The term Caribbean literature as used in the present discussion designates a wide body of writings from the Greater and Lesser Antilles and the Caribbean rimlands, a region that contains diverse nations, different languages, and various forms of worship. The political structures that govern the countries of the region have seldom encouraged contact and communication among the various Caribbean populations. Among the myriad island territories that spread across the region, plus the continental enclaves of Belize, Guyana, Suriname, and French Guiana, there have been right-wing military dictatorships, socialist governments, colonial possessions, semi-colonial structures, democracies, pseudo-democracies, and puzzling "free-associated" statehoods all occurring simultaneously. With the region's political balkanization, accentuated by the geographical disconnectedness reflected by the large bodies of water that intervene between the insular parts, it is no wonder that many scholars should feel apprehension about conceding to the region the capacity to give birth to a common literature. As a result, few have made systematic efforts to assess the works of, say, Maryse Condé from Guadeloupe, Frank Martinus Arion, a native of Curaçao, the Cuban Nicolás Guillén, the Surinamese Edgar Cairo, the Puerto Rican Ana Lydia Vega, the Martinican Aimé Césaire, the Guyanese Wilson Harris, and the Trinidadian Merle Hodge as part of one regional literature written in diverse tongues from the perspectives of different bodies of knowledge.

Admittedly, seeking to advance a comprehensive vision that encompasses literary activity across the region presents serious challenges to the literary scholar. The first challenge has to do with overcoming the temptation to view Antillean writing as an extension of the literatures of the European metropoles that brought Spanish, French, English, and Dutch to the region. The fact also that the individual European powers had distinct colonial styles, implemented particular forms of domination, and controlled differentiated portions of the Caribbean landscape may induce in observers the sense of an irreparable historical and cultural fragmentation that militates against a holistic appraisal of the region's cultural products. To assuage that disquieting sense one need only concede that the oneness of Caribbean writing lies in its "parallelisms" and "typological affinities". These terms, adopted by García Sierra and Sanz to describe the shared compulsions that link the region's texts, signal a "similar historical substratum" that accounts for the resemblances of texts which, though emerging from "a metropolitan plurality, are more similar to each other than to the respective metropolis" (1993: 8-9).

Fragmentation as Coherence

To view literary production in the Antilles on its own terms one may need to be equipped with centripetal vision, that is, have eyes that are socialized in autochthonous ways of seeing. The scholar, in other words, must have the readiness to grasp the region conceptually as a world that is pregnant with valid meaning, a native meaning, which, in turn, informs the body of writings produced there. Transcending the view that still looks at the Caribbean as "illegitimate, rootless, mongrelized" can foster a perception of the region's corpus of artistic writings as "one literature in several imperial languages", to echo the words of Derek Walcott during his Nobel Prize acceptance speech (Walcott 1993: pages unnumbered). The proper frame of mind will enable the scholar to overcome the frustration of experiencing the region as incurably fragmented.

Fragmentation need not be tragic. It can actually provide a principle of coherence in so far as it induces in the Caribbean artist a compulsion to sew the pieces together. "Break a vase," says Walcott, "and the love that reassembles the fragments is greater than the love which took its symmetry for granted when it was a whole." In the same speech, the poet adds: "This gathering of broken pieces is the care and pain of the Antilles, and if the pieces are disparate, ill-fitting, they contain more pain than their original sculpture, those icons and sacred vessels taken for granted in their ancestral places." In the Caribbean, Walcott ponders, one can hardly evade the command that urges artists to invest themselves in the "restoration of our shattered histories, our shards of vocabulary, our archipelago becoming a synonym for pieces broken off from the original continent." The awareness of fragmentation draws Caribbean artists to a common task: "That is the effort, the labour of the Antillean imagination, rebuilding its gods from bamboo frames, phrase by phrase" (Walcott 1993: pages unnumbered).

The pervasiveness of fragments imposes upon the scholar the need to rely on more than just one way of knowing to apprehend the Caribbean experience. During a major conference in his honour, Kamau Brathwaite spoke to that predicament in these terms: "I say you have to be everything to bring those fragments together because fragments by their very nature are everything... They are in fact everything, little seeds growing throughout the scattered diaspora, throughout the Caribbean" (Brathwaite 1992). Therein lies the transgression of disciplines and fusion of genres that we witness in the most central Caribbean authors. Brathwaite, as will become clear in the study of his work, fuses genres, breaks the boundary between artistic and intellectual expression, and defies the established norms of scientific communication. A similar conviction that the complexity of the Caribbean experience transcends the poor powers of any discrete discipline or art form has led Edouard Glissant to affirm emphatically that the exploration of the people's past in the region cannot be relegated to the historians alone (Glissant 1981: 133).

It follows from the foregoing observations that when approaching the cultural products of the region, the scholar must develop the rare ability to tolerate impurities, to conceive of a space of in-betweeness, where things enjoy a sort of ontological elasticity that permits them to be neither this nor that. A conceptually flexible framework alone can manage to converse with the multiplicity of components that have gone into the sociocultural formation of the people of the region and can enable the scholar to delve into the underlying congruity of visibly disparate elements. Critics approaching the Caribbean panoptically require an insight that transcends mere erudition in so far as the task involves a given attitude toward the subject matter under study. That is, they must wish to obtain meaning from the peculiar character of the region. Mervyn Morris, in his often cited poem entitled "To a West Indian Definer", elicits succinctly the complex character of the Caribbean world. The poet adduces the depth of the region's sociocultural plurality by simply listing the multitude of origins and options that one would need to consider in the construction of a vision of the Caribbean. Some of the lines say: "Africa England Portugal and Spain/ India and France China Syria/ Black brown pink and cream/ .../ Drought and hurricane, mountain soil and sea –/ All these" (Morris 1966: 87). By closing with the words "All these," the text draws our attention, not to the constituent elements in isolation, but to the global confluence, which has resulted in the process of creolization aptly described by Brathwaite in many ways since his pioneering *The Development of Creole Society in Jamaica* (1971).

Charting the Region, Imagining the Culture

What one makes of the global confluence of disparate elements in the Caribbean, whether one construes the assorted arrangement as a cohesive unit, and how one understands the cultural artifacts produced there, will largely depend on one's conceptual configuration of the region. From the current uses of the term Caribbean one can infer multiple definitions that range from a historical or ethnocultural sense to a strategic (Caribbean basin) or strictly geographical one (American Mediterranean), as surveyed by José Rodríguez Iturbide (1987: 7-20). Students of individual societies of the region may even doubt the existence of anything beyond single countries and be seduced by opinions like that of literary scholar León François Hoffmann. This Princeton University Haitianist contends that the concept of the Caribbean lacks validity in all but a purely geographical sense. He discards any other claim for the region as "more a myth than a reality" (Hoffman 1982: 26).

For some, the Caribbean forms a part of larger geopolitical or geocultural constructs such as the Americas or the Western Hemisphere, and that view shapes their way of charting the region's literary activity. We witness this integrative approach in a collection of essays that covers some Caribbean authors in a pan-American inquiry concerning whether the Americas have a common literature (Pérez-Firmat 1990). Caribbean texts also become subsumed in the hemispheric quest of Earl E. Fitz, who purports to present

"English and French Canada, the United States, Spanish America, and Brazil as constituting a community of literary cultures related to each other by virtue of their origins, their sundry interrelationships, and their socio-political, artistic, and intellectual evolutions" (Fitz 1991: xi). While the author occasionally mentions Caribbean writers in his panoramic study, he never sets them apart as belonging to a culturally differentiated region. He concerns himself merely with the geographically vaster notion of a New World literature (1991: 168).

Latin Americanists have normally had difficulty with the cultural autonomy of the Caribbean and have tended to visualize the region through a strong Hispanic prism. In 1950, the Cuban scholar Jorge Mañach understood the Caribbean simply as "a section of Latin America" that included, in addition to the Spanish-speaking Antilles, the territories of Mexico, Colombia, Venezuela, and Central America (Mañach 1951: 213-15). Nearly three decades later, the scholar Ileana Rodríguez presented literary production in the Caribbean as one "within the orbit of Latin American Literature." For her the geography of the region included "not only the island nations, but the east coast of mainland countries extending from the southern United States to Mexico, Central America and finally Colombia, Venezuela, and the Guyanas" (Rodríguez 1983: 13, 20). Latin Americanists, who have traditionally enjoyed a greater space and prestige in academia than Caribbeanists, suffer from an urgent wish to incorporate Antillean letters into the larger field of Latin American literary scholarship, a bent that now many recognize as counterproductive. As the Cuban scholar Margarita Mateo Palmer warns, the attempt to insert Caribbean writing within a scheme drawn from the study of Hispanic American and Brazilian literature may result in overlooking "its peculiarities and the pace proper to its evolution" (Mateo Palmer 1990: 7).

Interestingly, foreign policy spokespersons have exhibited less hesitation than literary scholars to declare the cognitive autonomy of the Caribbean. They have shown little doubt that the region can be grasped holistically. "Held in the embrace of two continents, the Caribbean is the key to both," noted W. Adolphe Roberts, calling it "our sea of destiny, the Mediterranean of the West" (Roberts 1940: 13, 19, 342). Cognizant of the Caribbean's strategic value, J. Fred Rippy thought of it as "one of the most important regions of the earth" and urged the United States never to permit its "domination by a strong aggressive power" (Rippy 1940: 4). "Sugar and slavery have been the two central factors in Caribbean history. Sugar, bananas, tourists, and military bases are the central factors today," claimed Paul Blanchard in the 1940s, denying to it the likelihood of begetting "new forms of political or economic society," and affirming that it would remain "a satellite region, taking colours from large and powerful nations" (Blanchard 1947: 8, 337). Robert D. Crassweller regarded the Caribbean as "enormous in the sense of the number and complexities of the land, peoples, and problems that are its substance," which appeared ideal for advancing U.S. policy toward the peaceful creation of a "Caribbean Community" (Crassweller 1972: 426, ix). Finally, a geopolitical analysis of the basin has imagined the area as a potential blaze upon the sea, an explosive arena for bloody wars if proper caution is not taken (Elisabeth and Seymour 1981: 156).

A common thread that runs through these texts is the perception that the Caribbean is important for the outside. Invariably, they stress the benefit or harm it has brought or can bring to the continental powers. They share a deep sense of the significance of the area as that which matters to the international community, which normally means the outside, and, more specifically, the particular world powers that have vested interests in the region. The centrifugal glance of these authors shows little regard for the Caribbean except for the profit or conflict that outsiders may derive from it. They collaborate in perpetuating a notion that assigns meaning to the region primarily in terms of its past, present or future connection with Western societies. Aside from that connection, their view reduces the Caribbean experience to a threnody of historical dispossession. The longevous legacy of the people who live, work, suffer, and create there fails to attract their attention. These authors articulate ideas typical of foreign policy spokespersons advocating the interests of empire, but their strategists' logic often becomes intertwined with the humanistic parlance of literary discourse.

During the 1940s, the celebrated Colombian essayist Germán Arciniegas offered a vision of the Caribbean that illustrates the occasional marriage of imperial foreign policy thinkers and literary sensibility. Arciniegas charted the Caribbean experience by merely tracing the glorious feat of the Europeans who courageously challenged the waters of the Atlantic to leave their epic mark on the region. His text moves from lyrical evocations of Amerigo Vespucci and Christopher Columbus through to the independence movements of the nineteenth-century Caribbean. Echoing the reasoning of a manifest destiny teleology, his book envisions Vasco Núñez de Balboa on a sunny afternoon gazing upon the Pacific and there conceiving the idea that centuries later would materialize into the Panama Canal: "the idea of a canal linking the two new seas was to become a dream that obsessed the minds of men for centuries. It is not too far-fetched to say that this bold conquistador, this son of the people, carried upon his shoulders the first ships that crossed the Isthmus" (Arciniegas 1945: 413). For the venerable Arciniegas, the story of the Caribbean amounts to little else than a sequence of regional repercussions of events and actions taking place in the Western metropoles and affecting the minds of Western men.

The definition of the Caribbean implicit in Arciniegas' centrifugal vision bears a striking resemblance to a more recent pronouncement by the famous United States author James Michener who in a novel entitled *Caribbean* undertakes to capture the history of the region and its people from pre-Columbian times to the 1980s. In introducing the book, the author grants that "European destinies were frequently determined by great sea battles in the Caribbean, especially those fought among the fleets of Spain, Holland, England, and France," thus assigning an important role to the region in the drama of "world history" (Michener 1989: 4). However, he hastens to deny validity to the practice of establishing a parallel between the Caribbean and the Mediterranean. Although geographically the parallel seems to obtain, since "both seas are landbound" and "are almost identical in size", Michener makes this distinction: "The lands bordering the Mediterranean gave rise to many outstanding civilizations and the three great religions, while the only great indigenous civilization that operated in the Caribbean area was the Maya in Yucatan, and even it was dying out before the explorers arrived from Europe" (p. 4). Michener's perception of the area's lack of greatness in pre-Columbian times extends also to what people there have achieved since 1492. That is why he finds it auspicious that "in recent decades businessmen predominantly from Canada and the United States have streamed down to invest their intelligence and money in efforts to make the islands tourist havens and international banking centres" (p. 4).

Epistemological Separateness

Perhaps Arciniegas and Michener can serve as useful examples of the mindset that scholars should avoid when seeking to understand the Caribbean as a literary region. Their inability to see Antilleans in their own right, as makers of history and producers of culture, bespeaks a measure of contempt. That it is possible, even for a foreigner to the region, to avoid such an inimical frame of mind becomes evident in a recent book by United States journalist Mark Kurlansky, a compatriot of Michener, who ventures to map the Caribbean destiny by searching in the annals of the region for the lived experience of the people. In his text, *A Continent of Islands*, he tries to see the Caribbean as it is perceived and lived by those inside: "Europeans ruined these lands, exhausted their soil on single-crop agriculture, drove their economies into dead ends. Caribbeans have fought hard to have nations, to be free men and women, to erase the stigma of slavery and take their place in the community of nations. But it was only when their Caribbean holdings were no longer profitable that Europeans relinquished them, just as slavery ended when the plantation economy was no longer profitable" (Kurlansky 1992: vii).

Kurlansky not only recognizes a direct link between Western prosperity and Caribbean poverty, but he manages to recognize, along with the trauma of destitution and dispossession, the courage of a vigorous multiethnic people perennially engaged in the business of survival. He has no difficulty in noticing that the long historic journey of Antilleans has necessitated a great deal of energy, endurance, ingenuity, strength, and productivity. Their legacy in this regard is no less great than the greatest of the most acclaimed civilizations: "In truth, there has always been a great deal going on: music, architecture, theatre, literature, painting – a people formed from a unique blending of races and cultures with a restless creativity and a rich ironic sense of humour that never fails them, even in the worst of times" (p. viii).

Once one has overcome the seduction of seeing the Caribbean through the imperial logic of foreign policy thinkers and strategists, and has gained access to a more or less centripetal vision of the region and learned to see Antilleans as speaking subjects, the next challenge for the literary scholar is to grasp that Antilleans themselves deserve credit as reliable interpreters of their own reality in the realms of life and letters. Many have been tempted to regard Caribbean culture as an early stage of a phenomenon that has yet to reach maturity. Jack Corzani, surveying the literature of the Francophone Caribbean, spoke of "a culture in the process of formation", which implies a conception of culture as a closed system, a completed entity, presupposing a teleological understanding of a particular point of evolution that must be reached before a culture can be thus denominated (Corzani 1978: 28). Since it would seem superfluous to refute this notion, whose ethnocentric implications are clear, we can simply counter it by affirming with Walcott that "Caribbean culture is not evolving" but is "already shaped" (Walcott 1993: unnumbered pages). However, we must deal with the fact that the notion of the Caribbean as a culturally underdeveloped area has thrived and may still infest the minds of some literary scholars. Therein lies the widespread hesitation to use indigenous discourses and tools of instruction when seeking to explain the region's cultural artifacts.

What one must keep in mind is that only Caribbean literature can explain Caribbean literature. As Earl Miner has reminded us, "there cannot be a poetics without a literature to describe " (1990: 13). Literary thought about a particular tradition springs specifically from a reflection on the artistic texts produced by that tradition. With that in mind, Miner in his *Comparative Poetics* has advocated an "intercultural comparative study" of literature which, by confronting us with the distinct systems of significance contained in diverse literary systems, not only can "assist in our understanding of their differences" but can also prevent us from "taking the local for the universal, the momentary for the constant, and, above all, the familiar for the inevitable (Miner 1990: 25, 238). Lubomir Dolezel's book

Occidental Poetics studies the "engagement with literature in Occidental culture" so as to trace the development of its two branches, "one called *criticism*, the other *poetics*" (1990: viii). In tracing the development of literary criticism and theory from Aristotle to Leibniz, to the Romantics, to French semioticians, to the Formalists, to the Prague School, Dolezel does a competent job of isolating a poetic system endemic to a particular culture area. Aristotle's *Poetics* is the "foundation stone of the study of literature in the Occidental cultural realm" and the text that lays "the foundation of Occidental *literary criticism*", but, as Dolezel reminds us, the philosopher's theory "is based on a thorough knowledge of extant Greek tragedies" (pp. 11,26,29). It follows that the poetics and literary criticism of other "cultural realms" ought to emerge from the specific texts they produce.

The ideas of Miner and Dolezel should suffice to discourage literary scholars from advancing global theories of Caribbean writing that are not informed by a system of significance taken from the region's texts themselves and the sociocultural contexts that inform those texts. Even when we focus on its cultural and intellectual interrelations with the West, we must not view the Caribbean as a passive receptacle of metropolitan influences. The Syrian poet Ali Ahmed Said, better known as Adonis, argues in his *Introduction to Arab Poetics* (1990) for the need to pay heed to the dynamics of Arab literary systems even when exploring such concepts as modernity. "Arab modernity can be studied only within the perspective of Arab thought, on the level of principles and actual historical developments, within the framework of specific assumptions, using its epistemological tools and in the context of the issues which gave rise to the phenomenon and have resulted from it," wrote Adonis, insisting that: "To study it from a Western perspective would be to distort it and distance oneself from the issues" (Adonis 1990: 83). Adonis makes a case that could easily apply to the Caribbean with little if any adjustment. The scholar of Caribbean literature, whether a native of the region or not, should begin by becoming familiar with the body of knowledge available in the region to explain Caribbean art and culture. Too many times commentators, including Caribbean ones, tackle their study of Antillean texts as if they were the first to do so.

The Caribbean through Borrowed Eyes

Among recent efforts to conceptualize the literature of the Caribbean as a whole, two in particular deserve close scrutiny for the favourable reception accorded to them as texts that aim to unveil global truths about writing in the region. They are Simon Gikandi's *Writing in Limbo* (1992) and Antonio Benítez-Rojo's *The Repeating Island* (1992) which lend themselves to an evaluation of the authors' success at meeting the serious challenge posed by the nature of their inquiry. In *Writing in Limbo*, Gikandi sets out to explore the "historical anxiety and ambivalence and the cultural and narrative forms Caribbean writers have developed both to represent and to resist the European narration of history inaugurated by Columbus and the modern moment," arguing that "Caribbean writers cannot adopt the history and culture of European modernism, especially as defined by the colonizing structures, but neither can they escape from it because it has overdetermined Caribbean cultures in many ways" (Gikandi 1992: 2-3). He proposes to investigate "the ideology and form of Caribbean modernism" in the light of "the hegemonic European idea of the modern" (p. 4).

Gikandi seeks to show "the essential modernity of Caribbean literature as apparent in the writers' anxiety toward their history" (p. 5). Caribbean writing, he argues, is motivated "by the need to inscribe Caribbean selves and voices within an economy of representation whose institutional and symbolic structures have been established since the 'discovery'." He also undertakes to reveal the political and theoretical implications of the "notion of creolization as an essential component of Caribbean modernism" (pp. 10, 16). Gikandi highlights the "modernist anxiety" associated with the linguistic predicament of Caribbean writers: the "parasitic relationship to the language community the poet opposes" and the drama of having "to map a Caribbean landscape" by means of "a European language already loaded with Eurocentric figures" (pp. 21, 15). *Writing in Limbo* occupies most of its pages in readings of texts by George Lamming, C.L.R. James, Samuel Selvon, Alejo Carpentier, Paule Marshall, Merle Hodge, Zee Edgell and Michelle Cliff with an eye on illustrating their modernist anxieties. In his conclusion, the author appears satisfied to have shown that: "It was in the language of modernism, the historical paradoxes of modernity, and the hopes and betrayals embedded in the doctrine of modernization that Caribbean writers sought a way of recounting colonial modernism so that they could effect a narrative of liberation. Only by subverting colonial modernism could these writers become modernists" (p. 256).

It is not clear whether in Gikandi's usage "modernist" means anything other than "contemporary". Nor does one learn, for instance, whether there exist any contemporary texts that might not be modernist either in the West or in the Caribbean. The author seems to use the words modernism, modernity, and modernization interchangeably, and to buttress his observations he appeals to a wide variety of Western thinkers. Fredric Jameson, Jürgen Habermas, Jacques Derrida, Julia Kristeva, Jean-François Lyotard, Michel de Certeau, Mikhail Bakhtin, Gilles Deleuze and Félix Guattari parade through Gikandi's pages without a clear pattern of theoretical preference. As a text that seeks to arrive at an understanding of Caribbean discourse, the book sins from an overdependence on Western secondary sources to legitimize its readings of the region's texts. At times, the author appears more committed to the history of Western ideas than to the project of investigating Caribbean texts as containers of autochthonous meaning. The Antillean books examined do not get a chance to yield the clues to their own explications.

In examining the recurrence of the theme of exile, for instance, Gikandi explains: "because exile was one of the most dominant tropes in the ideologies of high modernism – which tended to evoke cultural displacement as a form of artistic privilege – it was inevitable that those Caribbean writers who aligned themselves with the European avant garde would adopt exile and its rhetoric as the gesture that, by individuating and universalizing artistic production, would also liberate the writer from his or her 'compromised' literary traditions" (p. 34). Yet one wonders why the Caribbean writers studied by Gikandi would have needed to adopt the anxiety of exile and displacement from the European avant garde when they had their own experience to draw from. Gikandi himself relates that a good many of the major "literary and cultural documents in the Caribbean tradition... were produced in exile" (p. 33). Exile was and still is a constant element of the Caribbean experience, and the literary implications of that historical fact have been examined time and again, at least since Brathwaite's 1957 essay "Sir Galahad and the Islands". One would, indeed, be hard put to sustain the claim that exile, a consequence "of the plantation system and African slavery" and one of the "governing factors of Caribbean history", has become apparent in the region's literary texts as a result of the influence of Western aesthetic currents (Birbalsingh 1988: 11). The weight of the historical evidence would direct us instead to the writers' concrete existential plight as artists in exile. Adducing reasons that involve the quest for publishing opportunities, a larger readership, and other issues, Ivan Van Sertima estimated in the mid 1960s that virtually every major West Indian writer was living and working in exile in Britain, which "for most" was tantamount to a "banishment for life" and entailed the tragic risk of losing "touch with their origins" (Van Sertima 1968: 9-10).

Gikandi's close reading of individual texts, particularly his ideological exegeses of works of fiction by women authors, stands out as a virtue in his book. He argues cogently that in the novels of Hodge and Edgell "the unveiling of the lives of Caribbean women not only recentres them in history as custodians of an oral tradition, but also functions as an indicator of sources of domination that might have been lost or repressed in both the colonial text and the male-dominated nationalist discourse" (Gikandi 1992: 201). His discussions of Marshall's and Cliff's works suggest additional ways in which women writers from the Caribbean draw on orality and autobiography to decentre the colonial tradition and male-centred discourse. But, in general, the concerns raised by *Writing in Limbo* merely recount many of the standard issues in critical and theoretical discussions of Caribbean literature. The "modernist anxieties" that Gikandi encounters, namely history, language, creolization, colonialism, and the ambivalent attitude toward Western texts constitute standard *topoi* of Caribbean intellectual discourse. Approaching them through the prism of modernism may very well vary the critical terminology, but it does little else. The fact also that, except for Carpentier's, the texts examined come exclusively from the Anglophone bloc makes it unclear whether Gikandi's observations apply to the region's literature beyond the English-speaking West Indies.

In a similar vein, though brandishing a postmodern perspective whereas Gikandi adheres to a modernist one, Benítez-Rojo's *The Repeating Island* comes out of the author's perception that "the time has come for post-industrial society to start rereading the Caribbean, that is, to do the kind of reading in which every text begins to reveal its own textuality" (Benítez Rojo 1992: 2). Rejecting the notion that "the Caribbean is the union of the diverse" as a virtual reduction, he begins his rereading by advancing the "geographical fact" that the Caribbean area constitutes "an island bridge" that somehow connects "north and South America", which gives the region "the character of an archipelago, that is, a discontinuous conjunction (of what?): unstable condensations, turbulence, whirlpools, clumps of bubbles, frayed seaweed, sunken galleons, crashing breakers, flying fish, sea gull squawks, downpours, night-time phosphorescences, eddies and pools, uncertain voyages of signification; in short, a field of observation quite in tune with the objectives of Chaos" (p. 2).

Viewing the region through the lens of the new scientific field of Chaos, Benítez-Rojo finds that "within the sociohistorical fluidity that the Caribbean archipelago presents, within its historiographic turbulence and its ethnological and linguistic clamour, within its generalized instability of vertigo and hurricane, one can sense the features of an island that 'repeats' itself, unfolding and bifurcating until it reaches all the seas and lands of the earth, while at the same time it inspires multidisciplinary maps of unexpected designs" (p. 3). This island, however, does not correspond to any of the known Antillean islands. It is an island "as impossible to reach as the hypothetical *Antillas*" that befuddled the cosmographers in the past. The author allows himself this analytical strategy on the grounds that, like Hellas and the great Malay archipelago, "the Caribbean is not a common archipelago, but a meta-archipelago," and, as such, "it has the virtue of having neither a boundary nor a center" (p. 4). For Benítez-Rojo, the plantation is one of the most important machines (in Deleuze and Guattari's usage of the term) that frame the Caribbean historical experience. Similarly, viewing the area as the seat of an "aquatic" rather than a "terrestrial" culture, he sees Antilleans as one of the Peoples of the Sea: "and everything seems to indicate that they will continue to be so for some time, even within the interplay of dynamics that carry models of knowledge proper to modernity and postmodernity" (p. 17).

Benítez-Rojo accepts the notion, on a first reading at least, that the very existence of Caribbean literature is questionable "and that what in fact exist are local literatures, written from within the Caribbean's different linguistic blocs", although he himself purports in his rereading "to look at the rhythms proper to Caribbean literature" (pp. 24-25). He then ventures the notion that "the literature of the Caribbean can be read as a *mestizo* text, but also as a stream of texts in flight, in intense differentiation among themselves and within whose complex coexistence there are vague regularities, usually paradoxical" (p. 27). He contends that "the Caribbean text shows the specific features of the supersyncretic culture from which it emerges", a culture which developed against the backdrop of the tense but "not necessarily antagonistic" interaction of the "opposition Peoples of the Sea/ Europe" (pp. 28, 29).

With these general claims in mind, the author proceeds to examine the socio-historical processes whereby the Caribbean became dominated by the plantation machine. Privileging socioeconomic structures over culture as "the quickest route toward defining a substantial form of Caribbeanness," Benítez-Rojo would deem it "premature to venture an opinion about whether or not a Caribbean culture exists" before one has organized "the discourse of the Plantation" (p. 37, 39). He focuses primarily on the Hispanic Caribbean, declaring it beyond the scope of his book "to cover the history of the different colonial blocs" (p. 21). But even so, he argues that the proliferation of the plantation, which presented different features in each colonial bloc, made possible, nonetheless, "the existence of a pan-Caribbean society" in the same way "that a system of fractal equations or a galaxy is possible" (p. 72). He then offers an interesting reading of Bartolomé de Las Casas and of Nicolás Guillén. He advances an inquiry into *Contrapunteo cubano del tabaco y el azúcar* by Fernando Ortiz that proposes the book as an example of the Cuban ethnologist's "proto-post-modernity" (p. 156), revealing a process whereby "the Cuban trinity: tobacco, sugar, and alcohol" achieve centrality, thereby suggesting the basis of Caribbeanness "in the counterpoint of the myth of the Peoples of the Sea and the theorem of the West" (pp. 175-76). He also examines texts by Alejo Carpentier, Wilson Harris, Fanny Buitrago, and Edgardo Rodríguez Juliá.

The Repeating Island ends with an "Epilogue" which consists basically of a bibliographical review of the scholarship on Chaos that gave Benítez-Rojo the theoretical framework for his intellectual disquisition on the Caribbean. He argues in favour of the "models belonging to Chaos" on the basis that "they speak of dynamic forms that float, sometimes in unforeseen and scarcely perceptible ways within the Caribbean's huge heteroclitic archive" (p. 269). Anticipating the criticism that his work "does not encompass all of the Caribbean", he states that "due to the area's extremely complex cultural spectrum (a soup of signs), no one could really claim to be a full specialist in Caribbean culture" (p. 269). In his eyes, acceptable readings of the Caribbean fall within "the three great paradigms of knowledge that I've been talking about: those of the Peoples of the Sea, of modernity, and of postmodernity" (p. 270). And he insists that the postmodern perspective, whatever its drawbacks for assessing the "cultures of the so called Third World", is the only one that can "direct itself toward the play of paradoxes and eccentricities, of fluxes and displacements; that is, it offers possibilities that are quite in tune with those that define the Caribbean" (p. 271).

The Repeating Island is impressive for the ease and naturalness with which Benítez-Rojo displays his erudition regarding contemporary Western thought. An intellectual tour de force, the book is enticing, compelling one to admire the author's interpretive voyage and his flair for metaphorical renditions of historical realities. We know, for instance, that emigration has for long plagued Caribbean history, and many have pondered on the socio-economic forces that implacably separate Caribbean people from their homelands. But Benítez-Rojo detects in that cruel displacement a symbolic quest driven by the pursuit of an ontological essence: "Antilleans, for example, tend to roam the entire world in search of the centres of their Caribbeanness, constituting one of our century's most notable migratory flows. The Antillean's insularity does not impel them toward isolation, but on the contrary, toward travel, toward exploration, toward the search for fluvial and marine routes. One needn't forget that it was men from the Antilles who constructed the Panama Canal" (p. 25). His metaphorical logic construes an imperative of self discovery out of what Caribbeanists normally mourn as a bitter drama of uprooting and diasporic dispossession. His carefree, unencumbered theoretical stance invites a rebuttal of the sort that is contained in this sentence from Walcott: "The Caribbean is not an idyll, not to its natives" (Walcott 1993: unnumbered).

The value of Benítez-Rojo's book lies in his creative reading of individual texts, that is, in those pages that seem less subservient to postmodernist thinkers and less committed to the prism of Chaos. As a reading of the Caribbean, however, it cannot claim great virtue. Though a Cuban, Benítez-Rojo looks at the Caribbean through borrowed eyes, exhibiting a curious dynamic which relegates one's own land to the realm of the exotic. Showing more intimacy with the "postmodern perspective" than with Caribbean literature and culture, he proceeds as one for whom the Caribbean merely yields a forum wherein to rehearse some of the ideological and intellectual implications suggested to him by certain strands of Western critical theory. His greater commitment to the theoretical schemes employed than to the matter under study perhaps explains, for instance, the absence from his bibliography of all the major Caribbean thinkers who in the last decades have significantly enhanced our understanding of the Caribbean experience. But perhaps he should not be faulted for failing at a task that he has not attempted. He does clearly lay out the aim to suggest a model whereby "postindustrial society" can "start rereading the Caribbean", and we certainly cannot be expected to understand that by "postindustrial society" he means Haiti, the Dominican Republic or Trinidad. He means the outside.

Neither *Writing in Limbo* nor *The Repeating Island* overcomes the hesitation to accept the Caribbean as an area that has produced its own metadiscourse with which to speak about its own cultural artifacts. Scholars of Caribbean literature would concede that the region's texts, examined from within, offer clues to their own explication when seen against the backdrop of the lived experience of Caribbean people for the past five centuries. No one can deny the difficulty of mastering Caribbean culture, but too often intellectuals, including Caribbean ones, allow themselves too disproportionate a degree of ignorance about the region even as they can boast considerable erudition about the West. As a result, they tend to underestimate the validity of the knowledge produced by Caribbean minds. They show no regard for the value of the critical corpus that Caribbean scholars, thinkers, and artists have produced during the last seven decades. Their disregard for the region's intellectual production lurks behind affirmations such as these: "Caribbean literature does not yet exist. We are still in a stage of Preliterature", as we read in a now famous manifesto on Creoleness published by Martinican authors Jean Bernabé, Patrick Chamoiseau, and Raphäel Confiant (1990: 886). It matters little that they have echoed an affirmation previously made by Glissant, whom they have adopted as their "inspiration, their model and master" (Conde 1993: 128).

Perhaps Bernabé, Chamoiseau, and Confiant do have an earnest desire to contribute a discourse that will account for Caribbean complexity. But their adamic stance (a position that links them to Derek Walcott's phrase of "New World Adams"[1]) militates against their effort. "Neither Europeans, nor Africans, nor Asians, we proclaim ourselves Creoles," they state, arguing that "Creoleness", what they refer to as "the cement of our culture", can be defined as "the fact of belonging to an original human entity", one that derives from the distinct processes that have taken place in the Caribbean (Bernabé, Chamoiseau, and Confiant 1990: 886, 891, 894). They assert that Creoleness *will* serve as a means to "crystalize Caribbeanness, the ferment of a Caribbean civilization", and *will* manifest itself in the appropriation of the European language, leading to the emergence of Creole works of art. They define Creole art as that "art which, celebrating within its coherence the diversity of meanings, will preserve the mark which justifies its pertinence regardless of how it is understood, where it is culturally perceived, or to what issues it is associated" (pp. 900, 902-03). What is most clearly objectionable about this Creolist manifesto is its futuristic yearning for features that have long been second nature to Antillean writing. The nativization of the European language, the assumption of a distinctly regional identity, the celebration and incorporation of diverse heritages, the search for a counterdiscourse to official colonial historiography, in short, all the issues that the manifesto articulates as *desiderata*, have for decades been visible even in the authors' own Francophone side of the Caribbean. Besides, there exist indispensable sources in the scholarship from the area, such as Brathwaite's *The Development of Creole Society in Jamaica* (1971) and Pedro Mir's *Tres leyendas de colores* (1969), which have contributed decisive data and advanced crucial interpretive approaches to an understanding of the Caribbean from the point of view of creolization. Any writing about the subject that ignores precedents such as these should be read *cum grano salis*.

The assumption that one is starting *ex nihilo*[2] is hardly more permissible when writing about Caribbean literature than when dealing with North American or European letters. The Martinican authors reveal also the futility of venturing global conceptualizations of the region on the basis of knowledge of only one Antillean nation or even one linguistic area. Given the variety of cultural matrices that have shaped the lives and ideas of Antilleans and the variety of languages in which Caribbean literature expresses itself, perhaps it is only a comparative and, to a large extent, interdisciplinary approach that can hope to shed light on the socio-aesthetic imperatives that inform literary production in this particular part of the world. The efforts of most committed Caribbeanists point to the possibility of looking through the region's history of slavery, colonial oppression and economic exploitation to discern a world of human endurance and creation in the region, a world made homogenous by phenomena belonging in the realms of history, culture, economics, and politics which serve as "unifying factors", to use the words of Cuban scholar Emilio Jorge Rodríguez (1989: 27).

Toward a Native Vision of Wholeness

The challenge for Caribbeanists is not to achieve success at identifying a model for postindustrial society or any portion of the outside world to apprehend the region holistically. That has been done all too often. Texts penned by imperial foreign policy spokespersons meant to educate outsiders about the Antillean world abound in centrifugal models. What for our purposes can really make a difference would be to recognize unifying factors that may empower the people of the region to proclaim their own native vision of wholeness. Ultimately, different thinkers, scholars, and artists will undertake to elicit the oneness of the region by investigating whichever principles of coherence they deem most apparent, demonstrable, ideologically acceptable or theoretically feasible. The Puerto Rican fiction writer Luis Rafael Sánchez, looking at other writers from his own linguistic bloc, finds that "music, blackness, and wandering define the Caribbean according to three of the Caribbean's essential writers: Alejo Carpentier, Luis Palés Matos, and Pedro Mir" (1993: 22).

Sánchez is not alone in ascribing unifying value to the three factors he isolates. In fact, an ethnomusicological study by Kenneth M. Bilby contends that the Antillean world constitutes a differentiated musical region in light of the "present-day unity – broadly speaking – of Caribbean music" (Bilby 1985: 200). Similarly, the preponderance of African-descended people in the region has led many voices to look for homogeneity in blackness. We thus find studies like *Antilia retrouvée* (1983), a book by Haitian scholar Jean-Claude Bajeux, that brings together the works of Claude McKay, Aimé Césaire, and Luis Palés Matos, literary voices from three different linguistic blocs of the region linked by the experience and the socio-aesthetic implications of their shared blackness. Blackness, of course, hardly describes the totality of the Caribbean racial experience. In addition to Blacks, the Caribbean houses Europeans (from England, France, Spain, Portugal, Italy, and The Netherlands at least), Chinese, Indians, Javanese, Amerindians, Lebanese, Sephardic Jews, and many kinds of racial mixing – a wide variety of ethnic groups that are characterized by a great deal of interdependence, as Stephen Glazier argues (1988: 2).

A panoptic glance at race relations and racial designations throughout the region, as Harry Hoetink warns, may suggest that words such as *white*, *coloured* or *black* do not always name the same thing in all national settings (Hoetink 1985: 82). Perhaps then, one should not look for an unifying factor in any individual race but rather in the racial imperative that largely shapes the lives of people in the Caribbean. The "shared colonial victimization induced common attitudes of resistance and engendered unity of political purpose in Africans and Indians" says Frank Birbalsingh (1989: 7-8).[3] But the other groups of non-European ancestry also endured their share of "colonial victimization". The Whites too had their ethnicity thrust upon them by the phenomenal reality, that is, by the inescapable awareness that their superior social status rested primordially on their whiteness. The characters that populate the pages of Caribbean literature are inexorably conscious of their phenotypical characteristics, whatever racial classification they might fit into. They represent individuals whose history has rendered them inevitably racial beings.

Regarding "wandering", the third unifying factor cited by Sánchez, the movement of peoples between territories – from the ships of the conquistadores to the vessels of the Middle Passage to the massive migrations of Antilleans to Europe and the United States in recent times – is at the crux of the Caribbean experience. Above we quoted Van Sertima's and Gikandi's testimonies to the overwhelming proportion of Anglophone West Indian writers who have lived and worked away from their original home. Writers from the Spanish-speaking Caribbean have become increasingly involved with the drama of emigration. Not only is there a sizeable and growing body of texts written by Cubans, Puerto Ricans, and Dominicans in the United States, but also the works of writers who have not left the islands often deal with characters whose conflicts arise from or lead to issues associated with emigration or exile. In the Francophone Caribbean, too, as J. Michael Dash reminds us, "exile and return" or the "motifs of flight and return" are a constant concern of the writers (Dash 1994: 451).

Migration, of course, can be factual or mental, and in a sense the colonial condition has turned the Antillean man or woman into an existential migrant, an itinerant being, a person who wanders between worlds, between spaces, between traditions – which sometimes clash, sometimes come into strenuous harmony, but rarely cease to produce some tension. The Caribbean person, in the words of Gerald Guinness, is enmeshed in the "Here and Elsewhere" dialectic, a sort of "embrace" that "has always been a problematic one", but which he believes to be of great benefit to literary creation: "To live Here, physically or in one's imagination, and yet to have to cope with the constant push and pull of Elsewhere concentrates the mind wonderfully" (Guinness 1993: xii). In praising the gifts of V. S. Naipaul, Guinness highlights particularly the novelist's ability to navigate the tensions stemming from the "Here/Elsewhere" dialectic. He speaks of Naipaul as "our ace cultural trouble shooter, the man who shuttles between first and third worlds and between ex-colonizers and ex-colonized, to bring back reports of the continuing relationship between these estranged partners, still locked in symbiotic embrace long after the official divorce has been settled out of court. Naipaul's books are in a sense progress reports on the unavailing efforts of Caliban to throw off Prospero's spell" (p. 194).

Guinness' reference to Prospero and Caliban, and thereby to the colonial experience symbolized in that binary opposition, suggests also the value of history itself as another major paradigm that many view as a unifying factor in so far as it appears as a constant in Caribbean literature. There is already a sizable scholarship built around the exploration of the historical imagination in the region's literary production, a considerable portion of which tackles the interrelationship between myth and history. A recent example of that sort of undertaking is Barbara J. Webb's *Myth and History in the Caribbean*, which seeks to illustrate the harmonious interaction of myth and history in the region's texts. Webb undertakes a reading of Alejo Carpentier, Edouard Glissant, and Wilson Harris, three major Caribbean novelists and essayists who represent different linguistic sectors, to find that for them "the folk or mythic imagination is the key to artistic vision and historical understanding", and to establish that they have had recourse to myth in a common effort "to transform the void of historical rupture and fragmentation into an open-ended vision of possibility" (Webb 1992: 4, 149).

Webb's study is celebrated by Nepaulsingh as "a powerful little book" that collaborates in an "enormously important project", but it is treated with reserve by A. James Arnold who sees in it the "literary-philosophical reductions" typical of the modernists who too easily lapse into "myth and its literary derivatives" when confronted with the fractious history of the region (Nepaulsingh 1993: 206; Arnold 1995: 104). But there is much to be said for the historical imagination in Caribbean writing. Literary scholars ought to understand their job not as one of identifying a principle of unity in the historical events that have shaped the region but of exploring the comparable manifestations of the historical experience in the literary texts. Their area of perusal is the generalized engagement of the writers with what has taken place in their space. The events themselves may differ and the writers' philosophy of history may show striking disparities. A useful parallelism stems from their common necessity to speak to the present meaning of past events and their acute self-awareness as beings in the midst of historical processes. The density of the memory captured in the texts of writers throughout the region makes for an appreciable unifying element, and so does myth, if it is found to be widespread enough.

In addition to history, one may argue for the inclusion of religion and language among the major paradigms that permit the study of Caribbean literature as an intelligible unit. The omnipresence of religion, understood in its most general sense as the supernatural, what Lucretius called *superstitio*, reveals a major sphere of kinship among literary texts throughout the region. Kamau Brathwaite's *Barabajan Poems* (1994), which gathers pieces and reflections spanning much of the poet's career, largely illustrates the widespread view of the inseparability of the earthly and the sacred in Caribbean life. The literary works of Antillean writers like René Depestre, from his first book in 1945 to his *Hadriana dans tous mes rêves* (1988) which won him the Prix Renaudot, could not be conceived without constant meditation on the spiritual dimensions of life in the region. A list of all the Caribbean literary works that touch on religious matters, including those that do so in a negative way by denying or challenging the validity of the sacred, would absorb the greater bulk of the artistic writings produced in the region.

Similarly, the engagement with language, which in the Caribbean has been the source of tension but never of dismay for the literary artist, provides a pregnant field for exploration as a principle of regional coherence. Caribbean writers have not succumbed to the crisis of language that Western thinkers speak of in reference to their postindustrial society. A significant strand of Césaire's poetry presents us with a voice that "speaks to beget a world recreated in man's measure," as Joan Dayan says, "a welder of words" who gives his word power over things" (1983: 422-23). As Nepaulsingh asserts, "the prime function of language has always been, to the insular intellect, liberation, not imprisonment" (1993: 203). This sort of declaration is much in keeping with the spirit prevalent in J. Edward Chamberlin's *Come Back to Me My Language* (1993), a study of contemporary West Indian poetry that draws a celebration of language from the literary texts examined. The author concludes his inquiry with the affirmation that West Indian poets have given "to the rest of us, courage and understanding too. And a new faith in the power of language" (Chamberlin 1993: 274). The editors of *Voiceprint: An Anthology of Oral and Related poetry from the Caribbean* would seem to confirm Chamberlin's celebratory mood, pointing, in addition, to the fact that orality must of necessity figure in general accounts of an aesthetic for the region. They assert that "a West Indian aesthetic will embrace all ways of saying, all language registers, however different some of these may seem or be" (Brown, Morris and Rohlehr 1989: 23).

The reference to language registers alerts us also to a linguistic situation that rivals the racial situation in layers of complexity. In addition to English, French, Spanish, and Dutch, Caribbean languages include Papiamentu, Sranan Tongo, Hindi, various forms of West Indian Creole, and Haitian Creole, to name only the most prominent. Caribbean societies go from monolingual to bilingual to multilingual, showing also diverse relationships between European languages and linguistic formations endemic to the region. Linguists describe as either *diglossia* or *continuum* the typical interactions between the polar extremes of a European linguistic standard and an indigenous Creole formation (Alleyne 1985: 166). The question may arise as to whether one should not consider the possibility of "one, two or three literatures" arising out of the multiple linguistic registers. Thinking of the *diglossia* that typifies the Francophone Antilles, Ulrich Fleischmann raises such an issue regarding the "different and conflicting patterns of culture" that emerge from the coexistence of French and Creole (Fleischmann 1994: 318). However, the dominant impetus among the region's scholars and artists has been to look for an overarching link among the linguistic gradations of the continuum. Many have celebrated their sense of a gradual breaking down of the walls that – through class prejudice and cultural elitism – have normally segregated the literary expressions of Creolophone writers from those using standard European forms. The recognition now enjoyed by Louise Bennett in literary anthologies and histories of the Anglophone Caribbean bears testimony to that celebration.

The currency and popularity of dub poetry, which is presently the subject of performances in Europe, the United States, the Caribbean, and "countries all around the globe" denote a tendency towards a greater harmony between literate and folk linguistic expressions (Habekost 1993: 205).

Linguistic Creolization, of course, often assumes subtle forms. In the works of Depestre, the juxtaposition of the "français littéraire" and the local colour of Haitian usage produces the linguistic atmosphere of what the author has referred to as "l'usage maternel du français", regardless of whether or not morphologically recognizable Creole forms occur in his texts. Similarly, Brathwaite has convincingly argued for the presence of "nation language" in Anglophone West Indian writers who may not employ dialect forms in their texts. Indeed, in the Spanish-speaking Caribbean, the linguistic bloc deemed by the scholars as the most monolithic, many of the most salient works – namely *La guaracha del Macho Camacho* (1976) by the Puerto Rican Luis Rafael Sánchez, *Tres tristes tigres* (1968) by the Cuban Guillermo Cabrera Infante, and *Sólo cenizas hallarás* (1980) by the Dominican Pedro Vergés – achieve their aesthetic distinction by forging an idiom that convincingly deviates from a standard European linguistic norm and by their felicitous approximation of a regional Spanish.

Language, in other words, whether European or Creole, provides just as an engaging field of pan-Caribbean exploration as race, music, history, and religion. They all yield paradigms that aid in the investigation of the region's literary unity. The present list of unifying tropes does not profess to be exhaustive. Nor can the region claim to have invented the notions of music, race, wandering, history, religion, and language as issues of concern to literary artists. But we can speak of a particularly Caribbean kind of involvement with them. The particularity of that involvement cuts across language barriers and national boundaries, providing the grounds for holistic appraisals of the literary act in the region and permitting its study from a comparative and multidisciplinary perspective. The regional pervasiveness of the unifying factors noted here opens a world of possibility for scholars interested in a panoptic glance at Caribbean texts, and such a glance seems now more feasible than ever in light of the synoptic works – produced by women and men – that have become available over the last several years.

The most encompassing research tool ever to have been assembled, with the potential for shaping the configuration of and the debate on Caribbean literature henceforward, is the three-volume compendium *A History of Literature in the Caribbean* edited by A. James Arnold with J. Michael Dash and Julio Rodríguez-Luis as sub-editors, under the auspices of the International Comparative Literature Association. Born of nearly a decade of vigorous, passionate, and patient academic labour, Arnold's *History* really treads uncharted ground in its ambitious attempt to map "the literature of the entire Caribbean, the islands as well as the continental littoral, as one cultural region." Volume one covers the Hispanic and Francophone regions. Volume two traces the development of literary activity in the Anglophone and Dutch-speaking regions, and the third volume examines the whole Caribbean corpus cross-culturally and comparatively. Without fear of exaggeration, we can regard the goal of creating "a history of Caribbean literature that could be read across the linguistic divisions both for commonalities and for regional cultural differences" as an unqualified success (Arnold 1994: xiv). The very coming into being of the *History* constitutes palpable evidence of the unity of Caribbean literature, which, like Western literature, can absorb disparities, inconsistencies, and even contradictions without compromising its oneness. Of course, the study of this literature across the linguistic divisions would not have become feasible if there had not existed bodies of scholarship, literary history, critical discourse, and compilations attesting to the unity of texts produced within each of the linguistic blocs. The remainder of this chapter, therefore, will briefly survey holistic assessments of the region's literature within the Francophone, Anglophone, Dutch-speaking, and Spanish-speaking Caribbean, the literatures written in the local Creoles, such as Papiamentu and Sranan Tongo staying outside the scope of this work.

The Oneness within Linguistic Blocs

The discussion of linguistic blocs should begin with a disclaimer. This study will not do justice to the literary activities taking place in Curaçao, Aruba, Bonaire, Sint Eustatius, Saba, and Sint Maarten, the six islands formerly known as the Netherlands Antilles, nor in Suriname, due to the writer's insufficient knowledge of Dutch or the distinctive Creoles of those parts of the Caribbean. But also the lack of accessible material on the literature written there hampers adequate treatment of it. The fact that in what was for long the most thorough reference work on the literature of the Caribbean, the editor devoted to this part only forty-four pages while the English-, French-, and Spanish-speaking areas got an average of over 295 pages each gives an idea of the precarious state of the available scholarship on this area (Herdeck 1979). For long in the United States we had no available sources providing a systematic study of the literature of Suriname and the Netherlands Antilles. Published in 2001, the contrastive study of the Dutch-, Papiamentu-, and Sranan-speaking region of the Caribbean organized by the scholar Ineke Phaf for volume 2 of Arnold's *History* now constitutes a major milestone in addressing the former dearth of information. The visibility of the writers from these areas of the Caribbean began to increase in the U.S. academy with the publication of a special issue of *Callaloo* (21.3 [1998]), guest edited by Hilda van Neck-Yoder. However, prior to these developments, the work of some individual scholars who had ventured overviews on the literary production of this part of the Caribbean suggested that this literature displays significant "points of contact with the general spiritual consciousness" characterizing the entire territory (Debrot 1963: 1899). Likewise, the "Caribbean image-forming process" of the nation-building idea prevalent in the literature of the Netherlands Antilles and Suriname parallels the same "image-forming" and nation-building trend we find in the texts from the rest of the Caribbean (Phaf 1988: 168). An essay by Phaf (1990) on women writers from the Dutch-speaking Caribbean suggested a gender interaction that compares with the confrontation of the female discourse with the patriarchal structures that govern the intelligentsia elsewhere in the region. A reading of these sources convinces us that literary artists here face cultural and aesthetic problems similar to those encountered by writers in the other linguistic areas. I will, therefore, dare to assume that my claims concerning the other large linguistic sectors of the Caribbean may apply equally to this bloc as well.

Francophone Caribbean Literature

Commentators on Francophone Caribbean literature have long presented it as a corpus that differs from that of France. In the late 1940s, Léopold Sédar Senghor's famous *Anthologie de la nouvelle poésie nègre et malgache* grouped the poems of Léon-Gontran Damas (Guiana); Gilbert Gratiant, Etienne Lero, and Aimé Césaire (Martinique); Guy Tirolien and Paul Niger (Guadeloupe); and Léon Laleau, Jacques Roumain, Jean-F. Brièrre, and René Belance (Haiti), with poems from black Africa and Madagascar. What for Senghor served as a link between the Caribbean poets and the others featured in the anthology was that they all "assert their blackness with their talent" (Senghor 1948: 2). Like Senghor, literary scholars chronicling Francophone Caribbean writing have tended to see this body of texts in the context of Pan-African ideologies and to refer to them as "voices of negritude", thus assigning centrality to the question of race in defining their literary identity.[4] This tendency no doubt has its roots in the conspicuous role played by Caribbean writers such as Damas and Césaire in the negritude movement.

The approach which presents Francophone Caribbean literature as an undifferentiated component of the larger corpus designated as "literature of the Black world" has encountered sound opposition. Daniel Racine argued that an account of French Antillean poetry ought to include the likes of Saint-John Perse, a white man who "has extolled a common essence", just as one includes the black poets who marshalled the negritude movement (Racine 1974: 75). Racine's observation of the pitfall of dwelling on blackness in assessing French Antillean literature is well taken. As we have noted before, the region does not lend itself to a monolithic presentation of race. But the place of Perse in Francophone Caribbean literature is not unproblematic. One could argue that calling Perse's texts Caribbean would be the same as calling those of Albert Camus Algerian, those of Rudyard Kipling Indian, those of Phillis Wheatley Ethiopian or those of Jacques Derrida North African. With a well established spot in the history of French letters, Perse does have a place among Caribbean writers but not in quite the same way that Césaire and Alexis do. Perse is not Caribbean, says Glissant, since he "is not involved in this history, in that he was free to walk away from it" (1989: 227). Paradoxically, as Glissant himself argues, walking away is one of the manifestations of Caribbeanness.[5]

In addition to viewing Francophone Caribbean texts within the larger context of black literature, scholars have also placed them geographically among Francophone writing of the Americas, as Maryse Condé once noted (1972: 170). Condé had in mind panoramic surveys of New World literature in French such as that offered by the Swiss scholar Auguste Viatte that covers writers from the Caribbean along with those from Canada and Louisiana (Viatte 1971). In an earlier piece on the literature of Martinique, Guadeloupe, and Guiana, Viatte's manner of understanding the literary phenomenon as it occurs in the area becomes particularly clear. He characterized Perse as "uncontestably the most illustrious offspring of the Antilles" (Viatte 1963: 1369). His assigning the highest praise to the one Antillean-born writer who was grouped among European literary figures would suggest that he viewed Caribbean literary achievement strictly in terms of Western aesthetic value. Viatte singles out for excellence a writer who does not resemble the typical literary artists from the region, suggesting, in addition, that he did not associate Caribbean writing with an independent literary identity, especially since Perse won the Nobel Prize for literature in 1960 as a French writer. Viatte only granted to the texts from the French overseas departments the quality of an intermediary between France and Europe, the French-speaking parts of the American continent, and Francophone Africa (Viatte 1963: 1369).

Viatte revealed also a tendency among some scholars of Francophone Caribbean literature to separate the "Petites Antilles" (Martinique and Guadeloupe) and "la Guyane" (French Guiana) from Haiti, though he acknowledged a certain resemblance among them (1963: 1369). The splitting of the Francophone Caribbean into two separate cultural blocs has had one of its most articulate exponents in Jack Corzani, a French literary historian who has written a six-volume compendium on the literature of Martinique, Guadeloupe and Guiana. Corzani has argued that one cannot include Haiti in the same literary chronicle with the other Antilles except on the basis of blackness since the crucial events shaping the two parts of the Francophone Caribbean did not follow a common path. Haiti, with its independence in 1803, charted its historical evolution along a way that differed radically from those of Guadeloupe, Guiana, and Martinique, which have remained French colonies (Corzani 1978: I, 28). The same kind of reasoning may lurk behind the editorial decision of Gastmann (1978) and Herdeck (1979) to separate Haiti from the French Antilles.

Corzani does well in shunning negritude as an insufficient link to account for homogeneity in the Francophone Caribbean. Yet, the difference in juridical status can hardly be deemed a strong argument to set Haiti apart from the three "départements". The difference in political structure may not have made that much of a difference in the lives of people in the four societies. Haiti did acquire its juridical independence early in the nineteenth century, but it also has, just like the French departments, endured since then a most dire economic dependence on outside powers. In that respect, these societies have in comparable ways lived the condition of what Paulo Freire calls "object societies", existing thereby in a state of dependence upon the "director societies" of the West. The Brazilian thinker says that: "The action of the metropolitan society upon the dependent society has a directive character, whereas the object society's action, whether it be responsive or initiative, has a dependent character" (Freire 1970: 33). Even if Haiti abolished slavery and declared itself independent earlier than any other object society it did not erase the social problems and the mental structures firmly established by a long history of the colonial transaction in the island. Corzani himself would admit that the juridical abolition of slavery hardly sufficed to erase the vestiges of that institution (Corzani 1978: VI, 275).

One would also do well to remember that historically Haiti went through stages of (under) development that are comparable to those of Martinique, Guadeloupe, and French Guiana. The four societies became in the seventeenth century the seats of plantation economies, and the four have ended up as dependent societies in the twentieth century. The four saw the rise of anti-slavery and liberation movements in the early nineteenth century, though only Haiti was able to achieve national independence. But this independence was only consolidated in 1838 when Haiti's sovereignty was recognized by France at the cost of 90 million francs per year paid by Haiti to France as compensation for material losses suffered by the planters when the slaves decided to change their lot. Ten years later slavery would be abolished in Guadeloupe, Guiana, and Martinique.

By the end of the nineteenth-century France had already lost Haiti as a sphere of influence, having been supplanted by a younger imperial power, the United States of America, whose Monroe Doctrine was gaining momentum in the Western hemisphere. The United States felt the need to invade Haiti militarily in 1915 just as, in 1940, French forces, under Pétain proceeded to occupy Guadeloupe, Guiana, and Martinique. On January 1, 1948 the legislation whereby these three colonies became "départements" went into effect, and in 1957 the United States-supported François Duvalier seized power as President-for-life in Haiti. To this day the four nations have retained a comparable condition of semi-colonial economic and political dependence. Even a historical overview as scanty as the foregoing would suffice to make one doubt that the juridical difference in the status of Haiti constitutes a strong basis for dividing Francophone Caribbean literature into two cultural blocs.

Corzani discusses the keys that account for the "secrète unité" of French Antillean writing, having to do with the common history that has formed the people of the region, a people that has endured deracination, imposition of a alien tongue, inferiorization, and debasement (1978: VI, 282). But the same applies to the Haitian situation. Haitian writers, too, appear constantly preoccupied with their language and their culture. One also notes their frequent exploration of history or their effort to eradicate the traces of colonial oppression just as Corzani notes in the thematic concerns of authors from the overseas departments (Corzani 1978: VI, 276, 283). The frequency with which creative writers from the French departments have looked to Haiti for historical archetypes and regional symbols indicates their deep sense of cultural kinship.

Glissant's *Monsieur Toussaint* (1961) and Césaire's *Toussaint Louverture* (1962), two texts by Martinicans based on the life of the leader of the Haitian Revolution, come first to mind. Glissant has been particularly emphatic in highlighting the historical grounds that bind the peoples of the French departments with the people of Haiti: "Until the war of liberation waged by Toussaint Louverture, the peoples of Martinique, Guadeloupe, and Saint-Domingue (which then became Haiti) struggled together in solidarity. This applied as much to the colonizers as to the slaves in revolt and the freedmen (generally mulattoes) [...] Such was the case for Delgrès, of Martinican origin, who fell with his Guadeloupean companions at Fort Matouba in Guadeloupe, and whose example was so dear to the heart of Dessalines, Toussaint's lieutenant" (Glissant 1989: xl). Besides, certain *topoi* such as the figure of the maroon, have engaged the imagination of writers with equal intensity in both Haiti and the French departments. They both have "conveyed through the archetypal maroon figure a Caribbean idiosyncrasy of paramount import for the understanding of the region that is still searching for its identity" (Silenieks 1984: 124). Vere Knight would suggest that Haitian literature served as a decisive source for writers in the overseas departments. The dominant concerns of the negritude movement, she affirms, "come first of all from *Légitime Défense* and later from *Tropiques*, but they are familiar because they appeared some time ago in the literature of the Haitians" (Knight 1975: 82, 88). She reminds us that Damas had occasion to acknowledge the influence of the Haitian Jean Price-Mars on the principles upheld by the group.

There exist other persuasive indicators to question the division of the Francophone Caribbean into two distinct cultural and artistic sectors. For one thing, the data put forward by specialists indicate that the process of "nativization" of the French language that led to the development of Antillean Creole has occurred across the board (Prudent 1984: 21). Nor has the "nativization" of religion been less pronounced in one part than in the other. A scholar discussing the Haitian novel documents the omnipresence of "vodoun" there in terms that echo Condé's illustration of the recurrence of "Quimbois" among the women novelists she has studied in the French overseas departments (Hoffman 1982: 133; Condé 1979: 49). Another scholar, studying novelists of both sexes from both parts of the Francophone Caribbean, finds these writers equally concerned with the exploration of their immediate socio-cultural milieu and points to the creation of a set of images representing a "particular, personal vision of the Caribbean social context" as a common thread linking the works of the authors examined, namely Roumain, Glissant, Lacrosil, Zobel, Stephen Alexis, and Schwarz-Bart (Ormerod 1985: 137).

Condé finds the following: "Between the female novelists of the Lesser Antilles and those of Haiti, the distance has not seemed considerable to us [...] By the same token, our faith in the unity of the Caribbean has found comfort" (Condé 1979: 113). And, like her, many prominent French Caribbean literary artists have proclaimed the conviction evident in this rhetorical question posed by a character in Daniel Maximin's Guadeloupean novel *L'isolé soleil*: "All the Antilleans, are they not part of the same civilization?" (Maximin 1981: 212). This view of the Caribbean as a culturally homogenous totality, which numbers Glissant among its most eloquent proponents, has become well known in the Francophone Caribbean. Termed "antillanité", the notion came to occupy in the minds of notable intellectuals the place formerly accorded to the concept of negritude. Condé describes "antillanité" as another state of a cultural progression which seeks to emphasize the complexity of the Antillean heritage as distinct from negritude which characterized itself by "utter dissent" (1972: 175).

The utterances quoted above, from Viatte to Condé, reflect the two positions most often appealed to by writers trying to fathom the area. They either tend to emphasize the peculiarity of each nation, undermining regional unity, or to highlight the regional commonality, down-playing local specificities. Jean Benoist has referred to these polarized perceptions "contradictory temptations" (cited in Condé 1979: 5). Hoffmann's study of the Haitian novel so stresses the uniqueness of Haitian culture that he feels the need to deny the very existence of a Caribbean culture. For him the very concept of "la Caraïbe" can have validity only in a strictly geographical sense (1982: 26, 24-27). Since Hoffmann invokes the authority of Sidney W. Mintz' *Caribbean Transformations* to buttress his contention, perhaps it would help to clarify that in that text the prestigious social scientist indeed warns us against those who "by treating the region as homogeneous and undifferentiated, have created an image of sameness that reflects poorly the extent to which these societies differ", but he also cautions against the excessive specialization of those who "have been limited to particular cases, making generalizations very difficult." Mintz does not in any way question the cultural homogeneity of the region. He simply recommends that we avoid gross simplifications in any assertion of the unity of the Caribbean, particularly when upholding the notion of Caribbean nationhood, insinuating that we must separate culture from politics. He states that "commonality of origin, commonality of social form or of belief, commonality of fate, and a common territory may be thought of by some to underlie nationhood – but they emphatically do not equal it" (Mintz 1974: 264-65).

Proponents of Caribbean disunity may also stress what some perceive as the great "fidélité" of the people of the overseas French departments towards their "hérédité française" as a strong distinguishing feature in their history. But Condé, reacting to this argument, questions the validity of such a premise. She recalls the thousands of slaves who hurled themselves into the ocean from the slave ships, or who trained themselves to keep quiet, or who starved to death, or killed their children, or poisoned their masters, before accepting their lot. She lists many awesome events, including recent ones in Basse Terre, Pointe-à-Pitre, and Fort-de-France, which evince a tenacious legacy of resistance and a continuous thread of "marronage" against the French power structure as a vivid element of the area's history. "What fidelity are we talking about?" Condé asks rhetorically (1972: 173). Condé has actually traced the birth of an authentic Francophone Caribbean literature to the time "when the West Indians realized that if history had brought them under French rule, this did not mean they should be mere copies of the French people" – in other words, when they put an end to their "fidélité" towards the Gallic heritage (Condé 1968: 786).

The voices of regional unity in the Francophone Caribbean clearly have the upper hand in the debate. The most sophisticated among them have circumvented the sense of dichotomy by highlighting, as do the ideologues of "antillanité", the complexity of the region's culture and allowing for the possibility of variety within homogeneity. Able to transcend the contradictory temptations of polar extremes, they have come upon a third option, the possibility of a global sense of unity which can account for the internal diversity of the area. The most convincing approaches to the Caribbean focus on certain general mechanisms, mostly grounded in culture, that yield an undeniable coherence to the region, without presuming to erase whatever idiosyncrasies people from the various nations may have. Culture for our purpose here means no more than the way people do things in the midst of given socio-historical circumstances, the things they do constituting their cultural products, a definition that would fall within the purview of anthropological renditions of the concept (cf. Singer 1968: 527-43).

When one looks closely at cultural products coming from Haiti, Martinique, Guadeloupe and Guiana, their encompassing thread of commonality comes easily into view. Surely, these societies have their local specificities, as they should, but not so as to clash with their sense of unity.

Anglophone Caribbean Literature

Discussion of cultural and artistic homogeneity both within the West Indies and the wider Caribbean began in the Anglophone Caribbean rather later than in the French Antilles. For colonial education in the region, literature usually meant English literature exclusively, and the difficulties of inter-island travel meant that until air flights became more widespread there was little literary communication among the islands and British Guiana. Ideas for a West Indian federation that was not just a bureaucratic convenience of the colonial office go back to the early twentieth century at least. The activities of politicians such as the Grenadian T.A. Marryshow and his newspaper, *The West Indian*, and later of the trade unionists of the Caribbean Labour Congress approached the goal of unity from a popular perspective. But significantly the first influential Anglophone literary text that expresses a Caribbean identity is George Lamming's novel *The Emigrants* (1954), where it is only on the ship bound for England that the people from the different islands grow a sense of their commonality. As the JAMAICAN says to his fellow travellers:

> Me say to myself the two o' you come from different island but him talk the way you talk an' it ain't make no difference at all. De wahter separatin' you from him ain't do nothin' to put distance between de views you got on dis life or de next. Different man, different land, but de same outlook. Dat's de meanin' o' West Indies. De wahter between dem islands doan' separate dem. Many o' man in Jamaica would expound de same view, an' dere's a worl' o' sea between me an' you. (1954: 62-63)

In *The Pleasures of Exile* (1960), with its emphasis on writers such as Samuel Selvon, and himself, who gave voice to the "folk", in its historical sweep in paraphrasing C.L.R. James's *The Black Jacobins* (1938) and its seeking of cross Caribbean roots in the tonelles of Haiti, Lamming expresses a sense of Caribbeanness that crosses language boundaries. Other texts from this time expressed a localised country identity, such as J.E.C. McFarlane's *A Literature in the Making* (1956), which surveyed Jamaican writing to that date. Again, most of the earlier anthologies of Caribbean writing were mainly single country collections such as those by McFarlane (1929; 1949) from Jamaica, and N.E. Cameron (1931) from British Guiana. The texts that seek to chronicle Anglophone Caribbean literature as a separate, but unified corpus mostly date from the 1960s. Kenneth Ramchand, an early anthologist, adduced pedagogical reasons for justifying his compilation, arguing that since English literature offered a world essentially alien to the immediate reality of students in the West Indies, a collection which included West Indian writers would make it easier for young readers to respond to the contents of the texts. Ramchand, however, did not wish to engage in iconoclasm, so he made sure to clarify that in making his selection he did not "wish to lay down geographical and nationalistic boundaries in literature" (Ramchand 1966: 3). In an anthology that had appeared a year earlier, the late Andrew Salkey ventured his perception of the West Indian writer's awareness "that he may use the language of the English writer in order to discover the quintessence of his 'West Indianness'", though he did not think that West Indian writing had yet become an easily recognizable "way of writing" (Salkey 1970: 13). In the mid 1960s, in the Anglophone Caribbean literary arena, the notion still seemed to need asserting that there was a distinctly West Indian literature, and that it was not merely "a province of English letters". Some of this sense of beginning from nothing was due to ignorance of what had gone before; the published writing of Trinidadians such as C.L.R. James, A.H. Mendes and others in the magazines *Trinidad* or *The Beacon* was only republished in the 1970s. However, it is worth noting that in more implicit ways a pan-West Indian literary consciousness was present in three important literary institutions at an earlier date. The "little" magazines, *Kyk-over-Al* (1945-1961 and following) from British Guiana, edited by A.J. Seymour, and *Bim* (1942- with some years of non publication), from Barbados, edited by Frank Collymore, were both avowedly regional in their selection of material. Above all, there was the *Caribbean Voices* radio programme, which broadcast poetry, short stories and critical reviews from across the region between 1943-1958. Much of the anthology work of the 1960s was based on *Caribbean Voices* material or the work of writers who had emerged to view through it.

O.R. Dathorne figures among the first to have attempted to isolate some of the distinguishing features of the area's literature. He noted, among other things, the peculiarly regional nature of the material used by West Indian novelists. He pointed also to the "polygeneous mass of races that intermingle in the West Indian novel", distinguishing it from the narrower dimensions of standard European fiction, and identified the Caribbean writer's "definite striving for a historical sense" (Dathorne 1966: 9-11). Concerning the area's poetry, while finding much of it derivative of nineteenth century conventionalism, he perceived a poetic corpus with a distinct West Indian character, one in which "both English literature and language have been forced into a West Indianizing process" (Dathorne 1967: 15). He thus had no qualms about attributing an identity of its own to this literature.

John Figueroa in another famous compilation, based on *Caribbean Voices* broadcast material, reflected a good deal of the tension and the ambivalence typical of many general statements about Caribbean culture and art at the time in the English-speaking part of the region. Figueroa doubted the existence of a poetic corpus that one could call strictly Caribbean but admitted this poetry's concern with "what it means to be a West Indian", a concern which he found "difficult to separate from the racial, political and religious" condition of the area (Figueroa 1973: II, 9). Also, while he perceived nothing but futility in any effort to identify strictly West Indian themes, he acknowledged the linguistic peculiarity of West Indian writing, noting, for instance, that: "The 'structure' of the traditional English lyric, and the pattern of West Indian speech are likely to be at variance with each other" (Figueroa 1973: II, 11-13, 15). But the sort of ambivalence represented by Figueroa virtually disappeared by the beginning of the 1970s. Now most typical renditions of the area's literary art almost invariably assert its distinctness with confidence.

Salkey, overcoming his former hesitation, began to assert that the development of the outstanding poets of the area was inextricably "linked with and dependent upon our acquisition of the awareness of people, place and history in the Caribbean" (Salkey 1971: xviii). By the mid-1970s the cultural coherence of the region could be articulated with this fervour: "Out of the fragmented peoples of Caribbean social history has come a whole people with increasing awareness of their common heritage" (Livingston 1974: 7, 14). With Edward Kamau Brathwaite, Orlando Patterson, John La Rose and others, Salkey was active in the London-based Caribbean Artists Movement (CAM), which was influential both in asserting a cross-regional, cross-lingual sense of identity and in the cultural autonomy of the region.

In the 1980s, the certainty with which the unity and uniqueness of the area's literature is assumed can be gathered from the self-conscious tenor of James Berry, whose anthology aims "to take another step towards the establishment of West Indian writing, generally, in its own right" (Berry 1984: xii). Since then it has become natural to affirm with editor Paula Burnett that: "Caribbean literature is, of course, first of all by and for Caribbean people. Like any other culture, it gives expression to a particular people's experience" (1986: xxii). As this brief account suggests, the compilers of Anglophone Caribbean literature moved from a timid expression of uniqueness to the prevailing sense of categorical affirmation (Brown, Morris, and Rohlehr 1989: Markham 1989; Brown 1990).

The critics and historians of the area's literary achievement have followed a not dissimilar path. The English editor of the first book-length collection of critical essays on the literature of the Anglophone West Indies began his introduction to the book with the caveat that since history in the area has impeded the development of a coherent culture, one must view the achievements of Caribbean writers "against a background of disruption", yet at the book's close his afterword timidly allowed for the possibility that: "In some ways the literature covered in this book forms a unity" (James 1968: 1, 154). When the book was reviewed in London the impression it gave the reviewer was that the diversity of views included in it seemed consistent with the ambiguity that characterized literature and culture in the Caribbean, with writers who were inescapably beset by their chosen attitude toward "West Indianness" (Lucie-Smith 1968: 97). When *The Islands In Between* was reviewed in the Caribbean, it was assailed as a neo-colonial production by Sylvia Wynter in an important couple of articles in *Jamaica Journal* (Wynter 1968, 1969).

From the end of the 1960s, however, it became customary for critics and historians of Anglophone Caribbean literature to approach this corpus holistically. Gerald Moore discussed the centrality of non-English sources in the language and culture of these writers (1969/1970: xviii). Ramchand's study of the West Indian novel identified "the assimilation of linguistic properties" coming from "the oral usages of the folk" as a common thread shown by West Indian writers (1970: 114). In a later work, Ramchand raised the possibility that one could write national accounts that would demonstrate fundamental differences between writers in the region according to their different nations (1976). But in a more recent study he seemed to have settled for a view of Caribbean literature as a cultural institution whose unity is stronger than that of any political institution such as the West Indian Federation (Ramchand 1988: 95).

Looking at the novels of Edgar Mittelholzer, Michael Gilkes pointed to a "psychic division, a split in consciousness" evident in the novelist's vision and suggests that this can serve as a model for viewing Caribbean writing. I see the polarized options exemplified by Naipaul and Lamming as an illustration of this bifurcation (Gilkes 1975: 36). Later, though, in a general study of the West Indian novel, he arrives at the conclusion that Caribbean writing has resolved the split, having already "begun to move in the direction of a paradoxical mixture of the oral and the scribal, a nonlinear yet representational mode", thus coming to terms with "its paradoxical principle of diversity" which makes it, referring specifically to the novel, "both indigenous and universal" (Gilkes 1981: 157-58). This scholar's observations evince the totalizing claims now current in renditions of the literary production of the Anglophone Caribbean.

Furthermore, an array of critics has proclaimed not only the regional coherence but also the aesthetic autonomy of this literature. Decades ago, in praise of Derek Walcott's dexterous handling of the Western literary tradition, scholars would assert that "the greatest nationalist writers in French and Spanish as well as English, in modern Africa as well as the West Indies, have been those who have been able most fully to come to their own predicaments through the mastery of the European literary experience" (King and James 1968: 90). Many Caribbean intellectuals have in subsequent pronouncements superseded the aesthetic dependency implicit in such an affirmation. One could argue, indeed, that "the West Indian writer has been the most insistent, and certainly the most persuasive, articulator of a West Indian consciousness which defines a special cultural identity in the region and its literature, and which in the process endows that literature with a unifying principle and with a corporate national image" (Brown 1984: 8). Lloyd Brown's recognition of the region's literary artists' "deliberate self-definitions" and his proposed examination of this literary corpus "in the light of a growing West Indian consciousness" would point to a process of artistic de-Westernization rather than to the aesthetic dependency espoused by some (Brown 1984: 9). By the late 1970s the notion of West Indian letters as "a whole literature" had already become firmly established in the area's critical discourse (Baugh 1978: 11). Some trace the origin of this totalizing concept to "the period after the Second World War when a sense of community between the writers of various parts of the region was established" (King 1979: 7-8). In the 1980s, local critics sought further to emphasize the autochthonous nature of this literature by exploring its relationship with forms and expressions coming from the popular folk tradition. At a conference held on the Cave Hill campus of the University of the West Indies, Mervyn Morris highlighted the legacy of Jamaican Mikey Smith, whose "dub poetry" incorporates reggae rhythms, "usually in Jamaican creole, and often speaks out against oppression" (1985: 54). Another speaker pointed to the significance of "linguistic performances", theatrical-dramatic speech events, as they take place in the Caribbean, where their nature becomes inextricable from their "social context" (Creighton 1985: 56).

During the 1980s, in the Anglophone Caribbean, the critical discourse no longer wrestled with the issue of whether a literary corpus exists that may be deemed indigenous to the region and that pervades the whole English-speaking area. Rather, the concern was whether this literature requires special critical tools for its study and assessment as the collected volume *Critical Issues in West Indian Literature* (1984) demonstrates. Lloyd W. Brown, one of the contributors, argues for a "regionally relevant criticism" and urges literary scholars to go beyond the confines of English onto other linguistic sectors, aiming, that is, for "a broader regional exploration of Caribbean literature" (Brown 1984: 2, 5). Another contributor, the author of a very useful index of West Indian criticism, examines critical articles and book reviews by outside critics of West Indian literature to find them failing in the ability to recognize the subtle nuances bearing directly on the life of Caribbean people, with the result that they have tended to evaluate Caribbean writing strictly in terms of the Western tradition (Allis 1981, 1984: 8). The marked emphasis on the necessity to formulate an indigenous Caribbean aesthetics typifies the dominant trend in contemporary critical discourse in the Anglophone West Indies as the chapter on Brathwaite will show.

Hispanophone Caribbean Literature

The study of Hispanophone Caribbean literature presents levels of complexity that in some ways set its development slightly apart from the writings of the other linguistic blocs. Cuba, the Dominican Republic and Puerto Rico were the first Caribbean societies to have engaged in nation-building efforts. Seeking to break their ties with the Spanish empire in the nineteenth century, they preceded all other Caribbean societies, except Haiti, in igniting the process of separation from the European powers. At the same time they have been slower than their counterparts in the region in exploring possibilities for cultural self-definition outside the paradigms prescribed by Western culture.

Hispanophone Antillean thinkers anticipated those from the rest of the region in proclaiming the political and cultural unity of their three islands, but at the same time Hispanic Antilleans have tended to see themselves as part of the larger culture of mainland Latin America. In discussing the homogeneity of this literature, therefore, we cannot avoid dealing with the tension stemming from its relationship with the Latin American tradition. This need not be disabling, for, as Milan Kundera has intimated in relation to the Francophone Caribbean, "there are peoples whose identities are defined by the plurality, or rather by the duplicity, of their mediating contexts", and one could construe that "duplicity" or doubleness as a source of cultural strength (Kundera 1991: 48).

The dominant definitions of Latin American culture propounded by some of the most influential twentieth-century thinkers in the region have practically precluded the search for autochthonous expression in any source other than the West. In his celebrated *Seis ensayos en busca de nuestra expresión* (1928), the eminent philologist Pedro Henríquez Ureña presented the following view of Latin-American identity: "We not only write in the language of Castile, but we belong to the Roman world, the Roman family which constitutes a community, a cultural unit, descending from that world which Rome organized under its might. In the often repeated phrase of Sarmiento, we belong to the Roman Empire" (Henríquez Ureña 1960: 250). This statement captured the spirit of the intelligentsia's vision of Iberian-American regional unity. The prevalent thinking followed in the footsteps of José Enrique Rodó's famous essay, *Ariel* (1900), which extolled the virtues of "latinity" (latinidad) as the unifying force that held the nations of the hemisphere together. One thinks of a U.N. conference held in Buenos Aires in the 1940s to examine the topic: "Relationships Between the Cultures of Europe and Latin America." Some of the best-known Latin-American intellectual voices attended the event in order to exchange opinions with their European counterparts, who included figures of the stature of Jules Romains. A report of the conference indicates that a consensus prevailed regarding the affirmation by Alfonso Reyes that between European and Latin-American culture only "small differences, small shades" existed, which did not suffice "to differentiate two cultures" (Arias-Larreta 1965: viii).

Eurocentric definitions of Latin American culture have predominated in the intellectual discourse despite the legacy of José Martí whose 1891 essay "Our America" (Nuestra América) had promulgated the cultural emancipation of the region. A less prominent but significant trend has sought to promote an *indigenista* cultural heritage. Abraham Arias-Larreta, to whom we owe the report of the aforementioned U.N. conference, decries the inability of the Latin-American Westernized elite of the middle class to provide an authentic assessment of the region's cultural expression. In so doing, he appeals to "Indo-American" values, thus proposing a search for authentic cultural values based on symbols drawn from the indigenous peoples who lived in the area at the time when Christopher Columbus arrived (Arias-Larreta 1965: xii).

Whatever validity the notion of Indo-American identity may have for a definition of mainland Latin-American culture goes beyond the scope of our study. But the notion will not prove useful in describing the heritages available to the people of the Hispanophone Antilles. In the Dominican Republic, whose ethnic composition fairly resembles Cuba and Puerto Rico, over 80% of the population is either black or mulatto. The native pre-Columbian population of Santo Domingo had practically become extinct by the end of the sixteenth century, though literary artists continued to evoke the "Indian" as a symbol of Dominican patriotism, as Max Henríquez Ureña aptly observed (1945: 197). The African presence in Hispanic-Antillean culture did not become an issue in the literature until the twentieth century. Traditionally blackness surfaced only in the literary expressions of the folk and rarely without stereotypical treatments (Deive 1978: 151-74). Spanish-speaking Antilleans have lagged behind their counterparts in the rest of the Caribbean in the effort to highlight the African component of their culture. In fact, the Dominican case shows that often intellectuals have invoked pre-Columbian roots precisely to mitigate the overwhelming reality of the African presence.

At any rate, despite the vehemence with which Hispanophone Antillean scholars may have tried to define their cultural identity within the larger frame of Latin-American culture, they have not succeeded on the whole in earning credibility as producers of aesthetic objects in the eyes of the builders of intellectual discourse on the mainland. The briefest look at Spanish-American anthologies, compilations, and histories of literature will make it clear that cases such as those of the Cubans Nicolás Guillén and Alejo Carpentier, whose works have received continent-wide recognition and acclaim, are far from the norm. The norm, rather, is represented by the likes of Juan Antonio Corretjer, Aída Cartagena Portalatín, Fayad Jamis, Julia de Burgos, Domingo Moreno Jiménez, and Dulce María Loynaz, writers of superior artistic calibre whose names, though revered by their national audiences, seldom get included in the literary anthologies or histories produced in mainland Latin America.

The virtual absence of the Hispanophone Antilles in Latin-American literature texts would suggest a view of the islands as an area of lesser cultural expression. We shall not at this point undertake to show all the factors involved in the exclusion. But, clearly, these three nations, in addition to their common insular condition, share unique historical circumstances which separate them even from those parts of the Latin-American mainland nearest to them. In the realm of ideology, the recognition of a shared history and a common destiny for Cuba, the Dominican Republic, and Puerto Rico dates back to the nineteenth century when patriots of the intellectual and political prominence of the Cuban Martí saw the islands as the three Antilles that together are to be saved or together are to perish (Martí 1963: IV, 405).

Before Martí, the Puerto Rican Ramón Emeterio Betances had articulated the vision of Antillean unity that is succinctly expressed in his dictum "The Antilles for Antilleans" (Betances 1970: 115-16). Eugenio María de Hostos, the other great Puerto Rican patriot, had with equal fervour advocated Betances's notion of an Antillean Federation as the "final goal of our history" (Hostos 1942: 93-94). The Dominican military leader Gregorio Luperón had declared it erroneous and infamous "to be Dominican and not Antillean," that is, to conceive of a Dominican future without a commitment to that of Cuba and Puerto Rico (cited in Ferrer Gutiérrez 1940: 7). The Dominican Federico Henríquez y Carvajal, who in the latter half of the nineteenth century had befriended Betances, Hostos, and Martí still in 1945 decried the colonial status of Puerto Rico. Even then he held on to the hope that the Antillean Federation would one day come about (Rama 1975: 281).

A brief background to the fervour behind Puerto Rican, Cuban, and Dominican calls to regional unity would refer us to the political circumstances of the three islands in the late nineteenth century. Spain at the time was struggling desperately to preserve the last remnants of its formerly vast imperial domain in the Americas. Concurrently, the United States, under the foreign affairs policy known as the Monroe Doctrine, was seeking to consolidate its growing control over the Western hemisphere. Nowhere did the confrontation between the young empire and the aging one become more dramatic than in the Hispanophone Caribbean. Antillean patriots, then, while wishing for the liberation of their countries from the colonial domination of Spain, desired to avoid falling under the control of the United States. Thus, they understood that the three islands equally shared the peril of colonial subjection and judged it meaningless to struggle for the sovereignty of one nation separately from that of the other two. This historical conjuncture gave rise to the idea of the "Confederación Antillana", the necessary political union of the three nations.

The dream of the Antillean Federation, as we all know, did not come to fruition. American troops occupied Puerto Rico in 1898, claiming it as war booty earned in the Spanish-American War. Following U.S. military intervention, Cuba was honoured in 1901 with the piece of legislation known as the Platt Amendment, which, apart from granting the U.S. a military base in Guantanamo Bay, made any subsequent military invasion of the island by U.S. troops legal. And in 1907, the Dominican government was prevailed upon to sign the Dominican-American Convention, a treaty already in effect since 1905 which granted the United States absolute control over the financial life of the country through direct management of all customs transactions and a definite say on all that happened in the nation politically (Moya Pons 1995: 295).

The hope for political unity voiced by Betances, Luperón, Hostos, and Martí had, by the first decade of the twentieth century, met with disappointment. But the call for unity in the realm of cultural production remained vibrant, chiefly in literature. In 1932 the Puerto Rican poet Luis Palés Matos produced the first general statement on the socio-aesthetic unity of the Caribbean. Promulgating his credo of an Antillean poetic identity, he argued that the Spanish-speaking Antilles "have developed a homogeneous spiritual type" (Palés Matos 1978: 219). He based his case on the African presence in the islands, which he thought rendered their culture homogenous. In his own artistic practice, Palés Matos sought to explore poetic resources in language, rhythms, and themes that highlighted the African aspects of Antillean life. Likewise, the Cuban Nicolás Guillén prefaced his *Sóngoro cosongo* (1931) with a clear statement of what he viewed as the essentially mulatto nature of Cuban culture (cited in Marquez 1972: 20-21). Later, in *West Indies Ltd.* (1934), from the search of a sense of Cuban values Guillén expanded his cultural concern to encompass the entire Antillean region. This is evident not only in the title of his book but also in the *Lápida* that concludes the title poem, in which the speaker, vaunting his regional identity, signs: "Nicolás Guillén, antillano" (Guillén 1974: 66).

Enough grounds exist, then, to reassure literary scholars of a cultural identity that sets the three islands apart from the countries of Latin America. Roberto González Echeverría has put it in these terms: "Though the shores of the Caribbean basin are very much like the islands, what makes these latter a cultural entity of their own is that their modern history pivots on an equation relating the natural, social and political demands of the industry to the ebb and flow of population within a restricted area" (1980: 2). González Echeverría invokes the research of Manuel Moreno Fraginals to argue that the presence of a sugar industry "acted as prime mover in the elaboration" of the modern cultures of Cuba, the Dominican Republic, and Puerto Rico, insisting on the rise of "a Caribbean culture". He traces the phenomenon to the nineteenth century as the decisive moment that "set the Caribbean apart from the rest of Latin America" (pp. 2-3).

One should note, however, that while González Echeverría recognizes the cultural unity of the three Antilles and their separateness from mainland Latin America, he does not feel this justifies our speaking of a specifically Caribbean literature. He maintains, rather, that the literary production of the islands belongs to "Latin American literature, and ultimately... Western literature", though he acknowledges features in the region's literary corpus that "allow us to speak, however loosely, of a literature of the Hispanic Caribbean" (p. 17). This critic's hesitation is not itself unique. It actually follows the orientation of most Latin-Americanists for whom the use of Spanish ultimately determines the cultural identification of the islands with the larger Spanish America, regardless of whether or not they consider the cultural products of the islands worthy of inclusion among the considerable achievements of the Latin-American tradition. In González Echeverría's specific case, however, we detect an even more tangible reason for his hesitation. He simply does not believe, as his placing Antillean literature within the corpus of Western literature indicates, in the relationship between literature and culture. Otherwise his negation of a Hispanic Antillean literature would seem illogical in light of his affirmation of a Hispanic Antillean culture.

However, a history of scholarly discourse exists which has for long acknowledged Spanish-speaking Antillean writing as a differentiated corpus. A poetic anthology of the three nations published by Dominican poet Osvaldo Bazil in 1917 spoke favourably of the ideal of Antillean union and referred to "the ties that link" Cuba, Puerto Rico and the Dominican Republic "underneath the waters of the sea and in their History" (Bazil 1917: iii). Toward the middle of the century, an essay penned by Harriet de Onis (1952) would venture a discussion of the short story as a genre often preferred by Caribbean writers. By 1957 a scholar could already survey Hispanic Caribbean literature as a distinct body of writings, indeed, "the most homogeneous and, at the same time most forgotten" component of Spanish-American letters (Olivera 1957: 6). Similarly, the publication over the last few decades of anthologies bringing together the poetry and fiction of the area would suggest an awareness that the literary texts of the three nations somehow belong together (Fernández-Marcané 1978, Morales 1981, Colón Zayas 1984; Fernández Olmos and Paravisini-Gebert 1995).

Perhaps spurred by the popularity enjoyed decades ago by Afro-Caribbean poetry, a good number of studies have appeared which tend to assume the socio-aesthetic kinship of the literary production of Cuba, the Dominican Republic, and Puerto Rico (Wilson 1979, Hernández de Norman 1977, Pereira 1985). That background made it possible for a scholar to read the texts of the prominent literary figures from the three nations, namely Guillén, Palés Matos, and Manuel del Cabral as a collective attempt to establish the bases for a regional identity (Phaf 1985: 301). Indeed, it has become customary for critics to identify in Hispanic Caribbean literature "a role in establishing an identity, building a nation" (Pizarro 1988: 182; Phaf 1986: 5). Similarly, Julio Rodríguez-Luis describes a joint manifestation of the process of "modernization" through political tendencies peculiar to the national literatures of Cuba, Puerto Rico, and Santo Domingo (1988: 144). Today, with the cumulative effect of the groundwork bequeathed by political ideologues, literary artists, and literary scholars, the cultural unity of the Spanish-speaking Antilles and the socio-aesthetic homogeneity of their texts appear highly tenable.

Few issues highlight the gap between Latin-American literature and Caribbean literature more clearly than the existence in the continent of writers whose West Indian background sets them apart from their peers. One thinks, for instance, of Quince Duncan, Gerardo Maloney, and Cubena, three Central American-born authors of West Indian descent. Though writing in Spanish in Central America, they "have produced a literature that is West Indian" showing unmistakable affinity with the texts of the English-speaking islands to which they are linked by ancestral ties and cultural resemblance (Smart 1984: 40, 48, 109). Their West Indian cultural matrix would seem to impose upon them an idiom that does not resemble the dominant voices of the continent. That explains perhaps why we seldom read about them in books surveying Latin-American literature. Moreover, the virtual absence of Hispanophone Caribbean texts in accounts of Latin American literature can actually be interpreted as an admission on the part of mainland scholars and critics that what we have here is a separate tradition requiring a separate account. Unfortunately, the history of hesitation of many Cuban, Puerto Rican, and Dominican intellectuals to assert the Caribbeanness of their culture and their art has resulted in their frequent exclusion from pan-Caribbean anthologies and literary histories, whose authors have accepted the belief that the Spanish-speaking islands are separated culturally from the rest of their Antillean neighbours. But, as Margarite Fernández Olmos and

Lizabeth Paravisini-Gebert affirm, a look at their shared historical experience "reveals the error of that belief" (1995: 9).

Endnotes

1. See Derek Walcott, "What the Twilight Says" in *What the Twilight Says: Essays.* New York: Farrar, Straus and Giroux; London: Faber and Faber, 1998, and "Crusoe's Journal", in *The Castaway* (1965), for his New World Adams theme.
2. This is also a repeated tendency in Anglophone Caribbean writing. It is at the heart of George Lamming's *The Pleasures of Exile* (1960), which gives the impression that there was no Caribbean writing before his generation. In part this seems the result of intra-Caribbean miscommunication, in part the consequence of the disappearance or inaccessibility of earlier texts.
3. Unfortunately the unity of purpose Frank Birbalsingh wrote of lasted only half a dozen years. For the past sixty-five years, politics in Guyana have been mired in African and Indian rivalry for power.
4. The essay that brought negritude to international view was J.P. Sartre's preface to Senghor's 1948 *Anthologie de la nouvelle poésie nègre et malgache de langue française*, later published as *Black Orpheus*, trans. S.W. Allen, (Paris: Présence Africaine).
5. This would be one of the probably rare issues on which Derek Walcott would disagree with Glissant. See his admiration for Saint-John Perse as a Caribbean writer in "The Muse of History", *What the Twilight Says: Essays* (London, Faber and Faber, 1998), pp. 49-53.

2

TOWARDS A CARIBBEAN POETICS

> The West is not in a westward location.
> It is not a place. It's a project.
> Edouard Glissant (1981: 12)

The previous chapter ended with a discussion of the cohesion of Caribbean literary texts within individual linguistic sectors of the region. The present chapter will look at the prevailing arguments for pan-Caribbean cultural and literary unity in order to pin down the grounds for a regional poetics. We should begin with a few thoughts on how in the Caribbean, as in the West, cultural oneness need not correspond to linguistic unity. The Puerto Rican writer José Luis González has articulated a way of seeing the different languages of the Caribbean as a unifying, rather than a divisive, element. For him, we should see this multilingual situation as an element that "brings us closer together and unites us because it is the result of our common history" (González 1986: 41).

González's notion of language appears in the context of the discussion of Puerto Rican national culture, which he divides into popular and elite culture. Expressing a preference for popular culture, which he perceives as essentially Afro-Antillean, González describes it as the vehicle through which Puerto Ricans can achieve their integration into the rich Caribbean world to which they belong" (González 1986: 42). A consideration of national culture must acknowledge the duality of "cultura popular" and "cultura de élite," roughly corresponding to the culture of the people versus the culture of the upper classes. González presents a well-informed case to demonstrate that at the level of "cultura popular" the peoples of the Caribbean, irrespective of the language they speak, resemble each other in striking ways (pp. 21-22). One could probably trace the origin of González's idea of culture back to the thought of V. I. Lenin who entertained a concept of nationality and culture that is not contingent upon language exclusivity. For Lenin the gap between the upper classes and the people was so wide as to enable us to say that in each modern nation there are two nations and in each national culture two national cultures (Lenin 1983: 107; 1979: 86).

González, of course, is not the first to have upheld a view of Caribbean unity that transcends linguistic differences. Decades before him, Daniel

Guérin saw a regional sameness that he called “unité dans la misère”. The people of the region endured a sad historical plight at the hands of Western colonial powers. As they have shared common misfortunes, they have also exhibited common reactions. Accordingly, Guérin quotes Guillén, Lamming, and Césaire to illustrate how writers in the three linguistic areas have simultaneously and in unison pursued the elimination of the “inferiority complex” (Guérin 1956: 104). The German scholar Janheinz Jahn also glanced “across the barriers of water and language” to spot a literary expression that he termed “typically Caribbean” (Jahn 1954: 16). Though making the unity of the region too dependent on race, on what he calls “the Black Renaissance”, Jahn’s contention favoured the unitarian view of socio-aesthetic expression in the region.

Linguistic Diversity and Cultural Unity

In the mid twentieth century, Eric Williams, trying his hand at literary analysis, examined four major poets from the Francophone and the Hispanic Antilles: Jean F. Brièrre, Jacques Roumain, Palés Matos, and Guillén. Through the discussion of these poets he sought to demonstrate, with almost frenetic zeal, the outright impossibility of regional unity or even regional cooperation. Arguing that Caribbean cooperation would require the coming into being of various “miracles”, he emphatically proposed that even if cooperation did occur it would necessarily falter since “the two fundamental obstacles to its achievement would remain: the absence of a common body of knowledge, and the language barrier” (Williams 1952: 8). Clearly, Williams’s insistence on national isolationism as a somehow natural condition for the islands derived from his own political preference – made evident in his celebration of Puerto Rico’s relationship with the United States under Governor Muñoz Marín, “a cordial relationship on the basis of local autonomy”, which he offered as a healthy model for the other nations of the region (p. 14). Interestingly, however, the texts of the four poets he discussed do not really conform to Williams’s view of isolationism. Williams actually had to refute the unitarian views he found in their poems. He talked against their texts, not with them, and, consequently, tended to persuade the reader of the truth of what he set out to deny. Williams spoke here like the shrewd and accommodationist politician who a few years thence would become the Prime Minister of Trinidad and Tobago, not like the anticolonialist historian who some years before had produced the ground breaking *Capitalism and Slavery* (1944). Decades later, however, he would again favour the unitarian view of the Caribbean, proposing “the cultural integration” and the “closer collaboration” of the entire region as constituting “the great need of our time” (Williams 1970: 12).

Undeniably a long legacy of division has afflicted the Caribbean territories, as the case of the West Indies Federation should illustrate. Established in January 1958, after five years of considerable debate, it came to an end after the Jamaican referendum in 1961. Individual countries were hesitant to compromise their interests since they saw themselves as contributing more and gaining less in the federation (Watson 1979: 167-171). Indeed, one would have to agree that "nationalism, both economic and political, whereby costs and benefits are calculated solely in terms of their impact on a particular country" constitutes one of the most important obstacles that may impede the process of Caribbean integration (Axline 1979: 201). But it is also clear that this has to do with a characteristic of the local power structures. The inability of local politicians to advocate the integration of their countries into larger juridical units, which would probably endanger their own personal and class interests, should not be taken to negate the deeper common ground which unites the people of the Caribbean at the level of folk culture. Williams himself, who had confused one thing for the other in his discussion of the four poets cited above, had occasion to correct himself in later years.

The unitarian impulse in presentations of Caribbean literature has produced a good number of scholarly books, anthologies, bibliographies, or critical studies, some presenting theoretical grounds for justifying the unity, other simply expressing an intuition, but on the whole, making it ever more difficult to deny the literary homogeneity of the region on the basis of language differences. The existence of so many notable texts upholding the unitarian vision actually makes it permissible to see in them, to echo a reviewer of two such texts, a "declaration of the existence of a common Caribbean essence" (Smart 1981: 32).

Caribbean Literature and Race

The late G.R. Coulthard has been credited with laying "the foundation for pan-Caribbean literary criticism" (Smart 1984: 12). Coulthard's monograph *Raza y color en la literatura antillana* (1958) undertook a study of Caribbean literature from three of the major linguistic areas. The first book-length work on this literature to attempt a translingual approach, Coulthard's monograph shows an important point of contact between Caribbean literary texts across the board (1958: 173). The book explores essentially a thematic concern, namely the preoccupation with race and colour. The illustrations dwell exclusively on blacks or mulattoes since in the author's estimation blacks and mulattoes form the "similar ethnic base" of the Caribbean region (p. 63). However, Coulthard's point of contact is faulty since, like a subsequent study by Dathorne, it rests on the idea that the Caribbean somehow enjoys ethnic homogeneity (Dathorne 1981).

Any list of the prominent literary artists in the contemporary Caribbean would have to include not only blacks, such as Maryse Condé and Aimé Césaire, but also whites, such as Alejo Carpentier and Rosario Ferré, and East Indians such as Samuel Selvon and V.S. Naipaul. When it comes to race in the Caribbean we would do well to hear the warning of Trinidadian politician, Winston Mahabir, who condemns Eric Williams, his one time ally, for the practice of emphasizing one group at the expense of others during his administration (1987: 63). Besides, as Glazier (1985) and Hoetink (1985) would contend, not only does the Caribbean region have a truly multiracial population but also the terms of racial designation may vary from one nation to another in the region, or by comparison with current usage in the United States and Europe.

We cannot overestimate the emphasis placed on the relationship between race and literary creation in critical discourse. The author of a book on Langston Hughes, Roumain, and Guillén, attributes a common aesthetics to these poets on the grounds that they "broke with the cultural tradition of a white-oriented literary past to assert black consciousness in the language and the themes of their works" (Cobb 1979: 145). But one could equally well argue that their search for a black aesthetics had more to do with a condition of oppression within clearly delineated socio-historical contexts than with the biology of pigmentation. Nor does having an African descent automatically lead a writer to the adoption of a black aesthetics. Alexander Pushkin, a Russian court poet who suffered no racial oppression, did not find it necessary to brandish the banner of blackness in his works. Nor did Alexandre Dumas père, who enjoyed considerable popularity as novelist and playwright in France, feel compelled to vaunt his blackness despite his visibly mulatto features. In fact, in reading a novel of his like *Georges* (1843), whose central character is a mulatto, one has to concur with Hoffmann that the author there does not identity with the cause of black people (Hoffmann 1974: 22).

The Haitian scholar Jean-Claude Bajeux has employed the racial model in his search for a Caribbean commonality between Claude McKay, Palés Matos, and Césaire, whom he presents as "black Antillean poets". Cognizant of the pitfalls of a racial category, Bajeux justifies its use by placing it within a discrete socio-historical context. He argues for the validity of the model specifically because of the historical conjuncture in which blacks have found themselves throughout the colonial transaction: "The history written and interpreted by Westernness has identified, classified, and treated black people by reference to criteria of a racial nature" (Bajeux 1983: 284). Yet, even after Bajeux's sound caveat, the fact remains that one of his three "poètes noirs antillais", Palés Matos, though a foremost practitioner of "poesía negrista", was not himself a black man.

The proposition of blackness as a principle to account for pan-

Caribbean cultural and literary unity goes as far back as 1932 when, simultaneously with the publication of *Légitime Défense* by Francophone Caribbean writers, Palés Matos formulated his thesis of a genuine "poesía antillana."

The concept gained increasing currency particularly since Janheinz Jahn's idea of neo-African culture became widespread in various parts of the Third World. Jahn posited that the essence of African culture has survived centuries of separation and that it lingers in the souls of African descendants regardless of the distant points of the globe to which the diaspora may have taken them. In the "rumba" rhythm of Guillén's and Ballagas's poetry, for instance, he claims we can detect a connection with the religious dimension of certain African traditions (Jahn 1961: 90-95). The way blacks use words, he argues, has to do with the role played by "Nommo" (a Bantu term used to designate the creative Word) in traditional African society. Those possessing the African essence, even when inheriting their language from a Western education, tend to convert the European "Logos" into the African "Nommo". "So Césaire uses European words in an African way," says Jahn, who seems to trace most artistic expressions of black people, from the sombre notes characteristic of *the blues* to the sound of Afro-American work songs, back to the perennially inexhaustible heritage of an African tradition (pp. 152-223). Jean-Paul Sartre, in his *Orphée noir* (1948) had insisted that Negritude, to preserve its liberating function, must transcend itself. But Jahn, with a discursive enthusiasm that soars to the pinnacle of mysticism, maintains that the essence of African culture transcends geographical space and socio-historical circumstances. Directly answering Sartre, Jahn contends that "the critical significance of the African culture is not a phenomenon of one particular time" (p. 134). We do not wish to explore here whether or not Jahn's transcendental neo-Africanism would have any significance in a world devoid of racial oppression. What we can state with certainty is that the concept does not go far as the basis of the socio-aesthetic homogeneity of the Caribbean, a region that is discretely delimited by geography and history. As any list of pertinent compilations would indicate, black writers exist not only in the Caribbean but also in Latin America, in the United States, in Africa, and judging from the anthology of Alan Lomax and Raoul Abdul, practically all over the world for thousands of years (Lomax and Abdul 1970).

A category that is so diffuse, whose confines expand infinitely in time and space, simply cannot provide the key to explain a phenomenon that exists in a specific place in the midst of a particular historical moment. In the realm of cultural production, therefore, an aesthetics based solely on the excavation of "West Indian folk culture rooted in traditional African experience", as it has been posited by Errol Hill, simply cannot hope adequately to account for the autochthonous accent of artistic creation in the region (Hill 1983: 102). Blackness, which exists in so many parts of the world, does not suffice to tell us what is unique in the literature of the specific part of the world called the Caribbean or what differentiates it from the texts of other parts of the world. The peculiarity of the Caribbean would hopelessly dissolve into the ample expanse of the black world.

Speaking precisely of the Caribbean, Ngugi has warned that "to create a religion of skin colour is to despair of a solution for social injustice" (1973: 108). Besides, we should remain constantly aware of the fact that black is not the only Caribbean color. The Caribbean experience of other racial groups should not be exiled from our discourse. East Indian voices have insisted sufficiently on this and with good reason. In that respect, a compilation by Noor Kumar Mahabir has attempted to recapture and preserve a good portion of the East Indian experience in the durable container of narrative verse (Mahabir 1985: 43). The Trinidadian Samuel Selvon, highlighting the contribution of his ethnic community, has said that "perhaps the time is ripe to remind ourselves and others of what we have contributed and sacrificed for the upliftment of the society in all spheres of life" (Selvon 1987: 44). Likewise, another Trinidadian novelist of East Indian descent, makes it clear that "many of the problems and questions of *all* West Indians have their roots in identity" and that this issue affects Indians no less than it does Blacks (Khan 1987: 47).

While one cannot deny the predominance of blacks in the ethnic composition of the Caribbean, the concern with the issue of race and colour, in general, matters a great deal more than the specific issue of blackness in a definition of Caribbean culture. The unity of Caribbean literature transcends racial distinctions precisely in the act of absorbing multiple racial traumas. We thus find remarkable harmony in the aesthetic postulates and the literary practice of Alejo Carpentier, a Spanish-speaking white, and Jacques Stephen Alexis, a French-speaking black, who have with equal conviction explored the literary possibilities of "marvellous realism" (Ileana Rodríguez 1979: 66). As novelists and as critics both manifest a similar concern with developing a voice that expresses the peculiarity of the world they live in. Alexis maintained that art must make itself recognizable to people in a given milieu in order to have effectiveness (Alexis 1956: 267). Carpentier, on the other hand, though seeking to give his vision of "lo real maravilloso" a Latin-American scope, insisted in localizing his aesthetic search in cultural symbols coming exclusively from the Caribbean (Carpentier 1984: 78-79).

The Dominican Manuel del Cabral is as white as the Mexican Octavio Paz, and both write in the same language. Yet commentators of the poetry of the former unfailingly point out its "unmistakable Antillean voice" (Anderson-Imbert 1961: II, 173; Sánchez 1976: IV, 130). Nor can one read, for instance, the prose fiction of the Puerto Ricans René Marqués and Ana Lydia Vega without sensing their "antillanidad". The aesthetic characteristics perceptible in their works differ from those found in the works of the Argentinian Julio Cortázar and the Peruvian Mario Vargas Llosa though the latter share with the former their lightness of skin. The communication that takes place between Antillean readers and Antillean texts goes beyond pigmentation to a deep sense of rapport, a certain cultural intimacy. Roberto Márquez has said: "In reading the work of [Dominican] Pedro Mir, Puerto Ricans immediately sense they are reading something that directly relates to them on the level of national sentiment" (Márquez 1983: 77). Márquez refers to a familiarity born of a socio-aesthetic kinship whose source lies in cultural and historical variables that defy explanation by means of what Coulthard called the "similar ethnic base" of the area.

Latin-Americanists and Caribbean Literature

The reference to Latin America as a mediating context has complicated the discourse of identity in the Spanish-speaking Antilles, as we argued in the previous chapter. But the complication functions in two ways, as we can see from the words of Latin-Americanists about Caribbean literature. The literary section of the first annual conference on the Caribbean held at the University of Florida, Gainesville, yielded an instructive illustration of the problem. There the Cuban critic, Jorge Mañach, recognized "some degree of congruity" in the literary production of the Caribbean, a corpus "which bears certain common features, different from those of the southernmost countries" of the continent. He stated that these texts "are in Spanish and by peoples of the Hispanic American tradition", and that through the understanding of them, "we shall best reach the substance of Hispanic American culture" (Mañach 1951: 213, 215). Mañach perceived the Caribbean simply as "a section of Latin America" that included, in addition to the islands, Mexico, Colombia, Venezuela, and Central America. His view of Caribbean culture, consequently, had a very pronounced Hispanic bias. Among the other participants at the conference, which included such figures as Germán Arciniegas, John Armstrong Crow, and Jose Antonio Portuondo, only this last escaped the exclusively Hispanic vision of the region, conceding a brief mention in his presentation of such Francophone Caribbean writers as Césaire and Roumain (Portuondo 1951: 260).

Another important conference, organized by Latin-Americanists at the University of Minnesota in 1978, dealing specifically with Caribbean literature, showed the resilience of the Hispanic bias in attempts to theorize about the unity of Caribbean literature. Ileana Rodríguez, one of the organizers, presented literary production in the Caribbean as one "within the orbit of Latin American Literature" (Rodríguez and Zimmerman 1983: 13; 1980: 3). Her understanding of the Caribbean area covers an even greater geographical expanse than that of Mañach decades earlier (Rodríguez 1983: 20). With the task of seeking a coherent conception of the bases for integrating the Caribbean into Latin America as a whole, the conference participants did not generally succeed in escaping the Hispanic bias and may have even failed, as Hernán Vidal noted, to demonstrate "the underlying premise of an organic Caribbean unity" or even to show "that it was tenable" (cited in Rodríguez and Zimmerman 1983: 202).

What Vidal terms the conference's failure may be directly attributable to the urge apparently felt by most of the conferees to expand the geographical confines of the Caribbean into the innermost points of the Latin-American mainland or even, as in the case of Rodríguez, the southern United States. It is no wonder that the presentations that strike one as most persuasive are precisely those of authors who, like Guy Viêt Levilain, Lisa Davis, and Roberto Márquez, restricted their scope geographically to the archipelago, the coastal areas of Guyana, Suriname, Belize, and French Guiana. Levilain, a specialist in the Francophone Caribbean, limited his search to the "unity of the Antilles among themselves", and then between the "unity of the West Indies and the rest of the world", for which, he insisted, one must study Caribbean literature "comparatively" and employing a "multidisciplinary approach" (Levilain 1983: 167).

Davis concentrated her remarks on "the islands of the Caribbean archipelago" whose literature, she proposed, one must study translinguistically and with particular attention to "the colonial, dependent situation" which is "more or less the same throughout the Caribbean and shows up in the literature we read" (cited in Rodríguez and Zimmerman 1983: 25, 27, 204). Finally, Márquez, positing with the Cuban ethnologist Rogelio Martínez Furé "the existence of nothing less than an Antillean civilization", illustrated his idea of the socio-aesthetic commonality of Caribbean literature by listing a large number of writers from the various nations and language areas of the region, all of whom he found "ineluctably linked to each other as they are separated from Europe" (Márquez 1983: 97-98). Márquez not only left writers from the Latin-American mainland out of his list, but he even questioned the validity of the term Latin America as an ethnocultural designation of the whole geography of Central-South America and the Caribbean, whose varied ethnic, linguistic, and cultural composition would seem to defy the monolithic implications of the concept of "Latin" (p. 101).

Neither Davis, Levilain, nor Márquez shared the fear of balkanization that afflicts many Latin-Americanists. When devoid of their typical Hispanic bias, Latin-Americanists, it seems, earnestly dread the thought that by proclaiming Caribbean literature as representing a socio-aesthetic manifestation that differs from that of the continent, they might contribute to the further fragmentation of the Americas. Theirs is indeed a noble fear given the legacy of division that, spurred by the colonial interests of imperial economies, has historically plagued the peoples of the New World. Sometimes, however, a certain brand of Marxism, which seems to impose upon its adepts the urge to unify phenomena under large theoretical schemes even at the risk of ignoring crucial specificities, can further complicate the experience of Latin-Americanists vis-à-vis Caribbean literature and culture. When this happens, the requirements of the literature studied invariably tend to be subordinated to the demands of the theory employed.

At the Minnesota conference the scholar Marc Zimmerman exemplified this theoretical stance. He began with the conviction that the issue of "a Caribbean literature must be seen [...in the context of a] broader Marxist concern for the eventual constitution of a general literary theory as related to a global theory of culture under the spread of capitalism" and insisted that "without a proper definition and integration of the Caribbean, there can be no total view of Latin American literature" (Zimmerman 1983: 28, 30). He did not conceive the possibility that one could speak of the coexistence of two literary traditions, one Latin-American and the other Caribbean, just as one speaks of Canadian and United States literatures as two contiguous wholes. As a result, he raised questions whose formulation strikes me as awkward: "Can we speak of a Hispano-american literature that includes English, Dutch, French and diverse creole languages?" (p. 30). One wonders what the reason could be for calling such a literature "Hispano-american". At any rate, Zimmerman seems bemused by the division wrought on the area by the colonial past. He contends that an area so "highly diversified according to politics, language and degrees of cultural mix" could hardly yield a cohesive and autonomous literary culture: "Caribbean literatures will most emphatically relate to (even become subcategories of) the literatures of the European mother countries" (p. 35). Thus, in the light of the fractious history of the region, "Caribbean unity remains only a tendential reality, and our conception of a totalizing literature is just a model." He argues that we ought to satisfy ourselves with the hope that one day political unity in the region will come about, and then: "On that day of Caribbean unity, a firm and deep literary unity may begin to emerge" (pp. 46, 54).

Zimmerman's political determinism presupposes an immediate and direct relationship between art and socio-political structures. The Caribbean has indeed suffered political disunity, but this does not translate necessarily into socio-aesthetic division. The region's literary homogeneity corresponds to a shared system of significance based on culture and not on political transactions. Undeniably, artistic expressions usually reflect existing social structures, but they can also prefigure nonexistent ones, particularly when the bases for the existence of those conditions are perceived and desired by the artists. Marx himself had occasion to reflect on what he saw as a clear disparity between the "development of art" and the "development of society" with particular reference to the societies that produced the great classics of Hellenic literature or gave birth to the great drama of William Shakespeare. In both cases, Marx notes, the sophistication of the artistic achievement hardly accords with the degree of development reached by the society. But he has no problem in admitting that: "As regards art, it is known that certain periods of its florescence by no means correspond to the general development of society, or, therefore, to the material basis, the skeleton as it were of its organization" (Marx 1986: 46).

We need not fear that recognizing the congruity of Caribbean literature as a separate corpus from the texts of the Latin-American mainland may somehow constitute an assault on the desired unity of the Americas. Fernández Retamar, a Marxist critic interested in the unity of the Americas, has done a convincing job of delimiting the aesthetic confines of "la literatura hispanoamericana", thus making a clear division between this artistic corpus and others both in the West and in the Western hemisphere. The Cuban scholar says: "We need to think our concrete reality, indicate its specific traits," and only thus "will we know what we have in common, will we detect our actual links and will we be able to arrive one day at what in truth will be the general theory of general literature" (Fernández Retamar 1984: 70). He contends, in effect, that only after we recognize our own specificity can we establish our place in the culture of the universal. This line of reasoning suggests that the hesitation to concede to Caribbean literature a distinct socio-aesthetic identification as the autochthonous expression of a discrete culture rests on a groundless fear.

Simply, political disparity does not preclude cultural unity. Nor does the acceptance of a people's cultural and artistic uniqueness pose any threat to visions of internationalism. Levilain's reading of Césaire, Roumain, and Depestre, for instance, shows how in the exploration of their own socio-cultural specificity these authors have revealed their links with peoples the world over. In their universal concerns may be found the "great humanism the Antilles have given to the world" (Levilain 1983: 167).

Common Legacies: Aggression, Resistance, Survival

Many authors have approached the holistic exploration of Caribbean literature through a focus on the omnipresence of the theme of resistance. Selwyn Cudjoe's book *Resistance and Caribbean Literature* (1980) typifies this trend. His reading of texts in different languages by writers of various Caribbean societies at diverse historical moments leads him to see a common thread going through them. All the texts perused reveal to him the West Indian's "struggle for freedom and dignity, with resistance to any form of oppression that would deny him his right to be a person" (Cudjoe 1980: 275). Many prominent thinkers from the area would maintain that, through the centuries, resistance has had the force of an axis linking the Caribbean experience from pole to pole. Such is the claim of Glissant, for whom the maroon figure, an eloquent symbol of resistance, has a very special appeal precisely because, in his eyes, the maroon constitutes a constant of Caribbean culture. Violent resistance, associated with the concrete actions of maroons, not only has been a historically generalized phenomenon in the zone of "Caribbean civilization" but it has even served as a sort of prelude to intellectual resistance, "intellectual marooning", as Glissant says (1981: 69-70). Likewise, in a brief historical survey of the region's literary magazines, from *La Ronde* (1892-1902) to *Brigadas Dominicanas* (1962), across the linguistic spectrum of the region, including Dutch, Papiamento, and Sranan Tongo, Emilio Jorge Rodríguez stresses the significant role these publications "have played from various standpoints in the liberation struggle" (1983: 127).

Caribbean resistance has its roots in the socio-historical conditions of the region. Social scientists who have studied the area have much to say regarding the common lot which has befallen Caribbean people throughout its history. An odd kind of unity has resulted from the fact that, historically, outside forces have had a significant influence on the lives of people in the region. A Puerto Rican independentist writer would say that the imperial presence of the United States in the area has created among the various Caribbean nations a common goal of liberation (Cuesta 1974: 358-59), but, as the French historian Michel Dévèze shows, much of the economic and political evolution of the region has taken place in the wake of the battles waged by the metropolitan empires amongst themselves for economic supremacy. The Caribbean's dependent situation began with the "discovery" in 1492. In the late seventeenth and early eighteenth century, with the decline of Dutch influence in the region, France and England entered into a serious rivalry. These two younger empires, having become progressively stronger than their elders through their successful involvement in the slave trade and sugar commerce, now saw themselves equally bent on usurping the possession of territories then under the imperial jurisdiction of Spain (Dévèze 1977: 215 et passim).

Perhaps no other area in the New World, or even in the whole world, has served, as the Caribbean has done, as the arena for Western powers to test their might either by violent clashes or clever negotiations. Few descriptions so accurately capture the condition of the area as the term "imperial frontier" applied to the Caribbean by the Dominican Juan Bosch (1970). Bosch's term evinces the conviction, also expressed by Eric Williams, that the Caribbean has been subject to a succession of events related to the movements of the imperial economies of the West: "Whether their connections have been or are British or French, Spanish or American, Dutch or Danish", the Caribbean lands share "their common heritage of subordination to and dictation by outside interests" (Williams 1970: 12). The Caribbean, Williams argues, "differs profoundly from Latin America" precisely in that the former constituted the area "where both political and economic imperialism had been most deeply entrenched in the New World" (p. 507). The historical condition wherein West Indians have endured the state of what Paulo Freire calls "being for another" makes it natural for people in the region to link the discovery and affirmation of their cultural being to the fight for self-determination both through violent struggle and in the sphere of intellectual marronage. C.L.R. James looked to the two great Caribbean revolutions as pivotal moments in an uninterrupted historical development marked by resistance: "West Indians first became aware of themselves as a people in the Haitian Revolution. Whatever its ultimate fate, the Cuban Revolution marks the ultimate stage of a Caribbean quest for identity" (James 1963: 391).

The work of social scientists who have studied the area leaves little doubt that peoples of different races, whether in the role of oppressor or oppressed, whether bent on defeating a foe in an imperial clash or merely of clinging onto hope for survival, have for more than five centuries interacted to produce a circumstantial homogeneity in the Caribbean. Nowhere in the world, including Western Europe, whose homogeneity academics seldom question, has history so conspired to forge such a pervasive oneness out of so many otherwise disparate elements. Whatever the European powers that originally conquered them, the Caribbean territories have known, in the anthropological view of Jean Benoist, the same social organization, identical economic goals, and similarly constraining relations with the metropolis (Benoist 1972: 19).

The Caribbean world, even at the level of ecosystem, has characteristics of its own. The region consists of "a chain of territories, whose history, culture, environment, and general atmosphere are different in several important respects from those found on the mainland," says geographer David Watts (1990: xviii). The Cuban scholar Manuel Moreno Fraginals too has stressed that the region constitutes "an insular ecosystem of common climatic and geological characteristics, as well as, originally, similar flora and fauna" (1978: 42). The landscape, in other words, is sufficiently self-contained to differentiate itself from other landscapes. By the same token, the societies that have sprung up on the Caribbean's habitat, "in their essential sympathies," as Watts observes, "are neither wholly Latin American nor North American; and they are far from being any longer an extension of Europe in the New World" (Watts 1990: xvii). Historical forces have thrust a sense of oneness upon the region even in the shaping of the physical space. For, while "the precise nature of the environment in each island is different in degree to that of its neighbours", the human element has over the past five centuries so transformed that milieu that the result has been equalizing (Watts 1990: xviii). Today, the whole region fits this description: "Throughout most of the island Caribbean, the general tendency has been for the rates of growth of environmental instability and environmental deterioration to be augmented and accelerated over time" (p. 539).

This combination of social and natural phenomena makes one sceptical about Gordon K. Lewis' description of Caribbean nations as "lacking effective forms of community consciousness based on unifying forms and values" (Lewis 1983: 321). This negation is perhaps best addressed by making reference to a memorable essay published by Mintz entitled "The Caribbean as a Socio-Cultural Area". Still as valid today as when it first appeared in print, the essay articulates nine major features that explain the "regional commonality" of the Caribbean, drawing from much of the knowledge then available to scholars in the social sciences. Only the seventh of Mintz's nine-point checklist requires qualification. There he attributes to the region "the prevailing absence of any ideology of national identity that could serve as a goal to mass acculturation" (Mintz 1971: 20). This affirmation overlooks the recurrence of ideological propositions of national identity in the region from as far back as the nineteenth century with the proponents of the "confederación antillana" to the more recent manifestations of the same drive in such nation-building strategies as "antillanité". The very omnipresence of expressions of resistance, violent or intellectual, as attested to by artists and ideologues, must be seen as a function of the region's persistent exploration of ideologies of "national identity."

As demonstrated by social scientists, at any rate, the socio-historical cohesion of the Caribbean exists in spite of the area's balkanization due to the colonial transaction as well as the area's geography. One must recognize the scene of "superficial diversity" of which Franklin W. Knight writes, which is underlain, he says, by "a great deal of commonality, if not a patent community" (Knight 1978: 211). The perception of this commonality, expressed in the eighteenth century by Père Jean-Baptiste Labat who saw the Caribbean territories all "in the same boat sailing the same uncertain sea", resonates centuries later in the words of Dévèze who believes the Caribbean has "cyclones of its own" (Labat, cited by Knight 1978: 189; Dévèze 1977: 9). People who have looked at the region closely have generally seen it as a differentiated cosmos.

In the same way that it is not based on purity or on a monolithic constitution, the socio-cultural coherence of the Caribbean cosmos does not imply regional felicity. Guérin's perception of an "unité dans la misère" still pervades most descriptions of the Caribbean. While today most of the area's societies possess the status of independent nations, juridically speaking, they have invariably shared a dire economic dependence on outside powers whether it be on the United States, France, Britain, the Soviet Union or the Netherlands (Knight 1978: 211). But whatever the factors one chooses to document the Caribbean's regional commonality, what seems clear is that factors of various kinds have combined in the region to produce a people with a particular *Weltanschauung*, that is, "a more-or-less common way of looking at life, the world, and their place in the scheme of things", as Knight has put it (178: xi). It is in the socio-cultural coherence of the Caribbean world, the shared historical plight, and the resulting common way of looking at the world, that one must search for the literary unity of the Caribbean.

Oneness, Ideology and Class

Today most Caribbean literary artists write with the awareness, or at least the intuition, that theirs is a different world. When exactly this *prise de conscience* took place may vary from one language area to another, but most agree in placing the region's cultural awakening somewhere between the beginning of the twentieth century and the Second World War. Amon Saba Saakana highlights the Boer War of 1900, which seriously affected the Caribbean; World War I, which took many West Indians to the front; the Marcus Garvey movement; and the white Western world's economic crash of the late 1920s and early 1930s, which shook the foundations of Caribbean society. These crucial events aided the formation of a Caribbean self-image in the period 1900-44 which represents "an unbroken development of a nationalist and race consciousness in the Afro-Caribbean people as a whole" (Saakana 1987: 64). Guillén, for his part, localized the socio-cultural self-recognition of Cubans in the first decades of the twentieth century when literary artists began to see *negrismo*, not as the *fashion* it had been for the Europeans Gide, Cendrars, Picasso, Morand, and others, but as a cultural *mode*, thus evincing the acceptance of their *mestizaje*, the ethno-cultural fusion of their African and European heritages (Guillén 1966:74). Guillén's chronology coincides meaningfully with the most active period of the *postumista* generation in the Dominican Republic whose manifesto called for the valorization of autochthonous forms. The *postumista* tenor is illustrated in such lapidary statements as this: "The marbles of Pharos or of Corinth have not been made for our statues" (cited in Santos Moray 1978:275). Palés Matos's proclamation of *antillanidad* also dates from the same period, as do similar awakenings in the Francophone and the Anglophone Caribbean (Fanon 1966: 174; Brathwaite 1960b: 203-04).

The Caribbean *Weltanschauung* manifests itself in a regional poetic worldview – what I am calling a Caribbean poetics. The region's writers for the most part produce texts that speak with a typically Caribbean accent and invariably explore the question of what it means to be an Antillean. The particular variation of that question, or its specific formulation, depends on the personality, ideological positioning and class interests of authors, but their texts primarily revolve around issues pertaining to the immediate reality of the Caribbean experience. Whatever their individual manner of approaching the Caribbean legacy, their texts invariably address them. Form and content, theme and style, in short, their predominant aesthetic orientation, will revolve around the writers' approach to the perceived "problematics" of their socio-cultural heritage.

Whatever their race, their language, their nationality, or their class identification, Caribbean writers generally find themselves trapped, as it were, within the confines of their culture. Their aesthetics entails a cultural reflection whose complexity generally corresponds to the cultural complexity of the region. Derek Walcott, for instance, alludes to this in his description of the properties of "an island culture." He believes that "an archipelago, whether Greek or West Indian, is bound to be a fertile area, particularly if it is a bridge between continents, and a variety of people settle there" (Walcott 1970: 49). Caribbean literature occurs on the common ground of that culture, on a region that is insular and continental, that is pregnant with a long history of trauma and dogma, a cosmos marked by the sour and the sweet, dispossession and hope, a scenario of poverty and cruelty, against a backdrop of stunning natural beauty. The region has witnessed centuries of oppression and a creative legacy of strategies for survival, precariousness and rich potentiality, the violence of struggle and the solace of contemplation. It may be a chaotic world for some. Indeed, it has fostered disparate utterances in those assessing life in the region. But one need not rush to call this a contradiction. One need only concede that tension, hesitation, ambivalence, even the desire to escape, stem naturally from the region's traumatic history. One can then easily recognize the common compulsions lurking behind seemingly antithetical voices.

The Caribbean can withstand discrepant pronouncements, like those of, say, George Lamming and V.S. Naipaul. Lamming sees the area's history as active process. For him the struggle that begins with the slave insurrection of Haiti marks the start of a movement that has continued to characterize the region's historical development. The Shakespearean Caliban serves for him as a symbol that evokes "the continuing possibility" of that struggle. Taking Prospero's ownership of language as symbolic of his power over those around him, Lamming views the evolution of an authentic Caribbean culture as a continuous and necessary battle for language (1960: 6, 118). The deeds of those "languageless and deformed slaves", their experiential inscription in the cause of human dignity provide those modern Caribbeans who are their descendents with a genesis of language. Lamming, in fact, sees the achievement of West Indians as lying in their artistic and intellectual commitment to the historic mission of crushing "Prospero's old myth" (pp. 119, 125). For Lamming, language acquires newness when it serves the cause of liberation, and the slaves' actions of self-affirmation gave it validation by uprooting it from the sole domain of Prospero's oppressive usage.

From Naipaul we get an opposite reading of the Caribbean legacy. He sees the area's experience negatively as a passive process. His eyes perceive a historically fated area, one in which "there were only plantations, prosperity, decline, neglect: the size of the islands called for nothing else" (Naipaul 1962: 27). He glances at a place where people did not *do* things but where things merely *happened*. This, in Naipaul's view, makes it difficult to tell its history since: "History is built around achievement and creation; and nothing was created in the West Indies" (p. 29). Naipaul perceives a historical void in the very same space where Lamming points to a vibrant human legacy. He construes "a whole side" of West Indian letters as merely a "race war", discarding the search for group identity in the region as an impediment to the growth of "a mature literature", in the same way that he discards American Negro writing as based purely on "blackness", which he says "cannot be the basis of any serious literature" (Naipaul 1962: 68-69). He seems thus to turn the triumphant self-assertion of Caliban over Prospero's tyrannical ownership of language, as propounded by Lamming, into a myopically mistaken search, inevitably condemned to cultural and artistic failure.

The contrary articulations of Lamming and Naipaul seem rooted in very different perceptions of Caribbean reality and versions of the past (and future of the region). Lamming advocates the recovery of the human legacy of a people whose undertakings have not been preserved in the durable documents of Corinthian marble or heroic couplets. Naipaul, apparently incapable of detecting achievement and creation in anything other than huge edifices and extensive territorial conquests, voices a discourse that sneers at his people's lack of the aforementioned documents. But the reality that elicits their disparate reflections is one and the same. Both respond with equal force to the turbulent and not easily fathomable Caribbean experience. They are two brilliant West Indian minds equally vexed by the inescapable trauma of their history and culture.

Lamming and Naipaul merely choose two different ways to confront the problematics of their socio-cultural legacy. The former, recognizing himself as a colonial, cognizant of the way history has in many ways maltreated his people, proposes to "choose a way to change the meaning and perspective of this ancient tyranny" (Lamming 1960: 229). The latter, probably seeing his own intellectual and existential future unattached to the destiny of his people, has recourse to irony as the only vehicle through which to describe a world he seems unequipped to love. His chronicle of how as a young man he detested the steel band, whose sound is often associated with authentic West Indian culture, and his nightmarish experiences in England when, dreaming that he was "back in tropical Trinidad" he would wake up sweating feverishly from the terror caused by the phantom of his native land, suggests that in his view salvation depended on his ability to disassociate himself from the Caribbean world (Naipaul 1962: 41). But Naipaul's agony of escape brings him as implacably close to the socio-cultural context of the Caribbean as the mission of historical reconstruction brings Lamming. Both attitudes result directly from the legacy of the colonial transaction, which breeds cultural alienation as effectively as it provokes the militancy of cultural resistance. When we read their novels, we find that Naipaul's characters would be as inconceivable outside of the West Indies as would those of Lamming. Indeed, one can read Naipaul's novel *The Mimic Men* (1967) as a very specific, and pessimistic response to Lamming's *Of Age and Innocence* (1960).

Different ways of assessing the Caribbean heritage, different cultural ideologies, have emerged at various times throughout the Antilles. The Guadeloupean-born Saint-John Perse illustrates the complexity of articulating a vision of identity when different class origins come into play. Emile Yoyo, a scholar who asserts the poet's Caribbeanness, says that "Perse speaks of the Antilles in an Antillean language" in a book whose outside back cover admits: "Never before has a poet been so silent about his native country…" (Yoyo 1971: 17, 16). Indeed, some may, without denying the poet's Caribbeanness, resent the privilege implied in his detachment. Uttering such a view, a character in Maximin's *Lone Sun*, looking at La Joséphine, the Guadeloupe Estate where Perse was born, says this: "I understand how, in his child colonist's paradise, he could have written magnificent verses celebrating the harmonious world constructed on the backs of our slavery" (Maximin 1989: 182). As understood by Glissant, Perse experienced the dilemma of the white Creole in the Antilles caught between two worlds. For Perse, "The world is in the West and the word is in the West", but his work movingly reveals "this closed site where the poet places himself at the edge of his birthplace" (Glissant 1989: 227). For the Caribbean reader, Glissant affirms, "there is nothing so obvious as this inexorable separation, through which Perse both turns his back on us and is one of us" (p. 227).

Glissant understands that Perse, the child of planters, is as much an expression of the Caribbean as Césaire, the child of slaves. But the polar opposition in cultural ideologies does not always correspond to opposing racial backgrounds and class origins. Several dark-skinned Dominican authors of working-class origins have emphatically upheld strictly Eurocentric theories of national culture. In the previous chapter we quoted a Dominican for whom the Roman Empire epitomized the Latin American cultural identity; the same author, decades later, declared that: "Until 1916, the black population did not predominate in Santo Domingo, not even the mixture of black and white" and highlighted the preponderance of European-descended Creoles in the building of "Dominican culture in general" (Henríquez Ureña 1960: 250; 1982: 134). Equally pertinent in this regard are the contrasting viewpoints of Walcott and Brathwaite vis-à-vis the African heritage and the slave past.

A good portion of Brathwaite's work seeks to bring slave culture into visibility and to document the legacy of the uneducated folks, to assert their contribution to West Indian cultural identity. Walcott seems to challenge that effort in his nostalgic evocation of a time when "We recognized illiteracy for what it was, a defect, not the attribute it is now considered to be by revolutionaries. Language was earned, there was no self contempt, no vision of revenge" (Walcott 1970a: 7). Elsewhere he utters what sounds like an expression of gratitude to the British Empire for the European cultural legacy bequeathed to the West Indies through colonial education. "Our early education must have ranked with the finest in the world. The grounding was rigid – Latin, Greek, and the essential masterpieces, but there was the elation of discovery; Shakespeare, Marlowe, Horace, Virgil – [...] It was cruel, but it created our literature" (Walcott 1970b: 51). A Brathwaitian response to this evocation would probably contend that no amount of ancient hexameters or Elizabethan pentameters can ever compensate for the blood spilt or the dehumanization wrought by the colonial enterprise. When Martí, some eight decades before Walcott, grappled with the place of the European heritage in his vision of regional identity, he insisted on the necessary search for autochthonous values: "The history of America, from the Incas to the present, must be taught until it is known by heart, even if the Archons of the Greeks go by the board. Our Greece must take priority over the Greece that is not ours: we need it more" (Martí 1979: 173).

On the whole, positions by Caribbean thinkers and artists have reflected a gradual and progressive stance of self-assertiveness regarding their culture, their people, their world. Ideology or class origins aside, they have gradually moved toward the proclamation of their ontological emancipation in imagining their relationship with the Western metropolis. No longer will one find the obsequious vision evinced by the West Indian speaker in the 1940 poem "Coronation Ode to George VI", who accepts an identity of being for another in celebrating the native society strictly in terms of what it can give to the outside imperial parent: "Accept these products of our soil –/Jamaica's clear and sparkling rum,/Sweet spices of the Grenadines;/The ripe fruit of the Antilles;/And glorious wealth of Trinidad/Blest be your crown! Long be your reign" (Lambert 1940: 21). Today the predominant position construes regional identity and regional unity in terms of breaking the umbilical cord that ties the Caribbean to diverse empires: "in the extent to which we break the chains that tie us to different masters, what we share becomes more evident: We share the future" (Castro 1980: 84).

Oneness and Gender's Difference

The urgency to affirm the contingency of the Caribbean cosmos, its relationship of difference with respect to the West, has given much currency to the Prospero-Caliban dialectic. In organizing a discourse of Antillean liberation and cultural emancipation around Caliban's self-assertiveness, Caribbean thinkers have often preserved one tradition of oppression, that which excludes women from the realm of constructive action. Condé has noted, for example, that Fanon's categorical dumping of *Je suis martiniquaise* (1948) by Mayotte Capécia, as an example of the alienation he called "lactification complex", arbitrarily denied the text the benefit of the doubt as a "precious testimony" of the plight of a coloured woman in the West Indies of the 1940s (Condé 1993: 131). She notes further that most seminal Caribbean literary texts, such as *Gouverneurs de la rósee* and *Cahier d'un retour au pays natal*, feature "messianic male heroes" with the ambition "to change their societies" (p. 125). But women's texts normally face oblivion. Witness Suzanne Lacascade's *Claire-Solange, âme africaine* (1924), which "constructed a theory of the climate in order to prove the superiority of the coloured woman over the white one" quite "long before Césaire desperately tried to redeem the black man's image" (Condé 1993: 131). Condé argues that the obscurity surrounding Capécia's and Lacascade's names has to do with more than just literary merit.

Joan Dayan has made comparable observations regarding the minimal place accorded by Haitian literary scholars to the work of novelist Marie Chauvet, which indicts the crippling of women inside and outside the household, thus irritating the dominant male sensibility (Dayan 1991: 228). Haitian writers were more used to viewing women as the source of poetic inspiration than as fellow writers. The writings of males in the country abound in representations of women: "the poetry especially glorifies women as muse, ripe fruit, celebrated landscape, the essence of all things Haitian" (p. 229). Dayan has looked to Haitian vodou as a source of symbols and paradigms that may serve to offset the androcentricity of Caribbean literature. She would pose the "eccentric" goddess Erzulie "as ground for a new ethics of voice" that may counterbalance the figure of Caliban "as image for the black man's response to an alien language and abusive history" (Dayan 1989: 46). For her, "the vodoun tradition and the modern women writers of the Caribbean could lay bare the underpinnings of the male intellectual power structure and uncover where, in the name of Caribbean identity and revolution, it exploits and distorts the female culture that vodoun both sustains and preserves (Dayan 1989: 67).

Dayan would seem to concur with Condé, and with many other women literary artists and scholars, that West Indian society needs "a psychological revolution" to accompany or to precede "a political revolution" so that women may have their say without scandalizing their male counterparts. But, as things stand, whenever they "speak out, they displease, shock, or disturb" (Condé 1993: 131). The desideratum insinuated in their recriminatory observations would seem to be the advent of a complex, perhaps androgynous vision of society, one that incorporates the challenge of women's creativity. Condé cites a Bambara myth of origin to suggest the possibility of the female principle as a source of creative contingency: "after the creation of the earth, and the organization of everything on its surface, disorder was introduced by a woman. Disorder meant the power to create new objects and to modify the existing ones" (Condé 1993: 130).

Caribbean people are not exempt from the tensions suffered by other inhabitants of the planet as a result of the different places accorded to men and women in the social structure. One may see a contradiction in the fact that tensions should exist between males and females when historically they have had to endure together the weight of class and race oppression imposed by the colonial order. But the equality of their shared subjugation did not automatically translate into equality of shared liberation in post-colonial society, which has tended to be dominated by patriarchal nationalism. As a result, history, race, religion, language, and the other unifying paradigms we may consider, have become associated with the identity of the dominant male, and the dominant conception of the Caribbean experience has been perceived as a sequence of actions performed by men. As Carole Boyce Davies and Elaine Savory Fido observe, there seems to be "no history of women's participation in struggle in the Caribbean" (1990: xiii). To add a layer to the contradiction, sometimes women themselves use language that privileges what Arnold describes as "masculinist" renditions of history (Arnold 1994b). In a passage that celebrates the resistance of Dominicans against the U.S. military invasion of 1965, the most venerable Dominican woman poet of the twentieth century sings thus: "Three million say no/ they would have to kill every last decent man/ on this half of the Island" (Cartagena Portalatín 1995: 161). Paradoxically, these lines that circumscribe the patriotic resistance to "decent men" occur in "Yania Tierra", a poem of epic aspirations, that purports to evoke five centuries of women's participation in the events that have shaped the Dominican nation.

Since women's voices have been "historically silenced in the various 'master discourses'" of the region, it follows that female writers should assume an existential stance that may differ from that of their male colleagues (Davies and Fido 1990: 1). Their social condition associated strictly with their sex makes it uncertain whether one should place "race before gender" or "gender before race" when forging strategies of liberation or when charting Caribbean literature (Davies and Fido 1990: xv). Women write under compulsions connected with their voicelessness and marginalization, which sets them apart from their male counterparts. A study by Ileana Rodríguez on the intersection of gender, ethnicity, and nation has looked at Caribbean fiction to find a "denationalization of the representation of women" in the texts perused. The author gathers from the works examined the women's "consciousness of the negation of a feeling of nationality" as a "consequence of their exclusion as subjects of law in liberal republics, and of the plotting of the construction of nation as a series of male acts" (Rodríguez 1994: 196).

The oppression of women in the Caribbean, then, exhibits more layers of complexity than the oppression endured by men, and female writers cannot help but to reflect this. The social suffocation caused by the depth of their subjugation may perhaps explain Caribbean women writers' "persistent preoccupation with madness" (Mordecai and Wilson 1989: xii). One finds in their works the recurrence of a "female protagonist whose self-identity is so severely compromised that she becomes engulfed in a web of neuroses and phantasm" (Shelton 1990: 348). Similarly, women's banishment from the realm of the public, namely the conceptual construction of the nation and the articulation of the nationalist discourse, may lurk behind the frequent recourse that women writers have to the exploration of private spheres and familial arenas. However, one could also point to novels by Merle Hodge (1970), Merle Collins (1987) and Jan Shinebourne (1986, 1988), which though they portray women in patriarchal social contexts, also portray them as women whose agency far outweighs any suggestion of victimhood or neurosis. In the Spanish-speaking Antilles, poetry written by women tends "to deal with intimacies" (Rodríguez 1990: 345). But the same applies to the whole region and to the fiction they write, as we gather from the anthology *Her True-True Name*, whose editors highlight familial intimacies (relationships between women and men or mothers and daughters) among the predominant thematic foci of their collection of fiction by female authors (Mordecai and Wilson 1989: xiii-xiv). In the Dutch-speaking Caribbean, the texts written by women show a certain flexibility "toward any public and personal event" and a tendency to draw from their "rich oral history" (Phaf 1990: 363).

Clearly, then, Caribbean literature, viewed as an ontologically autonomous totality, consists of gendered parts, just as the human population of the region contains two gendered halves. A holistic approach to the regional corpus must remain acutely aware of the dialogue between women's and men's texts. For, since males and females have not experienced reality in the region identically, we cannot expect their literary works to imagine it or reconstruct it identically. When we look at the tropes and paradigms that pervade Caribbean literature, giving it the sense of oneness that we argue for in the present study, we must note that, in the hands of women, they are further problematized by the legacy of patriarchal structures with which their texts must converse. As Carmen C. Esteves and Lizabeth Paravisini-Gebert have aptly put it, the literary work of Caribbean women "both echoes and subverts [the] themes and tropes" that occupy the minds of their male colleagues (1990: xiii). The overall preference of female authors for the autobiographical mode corresponds to their privileging the realm of the private, which often comes accompanied by a confessional tone, showing thus a search for alternative strategies of expression at the level of both content and form. The in-depth exploration of these issues is possible now thanks to the labour of gender-conscious scholars who have contributed invaluable tools of analysis. The pioneering publication of pertinent bibliographies (Paravisini-Gebert and Torres Seda 1993; Berrian and Broek 1989), collections of scholarly papers and critical essays (Davies and Fido 1990; Cudjoe 1990), and selections of fiction works by women (Mordecai and Wilson 1989; Esteves and Paravisini-Gebert 1991) laid down important groundwork around which enlightened discussion has centred since the 1990s. The availability of those sources and other similar contributions compels us to reorder the organization of texts in the regional corpus. They provide intellectual tools that we can use to dissociate ourselves from phallocentric configurations of Caribbean literature. We are now in an ideal position to understand with Brathwaite that Caliban's search for a discourse of liberation needs to be aided by the strength contained in the legacy of Sycorax.

Commonality and Caribbean Poetics

Women or men, Caribbean literary artists exhibit a certain awareness of their differences and in many cases of their role as agents of cultural resistance in the region. They often recognize themselves as speakers on behalf of a people, representatives of a culture, engaged in "the search for an alternative tradition which builds a national and regional culture" as well as the forging of an art that draws "from the environment" to "produce the things that belong back to the environment" (Maxwell 1970: 25; Williams 1970: 18). In that respect, the critic Sylvia Wynter, who has pointed to an inextricable link between cultural self-affirmation and the exploration of political possibilities for the region, refers to West Indian literature as nothing less than "the expression of the breaking out of all the Calibans" against Empire (Wynter 1978: 22-23). Such is the awareness of their socio-historical significance as voices of a culture and a people that one could say with Condé that for Caribbean writers "I" means "we" or, as Glissant suggests, that writers see their private self as inseparable from the future of their community (Condé 1977: 13; Glissant 1981: 439).

Furthermore, just as they recognize the social value of their voice, Caribbean literary artists also proclaim the socio-cultural peculiarity of their own worldview. Not only do their texts reflect what a commentator on Glissant calls a "Caribcentric view of the world", but they also tend to assume the role of theoreticians in the exposition of the region's worldview (Yoder 1981: 27). In addition to his prominence as a literary artist, Glissant has been the foremost voice articulating the notion of *antillanité*, the Francophone rendition of Caribbean people's perception of their difference, their uniqueness, their regional commonality, and, above all, their peculiar way of looking at the world. Equivalent to the English *creolization* and the Spanish *antillanidad*, the concept of *antillanité* presupposes the conviction expressed by René Ménil that the region possesses its own culture, even its own civilization. Characterized primarily by the fusion in historical time of diverse elements, the Caribbean houses an essentially hybrid culture, one in which history has combined together "in an original syncretism all these elements coming from the four corners of the world without becoming any of the particular elements" (Ménil 1981: 32). Glissant himself, in response to the position that views this fusion as a sort of bastardization, presents it rather as a "fertile practice whereby the components enrich themselves" (Glissant 1981: 18).

The idea of Caribbean unity, the ability to see the oneness underlying the regional diversity is central to *antillanité/creolization/antillanidad*, even the more recent *creolité*. This perception recognizes hybridity, syncretism, synthesis, not as a liability but as an asset, not as a sign of weaknesses but as a source of strength. Glissant is also quick to admit that this unity, which he terms "a cultural reconquest", looks backward and forward, constituting simultaneously a discovery of what Antilleans are and a foreshadowing of their future liberation. The idea, he says: "resettles us in the truth of our being, it militates in favour of our emancipation" (Glissant 1981: 18). Articulating a comparable vision of Caribbeanness that reconciles "oneness" with "heterogeneity", Roberto Márquez has upheld the "fundamental similarity of cultural identity and historical experience that, assertions to the contrary notwithstanding, give the area its very organic and unique ethos" (1983: 96; 2010: 13).

Glissant's concept of *antillanité* has generated some criticism. Corzani has argued that it will have no future as a politics of liberation until "negritude" has accomplished its mission (1970: 30-31). Wilson Lima ascribed viability to it as a vehicle of liberation especially if it incorporates the creolization of the French language (1970: 43-62). Condé celebrated it as a political and at the same time cultural agenda for the region (1977: 70-71). Finally, Arnold in an essay on the *creolité* movement has charged, not without good reason, that *antillanité*, like negritude, "pushes literature written by women into the background", thus exhibiting a behaviour typical of an "avatar of the masculinist culture of the French West Indies" (Arnold 1994b). But what matters first and foremost for the present study is Glissant's effort to explain the region's socio-cultural oneness and its resemblance to similar endeavours in the Spanish-speaking and Anglophone Caribbean.

We can now venture a more discrete discussion of the aesthetic paradigms that serve to demarcate the Caribbean poetics. I shall attempt to map the Caribcentric view manifested in the region's literary production and Caribbean writers' shared socio-aesthetic foundation, that is, the "family resemblances" evident in literary works throughout the region. I contend that their common socio-cultural ground, their similar history, and common need to respond to the human legacy of their people underscore the existence of a regional poetics. The "faits littéraires", the texts themselves and nothing else, can provide the means to determine the regional aesthetic system so as to illustrate the area's poetics (Ménil 1981: 220). The work of scholars on Francophone Caribbean literature bears testimony to the existence of "a way of writing" (une écriture) that is indigenous to an Antillean literature (André 1981: 15). The identification of "a particular view of the world" through which an Antillean text yields "its true meaning" (son sens véritable) has a clear correspondence in Anglophone and Hispanophone texts (Ntonfo 1982: 231, 243).

Even when a critic says that: "Writing from the Caribbean region does not fit into any one category", apparently discarding the possibility of its classification, we can actually take the remark as an admission that it constitutes a separate "category" (Scarboro 1988 b: 1). Too many Western-educated critics still find it difficult to recognize the possible coexistence of unity and diversity or the unity existing outside of singularity and purity. Therefore, when confronted with Caribbean literature, a corpus characterized by syncretism, few realize that it appears to be *sui generis* precisely because it is a separate genus. Some, though, remain ambivalent, never quite denying and never quite asserting Caribbean literary unity. The Trinidadian scholar Michael Dash shows such an attitude. He may disclaim the existence of "even such a homogeneous entity as French Caribbean literature" in an essay in which he satisfactorily details the tendencies among Francophone Antillean writers who: "do reveal many interesting parallels" insofar as they "share some basic concerns" even when working "independently of each other" (Dash 1983: 110).

Dash has authored an essay on the "marvellous realism" of Alejo Carpentier, Jacques Stephen Alexis, and Wilson Harris to show how the three authors have similarly "turned to the myths, legends, and superstitions of the folk" to explore "a complex culture of survival" (Dash 1974: 88). He finds that these writers' "marvellous realism" offers a productive alternative to negritude in Third World literature. Significantly, Dash neglects to describe their aesthetics in Caribbean terms. He associates their poetics with the larger Third World context although the writers he uses are Caribbean and the elements that link their texts are inseparable from the Caribbean region. Elsewhere Dash explores the work of Césaire with a focus on "the possibilities for a non-European aesthetic", conceived as a venture into the "possibilities for the creation of a specifically West Indian aesthetic" (Dash 1974: 25). Finally, in a more recent analysis of aesthetic positions coming from Francophone Caribbean writing, Dash has explored a set of criteria that "go beyond French Caribbean writing to suggest an important process or mechanism in the Caribbean literary imagination" (Dash 1988: 129). He goes on to recommend a more linguistically encompassing search into the literature of the region "to locate the specific features of a Caribbean sensibility" (p. 129).

The conflicting claims in the texts of Dash reflect his hesitation regarding the homogeneity of Caribbean literature. His texts often argue two ways. If one may conjecture, Dash seems reticent to proclaim a Caribbean literary unity for fear of indulging in what he terms "ideologically determined perspectives on Third World literature", a tendency that he apparently loathes (Dash 1988: 114). Thinking it possible to write ideology-free criticism, he opts for a discourse whose claims run counter to the discourse of resistance upheld by many of the most prominent Caribbean voices. Therefore, while the likes of Lamming, Brathwaite, Wynter, Depestre, Césaire, Glissant, and Fernández Retamar, have elevated the figure of Caliban as a symbol of cultural emancipation in the region, Dash finds Caliban trapped in a sort of "ideological 'cul-de-sac'" and proposes, instead, the figure of Ariel with all of its metaphorical connotation of conservatism (1988: 128-29). Clearly, then, Dash's aversion to the presuppositions of one ideology leads him to uphold another set of ideological presuppositions. But, taken together, his observations add notably to the discourse on Caribbean literary unity.

The evidence of Caribbean literary texts themselves supersedes both ideological promulgations and/or the reticence of the critics. The culturally self-referential question of the meaning of West Indianness stands out in most literary texts of the region. An amalgam of socio-historical issues assault the imagination of West Indian writers, making their aesthetic explorations seem virtually inseparable from cultural reflection. Caribbean writing, in the apt words of Glissant, "will not divide itself up into genres but will involve all the strategies of the human sciences" (1981: 133). The fact that writers in the region so consistently experience the need to address their world, their people and their legacy in this specific part of the globe, is at the core of the socio-aesthetic kinship exhibited by Caribbean texts.

The shared need of Caribbean writers to wrestle with the human legacy in the region, fuelling them with the resources yielded by the environment and the experience of people there, is best illustrated by devoting the remainder of this chapter to look at three elements that are crucial unifying factors in the Caribbean literary imagination, namely language, religion, and history. Taken as paradigmatic *topoi*, these three offer a rich ground for an illustration of Caribbean poetics because they weigh heavily on a people's cultural experience and an individual talent's hassle with reality and the act of artistic creation. The three elements as we know them were originally codified in the region by wielders of the dominant discourse of the West in the course of the colonial transaction. While certainly not the only categories that could be used, the concepts of history, religion, and language will help to exemplify how Caribbean literary artists have addressed their inherited condition. For it is normally in the reworking of those concepts that they can have their say, most commonly express the uniqueness of their utterance, and achieve a diction of their own – one that collectively amounts to a Caribbean poetics.

The Nativization of Language

Caribbean poetics comes into being primarily as an exploration of language. Language in Caribbean literature is not merely a medium that makes the art possible nor a neutral channel to convey ideas and sensations. It is a strenuous vehicle of communication, a means of ontological positioning with respect to the environment, and a constant object of reflection. Caribbean writers must reckon with "the alienation produced by past and present oppression" and to search for the elements which may bring about a culturally and socially satisfactory self-definition (Pierre-Charles 1986: 150). The Nigerian novelist Chinua Achebe complains of having to use English to describe "situations or modes of thought which have no direct equivalent in the English way of life", echoing the similar plaint of Raja Rao decades before (Achebe cited in Gibbs 1986: 28; Rao 1976: vii). But both the Nigerian and the Indian novelists, educated in an European language, can conceivably choose the tongue in which to write their novels. Even if not always practical, they can opt to write in their native languages as has Ngugi who in the 1980s declared: "From now on it is Gikuyu and Kiswahili all the way" (Ngugi 1986: xiv). But Caribbean writers do not have such an option. They cannot regard the European tongue as a second language. The Creole linguistic formations that have flourished in various parts of the region invariably have a Dutch, French, Spanish, and English base or a combination of these even when the Creoles may exhibit demonstrable influences of African languages in "syntactic collocations, conceptual categories, residual tonal features and intonations, unstressing, and syllable structure" (Warner-Lewis 1979: 105). Whether writing in a standard European tongue or in a local Creole, Caribbean literary artists face the challenge of rendering their language consonant with the Caribbean cosmos.

In all linguistic sectors of the Caribbean region, literary artists confront the demand to nativize their language. Glissant thinks of this imperative as a crucial "proposition" affecting Antilleans, be they Creole users, Francophones, Anglophones or Hispanophones (1981: 281). The region's literature reflects its tackling of that proposition in the sort of creolization he calls "le rythme assonancé" (assonanced rhythm) identifiable "in the French writing of Damas, the English of Brathwaite, and the Spanish of Guillén" (Glissant 1981: 416). The scholarly data accumulated by linguists does provide ample evidence of the high degree of creolization undergone by Dutch, Spanish, English, and French in the Caribbean. In the Hispanophone Antilles, whether due to the influence of the African element, whatever may have survived of the languages of the indigenous population, or the preservation of certain Spanish archaisms suggesting a separate development for the Spanish of the islands, the bibliography on the field supports the conviction long held in the Caribbean "that the language spoken in the area had an individuality worthy of consideration" (González Echevarría 1980: 5; Henríquez Ureña 1982: 8, 133; Rivera de Alvarez 1983: 295, 473, 643, 880; Lawton 1971: 193). Nativization in the Hispanic Antilles did not result in "new languages" as it did in the other linguistic sectors where Sranan Tongo, Papiamento, French Creoles, and West Indian Creoles, for instance, having started as "pidgins", have evolved within the past three hundred years into bona fide linguistic systems, differentiated Creoles (Taylor 1971: 78, 79; Allsopp 1971: 130). "The indigenous Arawakan languages of the Greater Antilles died out during the course of the sixteenth century", when those who spoke them perished under the Spanish sword, forced labour, foreign disease, or suicide" (Holm 1989: 4, 306). Also, as R.W. Thompson has argued, the Spaniards, when populating their New World possessions, generally ensured that "their subjects of African descent did not greatly overwhelm in number those who spoke a European language" (Thompson, cited in Taylor 1971: 85). But Spanish underwent its share of transformation. Ricardo Otheguey has summarized the phonetic, morphological, and syntactical characteristics of

Caribbean Spanish (1973: 333-34). The linguistic John Holm finds justification for ascribing a semi-Creole to the area (1989: 309).

Enough linguistic nativization has occurred in the Hispanophone Caribbean to instill in writers there the need to explore in their works the distinctive flavour of their local language variety. Critics of the work of Puerto Rican authors Palés Matos, Ana Lydia Vega, and Luis Rafael Sánchez frequently point to these writers' *antillanidad* or Puerto Ricanness at the level of linguistic usage (Coin 1976: 74; Homar 1982: 74, 85). Dominican writers have drawn on the idiosyncrasies of local speech from as far back as the early nineteenth century. Some anonymous verses representing early samples of Afro-Dominican poetry and the folk poems of Juan Antonio Alix at the start of the twentieth century attest to an awareness of nativized linguistic forms (Rodríguez Demorizi 1979: 52-53, 267 et passim). The short fiction of Juan Bosch from his collection *Camino real* (1933) onward, Ramón Marrero Aristy's novel *Over* (1940), and Freddy Prestol Castillo's narrative *El Masacre se pasa a pie* (1973) demonstrate their authors' exploration of linguistic indicators to establish the local colour of their world and the native flavour of their characters. Likewise, in Cuba, from Lino Novás Calvo, to Guillén, to Guillermo Cabrera Infante, a major thrust of literary artists has been the effort to find in the island's peculiar use of Spanish a means to express the socio-cultural values that contain their *cubanidad*, that which can be regarded as unmistakably local. Novas Calvo's story "No le sé desil" comes easily to mind in this regard. A commentator on the language in Cabrera Infante's *Tres tristes tigres* notes its "peculiar lexicon: festive creations, jocular metaphors, popular terms, and characteristic Antillean – particularly western Cuban – grammar" (López Morales 1994: 19; Merrim 1980: 96, 99-100). One may note also Guillén's use of non-standard speech forms as well the lexical and morphological reflection of his commitment to "oral forms" in his poetry (Márquez and McMurray 1975: xii; Smart 1980: 363).

In the Anglophone Caribbean, the nativization of English has been central to the creation of "a distinctive, even nationalistic literature" (Midgett 1977: 219). R.B. LePage connected the region's literary maturity to the writers' ability to explore "vernacular usage in literature in depth" (LePage 1978: 129). He thought such an approach would give West Indian audiences access to "an indigenous literature in the indigenous language", echoing similar words by Gerald Moore (1978: 130). Selvon, in this context, has earned praise for having "consciously chosen Caribbean literary English", and for revealing through language the creolization of the Indian peasant, thus contributing significantly to the creation of a culturally authentic voice in West Indian fiction (Nasta 1988: 25; Rohlehr 1978: 153). The search for linguistic authenticity is at the core of the adoption of dialect which has serious cultural, political, and aesthetic implications. The use of dialect as a form of resistance goes back to "the original rebellion of the African slave", who defied the colonial regime just as in recent times their descendants have defied the middle class who tended to equate dialect with "incorrectness" since it represented "the speech forms of a lower class from whom they wished to be distinguished" (Brown 1984: 101; Saakana 1987: 44; Morris 1982: viii-ix, 1978: 137). Mervyn Morris in an essay on Louise Bennett regards dialect as limiting "in more senses than one", a sentiment shared by John Figueroa, who praises the work of Walcott precisely for employing, not a part, but the whole range of linguistic possibilities available to the West Indian writer, what he calls the "West Indian language continuum" (Morris 1978: 148; Figueroa 1978: 152). Except for such remarkable instances as Claude McKay's *Constab Ballads* (1912), and the occasional use in Una Marson's poetry collections written between 1930-1945, George Campbell's *First Poems* (1945) and the explicitly dialect work of Louise Bennett from the 1940s onwards, until the 1960s West Indian poets, unlike the novelists, tended to shun dialect or any distinctively West Indian usage of English. A quick glance at some of the volumes published at the time would indicate this. But in the post Brathwaite generation, nativization has become the norm, and it is now possible to associate the growth of West Indian literature from the mid twentieth century onwards with the fact that, as Evelyn O'Callaghan puts it, "our writers have not been using language as they used to" (1984: 125).

One of the oldest surviving texts in a Caribbean Creole language is a 1776 letter in Papiamento written by a Curaçao Jew to his mistress (Holm 1989: 314). As this detail may suggest, the linguistic situation in the Netherlands Antilles differs from the Anglophone and Francophone Caribbean in that the local Creoles, particularly Papiamento, which all social groups speak today, have suffered less stigmatization. Papiamento has enjoyed a considerably "high social prestige" (ibid. p. 315). In Suriname, Sranan Tongo, the lingua franca, has survived a history of class stigma (Carew 1984: 103). As a result, there has been a vigorous development and a continuous rise of Creole language and a Creole literature in Suriname (Voorhoeve and Lichtveld 1975: 75).

But the French-based Caribbean Creoles are the oldest of the local languages of the region, which partly explains the considerable growth of French creolophone writing from as far back as the early nineteenth-century (Prudent 1983: 29). Individual authors such as Paul Baudot achieved prominence writing in Creole at the time. Creole in Haiti constitutes the *lingua franca* for the overwhelming majority of the population whose exposure to standard French begins largely in school, for those children with access to an education. In 1955, the journal *Optique* (No. 22, pp. 71-73) discussed the "crisis of French" in the Haitian school system.

Reports alluded to "le français littéraire" often becoming a stumbling block for students whose mother tongue was different from their language of instruction, causing poor academic achievement and low graduation rates.

Already in 1905, the Minister of Education, Murville Férère, had formed a committee to assess the feasibility and utility of instituting Creole as the language of instruction in Haitian schools, with French taught as a second language. Férère's idea would come to fruition only in 1979 when Haitian law institutionalized it. Article 5 of the Haitian Constitution of 1987, promulgated the year after the departure of the Duvalier family, made Creole and French official languages of Haiti (Alexandre 1993: 189-91). But by the time such a development brought Creole to juridical parity with French, a Haitian literature had already come into existence, written mostly in French by authors who had to converse with the mother tongue either in friendly or unfriendly terms. The linguistic doubleness was always there even when the writers prided themselves on their perfect command of the language of Ronsard.

Not only in Haiti but throughout the Francophone Caribbean, the Antillean writer has experienced a split into diverse linguistic behaviours, a "dichotomy that gives a distinct guise to "la contradiction littéraire antillaise", as Roger Toumson calls it (1993: 80). Antillean writers can hardly avoid tackling the "contradiction" either head-on or obliquely. Toumson calls our attention to the linguistic offensive of Mariotte, the character from *Plat de porc aux bananes vertes* by André and Simone Schwarz-Bart, who discards "le français de France" as a mere pretension. Conversely, Chambord, the character in Berténe Juminer's *Les bâtards* (1961), endures the trauma of not knowing how to speak the Creole of his people and the sense of inadequacy at having to lapse into "the language of the whites", bordering on what he himself considers as "the limit of snobbism." The two examples speak to the complexity of the linguistic situation in the Caribbean and its strong rapport with literary activity. Describing the French overseas departments, Gilbert Gratiant has spoken of Creole as "the essence of the unique Antillean civilization" (1957: 255). I would be tempted to propose, instead, that the tension born of the linguistic doubleness, the fact of having to negotiate different linguistic forms, defines the Caribbean "essence" more fully than the role of any one linguistic mode.

The discomfort produced by the "duplicity" accentuates the Caribbean writer's sense of difference and the need to secure self-affirmation through nativizing their language. In their various ways, Caribbean literary artists seem to share the compulsion to handle the language inherited from Europe in a way that justifies them culturally and artistically. They must come to terms with their linguistic alterity vis-à-vis Europeans, hence their predilection either for Creole or for a subtly nativized rendition of the

European language. Gratiant's assertion that Antilleans achieve intimacy in their linguistic communication solely in Creole, a view that Jamaican linguist Jean Creary echoes, suggests the privileged place accorded to Creole in the hearts and minds of Caribbeans (Gratiant 1957: 254; Creary cited in James 1968: 18). Caribbean literature, of course, must reflect the need to nativize the word. The relationship between language and literature is a "dialectical" one, as Wellek and Warren have indicated, a relationship in which literature influences language as profoundly as language influences literature (1977: 174-75).

Nativization, of course, need not only occur through the adoption of dialect. The critic Gordon Rohlehr, for instance, advises Anglophone West Indian poets to appropriate the "*metrical* forms" employed by the calypso singer whose language "is pretty close to standard English, yet his organization of language is entirely different" (1970: 99). In the same way, the Haitian writer René Depestre, advocates "a maternal use of French, a Haitianized use of French" (1986: 192-93). Depestre explains that in his own literary practice Creole always informs his writing not only in the words he uses but at the level of "l'imaginaire," at the level of his "way of looking at life" and of his "most intimate aesthetics" (ibid. p. 193). Perhaps the very manner of using words for evoking the uniqueness of the Caribbean environment may add significantly to the nativization of language. A critic has examined Wilson Harris's "natural imagery" in precisely these terms, noting, for example, how in his texts: "Even the universal 'dew' is given added poignancy by its place in the tropical heat that so swiftly evaporates it" (James 1970: 85).

Linguistic nativization, then, can take place not only through morphological modification of the signifier, to use a Saussurean term, but also through accentuating the uniqueness of the signified. A new rhythmical arrangement produced by the syncretic mixture of the sounds emanating from diverse cultural sources and the new substance, socio-historically speaking, of the Caribbean world, should add fuel to the furnace necessary to recast the languages of the Old World. European languages, we can say, are rendered new in the Caribbean, particularly in the hands of Caribbean writers who are in touch with the socio-cultural specificity of their world. In a certain sense, this dynamic parallels a similar process in African literature. In the reading of one critic, African literature's originality resides in its elevating to aesthetic categories a world which until recently had not enjoyed such a privilege in the general development of written literatures: "It is in that respect that one can speak of African literature as that of an eminently new language" (Melone 1970: 12). The newness of the substance, in other words, has the power to transform the very essence of the old European words being used. Caribbean poetics exhibits either a knowledge or an intuition of such a dynamic.

The Religious Imperative

Caribbean writers "draw from a popular tradition of resistance that still lives in religion and language, tales, music, song, poetry, and drama," says Patrick Taylor (1989: 228). The first of the elements enumerated in Taylor's sentence, namely religion, will occupy this section. The Caribbean experience inaugurated in 1492 had a pronounced religious dimension. When at the start of the colonial transaction Europe met America, triggering the Middle Passage from Africa, not only human societies but also religious cosmologies clashed. With the arrival of the Spanish caravels, the trauma of the Arawaks and Caribs included, among several world-shattering things, having to deal with the Hebrew godhead and the rigours of Christianity, and often having to conceal their native *zemis*. One thinks of the Arawak guerrilla leader Guarocuya, known to the Spanish as Enriquillo. He grew up under the protection of a kind Spanish master who gave him a Christian upbringing and regarded him as a son. With the death of his guardian, he lost his social privilege and began to endure the treatment afforded any other "Indian". By 1519 the indignities had become unbearable, and he took to the mountains of Baoruco, where he led a band of aboriginal rebels against Santo Domingo's colonial regime. All military efforts to subdue the insurgents proved futile for over fifteen years. Finally, the colonial authorities had the wisdom to employ a more effective kind of offensive. They sent as an envoy Father Bartolomé de las Casas, Enriquillo's spiritual teacher, who had instructed him as a child in his first catechism. The rebellion came to an end. The head of the insurrection signed a peace treaty with the Spanish, with the result that his guerrilla forces became a military arm of the oppressive colonial structure.

Many have spoken of Enriquillo in literary and historiographical texts without stopping to ponder on the religious implications of the Baoruco rebellion. But the fact is that the Arawak warrior won the battle against the colonial masters in the military arena while he lost the war in the realm of the sacred. Had he been less vulnerable to the persuasive appeal of a Christian voice, had he, in other words, not been christianized, he might have taken the rebellion to its logical consequence. Perhaps the Arawaks would have survived the decimation that ultimately befell them. But, in any event, the point of evoking this episode is to stress the significance of religion as a crucial component of the Caribbean experience. It was not only the aboriginal population of the region that endured a spiritual trauma. The Africans brought here to fuel the colonial economy suffered it no less. The effort to deprive African slaves of their native spiritual world view led plantation society to perpetrate unspeakable cruelty against them. As the arrival of Africans continued, particularly in the British West Indies, even after the formal abolition of slavery, they were forced to repeat the cycle of adapting to another's world. They normally adopted Christianity to ease "the emotional burden of social ostracism" (Warner-Lewis 1979: 103). This usually meant entering into a state of spiritual duplicity. Their becoming Christian rarely meant "total severance from their own traditional worship and they continued to serve their deities under Catholic saints' names. Just as the saints carried a European label, they also carried a secret identity under a Yoruba name" (Warner-Lewis 1979: 103).

The conflicts that stem from competing belief systems have occupied the minds of artists and intellectuals for a long time. In his study of Haitian thought, Hoffmann has noted "the religious tensions between vodou and Christianity" as one of the threads that characterize the long history of Haitian intellectuals' attempts "to reconcile two worldviews", corresponding roughly to that of the majority of the people and that of the learned elite (Hoffmann 1990: 12). In Haiti, writers can hardly escape the religious imperative. The Haitian poet Carl Brouard once referred to vodou as "our sole originality" (cited in Hoffmann 1982: 270). While certainly not shared by the majority of Haitian writers, Brouard's assertion hints at the crucial position of religious issues in Haitian letters. A text such as the novel of Milo Rigaud, *Jésus ou Legba* (1933), while using the socio-political background of the American occupation of Haiti in 1915, dramatizes, in essence, the clash between Christianity and vodou. Invocations of the divine justice of the Haitian pantheon against the present domination of the Christian order abound throughout the text.

Edmund Wilson realized back in 1944 that to undertake a competent reading of the Marcelin's novel *Canapé vert* (1944) he needed sufficient background on the deities and symbols of vodou, despite his prejudiced perception of this folk religion (1970: vii; Dash 1988: 78-79). The two authors of that text, the brothers Philippe Thoby-Marcelin and Pierre Marcelin, make a similar demand on readers in all the other novels they wrote together. In *La Bête de Musseau* (1946), the character Horace suggests the coexistence of vodou and Christianity as two equally valid metaphysical alternatives. The character Diogène in *Crayon de Dieu* (1952) suffers the spiritual tension evoked by his position between the two religious systems. *Tous les hommes sont fous*, another novel by the Marcelin brothers, which appeared first in English in 1970, focuses on the disputes and confrontations brought about by the anti-superstition campaign launched in 1942 by the Catholic Church and the Haitian government to eradicate the practice of vodou among the Haitian masses.

Manuel, the main character in Roumain's *Gouverneurs de la rosée* (1944), solves the drought problem in the village of Fonds-Rouge by locating a source of water in a nearby mountain and coordinating a team to dig ditches and irrigate the arid soil. Manuel proves the efficacy of his people's own resources in confronting a problem before which vodou ceremonies had proven ineffective. He offers an alternative to the villagers' attitude of resignation and their entrusting the solution of social problems to the whims of the divine order. Manuel's attitude toward religion clearly corresponds to Roumain's own Marxist worldview, which he had articulated in his *A propos de la campagne antisuperstitieuse* (1942). While he decried the attacks of the Church against vodou worshippers, he foresaw a time when the progress of science and the continued development of their country would free the Haitian masses from their "mystical shackles" (cited in Souffrant 1978: 47).

By no means an adept of vodou, Alexis, also a Marxist, assumed a more ambiguous attitude, granting socio-historical significance to the vodou cosmogony. He seems to have regarded the loas, as the vodou deities are called, as essential elements of the physical surroundings, the local culture and the social milieu, along with the soil, the banana-trees, the cassava and the maize. In fact, his depiction of Bois d'Orme, the character in *Les arbres musiciens* (1957) who is a vodou priest, expresses a reverential attitude towards that faith. Alexis's respect for Christianity and vodou look very similar (Souffrant 1978: 69). But whether they view it as retrograde superstition or as a container of their national identity, Haitian writers must come to terms with vodou in their texts.

Condé's survey of Francophone Caribbean women novelists shows a similar tension between the official religion and "Quimbois", the folk religion of the French overseas departments. Women novelists throughout the French-speaking Antilles accord significant space to the religious situation of their countries, thus illustrating "the two faces of their society" (Condé 1979: 49). Condé's own prose fiction, in such works as *Ségou: Les murailles de terre* (1984) and its sequel *Ségou: La terre en miettes* (1985), chronicles the saga of religious experience and socio-political events in Africa and the Caribbean. Her *Moi, Tituba, sorcière… noire de Salem* (1986) invites readers into "a spiritual and ethical world" and confirms the pervasive presence of religious quests in the area's literature (Scarboro 1988: 8). The *quimboiseur* portrayed under various and sometimes disparate guises is an omnipresent character in the works of the most prominent writers there. Joseph Zobel, in such texts as *Diab'là* (1946), *Les jours immobiles* (1946), and *La Rue cases-nègres* (1950) portrays the *quimboiseur* as a dangerous being, associated with the forces of evil. But in the characters of Langoué from Glissant's *Le Quatrième siècle* and Jab-Herma from Michèle Lacrosil's *Demain Jab-Herma* (1967) we see the *quimboiseur* as an agent of the spiritual contribution of the folk to the people's struggle to assert their identity. Thus, this character has functioned as a "living symbol" (symbole vivant) throughout contemporary Francophone Caribbean writing (Ntonfo 1982: 162-71).

The profound religious sensibility that Arnold has noted in the works of

Césaire suggests that the concern with the sacred is not restricted to fiction writers. In explaining Césaire's notion of marooning (marronner), Arnold establishes a connection between subversion and the sacred, since the poet's subversion "sought transcendence in an Africanized syncretic myth that imitated the rituals at the root of all the former slave religions of plantation society – voudou, santería, macumba – in which these oppressed communities found collective survival mechanisms" (Arnold 1981: 229). The poet himself has said: "I believe I am a man of the sacred. The Martinican sacred, the French West Indian sacred exists; it has become trite, of course, it has become occulted, ignored, and sometimes so terribly distorted that we ourselves either misunderstand it or misjudge it, but I believe it is there" (cited in Arnold 1990: xxxvii).

A well-received Anglophone poetry anthology, under its chapter heading: "Gods, Ghosts, and Spirits," includes poems by the best-known poets from the area (Brown 1986: 87-95). This shows the concern with the sacred to be as strong there as in the other linguistic blocs. The novels of Roger Mais, *The Hills Were Joyful Together* (1953), in which Christian belief shapes the actions and attitudes of several of the characters, and *Brother Man* (1954), which features a Rastafarian protagonist, or Earl Lovelace's *The Wine of Astonishment* (1982), which focuses on the plight of a small congregation of Spiritual Baptists, exemplify the intimacy of Caribbean letters with religion. Jan Carew's *The Wild Coast* (1958) and Andrew Salkey's *A Quality of Violence* (1959), among innumerable others, provide further illustration. The works of Naipaul, the majority of whose characters reveal their attitude to Hinduism, and, as argued by a critic, "see their religion as something social rather than spiritual", testify no less to this religious sense (Ramraj 1987: 98). In the story "Turning Christian" by Samuel Selvon, Changoo the main character is persuaded that "only those Indians who turn Christian make any headway" (Selvon 1989: 16). As it turns out, it is "the white people religion", as Changoo's friend Gopaul calls it, that mediates between the main character and the black policeman Norbert in the end. The centrality accorded to religion in contemporary West Indian literature (which a study of this novel by Joan P. Bathersfield documents well) had already surfaced in the anonymous *Hamel, the Obeah Man* (1827), a book containing, in Brathwaite's view, the first complex portrayal of the black man's experience in the English-speaking Caribbean. Brathwaite celebrates the fact that the protagonist, a priest of the Afro-Caribbean religion known as Obeah, appears "in ideological opposition to a white missionary" (Brathwaite 1977: 153; Bathersfield 1977: 204).

The Hispanophone Caribbean has as strong a vein of autochthonous religious expression. Ñáñigo, Shango, and Santería are associated with Cuba (Willeford 1969: 218; Simpson 1970: 11; Bascom 1971: 522). In Puerto Rico, the popular belief system known as *Espiritismo*, apparently a supplement to Catholicism, has come to be regarded as a national expression, with manifestations that integrate elements of the spiritual traditions of whites, Amerindians, and blacks (Bran 1957: 340-47; Hollingshead and Rogler 1961: 17-21; Zenón Cruz 1975: 5, 206). In the Dominican Republic, anthropological research has revealed the existence of very strong folk religious forms, chiefly Dominican vodou and Gagá (Deive 1979: 171, 376; Rosenberg 1979: 17, 31, 226; Davis 1987: 75). Though considerably more timid than their Anglophone and Francophone counterparts, Spanish Antillean literary artists have also reflected the religious complexity of their region in their texts.

While many twentieth century Puerto Rican poets have dealt with religious themes, a good number have integrated specifically the elements of *Espiritismo* into their poetry (Pedrosa Izarra 1973: 74-93). Among the texts exploring Afro-Caribbean spirituality, two well-known poems by Palés Matos come to mind. In one, the speaker begins his evocation of the Antillean ambiance by alluding precisely to religious forms typical of the islands: "Cuba-Ñáñigo and song/Haiti-vodou and calabash" – Cuba-ñáñigo y bachata/Haití-vodú y calabaza (Palés Matos 1984: 488-91). In the other, "Ñáñigo al cielo", we hear the story of a ñáñigo worshipper as he endeavours to penetrate the Judeo-Christian heaven (Pales Matos 1984: 492-95). Ñáñigo is also the religion adopted by Menegildo Cue, the main character in Carpentier's novel *Écue-Yamba-Ó* (1933). Guillén, too, in *Sóngoro cosongo* (1931) evokes the Caribbean world by referring to the doubleness of the area's religious heritage: "On one side Saint Barbara/on the other Shango" – Santa Bárbara de un lado/del otro lado Changó (Guillén 1980: 105). In a poem from *West Indies, Ltd* (1934) we witness the ritual of the killing of a snake wherein the speaker repeatedly invokes the Afro-Cuban divinity Sensemayá (Núñez 1980: 424). Guillén draws here on the mystical power attributed to the word in traditional African religion: "In this instance, the word is charged with sufficient spiritual force as to produce the desired effect" (Williams 1979: 126). Similarly, two of the best-known Dominican poems, "Yelidá" (1942) by Tomás Hernández Franco and "Compadre Mon" (1943) by Manuel del Cabral, dramatize different aspects of the area's concern with the sacred. The former stages a theogony involving two distinct pantheons, Nordic gods on one end and vodou divinities on the other. The latter includes a rendition of the speaker's intervention on behalf of a woman who is being tortured during a vodou ceremony (Cabral 1987: 147-48). Both poems treat vodou negatively, reflecting the diabolical associations that the Catholic church has traditionally ascribed to it.

Hispanophone Caribbean writers, and particularly Dominican ones, have moved more slowly than their Anglophone and Francophone counterparts towards a positive consideration of folk religion. There the intelligentsia's reticence to search for the symbols of cultural identity in non-Western sources, has prevailed. The poet Félix María del Monte's characterization of vodou in the nineteenth century as a "diabolical, anthropophagic ritual" typifies the disdain of the upper classes for the religious forms of the folk (Deive 1979: 163). But the need in 1862 for a governmental edict banning that religion attests to the popularity it enjoyed among the lower social strata (ibid p. 163). Indeed, vodou occupies a central place in the cultural heritage of the Dominican people since the majority of the peasants, over 70% of the population, practice it in one form or another (Deive 1979: 376). From the folk poetry of Juan Antonio Alix, to the texts of fiction authors, to a poem by the contemporary author Rubén Suro, we can affirm that Dominican writers, in particular, and Spanish-speaking Antillean writers, in general, have to some degree shared with the other parts of the region an interest in exploring the socio-cultural significance of folk religion even when retaining a degree of Eurocentric bias. In sum, the pervasive concern with the sacred in Caribbean texts corresponds to the decisive role played by religion in the human experience in the area. It is to be expected, then, that Caribbean literatures should so often dwell on treatments of the sacred and wrestle with the spiritual imperative that pervades their historical experience.

The Historical Imagination

The central role of history in fuelling the West Indian literary imagination becomes evident even in the most casual glance at the region's texts. Derek Walcott's early play *Henri Christophe* (1950), Glissant's play *Monsieur Toussaint* (1961), Césaire's *La tragédie du roi Christophe* (1963), and the novel *El reino de este mundo* (1949) by Carpentier, among others, attest to the frequency with which characters and events from the Haitian Revolution have incited the region's writers. Perhaps West Indian history offers such a great wealth of dramatic material that writers here have little reason to fictionalize, as Vere W. Knight says (1974: 76). Sylvia Wynter has said it eloquently: "History, then, these things that happen, is, in the plantation context, itself, fiction; a fiction written, dominated, controlled by forces external to itself" (Wynter 1971: 95). From C.L.R. James to Glissant, another critic has noted, the major Caribbean writers "have all pronounced on the moral imperative to retrieve a history 'blanked out' by the official discourse" (Zimra 1988: 7).

In a similar way, Guy Tirolien in *Balles d'or* and Césaire in *Ferrement* both evoke the epic deeds of the Martinican hero Louis Delgrès. Glissant's *Le Quatrième Siècle* delves into four centuries of black experience in the Antilles. Patrick Chamoiseau's *Texaco* recreates a meaningful portion of the black Antillean's historic resistance. *Romancero aux ètoiles* by Alexis evokes the courage of Taino Queen Anacaona, victim of a massacre perpetrated by Santo

Domingo Governor Nicolás de Ovando in 1504. Jean Metellus, another Haitian author, has revisited the same figure in his play *Anacaona*. History, however, need not refer the reader only to the remote past. The exploration of recent twentieth-century political repression in her trilogy *Amour, colère et folie* (1969) forced Haitian novelist Marie Vieux Chauvet into exile (Paravisini-Gebert 1993: 74). Exploring the present manifestations of social structures whose genesis goes back to past events also satisfies the Caribbean search for history in literature. Contemporary fiction in Haiti, even after the Duvalier regime, continued to explore the devastating impact of Duvalierism. Joseph Ferdinand observes that this corpus "which has traditionally been nourished by the past, was now seeking to use the present, whose citizens seem like characters from a fantastic novel" (1984: 128).

In the Dominican Republic, prose fiction achieved maturity with Manuel de Jesús Galván's *Enriquillo* (1882), a novel based on the story of Guarocuya, the Taino warrior conventionally taken as the foremost symbol of Dominican nationality. The 1980 novel *Sólo cenizas hallarás (Bolero)* by Pedro Vergés can be read as "a scrupulously historical picture" of life in Santo Domingo the year after Trujillo's death (Cruz-Malavé 1988: 63). Without a doubt, as Margarita Fernández Olmos (1988: 87) recognizes to her delight, or does Doris Sommer (1980: 184) to her chagrin, contemporary Dominican fiction is largely engaged in historical exploration. The most prolific of Dominican fiction writers, Marcio Veloz Maggiolo, has authored works such as *La vida no tiene nombre* (1965), *Los ángeles de hueso* (1967), and *De abril en adelante* (1975), each of which undertakes to capture a distinct chapter in twentieth-century Dominican history. The most widely read Dominican fiction work *Los que falsificaron la firma de Dios* (1992), a roman-à-clef by Viriato Sención, treats contemporary political corruption in the country so vividly that the government-sponsored National Book Prize awarded to it by a literary panel was revoked with the public approval of President Joaquín Balaguer as reported on the front page of most major Dominican newspapers on May 7 1993.

In Puerto Rico, it is quite probable that the importance of the novels of someone like Enrique Laguerre "stems from their intrinsic value as social commentaries on diverse periods of Puerto Rican history" (Acosta Belén 1980: 184). Nor can a reading of the texts of Luis Rafael Sánchez, Emilio Díaz Valcárcel, José Luis González or René Marqués miss the examination of historical dynamics as an omnipresent element. In Cuba, Carpentier's "predilection for history" (Irish 1970: 98) is typified in his short novel *El acoso* (1956), which ingeniously recreates the atmosphere surrounding the struggles against the dictatorship of Machado in the 1930s. Two younger writers, Severo Sarduy in *Gestos* (1963) and Miguel Barnet in *Canción de Rachel* (1969) very successfully undertake the rewriting of Carpentier's text and in so doing present "their rival claims to historical authenticity" (Bush

1980: 161). Barnet's *Autobiografía de un cimarrón* (1966) recounts the stages of Esteban Montejo's life as a slave, as a maroon, and as a fighter in the ranks of the independence movement. Through Esteban Montejo the text chronicles the stages passed by Cuba from the late nineteenth century to the early twentieth. Edmundo Desnoes's *Memorias del subdesarrollo* (1966) dramatizes the angst of a bourgeois intellectual who did not abandon his country with the advent of the revolution of 1959 and had to experience, among other things, the turbulence of the missile crisis.

In the Anglophone Caribbean, the Morant Rebellion of 1865 in Jamaica, which provides the starting point for Vic Reid's *New Day* (1949), had also figured in Herbert G. de Lisser's *Revenge* (1918), though from an opposite, reactionary, perspective. De Lisser is charged with having treated past events "in a rather cavalier fashion" (Chang 1985: 16). Edgar Mittelholzer's Kaywana trilogy unearths over two centuries of Guyanese history. Lamming's novels, from *In the Castle of my Skin* (1950) to *Natives of my Person* (1974), exhibit the passage from a conflictive to a "fresher perspective on West Indian history" (Núñez-Harrel 1986: 32). In truth, few of the region's writers have escaped the lure of the historical imagination. This "predilection for history" need not manifest itself, of course, in pure historiographical writing. Mark McWatt, who sees a connection between the treatments of the myth of El Dorado by Harris and Naipaul and the West Indian writer's "obsession" with "the historical past", suggests that it can manifest itself also at the level of the imaginary (McWatt 1985: 46). The critic Kenneth Ramchand prefers the imaginative experience of fictional characters such as Mr. Biswas in Naipaul's *A House for Mr. Biswas* (1961) and the boy Francis in Michael Anthony's *The Year in San Fernando* (1965) to the more obviously "historical novels". But he also concedes that these imaginative portrayals "are concerned with contemporary reality" and consequently with historical processes, as are "nearly all West Indian novels" (Ramchand 1971: 101).

The convergence of the "historical imagination" throughout the area is such that it may well be almost redundant to speak of "the historical novel" as a separate genre in the Caribbean. Among the factors determining the omnipresence of historical exploration must be the conviction among Caribbean literary artists that the historiography they have inherited was shaped and ideologically constructed by the scribes of Western colonialism. These scribes, among whom may figure some Caribbean-born historians, tended to chronicle the region's past in ways that favoured the imposition and continuance of colonial social structures. The perception voiced by Wynter that the only history written and taught in the area "is the history of the plantation, the official history of the superstructure" gives rise to the perceived need for a more complete understanding and a more correct rendition of the lived experience of the region (Wynter 1971:

101). The understanding that just as the socio-political dynamics of local events were determined externally, the recording of those events has generally obeyed the command of a vision looking to the Western metropolis rather than to the West Indies themselves, has bred a widespread desire to undertake a general historiographical repair in the area.

West Indians, as has been affirmed, achieve their sense of self-recognition insofar as they are able to tell their story themselves (Mouralis 1983: 25). The telling of the region's history, then, requires considerable correction, addition and refashioning, and in this part of the world, history is not "the business of historians alone," as Glissant has emphatically affirmed (1981: 133).

The revision of history here goes hand in hand with the exploration of myth, the latter taken as the first given of the historical consciousness. These have been fused together in the region's literature to bring the true legacy of the Caribbean people to the foreground. For some, this entails an appreciation and reevaluation of the folk and their traditions. Brathwaite, for instance, has emphasized the "little traditions" of the folk in his definition of Caribbean culture since it is in the lower class strata that socio-cultural fusions most inexorably occur. With Wynter, I would challenge Sommer's belief that the raising of the Caribbean folk to the level of historical discourse necessarily verges on the "heroic folkish mythology of a Hitler" (Sommer 1983: 256, 265-66). The interplay of history proper with myth and legend occupies a legitimate and central position in the literary worldview that is reflected in Caribbean poetics.

Finally, in their engagement with history, religion, and language, Caribbean writers reflect an overwhelming concern with fathoming the human landscape in the region in its full complexity. The need to work out decisive issues concerned with ontological imperatives and their people's place in the larger scheme of things has magnetically attracted Caribbean writers to focus on language, religion, and history which, as we have said, are three central paradigms that can be used to chart a Caribbean poetics. In their use of and reflection on such paradigms, Caribbean writers present themselves thematically and formally in contradistinction to their counterparts in the Western metropolis. In their attitude to the West – in relation to which they exist as marginal writers – and their attitude to their local setting – in relation to which they function as spokespersons – Caribbean writers practice a *modus scribendi* whose uniqueness corresponds to their unique world. So far I have described and illustrated that *modus scribendi*, called here Caribbean poetics, in general terms. I shall now look more closely at the empirical illustration yielded by the works of Kamau Brathwaite, René Depestre, and Pedro Mir, three major writers of the region. In addition to the high calibre of their work, their texts allow for individual readings with differentiated emphases on language, religion, and history. Needless to say, Brathwaite, Depestre, and Mir are authors of elaborate *oeuvres* which are pregnant with interpretive possibilities and can withstand readings that diverge from the emphases stressed here. Taken together their works exemplify much of the richness and wonder of the Caribbean literary imagination and the indomitability of the creative genius of the human species.

3

KAMAU BRATHWAITE AND THE CARIBBEAN WORD

. .isn't it odd that the only language I have in which to speak of this crime is the language of the criminal who committed the crime?
Jamaica Kincaid (1989: 31)

Few *oeuvres* stress Caribbean literature's deep concern with language as sharply as that of the Barbadian Kamau Brathwaite. A poet, historian, fiction writer, and critic, Brathwaite became known in the early 1950s primarily through his contributions to *Bim*, which in addition to *Kyk-over-Al* was then the leading cultural journal in the Anglophone West Indies. He had already gained distinction as one of the leading producers of intellectual discourse in the area when his first published volume of poetry in 1967, *Rights of Passage*, brought him recognition throughout the Third World and to a lesser extent in the UK. A select list of his honours include the 1986 Casa de las Américas Prize for a collection of essays entitled *Roots*, which was republished in the United States seven years later by the University of Michigan Press (Brathwaite 1993), the 1987 Commonwealth Prize for Poetry, awarded by the London-based Commonwealth Institute, and the 1994 Neustadt International Prize for Literature. The Autumn 1994 number of *World Literature Today* (Vol. 68 No. 4) was devoted to his life and work. In 2002 he was awarded an honorary doctorate by the University of Sussex; in 2006 the Gold Musgrave award for Literature from the Institute of Jamaica and in 2010 the W.E.B. DuBois award. Today his prestige as a major contemporary poet has spread through Africa, the Caribbean, England, and the United States. A glance at the large body of criticism generated by Brathwaite's literary production reveals a common thread that frequently points to the element of sound in his texts. Decades ago a reviewer in England referred to Brathwaite's *Rights of Passage* (1967) as "very much a 'script' for recitation", and over twenty years later a West Indian critic observed that: "Acoustic effect and phonetic play have always been an important element in Brathwaite's poetry" (Lucie-Smith 1968: 100; Dash 1987: 88).

The pages that follow will provide a wide socio-aesthetic and cultural frame within which to view the implications of the soundscapes identified by critics in the poetry of Brathwaite. The recitative element, the acoustic effect, the phonetic play, the centrality assigned to sound in his texts, form part of a complex vision of art, culture, and society. That vision, as we shall see, corresponds to an overall philosophy of language that has aesthetic implications for virtually all facets of Brathwaite's literary practice. His poetry, prose fiction, historiographical essays, and literary criticism, all reflect a scheme of thought wherein the very substance of language as well as its referentiality is seen as a means of communication, a vehicle of cultural identity, a potential instrument of liberation from the vestiges of colonial education, and the principal ingredient of an aesthetics that delves into the socio-historical specificity of the Caribbean to uncover the elements of an authentic way of saying.

Culture and the Individual Talent

Brathwaite's idea of language is inextricably linked to his notion of culture and the artist's relationship to the community in a given socio-cultural context. His 1957 essay "Sir Galahad and the Islands" described what he perceived as a dichotomy in the attitudes of literary artists in the Caribbean regarding their native "island cultures". He distinguished those writers who chose to remain in the West Indies, whom he dubbed "Islanders", from those he called "Emigrants", the ones who felt they must leave "whether that migration is in fact or by metaphor" (Brathwaite 1957: 8). Among the former, he spoke positively of those who in their writings absorb their surroundings by claiming a "heritage". They reflect an attitude of alliance with the folk, the peasant tradition, evincing their recognition that they do "depend on" people, and in so doing augur a bright future for Caribbean letters (ibid pp. 8, 11, 13). George Lamming had earlier sketched out that view by claiming that the West Indian novel at its best is essentially rooted in peasant life (1960: 25).

While Brathwaite privileged the "Islanders" over the "Emigrants", he made a significant reference to the latter's distinctive use of language. Speaking of the fiction writers, he praised their use of narrators who "speak what is practically a West Indian language" (1957: 8). Brathwaite would further this point in his 1960 review of the anthology *Voices of Ghana* by Henry Swanzy. There he hailed the compiler's effort for "bringing in the voices of the people of the new nation making patterns of sound in hammer, engine, power saws, and the movement of earth and water" (Brathwaite 1960a: 131). Particularly he stressed the fact that the texts collected in the book were written in English by young Ghanaian writers "whose native language is not English" and who face the challenge of converting their "own forms and speech-rhythms into English", producing a sort of English which "while retaining its peculiar West African flavour" may be deemed "acceptable at any level by the critical intelligence" (ibid). What Brathwaite referred to as "the power and certainty of the writing", primarily "the way it celebrates and takes confidence from the culture and traditions of the land" in the Ghanaian anthology, appeared to him to have exemplary implications for West Indian writing (ibid 131-32).

Brathwaite's early criticism was prescriptive, along the lines suggested by the above dichotomy. He applauded, for instance, the achievement of the Jamaican V.S. Reid's novel *New Day* for its capturing "a feeling for the poetry of the spoken word, and an imagination capable of giving those spoken words life", an element which he found lacking in the novels of Edgar Mittelholzer (1960b: 207). Mittelholzer's novels, in Brathwaite's view, also lack "the actions of *people* in a given, recognizable society, acting under compulsions that we can understand" (ibid p. 206). Brathwaite requires in literature a "sense of social and moral values". The perceived absence of those values caused him to see a failure in John Hearne's *The Autumn Equinox* and their perceived presence made him hail the "peculiar distinction" of *A Quality of Violence* by Andrew Salkey (1960c: 217; 1960d: 219). Likewise, despite his positive words in praise of the "intuition" in Wilson Harris's poetry, he found it "limited through its inability to communicate at the level of religious significance" (1960e: 114).

The judgments Brathwaite has passed on the literary artists of the region are all linked directly or indirectly to his conviction that the "value of the artist's work is in the intercommunication between himself and his special public" (1960b: 206). In the essay "The New West Indian Novelists", he argued that when writers have their native public it is they who will best appreciate their style. When one writes as an "Emigrant" one becomes divorced from one's natural literary habitat and suffers the lack of "that special criticism and appreciation" which only the writer's own *home* public can provide (1960b: 206). Brathwaite declared in effect that "the final responsibility for the future and achievement of West Indian literature lies in the sympathy and sense of proportion of the West Indian reading public" (1961a: 280).

Brathwaite's early critical writings made the ability to communicate to a "home public" a part of the merit of literary artists. There must be a correspondence between the literary text, which is a cultural product, and the society and culture that inform it. A literary text, consequently, has its autochthonous audience, whose human drama it must address if it is to be considered authentic. V.S. Naipaul's *A House for Mr. Biswas* earns praise from Brathwaite because in it the novelist exhibits an acute awareness of the predicament of his own socio-cultural community, the East Indians of the Caribbean, "first brought here as indentured labour after Emancipation in 1838" (1963a: 16; 1968: 159). But the relationship between writers and their people must be genuine and not based purely on aesthetic and intellectual gymnastics. His essay "Roots" decries the practice of those West Indian novelists who derive their folk talk and rhythmic prose style from Anglo-American literature, "the Lawrence-Steinbeck-Hemingway tradition", contending that their use of "the people's speech" is not authentic since it does not arise from a real contact with the people" (1963a: 20). Since practically none of the writers referred to by Brathwaite could actually be said to form part "of the people", belonging as they do to the middle class, he conjectures that these writers' use of *folk* rhythms might actually be "a sign *and* symbol of their rejection of society" (ibid p. 20). Thus he proposes "a *prose* style which can catch the varying shifts and shades of narrative, action, and speech" in the West Indies in light of his conviction that a literary text that lacks an authentic relationship between writer and society cannot succeed artistically (ibid). Following that line of reasoning, he deems *The Scholar Man*, a novel by O.R. Dathorne, "a failure at all levels" (1965a: 68). At the same time, he praises Derek Walcott's *The Castaway* because there the St. Lucian poet succeeds in addressing "our great dichotomy: the split in most of us between Africa and Europe" without exhibiting the "frustration" or the "bitter choice" that seems to beset so many when confronted with the same realization (1966a: 140). Characteristically, the aesthetic valuation focuses persistently on the writer's relationship with the people, the society, the cultural habitat informing the creation of his or her text.

In Search of the Word

Brathwaite's literary practice as a creative artist during this early part of his career accords with the socio-aesthetic doctrine he had been expostulating in his critical writings. A short story entitled "The Black Angel" published in 1955 presents us with characters whose destiny follows the ups and downs in the town's factory, the sole source of employment for the people. While the town remains unnamed, the narrator's descriptions, even at the topographical level, place the setting unmistakably in the Caribbean. More importantly, the protagonist wins his battle against the unknown through the strength derived from the wisdom of the *folk*, symbolized here in Ta Mega, the "high priestess". Guardian of the spiritual well-being of the townspeople, she uses her "necromancography" to help him fight the forces of evil (1955: 84).

The narrative tension of another of Brathwaite's early fiction pieces, "Law and Order", is maintained through the cultural distance between the young sweethearts, Emma and Horace. The action takes place in a Ghanaian village where she is a native and he a foreigner. While strolling down the beach, they are harassed by a group of Ga fishermen, and it is up to Emma to confront the marauders, communicate, and negotiate with them. Though feeling that "after all this was a *man*'s palaver", Horace has to stay out of it because "he couldn't understand the language" (Brathwaite 1955b: 197). Here, as elsewhere in the story, what amuses most is the crisis of communication between Emma and Horace: her efforts to translate her culture to him, his almost unavoidable misconstruing of her rendition, and, consequently, their failure to say anything meaningful to each other. Here, as in "Cricket", a story published years later, language acquires centrality as a means through which to measure cultural authenticity. "Cricket", told almost entirely in Barbadian dialect, recreates an eventful match in the recent history of West Indian cricket. In enacting an encounter between a Caribbean team and a British team, the story symbolically dramatizes a colonial confrontation. The British invented cricket and brought it to the region, just as they brought the English language during the colonial transaction. Rendered mostly via a dialogue among the Creole-speaking characters, the dynamics of the match evoke the need felt by colonial people to prove their worth at the former masters' own game, "de very game they invent" (Brathwaite 1973a: 66).

When the Caribbean cricketers excel, they demonstrate their appropriation of the formerly British sport. Parallel to this, when the characters narrate the event in a West Indian vernacular we are also witnessing the nativization of English, the appropriation of the colonial master's language, another level of colonial confrontation. Using dialect means asserting the local culture, the culture of the folk. How the relationship between the colonial language and its nativized counterpart can affect human interactions in the Caribbean is suggested in an episode from "Christine", a text published in 1961 which appeared in print as a chapter from Brathwaite's still unpublished novel *The Boy and the Sea*. The contrapuntal effect of the dialogue between the two main characters, Adam and his teenage girlfriend Christine, dominates the narrative flow. They speak in a demotic language using recognizable forms of West Indian dialect. Playfully and with an unmistakable tenderness, the conversation revolves around their elders' supposed opposition to their romance. Only when Adam feels the need to scold Christine, do we hear him say: "Don't you know you shouldn't jump down like that from the branch of a tree?" – the only standard English sentence we hear him utter in their whole dialogue (Brathwaite 1961b: 249). This switch from the nativized speech to standard English indicates the characters' deep understanding of the linguistic codes available to them and their societal implications. Adam seems to sense that to sound for a moment rigidly prohibitive, he can do no better than to step outside the aura of intimacy and love which has been established through their Creole communication. To achieve a momentary distance from his sweetheart he reverts to the official language of the establishment, the standard English of the schools and the upper classes.

Brathwaite's theatrical writings illustrate his preoccupation with language and cultural authenticity no less than his prose fiction and his criticism. He wrote plays primarily while serving as an education officer in Ghana, a country with a complex linguistic situation. "English, the major language of education in this country, is not indigenous," says S. Addo in his introduction to four plays by Brathwaite (Addo 1964: iii). These plays, intended for primary schools, evoke the emblematic texture of Medieval mystery plays and derive much of their dramatic tension from their incorporation, both in form and content, of the linguistic situation and the socio-cultural reality of the people of Ghana. The collection includes *The Children's Gifts*, a reworking of the Nativity in an African setting, *Rabbit at the Well* and *Ananse and the Dinner Drum*, both of which draw on moralistic animal fables from African lore, and *The People That Walk in Darkness*, a recreation of another moment from the Nativity. The playwright allows for "improvisation sections" meant to be filled with words spoken by the children acting in their own mother tongue, as he recommends to future producers in his preface (Brathwaite 1964a: v). Three of the four plays feature a character who goes by the name of "the Linguist". In a characteristic scene from *The People that Walk in Darkness*, the birth of Mary and Joseph's child, made possible after defeating personified Darkness, is announced to a group of fishermen who are able to rejoice in the glorious news because the message is brought by angels who speak to them "in their own language" (p. 38).

Brathwaite's book-length play, *Odale's Choice* (1967a), takes up the Antigone story. The story here preserves the ethical dilemma and the existential predicament facing the heroine in the play by Sophocles which so delighted the mind of Hegel, who thought of it as "the most excellent and satisfying work of art" (Hegel 1962: 74). For the German philosopher, Creon and Antigone "stand fundamentally under the power of that which they battle, and consequently infringe that which, conformably to their own essential life, they ought to respect (p. 72). Hegel further observed that the play dramatized a clash between the two highest moral powers: "family love, what is holy, what belongs to the inner life and to inner feeling, and which because of this is also called the law of the nether gods, come into collision/– With the law of the State" (p. 325).

But, by placing the action against the backdrop of a tangible neocolonial setting, Brathwaite manages to incorporate into the drama a socio-cultural dimension and to season it with the conflict of varying linguistic codes. The social stratification of the characters is revealed in that the soldiers speak dialect while the higher ranking members of the power structure speak standard English. Thus, when the sergeant comes to Creon with the news that his edict has been violated, the head of state demands to be addressed in the official language: "For God's sake speak the language man! Don't talk to me in that damn pigeon all the time! Speak the language" (Brathwaite 1967a: 23). There is the suggestion also that Odale's challenge to the power structure may have the unexpressed support of people in the lower social ranks as represented by the character of Musa. Brathwaite's plays, like the other genres he has practised, seek to localize all human experience within very discrete historical circumstances. The characters have conflicts that correspond to the demands of a given society and their actions are coloured by distinct cultural variables. Language, whether it be the imposition of an official code or the affirmation of an alternative one, occupies a central position in the people's grappling with history, society, and culture. Even when dealing with an African setting, the plays bear relevance for the Caribbean and could probably be hailed for their "essentially West Indian or even suggestively regional" nature, to borrow the words of a reviewer (Marshall 1965: 71).

Poetry and Cultural Centredness

Brathwaite's poetry continues and expands the socio-aesthetic paths suggested by his texts in other genres, particularly since the publication of *Rights of Passage*, his first book-length poetic work to appear in print. His verse production before 1967 appeared in *Bim* and in various anthologies (Murphy 1970: 129). A good many of these early poems found their way into the poet's subsequent volumes (particularly *Other Exiles*, 1975). One could easily concur with Brathwaite's own assessment that his "verse until 1965 had no real centre" (cited in Murphy 1970: 129). For him the "centre" of his poetry came about only after he completed "the triangular trade" of his historical origins, that is, the passage from Barbados to England, from England to Ghana, and from Ghana back to the West Indies. His verse developed a definite direction, he affirms, after he acquired a "sense of belonging". And while he acknowledges a "European" influence through T.S. Eliot, he insists that his "major influence was perhaps the West Indian novelists who from the very beginning have been putting the speech of our people into our ears" (cited in Murphy 1970: 129). His explanation of how his verse production arrived at a point of aesthetic coherence clearly suggests a link in Brathwaite's mind between literary creativity and an awareness of one's socio-historical ontology.

Rights of Passage is the first part of a poetic trilogy that would subsequently appear under the title *The Arrivants* (1973b). Divided into four sections, the poem announces its theme in its epigraph from *Exodus* (16:1), which, in telling of the peregrination of the "children of Israel" upon their departure from Egypt, announces the journey which pervades the text. The first section, "Work Song and Blues", begins with a "Prelude" that sets the predominantly epic tone of the poem. Despite its peculiar line arrangement, the first stanza preserves a distantly perceptible echo of the Virgilian premium: "Drum skin whip/lash, master sun's/cutting edge of/heat, taut/ surfaces of things/I sing/I shout/I groan/I dream/about" (1973b: 4). *The*

Aeneid is the story of a historic voyage that traces in mythopoetic terms the origins of the people for whom the poem is written. *Rights of Passage* presents "an impression of the centuries of migration Westward across the Sahara, from Egypt to the West Coast of Africa", thus preparing the reader for the historic travel of the African people to their New World experience, which is a central concern of the poem (Rohlehr 1981: 23).

Early in *Rights of Passage* we come upon Brathwaite's stylistic exploration of a distinct sound quality to his subject matter. Passages such as: "Here clay/ cool coal clings/to glass, creates/clinks, silica glitters,/children of stars" (p. 5) draw on phonetic resources to convey meaning. Scholars have identified this practice as a common feature of Brathwaite's poetic production (D'Costa 1968: 25; Rohlehr 1980: 15-31). The preference for language that highlights sonority has thematic implications, particularly when Brathwaite develops the emphasis beyond being a resource of all poetry, to exploring its Caribbean specifics. Here he appears to believe that through the production of sound he comes closer to the sonority of the Caribbean world. The poet often uses sound to suggest an antidote to the destructiveness of silence. In the poem, the fight for life, for survival is frequently seen as a charge against silence. Silence evokes desolation in the African soil where the slaves were first seized: "...Flies/nibble and ulcer:/tight silver-/back swarms bringing/silence, the slender/proboscis of rot" (Brathwaite 1973b: 6). Images of death and destruction accompany silence: "...until sudden burst,/the buzzing black ones that were/silence, swirl through the/sunlight" (p. 6). Towards the end of the "Prelude", the first person singular which opened the poem transforms into a collective voice, saying: "Flame is our god, our last defence, our peril" (p. 8), enacting the bewailing of the slaves when faced with impending doom before the Middle Passage. This switch from singular to plural suggests a Protean transformation of the voice that occurs at various points throughout the poem. Implicit here is Brathwaite's notion of the harmony between the one and the many in a social group as the ideal relationship between an individual and his or her community.

The speaker in the poem "Tom" has a very clear sense of socio-historical identification, a definite idea of his origins, and a complete understanding of his place in his community. Derived from the central figure in the novel *Uncle Tom's Cabin* (1852) by Harriet Beecher Stowe, the character of Tom has been seen, particularly among African-Americans, as archetypical of the individuals who passively submit to oppression and who become champions of the interests of their masters (Malcolm X 1966). This poem, however, presents us with a view of Tom that shows the character's human depth and obdurate dignity. His apparent servility and submissiveness conceal a profound sense of resistance, to "mouth 'Massa, yes/Massa, yes/ Boss, yes/Baas' and hold my hat/in hand/to hide/my heart/hoping my children's eyes/will learn" (pp.15-16). Lloyd Brown has correctly pointed out that "considered as a whole Tom is as ambiguous as the circumstances of his conception. His habitual self-negation is actually a thinly disguised mode of defiant survival" (Brown 1984: 150). Tom's use of the first person plural indicates a clear awareness of his unique history as well as of his socio-cultural alterity vis-à-vis those in relation to whom he must live in subservience: "we who have achieved nothing/work/who have not built/dream/who have forgotten all/dance/and dare to remember" (Brathwaite 1973b: 13).

"The Spades", the second part of *Rights of Passage*, also begins with a "Prelude". It explores the various transformations of the African descendant in the New World and Europe and surveys some of the many human types that have arisen from the African diaspora. The multiple vocal characterizations that surface here struck Mervyn Morris as a "lack of unity of tone" (1967: 64), but it would seem more reasonable, however, to interpret these vocal shifts as an attempt by the poet to represent the "typical transformations of the Negro", as Edward Baugh put it, or, in the words of Gordon Rohlehr as "the several faces, masks, poses, and voices of the deracinated African in the New World" (Baugh 1967: 66; Rohlehr 1978: 64). This part of the book, at any rate, concerns itself less with historical reminiscence and more with an assessment of the contemporary descendants of the African slaves. Their presence is undeniable in the cultural centres of Africa, the Americas, the United States, and France: "in the fall we reached De-/troit Chicago and Den-/ver; and then it was New/York selling news-/papers in Brooklyn and Harlem./Then Capetown and Rio; remember how we/took Paris by storm: Sartre, Camus, Picasso and all?" (Brathwaite 1973b: 36).

The text entitled "Folkways" explores some of the known stereotypes constructed around these African descendants, including their sometimes demeaning self-characterizations. But most evident here is the concern with the music of the folk: "o' this work-song singin' you singin'/the chant o' this work chain" (p. 32). Through the allusion in the title and in the text to Folkways Records – the concern established by Alan Lomax to promote American Negro music around the world – we are reminded that music has often been one of the avenues of survival used by New World Africans. In lines such as: "quick bugle/train, black/boogie-/woogie wheels/fat/boogie/woogie waggons/rat tat tat" (p. 33) the language clearly aims to reproduce onomatopoeically what has been called "train blues". Also, the sombre languor of the blues is intended in these characteristic lines: "Ever seen/a man/travel more/seen more/lands than this poor/land-/less, harbour-/less spade" (p. 39). How these echoes of specifically Negro musical forms are central to Brathwaite's aesthetic plan in this book has been thoroughly demonstrated by Rohlehr (1980: 32-40).

But certainly music has not been the only vehicle of survival. There has also been outright, militant resistance. "Wings of a Dove", whose speaker identifies himself as a Rastafarian, covers this aspect of the African New World experience. Here the speaker recounts the plight of his people, their articulation of the oppressor in ethnic terms, and their appeal to a god who might favour them. The text begins with stanzas spoken in standard English, but as the speaker reproduces the voice of what he calls "my people", the tone of protest is heightened and a drastic change occurs in the morphology of the words: "Rise rise/locks-/man, Solo-/man wise/man, rise/rise rise/leh we/laugh/dem, mock/dem stop/dem, kill/dem an' go/back back/to the black/man lan'/back back/to Af-/rica" (Brathwaite 1973b: 43). Here is certainly an instance of what Louis James in a review of *Rights of Passage* referred to as Brathwaite's deliberate fracturing of "the conventional English cadences" to awaken the reader's attention to "the cadence of Caribbean speech" (James 1967: 41). But the practice has thematic implications as well. It presents language as being closer to the expression of the folk the farther it is from the standard forms of the schools and the upper classes. It insinuates also that the folk utter their wish for liberation in more militant terms than do those in the higher sectors of society. Marcus Garvey, one of the most intransigent leaders the black struggle has known, came from the folk. Similarly, Malcolm X, the most influential proponent of black nationalism in the United States, came from the lowest ranks of society. The possibility that those at the bottom, those suffering oppression in its crudest form, are quicker to speak an authentic speech of liberation seems to be behind the switch in linguistic codes from standard English to Creole forms in the above lines.

The last two sections of the book, "Islands and Exiles" and "The Return", dramatize the condition of dispossession and permanent exile of people in the Caribbean. A poem suggestively entitled "The Emigrants" describes the lot of Caribbeans who for want of a productive existence in their own lands often opt for testing their luck abroad. In the other Americas, the United States, and Europe, Caribbean people reverse the route initially charted by Columbus, and find that those shores do not hold in store for "these New World mariners" the wealth and the prestige that awaited the Admiral in the fifteenth century. It is only rhetorically that the speaker asks: "What Cathay shores/for them are gleaming golden/what magic keys they carry to unlock/what gold endragoned doors?" (Brathwaite 1973b: 52). These deracinated Caribbeans do not often fare well abroad, especially in the Christian West, where they are often met with outright hostility: "Once we went to Europe, and a rich old lady asked:/Have you no language of your own/no way of doing things/did you spend all those holidays/at England's apron strings?" (p. 55).

What is left for Caribbean people seems to be the option chosen by the speaker in "South". There he turns his eyes back to the archipelago, declaring: "But today I recapture the islands'/bright beaches" (p. 57). He rejoices in the natural beauty of the region and extracts from nature's very elements a source of historical hope: "And gulls, white sails slanted seaward,/fly into the limitless morning before us" (p. 58). That hopeful evocation of the area's potential gives the strength needed to assess realistically the otherwise hopeless situation of the West Indies as perceived by the speaker. He can then see the Caribbean soil as an intricate mixture of hope and frustration. From a picture of desolation, "the landscape with the broken homes" (p. 61), in the poem "O Dreams O Destinations" we move to "The Dust", where we find a moving portrayal of the wisdom of the folk. While evincing a measure of socio-historical misunderstanding about themselves as a people and about their affinity with the people who "speak so/in they St. Lucia patois" (p. 66) and while mouthing the conformism that often comes with Christian religious devotion, they instinctively sense things happening "widdout rhyme widdout reason" and feel dissatisfied with the prevailing order of things. Far from explaining their sorrows away, as their biblical training would encourage, they give vent to their doubt: "Why is that/what it mean?" (p. 69). Because of its sensitive delving into the experience of the folk, "The Dust" has been called a "near perfect expression of the life, music and philosophy of the people" (Pollard 1980: 41).

When looking panoptically at the region, the speaker in *Rights of Passage* does not fail to pass judgment on the disciples of Mammon among African descendants, those with a strong proclivity to imitate their former masters when governing themselves in the Caribbean. Through mass education, they preserve the same patterns of thought fostered by the former slave owners. Imitating the manners of the British and relishing their books, they, deprived of selves, go to school to learn how to be good British subjects. The pertinent question here seems to be: Where is the home of those who have been trained to be other than themselves: "In Paris Brixton Kingston/Rome?/Here?/Or in Heaven?" (Brathwaite 1973b: 77). The text poses a disturbing question and promises no easy answer. The speaker's historical past has not been easily visible to him and its legacy has often given cause for self-mockery and shame: "the old/unflamed remains/of Tom we sometimes/joke/about" (p. 78). He seems to see no other alternative but to define himself by his dispossession, which he, oddly enough, construes as an avenue of self-affirmation.

Rights of Passage closes with an "Epilogue" in which the speaker, after examining the journey of the children of the diaspora and their various legacies in the New World, declares that: "There is no turning back" (p. 85). The conclusion is neither sad nor happy but starkly true. Uprooted from their African abode, the slave descendants became deracinated through the colonial transaction. Living now for centuries in the New World, they cannot truly call Africa their home. Any search for a constructive existence in the present must begin with the conviction that the Middle Passage is irreversible. Clearly, we can read here a dismissal of the alternative proposed by Garvey's "Back-to-Africa" movement in the early twentieth century as an expression of a legitimate yet hopeless desire. This should not be seen, however, as a negation of the past in the search for origins, the valuation of cultural authenticity, and the coinage of a psychologically and aesthetically effective language. The point here, instead, seems to be that Africa provides not a *home* to which one returns but rather a source from which one draws understanding in order better to grasp the meaning of one's life in the Caribbean setting. As would later be said of the third volume of Brathwaite's trilogy, Africa becomes here a "fructifying interlude in the long task of finding a language and a ritual" befitting the Caribbean experience (Moore 1970: 186). One could infer from this the teleological notion that home is where one ends up, as opposed to the aetiological proposition: "Home is where one starts from" that we read in the "East Coker" section of T.S. Eliot's *Four Quartets* (1971: 129). In Brathwaite, destination takes precedence over origins, although the ability to go forward presupposes the empowerment that comes from knowing where one has come from. For someone who has to contend with an ignominious past of slavery, dehumanization, and dispossession, home is not "where one starts from" but rather a stage to which one *arrives*, after one has survived the misery of the earlier stages. The collective title of Brathwaite's trilogy is called, not incidently, *The Arrivants*.

The African Quest

The use of Africa as a source from which to draw understanding forms the core of *Masks* (1968), the second volume in Brathwaite's *The Arrivants*. "Only the fool points at his origins with the left hand," says the Akan proverb that serves as epigraph to the book. The book is divided into seven parts. Its first part, "Libation", begins with a "Prelude" that identifies the geographical and historical setting of the poem: "Out/of... the seven/ Kingdoms:/Songhai, Mali,/Chad, Ghana,/Tim-/buctu, Volta,/and the bitter/waste was/Ben-/in, comes/this shout/comes/this song". What we have here is a lyrical – though not romanticized – exploration of the African past from the ancient empires of old to the arrival of the Europeans. *Masks* has been the subject of various close readings, chiefly by Rohlehr (1981) and Maureen Warner-Lewis (1977). Our reading here focuses primarily on the poem's emphasis on tying the search for origins to a preoccupation with language and communication against an aura of religious significance.

Throughout *Masks* we find an emphasis on sounds and the rejection of its antithesis, silence. Particularly meaningful in this respect is "The Making of the Drum", which enacts the stages involved in the construction of the drum in ancient African culture. The ceremony surrounding the creation of the instrument symbolizes the awareness of these traditional people with regards to the need for an antithesis to silence. This is clear when we hear of the exigencies around the choice of wood for the barrel of the drum. It has to be the kind of wood whereby: "we hear the sounds/of the rivers;/vowels of reed-/lips, pebbles/of consonants,/underground dark/ of the continent" (Brathwaite 1973b: 95). In her reading, Warner-Lewis has found that sound (speech, song, music) and water are images of life and attainment whereas "silence and dumbness betray inactivity and death", consistently revealing a clear dichotomy throughout the poem and occasionally appearing as a juxtaposition (Warner-Lewis 1977: 19, 40). If one accepts this dichotomy as mythopoetically plausible, the meaning of this particular part of the poem emerges clearly. We can see that the drum is the most valuable object of these traditional people's craft because it is the vehicle through which the divine order can communicate with them. "God is dumb/until the drum/speaks," we hear (Brathwaite 1973b: 97). The drum serves as the language of ultimate communication. This first section concludes with "Atumpan", a text in which the actual sounds of the drum are reproduced ("kon kon kon kon/kun kun kun kun") to conjure Odomankoma, the sky-god Creator, who in turn speaks through the sounds of the drum (p. 98).

In general, the sonorous quality of *Masks* is achieved by a combination of onomatopoetic reproduction of drumming vibrations, the incorporation of ritual song forms and hymns, the introduction of various Akan words and phrases, as well as the exploration of Akan syntactical structures in English. One critic at least has, in an otherwise favourable review, objected to passages in the book that she finds more functional in sound than in sense, suggesting that the poem is bound by its rhetoric and exterior dimension (Risden 1967: 147). However, the more common view agrees with another critic for whom in Brathwaite the use of "sound itself" constitutes "another extension of the literary uses of language" (New 1978: 368). Warner-Lewis, for her part, sees sound and sense in the poem as inextricable, proposing that even those instances when the text is dominated by the "drum" sounds cohere into the overall "voice" of the poem (1977: 60). Even when the result appears to be what a critic calls "a hybrid prosody", the diction, syntax, and rhythm in *Masks* contribute to what Edward Baugh once called the "oneness of overall tone" (Lieberman 1969: 56; Baugh 1968: 209).

In the second section of *Masks*, "Pathfinders", the poem entitled "Ougadougou" [Wagadugu] significantly illustrates an important technique employed by Brathwaite. The words here are spoken by the Niger state as a persona. Talking in the first person as a character in a play, the speaker recalls in a spirit of self-recrimination the coming of warring visitors to the land: "Our errors before them; too soft,/too blandished, too ready for peace and for terror" (Brathwaite 1973b: 104). The states of Chad and Timbuktu also join the *dramatis personae*, and they too regret their lethal passivity. Finally, Volta, the personified river, symbol of the civilization that once flourished on its banks, speaks of a longing for the ancient glory of the empire (p. 109). In every case, the speaker (state, river, or person) comes summoned by the *mmenson*, the orchestra used on state occasions to relate history in ancient Akan tradition, to "recount now the gains and the losses" (p. 107), the past events of the land and its people. Through these various speakers, the poet allows himself the opportunity to rehearse diverse forms of telling in the text.

"Limits", the third section of *Masks*, explores the desolation of the ancient lands and their inhabitants. The collective memory, in desperation for a better time, appeals, for spiritual refuge, to the Egyptian past: "But the lips remember/temples, gods and pharaohs,/gold, silver ware; imagination/rose on wild unfolded wings" (p. 113). The speaker, however, reflects on the futility of overestimating a past which may also be filled with cruelty: "And Ra,/the sun/god's gold,/demanded blood/to make it sacred" (p. 114). It is, therefore: "Time to forget/these kings./Time to forget/these gods" (p. 114). One can read into these lines the suggestion that one must, when assessing the past, sort out the recoverable values from those that are to be rejected. Much has certainly been lost, abused, and misused, but, as the speaker in "Techiman" affirms, "the way lost/is a way to be found/again" (p. 119). The hope remains that the errors of the past can be averted in the future. Nor is it too late for repair because "Time's walking river is long" (p. 120).

The next two sections of the book, "The Return" and "Crossing the River", are particularly important because they enact the return of a New World African descendant to the original soil of the West African coast. The speaker evokes a pathos-filled encounter with the ancestral land and people. Their meeting becomes the most touching when it comes to verbal communication. When the New World Negro looks at the ancestral Africans, he sees their "white teeth/smooth voices like pebbles/moved by the sea of their language" (p. 124). They, of course, speak to him in the mother tongue: "*Akwaaba* they smiled/meaning welcome/*aye koo*" (p. 124). He is treated ceremoniously according to the demands of traditional hospitality. They realize that he has come "back a stranger/after three hundred years" and would wish to activate his memory: "here is a stool for/ you; sit; do/you remember?" (p. 124). He does not recognize them and their manner any more than they remember him. Here as elsewhere, the poem dramatizes the near amnesia which separates the survivors of the diaspora from their ancestral ways, as Warner-Lewis has appropriately observed (1973: 96).

The speaker here does not succeed, as Alex Haley in *Roots* (1976) claims to have done, in tracing his beginnings to an original progenitor in the

African continent. The return to the ancestral land leaves him with a sense of his disconnection. He utters this recognition: "I travelled to a distant town/I could not find my mother/I could not find my father/I could not hear the drum/whose ancestor am I" (p. 125). The disconnection from people and from the land manifests itself also in language (Warner-Lewis 1977: 56). For the fall of the glorious tribe in the past, as told by the speaker in "The Golden Stool", can be expressed as triumph of silence and death over the reign of the living word: "the priests cried:/die[...] Let the tongues,/lips' labials, rot;/withering words in the hot/wind. If/you must speak,/wear a black mask/of silence; ask-/ing no elder to lead you/again through the branch-/es, through the path-/ways of prayer,/to Onyame's now/leafless air" (Brathwaite 1973b: 145).

The final section of *Masks*, "Arrival", continues to dwell on the loss, but this time the speaker, who continues to be the New World African descendant, addresses contemporary African interlocutors. The arrival of the Europeans to the West African coast and the subsequent misery endured by their captives from the moment of uprooting through the various stages of the colonial transaction have coloured the intervening centuries. Reddened by the legacy of bloodshed and darkened by the oblivion resulting from the obliteration of ancient cultural traditions, history for the African descendant can hardly evoke pride and joy: "I wear this/past I borrowed; his-/tory bleeds/behind my hollowed eyes" (p. 148). The ancestral land also shows as much desolation as the New World abode: "Beginnings end here/in this ghetto" (p. 149). The African soil cannot help, nor can the ancient household gods since they, when the invaders came centuries ago, did "not save us from pride,/foreign tribes' bibles/the Christian god's hunger" (p. 149). Too long the machinery of destruction has prevailed, undoing the New World African people's sense of self and their creations, in the long colonial domination of the Europeans. In other words, "the termites' dark teeth, three/hundred years working,/have patiently ruined my art" (p. 150).

Despite the irreparability of his separation from the ancestral landscape and its people, however, the New World African and his counterparts in the old continent preserve a deeper memory that makes itself felt at the level of language: "welcome your brother now/my trapped curled tongue/still cries" (p. 148). Reference is made here to a sort of communication that transcends the centuries of uprooting and depredation. Perhaps the yearning for reconnection expressed here implies a reliance on the oneness of the peoples of the black diaspora with those who remained in the ancestral lands. This sense of an urge for communication between Africans and the children of the diaspora may have to do with a human experience which encountered equal misery at both ends of the Middle Passage. The last words in *Masks* are "I am learning/let me succeed" (p. 157). Spoken in the context of an invocation to Asase Yaa, the Akan earth goddess, those words would insinuate that it is in the areas of communication and understanding that the contact with the ancestral heritage can best equip the New World descendant of slaves. In this sense, the African journey of *Masks'* narrator justifies itself in the end as a journey of enlightenment and as a prelude to a "rediscovered voice" (Grant 1970: 187).

On Language and Home

Brathwaite's *Islands* (1969) completes the poetic trilogy *The Arrivants* and brings to closure the poet's "triangular trade". Just as the previous volumes dramatize the plight of the West Indian "emigrating" from the New World soil, going to Europe and then searching for "roots" in Africa, *Islands* brings the speaker back to the Caribbean. Divided into five sections, the poem begins with a part entitled "New World" which fathoms the spiritual climate of the region. The first poem, called "Jah", the name the Rastafarians of Jamaica use for God, illustrates this religious concern. The initial impression bespeaks a spiritual poverty prevailing in the area: "the land has forgotten the memory of the most secret places" (Brathwaite 1973b: 164). Then follows a prodding into the slave past to gather the remnants of a strong religious cosmology. We come upon the evocation of "Ananse", the Protean "spider-hero of the Akans; earthly trickster, but once with powers of the creator-gods" (p. 272). The epithets associated with the divinity ("dry stony word-maker, word-breaker,/creator"), whose close relationship with language is made evident, suggest to a significant extent that the search for a spiritual tradition in the area is closely connected to the search for an authentic speech.

It becomes clear in "Shepherd" that, as far as the speaker is concerned, the local milieu, despite the initial appearance, is rich in spirituality. "The streets of my home have their own gods/but we do not see them", he regrets (p. 189). All it takes to "see them" it would seem, is to enter into a sort of communion with one's surroundings so that one may be attuned to the language these surroundings speak. And they do try to communicate since: "the drum praises them/and the rope that loosens the tongue of the steeple;/ they speak to us with the voices of crickets,/with the shatter of leaves" (p. 190). The speaker utters his predications as a "shepherd" in the religious sense and more specifically as a "leader of the *pocomania* and other religious groups in the West Indies", as Brathwaite's "Glossary" explains (p. 275). His words, therefore, carry the weight of a collective regional voice. The general title of the second part of *Islands*, "Limbo" also sheds light on what we see here as an attempt to emphasize expressions which, like the religion of the folk, can be considered authentic Caribbean forms. For "limbo", though now frequently a kind of performance in Caribbean night clubs, has more authentic roots. Brathwaite's glossary describes it as: "a dance in which participants have to move with their bodies thrown backwards and without any aid whatsoever under a stick which is lowered at every successfully completed passage under it, until the stick is practically touching the ground. It is said to have originated – a necessary therapy – after the experience of the cramped conditions between the slave decks of the Middle Passage" (p. 274). It also refers to the state of liminality between continental African and African Caribbean identities, a limbo/liminal state also explored by Wilson Harris in his essay "The Limbo Gateway" (from *History Fable and Myth in the Caribbean and the Guianas* [1970])

"Caliban", another poem in the second section of the book, contains implications both for Caribbean religion and language. Caliban, inherited from Shakespeare's *The Tempest*, here becomes a spokesman for the region who clearly sees himself in contradistinction to the interests of the colonial power structure of the West. Curiously, *Une tempête*, Césaire's adaptation of Shakespeare's play, in which Prospero appears as "le colonisateur" and Caliban as "l'esclave nègre révolté", appeared in print the same year as Brathwaite's *Islands*, and Brathwaite was undoubtedly familiar with George Lamming's rethinking of *The Tempest* in *The Pleasures of Exile* (1960). At any rate, Caliban here begins with a bitter assessment of the dismal condition of his people in the Caribbean: "Ninety-five percent of my people poor/ninety-five percent of my people black/ninety-five percent of my people dead," he says (p. 191). A panoptic look at the region's history draws his eyes to pivotal moments which are also violent ones, and he asks: "How many bangs how many revolutions?" (p. 192). His survey of contemporary events yields a no less problematic picture. Present complexity is symbolized here by two opposing poles. The "limbo stick", on the one hand, smacks of socio-historical alienation: "stick is the whip/and the dark deck is slavery" (p. 194). The music, on the other hand, points to those elements in the local setting that contain the stuff of survival: "out of the dark/and the dumb gods are raising me/up/up/up/and the music is saving me" (p. 195).

To resist his indentured existence, Caliban must fight off a history that has deprived him of many of the symbols of his human integrity. Spiritual elevation becomes a potential vehicle of his liberation. But implicit in the choice of the Shakespearean character, who wields the ability to curse as a weapon of resistance against Prospero's domination, is the realization that his rebellion must also occur in the sphere of language. The choice of Caliban as a *persona* presupposes a confrontation which is no less dramatic than the one enacted in the poem, "Rites", a reworking in nation language of the short story "Cricket". In "Rites", as Kenneth Ramchand has pointed out, dialect and cricket are used in conjunction to suggest the drama of the islands (1976: 139).

In the third part of *Islands*, "Rebellion", the connection between history, spirituality and language is articulated in ways that are deeply meaningful for cultural authenticity in the Caribbean. The first poem here, "Wake", which has been described as "a highly formalized poem whose function is to summarize this journey from negation to self-affirmation", presents us with a speaker who seeks socio-cultural self-assurance through the spiritual equipment contained in language (Rohlehr 1981: 239). We hear him beg: "mother me with words,/gems, spoken talismans of your broken tongue" (Brathwaite 1973b: 210). It is in the absence of "the Word" that the moral poverty of the islands is most deeply felt. "For the Word is love/and has been absent from our butterflies./For the Word is peace/and is absent from our streets" (p. 212). The Word here, apart from its religious connotation, refers also concretely to language. As Rohlehr has indicated, it is for language that the speaker begs his Ibo ancestors, whose "incarnation must result in poetry" (1971: 196). For the speaker in "Naming" it seems an unequivocal equation that the absence of language necessarily amounts to an absence of meaning, for: "What is a word to the eye?/Meaning" (Brathwaite 1973b: 217).

Languageless peoples lack the power to name things and, in a certain sense, to make things happen: "The tree must be named./This gives it fruit/ issues its juices" (p. 217). The magical possibilities here attributed to naming recall the creative power of the Word in the African concept of *Nommo* as expounded by Janheinz Jahn in *Muntu* (Morris 1970: 19). Similarly unproductive is the use of language that cannot be called one's own. For the speaker in "Eating the Dead", this can lead to confusion and, eventually, to muteness, marking the triumph of silence: "My tongue is heavy with new language/but I cannot give birth to speech" (p. 221).

The political implications of the need and the quest for an authentic language are explored most meaningfully in "Negus". The title of this piece alludes to "one of Haile Selassie's titles which Rastafarians freely employ as a substitute for Jesus" (p. 260). The persona, placing himself in a post-colonial moment, speaks decidedly from the vantage point of one opposed to colonialism. In the modern period, the most overt signs of classical colonialism have been removed. But certain mental structures which get translated into cultural expressions still obey the command of a colonial social order. It is quite clear to the speaker, in that sense, that "it is not enough to be free/of the whips, principalities and powers/where is your Kingdom of the Word?" (p. 222). To direct one's destiny one must first be able to control one's language. Language is the ultimate confirmation of decolonization. Decolonization entails a possession, an appropriation of language. Therefore, the speaker declares: "I/must be given words to shape my name/to the syllables of trees/I/must be given words to refashion futures" (pp. 223-24). For Negus, as Rohlehr has aptly put it, "Independence must mean a new language, a redefinition of self and milieu" (1971: 197). The last line of "Negus", which ends in an invocation of Attibon

Legba, the vodou god of the crossroads, suggests that the struggle for the affirmation of "self and milieu" in the Caribbean has simultaneously political, linguistic, and religious dimensions: "fill me with words/and I will blind your God./*Att/Att/Attibon*" (Brathwaite 1973b: 224).

The fourth and the fifth sections of *Islands*, "Possession" and "Beginning", offer an inventory of the historical legacy of the West Indian region with the purpose of determining what can rightfully be owned. Towards the end of the poem one gets a suggestion of the youthfulness of Caribbean culture in the eyes of the poet and how such a view informs his artistic project. The emphasis on the past supposes an effort to create new possibilities for the future. One picks up the fragments of the lost heritages in order to better build a durable tradition. In this sense, a time that is past is an announcement of a beginning. Reconnection with one's surroundings and possession or appropriation of language must mark that beginning which corresponds to the refashioning of ones's future.

The speaker recognizes that the region has created various forms and types. In "Tizzic" we find an individual who seems to represent the lumpenproletariat. Indigenous to the socio-historical condition of the area, this individual enjoys a sort of alienating freedom that tends to perpetuate his oppression (Rohlehr 1981: 302). There is also "Vèvè", sign of the vodou religion and, consequently, symbol of the most authentic cultural forms forged by the Caribbean experience. The following lines are suggestive: "For on this ground/trampled with the bull's swathe of whips/where the slave at the crossroads was a red anthill/eaten by moonbeams, by the holy ghosts/of his wounds/the Word becomes/again a god and walks among us" (Brathwaite 1973b: 265-66). This is no mere resuscitation of the Western Logos, but a refashioning and validation of it via the power of Nommo as inscribed historically in the human experience of the people of the Caribbean. The revitalizing potential of this spiritual legacy has to do with the fact that, having survived the Middle Passage and the inhumanity of the colonial transaction, people here are just beginning.

Islands closes with a piece entitled "Jou'vert". The word refers to the dawning of each Carnival Monday in the West Indies (Rohlehr 1981: 313). In recreating the atmosphere of that festivity, the text suggests a possibility for synthesis between the liberated expression of certain regional types and the observance of authentic Caribbean forms. It proposes the grounds for a marriage between Tizzic and Vèvè under the aegis of the traditions of the folk. The carnival, an authentic expression of the creativity evident in what Brathwaite calls "the little tradition" of the folk, can serve for Tizzic as an outlet to his hedonistic energy since this expression uses music and dance. Simultaneously, since carnival employs religious symbols and forms of worship, it can induce Tizzic into contact with native spirituality in a way that demands less sanctimonious sobriety than would be possible in Vèvè

(Rohlehr 1981: 313 et passim). The location of these texts, at the end of the poem's last section, which is suggestively entitled "Beginning", indicates that it is from these autochthonous types and forms that one must start any attempt to appraise authentic Caribbean culture. Cultural authenticity alone can provide the arena wherein there can be: "hearts/no longer bound/ to black and bitter/ashes in the ground/now waking/making/making/with their/rhythms some-/thing torn/and new" (Brathwaite 1973b: 268-69). Brathwaite's review of Faustin Charles's volume *The Expatriate*, draws parallels with his own *Islands*. He observes in closing that: "Both books, published late in 1969, are concerned with the possession of the Caribbean through word, metaphor, and symbol" (Brathwaite 1970a: 65).

Brathwaite's publishing success with *Rights of Passage*, *Masks*, and *Islands*, and their collective republication in 1973 in one volume as *The Arrivants*, had little precedent for a poet of the region. Kenneth Ramchand credited the publication of Brathwaite's trilogy with having "at last brought poetry to the attention of the West Indian populace as something related to their lives" (1974: 197). The acclaim and popularity Brathwaite has enjoyed with an audience that encompasses readers from diverse class strata reveals the wisdom of his search for cultural authenticity. The trilogy brought him to the forefront of artistic discourse throughout the Third World, and his international reputation as a major poet began with *The Arrivants*. *Ancestors* (2001), a second trilogy, would further cement his pre-eminence as a major poet.

Shortly after the publication of the trilogy in one volume, three books of poetry by Brathwaite appeared in quick succession: *Other Exiles* (1975a), *Days & Nights* (1975b), and *Black & Blues* (1976). These lack the aesthetic cohesion of *The Arrivants*, their composition being in general less oriented by a systematic aesthetic programme. *Other Exiles*, for instance, simply gathers shorter poems spanning a period of 25 years of Brathwaite's poetic career. In general, the tone of the book is subdued. The voice sustains a predominantly personal vantage point and at times engages itself in questions pertaining to the drama of the individual artist. Despite the absence of a sustained thematic core, however, geographically the *locus* is the Caribbean. Likewise, while the systematic exploration of language as a vehicle of cultural authenticity hardly surfaces here, one can detect in the sonority of the words a music which "is euphony related to, and expressive of, meaning" to use the words of a reviewer (Silkin 1977: 230). Also, a good many of the poems included in the volume treat subjects related to local Caribbean history.

Days & Nights, containing basically a variation on a sequence of the same title that would appear in *Mother Poem*, the long poem Brathwaite was working on at the time, is a casual publication that ought to be seen as a fragment from a major poetic endeavour. *Black & Blues*, which competed for and won the Casa de las Américas poetry prize in Cuba in 1976, is also a gathering of shorter poems, many of which had appeared in earlier volumes, while others would find their way into later ones. But despite the assortment of texts in *Black & Blues* the organization of the collection gives it thematic unity. The experience evoked here is Caribbean and so are the voices through which the evocation happens. The voice that dominates the book at times speaks nation language, assuming the collective sound of the folk. Sometimes, inversely, a choric "I" expresses the sentiment of a collective consensus. Shango and Caribbean religion, Caliban and the history of the region, the tropical landscape, scarcity and dryness, beaches and sand, flora and fauna, the thirst for the word, most of the salient symbols of the local milieu are here. The following lines from "Harbour" evoke "self and milieu" in a way that evinces the contingent texture of the area's socio-historical make-up: "yet here in the cup of my word/on the lip of my eyelid of light/like a star in its syllable socket/there is a cripple crack and hopple/whorl of colour, eye/it is a cool harbour" (Brathwaite 1976a: 82). The speaker's tone is, as in the conclusion of *The Arrivants*, optimistic. The optimism derives from the realization that the existence of multiple options provides the opportunity for a creative future. At any rate, "it is a beginning" (p. 83).

The Woman's Caribbean

The next major poetic text published by Brathwaite, *Mother Poem* (1977a), as the first volume of the trilogy, *Ancestors* (his reinvention of *Mother Poem*, *Sun Poem* and *X/Self* in his Sycorax video typography), tackles the Caribbean experience with a focus on the plight of women. Localized in one specific island, Barbados, the text centres around the speaker's mother, who typifies women generally in Barbados as well as throughout the Caribbean. At the same time, the mother is also Barbados itself, a discrete historical *locus* in time and space, as well as all the other islands, "pebbles" floating in the unharvested sea of the Caribbean. Held together by a narrative voice that recounts the travails of the woman and the anxiety of her relationship with men (husband, son, preacher, boss, God), the poem occasionally intersperses monologues spoken by the mother herself. In general, the poem assigns the mother the role of preserver of culture, hope, humanity, and the word, anticipating the role given to Sycorax in Brathwaite's later work. Approximately one-half of the bulk of the book is written in nation language, "partly to create a voice for the speakers" and evoke the collective persona of the folk against the backdrop of a "search for an organic cultural tradition" (King 1980: 130).

At the beginning of *Mother Poem* the child-narrator speaks of the island-mother as a source of fertility: "my mother is a pool" (Brathwaite 1977: 30). Though having endured depredation, she has kept her hope. Among her various calamities, she has suffered the dehumanization of her man, for whom she pathetically bewails: "My husband/if you cud see he/fragile, fraid o'e own shadow" (p. 6). The official religion has not helped, so her telling of her present misery and grim future incorporates the language of Psalm 26 in a way that contradicts its biblical message: "and I will dwell in the house of the merchant for never" (p. 9). Her history has made her privy to her country's conflicting spiritual legacies. While attending to the requirements of Catholicism, she must also answer the calling of the more autochthonous form of worship. She appeals to the bell, a symbol of official Christianity, to gain access to the depths of the vodou cosmology: "is the bell, pastor john/leh me racket/is the bell, pastor john./leh me wreck it/till uh pour sounn in the Vèvè" (p. 15).

The mother's sense of socio-cultural self-recognition is clear. She sees herself in contradistinction to the colonizing legacy of the Christian West. She fears her children might get lost in the pit of alienating Western education, seduced by the crafty "Chalkstic the teacher" promising that for them "there would be the day" in order to beguile "another black hostage/ of verbs" (p. 24). Yet, she must remain occupied, ensuring the survival of the household by going to the "market bawlin' for fish" (p. 25). She, who now goes "selling half-sole shoes in the leather/department" (p. 36) as another way "of keeping her body and soul-/seam together" (p. 36), has been on the go since she, as a youngster, "left school/taking up sewing since she was fourteen" and now has to keep selling anything she can find to make a living (p. 38). The overall ambience of poverty and suffering recreated in this part of the poem is set against socio-historical and cultural opposites, with the Judeo-Christian capitalist tradition at one end and the native possibilities at the other. Lloyd Brown, in alluding to these polarities in the poem, has termed them "cultural complexities", that is: "standard English and island creole, Christianity and Afro-West Indian religious forms, the symbols of a deep-rooted, persistent colonialism and the musical modes (calypso, work-songs) of a vital, uncorrupted sensibility which the poet attributes to his Afro-West Indian folk" (Brown 1984: 167-68).

The sequence entitled "Woo/Dove" juxtaposes thoughts on the ways of the creator "who calls the lightning down", recalling the Lord's vaunting of his own almighty power when asked about the fairness of his designs in *The Book of Job* (Brathwaite 1977a: 41). Such is the background for a scene in which the mother, pressed by economic necessity, has to implicate herself in the virtual prostitution of her own child, whom she tries to soothe by saying things like: "it int hard, leh me tell you/jess sad/so come darlin chile/ leh me tell he you ready you steady you go" (p. 44). The fate that befalls the mother and her children is really a microcosmic representation of the lot of the people of the island. For, "all the peaks, the promontories" included, "there is more weed than food in the island" (p. 46).

The desolation which castrates the West Indian's potential to become more fully human, as Paulo Freire would say, is associated in *Mother Poem* with a human disruption that comes with capitalist exploitation. In that context, even the people's proclivity to love themselves or their land finds itself impeded since "the broken lives, broken eyes/shattered syllables of leaves/cannot love you" (p. 49). This desolation the mother, as a speaking persona, traces back to historical origins rooted in colonialism, whose remnants she sees in "the man who possesses us all/who has broken the heart of my father's hands" (p. 54). The mother, who has somehow managed to preserve a potential for rebellion, refuses to accept passively the docility of her men. She urges them on, assuring: "i will carry the wet twitching rag/bearing your face, conveying you futureless race/in its burst bag of balls to your doorstep" (p. 80).

The section of the poem entitled "Driftwood" suggests the possibility for the people of the region, the mother's children, of arming themselves with new strength, new meaning, freshly carved words. In essence, "they will wait: cutting their reeds/jagged eared knives working on wood/wreathing their own words" (p. 113). The mother evinces her self-recognition as the voice of a community which defines itself by its subversion against a dominant order. The resources used by the poet combine to highlight the contingent nature of the place, the situation, and the people appearing in the poem, what is called here "the manscape". The contingency pervading the texture of *Mother Poem* has been noted by Warner-Lewis, for whom the techniques of "line-internal rhymes", a certain "Biblical lyricism", the "oratorical crescendo of noun-phrase accumulation", and the echoing of "the phraseology of Rastafarian speech" all contribute to underline "the idiom of this anti-Establishment poetry". The critic connects this element of socio-aesthetic subversion to Brathwaite's nationalistic position which, as in Chinua Achebe and Ngugi wa Thiong'o, comes into view primarily through "an immersion in the language structures" of the metropolis and their recasting in the language of the people (Warner-Lewis 1985: 111-12, 114).

Mother Poem closes with the speaker's recognition of the possibility of empowerment for people in the region. There is reference to a recovery of water, antidote to the gloom contained symbolically in aridity, paralleled by a recovery or possession of the word, antithesis of silence, to announce the rebirth and replenishment of the long crushed vitality of the mother and her children, the land and its people. Thus, "let it be hand and clap and tambour/and she will praise the lord/so that losing her now/you will restore her silent gutters of word-fall/slipping over her footsteps like grass/slippering out of her wrinkles like rain" (p. 117). With its hopeful spirit and the expectation of a creative future for the "manscape", the poem's conclusion signals an insistence on identifying human potential in the midst of pervading ruins.

The optimism typical of Brathwaite's idiom derives from the poet's belief in the indomitability of the folk, represented in *Mother Poem* by the persona of the mother, whose "soul goes marching on" (p. 104), agent of resistance that she is. In a subsequent poem, *Soweto* (1979a), which deals with the moral annihilation to which the black majority in South Africa was put, the speaker manages to see beyond the devastation of the human landscape to point to existing – albeit not conspicuous – sources of liberating productivity: "and we know, somewhere, there/there is real fire" (Brathwaite 1979a). Another poem published in the same year, written as a tribute to Cuba's national poet, the late Nicolás Guillén, illustrates Brathwaite's tendency to express the possibility for hope in terms of Caribbean people's access to what can be considered culturally authentic. Addressing Guillén as "the *sunsum* of our ancestors", Brathwaite sings his solidarity with the Cuban poet, intimating a linguistic commonality that goes beyond the limitations of English and Spanish: "and the sea between us yields its secrets/silver into syllables into sheets/of sound that bear our pain" (Brathwaite 1979b). Brathwaite's choice of title, *Word-Making Man* for the poem to Guillén is worthy of note since he appears to have inverted the title of the anthology of Guillén's poetry *Man-Making Words* (1975) published by Marquez and McMurray, who in turn had taken it from a sentence in Ralph Waldo Emerson's *Journals*. Brathwaite's inversion of the words gives to human beings power over words.

The Caribbean and Manhood

Brathwaite's *Sun Poem* (1982a), the second volume of the trilogy that begins with *Mother Poem*, stresses the connection, indeed, the continuity between the plight of women and that of men. Using Barbados as its geographical focus, *Sun Poem* may be said to cover the same ground as *Mother Poem* but from the point of view of a voice that aims to capture the male experience in the island. The poem begins *ab ovo*, as it were, with a first-person narrator reminiscing the experience of things being born, stretching as far back as the beginning of time: "When the earth was made/when the wheels of the sky were fashioned/when my songs were first heard in the voice of the coot and the owl/hillaby soufrière and kilimanjaro were standing towards me with/water with fire/at the centre of the air" (Brathwaite 1982a: 1). The main character in *Sun Poem* is a boy called Adam, which brings to mind the Creation in the Hebrew tradition.

The setting of the poem is recognizably West Indian. Most of the action recounted here takes place around Browns Beach, a clearly defined Barbadian setting. Likewise, most of the poem consists of the boy's personal memories. He recalls discovering the sea on "that bright afternoon" (p. 8), his compulsion to master the water by making it go "chow" as it did when the expert "beach-boys jumped/and the water wore wreaths where they disappeared" (p. 12), his need to test his mettle before his peers by facing Batto "the shark of the sea-egg/season" (p. 15), his final self-assertion against Batto (p. 18), his boyish dreams induced by the sea (p. 21), and his wish to transcend the respiratory limitations of humans so he could breath under water like a fish (p. 29).

The greater bulk of the material in *Sun Poem* centres around Adam's *Bildung*, his upbringing and coming of age in the island, his bitter-sweet passage to adulthood. Growing up inexorably entails a loss of innocence, and for Adam the bitter reality of his surroundings must speed and increase the sadness of the loss. "[L]ooking back to the land/you would see that only the tallest trees were still/standing/but they were losing their colour/but they were losing their names/they didn't toss light anymore" (p. 41), he says, recalling a world of physical decay. The picture of an environment marred by deterioration is perhaps paralleled by the memory of a corresponding dismalness in the human landscape: "the afternoon of fathers going grey/soft in the head/in the belly/in the heart/and where it hurts him most/is filled with looking out of windows/waiting for the bells to ring/bring news of recognition" (p. 66).

There is much in the poem which could be read as autobiography, with Adam serving as the voice through which Brathwaite does his remembering. The sequence entitled "Fletches", in which the speaker reflects on two family photographs, has an unmistakably autobiographical tone. The speaker uses these photographic impressions as a vehicle through which to recapture the memory of his father (pp. 87-88). In "Indigone" his "inward eye" relives the experience of seeing his father grieving the death of his "further progenitor" (p. 94). Another sequence, the one entitled "Return of the Sun", reproduces in verse form the chapter called "Christine" from Brathwaite's unpublished novel *The Boy and the Sea*, which Warner-Lewis has described as an autobiographical text (1977: 1).

To say that the poem is largely autobiographical, however, does not limit the scope of its significance to the personal history of an individual. Here we find a practice that is typical of Caribbean writers, the tendency to connect personal experience with social observation. The picture recreated, remembered in *Sun Poem* relates to many men living in an oppressive social order, men who, powerless to deal with the roots of their oppression, resort to behaving in ways that replicate those forms of oppression, particularly against their women: "There is also the version of fathers/those who live on the dub side of mujeres" (Brathwaite 1982: 69). While the word "dub" may mean "money", as we gather from the *Dictionary of Jamaican English* authored by Cassidy and LePage (1980: 162), perhaps suggesting men's economic explcitation of women, it also references the dub side of reggae discs, with the implication that the fathers lead a life based on the women's song on the "A" side, a metaphor which points to a relationship of a rather more creative ambivalence. The very allusion to the genesis of everything at the beginning of the poem brings to the fore the larger implications of Adam's recollections. In this respect, a critic has accurately stated that "by identifying the man's cycle of existence with the heavenly cycle of the sun, Brathwaite universalizes the autobiographical details and avails himself of a cosmic imagery of light and colour which transfigures character, event, and situation and shifts the authority and effect of the poem from the autobiographical to the archetypal" (McWatt 1986: 64).

There is in *Sun Poem* a meaningful marriage between personal memories and historical reflection. The mountains mentioned as central to the creation, for instance, would indicate an intent on the part of the poet to present the beginning in more global terms than are offered in the *Old Testament*. In referring to Hillaby (Barbados), Soufrière (St. Vincent), and Kilimanjaro (Tanzania), these "landmarks of the Third World" (p. 98), the poem incorporates into the large cosmic scheme of the Hebrew scripture a geographical scope which is more consistent with the world as we have known it in post-biblical times. At the same time, growing up for Adam entails seeing himself as part of a larger community, a discrete people in a given regional reality, with specific historical, cultural, and spiritual legacies. The speaker learns of the time when "the *loa* came out of the sea" (p. 51) and of his own closeness with the local pantheon. "Sun have you forgotten my mother/sun who gave birth to shango my uncle/who was fixed in his place by ogoun the master of iron" (p. 53), he says in acknowledging his spiritual heritage of the Caribbean's folk religions.

Adam grows not only "up" but also "down to the darker soil of himself fitting himself to new feelings", coming to terms with the realization that, while "noisy on top", he "was silent having no words to nourish that darker feeling" and "finding for the first time that there was other sea behind the high hills of the island's other shore" (p. 39). Growing up (and "down"), then, leads to a historical "prise de conscience". He recognizes the legacy of past events, whose repercussions connect him with people back in slavery times. "Soon after the blacks arrived plantations prospered" (p. 53), he reflects. The reflection leads to an understanding of past sorrow, past subjection, past dehumanization, which must necessarily bring to mind the resulting history of rebellion, from the contemporary forms of anti-Establishment resistance symbolized in Rastafarianism ("*an we burnin babylone...*"), to the more traditional forms of subversion represented by Caribbean preachers who used the pulpit to speak "brave words" (pp. 55, 61). His sense of connection with a tradition of resistance makes him see a link with Hannibal, revered by the speaker as a courageous, if ultimately tragic, ancestor (p. 63). Hannibal, having challenged the military might of the Roman legions in antiquity, may, especially given his African origin, serve as a handy symbol if one is looking for alternatives to the hegemony of the traditions inherited from Western imperialism.

From the allusions to a legacy of resistance, the speaker moves to the precognition of a future with the potential for reconstitution and creation. The poem ends, in effect, with a further evocation of genesis. Instead of chronicling a completed event in the remote past, however, the vision of creation is rendered by means of using the present continuous tense, highlighting, thus, the notion of present beginning and future possibility. The closing lines, "and my thrill-/dren are coming up coming up coming up/and the sun/new" (p. 97), decidedly look forward in a spirit of hope. The use of the word "Sun" here, as in the title of the poem, suggests through phonetic association a threefold meaning: "Son" corresponds to the male child whose experiences are narrated in the poem; "Son" refers to the Afro-Cuban folk song form that is evoked in the last poem in the book; and "sun" is the heavenly body that keeps us warm and in the poem is associated with the Afro-Caribbean divinity Shango. The word "thrilldren," found in the texts that open and close *Sun Poem*, suggests both "children", marking beginnings and potentialities, and the "thrill" connoted by the moment of creation either human or cosmic. Through the association of personal, historical, spiritual, and cosmic levels of significance and the contextualizing of language in the Caribbean experience, Brathwaite achieves here a harmonious fusion of "manscape" and words.

Meeting of World Histories

Brathwaite's second trilogy, at the time without a collective title, ends with the volume *X/Self* (1987). Suggesting the indefiniteness of the voice, that speaks neither for a he nor a she, the text features a collectivized self, hence "X", which strikes one as an attempt to circumvent the pitfalls of individualism. An implication of the indistinct nature of the voice is that it conjures a speaker who reflects a condition of what Paulo Freire has called "dialogical" action, a state in which one has resolved the I/Thou contradiction and entered into a relationship of communion with one's fellow humans, all of whom become I's: "Subjects who meet to *name* the world in order to transform it" (Freire 1986: 167). This formulation resonates evocatively with the pronomial pairing "I and I" in the Iyaric language of Rastafari. Appearing four years after *Third World Poems* (1983), a volume which, consisting for the most part of poems gathered from his earlier books, does not merit a separate discussion, *X/Self* follows the historical explorations evident in parts of *Sun Poem*. But its tenor encompasses a wider spectrum – the Third World – and exhibits a more clearly subversive attitude vis-à-vis the Western tradition.

The voice that dominates the text in *X/Self* starts from a Caribbean reference point. But the vision of socio-historical connection expands to the vast panorama of which the Caribbean is but a component. "Rome burns/and our slavery begins" says a refrain that recurs throughout the poem. The refrain suggests an inevitable link between developments in the history of the West and the events that have shaped the destinies of the people of the Third World. From the start, the superimposition of various slices of historical experience – sometimes chronologically distant and, on the surface, involving disparate moments and events within a boundless geography – becomes evident in passages such as this: "there are no olives left in lebanon/in the camp of the visigoths vercingentorix the arvenin creole/chieftain/has met che has met kismet has met young doctor castro/ liberators are being guillotined from heaven/along the ho chi minh trail/ caesars daughter is pompeys wife" (Brathwaite 1987a: 6). The layers of historical experience here pasted together, as it were, give us a sense of the temporal connectedness of events one has grown used to seeing as separate and isolated from each other.

One has grown used to seeing the human experience encircled within very limited geographies and one has often failed to see either the links or the parallels that evince a global commonality among peoples in the world. Lines such as the following show a junction of human experience in the past along a geographically horizontal line of relationship: "cry babylon/ galileo galilei is free/far out across the lake of galilee/the aztecs wheel around their painted whips" (p. 9). The technique used here, as the author himself explains, is that of perceiving history as "one single, unfolding episode in montage: one image running into, echoing, continuing and extending another" (p. 122). At times the geography serves as a unifying arena to combine stages of past time, as is the case with the characters of Hannibal, Patton, and Rommel (p. 17), all of whom coincide in having led military campaigns in Africa. Arranged vertically in time and horizontally in space, the montage serves to expand the boundaries of chronology and geography. The thematic implication of this measure is that we can no longer see the experience of mankind in terms of a narrative that reduces everything to the history of the West, ascribing to all other human experience a merely tangential importance. Brathwaite's montage serves to reveal a picture showing a larger and more multifaceted mass of humanity than is made manifest in our history books, in which the "ascent of man" often appears to be equivalent to the rise of the West.

The expanded rendition of human history in *X/Self* sets the tone for critical analysis and occasional indictment. The sequence entitled "The fapal state machinery" [sic] explores the incestuous relationship between the Christian church and the powers of violence and exploitation through the centuries. It is the empire's adoption of Christianity as the religion of the state that comes to mind when we hear that: "in rome/god and his armies have become identified with each other" (p. 17). In "Mont Blanc", for instance, we come upon a reflection on the flourishing of Western technology and capitalism that recognizes modern advancements as indissolubly linked with the refinements of the forces of destruction: "industry was envisioned here in the indomitable glitter/[...]/there is more wealth here than with the bankers of amsterdam/more power than in any boulder dam of heaven/volt crackle and electricity it has invented/buchenworld nagasaki and napalm/it is the frozen first atomic bomb" (p. 31).

Certainly the historical re-reading that we get in *X/Self* seeks to dissect some of the most cherished cultural myths of Western civilization. We get here a rendition of the story of Charlemagne, unifier of Christendom and first Holy Roman Emperor, that is very far from the saintly nobility with which he is depicted in *La chanson de Roland*. In Brathwaite's poem, Charlemagne, "hope/of the christians/destroyer of muslims/defender of rome" (p. 24), made the glory of his name on the grounds that "he saved eu/rope from the so/called sterile fate of mulattoes" (p. 24). Fountainhead of the Christian West which would later evolve into the stage of capitalist imperialism, Charlemagne as a cultural symbol can be seen as antithetical to the aspirations of the people of the Third World. The introduction of Caliban here, contrapuntally to the words of the Emperor, brings to the fore the contingent nature of the Western project. For the West becomes the West fundamentally through its self-differentiation from non-Christian cultures and peoples.

It is very significant that Charlemagne, portrayed here "dying at aachen" and prophesying "the downfall of the empire", should foresee the imperial demise in terms of the destabilization of the language of domination: "the dialect of the tribes will come beating up against the crack/foundation stones of latin like the salt whip speechless lips/of water eating the soft stones of venice" (p. 29). Implicit in the highlighting of the relationship between the predominance of the Latin language and the hegemony of the imperial legacy of Rome in the Middle Ages is the unearthing of a precedent for the subversive overtones perceptible in certain uses of language in the Third World, particularly in the Caribbean. Drawing on morphological variation, rhythmical devices, and a sonority that often rests upon semantic transmutations, *X/Self* aims to present language in a way that is divergent from the language of domination. "The poem's language, sometimes verging on incoherence, articulates the pathos of the two-way linguistic inheritance of the West Indies: the givens of an alien, dominant lexicon (the imported, educated *langue de culture*) and the remnants of African usages still existing in the islands," says Joan Dayan in this respect (1988: 506).

In "Dies irie", whose title mixes liturgical Latin with Rastafarian dread talk, the speaker, clearly a voice of resistance, invokes the forces of justice in these terms: "day of thunder day of hunger/bring me solace bring me fire/give me penance give me power/grunt me vengeance with thy word"

(Brathwaite 1987a: 39). The word, we see, assumes the power of a weapon of redress. Consistent with that rationale, we see that those who are perceived as fighters for liberation earn the epithet of "sooth say/ers" (p. 69), as Malcolm X, Marcus Garvey, Martin Luther King, and Mahatma Gandhi are called in "Mai Village" (p. 69). In many respects the spirit of resistance to a power structure that seeks to undermine their sense of humanity is what most clearly connects the various peoples whose experiences figure in the poem. In Africa ("Nam") and in the Caribbean ("Cap" and "Citadel") people have had to struggle to maintain their dignity. The following invocation: "vieques porto bello choc guantanamo bahia O/black cat nany nanahemma do not desert us now" (p. 94) appeals to the legacy of subversion against empire as it has taken place in the Caribbean region. Resistance takes place in the spiritual arena as well, and the speaker in "Sun song", appealing to the local cosmology, invokes the restorative powers of the "spirit of the fire". He conjures thus: "i summon you from trees/from ancient memories of forests/from the uncurling ashes of the dead/that we may all be cleansed" (p. 98).

As *X/Self* draws to a close, there seems to be an increasingly perceptible relationship between spirituality, history, and language. First, the narrative voice recognizes the dual power of language to describe reality and virtually construct it. It is in language that "virgil invents aeneas as they set out for civilization", and it is in language that, the speaker complains, "you make of me mysteries foundationless histories" (p. 102). The word, therefore, ought to be appropriated by those whom it must serve. But that word must be changed, recast. It must be revitalized with the legacy of the folk, represented at one point by the figure of legendary jazz trumpeter Bunk Johnson, so that it may, its sense of justice restored, set history aright: "word/and balm/and water/flow/embrace/him/he will shatter outwards to your light and calm history/your thunder has come" (p. 111).

Characteristically, the volume ends in a hopeful outlook. Having appropriated the word, the central voice in the text offers a credo of empowerment. Abounding in historiographical and literary allusions, *X/Self* may be said to compare with Dante's *Divina commedia* and *The Cantos* of Pound in the wealth of its references. The text presents another stage, a global and more encompassing glance, in an aesthetic exploration that has marked Brathwaite's entire literary career. Decades ago a critic noted that Brathwaite's "most serious opposition is aimed at the Western Word, and his craft works carefully at expunging it from black modes of feeling and expression" (Ismond 1971: 58). Today that appraisal continues to seem valid although one should probably warn that in Brathwaite blackness too undergoes a process of creolization. Nommo too is nativized by the Caribbean experience as much as Logos. This caveat should also ward off the temptation to construe Brathwaite strictly as the spokesman of the African heritage, with Walcott, as champion of European values, representing his polar opposite (Ismond 1971: 59). In keeping with our argument in the previous chapter, Brathwaite and Walcott reflect two of the ideological options available to Caribbean thinkers in their attempt to tackle the awesome dilemma of culture in the region. Clearly, *X/Self* draws from diverse intellectual and cultural traditions just as Walcott's *Omeros* (1990) does. A fair treatment of this subject would avoid dichotomies. Reading *The Arrivants*, for instance, as "essentially a record of the stages of Brathwaite's life from feelings of exile", as does King (1980: 131), tends to undermine the public tenor and epic breath of the trilogy and reduces its meaning. Similarly, focusing on the aesthetic distinction between the two major West Indian poets, to celebrate Walcott and to slight Brathwaite's accomplishments, as does Walsh (1973: 63-65), is either an aberration of judgement, or a very conscious ideological position in defence of the Western aesthetic status quo (or "status crow" as Brathwaite terms it). Avoiding extremes, one should instead explore the aesthetic and philosophical creeds behind the differences that mark the works of the two poets off from each other, starting, perhaps, with glossing the significance of Brathwaite's collective "we" and Walcott's personal "I", as Anne Walmsley once proposed (1970: 157).

Independently of the relationship with Walcott, Brathwaite the poet continues to see himself as a rebuilder of the socio-historical reality in which he lives. Through a remodelling of the official language of the establishment, he undertakes to recompose the fragments of a scattered history with the intention of chronicling the experience of his people in a manner that may be deemed culturally authentic. That is the programme which informs the various facets of his literary creativity, and it is that programme that provides the prism through which he looks at the works of others. One may note that in the 1960s, he praised two anthologies of the literature of the region by Coulthard (1966) and Howes (1966) for their contribution to expanding communication throughout the Caribbean, thus helping to break "down the barriers of language, politics and custom that separate us" (Brathwaite 1966b: 223). Subsequently, his various entries on individual Caribbean poets for a dictionary of contemporary poets (Vinson 1980) indicated the persistence of his view of the literary artist as a griot through whom the community speaks. In reviewing Dionne Brand's *Winter Epigrams*, Brathwaite continued to assign value to literary works in proportion to the writer's effort to reconstruct his or her reality with an eye on empowering the voiceless sectors of society (1985a). In that respect, we can hardly concur with a reading by Dash that depoliticizes the poet by stating that any "attempt to extract either cultural or political prescriptions from Brathwaite's work" could lead to treacherous ground, insisting on the "rejection of man as the product of an ideology" as presumably "the most important single idea behind Brathwaite's work"

(Dash 1979: 226-27). Our reading suggests, instead, that Brathwaite insists on a theory of language, culture, and on a philosophy of history that have strong political implications in so far as they aim to liberate the Caribbean mind from the throes of a colonial heritage.

The West and the Word: Logos Denied

Writing on *X/Self*, Dayan has said: "Brathwaite's remembering of history in this remarkable sequence of poems demands a breakdown of the word and the fragmentation of identity. Whose word, how to say it, how to know it?" (Dayan 1988: 507). These words point to the most central concern in Brathwaite's writings throughout his literary career: the need to explore possibilities by means of which European languages are rendered indigenous to the people of the West Indies. Brathwaite thereby addresses an issue which may be deemed a constant of Caribbean literature. Reflection on language is at the very heart of most literary activity in the contemporary Caribbean. The poets have perhaps been the most sensitive in articulating the dilemma of language in the region. Early in the twentieth century Léon Laleau's *La flèche au coeur* (1926) included a poem that spoke of "this unequalled despair/To tame with the words of France/This heart that has come to me from Senegal" (ce désespoir à nul autre égal/D'apprivoiser, avec de mots de France,/ Ce coeur qui m'est venu du Sénégal, Laleau 1975: 504). And decades later Derek Walcott's *In A Green Night* (1962) would include a poem that addresses the duality in these terms: "how choose/Between this Africa and the English tongue I love?/Betray them both, or give back what they give?/How can I face such slaughter and be cool?" (Walcott 1986: 18). The fiction writers have been no less attentive to the issue of language. Ana Lydia Vega is well known for the delineation of character in her stories almost solely on the basis of highlighting the regional quality of their speech. Similarly, Luis Rafael Sánchez has successfully undertaken in his works the development of a "language of decomposition" whose result is a form of writing characterized by the recognizable diction of island Spanish, as Susan Homar makes clear (Homar 1982: 74, 85). But whether one looks at the literary artists, the critics or the theoreticians, most commentary on literature and culture in the contemporary Caribbean tends to consider the question of language as an intellectual problematic. Brathwaite's works succeed at giving effective voice to a preoccupation that is deeply felt throughout the area.

Language is also the area where Caribbean literature's relationship with the West becomes most tense. As in the Caribbean, much of contemporary thought in the fields of literature and the human sciences in Europe and the United States revolves around issues of language. The writings of a good many of today's most prominent intellectual celebrities in the West show a decisive emphasis on linguistic inquiry. To be sure, granting centrality to language in human affairs is nothing new. From Aristotle's *Politics* (I, 2, 1253a) to Charles Darwin's *The Descent of Man* (1874: 95) language has been adduced as evidence of man's superiority over the "lower" animal species. But, following the publication of Ferdinand de Saussure's *Cours de linguistique générale* (1916) and the subsequent arrival of Formalism, Structuralism, Semiotics, and the vogue of the intellectual currents normally grouped under Post-structuralism and Post-modernism, there appears to have been in the study of society and culture a global effort "to rethink everything through once again in terms of linguistics" (Jameson 1974: vii).

Today it is not deemed far-fetched to uphold Jacques Lacan's proposition that "beyond what we call 'the word', what the psychoanalytic experience discovers in the unconscious is the whole structure of language" (Lacan 1972: 289). Julia Kristeva, whose book *La révolution du langage poétique* (1974) owes much to Lacan's branch of psychoanalysis, explains the medium by means of which our "unified consciousness" perceives reality as a form of "syntax" (Selden 1985: 79). In a similar vein, Jürgen Habermas contends that an "ideal speech situation", which must precede all effective communication, affects our correct perception of reality. For him, in effect, "'truth' is a quality of propositional assertions contained within language use" (Giddens 1985: 130). But no one has been more influential than Jacques Derrida in arguing for a view of human society and culture that reduces all meaning to linguistic constructs. Positing with Heidegger that all humanism remains metaphysical because it is trapped in presuppositions contained in language, Derrida expresses serious doubts about our ability to apprehend reality. He denies the existence of any "extralinguistic way to determine whether the world has a stable or consistent nature that language could mirror" (Hoy 1985: 52).

So, producers of intellectual discourse in the West are as preoccupied with the problematic of language as is Brathwaite and many other Caribbean authors. But in the West the preoccupation has to do with particularly Western developments that have caused many thinkers to perceive language as fraught with an inherent undecidability. Philosophical and psycholinguistic positions have cast doubts on the functionality of language to ensure a mimetic reproduction of reality, to the point that logocentrism has lent itself to denunciations. But in the Caribbean, the preoccupation has its origin in the concrete reality of the colonial transaction, in quite tangible historical and cultural conjunctures. European languages were brought to the Caribbean and imposed on the indigenous populations and the enslaved Africans so that these captives could understand and obey the command of their masters. "The development of language in the West Indies," says Peter Roberts (1988: 5) referring to the

Anglophone area, "has been completely dominated by the structure of society" in a plantation economy that stratified people sharply into planters and administrators, poor whites, house slaves and artisans, and field slaves. After a while, the white people in the region, from the contact with the local setting and the separation from the metropolitan milieu, developed a distinct, Caribbean-sounding language.

From a European perspective, the language of the slaves and indentured servants was deemed "bad" or "broken". But even that of the whites was considered of a lesser status. The region often appeared to outsiders as a languageless place. The rise of Caribbean letters in the twentieth century, then, ought to be seen as a linguistic battle, a brandishing of the word whereby the people of the area assert their being. Unlike Western intellectual discourse, contemporary Caribbean literature extols the virtues of logocentrism, probably due to the association between language and ontological self-assertion for the people of the region. Also connected with this attitude to language is the "verbal flamboyance" of many Caribbean popular cultural forms that scholars trace back to African traditions (Warner-Lewis 1979: 112-14). The acclaim garnered in Caribbean popular culture by individuals who are "good at using words", or "men-of-words", and the prestige enjoyed by displays of "quickness of wit and for eloquence" may illustrate "a continuity between New World speechmaking practices and African expressive patterns" (Abrahams 1983: 2, 21).

The affirmation of language in the Caribbean, then, has serious cultural implications for Brathwaite's search for authenticity. The liberation of the Caribbean mind from the burden of its colonial legacy necessarily leads to the arena of language, given the role of the European language in consolidating the colonial regime. Upon the publication of Antonio de Nebrija's *Gramática de la lengua castellana* (1492), the first grammar of a modern European language, the Bishop of Avila is reported to have presented it to Queen Isabella of Castile with these words: "Language is the perfect instrument of empire" (Hulme 1986: 1, 267). The Iberian philologist Marcelino Menéndez y Pelayo, who held an imperialist view of the world, also saw a clear correspondence between language and empire. Menéndez y Pelayo saw it as the distinct "privilege" of classical languages (Greek and Roman) that they "extended their empire through very distant regions from those where they were born", and he compared the expansion of Spanish and English in the Americas with that of Latin and Greek in antiquity (Menéndez y Pelayo 1911: 11-12). For him, Spanish-American literature reflected the "genius of the Spaniards", from which he derived imperial consolation in light of "the secondary position we now occupy in the control of the affairs of the World" (ibid p. 12).

Western discourse appealed to language to vaunt its superiority over non-Europeans and to justify their subjection. David Hume, who believed "negroes, and in general all other species of men... to be inferior to whites", once discarded the rumour of a Jamaican Negro who showed a literary gift on the grounds "'tis likely he is admired for very slender accomplishments, like a parrot, who speaks a few words plainly" (Cited in Gates 1986: 10). For Immanuel Kant, who regarded the fundamental difference between blacks and whites to be "as great in regard to mental capacity as in colour", the fact that a statement was uttered by a Negro served as "a clear proof that what he said was stupid" (ibid, pp. 10-11). We know that for Hegel, Negroes, in whom he saw "nothing harmonious with humanity", could only be morally and spiritually elevated through the institution of slavery which for them, he said, meant "the occasion of the increase in human feeling" (Hegel 1956: 93, 98). In Hegel's mind, as Henry Louis Gates, Jr. has suggested, the subhuman condition of the Africans was connected with their lack of "systems of writing and the perception that they had not mastered the art of writing in European languages" (Gates 1986: 11).

European spokespersons often alluded to verbal products when the need arose to proclaim what Victorian England often referred to as "the genius of the race" (Brantlinger 1988: 7). Lord Macaulay's insistence that "a single shelf of a good European library was worth the whole native literature of India and Arabia" and that in historiographical texts, expository discourse, and scientific treatises "the superiority of the Europeans becomes absolutely immeasurable" seems motivated by the need to affirm Western man's exclusive ownership of the word (Macaulay 1952: 722-25). Aimé Césaire's *Discours sur le colonialisme* (1955) quotes a good number of such proclamations in which the celebration of the West, and thereby the depreciation of non-European peoples, is expressed within the framework of Logos (Césaire 1969: 180-82). Max Weber had in mind precisely the European man's presumed superiority in the realm of Logos when he declared that "in Western civilization only, cultural phenomena have appeared which (as we like to think) lie in a line of development having *universal* significance and value" (Weber 1958: 13).

Similarly, cases of linguistic dexterity in non-Europeans occasionally necessitated explanation and justification to the Western colonial mind. Gates cites the instance of the publisher of Phillis Wheatley's *Poems on Various Subjects, Religious and Moral* (1773) who judged it wise to preface the small volume with a letter by John Wheatley, "the Author's Master", certifying that the slave girl had indeed "attained the English language". In addition, he included a document signed by 18 respectable Bostonians, headed by the governor and the lieutenant governor, to vouch that, "brought an uncultivated Barbarian from *Africa*", Phillis, the girl identified as the author of the poems in the book, having "been examined by some of the best judges", was "thought qualified to write them" (cited in Gates 1986: 7-8). By the same token, the skill of a Negro in the handling of verbal structures served also as a weapon for Europeans who disapproved of racial oppression. Fritz Müller, the German naturalist, in praising the poetry of the Brazilian Joâo da Cruz e Sousa, had this to say: "This Negro represents for me one more support for my long held opinion against the prevailing point of view which perceives the black man... as inferior and incapable of development by his own abilities" (Cited in Muricy 1961: 24). Language, then, functioned as the area within which one's humanity may be attributed or denied.

Brathwaite's search for and affirmation of a Caribbean language, then, ought to be seen against the backdrop of a discourse tradition that has denied his people a place in the realm of Logos and has often, as a result, doubted their identity as rational beings. An early literary image of the Caribbean produced in the West, the successful comedy *The West Indian* (1771) by Richard Cumberland, manifests a perception of the area as one dominated by savage impulses. In England, Belcour, the white West Indian, is anxiously awaited by Stockwell, his father, who, about to catch a glimpse of his foreign son, hopes him to be "wild, perhaps, as the manner of his country is, but, I trust, not frantic or unprincipled" (Cumberland 1964: 348). Critics of Cumberland's play have recognized that the notion of the Caribbean as an irrational domain is crucial to the dramatic situation. Standard descriptions of Belcour normally highlight the effect of his birthplace on his personality: "a youth of air and fire, of English parents but of tropical birth" (Williams 1917: 75). Belcour's "social fault", another critic sustains, is "substantially explained by his being the product of an uncivilized society" (Dircks 1976: 34).

Belcour's Caribbean birth, then, accounts for his irascibility. That he is white does not exempt him from Caribbean irrationality, it seems. Another eighteenth-century author, the British historian of Jamaica, Edward Long, provides an insight on how in the field of language the "White Creoles" were infected by the "unintelligible jargon" of the blacks. They "learn it from their nurses in infancy and meet with much difficulty, as they advance in years, to shake it entirely off and express themselves with correctness" (Cited by Ramchand 1970: 33). In fact, according to the report of Lady Maria Nugent in her famous *Journal*, many "planters had to send to England for governesses" so as to minimize the effect of black dialect on their children. She, who was sure that "Creole language is not confined to negroes", told of local ladies who spoke "a sort of broken English, with an indolent drawling out of their words, that is very tiresome if not disgusting" (cited in Ramchand 1970: 36; Brathwaite 1971: 302). Long and Nugent, their value judgments aside, shed some light on the historical background to the longevous coexistence of "two very closely related vernaculars, one bearing all the elements of prestige, and the other socially unacceptable", a linguistic and class division that remained current in post-colonial times

(Bailey 1967: 7). Ramchand has argued that Standard English has retained a powerful influence. Though spoken only by a minority, it remains the unknown form by which even the illiterate measure social standing (Ramchand 1970: 39).

The sense of Antilleans as linguistically anomalous beings can find its way even into a document as neutral as a foreign language textbook. Ruth Hernández Torres has looked at a the textbook *Parole et pensée: Introduction au français d'aujourd'hui* (1977) by Ivonne Lenard, which in the conversational sections includes an Antillean among the cast of characters. Hernández analyzes the portrayal of Michel, a young man from Martinique, in his interaction with the other characters, who are either white American or French. She detects a gradual obliteration of the Antillean and his characterization as a "linguistically suspicious being". Among his various differentiating traits, we learn that he has a "funny" accent. The assumption of the Antillean's odd relationship with language lurks in this comment: "Michel has an amusing accent for the rest of the group" (Hernández Torres 1985: 116). But the assumption may appear even in laudatory appraisals such as the preface written by André Breton to the 1947 edition of Césaire's *Cahier d'un retour au pays natal*. There Breton celebrated the Martinican's poetic accomplishment with these words: "...here's a black man who handles the French language like no white man today can handle it" (1983: 80). The praise was most likely genuine, but one should not ignore Fanon's contention that even though Breton may be stating a fact, there should be nothing to underline regarding the poet's handling of the French language since Césaire was a native of Martinique, a French-speaking country, and a university graduate (Fanon 1952: 50).

Curiously, one finds the British poet Robert Graves praising a major Anglophone West Indian poet in similar terms: "Derek Walcott handles English with a closer understanding of its inner magic than most (if not any) of his English-born contemporaries" (cited in Dawes 1977: 5). There is a revealing similarity between the words chosen by Breton and Graves in their praise. Both dwell on the singularity of the Caribbean poets' dexterity in the use of the language of the metropolis. In his observation Fanon was worried mostly about an association in the mind of the West between race and linguistic ability, which can certainly be inferred from the words of Breton. But in addition to the racial reading there is a regional one. Both Césaire and Walcott come from a region that has been regarded as a languageless world. If we understand that the language of the West Indies was deemed "bad" when used by Negroes and "corrupted" when used by white Creoles, we can see how in the Western mind the attribution of linguistic dexterity in a European tongue should be the highest form of praise to be lavished on an individual from the region. Thus Breton and Graves are overwhelmed by the achievement of the two Caribbean poets not so much for their command of metaphor, imagery, and characterization or the depth with which they approach their subject matter but for their competence in handling the European language.

Before Graves and Breton, Menéndez y Pelayo had occasion at the turn of the century to assess Spanish-speaking Caribbean writers on the basis of their handling of the language of the empire. Surveying Puerto Rican poetry he only lavished some praise on two authors, a woman poet whose work showed a "delicate and correct inspiration", and Francisco J. Amy, a poet whose work the standard dictionary of Puerto Rican literature describes as "correct and sober" (Menéndez y pelayo 1911: 356; Rivera de Alvarez 1974: 61). The two poets who in the eyes of the eminent Peninsular scholar stand out in Puerto Rican poetry both distinguished themselves for the "castizo" element in their style, that is, their correctness and good use of the Spanish language. Perhaps the Western perception of the inhabitants of the region as a people to whom language did not come naturally may have influenced West Indians themselves. Fanon has offered compelling insights into a form of cultural alienation that manifests itself in the hyper-correctness of black Antilleans when speaking the French language (Fanon 1952: 50). It could very well be that when using the master's language, the former slave, educated in the master's school, yet aware of the master's proprietary claim on Logos, proceeds as one who needs to walk a straight path. Perhaps it is the sense that they are being watched by the "legitimate" users of the language that causes middle-class Antilleans to strive for the linguistic impeccability that Fanon observed.

The foregoing background to the language situation in the Caribbean shows the relevance of Brathwaite's focus on language as the arena within which to define and assert cultural authenticity for the people of the region. It is also logical that for him Creole should appear as the most meaningful form. For in Creole, the European words have already been recast into an indigenous morphology, and new, local meanings have been added to the old, Western lexicon. In Creole, which may be seen as the people's appropriation of the language of the former colonial masters, Caribbean culture also achieves originality, which has little to do with purity and much with cultural paradigms that determine patterns of inclusion and exclusion of borrowed elements. At the same time, Creole constitutes an incontestable testimony to the legacy of resistance of the lower strata of the population, "the folk", the most genuine depository of the local culture according to the poet. Brathwaite would sustain, with Sylvia Wynter, that, language being the area of the plantation where the slave most dramatically "negated his being", the rise of "dialect and Creole forms was an original act of self-preservation and rebellion as important as the innumerable slave revolts" (Wynter cited in Homar 1982: 40).

Caliban's Word: Logos Recast

Because of the association between language and cultural resistance, the character of Caliban appeals to Brathwaite not only as a symbol to be used in his poetry but also as a paradigm by means of which to explore historical processes in the region. The study of the Jamaican slave rebellion led by Sam Sharpe in 1831 brings to his mind the Shakespearean paradigm. The confrontation of opposing forces of the masters and the slaves, mediated by the pacifying presence of freed and/or educated slaves is metaphorically represented here by the confrontation between Prospero and Caliban, with Ariel playing the mediator. What the revolt enacts for Brathwaite is "a crucial moment of competing orientations within the developing creole matrix" of Caribbean culture (1977b: 41). For him, Caribbean culture evolves from Caliban's effort to "discount the omnipotence of Prospero's magic" and avoids the influence of Ariel, the master's servant. The line of rebellion that goes in the region from the Haitian Revolution to Sam Sharpe indicates that in 1831 "Caliban was already (had in fact been all along) creating for himself a language of resistance/revolt based upon his own mythology of survival" (p. 46). Brathwaite acknowledges in this work the aim to highlight "the attitudes, opinions, and observations not only of the elite – leaders, martyrs: those trapped in print – but also of the little fellas, the folk" (p. 60). In this sense, he himself as an intellectual embodies the language of resistance that he ascribes to Sam Sharpe, whose uprising constitutes the revolt of Caliban.

In his analysis of Sam Sharpe and elsewhere in his works, Brathwaite understands such confrontations as examples of a process he has called creolization. Creolization, put briefly, is the third cultural option resulting from the clash between competing orientations. It is the recycling of heritages that has produced a genuine Caribbean culture. Coming from a confrontation, it is inscribed in a legacy of resistance.[1] How creolization manifests itself in language in the West Indies was most clearly articulated by Brathwaite in 1979 in a lecture given at Harvard. It was there that he first lifted the banner of what he has since then been calling "nation language", a medium which he has defined as "the submerged area of that dialect that is much more closely allied to the African aspect of experience in the Caribbean" (1981a: 21) Brathwaite credits Glissant's 1976 essay "Free and Forced Poetics" with having first articulated the concept of nation language (Glissant 1989: 120-34). He attributes to Glissant the understanding that "nation language is a strategy: the slave is forced to use a certain kind of language in order to disguise himself, to disguise his personality, and to retain his culture" (Brathwaite 1981a: 23). His embracing of Glissant's view is motivated no doubt by the Martinican author's linking of nation language and the history of resistance in the region. For nation language derives primarily from the folk, descends from an oral tradition, and is linked with folk musical forms such as calypso and folk religious forms such as kumina and shango (Brathwaite 1981a: 24-25).

Much of the lecture is devoted to illustrating the presence of nation language in West Indian poetry, not only in the popular tradition represented by the likes of Louise Bennett, Mighty Sparrow, Don Drummond, Michael Smith, and Bongo Jerry, but also the more mainstream tradition that goes from Claude McKay, to George Campbell, to Frank Collymore, to John Figueroa, to Derek Walcott. His survey indicates that at a certain level it is possible to nativize one's language while still using standard English. Nor does he legislate that West Indian authors refrain from finding their models in Western literature. What he claims is that in order for outside voices to be absorbed by literary artists in the region they must somehow offer elements that accord with the needs and the inclinations of the local idiom. T.S. Eliot became influential in the Caribbean, he explains, because "the notion of the speaking voice, the conversational tone" found an aesthetic predisposition in Caribbean literature's tendency to reproduce the tenor of the spoken word (Brathwaite 1981a: 33).

Regarding the relationship between nation language and dialect, the republication of the lecture as *History of the Voice* (1984a) makes it even more clear that one need not write in Creole in order to produce nation-language texts. Even when morphologically faithful to the European language, the standard English of the West Indian writers cannot escape the influence of the "submerged culture" of the folk. This becomes evident at the end of Brathwaite's text, which, like the original lecture, closes with a poem by Anthony McNeill but described with words that were not there originally. Written in standard English, the poem is here spoken of as a "nation-language poem that doesn't even have to use a verb of nation", thus establishing that nation-language is not reducible to dialect (Brathwaite 1984a: 50). Creolization of language corresponds to the socio-cultural dictates of the Caribbean milieu. The immediacy of the local reality compels what René Depestre has referred to as "un usage maternel" of the European language (1986: 192). With this expansion of the concept of nation-language to include writers who do not use dialect, Brathwaite makes sure to acknowledge the contribution of those West Indian writers who, while expressing themselves in standard English, have aided in the development of an identifiably Caribbean diction in literature.

The Caribbean Voice

As a historian of the voice of Caribbean people, Brathwaite, a modern Caliban, wholeheartedly identifies with that voice. A reviewer of *History of the Voice* has in this respect indicated that Brathwaite's "work is the symbol of the human situation: we need to both reach out and defend our own, to be willing to embrace everything and determined to make strict and firm boundaries to our accommodation", which means that he at once serves the "function as a vision of the creator and the voice of a particular group with a specific agenda coming directly from a historical and racial experience" (Savory 1985: 75). This creates the dilemma caused by the need to achieve a balance between historiographical objectivity and a moral commitment in his desire to unearth the legacy of resistance and the surviving testimonials of his people's cultural authenticity. Just as for Glissant, for Brathwaite discovering the past is inseparable from creating what ought to be the future. He has, in fact, judged it dishonest "to try to hold that it is possible to be an impartial critic in cases where one's historical and historically received image of oneself is under discussion" (1985b: 34). In furthering the concept of creolization, then, Brathwaite proposes at the same time a method for exploring the Caribbean past and a strategy for enhancing and retaining cultural authenticity.

Brathwaite first proposed this vision of creolization in the historiographical work *The Development of Creole Society in Jamaica: 1770-1820* (1971a), which was accepted by the University of Sussex as a doctoral dissertation in 1968, precisely the time when his first poetic trilogy, *The Arrivants*, was coming out in print. He defines "creole" there as "born in, native to, committed to the area of living" with the overtone of "authentic" and "culturally autonomous" and applying equally to blacks and whites (Brathwaite 1971a: xv). His definition allows for the "juxtaposition of master and slave, élite and labourer, in a culturally heterogeneous relationship" (p.xvi). While the "creole culture" documented in this book is localized in Jamaica in a very discrete historical period, Brathwaite would hereby have us see "the forms, institutions and attitudes of West Indian society during the slavery period as essential to today's concern with racial and cultural identity" (p. viii).

Among the merits of this book is that in it, as a reviewer observed, Brathwaite the historian connects with "the poet and literary critic" in rejecting "the nihilists and existentialists of the Caribbean scene"[2] who, mining more or less the same ground, have "found a 'nonsociety,' or worse" (Mathurin 1971: 120). In other words, Brathwaite rejects the widespread perception of slave society as merely a planter or "absentee" planter society in which slaves did nothing but produce profits for their masters. Instead, he highlights complex cultural dynamics that were at work even then. In the words of Mathurin, he "has been impressed more by the presence, than by the absence, of ruins" (Mathurin 1971: 120). He argues here for a vibrant "folk culture" contemporaneous with the dehumanization brought about by the experience of slavery. From the African orientation of Jamaican folk culture, as reflected in surviving customs connected with birth, death, sexual and domestic unions, religions, music and dance, song, carnivals, and dress, Brathwaite adduces cultural formations among the slave folk which, "though usually autochthonous", are profoundly informed by African traditions (Brathwaite 1971a: 213). Creole linguistic forms, for instance, are informed by the African sense of Nommo that Janheinz Jahn talks about. This is explained by the fact that: "It was in language that the slave was perhaps most successfully imprisoned by his master, and it was in his (mis)use of it that he perhaps most effectively rebelled. Within the folk tradition, language was (and is) a creative art in itself; the word was held to contain a secret power" (p. 237). The passage of Nommo from West Africa to the West Indies, however, was no mere transfer. For "nommo was quickly creolized by Anancy into a secular device", thus providing the grounds for the genesis of an authentically Caribbean language (p. 237).

Brathwaite uses the bulk of his documentation to show that Jamaican slaves had a "cultural life that was as valid and meaningful as their masters'" (p. 244). The two great traditions of Africa and Europe fused into the third option of "authentically local institutions, and an Afro-creole 'little' tradition among the 'slave folk'" (p. 309). The result is the syncretic culture of the Caribbean. This understanding of creolization in Caribbean culture has a restorative value in that it allows Brathwaite to piece together the various fragments of the human experience in the region. Dispelling the notion that the Middle Passage was *only* a traumatic experience marked merely by plunder and utter loss of history and tradition, he undertakes to chronicle the survival of the legacy of the slave folk and to suggest ways in which it, having been recycled by the contact with the legacy of the masters, can offer "a pathway or channel between this tradition and what is being evolved, on new soil, in the Caribbean" (Brathwaite 1981b: 7).

The concept of creolization helps to trace the "history of the voice" in the Caribbean from a time that precedes the emancipation of the slaves and in a way that transcends racial essentialisms. Specifically in regards to literary creativity, for instance, one can go back to the period of slavery to "the poetry and prose fiction written… by persons, not necessarily native, but creole to the extent that they had intimate knowledge of and were in some way committed by experience and/or attachment to the West Indies" (Brathwaite 1970b: 47). Brathwaite has paid a great deal of attention to *Hamel, the Obeah Man*, an early nineteenth-century anonymous work of fiction whose main character, a black man, is a practitioner of obeah. Though written by a white man, as the scholarly consensus assumes, this work touches upon the dilemma of competing cultural orientations besetting people in the region. It lends itself, therefore, to a reading in terms of the colonial confrontation that has characterized Caribbean history from 1492 to the modern period. Consequently, Brathwaite reads it in terms of the Shakespearean paradigm: "At the end of the novel, Fairfax, the disinherited Prospero, has regained his kingdom; but Caliban, speaking his master's language by adhering to his culture, has gained his independence; fully aware at the same time, of what that independence has cost" (1970b: 72).

The various stages of creolization in Caribbean history may also be said to be tied to the attitudes of West Indian writers toward the African legacy from slavery to the present, post-independence period (Brathwaite 1974b: 81). In the field of literature, as in every other area of human endeavour in the region, what the poet-historian would have us see is the complex movement from "acculturation" to "interculturation". He would insist on the historical passage whereby the Caribbean moves from a stage in which a dominant culture seeks to absorb another to one in which we see "a more reciprocal activity, a process of intermixture and enrichment" (Brathwaite 1985b: 11). One must keep in mind that in positing creolization as the "cultural norm" of Caribbean society Brathwaite is revealing the difficulty of finding wholeness in the area. The norm itself may not be "whole or hard…, but cracked, fragmented, ambivalent, not certain of itself, subject to shifting lights and pressures" (p. 6). Therefore, he debates what he perceives as the "either/or distinction" upheld by Sylvia Wynter in proposing the notion of "indigenation," which for her, Brathwaite argues, "represents the more secretive process by which the dominated culture survives; and resists" (p. 16). He believes that the emphasis on the dichotomy can hardly yield a productive result.

In his important publication, *Contradictory Omens* (1974/1985) Brathwaite recognizes the various areas of division that exist in the Caribbean. Referring specifically to the English-speaking West Indies, he speaks of four major orientations: Europeans, Euro-creole, Afro-creole, and Creo-creole, with the Madeiran Portuguese, the Chinese, and the East Indians being designated under the fourth "orientation" (pp. 25, 44). This sort of diversity has on occasion translated itself into ethnic polarities and the perception that the agenda of one group may clash with that of another. But he maintains that the socio-historical dynamics that have acted upon the area – slavery, mercantilism, racial superiority/inferiority syndromes, and the like – have created a sort of common ground that informs the human experience horizontally throughout the Caribbean "manscape". He disassociates himself from "the idea of people sharing common divisions instead of increasingly common values" (p. 25). Arguing that one should concentrate on the hybridization that results from the encounter between the dominant and the dominated cultures, he posits that "the objective of all groups in this endeavour… should be similar and ultimately cooperative" (p. 54), arguing that their acute differences exist against the background of an awesome equalizing fortune. No matter what the specific group one belongs to, he says, "we remain part creole, part colonial, seeking many-ancestorial conclusions" (p. 55).

In the essay "Caribbean Man in Space and Time" it becomes clear that Brathwaite favours above all else the sort of scholarship which in his estimation highlights the dynamics which have created a Creole personality in the area. "Caribbean creole society may therefore be seen as reacting to an electro/magnetic norm, producing euro-creole, afro-creole, indo-creole or sino-creole characteristics," he insists (Brathwaite 1975c: 5). At the same time, he points out the weakness of "plantation studies" for generally ignoring "maroon societies" and often leading to a "pessimistic view", trapped as they often are in insurmountable dichotomies. He proposes, instead, a closer look at what he has called "the inner plantation". This may mean, of course, that the student of the area would have to research using documents which are less than conventional. "The archive of course is there, all around us: in the speech and actions of us," he says and adds: "This is why our concept of scholarship must include the creative arts" (p. 9). In this revision of the concept of scholarship, Brathwaite again ascribes crucial importance to the Caribbean word, embedded as it is in the language of the folk. There, as illustrated in his example of the words of a Kingston-based, Jamaican Kumina Queen, "this reality and language represents a truly cultural unit, interacting with other groups and through them, with the society as a whole" (pp. 10-11).

Brathwaite's own preferred method of research seeks a "connection with the inner metropole, with the ancestors, with the outer plantation, and with the neglected maroons" (p. 11). And just as he would recommend his method to other students of the history of the area as the surest means to understand the Creole culture of the Caribbean, similarly he would recommend it to those wishing to understand the literary texts written in the area. His major objection to the critical essays included in Louis James's *The Islands In Between* (1968) is that the contributors there, "a body of critics trained to respond almost exclusively to European influences, and whose main concerns are with 'the artist' and 'the individual'," fail to see that "West Indian culture must be defined in terms of the process of creolization" (Brathwaite 1969a: 272, 271). He insists that, not only have "West Indian writers, on the whole, abjured individualism," but he denies that the exclusive "application of Eurocentric cultural norms" would thrive in a meaningful assessment of Caribbean writing (ibid 271-72). He contends that even in the works of writers likes Naipaul, an "apparently Eurocentric East Indian" who of necessity remains a Caribbean, "West Indian writing, as a collectively regional enterprise, has been unambiguously concerned... with an examination of West Indian society" (ibid 276).

Toward a West Indian Aesthetics

From his refutation of the critics in *The Islands in Between*, as well as from his other texts, we can adduce Brathwaite's belief that art speaks for the sociocultural norm that informs its creation even without any conscious awareness of that process on the part of the artist. All intellectual discourse obeys such a dynamic. His analysis of *Rap on Race* (1971), the published text of a well known dialogue between Margaret Mead and James Baldwin, leads one to see each of the speakers as the inescapable persona of his/her social constituency. Although Mead repudiated racism as much as did Baldwin, in their conversation they cannot avoid waging an unconscious battle. Though meaning to relate to each other, they speak against each other. Their dissonance results from the fact that, whether they know it or not, Mead *represented* the dominant sector and Baldwin the dominated one. Brathwaite puts it this way: "Both beautiful psyches are trapped in primordial forces over which they have no control. Throughout their nearly eight hours of conversation, whatever the agreements, whatever the disagreements, Mead is unwittingly trying to persuade Baldwin to accept a definition of himself and his social nexus on *her* terms; while he tries to agree *and* disagree at the same time" (1972a: 59-60)

Brathwaite's comment on Paule Marshall's *The Chosen Place, The Timeless People* (1969) to the effect that if the novelist had "been a West Indian, she probably would not have written this book. Had she not been an Afro-American of West Indian parentage, she possibly could not have written it either" further indicates the inseparability of artist and socio-cultural norm in his mind (1970c: 175). That is why, in his attempt to articulate an aesthetics that could be considered indigenous to the region, he has paid particular attention to cultural elements that either have their origin in the Caribbean or are, for socio-historical reasons, congruent with the Caribbean sensibility. His first sustained effort in this direction is the three-part essay "Jazz in the West Indian Novel" in which he advances the view that the Anglophone West Indian novel and jazz are aesthetically linked by their common ground in a folk culture (Brathwaite 1967b: 276).

The use of jazz as an archetype connects with the concept of creolization in that, in Brathwaite's view, it provides the context of an expression that is simultaneously European and African. The sound of jazz is paralleled by the West Indian novelist's possession of Logos. Brathwaite seeks to illustrate this by surveying characteristic Caribbean novels that exhibit a prose style marked by predominantly rhythmic elements and what he conceives as the authors' "personal urge for words". He cites "the cadence and intonation of Trinidadian speech" perceptible in works by Samuel Selvon and Earl Lovelace as well as the word, speech rhythm, and strong imagery in *The Leopard* by Vic Reid as among the basic jazz elements of the West Indian novel (ibid pp. 279-83). The improvisational element of jazz, he tells us in the second part of the essay, can be found in such works as Neville Dawes's *The Last Enchantment*, just as the element of "call-and-response", which links jazz to a folk/oral tradition, appears visibly in *New Day* by Vic Reid, which strike him as "an expression of a West Indian 'creole' experience" (Brathwaite 1967c: 43, 46, 51). The third part, devoted primarily to a reading of Roger Mais's *Brother Man*, undertakes to show the novel's relationship to New Orleans jazz in "its peculiar sense of union and unity, its contrasting 'duets', its 'improvisation' and correspondences and above all, its pervading sense of community (its collective improvisation)" (Brathwaite 1968b: 122). Elsewhere Brathwaite contends that in *Brother Man* the reader gets through "language change to the cardiograph of the people themselves" in so far as its "two language-styles also set the novel firmly in its cultural context where bi- and inter-lingualism is a feature of our culturation" (1974b: xiii-xiv).

Kenneth Ramchand is probably right in challenging the concept of "jazz novel" for its lack of rigour in a conventional academic sense (1970: 53-54), and later Kwame Dawes in *Natural Mysticism: Towards a New Reggae Aesthetic in Caribbean Writing* (1999) was to critique Brathwaite on his own nativist terms for not using a Caribbean model which was closer to hand. One should keep in mind, though, that Brathwaite has been cautious not to suggest that this model provides a descriptive rendition of what West Indian novels have been doing. Rather, the idea of jazz constitutes "an aesthetic model (a way of seeing; a critical tool)" whose importance lies fundamentally in that it may suggest to us a way of viewing what the novelists write "and relating it to our indigenous cultures," and that it can provide us with "a creole way of seeing" (Brathwaite 1968b: 124-25). He admits, in fact, that *Brother Man* and Andrew Salkey's *A Quality of Violence* are probably the only existing jazz novels in Caribbean literature. Brathwaite does not conceal the fact that in advancing the notion of jazz as a critical tool he was moved by the need, not only to devise a method that can better reveal what has been done in the Caribbean but also to develop a more creative, more culturally authentic way of assessing the Caribbean legacy. If, as he himself concedes, the literary texts themselves do not support the idea of a "jazz novel" in the Caribbean, its critical utility remains useful at the metaphorical level.

Brathwaite's more recent essay, "The Love Axe/L: (Developing a Caribbean Aesthetic, 1962-1974)", constitutes a substantial contribution to critical analysis of the arts in the region.[3] A view that becomes obvious in this piece is that aesthetic ideas, and for that matter all intellectual production, have a meaningful relation with all other aspects of the human experience in the Caribbean. The author places the Cuban revolution side by side with the scholarly contributions of C.L.R. James, Eric Williams and Elsa Goveia among the "founding factors of the New Movement" that has ushered in the aesthetic orientations current in the Caribbean at the time of his writing (Brathwaite 1977c: 55). He adduces, for instance, the ideas of Walter Rodney, the publication in Jamaica of the cultural, militant journal *Bongo-Man*, the rise of the Rastafari as a visible cultural/spiritual model, and the continued "Westindianization" of the University of the West Indies as elements which have fostered what he calls a "new value system" and which he finds best exemplified in the criticism of Sylvia Wynter. Illustrative of Brathwaite's intransigence in his desire to nativize the tools of cultural analysis is the conclusion to his review of Rodney's *How Europe Underdeveloped Africa*: "My maroon comments here concern not this brother's achievement, which quietly shines forth, but the feel and texture of this particular work: the need for some dialect to go along with the dialectic" (Brathwaite 1973c: 99).

Brathwaite admires Wynter primarily because, despite whatever agony as an *individual* she may have endured, she has nonetheless contributed to the *collective vision* and, with a "sense of responsibility and inter-relatedness" that is "fundamental to any definition of our aesthetic", has succeeded in developing the notion that "the concern of the West Indian writer should be with the anonymous mass of our people" and has opted to focus on a "consideration of folk, rather than colonial, culture" (Brathwaite 1977c: 64-65; 1977d: 100, 102). He expresses a similar favour for the work of Gordon Rohlehr, a critic who has shown a deep concern with the process of creolization of Caribbean culture and who has set up an "aesthetic link... between 'folk' forms and 'art' forms" (Brathwaite 1977d: 106). In a larger sense, this explains Brathwaite's positive appraisal of Dell Lewis's application of the concept of *yard* to the analysis of West Indian literature. These critics, in effect, share Brathwaite's own aesthetic conviction that writers, whether they are poets, dramatists, novelists or critics, ought to deal with "human/communal relationship" rather than with the merely "literary" (1978a: 184). The critics celebrated by Brathwaite have earned his praise because they are creative thinkers who, in his judgment, are concerned "with a total roots-oriented (re-)definition of ourselves: an aesthetic: word act, vision, value system" (p. 186).

For Brathwaite valid critical assessments of Caribbean culture and art are those that, focusing on the process of creolization and recognizing and identifying with the "little tradition" of the folk, can define the Caribbean experience without indulging in bitter dichotomies. Nor is the prism through which he looks at the work of literary artists any different. His view of Caribbean culture is inseparable from his aesthetics. The thrust of his writings is to document, by conventional or unconventional means, the creative past of his people and to show, in contradistinction to Naipaul's dictum, that much has been created in the Caribbean. In this sense, he perceives his aesthetic exploration within a larger agenda whose main objective is to reconstruct local history and to strengthen the authenticity of the local creole culture.

Brathwaite has done considerable work as a bibliographer, collector, compiler, and recorder of various aspects of the Caribbean heritage. Witness his application of historiographical scholarship to shed light on the legacy of resistance bequeathed by Jamaican slave rebels Nanny (1720-1742) and Sam Sharpe (1801-1832) and raise them to the level of national heroes (Brathwaite 1977e). Similarly, he has compiled bibliographical checklists of Jamaica (1979c), Barbados (1979d), the Caribbean (1977f), so as to fill the information gap regarding the publications that are pertinent to literature, history, and culture in the area. He has chronicled the history of serial publications such as *Kyk-over-Al* that have made significant contributions to the cultural dialogue in the area (Brathwaite 1966c: 55-57). And he has captured the "thought/word/belief" of Mrs. Imogene Kennedy, "Miss Queenie", a woman who is herself a document of the spiritual heritage of the folk, a "queen or priestess of the Afro-Jamaican religious/culture complex known as 'Kumina'" (Brathwaite 1978b: 46).

Brathwaite appears aware of his own influence when, introducing the texts of thirteen contemporary young poets, he celebrates in them "the revelation of the *word*" and finds that in their poems: "The language has been unwhitened; the horizons are at the same time wider and more parochial" (1979e: 4-5). It is the triumph of creolization in the language of Caribbean poetry.

We can summarize the thrust of his works by borrowing words he himself used in prefacing a poetry collection that appeared in *Savacou*, a journal he edited for many years: his "work tries to create a world and he writes towards what he conceives to be a common future of wholeness" (Brathwaite 1970d: 5). In a personal retrospective of his own artistic development he has traced his socio-aesthetic awakening to his reading in 1953 of George Lamming's *In the Castle of My Skin*. At that point: "The words, the rhythms, the cadences, the scenes, the people, their predicament. They all came back. They all were possible" (Brathwaite 1970e: 37). He has composed, in the words of Jürgen Martini, a "terrifyingly complex and Caribo-centric" conception meant to "force the Eurocentric critic to abandon all previous ideas about European aesthetics, literature, and culture" (Martini 1984: 380-81).

Doris Monica Brathwaite, making good use of what she termed "inside" or "privileged" information, managed before her untimely death in 1986 to complete a chronological bibliography of her husband's work (1988: viii) and a checklist of his prose and poetry (1986: iv).[4] Unfortunately, both texts came out posthumously, but together they cleared the way for other scholars to examine the development of Kamau Brathwaite's literary production from his beginnings in the late 1940s to his current practice as one of the most dynamic writers of our times. One gets the sense that in classifying Brathwaite's writings, Doris's identification with her subject, as "a witness of the Middle Passage" whose experience has been "so clearly forced into the kind of utterance that I think is his", arises from a deep concern with the future of Caribbean literature that goes beyond the understandable support for the work of a spouse (D. M. Brathwaite 1986: iii; 1988: viii). Indeed, only three years after their marriage, in her review of V.S. Naipaul's *The Middle Passage*, whose assessment of the West Indian situation she characterized as "bare and insensitive with little hope or promise", already she showed a distinct affinity with her husband's view of the literary artist as spokesperson for a culture and a people (D. M. Brathwaite 1963: 73).

Doris Brathwaite's bibliographies attest, at any rate, to Brathwaite's vibrant literary career and lifelong dedication to creating models to bring to the surface the images, symbols, and forms of expression that best convey the texture of the Caribbean experience. Through his poetry, lectures, plays, criticism, compilations, as well as historical and cultural monographs, Brathwaite has stressed the need to unearth and assert the *ways of saying* that truly correspond with the Caribbean's history of fragmentation and its people's need to contrive "a common future of wholeness."

Western Market, Caribbean Alterity

As a poet, historian, critic, cultural activist, and teacher Kamau Brathwaite has posited that the Caribbean, crucible of various interleaved traditions, has produced its own cultural forms that not only speak with an indigenous creole voice but have the capability of posing an alternative existential model to the Western tradition. As such he has emphasised the collective relationship between the writer, other writers, a Caribbean readership and the wider non-literary world of the folk that has preserved the pool of Caribbean cultural resource. But it is also important to recognise that Brathwaite's literary credo rates originality very highly. He represents the quintessential artist whose commitment to genuine expression has led him into a daring succession of imaginative leaps. Each leap has entailed a grave risk that he has confronted boldly. Like Pablo Picasso, he has allowed the momentum and the internal logic of his aesthetic quest to guide his steps, even at the risk of frustrating the predilections of mainstream scholars or the established taste in the literary market. Unlike Picasso, however, Brathwaite works with language, which is a far thornier vehicle of expression than the most potentially factious of the media used by plastic artists. Words are vessels that carry discordant ideologies, social values, religious beliefs, and intellectual paradigms more overtly – hence more hazardously – than the shapes painted on a canvas or chiselled from a block. Thus, while Picasso succeeded in eventually securing a general audience for each new stage of thematic and formal innovation, Brathwaite, on the whole, after many decades of creative perseverance, still faces the frigidity of dominant sectors of the Western academy and literary market and sometimes hostility from within the more aesthetically conservative sections of the Caribbean literary and academic community.

While, for instance, the poet attained almost instant recognition in Africa and the Caribbean when his first book appeared in 1967, the favourable reception did not automatically spread over to England and the United States. A *Times Literary Supplement*'s commentator discarded *Rights of Passage* as a book that "makes very flat reading", granting only that, "given the right voice, the right production, and the right mood", it might conceivably "make a powerful radio performance, at least in part" (TLS 1967: 125). Another British reviewer approved of the text as a good example of Commonwealth poetry, but one cannot help thinking that if in his mind that praise had meant much he would not have needed to add this caveat: "I mean no disrespect to Mr. Brathwaite" (Symons 1967: 479). Among the American *litterati* who commented on the book, one simply contrasted the author to Whitman, Pound, and Williams, three authors of successful "epic-length" poems, stating that he, unlike them, lacked "style", which is indispensable for anyone writing an epic without a "narrative involving several characters besides the author". As a result, he found in the book merely "sociology and journal entries in a generalized, contemporary, sometimes jazzy free verse, and that is not enough" (Turco 1967: 32). Strikingly, twenty five years later, a *Choice* reviewer writing on *Middle Passages* (1993a), the latest anthology of Brathwaite's poems, utters comparable reservations and much of the criticism evoked by *Rights of Passage* in the past. This author starts out pitting Brathwaite against Walcott, who "has developed his technique" and has attained recognition "as the greater poet", then proceeds to discard Brathwaite's "Sycorax video style", and concludes that "this collection does nothing to enhance the poet's reputation – and it demonstrates the now great chasm between Brathwaite and Walcott" (McLeod 1993: 1460). Decades of creative insistence, in short, have not sufficed for Brathwaite to receive the legitimizing approval of the West.

However, Laurence Breiner, another American critic who has made a deep study of Caribbean poetry, writing on *X/Self*, has lamented the scarce visibility accorded to Brathwaite in the United States as compared with the great prestige enjoyed by Walcott, whom "one anthology even adopts… as a 'New York poet'" (Breiner 1989: 316). Moved by his sense of fairness, this scholar would wish for the "two masters" of English-speaking Caribbean poetry to receive equal recognition in this country. But the barriers which militate against the prevalence of such aesthetic equity are formidable. They manifest themselves in ideological, cultural, and even epistemological imperatives. In all fairness, individual American readers with the sensibility of a Hayden Carruth have since the 1970s often hailed Brathwaite as "a poet of real accomplishment by any standards, to whom we must give not only our attention but also our admiration" (Carruth 1974: 320). But Carruth's appraisal is hardly predominant. For the most part, Brathwaite's writings have appealed in the United States to people interested in the black experience globally or to those who, like Breiner, have discovered Caribbean literature as a field of study.

The meagre presence of Brathwaite's texts in the American literary arena, as compared with the considerable celebrity of Naipaul and Walcott, can be explained by the nature of his own search for authenticity and the choices that he, as a Caribbean writer, has had to make. Of the two paths normally available to writers from the neo-colonial Third World, he has chosen the road less travelled by, to use a Frostian turn. Gifted intellectuals and artists from the old colonies invariably have to contend with the fact that they depend on the West to attain international visibility. Due to the economic and political dependance of their native countries, as well as the lack of cultural self-respect characterizing the national bourgeoisies in those lands, Caribbean writers can seldom fulfil their professional aspirations exclusively on the basis of local success. Their nations lack a dynamic publishing industry via which successful authors can participate in the literary market worldwide. Indeed, their publishing industry can seldom afford to free them from the burden of subsidizing their own books. As they cannot subsist solely on their national readership, they end up yearning for a space in the Western metropolis.

Literary success in the West promises proportionate material reward that can help writers occupy themselves more fully with the demands of the craft and less with the absorbing business of earning a living. But Caribbean writers may need more than just talent to succeed in the West. They also may have to curtail their vision and suppress their alterity. They need to be able and willing to accept the Western reader as their interlocutor, which generally means that linguistically and epistemologically their texts should endeavour to project a vision that the West can find understandable and palatable. They must become dexterous cultural interpreters with the skill to translate the native cosmos to their Western interlocutor. The feat requires not only literary genius but also a carefully crafted strategy of communication. For the writer comes from one world and the reader from another. The inside must speak to the outside. But the speaker must contrive a vocal texture that will not disturb the outsider's way of hearing. The insider must reveal a good deal of the mysterious interiority of the native cosmos for the outsider to feast upon, but the rendition must be codified in the system of signs that govern the interlocutor's view of the world. Naipaul and Walcott have mastered the skill of translating the inside without straining the Western outsider's ears. Brathwaite, on the other hand, has opted out of that strategy.

Elaine Savory has highlighted some of the implications of the reticence exhibited by the Western literary market with respect to some texts by Brathwaite. She examines this writer's publishing history to surmise that "whereas at every stage, (fortunately), there has been at least one publisher willing to take the risk, from time to time the work has been held up or rejected and the reason given or implied seems always connected to the prevailing expectations of the predominantly Western marketplace for the book" (Savory 1993: 3). The publishers' caution transcends the mere logic of supply and demand. Indeed, Savory links it to Brathwaite's defiance of "the continued dominance of discourses deriving from Western intellectual history and the discussion of so-called Third World or Minority Cultural products still contained within Western referential signposts" (Savory 1993: 26). How this predicament of the Caribbean writer vis-à-vis the publishing industry manifests itself in the Hispanic and Francophone parts of the region will become clear in the discussion of René Depestre's increase in popularity with French readers (Chapter 4) and Pedro Mir's limited impact outside the confines of his own country (Chapter 5).

Brathwaite shows no interest in tempering his cultural and historical alterity vis-à-vis the West. He has flaunted it, instead, by seeking in the realm of his difference for the elements of his authenticity. At the level of form, his texts, since *Rights of Passage*, have sought to explore various uncommon dispositions of the words on the page. For him, the forging of an authentic voice necessitates the reshaping of conventional syntax and orthography. Thinking of the formal arrangement evident in *Rights of Passage*, his French translator speaks of "irregular verses, asymmetrical stanzas, innumerable breaks at the ends of lines, a syncopated rhythm, dislocated syntax, truncated style" (Mollica 1986: 12). By the same token, thinking of *Middle Passages*, critics continue to note the poet's delving into the communicative possibilities of graphic effects: "line breaks, shape poetry, contractions, and pastiche elements, all creating their maximum effect through explosions of imagery coupled with an astonishing verbal tenderness" (Dabydeen 1993: 426).

But in addition to the configuration of the words on the page, Brathwaite has taken even riskier steps in recent texts such as *Trench Town Rock* (1992a), *DreamStories* (1994a), and *Barabajan Poems* (1994b) by challenging the very "Western idea of the book through his video style of changing font style and sizes, his use of computer windows in the text, and his interpretation of the form of the journal or diary, journalistic reportage, interview and poem" (Savory 1993: 19-20). In the unyielding search for an authentic voice, he has put himself in jeopardy as far as the metropolitan market is concerned. Poets from the old colonies who "become radically unexpected", as Savory puts it, do so at their own peril: "If poets pursue the goal of decolonization or of preservation of a sense of a particular cultural community, especially in the so-called Third World, then they run an increased risk of becoming un/'market'/able" (Savory 1993: 4). Brathwaite has paid the price of his insurrection. For the most part, the West will not normally sponsor the literary products of a writer whose poetics embodies the outright shattering of Western paradigms. One cannot reasonably expect the West to embrace poetic systems that deny its centrality.

Calibanism and Form

On the whole, Brathwaite's writings make up a testament of dissidence with respect to the West. His literary practice occurs as a reaction to the awareness that "here in the Caribbean we have people without apparent roots; all the result of this dis/traction, this destruction", a "*history* of catastrophe" which "requires a *literature of catastrophe* to hold a broken mirror up to broken nature" (Brathwaite 1985c: 456-57). Brathwaite's effort to recast the word into a nativized mould has continued undiminished, showing a growing emphasis through the successive volumes that make up the two trilogies. The collections published independently of the trilogies, particularly those, like *Middle Passages*, that bring together poems from much of the length of Brathwaite's career, permit a rapid glance at his skilful versatility in drawing from a wide variety of linguistic registers to devise a genuine vehicle of expression. That is the case with *Jah Music* (1986a) and *The Visibility Trigger* (1986b), which comprise texts from previous volumes as well as uncollected verse from periodical publications. The poems in *Jah Music* centre around the relationship between music and spirituality. Those in *The Visibility Trigger*, a selection of five long poems translated into French with the English original on the opposite page, span many of Brathwaite's major historical and cultural themes.

Perhaps the most unusual of Brathwaite's poetry books is *Sappho Sakyi's Meditations* (1989a), a reprint of a poetic sequence published originally in the 1950s, which appears now together with a later revision of the same texts. In both the older and the newer versions we encounter a speaker who fathoms the wisdom and the genius of the animal kingdom and from time to time takes a comparative glimpse of human society. At one point the speaker envies the peaceful orderliness enjoyed by fowls of the air: "How lovely is the life of birds/Who sing, not sweat, for mates/Who wage no wars/Or words" (p. 12). Then, in a section that deals with driver ants, the comparative glance leads to the realization of our similarly dismal unenlightenment: "Like you, they are totally blind" (p. 13). Similarly, the toiling of the poet is evoked in this simple simile: "But bees still work/In honey as you work/In words" (p. 20). What most strikingly sets this small collection apart from the rest of Brathwaite's poetry is that it retains the standard English grammar, diction, and phraseology predominantly employed in the original version of the sequence three decades earlier. Yet, in the expert reading of Rohlehr, the sequence marks the emergence of "the distinctive Brathwaite style and sound" (cited in Breiner 1993: 12). In a sense, the collection shows that in the effort to bring forth an authentic voice, Brathwaite has not necessarily discarded the verbal modulations associated with the Queen's English or standard Caribbean English, but has mastered the full range of what has been called "the West Indian language continuum." It shows also that for this poet discovering "the centrality of the voice and sound in African forms of self-expression" does not mark a "turn away from scriptured forms to oral ones", as Simon Gikandi has claimed, but rather it generates a seamless integration of writing with orality (Gikandi 1991: 727).

As Brathwaite's poetic output has continued to grow, he has intensified the search for expressive possibilities, emphasizing the transformations of the words on the page. We get a sense of this in *Shar: Hurricane Poem*, a lyrical and threnodic evocation of the destructive onrush that Hurricane Gilbert visited upon Jamaica on Monday, September 12, 1988. The second stanza begins thus: "And all this. all this. reduced to all this to so little. this./to so almost nothing like this in the shattered cess of the storm. to this/ nothinglessness in the thistle & cease. less like cease. less/drip. from the sky/ of my roof" (Brathwaite 1990). The words here tend to disintegrate as if to emulate the devastating shatter enacted in the poem. Gilbert practically destroyed Brathwaite's Irish Town house, the violent wind loosening the roof from its hinges, a mud-slide flooding the library and damaging much of his Caribbean literature holdings. Brathwaite's sister, Mary Morgan, has recalled "the terrible experience" briefly in a family chronicle entitled *A Gathering of Threads*. Regarding her brother's losses, she writes: "The road back from Gilbert was hard – for some, like my brother Kamau, with work on his house and the land-slid road still to be completed, it has seemed cruel, lonely, heart-breaking" (Morgan 1991).

From Mrs. Morgan we learn that Brathwaite named the poem *Shar* in homage to her daughter Sharon Marie Morgan Lake, who died on July 28, 1990 at the age of twenty eight. Speaking at a conference in honour of her brother, Mrs. Morgan explained *Shar*'s marked emphasis on song as her brother's tribute to his niece Sharon, who "really liked to sing" (Morgan 1992). Indeed, as the poem draws to a close, the singing actually overshadows the sorrow for the hurricane victims and the overall loss. Perhaps most pertinent to the present discussion, the prevalence of song in the latter half of the text is paralleled by the growing size of the print on the page. The raising of the voice, nearing a shouting pitch, has its visual correspondence in the enlargement of the letters to suggest the sound amplification.

The poet's intensive exploration of the visual dimensions of poetic communication makes his next daring formal innovation, his "Sycorax video style", appear as a natural development. His use of computers presupposes the realization that this new scientific contrivance should serve as an ally rather than a foe of poetic expression. "Letter Sycorax", an epistolary text appearing in *Middle Passages* (1993), provides the intellectual framework that informs the style Brathwaite has ventured to rehearse in this new literary phase. Addressed to "Dear mamma", the poem reveals a sense of awe at the possibilities that make themselves apparent with the discovery of the computer as a writing tool: "is one a de bess tings since cicero" (Brathwaite 1993a: 97). To the new technological innovation corresponds a conceptual reconsideration. Thus, the speaker is now able to rehearse previously concealed choices contained in the relationship between Prospero and Caliban, the Shakespearean paradigm that has so pervasively captivated the author's imagination. In other words, the speaker declines to draw her self-awareness from the mere opposition to Prospero, to "curse/wid im own/curser" (p.107), and prefers a more self assertive outlook on history and self: "but is like what i try./in to sen/seh &/seh about muse./in computer/& mouse&/learn./in prospero ling./go & ting/not fe dem/not fe dem/de way caliban/done/but fe we/fe a-we" (p.106). The combination of "Letter Sycorax" and the more linear texts that make up *Middle Passages* puts us in touch with Brathwaite's continued "endeavour to articulate personal and communal feelings, to reconcile literary and oral traditions in Caribbean poetry" as well as with both his way of assessing "the contemporary post-colonial scene and the sixty-two-year-old poet's own sense of being in transition" (Parker 1992: 27).

Brathwaite does not circumscribe his video style to the writings in verse. He applies it extensively in the seven "prose" pieces that make up his *DreamStories* (1994a), a volume that delves into unconscious journeys through the experience of dreams. The book opens with "The Black Angel", a reissuing in video style of the conventional short fiction piece that Brathwaite had published in 1955. The current version abandons customary conventions of punctuation, sentence structure, and paragraphing. Idiosyncratic spellings, broken and abbreviated words, letters from the Greek alphabet, slashes, parentheses, and other symbols recur, including computer-generated graphic designs. Similarly "The 4th Traveller", a story which recalls Dante's descent into the netherworld, is also the revised version, with newly incorporated visual effects, of a story the author had published some years earlier (Brathwaite 1989b). In "Dream Chad" we come upon alternating small and large print, words in bold and italic letters, several fonts competing on the same page. The visual noise caused by the graphics perhaps accords with the emotional tension of the narrator who at the beginning struggles to compose a story that the computer's mind – "some spirit in the machine" (p. 48) – insists on erasing and ultimately transforming. In "Dream Haiti" and "Grease" the placement of the words on the page resembles the line disposition of verse more closely than the sentence arrangement characteristic of prose, stressing a feature Brathwaite had used in "The Crossing" (1989c), a story that captures moments of a lost childhood. *DreamStories* closes with "Salvages", which combines many of the visual effects employed in the other six stories. On the whole, Brathwaite's strategy in this collection seems to be aimed at "rendering in language the shapes of the narratives that lay immersed in the dream's formless flow", as indicated by Rohlehr, who sees a parallel between the "dream journeys" dramatized in the stories and the writer's "journeys into language and format" (Rohlehr 1994: viii). In so far as these texts gives vent to paranoias, phobias, and desires, instigated by the immediacy of Brathwaite's major losses and personal traumas since the death of his wife in 1986, *DreamStories* shows a new emphasis on private pain as firewood to fuel the literary imagination.

Transgressing Turfs

Using the visual virtuosity of the video style, which reaches an unchecked intensity in the writing that arises from deeply personal and painful experiences, Brathwaite ventures into texts that transcend generic barriers. Such is the case with *The Zea Mexican Diary* (1993b), a text based on his journal entries starting with the shock of learning that his wife was terminally ill, and continuing "helplessly & spasmodically" through her death, plus extracts of letters to his sister Mary, and other pieces occasioned by the burial and the sorrow. The text, divorced from its visual effects, exudes a sense of troubled serenity, but in the stridency of those effects one gets a sense of the narrator's repressed grief before Doris dies. That is what the *Village Voice* reviewer probably meant when he or she wrote that "the author zigzags across the boundaries of poetry and prose, altering punctuation and spelling with an intuitive sense that captures the subtle and pained cadences of his experience" (VLS 1993: 11). Starting on section V, which relives the events that follow the death of Zea Mexican (Doris), the typographic variations, letter sizes, and different fonts change rapidly as if to reproduce visually the erratic, directionless state that comes with desperation and the awareness of utter, irreparable loss.

The same visual intensity pervades *Trench Town Rock* (1992a), a turbulent composition based on Brathwaite's traumatic experience of having his house ransacked on October 24, 1990 by armed robbers while he, gagged and tied, powerlessly awaited the gun's mortal "click". When the muggers left, the images that remained recalled Gilbert's havoc two years before: "-my room like the sea-the debris & litter all over the beaches-bibliography files & my poetry manuscript folders all trampled & curled by the breakers-books hit by like a hurricane-what more can I tell you?" (Brathwaite 1992a: 188). Profoundly personal, *Trench Town Rock* is also deeply social. Indeed, before getting to the individual catastrophe, the text amply evokes, via typographic variations, interviews, news reports, and other discourse combinations, the omnipresence of violent crime in Kingston. The story of his own travail comes in a section entitled "My Turn", suggesting that for anyone in the society to become a victim is just a matter of waiting a turn.

Sandra Pouchet Paquet has said that the aesthetic illustrated in *The Zea Mexican Diary* "privileges private expression of grief in a public forum" (Paquet 1993: xi). Our reading here, would suggest, besides, a tendency to reveal the collective implications of personal sorrow. In a text triggered by his perception of "the brutal and frightening neglect" inflicted on him by his campus community at the University of the West Indies, following the death of his wife, Brathwaite himself endeavoured to place his individual misfortune in a larger social frame. In a letter dated November 22, 1986, the distraught writer, though fraught with the lonely bitterness induced by his feeling of abandonment, not only ventilated his disillusion, but he also transcended the strictly individual nature of his pain: "I am only one symptom of what is happening to our society. We are so bombed out, burnt out, raped out, knifed out, shot up, robbed out that I wonder if we are still a society at all" (cited in Rohlehr 1992: 218).

Brathwaite's fusion of different forms of discourse and genres entails a breaking of the boundary between artistic and intellectual expression, as well as a defiance of the established norms of academic communication. As illustrated in *Contradictory Omens* (1974), and most of the "scholarly" or "academic" works, written or spoken, that he has produced over several decades, Brathwaite the historian or literary critic has drawn substantially from the formal and linguistic innovations he has developed as a poet. The transgression of disciplines and the fusion of genres have the weight of a necessity. For him one simply cannot apprehend the Caribbean experience by discrete ways of knowing: "I say you have to be everything to bring those fragments together because fragments by their very nature are everything. That's the secret of the scattered fragments. They are in fact everything, little seeds growing throughout the scattered diaspora, throughout the Caribbean" (Brathwaite 1992b).

The marriage of discourses reached a high point of seamless significance particularly in his "Metaphors of Underdevelopment: A Proem for Hernan Cortez" (1985a), a text that combines prose and verse to chronicle the historical conjunctures from antiquity to modern times that have framed the Caribbean experience. The text advances many of the paradigms, characters, and passages that would subsequently go into the composition of *X/Self*. In section VII of the text Brathwaite announces an aesthetic purpose that succinctly articulates the marrow of his dissident stance: "to create X/ SELF: a literature of subversive underdevelopment: from MAMMON of UNPROSPERO: to its creative opposite: NAM, SYCORAX, MABRAK" (1985a: 460). The proper names in the passage are all heavily loaded with meaning in Brathwaite's vision of the Caribbean's relationship to Western culture. They represent an utter refashioning of the conceptual and interpretive models bequeathed to the islands by the colonial transaction, and the fusion of discourses exhibited in the text shows the formal facet of the socio-cultural transformation he has espoused.

This literary subversion proclaimed in "Metaphors of Underdevelopment" manifests itself most comprehensively in *Barabajan Poems* (1994), a compendium assembled from diverse and seemingly disparate discourses and materials. This book of "poems" actually starts out as a lecture on "The Poet and his Place in Bajan Culture" given by Brathwaite in Barbados on December 2, 1987, upon the invitation of the Governor. The text, as it immediately becomes evident, is a sort of "biographia literaria" that allows the reader a privileged glimpse of "the stones & steppes in the heart of the poet who sings from the dirt that he ate in his yard from the dream that he drinks from his mother's milk" (Brathwaite 1994: 24). The prose contains all of the visual features of the video style displayed in the more "fictional" *DreamStories*. At the same time, verse excerpts and whole poems from the two trilogies and the other poetry volumes intercede to help advance the account of the life unfolding here. In the process we learn about one man's intellectual emancipation, his discovery that "like the hurricane, our seas don't usually speak in pentameters" (p. 115), and his ensuing realization that "to create our sense of self of hope of history/we need to have our own-own true-true poems And that is what consumes me all these years" (p. 116). We learn, besides, of Brathwaite's descent into self, his discovery of the motherly water running invisibly underneath his native island.

Convinced that an island without water is strange, Brathwaite has come to believe with equal conviction that: "No culture can exist without the gods of that landscape", so for him seeing a Barbadian woman at a Christian church pass mysteriously from the worship of the Hebrew God to the worship of the Antillean Shango illustrates the vitality of the submerged culture (Brathwaite 1992c: 36; 1992d: 33). Witnessing the surfacing of the gods of the Middle Passage has an empowering effect on the percipient, who, armed with the unextinguished force of native deities, can successfully repossess them on the "Igbo Bajan landscape" (1994b: 205). *Barabajan Poems* lets us peek also at a 1971 ceremony of initiation in Kenya where Brathwaite received the Kikuyu name *Kamau* from Ngugi wa Thiong'o's grandmother, which marked a turning point in his arduous quest for spiritual renewal (1994b: 236).

The pilgrimage disclosed in *Barabajan Poems* has not lacked obstacles. A case in point is the writer's recollection of the Association of Commonwealth Literature and Language Societies (ACLALS) conference held in January 1971 at the University of the West Indies, Mona, where Brathwaite and some of his intellectual kin were branded "cultural gorillas" (p. 322) for presumably creating an atmosphere which displeased some distinguished guests like Naipaul, who was the keynote speaker. In sharing that disappointing moment in his career, the author reminds us of the hurdles and the stress involved in the pursuit of authenticity. For, in the Caribbean, too, due to the vestiges of the colonial heritage in the mind of the academic establishment, a writer who has been legitimated by the West normally inspires more respect and adulation than one who has challenged Western cultural pre-eminence.

Brathwaite, one might say, knew all along that his artistic and intellectual project would have to contend with adverse forces that were well entrenched in Caribbean society. He showed an early awareness when, having just returned from eight years of service in Ghana, he served as Resident Tutor for the Extra-Mural Studies Department at the University of the West Indies in Castries, St. Lucia, in 1962. Beginning to formulate a centripetal approach to West Indian life and culture, he launched a critical look at two local institutions that remained still embedded in the emulation of British models: public radio and higher education. He disparaged the prevailing practice of treating the airwaves as mere "loudspeakers for advertisement", and advocated, instead, a use of radio that would encourage listeners to empower themselves by means of their own resources. Consequently, he decried the local stations' undue "reliance on BBC material (much of which is of questionable value for our needs)", contending that their excessive consumption of British programming probably implied overestimation of "overseas products and distrust of the local" (Brathwaite 1963b: 35-36).

Regarding higher education, he ascribed great importance to the University of the West Indies for its potential to help in the development of society by producing technical knowledge, training leadership for the region, fostering public opinion, and furthering the road to nationhood. But, most importantly, for him the University could play a crucial role as an organism in which the individual could find "his most perfect self-expression." He then affirmed the need to engage in the quest for self-knowledge and cultural authenticity: "we in the West Indies – must insist on the importance to us, as West Indians, of the University of the West Indies… It is only in the West Indies that the individual can learn about the West Indies: can absorb what West Indian means" (Brathwaite 1963c: 18). Looking retrospectively at his work over the decades that have elapsed since this pronouncement, one cannot help marvelling at the consistency with which he has adhered to the cultural directives he then prescribed to the radio industry and the University. At the same time, we must marvel at the durability of the predominant cultural attitudes Brathwaite set out to combat decades ago. As *Barabajan Poems* reminds us, they still loom large in the Caribbean.

Searching for Sycorax

Since *Barabajan Poems* ventures a panoramic account of the writer's life, which includes his growth and re-education, it also affords us a convenient glimpse at some significant shifts in emphasis during his long creative journey. We note, therefore, that thoughts and episodes touching on spiritual self-awareness, like the poet's baptism in Kenya or a woman's possession by Shango, occur with increased frequency in the latter half of the book. Indeed, it is evident that a concern with the presence of the sacred has broadened in an all-encompassing scope in the latter half of the author's career. Since the late seventies, Brathwaite has ever more emphatically undertaken to uncover the spiritual dimensions of his quest for cultural authenticity. He has endeavoured to construct a vision of history, culture, and religion for the Caribbean that stresses the spiritual legacy of the African heritage, focusing on the intricate historical process whereby the Middle Passage turned African spirits into "gods of the New World Caribbean". These gods, he contends, show themselves in their ontological complexity as human, vulnerable, powerful, natural, and familiar, hence diverging drastically from the divinities brought to the Caribbean by the Christian West (Brathwaite 1982b: 43).

René Depestre's *Un arc-en-ciel pour l'Occident chrétien* (1967), a text based on the deities of the Haitian pantheon, a "poem so firmly rooted in vodoun", awakened Brathwaite's interest precisely because there he saw a major Caribbean poet reconnecting with the "gods of the New World Caribbean" (Brathwaite 1984b: 43). However, he criticises Depestre for not carrying the vodoun, creole logic of his text all the way through. He finds that "despite the generosities of at least the first 3/4 of *Arc*", the Haitian poet succumbs in the end to Western reflexes at the level of frame of reference and language: "Now language, as all (ex)-colonials know, is Caliban's big problem/monster. How to rename. And rename with organic and symbolic resonance" (Brathwaite 1984b: 46). Depestre, he seems to suggest, lost the opportunity to achieve the liberation of renaming because of his ultimately tentative embrace of the indigenous gods. Renaming in Brathwaite has revolutionary implications to the extent that it entails a reappropriation of self for both the individual and the community. It implies a coming into contact with one's *nam*, "the indestructible and atomic core of man's culture… the kernel of his name" (Brathwaite 1982b: 18).

The recognition of and identification with autochthonous spiritual forces form part of the quest for authenticity and mental liberation in the Caribbean, Brathwaite contends. Thus his cosmology often elevates historical individuals to the rank of *zemis* or *loas* (generic titles for ancestral Caribbean divinities) for embracing the deliverance of their people as a primary mission. Rohlehr reminds us that: "Brathwaite advocates maroonage as an absolute necessity, and invokes the spirit of Nanny Nanahemmaa – Jamaican Maroon Queen Mother – who, like Toussaint…, has become a *loa* or *zemi* because of the quality of her historic resistance to the plantation's militia" (Rohlehr 1989: 33). We have here a political philosophy whose view of liberation for the Caribbean person incorporates a spiritual dimension. As Brathwaite insisted in a lecture delivered at the University of Mysore in India during his tenure there in 1982, the Caribbean cannot afford the sort of emancipation that attends to the body only and not the soul, hence his advocacy for: "a different kind of Caliban, not the Caliban who is concerned with physical revolt only, but a Caliban who is concerned with metaphysical revolt, the revolt of the spirit, the reconstitution of the mind, which is something that becomes more crucial in the development of the Third World than simple physical revolution" (Brathwaite 1984c: 45).

Since Brathwaite understands the Caribbean as partaking of "the culture of the circle", which was made possible by "the capsule" that came to the region along with the gods of the Middle Passage, we find here a cultural history imbued within the history of the gods. Brathwaite develops these ideas most systematically in *Afternoon of the Status Crow* (1982c) and a slightly modified rendition of that text that appeared in Bremen as "Caribbean Culture: Two Paradigms" (1983b). Here we find Toussaint associated with Legba, the vodoun god of the crossroads, and represented as the ultimate maroon. In this portrayal, Toussaint embodies the qualities of the *alter/native*, meaning the native who has recognized his otherness and has sought to draw strength from it by coming into contact with his *nam*. The maroon, who for reasons of survival has needed to resort to concealment and disguise, has the advantage of preserving the autochthonous culture despite the fragmentation perpetrated by Prospero (Brathwaite 1982c: 26). But even maroons need to undergo a process of intellectual emancipation lest they fail to connect with their own native source of energy wherein lies the key to their survival. Toussaint's demise came about as a result of his "love of Europa", his desire, "in victory, to emulate the Other's Model" (Brathwaite 1983b: 42).

Therefore, the Caribbean requires an indigenous model to deal with a catastrophic history in a manner that points the way out of fragmentation. To claim explanatory power, however, the model would need to deploy images, symbols, and names that break away from the modes of perception taught by the culture that inflicted the fragmentation upon the region. The effort must aim at a drastically different philosophy of history, one which privileges the logic of the capsule over that of the missile. Brathwaite's own "Caribbean Aesthetic Dictionary" defines the "missile" as a pointed image symbolizing Western destructive technology and imperial imagination and the "space capsule" as an "image trying to explain how culture(s) can be transported/transplanted" (Brathwaite 1983b: 54).

A culturally centripetal Caribbean philosophy of history would separate itself from Hegelian dialectics with its teleological inexorability and would uphold, instead, Brathwaite's concept of "tidalectics", a far more humane notion. Contrary to dialectics, his notion permits us to see achievement in the Caribbean: "'success' of dialectics: synthesis. For dialectics is another gun: a missile: a way of making progress:/farward/but in the culture of the circle 'success' moves outward from the centre to circumference and back again: a tidal dialectic" (Brathwaite 1983b: 42). In an interview with Nathaniel Mackey, Brathwaite has further explained the concept of tidalectics as "dialectics with my difference. In other words, instead of the notion of one-two-three Hegelian, I am now more interested in the movement of the water backwards and forwards as a kind of cyclic, I suppose, motion, rather than linear" (Mackey 1991: 44). Tidalectics accords with the culture of the circle, which is typical of traditional societies in Africa and the Caribbean, just as dialectics corresponds to the culture of the missile, which is consistent with the expansionist societies of the West.

Brathwaite has buttressed his cosmic vision by reference to Gary Snyder's somewhat idiosyncratic distinction between ecosystems cultures and biospheric ones. The former draw their "economic base of support" from "a material region, a watershed, a plant zone, a natural territory" whereas the latter "spread their economic support system out far enough that they can afford to wreck one ecosystem, and keep moving on" (Snyder, cited in Brathwaite 1985d: 54). Snyder's paradigm fits perfectly into Brathwaite's notion of functional shapes. Biospheric cultures, with the rocket as icon, follow a missilic logic that bids them to expand and conquer. Ecosystems cultures, with the drum as their icon, follow a circular logic that induces a return to the mother. Logically, then, these antithetical types of culture must breed different *ways of seeing* and different *ways of saying*. Dialectics, for instance, accords with the forward thrust of expansionist, imperialist Western culture just as tidalectics corresponds to the traditional, marginalized, Caribbean culture.

The elements of such an indigenous philosophy of history can foster an alternative to the view that has compelled the likes of Naipaul to give in to the seduction of fragments and devastation to the point of seeing merely a history of "West Indian futility". The alternative model can sharpen the percipient's eyes to the "submerged culture" of the Caribbean. The confluence of ancestral cultures from Amerindian, European, African, and Asian matrices may come to the surface. The heritage of the maroons, "the first successful alternative communities in the Caribbean", whose creativity bequeathed an enduring legacy, from the Haitian Revolution through to the boom of reggae, comes into visibility (Brathwaite 1984c: 57). Similarly, Sycorax, the least known of the archetypes coming from *The Tempest*, emerges to possess the spotlight. Brathwaite conceives of Sycorax as follows: "She possessed the island and she gave birth to her son Caliban, she was then imprisoned and indentured to Prospero. The woman herself, Sycorax, was banished, she was imprisoned, but the point about her is that she became submerged. She does not appear" (Brathwaite 1984c: 44).

The privileging of Sycorax in Brathwaite's metaphors of historical awakening comes from the understanding that in the Caribbean the submerged mother holds the key to cultural authenticity. Caliban's mental liberation cannot happen without a return to the vital source of "his own mother's milk" and "his own mother's language". Caliban has the awesome task of undoing the alienation inflicted upon him by a lifelong process of mental conditioning in Prospero's schools, mass media, and the other instruments of socialization. Therefore, if he is really committed to his liberation, Caliban, "the colonized", has the responsibility "not only to revolt against that imposition but to discover his own coral, his own roots" (Mackey 1991: 47). He must, in other words, seek refuge in Sycorax, "the carrier, the keeper, the protector of the native culture", whose banishment, with all its disadvantages, has nonetheless enabled her to preserve "in a submerged manner the very essence of the native culture" and to hold on to "the secrets of a possible alternative culture for the Caribbean" (Brathwaite 1984c: 44).

The Alter Native's Authenticity

By means of these explorations (the design of a cultural history that unites divine expressions with social imperatives, the forging of a word that conveys the autochthonous sound and sense of the Caribbean experience, and the constitution of a philosophy of history that accords with the logic of the region's "manscape"), Brathwaite has, as a writer, embodied the outlook of the *alter/native*, the emancipated Caliban. In arriving at this worldview, Brathwaite may have received some influence from Wilson Harris whom he admired already back in the 1960s when the Guyanese writer had begun to articulate similar views. His literary emancipation has entailed more than just the building of a counter-discourse to strike back at the West, for that would have meant stopping at the curse, like the unenlightened Caliban: "If Caliban instead of learning how to curse in pidgin had listened to his mother's voice; if he could speak her in their *language*/He might have had a better chance when the chance for revolt came his way" (Brathwaite 1983b: 35). An effective revolt needs to transcend oppositional thinking, the sort of mental scheme whereby one becomes a self only by negative reference to an adversary. For such thinking makes one ontologically dependent on the other, thus inducing a distorted sense of identity.

Brathwaite has laid the conceptual groundwork for assessing Caribbean discourse outside the framework of Western culture's dominant modes of thought. Having himself undergone a process of "de-education", he has postulated an aesthetic model that is equipped with the necessary resources to free the Caribbean mind from the tyrannous dependance on Western images, models, and forms. Since one cannot get around the fact that "if you are moving into a definition of aesthetics, we need to have terms which make sense", he has worked vigorously on the construction of an indigenous lexicon, "a critical system which is using terms of critical value different from what you would find in the *Times Literary Supplement*" (Brathwaite 1992c: 30; 1984c: 71). Like Glissant, he upholds a conception of Caribbean culture that looks backwards to the past while it points forward to the future. His project, therefore, has the twofold function of simultaneous discovery and creation.

In his search for an authentic Antillean expression, Brathwaite has sought to piece together the history of the voice for his people, but he has also invested much energy and imagination in the task of inventing that voice. The repetition, recurrence, and recasting of ideas or verbal performances in many of his works suggest the urgency with which he has assumed the task of unearthing and creating. The frequent reworking and republication of previously printed materials may have to do also with what Anthony Kellman has called "a retrospective style" that "shows a continuity of vision, of artistic concern" (Kellman 1988: 648). As Brathwaite himself explains it, the occasional return to earlier material is part of his technique to not only revise "but to go on working", in keeping with his "sense of seamlessness of organon, or the organic, and therefore all of my work fits into a constant pattern which keeps on growing" (Brathwaite 1992b).

Brathwaite recalls that as a youth in Barbados, before going on a scholarship to England, he and some peers had to design their own course of study to prepare for a competition, and he deems this an important event. That period of self-education "made the difference" in that it gave them from "the very beginning a different sense of literature" and enabled them to circumvent the officially prescribed road to literary learning: "we did not go to the golden treasuries, and the kinds of Wordsworthian daffodils that were available" (1992b). The experience of self-education permitted them to draw selectively from the Western tradition, choosing particularly those voices, such as that of T.S. Eliot, which they could use to tune their own: "by teaching ourselves we are able to establish a whole, for the first time, sense of being Barbadian, Caribbean" (1992b). Behind the recollection of that lucky period of self-education lurks the sense that the official culture of the Caribbean, generally designed, at first, by the colonial authorities, and, in post-colonial times, by some of Prospero's best behaved pupils, puts the native student in an intellectual straightjacket and culturally alienates him or her. The self-taught student, however, has the chance of averting such mental incarceration.

On the whole, Brathwaite's quest for authenticity has yielded fruit. His own work exudes a sense, a sound, and a texture of things autochthonous. Nor has he toiled in vain as regards his influence on younger generations of writers. One such writer, Linton Kwesi Johnson, bore this out by his admission of indebtedness to the older poet during a reading at the end of "Kamau Brathwaite and the Caribbean Word", a day-long conference in his honour held at Hostos Community College, City University of New York, on October 24, 1992, on the exact second anniversary of the traumatic event evoked in *Trench Town Rock*. This conference, which attracted numerous people from various parts of the United States, gave a clear idea of the extent to which his work has spoken eloquently to people from diverse national, cultural, and regional backgrounds. An enthusiastic and mixed audience of students, scholars, community people, and distinguished personalities such as Dame Nita Barrow, Barbados' Governor General, the American novelist Paule Marshall, and the African writer Abiola Irele, crowded the Hostos Convocation Hall for ten hours straight.

In his closing remarks, moved by the great enthusiasm and the overwhelming show of admiration generated by his work among the large audience as well as from the international array of speakers who participated in the programme, Brathwaite said that after many years of literary effort, only on this eventful day did he realize "that the work appears to be making sense." His work has certainly made sense to people in the Third World. In the United States and England it has made sense too, if only to the less dominant sectors of those societies. As this chapter set out to show, the alternative aesthetics and intellectual dissidence of Brathwaite's texts have tended to preclude the favourable reception of mainstream readers and academics generally. His work may actually repel establishment readers in the same way that it attracts those from the less empowered sectors of society. Consolation is hardly warranted in this case. For in England and in the United States, as everywhere else, the less empowered, who necessarily want to change the world, greatly outnumber those at the centre of power, who naturally wish to keep it the same.

Endnotes

1. But see the work of Shalini Puri in *The Caribbean Postcolonial: Social Equality, Post-Nationalism, and Cultural Hybridity* (2004) which critiques the tendency for an uncritical acceptance of the ideas of "creolisation" and "hybridity" as positive cultural markers (as opposed to the crimes of Afro-centrism or other essentialisms). Puri points out that serious inequalities of class and race lie embedded in these terms.

2. The reference is to novelists such as Garth St Omer, and particularly to Orlando Patterson's *An Absence of Ruins* (1967), which contains a parodic critique of what Patterson evidently regarded as petit-bourgeois cultural nationalism in the Caribbean novel. Patterson crossed swords with Brathwaite as a fellow member of the Caribbean Artists Movement (CAM), evidently regarding him as the chief ideologist of this tendency. St Omer and Patterson were seen as not only insufficiently Caribbean because of their interest in the French existentialists, but also nihilistic in their scepticism about the nationalist project.
3. *LX: The Love Axe/L* is a vast, and as yet still in press, expanded version of the essays first published in *Bim*.

4
STAGES OF THE SACRED IN RENÉ DEPESTRE

> "The fact that the gods were anthropomorphous goes to show that religious thinking did not spring from a contemplation of the phenomena of nature, but sprang from the social struggle."
> Maxim Gorky (1982: 310)

René Depestre, one of the most prominent Haitian literary artists living today, belongs to a select group of Francophone Caribbean writers who have achieved distinction in France and much of the French-speaking Third World. Like Edouard Glissant, Maryse Condé, Simone Schwarz-Bart, and Patrick Chamoiseau, Depestre has received coveted literary prizes awarded by the French literary establishment such as the Prix Renaudot and the Prix Goncourt. While Depestre's writings since the latter half of the 1980s show an increasing leaning towards conservatism, scholars and critics in Haiti, Europe, and the United States, looking at the first four decades of his career, have celebrated the undaunted social commitment then apparent in his work (Berrou and Pompilus 1977: 275; Kesteloot 1967: 164; Shapiro 1970: 226; Couffon 1986: 84). Years ago, Depestre offered an assessment of his literary creed that closely resembled the consensus of his critics in that it linked his position as a literary artist with the social reality immediately pertinent to him as a Haitian revolutionary. He associated his early poetics to his awareness of the precarious situation of the Haitian proletariat: "This is for me a human drama, corresponding to the drama of the whole of my people, kept until now from the most elementary beauties of human existence" (Cited by Kesteloot 1971: 269). The recognition of a social reality which needed correcting had for him the force of a "commande sociale" since he began writing poetry as a teenager in the mid-1940s. According to his own testimony, Depestre composed his first verses moved not only by the overwhelming tropical beauty of his native city of Jacmel, but also awakened by the perception that "there was the surrounding misery that I wanted to express, to denounce" (Couffon 1986: 18).

In the social commitment of his literary beginnings Depestre shared the inclinations of older Haitian writers such as Jacques Roumain, who founded the Haitian Communist Party, and Marie Vieux Chauvet, who consistently indicted conditions of oppression in Haiti. The majority of Depestre's texts exhibit the traits of cultural resistance which scholars acknowledge as a principle of coherence among the various literary expressions of the Antilles. The most graphic example of the role of art as a vehicle of resistance in the Caribbean was perhaps the publication of Depestre's own first volume of poetry, *Etincelles*, which along with the founding of *La Ruche*, a revolutionary cultural journal bringing together the efforts of the most progressive young intellectuals of the country, contributed to igniting the events culminating in what Haitians refer to as the Revolution of 1946 (Berrou and Pompilus 1977: 258; Garrett 1963: 191; Dash 1981: 160; Baridon and Philoctète 1978: 18). This episode offers an instance of cultural resistance in its most political form; the Francophone Caribbean has witnessed innumerable examples of cultural resistance that do not necessarily become translated into political events.

Depestre has been situated within the general context of négritude, the literary movement championed by Aimé Césaire, Léopold Sédar Senghor, and Léon Damas (Baridon and Philoctète 1978: 18; Shapiro 1970; Kennedy 1989). Some scholars have approached his works in terms of its relationship with the Surrealist movement. The Trinidadian critic J. Michael Dash has explored the ways in which the socialist bent of Depestre's poetics, along with that of his literary generation in Haiti, "combined without any contradiction whatever with the revolutionary poetics of Surrealism" (1981: 159). Dash argues that the young poet, inspired by the visit of André Breton to Haiti in 1945, encountered in Surrealism "a poetic language which could convey the violent frenzy of the times" (ibid). Likewise, discussing the use of vodou in a 1967 text of Depestre's, Jacqueline Leiner insisted on the poet's interest in Surrealism, contending that his attraction to the Haitian popular religion stemmed from its similarity to Surrealism (Leiner 1977: 44). Reasoning along the same line, Jean Claude Michel has included both Depestre's "Póesie de révolte" and his interest in vodou among the instances of "le merveilleux" that so attracted the attention of Surrealists in general (Michel 1982: 138-54).

Until 1967, when Depestre published his now famous "Poème-mystère vodou", critics of his work paid little if any attention to religious matter in his poetry. The scholar Joan Dayan [aka Colin Dayan], who translated the text into English, read the poem as breaking away from his first twenty years of literary production (Dayan 1977: 3). But a different reading of Depestre's complete *oeuvre* can reveal a continuous involvement with the sacred that shows up in different guises in keeping with his successive ideological stages over more than five decades. An examination of his work with an eye on the spiritual imperative can help us trace the various roles accorded by the poet to the sacred in an intellectual project aimed at encompassing not only the temporal social structure but also "the upper spheres of knowledge", to put it in the words of Tituba, the memorable character in the novel by Maryse Condé (1992: 10). The imagery, the symbols, the language, the tone, and the *topoi* recurring in Depestre's texts manifest a religious worldview that combines the elements of a Christian liberation theology with Marxism and vodou to articulate a vision of utopia in the Caribbean. Espousing a programme of cultural resistance that covers the entire human experience, Depestre's poetic ideology allows for the harmonious interaction of the human and the divine, the visible and the invisible. When in the mid 1980s Depestre parted with the ideals he had formerly envisioned as connatural with an imminent socialist cosmos, he retained an attachment to the realm of the sacred, even if devoid of the humanistic fervour that had formerly characterized his poetics. He may have traded political ideologies, but through the spiritual imperative, he maintains an intimate aesthetic affinity with the prominent literary artists of the West Indies. His delving into the mysteries of religion accords with an element not only of Haitian literature from Virginie Sampeur to Marie Chauvet to the present, but also of the literature of the whole Caribbean region, as represented by Condé, Glissant, Myriam Warner-Vieyra, and Alejo Carpentier, to name just a few.

Christian Beginnings

Depestre's poetry from *Etincelles* (1945) through *En état de poésie* (1980) exudes a confidence in the perfectibility of humankind, an ardent faith in the possibility of a better world, and an indomitable adherence to the notion of a global kingdom of love. The lyrical voice in those books preaches against the selfish individualism bred by capitalism as an obstacle to the realization of the ideal society. Perceiving a world in which beauty and tenderness do not prevail, Depestre elaborates, in verse and prose throughout the first thirty-five years of his career, what one can read as a socio-religious gospel. His gospel differs from the teachings of the Catholic Church in that it preaches not contemplation but social action on behalf of a new order, something akin to what has become known as "the theology of liberation". While differing in approach and method, the tenor of a large part of Depestre's work is comparable to that espoused by the Nicaraguan poet Father Ernesto Cardenal, former Minister of Education in the embattled Sandinista government of the 1980s. An exponent of liberation theology, Cardenal sought to marry his belief in Christianity with the yearning for a socialist society: "a society in which we no longer exploit one another, in which it is not what you take away from but what you give to others that makes you somebody... The true atheism, the true denial of God are for me ESSO and Standard Oil ... that make their money producing napalm" (Cardenal 1978: 31, 52). During the 1960s and 1970s many would seek to reconcile the ideas of redemption, in the Christian sense, and effective liberation in the political arena (Concatti

1968: 67). As Herbert Marcuse noted in that regard, "Marxian theory" found an ally, especially in Latin America, "in those tendencies, groups, and individuals committed to the part of the Christian teaching that stands uncompromisingly against inhuman, exploitative power" (1970: 10).

At the tender age of sixteen, while attending secondary school at the Lycée Pétion, Depestre is reported to have addressed his peers with these words: "Young people ought to be Christian; they should pray" (Berrou and Pompilus 1977: 257). Claude Couffon, whose book *Depestre* (1986) is based primarily on interviews with the Haitian poet, attributes to him a "crise mystique" at the age of 17 and a marked interest in becoming a priest (1986: 195). Whatever the particular circumstances under which he may have undergone those experiences, their occurrence matters as an indication of his early proclivity to holding strong beliefs, an early devotion to systematic doctrines. Also crucial is the fact that Depestre as a child was in constant contact with the supernatural. He attended vodou ceremonies regularly and grew up informed by the animistic worldview of that popular religion. He admits, for instance, to having felt a tremendous respect and a mystical adoration for all trees in his backyard, and to having harboured worshipful sentiments especially for a commanding flamboyant (Couffon 1986: 10).

It is no coincidence that with such a background, we find in Depestre's poetry an acceptance of a supra-sensory realm. His language and his themes evoke situations in which our everyday concrete experience of the world dissolves into an immaterial, intangible plane of perception. Violating the usual separation between the spiritual and the material worlds, he creates a poetic vision that places the world of divine beings within a socio-historical context, corresponding specifically to the Caribbean world. The sense of religion that we associate with Depestre's vision accords generally with Emile Durkheim's definition of religion as "an eminently collective thing" which consists basically of "a unified system of belief and practices related to sacred things" (Durkheim 1915: 52). Durkheim concedes that the sacred is not limited to personal things but can extend to objects in nature, to rituals, and to words and expressions (ibid p. 62). Mircea Eliade further expands the definition by stating that the sacred is essential to all religions and positing that: "In a desecralized world such as ours, the 'sacred' is present and active chiefly in the imaginary universes. But imaginary experiences are part of the total human being, no less important than his diurnal experiences" (Eliade 1963: 30; 1969: 126). As we survey Depestre's work we shall see the poet's insistence on erasing the dividing line between the imaginary and the diurnal.

The poetic lexicon used by the speaker in *Etincelles* seems impregnated by the hopeful sentiment of an unequivocal new Jerusalem. "Me voici", the first poem in the collection, begins with this self-definition: "Me voici/ citoyen des Antilles/ l'âme vibrante/ je vole à la conquête de bastilles nouvelles" – Here I am/citizen of the Antilles/my soul throbbing/I speed to the conquest of new Bastilles. The conquest of the "new Bastilles" derives its guarantee from the orientation of the speaker's search: "je cherche la vérité" – I am looking for truth. The emphasis on hope corresponds to the speaker's access to a newly found system of knowledge. The speaker has entered into contact with a fresh or renewed belief, the practice of whose precepts starts with plunging into "the cosmic adventure of poetry." The general tone of the voice expresses the passion of one who has experienced a spiritual rebirth. Spiritual rebirths usually come accompanied by a rejection or at least a reconsideration of the precepts one lived with before the change. Thus in "Confession", the third poem in *Etincelles*, we encounter the rejection contained in this pronouncement: "on inventa la bible/ on inventa les chaines/ on inventa mille façons/ d'inoculer/ la soumission dans toutes mes cellules/ mais depuis j'ai su la vérité." – They invented the bible/they invented chains/they invented a thousand ways/of injecting/my every cell with self-surrender/but then I learned the truth. The speaker declares himself possessor of the truth, a truth which he has acquired in spite of the darkness of thought inculcated in him by the prevailing belief system before his present state of revelation. His new knowledge derives from a spiritual source other than the Bible, the sacred text which informs the Christian faith, the creed which in the form of Catholicism constitutes the official religion of Haiti. In equating the sacred text with "chains", and other means of inducing submission, the speaker ascribes to its theological teachings the power to enslave, oppress, and keep individuals from the truth. He declares himself free from the manacles of such a theology, and he claims a superior standpoint which equips him with a critical perspective, rendering him capable of revising some of the traditional symbols of Christianity.

We see further evidence of the speaker's enlightenment in the fifth poem of the collection "Mon ami: voici ta Noël", where he decries the partnership between Christianity and the values of the consumer society in Haiti. Christianity is here symbolized by the traditional celebration of the birth of Jesus (Noël) as practised in Haiti. The speaking voice addresses itself to a friend to question thereby the idea of Noël. He first denounces its corrupted commercialism, "la Noël des vitrines luisantes" – The Christmas-time of gleaming shops, and then mocks the bourgeois social festivities ("des coups de canon,/ des sermons ridicules,/ des messieurs à faux-cols,/ qui dilapident l'avenir de tes enfants" – Of canon-shots/of stupid sermons/of starch-collared gentlemen/who wear away the future of your children). In criticizing the opportunistic commercialism of traditional Christmas celebration in Haitian society, the speaker yearns for a sort of *Ur-Noël*, one untainted by consumerism, one closer to the original form of Noël. But since commercialist contamination has rendered the tradition destructive, one must reject it and replace it with values that more closely resemble the original purpose of the "petit Jésus" – one no longer to be found in the official symbology surrounding Noël. The last stanza concludes the lesson to his friend with a tone of exhortation: "Ta Noël, mon ami/ sommeille dans ta conscience/ dans ta rancoeur/ dans tes espoirs/ dans tes points d'interrogation/ en face du monde que l'on t'a fait/ dans le débordement des tes haines accumulées" – Your Christmas-time, my friend/lies sleeping in your conscience/in your bitterness/in your hopes/in all your question-marks/that stand before the world they made for you/in the overflowing torrent of your hatreds long held back.

A more encompassing revision of the symbols of the official faith appears in the poem entitled "Visions mortes" in which one finds a rationale for the adoption of a new system of belief. The speaker here makes Christianity, through many of its most evocative images (angels, saints, legends, catechisms, cathedrals, etc.), responsible for his previous ignorance. Visions of "anges aériens" – airy angels and ""Saints triomphants" – triumphant saints" had clouded the buried dreams of his befuddled childhood as well as the "la nuit sombre de mon adolescence" – sombre night of [his] adolescence. But the revelation of human suffering has surpassed in his mind the influence of gothic domes, catechisms, and chapels and brought him to the realization that only in the search for social redress can one find redemption. His previous ignorance consisted in the inability to grasp the "clarté essentielle" – essential truth of human existence, namely the recognition of global human suffering. With his new awareness, he can now overcome his previous attachment to "visions mortes" – dead religious images". He thus rejects the orthodox Christian principles which prohibit our engaging in the praxis of social struggle and would have us passively accept human injustice with "la froide acceptation de l'illustre crucifié" – the cold resignation of the man on the cross.

Depestre's preoccupation with religion is a crucial component of *Etincelles* as one can gather from the above quotes, as well as from similar references that occur in varying degrees in many of the twenty poems which make up the thin volume. In general, the ambivalent attitude toward the official faith moves to a criticism of Christianity's apparent indifference towards social evils. Convinced of the need to redress human suffering, the speaking voice in the book appoints himself advocate of those Roumain had called "les damnés de la terre" in the poem "Sales Nègres", which appeared in the posthumous volume *Bois d'Ebéne* (1945). Depestre's speaker declares himself ready to use on behalf of "the wretched of the earth" the weapon he best knows how to wield, namely poetry, hence the inclination to revise Christian symbols. His main complaint against Christianity here seems consistent with the Marxist contention that: "The social principles of Christianity preach cowardice, self-contempt, submission, dejection, in a word all the qualities of a 'canaille'" (Marx and Engels 1964: 84). As

Friedrich Engels put it in the *Anti-Duhring*, "Christianity knew only one point in which all men were equal: that all men were equally born in original sin – which corresponded perfectly to its character as the religion of the slaves and the oppressed" (ibid p. 145).

The affinity with the Marxist characterization of Christianity is not accidental since by the time he published *Etincelles* in 1945, Depestre had already espoused the ideals of socialism. A committed junior member of the Haitian Communist Party, he began to develop his poetic vocation simultaneously with his dedication to bring about structural changes in Haitian society (Berrou and Pompilus 1977: 256). Indeed, in spite of his precarious financial situation, coming as he did from a family which often endured hunger, he invested the $2,000.00 collected from the surprisingly successful sale of *Etincelles* in publishing the journal *La Ruche*, whose first issue appeared in December 1945, to advance the revolutionary ideas then prevailing in his circle (Couffon 1986: 24-25).

The influence of the group behind *La Ruche* can be deduced from the nervousness with which the Haitian government responded, banning the publication of the journal and temporarily incarcerating its young editors. The arrests, coupled with the general discontent prevailing among the majority of the Haitian population, led to strikes by students and workers and eventually to the demise of President Elie Lescot (Baridon and Philoctète 1978: 17-18). Assessing these events, the Haitian poet René Belance, a contemporary of Depestre, has referred to him as "a national hero who made the Revolution at nineteen" (cited in Dayan 1977: 17). That the revolt known as the Revolution of January 1946 did not bring about any essential structural modifications of Haitian society became clear to the young leaders immediately. Depestre himself has pointed this out on a number of occasions. Very soon the spot vacated by the arch-conservative Lescot was occupied by the military authorities whose machinations resulted in the coming to power of the even more conservative Dumarsais Estimé on August 12, 1946.

The Gospel of Truth

The year after *Etincelles*, Depestre published a second collection, *Gerbe de sang*, which many have read as a document of Depestre's disenchantment with the result of his political efforts. Naomi Garret finds in *Gerbe de sang* an entirely disillusioned Depestre: "no longer does he believe in justice, reason or any of his former ideals" (1963: 195). Garret commits herself so deeply to the idea of the young poet's disillusion that she saw it reflected even in his presumed loss of the desire to write. In 1963, her study of Haitian poetry affirms that Depestre "has not published a volume of poetry since *Gerbe de sang* (Garret 1963: 195-96). The truth is, however, that Depestre had added three published volumes to his poetic production when Garret's book appeared. With respect to the aesthetics of *Gerbe de sang*, Dash has noted in it the predominance of Surrealist stylistic devices and a notable deviation from the path marked by *Etincelles*. He states that the language of *Gerbe de sang* "shows evidence of an enigmatic visual imagery which is deliberately ambiguous and makes few concessions to the reader's understanding" (Dash 1981: 170). It must be stressed, however, that while the volume shows an undeniable change of mood, manifesting stylistically and thematically the rejection of established norms typical of Surrealism, one should not overlook the persistence of a voice which continues to express hope in the future and a desire to reconstruct the world via the resources attributed to the higher spheres of knowledge.

What has been termed disillusion can alternatively be thought of as reflecting a more mature stage in the poet's intellectual growth. Perhaps now, having seen the failure of an enthusiastic popular revolt, he understood the world as a much more complicated structure than he had thought a year before. That much at least one can derive from his own account: "*Etincelles* had been the fresh and passionate expression of an adolescent who discovered with faith the world of action. *Gerbe de sang* was the cry of someone who has received a baptism of fire and who takes leave, wounded, of adolescence" (cited in Couffon 1986: 28). Rather than a shift from optimism to pessimism, the change of mood in the volume attests to an ideological progression. A careful reading of the text does not corroborate the utter loss of hope perceived by Garret although in it Depestre has clearly drawn on Surrealism for stylistic and thematic devices.

The rejection and denial of organized society in *Gerbe de sang* occurs so that a new, more humane social order may come into being. The last lines of "Avant-Propos", the first poem in the collection, preach a gospel of hope: "L'amour a passé dans le camp ennemi/N'en parlons plus/ Recommençons le monde avec nos/ seules ressources" – Love has gone to the enemy camp/ Let us say no more/Let us begin the world anew/with resources of our own. The book abounds in poems such as the one significantly titled "Pour annoncer l'Aurore", in which the speaker, while regretting the duress of the present, exemplified for him in the precarious social condition of his people, finds room for a rebirth of hope and the assurance of their coming freedom: "chante liberté Liberté chante" – let freedom ring. Freedom ring" (p. 20). The conviction that ideas are validated primarily in the field of social action appears here as it did in the previous book.

In some parts of *Gerbe de sang*, as in the poem titled "Ressouvenance", it becomes clear that the speaker's hope in the future derives its foundation from the redressing power of armed struggle: "nous sommes enfants de barricades/ pour notre soif chaque fusil est fontaine/ pour notre fatigue toute pierre est sommier" – We belong in barricades/for our thirst every gun is a spring/for our fatigue every stone is a bed, p. 24). Again, as in *Etincelles,* we come face to face with a speaker who sneers at the passivity of Christianity before human evil. At times, we come upon a celebration of the oppressed's endurance in withstanding suffering, connoting a relationship between suffering and salvation that recalls the religious practice of penitence. Only in such a frame of mind can the speaker in "Cellule No. 1" afford to rejoice in the penury of his prison cell, and ascetically conclude: "les bourreaux peuvent dormir en paix/ la prison cette nuit est un lieu d'espérance" – the executioners may sleep in peace/this prison tonight is a ground of hope.

In "Nouvelles créations" Depestre uses religious imagery and vocabulary with renewed intensity, creating a speaker who imagines himself as a new Adam who invites his beloved, a new Eve, to undertake with him a repopulation of the Earth. The implication is that this time around it will be done correctly: "nous savons de nous-mêmes que nous avons/ le monde à repeupler/ et l'Humanité qui naîtra de nos entrailles en feu/ n'aura pas de fautes à reprocher à ses premiers parents/ toi et moi" –We know that we ourselves have/the world to refill/and the Humanity that will come from our fiery loins/will have no fault to blame on her first parents/you and me (p. 33). The world visualized here consists of the "creation" as narrated in the "Book of Genesis" minus the evil and the sorrows caused by man's unfortunate fall from divine grace. He invites his beloved to cooperate in creating a Garden of Eden which will remain with us, where human goodness will not be marred by original sin, where humans will not be fallen creatures. Cognizant of the possible incredulity of his beloved, he proceeds to assert the feasibility of his vision by assuring her that their idyllic project will succeed since it will be guaranteed by the one seemingly infallible element, namely: "l'Amour que nous proposons à tout le reste de la Création" – the love we shall propose to all the rest of the Creation (p. 34). His reliance on the power of love as the supreme, most efficacious, most constructive human pursuit recalls the words of Saint Paul: "Love bears all things, believes all things, hopes all things, endures all things. Love never ends... so faith, hope, love abide; but the greatest of these is love" (Corinthians I, 13: 7-13).

The voice in *Gerbe de sang* consistently reaches the impassioned elevation of religious fervour. The speaker constantly addresses himself to the oppressed, urging them to grab the reins of their own political destiny. The dominant tone is of high-sounding indictments hurled against the entire status quo which sponsors human oppression, particularly when condoned by Christianity. The poem which most eloquently synthesizes most of these thematic concerns is "Croisée des routes", which presents us with the meeting ground for all the levels of Depestre's subversive vision. The speaker here identifies himself as a black man from the Caribbean, one who recognizes himself as the victim of oppression, cultural as well as political, who openly advocates the cause of the lowly. The dominant tone is militant, but the poem combines violence with meditation, achieving a certain complexity in evoking the speaker's socio-historical predicament. Highlighting his difference, he introduces the dichotomy of the "ils", referring to Western civilization, and "moi", referring to himself as a black Caribbean, echoing the opposition previously postulated by Césaire in *Cahier d'un retour au pays natal*. The speaker defines himself according to his difference from the "ils" ("Ils ont construit des villas de marbre" – They have built marble edifices (p. 103)), placing their cultural, political and technological achievements as well as their racial supremacy at one pole, with his self-characterization representing the opposing pole: "Moi je ne sais rien... Je suis nègre" – Me, I know nothing... I am black (p. 104). As the antithesis is further developed, it becomes clear that the "ils" in their position of power bear the responsibility for the ignominious socio-political situation of the "moi". Moreover, they, the oppressors, have used religion to blind their victims: "Le seul livre qu'on me laisse/c'est la bible" – The only book they allow me/is the bible, nullifying the speaker's potential for creativity and freedom (p. 104). Consequently, in his self-characterization as at a polar extreme to the "ils", he must recognize himself as heir to a non-Western spiritual legacy. Hence: "Je n'ai que des hougans pour ancêtres" – I have merely hougans as ancestors, referring to the name of vodou priests.

Such a recognition leads to the inevitable de-christianization of the speaker, who, hostile to the indifference or the social inefficacy of the "petit Jésus", appeals to a more historically tangible spiritual being. He says: "J'ai rencontré Lénine/ Et pour un regard d'épouvante/ il m'a rendu des antécédents sans limites/ il m'a rendu mon orgueil Il m'a rendu l'amour..." – I came across Lenin/And in a frightful glance/he returned my limitless past/he restored my pride and gave love back to me (p. 105). He presents his discovery of the intellectual and political legacy of Vladimir Ilich, then a venerated Soviet leader, as bordering on divine revelation. The speaker experiences a decisive transformation in his encounter with this secular messiah, this saviour of his soul. In such a state of spiritual elevation, he gains unrestricted access to a vantage point from which he can see the future. The vision appears to him with as much clarity as did John's in *The Apocalypse*, and, therefore, his prediction carries as much certainty as that of the Evangelist: "et on dira/ *Voici le premier jour de la vie/ Voici la terre à la veille de l'amour*" – and we will say/Here is the beginning of life/Here is the earth on the eve of love (p. 107). He perceives a new beginning marked by possibility.

Gerbe de sang, then, insists on spiritual salvation as much as it does on social liberation, there being for Depestre no apparent distinction between the two. Here is a voice aiming to change the world, to refashion it as more just, populated by men and women of good will and ruled by the precept of love. The kingdom of love will clearly not come through the passive contemplation encouraged by Christianity but rather through dedication to social action. In keeping with such a contingency, the language here oscillates between the calmness of meditative prayer and the incantatory amplification of an impassioned sermon. While the frequent anaphoric repetitions and the many passages marked by monotonality in the book may derive from Surrealist practice, they contribute, nonetheless, to heightening its emotional fervour. The diction attains at times the rapture of highly devout religious pronouncements. This kind of blending of a religious sensibility with revolutionary zeal is much less commonly found in Anglophone Caribbean writing of the time, though the first modernist poet of Jamaica, George Campbell, sings "I dreamed/Jesus kissed Lenin on the Lips/ For the Russian Revolution" in "I Dreamed" (*First Poems* 1945). But as Neville Dawes, a real Jamaican Marxist, observed, this was "an adolescent dream" coming from a poet whose politics, attached to N.W. Manley, were those of a bourgeois nationalist kind (Dawes, 2012 [1981]: 334).

The virtual deification of Lenin suggests the great enthusiasm with which Depestre adhered to the ideals of Communism. It was his association with the Communist Party of Haiti which precipitated his trip to Paris in the summer of 1946, beginning what became for him "un interminable exil" (Couffon 1986: 28). There he came into close contact with the work of some of the salient literary figures of the day: Tzara, Breton, Desnos, Soupault, Aragon, Eluard, Char, and Michaux, most of whom he had occasion to meet. He found in them a special correspondence with his own sentiment of rebellion which he recognized from an early date as "eminently Haitian" (p. 30). By virtue of his particular cultural roots he considered himself to be in a position to widen the scope of their rebellion, to give it "an intercultural ingredient" (p. 30).

Sacralizing the Secular

In Paris, Depestre also came into contact with the leading intellectuals of the French-speaking black world, meeting Césaire, Fanon, Damas, and Senghor. He also participated in the founding of the journal *Présence Africaine* in 1947 (Couffon 1986: 31). Césaire recorded his admiration for him in a laudatory preface to Depestre's third book, *Végétations de clarté*, published in Paris by Pierre Seghers in 1951, following the young poet's deportation from France along with Edith Gambor Sórel, the young Romanian woman he had married less than two years before (ibid p. 35). Césaire's "Préface" hailed the slim volume as an exemplary "testimony for all of today's young poetry" (Césaire 1951: 9). He primarily commended Depestre's ability to transport a current or immediate event to an authentically poetic realm. Césaire thus describes the subject matter of the book, which consists of eulogies or celebrations of contemporary figures. Five of them sing of individuals who are admirable to Depestre, and Césaire. The sixth, the elegy "Tombés au champ de la clarté", mourns the death of eighteen black miners assassinated in Nigeria while on strike protesting their low salaries.

This, the third poem in the book, pervaded by the slow rhythmic pace of a threnody, is particularly interesting in that it presents us with a speaker whose outlook enables him to interpret the deaths of the Nigerian miners in a positive light. The closing lines suggest a historical redemption: "l'avenir déjà s'aiguise à la meule sourde de votre mémoire/ et couvre vos corps noirs de son champ de clarté" – the future is already sharpened by the deaf grindstone of your memory/and wraps your black bodies with its aura of light (Depestre 1951: 25). The rationale behind this hope is that the miners, in dying for a noble cause, have left behind a legacy of righteous action. In so doing they bequeathed a portion of light to those who remain engaged in social struggle, thus necessarily advancing the cause for which they died.

The remaining poems sing the glory of Joseph Stalin, the Soviet leader, Maurice Thorez, secretary general of the French Communist Party, Nazim Hikmet, a Turkish poet imprisoned for his communist ideas, Raymonde Dieu, political activist, and Henri Martin, a soldier in the French army. With a candour even more intense than before, Depestre celebrates in these individuals their having trodden the path of light (clarté). A suggestion of what that means may be gathered from the epigraph to the book which is a passage by Aragon defining the Communist as one who has seen the world so clearly that he cannot forget it, and henceforward nothing for him is of more consequence than this light, "not even his primary interests, not even his own life (cited in Depestre 1951: 13).

Light metaphorically evokes the notion of truth, goodness, justice or any other of the pursuits which the speaker deems necessary for the kingdom of love to come about. It is a state of revelation in which he can enjoy the clarity of vision of a "son of light", to use New Testament terminology. "The Gospel According to John" quotes Christ as saying: "While you have the light believe in the light, that you may become sons of light" (12: 36) and "I have come as light into the world, that whoever believes in me may not remain in darkness" (12: 46). Images of light, translucence, and clarity pervade Depestre's little book, and these are combined in many cases with imagery representing the "force and splendour" of nature (Berrou and Pompilus 1977: 266). The poem to Stalin, for example, relies heavily on nature imagery, and in the one to Thorez the light brought by Communism assumes the form of a dove (*colombe*): "Je te chante, vaillant secrétaire de la colombe" – I sing to you, brave secretary of the dove (Depestre 1951: 22). Likewise, in the poem to Hikmet, the speaker attributes the repression and imprisonment suffered by the Turkish poet to the government's fear of the possible repercussion of "l'accolade du poète et de la colombe" – the embrace of the poet and the dove (p. 28). The embrace between those two liberating forces would be lethal to the oppressive power structure, he assures us, recalling the power attributed to poetry in *Etincelles*. Such appears to be the fear inspired by poetry that in this poem to Hikmet we hear that in Turkey "la poésie a été mise hors la loi" – poetry has been outlawed (p. 26).

We find in *Végétations de clarté* much of the elevated and incantatory tone of Depestre's previous books, with prayer-like repetition and the phonetic amplitude of a sacred chant. This, of course, accords with the high level of devotion manifested by the speaker. Particularly in the poem to Stalin this religious fervour is unmistakable. He raises Stalin, to the level of a being who intermingles with and becomes inseparable from the elements of nature. With an omnipotent and ubiquitous subject, source of infinite power and goodness, the adoration due him must also be infinite. Thus, he celebrates Stalin in these words: "Je chante cet homme qui nous est plus cher que nos/ yeux qui est à nous comme l'air que nous respi/ rons et tous les peuples de la terre ouvrent leurs/ poumons sur l'oxygène de ses leçons d'amour" – I sing to this man whom we cherish more/than our eyes who is for us like the air we breathe/and all the peoples of the earth open their/ lungs to the oxygen of his lesson of love (p. 16).

While attributing to his subject unmistakably divine qualities, he insists that this saviour comes from a different stock, of concrete, earthly humanity: "Ni Jésus ni Mahomet ni un quelconque produit de/ l'imagination mais un homme jusqu'au cou dans la/ réalité, mêlé à son peuple comme la rivière à/ ses alluvions" – Neither Jesus nor Mohamed or anyone produced by the/ imagination but a man with reality up to his neck, blended with his people/ like the river with its floods (p. 16). However, as the description progresses, we sense that this man has risen to a level beyond the ordinarily human. Only this justifies the rapture of the conclusion: "Gloire à Joseph Staline/ notre capital/ le plus/ précieux!" – Glory to Joseph Stalin/our most precious/possession! (p. 17). This glorification of Stalin is undoubtedly objectionable in light of his subsequent demythification in the West, and at least one critic has decried Depestre's "disappointing Stalinism" (Dash 1988: 94). But this needs contextualization lest we succumb to the temptations of anachronistic reasoning. When *Végétations de charté* appeared in 1951, Stalin was still in power. It was only when, five years later, after he was dead, at the 20th All-Union Party Congress, in February 1956, prompted by Nikita Krushchev and other Soviet leaders, that the charges of tyranny and terror against Stalin began to receive widespread international attention. Until then no consensus existed among intellectuals and artists either in the West or in the Third World regarding Stalinism as an opprobrious legacy, though the debate had already emerged. Albert Camus in *L'homme révolté*, published in the same year as Depestre's volume, declared the failure of the Marxist doctrine in the Soviet Union. He decried the fact that, contrary to Lenin's proposition regarding the eventual disappearance of the state, there: "The proletarian State, after more than thirty years, has given no sign of progressive anaemia" (Camus 1951: 286). He posited that all revolutions lead inevitably to the deification of the state. He categorically grouped Stalin with Mussolini and Hitler as rulers equally engaged in the practice of "State terrorism" (p. 221). But Camus represented the views of an intellectual elite that generally opposed Marxism and did not believe in revolution.

Those views, however, were not the only ones prevalent at the time. The quarrel between Sartre and Camus attests to that. The French Communist Party, for instance, never publicly denounced the Soviet state. Others expressed ambivalent attitudes. Some felt that even if "the Soviet régime is not authentically revolutionary", it had the virtue of "being the only system of government which even attempts to be so" and that while one could "disapprove of certain methods used", one had to "applaud the purpose of the enterprise" (Cruickshank, 1960: 124). Depestre's Stalinism, then, was only as "disappointing" as that of a good many thinkers and artists in 1951. The Haitian poet, one must remember, was twenty-five years old at that time and had, only a few years before, passionately embraced the ideals of Communism. If writing a poem that venerates Stalin makes him a Stalinist, then his embracing Stalinism meant that he chose one of the few ideological options then available to people on the left. The older and presumably wiser Césaire, who would later denounce and dissociate himself from the Stalinism of the French Communist Party in the admirable *Lettre à Maurice Thorez* (1956), had shared Depestre's 1951 views of Stalin. The uninhibited praise he lavished upon Depestre's *Végétations* indicates no less. One could more appropriately criticize Depestre for his unqualified and hyperbolic celebration of political leaders and political creeds in general, not for embracing specific ones. For such an uncritical stance bespeaks a naive vision of political phenomena and triggers expectations of outcomes so ideal that no system can live up to in the crudity of concrete reality. Such a mindset leads too easily to disenchantment when bitter reality sets in to frustrate the cherished ideals. That may, in fact, explain Depestre's pitiful renunciation of socialism starting in the mid 1980s. In the 1950s, Stalin gains from Depestre the same apotheosis previously accorded to Lenin. This is one of many cases in which we see him making secular leaders the subject of religious adoration.

The Quest for a Homeland

Early in 1952 we find Depestre in Czechoslovakia. From there he made an unsuccessful attempt to return to his native land to engage in activities that would spark the Haitian people to rise against the tyrannical government of Colonel Paul Magloire (Couffon 1986: 39). A necessary sojourn in Cuba, where he and his young comrades had to stop before launching the revolutionary expedition, frustrated the enterprise. The police of General Fulgencio Batista arrested them and shipped them back to Europe. Depestre records these experiences in a book published in October of the same year, *Traduit du grand large*. The book consists of a continuous narrative poem of about fifty pages divided into fifteen sections. The voice evoked here is that of a Haitian in exile, who, while affected by an overwhelming nostalgia, nonetheless has been enlightened by the distance separating him from the native soil. As a result of his travels, he can now reflect on the condition of the countries he has visited or learned about and can look at the suffering of his people within an international context. Haiti serves as the pretext for the book, as the subtitle "poème de ma patrie enchaînée" (poem to my captive fatherland) indicates, but the subject matter is really the suffering of the proletariat everywhere. The book displays an ideological fervour reminiscent of Martin Carter's 1954 collection, *Poems of Resistance from British Guiana*, though Carter's politics is firmly without religious sentiment. Depestre's panoramic view includes a wide range of countries and peoples involved in struggles for freedom and justice: Spain, Italy, the United States, Vietnam, Malaysia, India, Burma, Turkey, Egypt, Tunisia, Senegal, Iran, China, Argentina, Brazil, Chile, Cuba, Madagascar, and Romania, among them.

In referring to areas that had suffered Western colonialism, poems inevitably reflect on questions of race and colour. This becomes particularly meaningful in light of Depestre's Romanian wife, nicknamed Dito, whose skin colour is that of the colonists who have exploited and oppressed the peoples of the Third World. The apparent paradox leads to this realization: "Mais nous savons O mon Dito/ Nous savons O mes peuples nègres/ Que le pigment de la peau/ N'est que le bouclier/ Qui dissimule le teint sans couleur du capital/ la neutre carnation de la misère" – But we know, Oh my Dito/We know Oh my black peoples/That the colour of the skin/Is nothing but the shield/That hides the colourless dye of capital/the neutral flesh tint of poverty (Depestre 1952: 31). The colourless dye of capital and nothing else, he suggests, has rendered ethnic distinctions insignificant. The economic roots of exploitation, then, merit more attention than racial issues.

Adhering to a typically Marxist analysis of history, the conviction expressed in this poem is that human happiness rests in the abolition of class society. In socialist Romania he perceives a placid world: "Au pays de mon Dito gouverne la lumière/ d'ouvriers et de paysans" – The land of my Dito is ruled by the light of workers and peasants (p. 34). He also admires the struggle of the Korean people, whom he sees as seeking the light in fighting against imperialism (pp. 36-38). Nor does he doubt that soon the entire world will share an equal access to the kingdom of light: "L'homme est en train de devenir une colombe pour la/ clarté de l'homme" – Man is soon to become a dove for the enlightenment of Man (p. 34). More specifically, the day will come when the earth will enjoy total harmony, as in Paradise: "Viendra le temps où les mains des peuples/ Seront les unes pour les autres/ Les plus terrestres des paradis" – The time will come when the people's hands/will join together/A most earthly paradise (p. 52). Nor will getting admission into this Paradise depend on one's following steps comparable to those recommended by the Christian faith to enter heaven. "Personne n'aura besoin de jeuner/ Ni de vivre de piété d'hostie et d'eau bénite" – There will be no need to fast/Nor pursue the piety of wafer and holy water (p. 52).

As he continues to develop his credo, the poet here assigns to "reason" an essential role in guiding our world: "Le pouvoir de la raison conduira la nature" – The power of reason will rule over nature (p. 52). Reason is to be understood as the type of thinking contained in the universalist ideals of Communism whose most revered prophet is evidently Vladimir Ilich: "Lénine frère de lait de la liberté/ Traversa l'Europe à la vitesse solaire de son coeur/ Pour aller poser la première pierre du règne infini de l'homme" – Lenin blood brother of freedom/Went across Europe at the solar speed of his heart/To place there the first stone in the ultimate kingdom of humankind (pp. 53-54).

As to poetry's role in bringing about "the infinite kingdom of humankind", the speaker in *Traduit du grand large* characterizes his own poetic voice as a vehicle of light and of love. In the concluding section, addressed to Haiti, he says of his song: "Voici le chant de ton poète de choc" (p. 57). The term "poète de choc" implies poetry's concrete role, akin to that of a task force, in fulfilling the dictates of the poet's credo. In absolute solidarity with those in need of justice, the poet here presents himself as an evangelist effectively engaged in the liberation of the oppressed and in bringing us closer to the kingdom of light. Having declared the inefficacy of Christianity in satisfying the aspirations of the needy, and having proclaimed the gospel of social action guided by the light of his socialist credo, the speaker retains his native popular religion as a viable spiritual source. Among the various services he, as a poet, will render his native Haiti, will be the restorative function of his song, which: "sera sous les tonnelles de ton plaisir mêlant les gammes de sa passion/ Au vodou ruisselant de ta sensualité" – will be in the arbours of your pleasure blending the gamut of its passions/ with the streaming vodou of your sensuality (p. 55).

The above lines illustrate a willingness to reconcile the gospel of social action with the realm of the "sacred". Depestre's rejection of Christianity does not correspond to an utter renunciation of religion. We find in his early poetry constant allusions to "anointed" individuals, such as Lenin, the imagery evoking liturgical ceremonies, the references to states of revelation, the elevation of the diction, the passion, and the devoutness of the voice. It is only the social passivity or the indifference of Christianity that he decries. He favours a form of religion which "being a collective enterprise, is concerned with directing the cosmic forces toward a collective public good," to use Maya Deren's definition (Cited in Dayan 1977: 101).

At the end of *Traduit du grand large* Depestre gives the places of composition of the poem as follows: Haitian Coast, Rome, Paris. Elsewhere we learn that these locations correspond to his travels following his expulsion from Cuba and the frustrated revolutionary expedition to Haiti. Sent in a ship to Europe, he was not allowed to live either in Italy or France and had to seek refuge in Eastern Europe (Couffon 1986: 47). As he would relate later, in his "Lettre de Cuba", the experiences of his early exile and the rejection he endured at the hands of some of the Western nations gave him the occasion to clarify what he came to understand as the antithetical components of the Christian West. He saw at least two conflicting Western traditions: "the civilized and humanist, bathed in the tender universal light of Shakespeare, da Vinci, Goethe, Hugo, Tolstoy, Beethoven, Marx, Einstein, etc", on the one hand, and "the barbaric, racist, colonialist known and detested on three continents because it invariably turns towards the worst excesses of money and egoism", on the other (Cited in Dayan 1977: 19).

In Louis Aragon, Depestre thought he had found the "civilized and humanist" aspect of the West. Aragon, whose political views he came to share and in whom he at one point declared to have found his true literary model, was at the time upholding a poetics that Depestre found attractive. Aragon embraced a theory of national poetry that "proscribed free verse, pilloried formal individualism, and generally tied the traditional prosody of France to the interests of the revolutionary working class" (Arnold 1981: 180). His preface to Eugène Guillevic's book of poems *Trente et un sonnets* (1954) illustrate Aragon's thought on this matter, and his own poetic works from *Les yeux d'Elsa* (1943) to *Les yeux et la memoire* (1954) undertake to put his theory into practice. On the whole, they show a return to "traditional French prosody with some interesting modifications" (Arnold 1981: 180). In a letter addressed to Charles Dobzynski, later made public by *Les Lettres Françaises*, Depestre pronounced himself a most ardent disciple of Aragon's teachings. At one point the letter reads: "I am about to resolve, thanks to Aragon, the conflict wherein my formal individualism has floundered/... I am convinced that with hardwork and meditation I will succeed in the coming months to raise the level of my poetry, following Aragon's lessons" (cited by Montas 1955: 46). Depestre finds Aragon's aesthetics exemplified most successfully in the French poet's *Les yeux et la mémoire*, the importance of which he expresses by saying: "the book has not left my bedside since I bought it and began with it my poetry lessons" (cited in Montas 1955: 48). Announcing his pursuit of the study of "la grande aventure de l'alexandrin" and other traditional forms, Depestre illustrates his new poetic credo with fragments of a poem he was composing at the time. Depestre goes as far as to prescribe Aragon's poetic formula as the course which Haitian poetry ought to take (ibid pp. 47-48).

Such an apparently uncritical acceptance of a poetic theory positing a return to traditionalism by someone who already in 1955 could be called "one of the masters of Haitian poetry" was sure to cause some reaction from Caribbean writers, most of whom saw themselves in opposition to Western traditionalism (Montas 1955: 48). Césaire reacted immediately with a poetic epistle entitled "Réponse à Depestre poète haïtien (Eléments d'un art poétique)". In it Césaire questions Depestre's submission to Aragon's poetic doctrine and characterizes Depestre's attitude as perhaps arising from a lack of confidence in his own national tradition: "est-il vrai que tu doutes de la forêt natale" – is it true that you doubt your own native forest (cited in Montas 1955: 50-51). Clearly, Césaire heard in Depestre's declared alignment with Aragon's version of realist and revolutionary poetry the same sort of cultural assimilationism which the Martinican poet in his *Cahier d'un retour au pays natal* had tried to counter. So, he invites the Haitian poet to discard the traditional forms of French prosody, which he considers a lifeless source: "Laisse-la Depestre laisse-la/ la gueuse-vie solennelle d'un air mendié" – Leave it Depestre leave it/the solemn beggarly life with its mendicant ways (ibid). He urges the Haitian poet to assume a more fitting attitude of cultural subversion: "Marronnons-les Depestre marronnons-les/ comme jadis nous marronnions nos maîtres à fouet" – Let's Maroon them Depestre let's maroon them/As we once did maroon our lash-bearing masters (ibid).

The subtext informing Césaire's poetic epistle is clearly his quarrel with the French Communist Party, of which Aragon was a leading member. Aragon sat on the central committee of the party, and in that capacity he had occasion to advance the party's preference for socialist realism. Césaire had come to disagree with some of the party's directives in political and cultural matters. Césaire's position would be made public in 1956 in his *Lettre à Maurice Thorez*, in which he broke with the party. Politically, he denounced the party's reluctance to repudiate the legacy of Stalin and "the methods that drove him to crime", its reluctance, that is, to proceed along "the road of de-Stalinization" (Césaire 1956: 6). Culturally, he had come to understand that colonial people had problems of their own that could not be satisfactorily addressed by giving them some obscure place in the agenda of the party, which could only treat them as a negligible part "of a more important whole" (p. 8). Insisting on what he called the "uniqueness of our culture", he saw in the French Communist Party a "colonial paternalism" that he found unbearable (p. 11). When he learned of Depestre's subservience to Aragon's aesthetic dictates, Césaire must have seen it as a case of a colonial writer giving in to the self-assumed "omnilateral superiority of the West" (p. 11), at the expense of his own cultural "particularité", what in the epistle he calls "the native forest".

Césaire's response was not entirely justified. While embracing Aragon's views, Depestre in his letter did not fail to recognize the need to integrate "the cultural patrimony we inherit from Africa" as harmoniously as possible with "the legacy of French prosody", suggesting a potential hybridization rather than cultural assimilation (cited in Montas 1955: 47). As Arnold's major work on Césaire shows, Césaire simply jumped at the opportunity to use Depestre's declaration as a pretext to voice his own disagreement with Aragon's normative aesthetics. At any rate, the confrontation between the two Caribbean poets had considerable repercussions, particularly in Haiti where the writer Lucien Montas published the article "René Depestre et les problèmes de la poésie nationale", which reproduced fragments of Depestre's letter to Dobzynski as well as Césaire's response, inaugurating a heated debate on national poetry in the Haitian literary arena. Lasting for over a year, mainly through the pages of the Port-au-Prince journal *Optique* whose monthly issues since August 1955 through February 1956 carried statements on the matter, the debate motivated the theoretical insights of many of the leading literary figures of Haiti. It afforded Depestre himself the opportunity to further clarify his position regarding the art of poetry within the context of nationality and culture.

Depestre expounded his revised views in his long essay: "Réponse à Aimé Césaire: Introduction à un art poétique haïtien". In an attempt to undermine Césaire's advice to Haitianize his poetry, which Depestre read, perhaps too conveniently, as an insistence on racial values, he argued that the national character of any given culture lies neither in language nor in race but in the discrete conditions of each country's historical development (Depestre 1955: 45). Resorting to the analytical machinery of historical materialism, he proceeds to dismiss the concepts of "poésie noire" and "négritude" as respectively a myth and a metaphysical notion. While admitting certain commonalities among the black peoples of the world and recognizing in the African past a more or less coherent set of perceptions and manifestations of "the sensibility and psychological make-up of the Haitian people", he rejects any racial essentialism as valid for the definition of Haitian culture, and proposes, instead, a definition based on "the movement of class struggle" (Depestre 1955: 46, 48).

The "supreme goal" of poetry being to advance the human species to a world governed by "peace and love", Depestre argued that one ought to define poetry both according to the "nobility" of its themes and the inventive rigour of its stylistic elements, two aspects which he considered to be "dialectically inseparable from the unity of the work of art" (pp. 62, 50). What matters, he argues, is not what resources one draws on but how and to what ends one employs them. He challenges, in other words, Césaire's dismissal of traditional French prosody. In doing so, however, Depestre has occasion to rethink his own unconditional alignment with Aragon's rigid legislation of regular verse and comes to the conclusion that what the French poet called "formal individualism" could occur regardless of the stylistic devices one has recourse to if one's poetry was marred by what he terms "ideological misery in the content" (p. 61). The response to Césaire, as we can see, gave the Haitian poet the opportunity to articulate in prose the vision he had already made manifest in his poetic praxis, having been guided from the beginning by a "passionate meditation on the future of human liberties" (p. 61) But we can also add that with these aesthetic pronouncements he came to integrate at the theoretical level the seemingly opposing realms of the traditional and the innovative, suggesting the ideological coming of age that is reflected in the thematic variety and intellectual complexity evident in *Minerai noir*, Depestre's next book of poems.

Love and Radical Humanism

Minerai noir opens with an evocation of the suffering of black people at the hands of Western colonialists. The title alludes to the way people of African descent served to fuel Western economic progress through the highly profitable institution of slavery. Many poems in the collection illustrate that suffering. Other poems illustrate a sort of suffering which is not explicable within an ethnic frame alone: the hunger pains of a child in the autobiographical "Mon cinéma d'enfant noir", or the sorrow of mothers enduring the loss of their children in the very moving "Complainte des mères malheureuses", for instance.

Depestre's commitment to the gospel of love, as manifested in his meditation on global human suffering, figures significantly in *Minerai noir*, which also exhibits a special insistence on world peace. In "Le maïs qui leve", for instance, the speaker equates the struggle against oppression and human exploitation with the cause of peace: "O Peuples levez-vous tous car seul votre sève/ Populaire a la force d'allaiter dans son sein/ Cet amour de la paix qui par mes poumons respire!" – Peoples of the earth rise up, you all, for only your/popular vigour has the strength to suckle in its breast/This love of peace that breathes through my lungs (Depestre 1957: 33). Addressing himself to the season of rebirth ("Oh camarade Printemps"), he commands Spring to ally itself with his song so that together they can outlaw the "atomic shame" ("la honte atomique") which threatens the survival of our species (p. 34). He himself in his role of poet claims a special mission in averting the disaster and implies that if he were to remain silent ("Oh si je me taisais quand le mal nucléaire/ Autour de moi fait rage" (p. 36)), he would deserve the worst kind of punishment imaginable, namely the contempt of his fellow human beings and his absolute oblivion.

The love of peace and the struggle for it presupposes a love of human freedom, which is never obtained, the speaker suggests, by passive means. In "La liberté raconte sa vie", personified Liberty herself is the speaker. She puts it quite clearly: "Chaque étape de ma vie a eu ses martyrs./ Héros tombés avec mon soleil sur leurs lèvres" – Each stage of my life has had its martyrs/Heroes fallen with my rays on their lips (p. 43). But the love of humanity that Depestre sings in *Minerai noir* appears not only in general philosophical concepts such as peace, freedom, and justice, but also particularized in the voice of a man singing with passion of the virtues, the mystery, and the grandeur of the opposite sex. In such poems as "Le large d'Edith" and "Dito", for instance, we recognize the husband singing the merits of his wife who has shared with him the travails of exile. The autobiographical "Sous les ponts de l'amour", likewise presents us with the personal voice of a speaker recalling with tenderness the discovery of carnal pleasures earlier in his life. In the last poem of the book, "Les gués de l'amour", he recreates in a highly lyrical mode the memory of a beloved of insurmountable and evasive beauty.

The presence of the personal voice and the elevated lyricism pervading many of the poems in *Minerai noir* suggest the sort of all-embracing aesthetic orientation voiced by Depestre in his response to Césaire. In any case, the book shows a change of tone in the sensibility of the speaker, with a virtual absence of the declarative statements, the slogans which characterized his earlier books. Even when addressing white racists, his condemnation acquires a corrective rather than a vindictive intent. He wishes he could, the speaker says in addressing a white supremacist, "rétablir le cours humain/ de la beauté dans ton coeur!" – restore the human course/of beauty in your heart (p. 41). This relative change of sensibility corresponds to the widening in ideological scope Depestre articulates in the above essay, a tenacious gospel of love expressed in a vocabulary stemming from Marxist radical humanism. This refers, of course, to that aspect of Marxist philosophy that reduces all meaning to human meaning: "Theory is capable of gripping the masses as soon as it demonstrates 'ad hominem', and it demonstrates 'ad hominem' as soon as it becomes radical. To be radical is to grasp the root of the matter. But for man the root is man himself" (Marx and Engels 1964: 50). That Depestre at the time viewed poetry within a global concern for the future of humanity is clear not only from his theoretical position and his poetic praxis but also from his comments on other poets. One need only look, for instance, at his evaluation of the

Senegalese David Diop as "a carrier of hope" (Depestre 1956: 111). He admires the total absence of any "appeal to the power of hatred" in the work of the Ivory Coast poet Bernard B. Dadié (p. 112). And he celebrates "man's universal hope of freedom" in the work of Jacques Rabemananjara, the Malagasy poet (p. 114).

The Cuban Experience

Depestre's next book of poetry, *Journal d'un animal marin*, appearing eight years after *Minerai noir*, further enriches his radical humanism with the exploration of some concrete symbols of human good and the elaboration of a much more socio-historically specific religious discourse. With the serenity of his previous book, the poet continues to develop his global reflection on the need to struggle for humanity's well-being. Depestre was nearing forty years of age, which perhaps explains his pronounced mood of regret, stemming not only from homesickness for his ever more distant native land, but also from the nostalgic evocation of his younger years. A particularly moving text, "La dernière hirondelle" – subtitled "Poème de fin d'amour" – dramatizes a marital separation. It alludes to Dito, whom Depestre had divorced in 1961, in a farewell that evokes nostalgia rather than resentment. A good many of the poems included in this collection engage the speaker's male voice in commemorating the individual women who shared different moments of his past life. These lines from one of them, in which he voices his fascination with the rhythmical movements of a woman he danced with in Moscow, illustrate the predominant tone of his homage to women: "Ta danse était mon vaudou/ Mon cri de paix et de guerre/ …Ta danse était une grande sagesse/ Une nouvelle religion une prophetie… O bénédiction de ton corps contre le mien… Une espèce cosmique naquit de notre danse" – Your dance was my vodou/My declaration of peace and of war/… Your dance was a source of great wisdom/A new religion a prophecy… Oh blessing of your body against mine… A cosmic breed was born from our dance (Depestre 1964: 34-35).

The homage to individual women expands into a general celebration of the entire gender in "Blason du corps féminin", where the female body elicits an exaltation which could have been called Whitmanesque if it had encompassed both male and female bodies. One thinks, of course, of Whitman's exuberant celebration of the human body, male and female, as well as the bodily functions in "I sing the Body Electric" in the CHILDREN OF ADAM section of *Leaves of Grass*. Clearly, a gender-conscious reading would almost inevitably discern objectionable traits in Depestre's celebration of women. Here as elsewhere in his works, the female appears merely as a vehicle that serves the protagonist, who is always a male, to revitalize himself in order to realize his dreams and aspirations. Depestre for the most part has created no meaningful female protagonists, only female characters who either complement male ones or serve as a catalyst for male desire. In this respect, the poem "Élégie Païenne", a song for all the women ever loved by the speaker, synthesizes the frame of mind adopted by Depestre in his characterization of the opposite sex. Assigning a significant place to the erotic dimension of human love, the speaker launches an overt exaltation of human sexuality through women as the quintessential fountain of carnal pleasures. The word "pagan" in the title indicates the religious context within which he wishes to place his celebration of the flesh. He seeks not the blessing of Christianity, whose "jealous gods" abhor the body, but presents it as a challenge to that creed: "Mon chant défie les dieux jaloux/ Qui ont un jour maudit/ Ta gloire sur la terre" – My song defies the jealous gods/Who one day cursed/Your glory on earth (p. 56). In placing his devotion to the glory of the flesh in opposition to the religious ethics of Christianity, he declares his affinity with "pagan" values whose theology does not malign sexual intercourse.

The emphasis on love, universal love of humanity, we can say, appears in *Journal d'un animal marin* dramatized in its multiple manifestations. The poet still speaks in the voice of one who, confident of the importance of his service in fighting injustice, will devote his energies to the cause of the destitute. Such, indeed, is the self-giving tenor of the speaker in "La Rivière", in which a personified river explains his own birth in terms of a devotion to the cause of the needy. This river was not always a river. Its present state is the result of a most noble metamorphosis for humanity's sake: "Il y a tant d'assoiffés dans le monde/ Pour eux me voici changé en rivière" – There are so many people thirsting in the world/On their behalf, here I am turned into water (p. 14). But the emphasis on this global love becomes more concrete, and hence more apprehensible, in particularized manifestations such as in the appreciation of women and the aforementioned nostalgia for past pleasures. Many poems in the book also touch on the complexity of human existence, the passage of time, solitude, and the brevity of life. Amidst all of these reflections, however, we find an indomitable spirit, ready to undermine the limitations imposed upon us by our very humanity. In "Sur la mort", while pondering the inevitability of death, the speaker ends with a stubborn reaffirmation of life and the beauty of the world (p. 78-79). Likewise, in "La vie suit son cours", he meditates on the ability of life in general, the totality of the great cosmic order, to move on regardless of pain and joy (p. 20). The speaker must go on in his concern for the future of the species, and he reaffirms his advocacy for world peace in poems such as "Un cri de paix".

Journal d'un animal marin praises individuals such as Lenin, Eluard "directeur de la neige" (director of the snow), and the Chinese musician Nieh Er on the grounds that each in his own field of endeavour has made a significant contribution to the global cause of humanity. The cause, then, aims at a universal appeal. Yet the speaker voicing these universal concerns remains recognizably Haitian. In "Le mur du son", for example, we hear him wondering about the historical meaning of a sense of rhythm that inhabits his heart. In another poem he discovers a nurturing, hope-giving quality in the sounds of Haitian drums, which impregnate him with the expectation of an imminent new age for his people: "O forêt qui as soif/ O tambours haïtiens/ Patience frères/ La rosée est en route" – Oh thirsty forest/Oh Haitian drums/Patience oh brothers/The dawn is on its way (p. 42). Clearly, here as elsewhere, the speaker situates his gospel of universal love within a socio-culturally Caribbean context, making it more tangible, especially with the integration of imagery derived from the local milieu such as the forest, the drums, and the Haitian gods.

Cuba became a central source from which to draw abundant socio-cultural imagery for Depestre, who settled there in 1959, after having lived for over a year in Haiti. Depestre had returned to Haiti on December 23, 1957, with the intention of regaining his "home" during the first months of the government of Doctor François Duvalier. But he soon incurred the displeasure of the governmental authorities for his revolutionary ideas, which he expressed in some public statements (Couffon 1986: 56-57). His return to Haiti was greeted with enthusiasm as witnessed by the triumphal reception accorded to him in Port-au-Prince (p. 56). His refusal to accept a post with the government and other dissident positions soon led to his being placed under house arrest. When, on January 2, 1959, the revolutionary forces of Fidel Castro entered Havana, marking the victory of the revolution, Depestre was quick to publish an article urging the Haitian people to support the Cuban revolution (p. 59). Shortly thereafter he was invited to Cuba by Nicolás Guillén, whom he had met in Europe. He arrived there in March 1959, to remain until September 1978 (pp. 60-82). Once he broke with the political authorities in Haiti, a governmental structure that he would later characterize as a "papadocracy", Depestre found in Cuba a physical as well as a spiritual refuge (Depestre 1976: 56-64).

Frequently in *Journal* we find a speaker for whom everything in Cuba merits celebration. Overjoyed at seeing the rain fall on the Cuban soil, he exclaims: "Donne-moi une goutte de cette eau cubaine/ Une goutte de cette nouvelle aurore" – Give me a drop of this Cuban water/a drop of this new dawn (Depestre 1964: 47). In another poem "Un haïtien parle de Cuba", the speaker expresses a different sort of enthusiasm, which elevates him to a practically mystical dimension. A Haitian fearing American aggression against the young revolution, he indicts the potential intruders and assures the Cuban people that no one will dare profane the sacred shore of the place "où commence la tendresse du monde" – where the tenderness of the world begins (p. 66). Considering the date of the poem, 1962, the possibility of the

U.S. military expedition alluded to in the text seemed very real for Cubans at the time. The year before the U.S. had equipped and financed the infamous and unsuccessful Bay of Pigs invasion. Then, in October 1962, the Missile Crisis brought constant threats of U.S. aggression against the Caribbean island. Viewing revolutionary Cuba as the most eloquent symbol of a new dawn for the human race, Depestre's speaker cannot conceive of its possible defeat, no matter how powerful the enemy. Aided by the power of justice and truth, it will withstand any incursion, no matter how violent. The heroic people of Cuba will hold the enemy, but even if their human power should not suffice, the botanical world will join the constituents of this worthy cause: "Je sais que les palmiers sont/ Des miliciers aux ordres de Fidel/ Que le sucre est prêt à se changer/ En poison dans la bouche de l'ennemi" – I know that the palm trees are/Warriors in the service of Fidel/That the sugar is ready to transform itself/Become poison in the mouth of the enemy (p. 67). Even the four elements wear the colours of the revolution: "Je sais que les quatre éléments/ Vétus de vert olive ont déjà/ Formé des milliers de bataillons cosmiques!" – I know that the four elements/Dressed in olive green/Have already formed thousands of cosmic platoons (p. 67).

The background to the almost frenetic enthusiasm expressed in that poem resides in the great symbolism the Cuban revolution had for Depestre as well as for many other Third World thinkers and artists. It was the coming of socialism, the bringing of light, to the Caribbean soil, the arrival of a system containing the possibility of ending human suffering, of recreating the world according to the dictates of the gospel of love. It was utopia become history in the Caribbean, and the victory of the soldiers of the revolution over the United States-supported invaders of the Bay of Pigs further amplified the epic proportions of the event and elevated the protagonists of the insurrection – Fidel, Camilo, and Che – to an almost superhuman level as angels of world revolution. In the opening to a book of essays, the poet evokes Ernesto Che Guevara as someone whose voice, words, and countenance gave dazzling proof of having successfully integrated "in a singular crystal all his psychological ingredients and to chisel his personality into a diamond of the first order" (Depestre 1974: 10). The tone of devout adoration gives an idea of the extent to which the protagonists of the Cuban struggle rose to mystical dimensions in the eyes of the poet. Depestre was deeply moved when he came to Cuba and actually witnessed that historical moment: "I had the feeling of being the privileged witness of a great historical event" (Couffon 1986: 62).

The Cuban milieu, then, with its highly dramatic situation, with its tense historical circumstances, and the heroic stature of its characters, provided Depestre with the necessary imagery and symbology, ingrained in the local context, to render his gospel of love poetically concrete. From this point of view, *Journal d'un animal marin* marks a point of maturity in

Depestre's poetics. Valentin Y. Mudimbe has perceived in it a tension stemming from the poet's twofold aspirations: on the one hand, the pursuit of a "reconciliation of a literary vow and the lived experience" and, on the other, the desire to unify "political aspirations with a poetic creed" (Mudimbe 1971: 86). But we would add that what allows Depestre to give cohesion to his poetics is precisely the harmonious integration of those seemingly incompatible aims. The biographical and the literary, the political and the aesthetic, the universal and the culturally specific unite without contradiction to produce a poetic discourse of radical humanism. Always underlining these is a socialism that expresses itself in religious images and symbols, proceeding this time from a primarily local milieu.

Consistent with the hopeful prospect signified by the triumph of the revolution in Cuba, the dominant tone of *Journal d'un animal marin* is urgently optimistic. The speaker chooses to see all aspects of life in a good light. He declares everything to be possible, ascribing supernatural powers to noble humans, claiming the favour of the entire cosmic order for worthy social causes, celebrating all things, and expecting the best for humanity. His mood is unmistakably cheerful and festive. Even when facing prospective evil, as in the aforementioned "Un haïtien parle de Cuba", he sounds convinced that evil will not thrive. Exuding as it does a most invigorating "joie de vivre", this book is exuberant with celebration and rings with the subversive sound of laughter. Depestre places considerable emphasis on the close tie between joy and liberation. This element of discovered and appropriated joy perhaps more than anything else contributes to making the insistence on presenting the female body as a source of carnal delight less vulnerable to the charge of phallocentric representation. When the erotic text does not promote a vision of liberation, as may happen with some of Depestre's later work, one can argue that pornography occurs.

The Gods of the Native Forest

The religious imagery and symbols of the Caribbean milieu, towards which Depestre's spiritual discourse had been moving gradually, becomes the primary raw material for *Un-arc-en-ciel pour l'Occident chrétien* (1966), the text that has generated the most critical attention of all of his works. It has elicited critical approaches as varied in scope as one that reads it for the interaction of vodou and Surrealism (Leiner 1977) and one that studies the "bestiary" in the text (Degras 1983). *Un arc-en-ciel* has been translated once into Spanish and twice into English. Of the two English translations produced in the United States, one by the poet Jack Hirschman (1972) and the other by the scholar Joan Dayan (1977), our discussion will draw from the latter. As indicated in the subtitle, "poème-mystère vaudou", the text gravitates around the acts and words of a set of Haitian divinities in their interaction with a white Alabama family that represents the Christian West: "an exorcism through voodoo, the induction of the water-based grandeur of Blackness into the Southern-white dynastic decay" (Hirschman 1972: 5). Divided into seven interconnected parts, the poem combines prose and verse, narrative and lyric with the dramatic resources of monologue and dialogue.

Un arc-en-ciel opens with a "Prélude" whose speaker brandishes his militancy: "Yes I am a tempest-nigger" (Depestre 1977: 109). He thunderously declares his spiritual rebellion: "The little Christ who was smiling in me/Last night I drowned him in alcohol/Likewise I drowned the Tablets of the Law/Likewise I drowned all your sacred sacraments" (p. 111). The speaker addresses the Alabama family, whose composition (a West Point cadet, a Yale University student, a future American Ambassador to Panama, a businessman, and the widow of a colonel killed in Korea fighting the "reds") represents a set of pillars of Western imperialism. He denounces the contradictory nature of their spiritual legacy: "A family calling to the rescue/Jesus and Ku Klux Klan together/H bomb and Electric Chair/And the Statue of Liberty" (p. 115). Therefore, he advocates the annulment of the Christian spiritual tradition "Tonight all your ideals are destined to silence" (p. 119) and invokes the restorative powers of a more morally edifying spiritual order, namely the "green gods" of Haitian vodou. Referring to one of these Haitian deities (loas), the critic Julio Finn has described the process in the first section of the poem, noting that the "Loa Zaka dethrones Christ in order to fulfil the work Christ could not: to perform the miracle of lifting sin. Voodoo will succeed where Christianity has failed" (Finn 1988: 129).

The apparition of these Caribbean divinities, each of whom recites a monologue of personal introduction combined with some demand or accusation addressed to the Christian capitalist Alabama family, constitutes the second section, called "Epiphanies des dieux du vaudou" – Epiphanies of the Voodoo Gods. That these gods claim access to a superior sense of justice and truth becomes clear particularly in the next section, "Le bain du petit matin" – The Early Morning Bath. Here, with the speaker serving as mediator between the vodou divinities and the white Alabaman family, a ceremony ensues by means of which the deities attempt to purge the family's sins. In a scene reminiscent of ancient Greek libations, the *loas* intend to pour into the bath of the Alabamans "the dewdrop of Haitian wisdom" (p. 162), purposing to rid them of their evil. This liturgical ritual is supplemented by another epiphany, that of the seven female loas in "Cantate à Sept Voix" (Cantata for Seven Voices), the fourth part of the poem. Their appearance on stage serves to develop the symbology of the rainbow referred to in the title of the poem and makes use of the mystical significance of the number seven which is foregrounded in this section. Addressing the oppressed condition of blacks through the centuries, the seven female loas opt to weave their own version of the rainbow by singing the glory of seven legendary black men who gave their lives fighting for the liberation of their race. Each charged with the glorification of one chosen hero, they devote seven odes to Mackandal, Toussaint Louverture, Dessalines, Antonio Maceo, Charlemagne Péralte, Patrice Lumumba and Malcolm X, respectively, making up the next section of the book: "Les sept piliers de l'innocence" – Seven Pillars of Wisdom.

The political significance of the seven heroes celebrated by the female loas suggests the integration of the spiritual and social realms characteristic of vodou. It is this aspect which makes the symbols and images of this popular religion so naturally coherent with Depestre's poetic worldview. In the glossary to *Un arc-en-ciel* he defines vodou as the popular religion of Haiti – a syncretism of African religions and Catholicism – and ascribes to it an important role in "the formation of the national culture of the Haitian people" (1967: 139). Shortly thereafter he would write in another glossary that "Vodou is one of the aspects of the ideological and cultural *marronage* [marooning] practised by the slaves to prevent the total shipwreck of their human *identity*" (Depestre 1968: 157). Looking at the poet's own definition of vodou, we can gather that in incorporating it into his poetry he has undertaken the same sort of subversive action attributed to that religion. To glorify vodou, as a commentator on the collection has put it, means to exorcise "the shame, the humiliation of slavery and colonial domination" (Degras 1983: 68). In his response to Césaire more than a decade before Depestre had characterized the exultation of vodou encouraged by the Martinican poet as a "contemplative and fatalistic attitude" of religious alienation (Depestre 1955: 54). He had only partially accepted the value of this faith as "the predominant religious expression of the class struggle in Haiti" (Depestre 1955: 55). But now he presents the Haitian divinities "as vibrant beings, full of revenge" in opposition to the "uselessness of Jesus Christ," to put it in the words of Keith Q. Warner (1974: 51).

The socially subversive quality of vodou was examined by Alfred Métraux in his classic *Le Vaudou Haïtien* (1958) as well as by others who have attributed to it a significant role in the late eighteenth-century insurrection of the Saint Domingue slaves which culminated in their emancipation and the subsequent birth of the Republic of Haiti (Mennesson-Rigaud 1958: 45-67). The black slaves of Saint Domingue, subjected to the most atrocious living conditions, were exploited to the extent that their life expectancy once on the island did not exceed nine years (Métraux 1966: 47). For them to be able to worship the gods and spirits of African ancestors, even at the risk of provoking the ire of their Christian masters, meant, "at once, a refuge and a form of resistance to oppression" (ibid. p. 46). Such was the socially subversive nature of this faith that, as Métraux informs us, one of the military heroes of the Haitian revolution has found a place among the inhabitants of the divine realm. He tells us of vodou ceremonies in which the *loa* Dessalines makes his appearance, causing an impassioned song by a chorus of "servants of the gods" in whose martial tune one catches "a distant echo of the revolutionary struggles" (Métraux 1957: 143).

In light of the revolutionary associations of vodou, Depestre found it useful to nourish his poetry and give his humanism a concrete cultural context. The very affirmation of this folk religion constitutes an act of rebellion against the view of human culture that equates universal values with the Christian West as well as against the religious order of the colonial regime. For religious teachings did play a crucial role in inculcating passivity and acceptance in the minds of slaves. Article 2 of the *Code Noir*, for instance, prescribed categorically that every slave owner should provide his slaves with Catholic instruction (Métraux 1957: 47). The clerical and political authorities of Haiti agreed at the time that a Christian religious education would succeed in restraining any desire to escape, poison or rebel since in this creed: "no one can be sanctified but by fulfilling the duties of his state in the condition and the situation in which Providence has placed him" (Métraux 1966: 48). But to achieve their end the colonial authorities had to repress the folk religion of the slaves. The repression by the clerical and political authorities in Haiti from colonial days carried on well into the twentieth century (Métraux 1972: 335-44).

In the classic *Ainsi parla l'oncle* (1928) Jean Price-Mars endeavoured to defend vodou against the then prevalent characterization of it as an expression of sorcery and fetishism of a diabolic nature. The seriousness with which he wanted to combat prejudiced appraisals, especially by travel writers during the U.S. occupation of Haiti, and to claim for vodou the status of a bona fide religion is clear in statements such as this: "More than twenty years of research allow us to affirm with all certainty that vodou is not a cannibalistic sect" (Price-Mars 1973: 222). Likewise Métraux, in tracing the major divinities of the Haitian pantheon back to solid religious systems originating in Africa, aided in the battle waged since the 1920s by Price-Mars against those who, like Edmund Wilson, contemptuously derided the Haitian folk as "Voodoo worshipping peasants" (Métraux 1966: 46; Wilson cited by Dash 1988: 78-79). Dash has shown a connection between deprecatory characterizations of vodou and the image of Haiti as a savage, untamed, wild realm used by U.S. travel writers to justify the "civilizing" presence of United States military forces during the occupation between 1915 and 1934 (Dash 1988: 32).

Reference sources in use in the West long persisted in subscribing to definitions that construe vodou as an anthropophagic cult. The 1906 edition of a British encyclopedia gave this picture: "human sacrifices are still offered, and the heart and lungs of the victim are said to be eaten raw, while the flesh is salted by priestly families; the blood is drunk while yet warm, and tubes are inserted into the veins of the half-dead victim for sucking out his life, which thus adds to the vitality of the drinker" (Forlong 1906/1964: 492). The erudite *Encyclopedia of Religion and Ethics* defined vodou as "devil worship" and "fetishism" whose "chief sacrifice is a girl child", and the practice of which poses grave danger for "white people" (Hastings 1927: XII, 640-41). *Encyclopedia of Religion and Religions* attributes to it such qualities as "devil worship, Phallicism, and magical and obscene practices" (Pike 1951: 392). The more recent *Dictionary of Comparative Religion* retains the diabolical characterization, conceding only that in present practice vodou practitioners have substituted a white kid for the girl child (1970: 664). Dayan has documented the pervasive representation of vodou in the American press through images that foster a "climate of fear and terror" well into the 1980s (Dayan 1988: 329). A graphic illustration of that persistence is the headline "Voodoo, Porno, and Cocaine" on the front page of New York's *Daily News* for December 23, 1989, for an article that, in chronicling the U.S. invasion of Panama, undertakes to demonize General Manuel Noriega. Clearly, then, asserting vodou in *Un arc-en-ciel* constituted a challenge to the cultural biases of the Christian West.

The various prose fragments which compose the sixth section of *Un arc-en-ciel*, "Aphorismes et paraboles du nouveau monde" – Aphorisms and Parables of the New World, abound in sarcastic and lugubriously funny observations regarding the way in which the West has availed itself of Christian practices to achieve the subjection of blacks in the Americas: "In the last century, seven million bags of coal were baptized before Christian altars (Depestre 1977: 215). At one point the speaker implicates the Christian godhead in personally allowing black women to be raped by their white masters: "As for God, he found these clandestine nuptials charming" (p. 219). Depestre condemns the Western divinity's complicity with the most execrable human actions. This condemnatory attitude dominates until the beginning of the seventh and last section of the poem, "Pour un nouvel âge du coeur humain" – For a New Age of the Human Heart. Here the narrator translates for his Haitian divinities the message he reads in the words and actions of the Western deities, revealing, above all, their alleged dedication to destruction.

In the first third of the closing section, the speaker stages the action in Omaha, which, as the poem's translator notes, is the place in Nebraska that serves as headquarters of the Strategic Air Command, where U.S. nuclear bombs are stored (Dayan 1977: 254). The idea is to show to his loas how in this spot the Christian West conspires, as it were, against the future of humanity: "Here man/Passionately prepares the end of man" (p. 225). But in spite of the destructive designs of the "atomic gods" of Omaha, makers of "soleils homicides" – homicidal suns – as exemplified in the H Bomb, the speaker does not surrender to fatalistic anxiety. Invoking the mysterious power of "Notre Dame des cendres" – Our Lady of Ashes, associated with Aphrodite and with the female principle of Haitian vodou, he manages to remain: "carrier of faith/ [Of] an unconquerable faith unconquered" (p. 235). The poem concludes with an affirmation of faith in the possibility of a rebirth for mankind. The speaker makes the sign of the cross and pleads with the Christian West to aid in the rebirth: "In the name of revolt/And of justice/And of tenderness" (p. 237). "Revolt, justice and tenderness are three recurrent themes in the thought of Caribbeans, three concepts without internal contradiction for they belong to the dialectics of love and revolt and are part of a socialist humanism, a militant humanism," says a scholar accentuating the ideological implications of Depestre's conclusions to *Un arc-en-ciel* (Levilain 1983: 165).

Un arc-en-ciel reaches the pinnacle of religious elevation with a discourse that remains socially engaged and culturally discrete. Théophile Obenga sees it as the supreme achievement of Depestre to have poeticized at a universal level the strong and secular tradition of the vodou ceremonies of Haiti (1984: 120). Obenga's judgment resonates with the spiritual rapture the text inspired in the poet Jack Hirschman, its first American translator: "It was amidst the auras and lights of Jewish mysticism that one day lead me to the discovery of this book, a day in 1971 during the trial of Angela Davis and inclusive of the terrific work of light that was being carried on at the time" (1972: 6). With a clear intuition of the integrative project implicit in Depestre's poetics, Hirschman found in the book "the secret music and meaning of a shared world of poetry and philosophy 'grounded' in the high politicities of our time" (ibid.).

The ideals of the socialist revolution and the spiritual quality of the Caribbean past yield for Depestre a wealth of poetic potential which he objectifies in the integrated popular religion of Haiti. This folk religion lends itself most adequately to Depestre's politicized treatment since, as Dayan has succinctly expressed it, "the essential nature of voodoo is its uncompromising spirit of revolt, predicting a complete revolution of human existence through the magic power of the mind and through its actual, positive power of synthesis" (1980: 79). Dayan's line of thought challenges the view that "the utilization of vodou by a Marxist poet can only be ludicrous, sacrilegious" (Cailler 1979: 58). Bernadette Cailler too rapidly assumes the irreligious nature of Marxism, thinking probably of the Marxist dictum that terms religion "the opium of the people". Interestingly, in Marx's own text, that phrase comes a few sentences before the statement: "Man makes religion; religion does not make man" (Marx and Engels 1964: 41). In volume 1 of *Capital* Marx says that "The religious world is but the reflex of the real world" and Engels's *Bruno Bauer and Early Christianity* argues that even Christianity in the past constituted a revolutionary force (Marx and Engels 1964: 135, 202). In their joint review of Daumer's

The Religion of the New Age both thinkers posit that "with every great historical upheaval of social conditions the outlooks and the ideas of men and consequently, their religious ideas, are revolutionized" (Marx and Engels 1964: 94). Despite Cailler's assumption of incompatibility, one should not overlook the place accorded to Marxism in the theology of liberation.

One can argue, along with Souffrant, that there is a religious side to the worldview of avowed Haitian Marxists such as Jacques Roumain and Jacques Stephen Alexis (Souffrant 1978: 42-47, 68-73). Nor can one deny that "Socialism is an all-embracing theory of life, and that it has an ethic and a religion of its own," as William Morris put it (1915: 255-56). European Marxism has been historically hostile to religion, but Depestre comes from a region with different epistemological imperatives. By the time of his vodou poem, he had already come to terms with his cultural "singularité", and the text attests to a desire to nativize his Marxism. The spiritual imperative is simply too strong in the Caribbean for a culturally-conscious poet, Marxist or not, to ignore it. A less dichotomous reading than that of Cailler could find *Un arc-en-ciel* a considerably creolized version of Marxism as much as a creolized rendition of the sacred.

What may constitute the most serious question is not the propriety of an intermixture of Marxism and religion but the fitness of vodou itself in the construction of a discourse of liberation. From General Soulouque, who ruled Haiti as Emperor Faustin I during 1847-59, to President Antoine Simone (1906-11), to Dr. François Duvalier, Haitian leaders have as successfully placed vodou at the service of repressive political regimes as it has served the cause of liberation in revolutionary times (Taylor 1989: 118). Patrick Taylor argues that the lack of anything "intrinsic to the vodou narrative order" requiring the believer to "enter into a struggle for liberation" explains its political malleability (1989: 118). He claims that vodou's "real ambiguity" lies in that "its mythic structure orders both resistance to oppression and accommodation with the oppressor" (p. 122). According to Taylor, vodou lacks "the narrative of liberation", but has a "tragic structure" instead, one that assumes the "fatality of evil" and harbours an implicit crisis that bars "the way to truly transformative action" (p. 125). The tragic structure of vodou's mythical narrative "does not presuppose the necessity of freedom. Though the loa will emancipate their followers if requested", they lack an inherent commitment to emancipation *per se* and make "no call for liberation as a universal demand or categorical imperative" (p. 125).

On Depestre's behalf, one can say that *Un arc-en-ciel* privileges the liberating side of vodou particularly through the contrast with the oppressive side of Christianity. But we should remember also that the Haitian reality, visible and invisible spheres included, forms part of a larger neocolonial, capitalist arrangement. Duvalier, for example, managed to exert as much influence over vodou and enlist the services of so many hougans as a result of the concrete power of coercion that United States economic and political support afforded him (Dayan 1988: 329). But the testimony of scholars would suggest that vodou has the ability to survive political co-optation just as it has historically survived the onslaught of Catholic authorities. Vodou historically succeeded at "incorporating and consuming… the trappings, prayers, and representations of Catholicism… to survive attempts to threaten, weaken, or destroy it" (Dayan 1991: 47). The "absence of any unified superstructure in its pantheon" gives it the quality of "a continuous, heady drama of transmutation", to say it in the words of Dayan, who highlights vodou's "adaptability and absorption" as an effective "subversiveness" that turns "everything into material for change", ensuring its capacity to fend off "all kinds of extermination campaigns" (1988: 322).

Politically repressive regimes, as Dayan shows, have either persecuted vodou or privileged its negative side. Thus, the family loa and root loa (*loa héritage* and *loa racine*) take precedence over the bought loa (*loa acheté*), known also as *bokós*. The difference between the two is simple: the former foster "healing or preservation" whereas the latter "answer the call of greed" (Dayan 1991: 52). Vodou believers can tell the difference. They disdain *bokós* as "travaillant des deux mains" (serving with both hands), working for the loa with one hand and for the devil with the other (Dayan 1988: 320; 1991: 49). The positive and negative aspects of sorcery exist all around us. In describing her character Tituba as a "positive sorceress", Maryse Condé puts it succinctly: "In any given community, you have two types of individuals relating to the invisible forces. The first type is working for the benefit of the society, i.e., working, as they say, with the *right* hand. The second type is working evil on the individual and the community. It is said that this type is working with the left hand" (Condé 1992: 206). In the case of Haiti, vodou becomes an obstacle to collective liberation when those who work with the left hand preponderate. Dayan's reading would seem to challenge Taylor's search for the cause of vodou's dubious record in the narrative structure of the religion itself. Most likely we should look, instead, into the narrative structure of Haitian historical reality, a racialized and demonized nation within the confines of neocolonial, dependent capitalism. Ultimately, though, the characterization of vodou as a liberating faith in *Un arc-en-ciel* needs no other legitimation than Depestre's belief in the power of poetry to remake the world. The poet has at his disposal the authenticating power of metaphor.

Caribbean Gods Empowered

The power of metaphor allied with the poetic justice that Marxist revolutionary ideals encourage further equipped Depestre to manipulate the Haitian folk religion in a later work, written to commemorate the first anniversary of the death of Ernesto "Che" Guevara. Entitled *Cantate d'Octobre à la vie et à la mort du Commandant Ernesto Che Guevara*, the work reads as a devout account of the passion, the death, and the resurrection of the hero. Again combining dramatic techniques with lyric and narrative, the book tackles once more the mystical value of the number seven both in Christian and in non-Christian traditions. Seven are the parts of the poem and as many ("Lécher ses sept blessures" – To lick his seven wounds) the wounds inflicted on the hero by his killers (Depestre 1968: 13). In a highly lyrical dialogue by two minstrels, one male and the other female, and a chorus, a section called "Une atroce nouvelle arrive de la montagne" – An awful piece of news has come from the mountain, exposes us to the voices of a child, the Third World personified, Europe, and North America, all bewailing: "Ils ont tué notre Che!" – They have killed our Che (p. 15). We hear of the earthshaking impact produced throughout the world by the death of the revolutionary leader, described in the second part of the volume as a "Ulysse d'Amérique" – New World Ulysses – with the revolution as his Penelope and Cuba as his Ithaca (p. 16).

The text re-enacts the actions of Che and Fidel during the turbulent moments of the revolution, incorporating actual words from the published speeches of the two leaders. The conversants, including two sirens, in addition to the speakers already mentioned, represent the opposing forces of good and evil. Two distant voices, one African and the other Asian, highlight the heroic dimension of Che and Fidel, praising above all Che's enthusiastic dedication to the revolutionary cause: "Un seul feu habitait ses veines:/ Repartir vers d'autres guérillas de l'homme" – One sole fire ran through his veins:/To set out for humanity's other guerrillas (p. 25). The poem dramatizes Che's overcoming of the seductive voice of the "evil" siren, the one inviting him to remain in Ithaca (Cuba) enjoying the benefits of his precious toil, to continue his mission in other lands, a devotion which brought him to the mountains of Bolivia, where he met his death.

This characterization of Che derives much of its dramatic tension from the biographical details surrounding his departure from Cuba in 1966. Che had fought alongside Castro in the Sierra Maestra mountains of Cuba. After the revolutionary troops marched victoriously into Havana on January 2, 1959, he became a prominent member of the government. Born in Argentina, Che became a Cuban citizen, represented Cuba on many commercial missions and delegations abroad and headed many important ministries as well as other State institutions. In the autumn of 1966, after having dropped for a period out of public life, Che travelled to Bolivia, where he led a guerrilla group in the Santa Cruz region. On October 8, 1967, the Bolivian Army captured him and subsequently shot him to death ("Guevara, 'Che'" 1979). His farewell address on leaving Cuba evinces the degree of Che's devotion:

"I formally give up my duties in the leadership of the Party, my ministry, my rank of Commandant, my Cuban citizenship... Other lands of the world require the input of my modest efforts... In the new battlecamps I will carry with me... the sense of fulfilling the most sacred of duties: to fight against Imperialism wherever it might be... I leave to my children nothing material, and I am not sorry" (Guevara 1985: 697-98).

In Depestre's homage to Che the death of the revolutionary leader is presented as a relief to the "enemies of poetry", meaning the heads of state of the eighteen Latin American nations. The enactment of their self-congratulatory conversations with the Pentagon, via telegraph, appears as the third section of *Cantate*. The messages were intercepted, we hear, thanks to the supernaturally communicative power of poetry. This power enabled "une équipe de poètes latinoaméricains" – a team of Latin-American poets – to concoct a "sorte de radar spirituel" – sort of spiritual radar. Thus they have revealed the euphoria of Washington and the Latin-American right-wing governments with respect to the death of the guerilla leader. Their delight at their apparent victory becomes strident in "La danse des épées de la peur" – Dance of the Swords of Fear – the fourth part, evoking in the speaker the utmost abhorrence: "Comme ils se roulent par terre dans le sang/ de notre Che!" – How they roll in the ground with the blood of our Che! (p. 101). This indignation parallels that of devout Christian onlookers having to witness the profanity with which a bunch of salaried Roman soldiers play dice at the foot of the cross. Here it takes the insight of innocence, personified in a child, to apprehend the message of hope written by the revered dead: "Je vois que le Che est un matin/ Sans fin qui commence" – I see that Che is a morning/That begins endlessly (p. 117).

What follows in the sixth part, "Testament d'Ernesto Che Guevara", is a laudatory appraisal of the ideological and practical legacy of Che pronounced by the original minstrels and the chorus. The final part stages – using the resource of the Haitian pantheon – the effective apotheosis of the no longer human hero Their dialogue recalls the assembly of the gods in book XXIV of *The Iliad* where Zeus and the other Olympians discuss the fortune of Hector's murdered corpse (Homer 1951: 476-78). The loas of vodou, touched by the misfortune represented by Che's death, gather to discuss its meaning and its consequences for humanity. Each of the divinities, from Atibon-Legba to Ogou-Ferraille, sings the virtues and moans the loss of the revolutionary leader. After ascertaining the great love borne him by the peoples of the continent, they reach the consensus which is expressed by Ogou-Badagris: "Un nouveau loa vient de naître!" – A new loa has just been born (p. 79), announcing Che's ascension to the divine realm. Incited by the induction of the new loa, Ogou-Ferraille launches a self-recriminatory assessment of the way in which they, the vodou gods, have for long remained socially inactive, dishonouring their good record of past revolutionary involvement: "Nous ne sommes plus des loas debout comme à Vertières" – We are no longer loas in action as in Vertières (p. 153).

The reference to Vertières evokes the geographical setting of the decisive battle between the French army and the insurgent slaves on November 18, 1803, but also the name given to that historic battle in which the invading Napoleonic forces surrendered to the revolutionary troops led by the former slave, General Jean Jacques Dessalines (Depestre 1968: 158). Ogou-Ferraille's speech alludes to the role played by vodou worshippers in the victory that took place at Vertières. He concludes with the assurance that with Che as a member of the divine assembly the loas will regain their place in social action. They, once more, will play their part in influencing the course of history in the Americas: "Le Che est un cri végétal. C'est ce qu'on entendra/ lorsque tous les arbres d'Amérique se mettront ensemble/ à pousser des cris de guerre!" – Che is a cry of nature. We shall hear it/When all of America's trees will join together/in screaming war-cries (p. 153). Through Che's emergence as a new loa, the vodou gods will overcome their "fossilization" and undergo a "rebirth" in the "popular spirit of resistance and rebellion" which the Haitian folk religion expressed in revolutionary days (Levilain 1983: 189). As the *Cantate* concludes, with its wealth of lyrical effects and the sustained thread of intertwined pathos and hope, one is left with the impression that Che, having after death ascended to the divine realm, is now capable of waging a more effective war against the forces of evil than when he lived among the mortals.

Cantate consolidates Depestre's fusion of socialist teleology with religious imagery and symbology. Above all, he asserts in an overt manner the harmony between his radical humanism and the cultural specificity of his subject matter, ingrained in political and spiritual circumstances deriving from the Caribbean milieu. He shows that the regional particularity of the content of his poetry need not rob it of its claim to universality in keeping with the words of a compatriot and comrade: "all cultures are equally capable of renewing the sense of beauty in the eyes of all humans" (Alexis 1965: 262). For the same reason, Depestre applauds the project of poets like Langston Hughes whose work seeks to record in depth the plight of black Americans. He finds that, in focusing on "the tragedy of his people, which is a human tragedy of our times", Hughes possesses "the feeling of the universal brotherhood of people and things" (1966: 186). The comment is not casual. Hughes had needed to reckon with the all too frequent charge that black American poetry lacked "universality" in so far as it drew almost exclusively on the plight of blacks (Hughes 1971: 175). Clearly for Depestre the subject matter of *Cantate*, which glorifies the exploits of a Caribbean hero, speaks about the human condition beyond borders and times.

Toward a Socialist Negritude

From the time of the publication of "El que no tiene Congo", a short story chronicling the drama of a Haitian immigrant facing and eventually overcoming racism in Cuba (Depestre 1967b), Depestre took to writing mostly fiction and essays aimed initially at explaining the local milieu by tracing the origins of present conditions and exploring and suggesting possibilities for the future. His prose largely supplements and, consequently, serves as a gloss for his verse. His collection of essays, *Pour la révolution, pour la poésie*, published first in Spanish in 1969, devotes the majority of its pages to an examination, poetical and political, of the present reality of the Third World. The study of Haiti takes a special place here with particular emphasis on the liberation movement whose triumph on November 28, 1803 marked, he suggests, a movement of moral ascendancy "for blacks as well as for whites" (Depestre 1974: 33). Delving into the historical depths of Haitian reality, he has occasion to dissect the notion of "négritude" which he accepts as "a concrete awakening towards oppression" but rejects any essentialist attribution to racial characteristics used to define a major portion of humanity (p. 65). He discards the essentialist branch of the concept as a dangerous notion which can be used, as Duvalier used it, to the detriment of blacks themselves. He affirms that the Negritude upheld by Duvalier "is nothing but an Antillean form of Fascism, a totalitarian neo-racism whose main victims are the millions of black peasants and black workers of Haiti" (p. 69).

Rejecting the attitude that "encloses the black man in his blackness and the white in his whiteness", which he detects in the approach of the Belgian literary scholar Lilyan Kesteloot, Depestre finds value in Sartre's position in *Orphée noir* that négritude must transcend itself to become a global cry for universal humanism (p. 79). This means that it must transcend colour and race and embrace the universalist ideas of the revolution: "The new black Orpheus will be revolutionary or it will not be at all" (p. 88). The poet upholds the conviction that black liberation is nothing but a component of a larger pursuit from which it cannot be extricated, namely human liberation. His heroes, therefore, may come from any corner of the globe where people are fighting to assert their humanity. This explains Depestre's perception of the struggle of Ho Chi Minh in Viet Nam as directed "against all the injustices of his country and of the world" (p. 108). The sort of ethnic self-assertion visible in the ideas informing Négritude, Pan Arabism, African Personality, the Harlem Renaissance, and others of what he calls "ideologies of decolonization" has for Depestre an important value only initially, in playing their fundamental role of "cultural marooning", but certainly not as an end in itself (p. 114). These affirmations clearly explain the "contre-negritude" attributed to Depestre by Souffrant (1978: 155).

Third World intellectuals, artists or thinkers, are for Depestre individuals engaged tirelessly in the search for an authentic cultural identity for their people. Their work, in this sense, "yearns for a human totality, like the masses, like the revolution that connects them up with the doubly disalienating circuit of particularity and universality" (Depestre 1974: 133). As we can gather from these words, an affirmation of ethnic or regional values will not succeed without the global liberation of mankind, which will come only through the vehicle of revolution. This conviction leads him to propose a modified version of the Cartesian "cogito" in these terms: "I make the revolution; therefore, I am; therefore, we are" (p. 132). Making no separation between moral and artistic goals, he applauds the work of writers who, in his view, have advanced the cause of human liberation, hence his celebration of the message of hope in the work of Eluard and his regret that Breton, who contributed tremendously to the "emancipation of poetry", did not transcend the purely artistic revolution (pp. 255, 213). The terms in which Depestre praises certain Western authors do not differ essentially from his appreciation of, say, Aimé Césaire whose work contains "the good law of tenderness and generosity and human compassion" (p. 156). This by no means minimizes the specific socio-historical condition of Caribbean people or denies their condition of double alienation. For he concedes that to advance the cause of humanity in the region means, first of all, to break free from colonial or neocolonial bonds in the local context. He welcomes the decolonizing thrust of Caribbean literature, among other things, for its role as a literature of identification (Depestre 1972: 23). But he also proposes that this decolonizing search for an authentic identity cannot be divorced from the more global liberating ideals of socialism, for, as he would put it later, there is no decolonization, if it is not a socialist one (Depestre 1975: 100).

The Politics of Caribbean Theogonies

Caribbean people appear in the work of Depestre in charge of a double mission of liberation. On the one hand, they must assert their socio-cultural specificity (particularité), and, on the other, they must remain crusaders for the good of global humanity (universalité). The characters from his fiction generally appear involved in circumstances which reveal the complexity of living between competing cultural traditions. Alain, the main character from "Roséna dans la montagne", one of the stories in his collection *Alléluia pour une femme-jardin*, is a young Haitian who hopes to find in the priesthood "the only way to attract the attention of Christ toward a land without tenderness and consolation" (Depestre 1973: 10). This leads him to seek the tutelage and the reputed wisdom of Father James Mulligan, an Irish missionary in Haiti. But he is more enlightened, however, by the folk wisdom of the exuberant Roséna

Rezel who awakens him to the license of his own Haitian deities: "And our loas, who are also gods, why do they make love," she asks (p. 20). He then recognizes that Father Mulligan's Christianity entails a rigid repression that outlaws sexual intercourse. Reconciled with the legitimacy of his own local pantheon, Alain rejoices in his discovery of sex. The two lovers are then violently confronted by the priest who wants to chastise them for succumbing to the demands of the flesh. They end up castrating Father Mulligan, after which they abandon the house of Christian worship, escaping presumably into the freedom of their own spiritual world (p. 42).

Alain becomes liberated through an affirmation of his particularity. The characters in the other stories, including the title story "Alléluia pour une femme-jardin" privilege the Haitian milieu socio-culturally and historically, generally evoking also the "real geography" of the Caribbean region (Brahimini-Chapuis and Belloc 1986: 233). But the tension between conflicting cultural matrices occurs even when the action of the story takes place outside the Caribbean. Olivier Vermont, the main character in "Mémoires du géolibertinage", is a Haitian student in Paris who achieves a partial liberation by radically distinguishing himself from Western values. He reduces the Christian West to "a desert of evil, hypocrisy, and bestiality" that has thrived on plundering other cultures and has consequently turned the narrator himself into "a zombi among one thousand five hundred millions of other zombies in Asia, Africa, and Latin America" (Depestre 1973: 92). In this case, however, the descent into the spiritual depths of his cultural self, achieved while in a sort of trance, does not culminate in effective liberation. Having tasted the experience of justice and absolute freedom, led by a vodou deity to the absorption of the energizing power hidden in the female sex, he awakens to the realization that his descent has not changed the imminence of his social reality. The text closes with a reflexion on the weakness of the narrator's "humble gods of underdevelopment" (p. 113).

Depestre's first novel, *Le mât de cocagne*, more sharply than any of his previous works, dramatizes a Caribbean theogony with implications for Third World intellectuals who, vexed by the complexity of their conflicting heritages, must strive to recognize a cultural fountain of their own to pursue their liberation. *Le mât de cocagne*, published by Editions Gallimard in 1979, appeared first in Spanish translation as *El palo ensebado*, published in Havana (1975). An English version, based on the Paris edition, exists under the title *The Festival of the Greasy Pole* (1990). In the interest of remaining faithful to the chronology of Depestre's stages we should refer throughout this discussion to the Havana edition as reprinted in Santo Domingo in 1977. The Gallimard version, as the United States translator notes, differs from the early Spanish text in significant ways. For "the version eventually published in France" Depestre undertook to eliminate "the more cumbersome indices of the historical reality behind the action in order to achieve greater 'dramatic intensity'" (Coates 1990: xxxiv). Put more directly, the Haitian author "reduced the amount of detail and, perhaps, of cultural baggage expected of the reader, in favour of creating narrative economy in his ironic recreation of 'Papadocracy'" (p. xxxvii-xxxviii).

This bibliographical history of Depestre's first novel is important because it shows the author by 1979, the year after abandoning Cuba, already engaged in the process of accommodating the rendition of his native culture to the needs of a Western readership. In discussing the novel by Maryse Condé *Traversée de la mangrove* (1989), the Martinican writer Patrick Chamoiseau criticized the effort of cultural translation as a gesture that smacked of the effacement of the native public. He says, "all the footnotes that explain what we already know make us think, dear Maryse, that you are not addressing us, but some other people... How can we construct our own literature if we fail to speak profoundly to ourselves, if, at the very moment of writing, we address another people, another culture, other needs" (Chamoiseau 1991: 394). Whether or not one deems Chamoiseau's opinion too severe, his words point to the relationship of literary artists to their home public and its implication for cultural authenticity. Depestre's reworking of *Le mât de cocagne* to make it more accessible to the Parisian reader probably begins to announce the epistemological break that would become evident in his production during the latter half of the 1980s.

At any rate, when Depestre wrote the original version of *Le mât de cocagne*, he was free of the compulsion to translate the Caribbean world to the French, and since the Spanish edition reflects the aesthetic development and the ideological mindset of the author at the time, its use in our discussion here accords with the chronological approach we have favoured in this study. In the novel Henri Postel, the main character, must choose one of three equally perplexing alternatives. He could passively submit to the "zombification" to which the ONEDA, the centre of power of the totalitarian regime of Doctor Zoocrate Zacharie, has subjected him on account of his former opposition to the government when he was a senator. He could secretly travel to Canada, thus escaping the mentally and physically crippling effect of his compulsory job as the grocer of "Noah's Ark", a retail store designed by the "onedozoocratie" for the express purpose of stifling in him any potential for rebellion. Or he could confront the frightful machinery of the tyrannical state, a thinly disguised representation of Papa Doc's Haiti, with all the danger that this option would entail.

Postel opts to defy the government as this seems the only really meaningful option. For that he undertakes a systematic reappraisal of his ideological baggage, the result of his formal training in Political Science at the Sorbonne, in the context of the discrete socio-cultural characteristics of his people. He resolves to join a popular competition ("le mât de cocagne"), a public amusement consisting of climbing a greased pole with a prize attached to the top. His involvement in an event that generally catered only to the lowest strata of the population results in the perception by the grass roots of his country (labourers, artisans, domestics, employed and unemployed) that his gesture is somehow interpretive of their aspirations (Depestre 1977: 211). But, most importantly, he comes to terms with the fact that the people who rally with him, chiefly Sor Cisafleur, Horace Vermont, and Elisa are fervent believers in vodou, a "superstition" of which his advanced French education has made him sceptical. After reflecting on the relative merit of racial affirmation in the history of his country, marking the evolution from a time when "everything was white: God, his money, his ideas, his sword, his commandments" to the time when God could be black or mulatto, he agrees to yield to the treatment prepared by the Priestess of Erzuli to exorcise the lethal diabolic spell which a government ally has cast upon him (1977: 150-56). It is also through the service of the "vaudouisants" that he recovers from his physical decrepitude. In contact with the flesh of the sensuous Eliza – which for him functions "as a marvellous blood transfusion" – Postel rediscovers his long dormant sexual vigour (p. 170).

Even if Postel does not quite believe in vodou, he does undoubtedly benefit from it since "his followers and administrators" do believe in and derive strength from it (Metellus 1979: 12). He needs to rationalize his acceptance of their service, but this contributes decisively to his final redemption. At the end of the novel, Postel, cheered by the grass-roots crowd and with his newly acquired strength, reaches the top of the greased pole. There he finds a gun which he at once fires at Clovis Barbotog and other government officials who have come to the competition to see him defeated and buried as the people's last gesture of opposition to the "onedozoocratie". Postel's violent act, followed immediately by his death, fuels the population's dormant desire for freedom, resulting in a three-day-long bloody combat between the government forces and the people. His death notwithstanding and whatever may be the eventual result of the battle, Postel obeys his "commande sociale" by warding off his own "zombification" and inciting the people to combat theirs.

Postel embodies the plight of the Caribbean intellectual who must embrace the spiritual baggage of his local culture in order to authenticate himself vis-a-vis the postulates of the official culture which has cast the "universal human being" in a purely Eurocentric dye, to echo words written elsewhere by Depestre (1980: 40). Postel, like Depestre, lives in a world in which he is forced to recognize the need to assert the humanity of his people. Having been robbed historically of his "psychological integrity" and his "most secret beauties of human being", he can only assert himself by utilizing his self-affirmation as a weapon against the cultural or ideological power structure responsible for his sad state of "zombification". That the neocolonial political structure of Dr. Zacharie's regime derives much of its strength from its association with Western capitalist powers, together with the use of henchmen who work "with the left hand" in their dealings with the invisible forces, accentuates the parallel's with the Duvalier dictatorship.

Speaking of intellectual activity, Depestre has described the principal Caribbean authors as maroons vis-à-vis Western culture (1972: 27). Postel is clearly one such maroon. But, as we have said before, Depestre did not believe that self-affirmation alone would suffice to bring about the desired "de-zombification". For this reason, his hero does not stop at a fervent embrace of the autochthonous culture of the uneducated masses or by surrendering to the spiritual services of the native religion. He also takes his rebellion to the tangible arena of social action, directly contributing to the effective awakening, at least momentarily, of the masses. In the revolutionary significance of his martyrdom, the protagonist in *Le mât de cocagne* achieves a moral victory comparable to that of Che in *Cantate*.

Saint Eros and Revolution

Eight years after *Cantate*, Depestre published another volume of poetry that restates the major thematic strands of *Le mât de cocagne*: religion, love, poetry, and revolution. Entitled *Poète à Cuba* (1976), the volume, in its very structure, begins to reflect a dialogical interaction among the ideological and literary values once cherished by the poet. This seems to foreshadow his rethinking of previously held ideals which in later work will be highlighted, suppressed, or recast. The first section of this three-part volume, "Images d'une anti-autobiographie", consists of poems primarily exploring childhood and the relationship of the poet to his craft. The second part, significantly titled "Evangile selon Saint Eros", comprises a series of texts singing the "gospel" of love against a general background of popular religion. Love is first concretized in the grandeur of women: "Comme les anges par les nuits/ De pluie pleureraient/ Comme les dieux vieilliraient vite/ Si la femme n'existait pas" – How the angels at night/Would weep showers of tears/How the gods would age/If woman did not exist" (Depestre 1976: 79). The valuation of the female half of humanity, religiously inspired, occasionally borrows from the language of prayer: "Bonjour Notre-Dame de la pluie/ Notre-Dame du feu bonjour!/ Femme rafraîchissante..." – Good day Our Lady of the rain/Our Lady of fire good day!/Revitalizing woman (p. 89).

The love of women in *Poète a Cuba* is objectified through the necessary vehicle of sex but within an atmosphere of spiritual devoutness and a tone of religious elevation. "Magie au Moulin d'Ande", for example, recounts an erotic encounter with Anne, a woman whose supreme beauty and sensuality enables the speaker to see God. Likewise, in "Vatican VII", the speaker narrates his sexual intercourse with Sister Teresa, "une petite soeur de charité" – a little sister of charity (p. 97), whose sanctity elevated their carnal union to a ceremony of religious worship. As one would expect of Depestre, the celebration of love through women and the carnal union of the couple is linked with revolution as the means of human liberation and, consequently, as the ultimate expression of love: "Ton fusil dans une main/ Ton droit à l'orgasme dans l'autre/ Cours nu vers le soleil/ Lève tes barricades/ Fais ta revolution" – Your gun in one hand/Your right to orgasm in the other/Run naked toward the sun/Raise your barricades/Make your revolution (p. 94). The text exudes an effort to reconcile the sense of self-denial implicit in the fight for revolution in a world ruled by the capitalist order of the Christian West, with an absolute and almost anarchic freedom for the body.

Poète à Cuba lends itself to a discussion of the relationship between literature and politics in the context of revolution. Depestre had participated in one such discussion with a distinguished group of Cuban and Latin American intellectuals that included the poet Roque Dalton, the novelist Edmundo Desnoes, and the essayist Roberto Fernández Retamar. Their reflections later appeared in book form as *El intelectual y la sociedad* (1969). Depestre's remarks on that occasion stand out because he, while still very much committed to the revolution, daringly argued that literature does not have "a pedagogical end", and that it has, therefore, "no direct power over the masses as, for example, journalism and political oratory do" (Dalton, et al. 1988: 69). He contended that "the relationship between literature and revolution is very complex, and neither literature nor revolution has ever gained from attempts to simplify it", emphasizing also that literature "does not only have immediate social goals" (Dalton et al. 1988: 70-71, 74). Depestre placed a strong emphasis on the notion that literature communicates by means of different strategies from those employed by the Party and its leaders to disseminate the teachings of the revolution. "Literature has recourse to images, symbols, allegories, dreams, that are not reducible to the revolutionary ideology," he insisted (Dalton et al. 1988: 86).

Perhaps the farthest in spirit from Depestre among the participants in the conversation was Desnoes for his willingness to admit that the idea that "in Cuba there existed an absolute freedom of unrestrained expression" was "an illusion" (Dalton et al. 1988: 26). He qualified the possibility of freedom to the exigencies of a society in the process of recreating itself for the benefit of the collective. He stated: "Freedom is conditioned by the revolution… It is not an individual but a social freedom; not the affirmation of my freedom against society but for society" (Dalton et al. 1985: 27). One can see that Desnoes diverged slightly from Depestre who, convinced that literary discourse behaved differently from pedagogical discourse, would seem to conceive of no limits to what one could express. *Poète à Cuba*, where one can read such lines as "Je ne serai pas un cocu du socialisme/L'Etat, c'est moi, je baise donc je suis" – I will not be Socialism's cuckold;/I am the State; I get laid, therefore I am, clearly trod delicate ground and may be taken as libertine assertion of individuality against state authority. Indeed, Depestre evidently incurred state displeasure by his ideological provocation against established norms in Cuban society. Years later he would bitterly recall that the Central Committee of the Cuban Communist Party asked him to make changes in the manuscript. "I would not accept the automutilation imposed by these police of dreams," he has said, explaining that he opted to publish the book in France instead (Dayan 1993: 138-39). The conflict around the publication of *Poète à Cuba* underscored a conceptual tension between Depestre and the Cuban authorities, foreshadowing his final departure from the island in 1978.

But, for the most part, *Poète à Cuba* continues to advance Depestre's socialist creed. The last third of the volume reworks in verse many of the aesthetic positions delineated in his book of essays *Pour la révolution, pour la poésie*. Suggestively titled "Poésie et Révolution", this section generally insists on the value of poetry as a means to bring about the new dawn of man, a concept which he had upheld consistently since his response to Césaire two decades before. He condemns poets whose verse is devoid of social meaning especially since, in his view, our times so much need their commitment. In "Un appel aux poètes d'Europe" (An appeal to European poets), dedicated to Régis Debray, he advises contemporary European poets to assume such a committed role, since: "Notre époque est un enfant abandonné/ A la porte de chaque véritable poète" – Our age is a child abandoned/At the door of every true poet (Depestre 1976: 127). The poem's conclusion suggests that poets have a responsibility for the course our world should take and that they must embrace the cause of revolution to prove worthy of their art.

Illustrative of Depestre's view of the necessary relationship of poets to their history is "Ruben Dario: entre cygne et fusil", a poem that assesses and possibly updates the aesthetic preferences of the well-known Nicaraguan poet. The speaker conjures the presence of Dario to sit at the table with Fidel. The Cuban leader enlightens the venerable poet with these words: "l'Amérique aux yeux tristes/ cherche comme Cuba le vent et la mer libre" – Sad-eyed America/Seeks like Cuba the wind and the sea of freedom (p. 151). Dario, the most outstanding exponent of Modernismo in Hispanic America, was distinguished by his socially detached aestheticism. Many of his books, influenced by the French Symbolists and Parnassians, draw substantially from Western and Oriental mythology, showing a predilection for what is distant geographically as well as temporally. His detachment from his immediate historical reality was clear in pronouncements such as these: "Is there perchance in my veins a drop of African blood, or of Chorotega or Nagrandano Indian? Perhaps, despite my marquis' hands. But in these my poems you will find princesses, kings, imperial grandeur, visions of distant or impossible countries. What else could I do? I despise the life and the time in which it was my lot to live" (Darío 1977: 180). Darío's outlook is exemplified in "Sonatina", the poem specifically alluded to in Depestre's text. Having been brought to the present and put in contact with the current situation of the continent, Depestre's Darío lays down the socio-historical despondency that is symbolized in the image of the swan. As a result, "Il fait que le cygne et le fusil/ Se changent en une même étoile" – He causes the swan and the gun/To fuse into one sole star, achieving thus the aesthetic unity of poetry and revolution (Depestre 1976: 151). Depestre also acknowledges other poets who have accomplished the desired unity successfully and of their own accord, such as Alejo Carpentier, Nicolás Guillén, and Roque Dalton, who are celebrated in the last section of the book.

Toward a Gospel of Poetry

Depestre left Cuba in September 1978 in the company of his Cuban wife, Nelly Campano whom he had married fifteen years before, as well as his two sons Paul-Allain and Stephan (Couffon 1986: 67). He had spent in Cuba the "most interesting" years of his life and "without a doubt the most fertile" period for his poetry, as he himself reports to Couffon (1986: 60). The departure from Cuba – a break "without anger" according to Couffon (p. 82) – marks a clear transition in the intellectual and ideological leanings of Depestre's work. His insistence on the positive social value of poetry in the last third of *Poètè a Cuba* remains, but with amplified devotion and decreased political militancy in the volume of verse *En état de poésie* (1980), a book that appeared while Depestre served in the UNESCO secretariat in Paris. The small book contains a sedate and meditative rephrasing of his faith in the medium of poetry. Far from limiting it to the domain of a literary craft, he describes poetry as an all-embracing spiritual condition, the "poetic condition" alluded to in the title: "le seul état de la vie qui permet de marcher pieds nus sur des kilomètres de braises et de tessons ou de traverser à dos de requin un bras de mer en furie" – the only mental state that enables us, barefoot, to walk over miles of live charcoal and broken glass or to cross a violent sea riding on a shark (Depestre 1980: 9). A state which "est commun à tous les hommes" – common to all humans – and is guided by an unbending sense of justice, the poetic condition does not hesitate to protest and oppose human oppression (p. 11). Thus, it will naturally cry: "Haro sur l'apartheid radoteur et physiquement armé!" – Down with apartheid, senile and physically armed! (p. 14), its ultimate aim being the triumph of "tendresse" (tenderness) among us all (p. 25).

The predominant devotional attitude combines a global cry for human tenderness with the exploration of Caribbean and Third World difference. The "moi", represented here in the character of Caliban (p. 18), is opposed to the "ils" of the Christian West, which is the object of an indictment in "Christ and Co" (p. 39). The speaker condemns the West, as in *Un arc-en-ciel*, for its legacy of destruction: "La culture occidentale/ offre au monde/ sa dernière conquête: la bombe à neutrons" – Western culture/offers to the world/its latest achievement:/the Neutron bomb (p. 51). This leaves Third World people with the alternative that had been encouraged by Césaire in the poetic epistle of a quarter-century before. They must assert their difference: "Me voici/ Caliban/ l'homme-four de la Caraïbe" – Here I am/ Caliban/furnaceman of the Caribbean, and embrace the natural rebellion of their people, maroons by socio-historical necessity: "Nous buvons chantons dansons rions/ nous marronnons au four le temps/ de Prospéro!" – We drink we sing we dance we laugh/we maroon Prospero's time to ashes (p. 34).

The tension between the apparently antithetical cultural poles of the Caribbean and the West is resolved in the harmonizing power of poetry, which allows one to speak of humanity in general while narrating the drama of oneself. Thus the speaker declares his solidarity with the species with this conviction: "ma joie est de savoir que toi est moi/ et que moi je suis fortement toi" – my joy comes from knowing that you are me/and that me, I am inexorably you (p. 28). One recalls Victor Hugo's reassurance to his reader in *Les contemplations* (1856), a book in which the poet speaks constantly of himself, that though referring to himself he was speaking of them also: "Alas! When I speak to you of me, I speak to you of you. How could you not see that? Oh! foolish ones, who think that I am not you!" (Hugo 1922: 6). Depestre's radical humanism, his universal solidarity with the members of the species, combines with an evocation of nature in *En état de poésie* that remains recognizably Caribbean. Guava, mango, tamarind, and other tropical trees in the text bespeak the environment of the poet's native city (Depestre 1980: 30). In its assertion of the Antillean particular, the book champions its elevation to the human universal. Thus, in "Rage de vivre" the speaker, undertaking a mental voyage back to his early childhood in Jacmel, evokes the local image of: "un amandier/ où je découvre enfin la rage et l'art de vivre/ tout près de l'ordre esthétique des grands arbres" – an almond-tree/where I at last discover the fury and the art of living/very near the aesthetic order of the great trees (p. 32). These lines imply that the regional peculiarity of the Haitian milieu partakes of the universal in the "aesthetic order", an idea that accords with the poet's notion of radical humanism, as discussed above, which *En état de poésie* upholds further through the preaching of a transracial faith, "profession de foi transraciale" (p. 54), and the harmonizing of Caribbean self-recognition with the call for global human tenderness. Human tenderness appears as the only pursuit worthy of the initiated into the poetic condition. The spiritual attitude of the true poet entails an unbending commitment to the cause of humanity. Only with such a stance can one call oneself truly a poet, since: "On est poète/ quand on a des pieds/ à donner sans repos/ aux bonnes nouvelles/ de la tendresse" – One is a poet/When one submits one's whole self/restlessly/to the good tidings/of tenderness (p. 58).

En état de poésie draws many of the ingredients of its discourse from a metaphorical access to a higher sphere of knowledge. The vocabulary, the images, and predominant symbols endow the speaking voice with a claim to an invisible reality, one that goes beyond the ordinarily human. Poetry in this volume turns into an avenue of contact with the sacred. Throughout Depestre's previous work the sacred makes its presence felt in diverse ways. Admirable characters are sanctified either by means of liturgical practices similar to Christian ceremonies or by associating them with divine beings of Christian or non-Christian origin. Divine beings make their appearance and engage in human affairs, assisting in the social transformations which the poet deems essential. When they remain indifferent, they appear anyway and suffer the poet's indictment. Referring regularly to the elements of vodou, the poet imagines a universe in which divinities share the aspirations of the people and seem to orient their actions along the lines of socialist ideals. The gods come down to earth, and revered human beings rise, like the Greek Herakles, to the level of divinities. Radical humanism, the desire for a new Eden devoid of all social injustice, the belief in revolution as the inexorable means to the Summun Bonum for the future of our species, and the sanctification of carnal love, are all underlined by the spiritual imperative that shapes the voice of an increasingly devout speaker in poem after poem. With *En état de póesie* Depestre forges a speaker who has attained a further level of anointment, a "poetic condition" that appears as a prerequisite for advancing the global cause of humanity, a creed that can best be described as an ardent gospel of poetry.

Throughout his oeuvre, as ought to have become apparent by now, Depestre presents us with a world in which the intangible acquires cultural, historical, and political reality. Theoretically he has justified this poetic usage in his response to Claude Roy's preface to *Poète à Cuba*. There he argues, en passant, that the revolutionary poet, "someone who burns with reality, truth, imaginariness", need not be confined to the immediately tangible to express the complexity of perceptions. Instead, the poet "must explore the real and the imaginary together, according to social need and individual desire" (Depestre 1976: 20). In fact, he has come to suggest that an artistic representation of Haitian reality will necessarily convey the interpretation of the natural and the supernatural, that quality which Alejo Carpentier in the preface to *El reino de este mundo* (1949) described as the country's "sortilège" (Carpentier 1984: 76) The last pages of Depestre's *Bonjour et adieu à la négritude*, a collection of essays, reconfirm his view of this wondrous aspect of his native land (Depestre 1981: 237-46). Consisting basically of revised versions of essays published earlier, this book tenaciously retains his all-embracing humanism, holding on to what a reviewer has termed "the right to his difference in and through his identity" (Cortanze 1981).

A Gendered Vision of the Magical

Writing in the *UNESCO Courier*, Depestre once emphasized the peculiar spiritual characteristics of the Haitian milieu, describing his native soil as possessing a "bewitched reality" which allows for the interpretation and commingling of "the natural and the supernatural, the picaresque, the erotic, the ineffable, the absurd, the comic, the magical and the entrancing" (Depestre 1979: 29). Haitian literary artists, therefore, cannot overlook the seductive attraction of the spiritual richness encircling their world. Indeed, the swiftest glance at Haitian letters would show a constant fascination with the invisible from the nineteenth century to the present. Depestre's own attempt at surveying Haitian letters traces its origins to the creole oral chants of the slaves and their folk narratives embedded in "the rich vodou mythology" (Depestre 1971a: 318). It is noticeable, though, that Depestre's overview of literary production in his native land makes no mention of even one female author during the 164 years of Haitian literature that he purports to chronicle. Another overview in which he sets out to discuss the literature of Guadeloupe and Martinique also omits reference to the work of Antillean women writers with the exception of Mayotte Capécia, whose *Je suis martiniquaise* he cites as "the ultimate expression of a woman's alienation", illustrative of how far "a woman could go to escape from her skin, to be a French woman of colour" (Depestre 1971b: 348-49).

Clearly, Depestre's rendition of Francophone Caribbean letters did not concede to women an active role as producers of discourse or protagonists of change. His overviews, articulated in 1968, certainly evince the conviction that the revolutionary struggle would bring about a deracialized vision of literature and culture. He holds on to the ideal of a transracial, decolonized conception of artistic and cultural production even after he ceased to espouse the dogma of revolution. Speaking in Japan as a spokesperson of UNESCO in the 1984 meeting of PEN CLUB International, he would still sustain "the contingency of the local and the singular" as crucial to the formation of a "planet-wide consciousness" and would fervently advance the necessary recognition of "endogenous creativity" as prerequisite for the development of any true literary exchange internationally (Depestre 1986a: 25, 1986b: 158). But he fell short of aspiring to a degendered understanding of literature and culture, which becomes a disconcerting omission especially for a writer committed to the exploration of the sacred, which in the Caribbean is a spiritual space occupied equally by males and females.

Condé fittingly picked Tituba, a female character, to dramatize "the clash between two belief systems: the slaves' animistic and positive sorcery, one which is the product of the right hand…, and the European belief in malevolent sorcery" (Manzor-Coats 1993: 741). Condé herself has explained her character portrayal by reference to the inextricable connection between woman and the sacred in the region: "I wanted to turn Tituba into a folk heroine of the West Indies, and as you know, the folk heroines from our region are healers. I gave her a power that perhaps she did not have in reality" (Clark 1989: 129). In that respect, a consideration of Depestre's overlooking the presence of women in the region's letters and his relegating women to a secondary, sexual role in his texts would lead us to concur with women scholars who have objected to his "implied attitude to woman". One can hardly deny that he reduces woman metaphorically to a "half-acre of bush to be captured. The literal meaning of *femme-jardin* is an exploitative one: the woman a man keeps in useful proximity to fields cultivated in scattered locations" (Jones 1981: 29). But Haiti alone provides ample illustration of women's involvement with literary production and their concern with the sacred. Virginie Sampeur (1839-1899), Haiti's first-known female literary artist, wrote mostly verse and is thought to have burned most of her writings at the end of her life (Charles 1980: 26, 72). But one of her few extant short fiction pieces, "A Drama" (1898), deals precisely with a couple whose wedding has a tragic end as a result of the vengeful intervention of a woman "who specialized in sorcery" (Sampeur 1993: 59).

The work of Marie Vieux Chauvet (1916-1973), one of the most accomplished fiction writers in the history of Haitian literature, invariably touches on the spiritual options available to her characters on the Haitian soil. Lotus, the mulatto woman who is the main character in *Fille d'Haiti*, finds herself inadvertently and progressively moving towards a close identification with vodou practices. Her maid Gertrude alerts her to instances when she appears to be possessed by the loa and her behaving in a manner that anyone might take her for a *mambo* (the name given to vodou priestesses, the name hougan being reserved for the men) (Chauvet 1954: 90). Chauvet's *Le danse sur le volcan* (1957), which appeared in English as *Dance on the Volcano* (1959), in its recreation of the life of two women who lived in Saint-Domingue in the late eighteenth century, allows a passing glimpse of the role of vodou as "a powerful force in the hands of the *maroon* leaders, a stimulant that could revive the strength of the most resigned and defeated slaves" (Chauvet 1959: 42).

A light-skinned middle-class woman from a prestigious family, Chauvet had the sort of refined education that would not foster an identification with the religion of the folk. Therein may lie the reason why her characters normally have to discover vodou. *Fonds des Nègres* (1960) dramatizes the poverty suffered by Haitian peasants as perceived by Marie-Ange Louisius who has come from the capital and identifies with their plight. The city girl eyes the peasant's vodou worship with scepticism, even linking their misery to their superstitious contemplation, but when she attends a vodou ceremony, she discovers that: "The drums lured her. Their beat ran through her blood, through her flesh" (Chauvet 1960: 4, 157). Similarly, Claire, the rich planter's daughter in the first part of *Amour, colère et folie* (1968), grew up thinking of vodou as "a shameful religion practiced only by the poor", only to discover that her father "serves the loas too" and that he expects her to do the same, against the advice of her Christian mentor Father Paul (Chauvet 1968: 116-18). The same theme of self-discovery through the discovery of the world of the tonelles by a young light-skinned woman of the middle class is also present in George Lamming's novel, *Season of Adventure* (1960). Depestre's sense of Haiti's "bewitched reality", then, informs the writings of many of his female compatriots, as the references to Sampeur and Chauvet should suggest. Even so, a patriarchal ideology prevented him from seeing that women, too, had to contribute to the exploration of the peculiar reality in his native land that gave rise to a unique kind of art, the uniqueness that he recognised in Haitian painters whom he calls "great itinerant loas of joy and pain" (Depestre 1984: 36).

His masculinist worldview notwithstanding, throughout his oeuvre, Depestre has presented us with a divine order that takes sides, one in which deities are maroons engaged in the same campaign of resistance that the poet himself has championed in most of his works. In his work, as in that of many Caribbean writers, we do not witness the death of God but rather the metamorphosis of the Western God into the historically conscious gods of the Third World. This connects powerfully to the work of Kamau Brathwaite on the "death of god" as a symptom of western mercantilist nihilism in contrast to the survival of the gods of Africa amongst those who were mercantalism's victims (Brathwaite, 2013). For Depestre, a god cannot appropriately protect both the oppressor and the oppressed. At various points Depestre's metaphorical cosmos implies a certain complicity between the Christian God and Western Capitalism in despoiling the countries which we have come to call "underdeveloped." Such a divine favoritism, as manifested in the actions of the Church, the institutional representation of God on earth, gives the impression that God's allegiance has been to the colonizer and not to the colonized. Thus the poet opts to explore the possibility of a spiritual realm which advocates the cause of the disinherited. Just as the Hebrews of the *Old Testament* call on their own

God, "the God of Jacob", to deliver them from their Egyptian captivity, so Depestre, like many other Caribbean artists, calls upon a divine order that he can consider his own to embrace the revolutionary cause which will eventually bring about equality among humans within and without the Third World. However, as we move into the next stage of his literary trajectory, we see Depestre lessening the emphasis on the role of the sacred in mediating social relations on the earth.

Depolitization of the Gods

As we examine Depestre's literary production since *En état de poésie*, with a focus on the position of the sacred, few features will seem so striking as the virtual depolitization of the vodou gods. The definition of the Haitian religion offered by the writer in one of his latest glossaries renders it as "an agrarian cult that plays in Haitian society the same role as that of pagan cults in ancient societies; it comprises a rich mythology" (Depestre 1988: 195). This definition ceases to privilege the elements of political dissidence, cultural resistance, *marronnage*, and affirmation of human identity, which had been consistently associated with Haitian vodou in the glossaries that appear in *Un arc-en-ciel*, *Cantate*, and *Le mât de cocagne*. Writing by then in his late sixties, Depestre seemed to have undergone a profound ideological transformation. The two volumes of verse that appeared under his name after *En état de poésie* are essentially anthology selections of his earlier poetic work. *Journal d'un animal marin: Choix de poèmes 1956-1990* gathers selected texts from seven of his volumes of verse. Restating the title of his 1964 book, the collection provides, in the words of a reviewer, "an excellent introduction to the work of the great Haitian poet" (Linkhorn 1992: 852). One might regret, however, the absence in the anthology of a good many poems from the early volumes. The only eight previously unpublished poems included in the collection are telling as documents of the poet's reconciliation with his condition of permanent exile (Depestre 1990: 103-18). This is significant in light of the ambivalent views on exile that he had expressed in two important interviews (Jonassaint 1986: 211; Dayan 1993a: 141).

Anthologie personelle, Depestre's other poetry collection, carries a prologue that puts his new political creed clearly in perspective. He leaves little doubt there that he no longer believes in the "messianic myth" of the salvation of humankind through the socialist revolution, which he now perceives, based on the experience of Moscow, Pekin, Prague, Hanoi, and Havana, as "the Soviet projection… of terror and iniquity" (Depestre 1993: 10). Voicing a virtual *mea culpa*, he decries his own share of "responsibility in the tragedy of the international Communist movement" for having so "rashly, unreasonably lived in the fascination of the revolutionary myth"

(p. 10). There is something sad about Depestre's recanting his former beliefs. Renunciation can hardly compare with the lofty passion of belief. And our reading of his work would suggest that it was belief that fuelled his admirable poetic corpus. Nor can one help sensing in his accent of regret an echo of the self-reproaching "rénonce" into which the Catholic church coerced vodou believers during the various antisuperstition campaigns that the folk religion of Haiti has suffered.

It is in this context that one can make sense of Depestre's second novel *Hadriana dans tous mes rêves* published in 1988. The plot is simple. Hadriana Siloé, a 19-year-old white beauty, is scheduled to marry the young Haitian Hector Danoze on Saturday 29th of January 1938. People in the city of Jacmel, the geographical setting of the story, have high regard for the young woman. In the announcement of her wedding in the local press, for instance, she is spoken of as "Hadriana, only daughter of the distinguished couple Denise and André Siloé, is the princely gift with which the France of Debussy and Renoir has regaled our country" (Depestre 1988: 37-38). The day of the ceremony she drops dead at the altar just as she accepts her matrimonial vows. Hadriana's death, we learn, occurs through the agency of forces of evil intent on taking possession of her soul (*zombification*). Her disappearance from her tomb shortly after the burial confirms the intervention of supernatural entities (p. 91).

Hadriana's death so shakes the foundations of the city that over thirty years after the event the narrator can establish a link between Hadriana's departure and Jacmel's socio-economic decline (p. 122). Patrick Altamont, the narrator, a childhood friend and admirer of the deceased, as he travels around the world retains the assurance that he will one day meet Hadriana again. Then in 1977, at the Mona Campus of the University of the West Indies, Kingston, Jamaica, where he is serving as visiting professor, she walks radiantly into his classroom with the same beauty of thirty-nine years before. His dream fulfilled, he enthusiastically welcomes her arrival with the word "Hosanna!" (p. 138). Their reunion culminates in a sexual encounter, after which Patrick asks Hadriana to reveal the story of her "aventure de zombie" (p. 139). The telling of Hadriana's prodigious experience in the "underworld" makes up the last third of the book. There we learn how in her *post mortem* existence she mingled with such figures as Toussaint Louverture, Bolívar, and Stalin (p. 164), her difficult escape from the servants of Baron-Samedi who sought to control her soul (p. 181), her return to the world of the living, her arrival at a gathering of peasants preparing to migrate to Jamaica, her being confused by them with the loa Simbi-la-Source, and her agreeing to accompany them to Jamaica, where, having decided to break her links with her "passé jacmélien", she has resided since her famous "évaporation" (p. 189). The book concludes with a short epilogue spoken by Patrick, in which he refers to the ten years that have passed since he and Hadriana have lived as a "happy couple" (p. 191).

As suggested by these references, the book maintains the tendency to frame the *sacred* within the socio-cultural confines of the Caribbean. Vodou continues to appear here as a religious system that exists in direct opposition to Christianity. When Hadriana dies, for example, a debate ensues among the mourners as to which spiritual tradition should prevail at the wake. As a result, "Thenceforward a fierce struggle ensued between the two systems of belief that have for ever competed in the Haitian imagination: the Christian faith and the vodu faith" (p. 48). Equally adamant about the legitimacy of their rituals, mourners from both faiths "contend ruthlessly for the body and soul of the girl" (p. 52). They end up, in effect, breaking into separate factions to honor their beloved Nana, the name given to Hadriana by the people of Jacmel. Thus, one group invokes Ogou (p. 76) while the other invokes Jesus (p. 86). For they all seem to concur that the death of their Hadriana touches everybody alike: "Every body wept, catholic priests and vodou gods included" (p. 89).

However, the book differs from Depestre's earlier work in its somewhat gratuitous treatment of the sacred. The montage of the divine realm here seems to seek no corrective ends. The gods do not take overt social positions regarding human affairs. Without the mission to advance a historical teleology, the sacred exists here for its own sake. Besides, the recurrence of phrases such as "surréalisme quotidien" (p. 17), "la Walpurgis caraïbe" (p. 77), "le réel merveilleux Haïtien" (p. 92), as well as the instructional tone of sections like the one where the narrator explains the process whereby the *bokor* turns a person into a zombi (pp. 96-98), or when he traces the historical origin of the zombi in the Haitian imagination, all seem to suggest that the author is desperately appealing to an audience that needs cultural translation. Depestre's own words in an interview with Joan Dayan indicates this: "I am not only addressing Haitians, and so, I must give information that will help other readers… So, since I live outside of Haiti, I wanted to give my readers, who are not Haitian, a certain sense of a reality they would not otherwise know" (Dayan 1993a: 146). In other words, rather than affirming the Caribbean milieu, the book seems intent on making it accessible to the hegemonic culture. Depestre no longer stands here as a radical celebrant of the legacy of his marginal culture but rather as a mediator between the two worlds. Hadriana, who is hailed by the people of Jacmel as their supreme beauty, happens to be a white woman. Many instances of the vodou experience in the novel are translated into Western images such as "Walpurgis", "Thanatos et Eros" or the *Nabucco* of Verdi (pp. 77, 89). And, in general, the novel exhibits an interest in casting the convergence of the sacred and the profane in the everyday life of Haiti in terms that a Western audience may easily understand and accept.

Hadriana dans tous mes rêves resembles in many respects the reputedly "objective" rendition of life in a small village of the Central African Republic offered by René Maran in his novel *Batouala* (1921). Maran's book in such characteristic passages as the "Ga'nza", the circumcision and excision ceremony that is described in chapter six, portrays, in exuberantly graphic detail, the ways of the pre-scientific African for cultivated French readers to feast their eyes on (Maran 1987: 79-90). Not coincidentally, just as Maran's work received the Prix Goncourt in 1922, Depestre's got the Prix Renaudot in 1988 from the French literary establishment. The novel received other prestigious literary awards and sold nearly 200,000 copies within two years of the publication date (Dayan 1993b: 157). Dayan has persuasively argued that the novel's success had to do with its touching a desire for the exotic in French readers (Dayan 1993b: 163-64). She has also evaluated the political implications of an exoticism that invites the mythologizing of Haiti, a country that has endured more than its share of demonization (Dayan 1993b: 167).

Hadriana marks what Althusser, in examining the development of Marx's thought, referred to as "an epistemological break" (Althusser 1979: 32-34). The novel exhibits a departure from the major ideological tenets evident in Depestre's previous works as discussed above. The departure is corroborated by the testimony of the Haitian writer Jean Jonassaint who, after many unsuccessful attempts, managed to interview Depestre in 1982. Already then he found that: "Depestre has changed a lot, perhaps it's only appearance, but today, in Paris, a high-ranking officer of UNESCO, a member of the Gallimard team, René Depestre is no longer available, at least very little for the Haitians, I believe" (Jonassaint 1986: 86). The interviewer reasonably accepts an explanation of the perceptible change as a switch in emphasis from political goals to literary pursuits: "He wants to win his bet as a writer, his revolutionary dreams having regretfully failed, he says" (Jonassaint 1986: 186). But Depestre's own words, particularly the explanation of his moving away from the *contestaire* spirit in his art, suggest a deeper transformation. He affirms: "I integrate the revolt into another level of creativity. I integrate it into a greater wisdom, into the human spirit, the experience of living. I no longer see things in black and white; I'm no longer Manichean. I have lived my ideology fully. I have seen the limits and the merits of the doctrine I upheld as a young man. I totally refuse to consider the antagonisms between North and South, East and West as the only antagonisms that exist in the world" (Jonassaint 1986: 208). Clearly what we have here is a new Depestre, someone who experienced a dramatic change of heart. In the interview with Jonaissaint, though ideologically changed, he had not become resentful of the years he spent singing the cause of revolution, cultural identity, Third World liberation, and nationalist struggles against imperialism. By the time of his interview with Dayan eight years later, after the fall of the Berlin Wall, he had become a voice of bitter conservatism (Dayan 1993a: 144). The prefatory words he writes for *Anthologie personnelle* exhibit a scornful rejection of his former affiliations and beliefs.

The Triumph of Saint Eros

Depestre said "bonjour et adieu" to negritude early in his literary career. Following his departure from Cuba, he has also parted with revolution. A poet who first broke into verse compelled by a social call, he has lost faith in all of the political discourses that preach collective liberation. As we have seen, the vodou gods that now populate his texts have ceased to voice metaphorical agendas for the betterment of human society. In *Hadriana dans tous mes rêves* they go about unmoved by earthly suffering. As political ideals have vanished from Depestre's literary discourse, human interchange through sexual contact has grown in prominence. Saint Eros, in other words, has come to monopolize Depestre's prayers and to circumscribe his worship to the temple of the flesh. *Eros dans un train chinois* (1990), a subsequent collection of short fiction, reads as a sexual extravaganza. Made up of ten bawdy tales, the volume features characters whose primary compulsion is the realization of carnal desire. The first story in the book, "Faisane dorée", tells of the mental voyage of a "monsieur Depestre", a visitor to Maoist China in 1961, as he imagines ways to possess the female comrade who serves as his tour guide during the sojourn. "L'invité d'un soir de juin", the sixth story in the collection, recounts one night in the life of Alain Soleiller, who returns to Haiti in 1958 after twelve years of living abroad. Reunited with his old friend Laurent Sterne, who has married the ravishing Gladys, he accepts an invitation to go dancing with the young couple. The tension brought into the couple's communication by Alain's presence and his lusting for his friend's wife form the core of the text. The last piece, entitled "L'oeillet ensorcellé", deals with the adventures of Vincey Lozeroy, nicknamed General Mephisto, a young man endowed by nature with a penis of Gargantuan proportions. Mephisto's prowess in copulation culminates in his astonishing sexual bout with the petite Josefina Finamour, a young Cuban woman who proves to be his match. After nine days of continuous intercourse, she grows "at least nineteen centimetres" to become "a tall blonde at the side of the glorious General Mephisto" (Depestre 1990b: 167). Since the book gives vent to a great verbal virtuosity regarding nomenclatures for male and female genitalia, it carries a glossary that not only defines them but also narrates "the extraordinary adventures of the sexual organs" (Depestre 1990b: 169).

Eros dans un train chinois has elicited mixed reactions. A reviewer in the United States finds the stories in the collection "perceptive; many of them are extremely funny" while speaking bashfully about their content and noting the advantage of their being written in a foreign language since "one can read them in an airplane or a waiting room without raising eyebrows" (Hartwig 1992: 1078). Milan Kundera, however, greets the book precisely for its overt display of unchecked libidinous impulses. He applauds Depestre's unmitigated eroticism: "all his women gush with sexuality to such a degree that the street signs turn around to leer at them. And the men are so lascivious that they'll make love during a lecture, an operation, in a space rocket, on a trapeze" (Kundera 1991: 46). Kundera praises the lack of adornment, the moral, existential, and psychological neutrality of "a world where vice and innocence are one and the same," commending Depestre for putting on "the map of human existence the previously unexplored reaches of innocent and joyful eroticism, the near-impossible paradise of unbridled sex" (p. 46). But it seems probable that Caribbean readers will find less to celebrate in what a critic has already dismissed as Depestre's incursion into "la drôlerie érotique" (erotic jesting). Regis Antoine in fact resents the commercial success of *Eros dans un train chinois*, a book "without great literary merit" that now forms part of the widely-read Folio series and has received the enthusiastic favour of the same French public that ignored the "major texts" written by Depestre such as *Un arc-en-ciel pour l'Occident chrétien* (Antoine 1993: 91).

Besides eliciting charges of frivolous self-indulgence, the heavy concentration of venereal exploits in Depestre's texts raises at least one aesthetic question: If the text does not transcend the representation of the sexual act, if the controlling idea is the pursuit of orgasm, in what respect does it differ from downright pornography? But there is also the sociology of bedroom action. Depestre's erotica presents us mostly with the male narrator who achieves or yearns to achieve self-realization through the possession of a woman's body. Devoid of the opportunity to attain ontological independence, Depestre's female characters exist primarily as objects of male desire or as fuel for male erotic fantasy. Depestre has sought to dispel any association of his work with an "erotic literature imbued with elements that degrade women", insisting that he as a writer celebrates "la condition féminine" (Jonassaint 1986: 194). Yet, even when he traces his love of the erotic to his contact as a child with "many stories about women" (beaucoup d'histoires de femmes), one sees that women remain relegated to the status of subject matter. When he construes the telling of "histoires de femmes" as "one of the components of Haitian sensibility", it seems clear that he means the sensibility of Haitian men (Jonassaint 1986: 197).

Depestre's own characterization of the treatment of women in his texts fails to satisfy Dayan's concern, dating back to her 1986 study of *Alleluia pour une femme-jardin*, that "in his attempt to recapture the singular identity of his Caribbean brothers, Depestre in fact dispossesses the female in his culture", and that in his "particular celebration" he "both idealizes and disempowers the real flesh-and-blood woman" (Dayan 1986: 583, 581). Indeed, we might read a measure of mockery of women as intellectual beings in instances when Depestre's male narrator can only focus his mind on the woman's breasts and hips even while she, as in "Faisane dorée", makes an earnest attempt to elucidate for him the nature of Maoist thought or to evoke the heroic struggle of her people against the onslaught of imperial enemy forces. Too many of Depestre's male characters speak and behave as if they were convinced that all of women's aspirations can be taken care of by them in the bedroom. In announcing *Les aveugles font l'amour à midi*, the closing volume of the erotic trilogy, Depestre promised to stay clear of reductive assumptions regarding "la condition féminine", striking the cord of a complex and humanizing celebration of women. By 2007, when the Parisian publisher Seghers published his collected poems (*Rage de vivre. Oeuvres poétiques complètes*), the projected volume of erotic fiction had not appeared.

But beyond the erotic arena, one cannot prophesy much regarding the direction that Depestre's work might take. With an outlook that sneers at humanistic utopias, a worldview that rejects all commitments to collective liberation, Depestre has become an atheist in the saddest sense. One feels tempted to say "yes" in response to Dayan's question: "Has Depestre been zombified by French fame?" (Dayan 1993b: 175). Perhaps it is even gloomier than that. His market success has come precisely after he ceased challenging the ways of the Christian West and the workings of empire. He gave up revolution, renounced his former dissidence, gave up on anticolonial discourse, dissociated himself from the concept of the Third World, and made peace with the West. Now his hope lies in "the intelligence of the French public and in France, because it is a country of culture" (Dayan 1993a: 153). In abjuring his former political commitment, he has by implication admitted to wrongdoing. The French literary establishment and the market have, in turn, legitimized him with celebrity. His material well-being secured, cultivating his own garden in the pastoral comfort of a majestic house in southern France (in a way not dissimilar to Sir V.S. Naipaul's life as an English country gentleman in rural Wiltshire), he has entered into partnership with the very structures he had spent a whole literary career antagonizing. The empire can now claim its gory victory over the Haitian loas. The Christian West has miserably defeated the gods of the native forest. When his collected poems came out in 2007, he also made it known that he would write no more poetry. The journalist covering the news of the publication for *Le Magazine du Carcassonnais et de l'Ouest Audois* (Michel Sawas, 25 April 2007) refers to the eighty-year-old Depestre as "un 'grand nom' de la littérature" when not identifying him by name, and as "le Lézignanais" for

Lésignan, his current place of residence in the Langedoc. Haiti appears long forgotten.

In the end, however, when all is said and done, Depestre cannot obliterate the fact that he owes his renown outside of France to the important literary work that he produced in those decades when he voiced the dissent of the disinherited about the indignities perpetrated against them by larger forces. Therein lies the great significance of his contribution. His current ideological state does not alter in essence the validity of his service. His change of heart does not erase his previous effort to forge a mythopoesis that, creatively incorporating religion as a depository and vehicle of the human experience for people in the area, positively affirmed the artistic value of autochthonous Caribbean expressions. Nor do his conservative pronouncements make him less representative of Caribbean poetics. The examples of George Lamming and V.S. Naipaul, two typically Caribbean and ideologically antithetical writers, indicate the plurality of political positions that have gone into the building of a diverse but coherent literary corpus in the region.

Taken together, Depestre's works have undertaken a constructive exploration of the sacred as a means to highlight the socio-cultural specificity of Caribbean life and its contingent relation with the hegemonic culture of the West through the history of colonialism and the region's resistance to it. Depestre's texts provide an artistic illustration of the uniqueness of Caribbean life. He has successfully set out to bring into visibility a religious realm that accords with the discrete reality of the Caribbean experience and that informs the minds of people throughout the region. His works have done a great service in affirming the cultural authenticity of the people of the Caribbean. It is his privilege to go wherever his new interests will take him. But the Caribbean will remain indebted to him for having devoted several decades of literary practice to exploring the relationship of religious expression and cultural marooning in the region. Like other important Caribbean authors, Depestre has contributed notably to "the decolonization of the soul" in the region (Levilain 1978: 55).

CHAPTER 5

PEDRO MIR AND THE HISTORICAL IMAGINATION

> History, then, these things that happen, is, in the plantation context, itself, fiction; a fiction written, dominated, controlled by forces external to itself. It is clear then, that it is only when the society, or elements of the society rise up in rebellion against its external authors and manipulators that our prolonged fiction becomes temporary fact.
>
> Sylvia Wynter (1971: 95).

The work of the Dominican poet, fiction writer, and historian Pedro Mir emphatically illustrates Caribbean literature's engagement with history. Born in 1913 in the southerly city of San Pedro de Macorís, he published his first poems in 1937 through the agency of Juan Bosch, who had already achieved distinction in Dominican letters. When he died in 2000, no Dominican author living in the country had enjoyed more popularity and reverence than Mir among both literary and non-literary readers in virtually all sectors of society. The agreement by the full multipartisan legislature of the Dominican Congress in 1982 to confer upon him the title of National Poet suggests the high regard in which his native audience has held him. He received recognition both at home and abroad. Hunter College of the City University of New York awarded him an honorary doctorate in June 1991, and in February 1992, Hostos Community College, another campus of New York City's public university system, devoted a day-long conference to his literary career. Mir received the Dominican Republic's National Prize for Literature, the country's highest distinction for literary artists (Torres-Saillant 1993: vii) in 1993, the same year when the Washington publisher Azul Editions put out a bilingual collection of his poetry under the title *Countersong to Walt Whitman and Other Poems* (Mir 1993). The following year the prestigious Mexican firm Siglo XXI Editores published his collected poems as *Poesías (casi) completas* (Mir 1994). Especially since 1993, when he became 80 years of age, Mir was the object of numerous tributes and homages, especially in his home country and in the neighbouring island of Puerto Rico.

However, as a scholar has noted, Spanish American literary histories and anthologies have generally omitted mention of Mir's work (Ortega 1987:

101). In 1972 the Mexican poet Jaime Labastida introduced his selection of Mir's poetry for Siglo XXI Editores wondering why the name of Mir did not appear beside those of Pablo Neruda, Nicanor Parra, Nicolás Guillén, and the other important contemporary Latin American poets. At the time he could conceive of at least two possible explanations: the fact that Mir's texts have been published in the Dominican Republic in editions of limited circulation, and his coming from a country without the worldwide visibility that might propel his poetry outside of the national borders (Labastida 1975: x). Labastida's selection, published with the express purpose of gaining a continental readership for Mir, is probably responsible for much of the visibility the Dominican poet achieved outside his country since the mid 1970s (Labastida 1975: xiv). But the fact that for his introduction to Mir's collected poems as published nearly twenty years later by Siglo XXI Editores, Labastida has retained the same remarks he wrote twenty years before indicates that in his mind one could still speak of Mir as an unknown poet (Labastida 1994).

Mediating Cultural Contexts

Though Mir began publishing in the 1930s and enjoyed some literary and intellectual visibility in the 1940s, his work became widely known in his native land starting in 1962 when his return from a fifteen-year-long exile met with ardent enthusiasm. Throughout the 1960s his poetry recitals in Santo Domingo, mostly in workers' clubs, attracted thousands of people "who recognized themselves" in his poems, and the repeated reprintings of his long poem *Hay un país en el mundo* have made him into what Pedro Conde has called "one of the most striking literary successes" in the history of Dominican literature (Conde 1985: 47, 51). A question may come up regarding the oddity of a Dominican writer who, a literary celebrity at home, should remain little known in the Caribbean and continental Latin America. But the phenomenon is not unusual in the region, as can be seen in the case of Martin Carter, a great Guyanese poet, who stayed in Guyana all his life, whose reputation only began to extend beyond his native country after his death in 1997. Part of the explanation in Mir's case lies in the secondary position accorded to the literature of the islands in general and the Dominican Republic in particular by the Latin American literary establishment. Perusing Latin-American literary compendia one soon verifies that Dominican literature is the least regarded of the literatures of the Hispanophone Antilles.

But the lack of visibility that Mir suffers in the Caribbean itself has to do with the misapplication by Dominican literary scholars and critics of the relationship of their culture to the mediating contexts of Latin America and the Caribbean (Torres-Saillant 1994: 50). Trained in the traditional Western-centred view of Latin-American literature, they have, rather strangely, entered into self-destructive complicity with the builders of the canon in the continent. Dominican intellectuals have been slower than their counterparts in the other Hispanic Caribbean nations in claiming their cultural link and affinity with the other peoples of the region. Puerto Rico can boast of an important intellectual current in the twentieth century, going at least from Luis Palés Matos to José Luis González, which has tenaciously articulated Puerto Rican culture in terms of the regional, Caribbean tradition. Cuba, at least from Nicolás Guillén to Emilio Jorge Rodríguez, has also systematically asserted the Caribbean texture of the island's culture. But Dominican intellectuals have not yet caught up with their Cuban and Puerto Rican counterparts in this respect, consequently encouraging exclusions of Dominican authors like Pedro Mir from pan-Caribbean anthologies and histories.

Mir's work lends itself remarkably to an exploration of Hispanophone Antillean cultural "duplicity", to use Kundera's terminology (1991: 48). Cuba, Puerto Rico, and the Dominican Republic serve as cultural crossroads where the Caribbean and Latin America intersect, and Mir can be read with a focus on these two mediating cultural contexts. Labastida stresses Mir's quality as "a great political poet, typified by the denominator of a plural subject", explaining the poet's identification with the Latin-American proletariat regardless of ethnic origin (Labastida 1975: xi). But, while one cannot contest the plurality of Mir's subject and the global Latin-American relevancy of his poetic discourse, a more discretely regional vision becomes apparent in his work. The poet himself would seem to insist on his Caribbean identity. The speaker in the proemium to his long poem *Contracanto a Walt Whitman* (1952) highlights his birth on Quisqueyan (Dominican) soil, to a Borinqueña (Puerto Rican) mother and a Cuban father. In Jonathan Cohen's English translation the opening lines read thus: "I,/a son of the Caribbean,/Antillean to be exact./The raw product of a simple/Puerto Rican girl/and a Cuban worker,/born precisely, and poor/ on Quisqueyan soil" (Mir 1993a: 47).

The presence of an Antillean assertiveness in Mir's poetic diction has caused Labastida, whose primary interest is to establish the Dominican poet as an author of continental calibre, to qualify Mir's continentality in these terms: "And, of course, his primary concern is... Santo Domingo, and then the Caribbean, but Latin America also" (Labastida 1975: xii). In other words, Mir's affiliation with Latin America comes after his self-recognition as Antillean. Roberto Márquez, who includes Mir in an anthology of Latin-American revolutionary poetry, has placed Mir's work in relation to the Antilles and the continent: Mir "is a Caribbean poet in the militant troubadour tradition of Guillén, Césaire, or Jacques Roumain; he is also a poet whose allegiance to the Dominican Republic and the

Caribbean encompasses a broader allegiance to Latin America and to all the wretched of the earth" (Márquez 1974: 208-09). Mir's immediate socio-cultural matrix is the Caribbean, and his affiliation with Latin America and other parts of the world fits into the internationalist vocation typical of other Caribbean writers such as Roumain, Depestre, or Condé.

In reading Mir as a Caribbean literary artist, this chapter will focus primarily on his persistent concern with the historical processes which have determined the present political and cultural configuration of the region. He devoted the bulk of his over five decades of literary activity to the clarification of historical phenomena which have occurred in the region from the time Columbus and his entourage first set foot on Antillean soil in 1492 until the contemporary era. He untiringly journeyed to the lived experience of his people in the region's past to find the raw material for his literary work. Mir, in short, epitomizes the pervasiveness of the historical imagination among Caribbean writers. His preoccupation with reconstructing and correcting false images of the Antillean past makes him akin to such authors as Césaire and Reid. Césaire's *La tragédie du roi Christophe* (1963) and *Toussaint Louverture* (1962) and V.S. Reid's *New Day* (1949) and *The Jamaicans* (1976) explore the legacy of rebellion and resistance in the Caribbean experience. Likewise, Mir from the early 1940s to the 1990s methodically examined the path charted by his people in their continuous struggle to overcome internal and external onslaughts on their human integrity. Like other Caribbean writers, Mir's dedication to historical material finds expression in more than one genre, as he moved from poetry, to fiction, to criticism, to historiographical essays.

History: These Things That Happen

Mir's literary career is, then, nourished by what Derek Walcott has called "the muse of history". However, Mir's project of historical reconstruction and correction might meet with disapproval from the Saint Lucian poet and playwright. Walcott has regretted the New World writer's subservience to a documentary past. In his words: "In the New World servitude to the muse of history has produced a literature of recrimination and despair, a literature of revenge written by the descendants of slaves or a literature of remorse written by the descendants of masters" (Walcott 1978: 39). Fearful that the documentary recollection of the past might be too imbued with "the memory of hero or of victim", and convinced that a literature which "serves historical truth" either "yellows into polemic or evaporates in pathos", Walcott advocates a view of the past that through mythical channels can trace the human condition back to a remoter, Adamic beginning (Walcott 1978: 38, 39). For Mir, the search for historical truth is not negotiable. Besides, his dedication to a documentary recovery of the past, contrary to Walcott's fear, always transcends bitterness and invariably serves as a prelude to the announcement of a new dawn.

In Mir the past always points to the future, a future which is rich in possibilities. His work also demonstrates Maryse Condé's argument that between history and memory there need not be a real dichotomy. In an interview with Mohamed B. Taleb-Khyar, she states: "in *Ségou*, I was writing history. I was trying to explain the decline and fall of an African kingdom and of Africa, of the Black people, in a way. But, in *Traversée de la mangrove*, I'm writing memory. I'm in a small village among people who are not heroes, who are just ordinary men and women, and whose life seems totally meaningless" (Taleb-Khyar 1991: 357). Indeed, Mir's writings illustrate how history and memory complement each other in the recollection of the past. His characters, like those in the works of the Haitian novelist Marie Chauvet, are usually ordinary individuals who cannot be traced to any of the figures who populate the history books. Instead, they represent residues in the collective memory of the people, though they invariably fit into a frame that accords clearly with distinct stages of the larger Dominican experience. Mir, like Chauvet, reflects the manner in which Caribbean literature endeavours to fathom the history lurking behind the memory. At the same time, in Mir's work the search for historical truth does not dispense with the instruments of mythopoesis, so that the muse of history does not necessarily lead to revenge or remorse. Historical truth, too, Mir shows, can provide a vehicle toward the Adamic.

As the main thrust of my readings of Mir's work is to emphasize the omnipresence of history in Caribbean literary writing, the discussion of his career begins with a look at the conventional historiographical texts he has produced. Like many of his Caribbean colleagues, Mir has not only used history in his art, but he has also tried his hand as a historian. Mir completed his first historiographical work, *Tres leyendas de colores*, in 1949, the same year his first published volume of verse appeared. Though the book remained unpublished for twenty years, due to the loss of the manuscript and other circumstances that the author narrates in his preface, when it finally came out it broke new ground in Caribbean historiography by tracing the roots of current issues of class and race in the region to events that took place during the first thirty years of the colonial period among whites, aborigines, and blacks. The book deals with the genesis of the Caribbean, the origin of the ethnic and cultural fusion that gave the region its distinct character. It narrates what the subtitle refers to as "the first three revolutions in the New World", all of which took place in Hispaniola within years of Columbus's arrival in the island in 1492.

Tres leyendas starts out with a study of the Admiral's male attendant, Francisco Roldán Ximeno, whose lowly social rank as a squire, the author tells us, predisposed him to become a contingent element with respect to Columbus and his ruling social structure. When the Spaniards hit shore, the contradictions arising from social class stratification made themselves felt, and Roldán became, by virtue of his social station, the voice of the less advantaged among the settlers. He played that role because: "He met all the necessary requirements to do so: he had been a servant. He boasted no title of nobility nor family shield. In short, he was the people" (Mir 1978: 37). By 1496 the rebellion of the "roldanistas" in La Isabela, the very first Spanish settlement in the Americas, had risen to such revolutionary heights that it even encompassed issues pertaining to the freedom and well-being of the aboriginal population (p. 50). Roldán, in articulating the interests of the insurgents, served as "an instrument of the people", Mir says (p. 72). Here, and throughout the book, Mir advances the idea that when the people require a voice to express the concerns of the collective, they pick leaders, liberators, national heroes, and even poets (p. 31). The birth of the Encomienda as a system which divided the land into private lots, each containing a number of native hands to till it and make it yield, may have occurred precisely as a consequence of the success of Roldán's insurrection (p. 81). The new institution appeased the "roldanistas" who were given a share of the colonial pie and then exacted satisfactory benefit from the forced labour of the indigenous population. The contradictions among the settlers, then, were resolved at the expense of the aborigines who, lowered to what Mir calls "the category of the people", had then to become the contingent element (p. 119).

The second part of the book tells of the uprising of the aborigines. Mir concentrates here on the story of Guarocuya, the son of an Arawak chief who grew up under the protection of an Encomendero named Valenzuela. Named Enrique and often called by the endearing diminutive of Enriquillo, he received his education in a Franciscan convent and "was almost a Spaniard" (p. 130). The death of his kind master, the loss of his considerable privileges, and the abusive ways of his new master awakened him to the condition of subjection of his people. He thus became in 1519 the leader of an insurrection in the mountains of Bahoruco (p. 132). Mir minimizes the personal nature of Enriquillo's grudge against the Spaniards, stressing that his action ceased to be personal as soon as his people gave it momentum by accepting it as their action also (p. 145). Enriquillo, however, did not prove to be an authentic leader. An Ariel *par excellence*, by virtue of his upbringing, he capitulated as soon as Prospero restored his blessings.

When the Spaniards offered to repair all his wrongs, even honouring him with the noble name of Don Enrique, he negotiated an infamous peace arrangement. The arrangement included helping the Spanish authorities to capture other insurgent aborigines throughout the island as well as hunting down black maroons at a price *per capita* (p. 156). Mir argues that

Tamayo, a truly radical insurgent Taíno leader who came under the aegis of Enriquillo, absorbed by the latter's prestige, would never have blemished the annals of history with such a treaty. He explains too that Enriquillo's treacherous actions did not dissuade subsequent historians from placing him at the pinnacle of heroism and portraying him as a symbol of the Dominican nation. The idea is simple. A historian with the mentality of Ariel will find virtue in the Ariels of the past. It should surprise no one, then, that Manuel de Jesús Galván, the main architect of Enriquillo's apotheosis, should also be one of the intellectual engineers of the annexation of the Dominican Republic to the Spanish Empire in 1861, the moment when an entrenched Dominican oligarchy exchanged the nation's sovereignty for their own well-being. Mir puts it succinctly: "Galván was a modern-day Enriquillo" (p. 166).

The third part of *Tres leyendas* tells of the 1522 uprising of the black slaves in the island. No figure of the stature of Roldán or Enriquillo stands out in this struggle. The hero here is anonymous, which, Mir says, is a more authentic identity for the people, since: "To be anonymous is to be unanimous. To have no name is to have everybody's name... Anonymity is plural" (p. 199). Mir sets out to show in his reconstruction that the blacks did not submit to their enslavement in Hispaniola peacefully, though when they rose against their masters, they too, like the aborigines, suffered defeat. Their defeat, however, had repercussions that affect us even to the present moment, Mir argues, for with their subjection in Hispaniola, slavery for the first time in human history became a racial institution (p. 219). He shows that the ideological superstructure that developed around the justification of racial oppression and inequality, the pronouncements from Las Casas to Renan, to Gobineau, to the Ku Klux Klan, can be said to start with the defeat of the black insurgents in Hispaniola.

It began with the "Ingenio Poderoso" founded by Bachiller Gonzalo de Velosa in 1516 in the village of Yaguate. Velosa's was the first successful plantation in the New World and the first arena where the use of blacks in the sugar plantation revealed its economic viability. The equation blacks=sugar plantation was born from this successful experiment. The industry bloomed, and so did the traffic, particularly under the reign of Emperor Charles V. The need for hands would from then on be satisfied not just by *slaves* but specifically by *black slaves* (p. 195). The institution having acquired a distinct colour, the activities of the Middle Passage intensified, marking the destiny of Africa, Europe, and the Americas forever. Modern racism, born in the historical laboratory of Hispaniola the moment the economic viability of race oppression was ascertained, accompanies us until the present day. Mir's argument gains significance if one thinks of some ancient examples. Horace, the son of a slave, became respectable as a Roman poet who frequented the court of

Augustus Caesar. Terence, an African, became prominent as a dramatist in the same Roman society that had enslaved him. Such a movement up from slavery was possible in the eras before the institution had acquired colour, before the equation blackness=slavery had come into being. Once the equation was made, slaves could not so easily shake off their bonds even when they legally acquired their freedom. The fusion of slavery with pigmentation disabled former slaves from full citizenship because though one could get rid of one's chains, one could not shed one's skin. As a result, in the United States, nearly one hundred and fifty years after emancipation, the possibility of a black person becoming President of the country had met with incredulity from both blacks and whites until 2008, when Barack Obama, the son of a white American woman and a black man from Kenya earned the favour of the electorate. Mir would urge us to look to "Ingenio Poderoso" for the causes of our perplexing racial present.

Tres leyendas tells, in effect, how in the island of Hispaniola the Caribbean began. Resistance as a permanent characteristic, racial mixture, the plantation, nativization of all incoming institutions, those of the masters as well as those of the slaves, had their start on this island. In other words, Caribbean creolization, as has been advanced by Brathwaite, had its beginning here (Brathwaite 1971: viii, xv, xvi). Mir also highlights the crucial role played by the Caribbean in shaping the modern world, which owes so much of its present physiognomy to institutions and economic forms that started in the region. He anticipates the declaration by Tzvetan Todorov that "it is in fact the conquest of America that heralds and establishes our present identity; even if every date that permits us to separate any two periods is arbitrary, none is more suitable, in order to make the beginning of the modern era, than the year 1492, the year Columbus crosses the Atlantic Ocean" (Todorov 1984: 5). One hardly needs to be reminded that the process described by Todorov began in Quisqueya, in the very heart of the Antillean world.

Rafael Altamira's posthumous preface to *Tres leyendas* praised the book for its innovative historiographical form (Mir 1987: 7). Mir actually constructs a narrative that often crosses over to the realm of the literary. In the recreation of certain historical scenes, such as the meeting of Roldán with Alonso de Ojeda (p. 93) or that of Enriquillo with Hernando de San Miguel (p. 143), the author emulates the plasticity of cinematography. Certain moments such as the encounter between Don Bartolomé Colón and Roldán (pp. 48-9) are rendered by means of theatrical effects. Many narrative passages exhibit a novelistic flow, and literary allusions abound throughout the text, such as the comparison of Roldán with Sancho Panza (p. 35) or the recurring reference to John Donne's words "no man is an island" to explain the collective will that produces a leader (pp. 72, 145).

Also, like the self-conscious narrator of many novels, the narrator in this book at times reflects upon his own telling of the story at hand (p. 81). Stylistically, the book does not submit to the conventions of historiographical discourse. We see here a two-fold purpose. First, by incorporating artistic devices in the narrative Mir accentuates the interdependence of historiography and literature. Mir believes that, to put it in the words of a fellow poet, "History explains literature, and literature explains history" (Incháustegui 1977: 121). Secondly, by going beyond the boundaries of formal historiographical discourse, Mir expands his scope so as to include the human experience that the official historians normally omit. His attempt to reconstruct the unwritten history of the people among the Spaniards, aborigines and blacks suggests an interest in amplifying the scope of the discipline along corrective lines. This concern would later find eloquent articulation in Brathwaite's project to unearth the "little culture" of the West Indian folk.

Mir's next historiographical work, *El gran incendio* (1969), starts where *Tres leyendas* leaves off. Also drawing on literary narrative techniques, the book tells how a great fire in 1605 reduced a sizable portion of Hispaniola to ashes. Juan Antonio de Osorio, then Captain and Governor General of the island of Santo Domingo, had ordered what was in fact arson. He had the duty to stop at any cost the illegal commerce that had flourished in the northern part of the island, beyond the control of the Spanish authorities. Practically all other major European powers had a vested interest in the clandestine commercial activity that took place on this very first Spanish colony in the New World (Mir 1974: 84). In a desperate measure to curtail the ongoing "illegal commerce" and thereby retain its economic and political hegemony on the island, Spain, through Governor Osorio, set whole cities afire. Puerto Plata, Bayajá, La Yaguana, and Monte Cristi were wrapped in flames (p. 107), and the great conflagration spread over one half of the island's territory (p. 124).

Mir undertakes to show the global implications of the fire. At the time, Spain had a backward-looking economy that was still feudal in structure, and he points out that it was incipient Western capitalism, with Holland at the forefront, that had come to the very shores of Santo Domingo to challenge Spain's hegemony. Santo Domingo served as the arena for the confrontation between those two historical currents, and the fateful fire was an extreme manifestation of their clash (pp. 50-51). The fire symbolized the obstinacy of the feudal tendency which thereby managed to frustrate the first "balbuceos" (stammering) of capitalism in the New World (p. 134). Indirectly, however, the flames, by expelling all inhabitants – rich and poor – from the scorched territories, vacated the grounds that would later become the "terrenos comuneros" (communal lands). By the same token, a portion of the depopulated territory eventually became the seat of a French colony, Saint Domingue, which would develop side by side with the remainder of the Spanish colony of Santo Domingo (pp. 144-5). The Spaniards not only coexisted with the French on the island, but, in the course of time, the two colonial powers ratified the partition by means of a treaty signed in the Spanish city of Aranjuez on June 3, 1777 (p. 151).

Again in *El gran incendio*, Mir both shows the Caribbean region as imperial frontier for Western colonial powers, and traces the historical origin of two Caribbean nations. From the territorial bifurcation that followed the great fire would rise the people of Haiti, on the French side, and the Dominican people, on the Spanish side. Mir thus sheds light on the outside pressure the people of the region have had to contend with through the ages. At the same time, one can see that Haitians and Dominicans, speaking different languages and having experienced varying colonial models, share not only a common territory but also a common legacy of struggle and resistance. Elsewhere Mir examined the potential for unity that derives from this commonality, pointing to various moments in the history of both societies when unification seemed feasible. Unification, of course, did not occur, because, in the first place, as Mir argues, of the divisive interference of the two colonial orders, and, later, the short-sightedness of leaders from both sides of the island, chiefly Jean-Jacques Dessalines, Louis Ferrand, and Juan Sánchez Ramírez (Mir 1973: 176). Yet Mir insists that the feeling of "confraternidad" (fraternal solidarity) between Dominicans and Haitians, resulting from the common "raíces históricas" (historical roots) and the common lot they have subsequently experienced, has survived through the centuries, even against the wishes of the upper classes in both nations (1973: 178).

Mir's next book-length historiographical publication, *Las raíces dominicanas de la Doctrina de Monroe* (1974), focuses on aspects of the relationship between the United States and the Dominican Republic. It further illustrates how Western powers have followed lines of political development that have been dictated by the dynamics of their contact with the Caribbean region. As early as 1854, ten years after the juridical birth of the Dominican Republic, the United States initiated diplomatic actions aimed at the acquisition of Samana Bay (Mir 1984: 33). The Dominican president General Pedro Santana's plan to cede the bay to the Americans elicited the protest of the other imperial powers that had an interest in the Dominican land (p. 39). The negotiations did not prosper, and Santana found himself some years later, in 1861, negotiating the annexation of the whole country to the Spanish crown. Spain occupied the land militarily, thus giving rise to the chapter known in Dominican history as the War of Restoration. Spain had strategic reasons for wanting to repossess Santo Domingo because of the country's proximity to Spain's two other colonies in the region: Cuba and Puerto Rico (p. 54). Santana, too, had his reasons for engineering the transaction; as a representative of the landowning class, he belonged to a tendency with a very long history of attempts to hand over the sovereignty of the nation to foreign imperial bidders.

After two years of violent confrontation, Dominicans succeeded in expelling the invaders and restoring the country's independence (p. 66). But by 1868, another agent of annexationism, Buenaventura Báez, occupied the presidency. In the meantime, in the United States the Civil War had subsided and the interest in Santo Domingo revived, particularly the interest in "Samana Bay with a view of securing it for a naval station" (Thomas 1923: 217). However, President Andrew Johnson's project to purchase the bay met with opposition in the House and did not receive approval (Thomas 1923: 217). His successor, President Ulysses S. Grant, though, was more aggressive in pushing the Dominican question. Grant's "famous passion for the acquisition of Santo Domingo," as Dexter Perkins put it, matched perfectly with Báez's almost lascivious desire to sell the country to a convenient bidder (Perkins 1955: 158). Grant and Báez did not succeed in getting the treaty of annexation of Santo Domingo ratified by the U.S. Senate, but Mir argues for the significance of the fact that in his appeal to American legislators Grant declared on May 31, 1870 that the annexation of Santo Domingo was "an adherence to the Monroe Doctrine" (Mir 1984: 72-3). The "doctrine" had acquired its legendary status as a principle of foreign policy, pertaining to "national security", and even received its formal appellation, in connection with the Dominican situation. President James Monroe had made his statement in a speech back in 1823, but only in the subsequent attempts to secure the Dominican territory in whole or in part, by annexation, purchase, rent, or mortgage, did those words get invoked and reformulated as U.S. foreign policy.

The Monroe Doctrine, which the U.S. adopted "a propos of the Dominican situation" (p. 77), had a sequence of manifestations in the Dominican arena. Among them was the Convention of 1905, which would lead to an arrangement whereby the American government assumed administrative responsibilities for Dominican customhouse transactions and other aspects of financial life in the country. For Mir, the Doctrine manifested itself in the invasion of 1916 and extended even to that of 1965 (p. 101). But despite the persistence of the doctrine and the devotion to annexationism exhibited by the Dominican ruling classes, the people, the popular masses, have historically managed to exert themselves and prevent the cession or transfer of their territory (p. 31).

The path trodden by the Dominican people in their historic self-defence against internal and external aggression is precisely what occupies Mir for the three volumes of his most ambitious historiographical effort, *La noción de período en la historia dominicana* (1981-83). He finds here that the communal lands, with their origin in the great conflagration examined in *El gran incendio*, constitute "the absolute historical base" of the people of the Dominican Republic, the core that serves as "the crucial backbone to all of the country's history" (Mir 1981: I, 201, 211). He proposes that one can identify the master narrative of Dominican history by tracing the "gigantic feat" of the Dominican people in its continuous attempts to ward off internal and external hostility (Mir 1983: II, 291). The Dominican people, Mir affirms, while not abounding in innumerable heroes performing great individual exploits, has forged its own history in the most anonymous, and therefore, most intrinsically popular, manner (Mir 1983: II, 621). He celebrates the anonymity and tenacity of the Dominican people, which has demarcated the contours of its humanity precisely in its struggle against the mendacity of the elites and managed to survive in spite of its leaders.

Mir's historiographical essays minimize the subjection of the slaves *qua* slaves in the trajectory of the Dominican people. He suggests that even when men and women are identified as slaves in historical documents, one ought to see them in the category of "the people". His discussion of an 1812 slave rebellion – which numbered both slaves and freemen among the insurgents – shows Mir's insistence on depicting the nature of Dominican slavery in somewhat benign terms (Mir 1983: II, 357). His grounds for sustaining such a view are that after the fire of 1605, the Spanish colony on the island never developed the plantation economy that flourished in the French colony and that, therefore, slavery did not play a central economic role in Santo Domingo as it did in Saint Domingue. In addition, the economic stagnation that beset the Spanish colony throughout the seventeenth century often reduced both master and slave to the same level of pauperism (Mir 1981: 166-67). Mir here subscribes too rigidly to the demands of class analysis, which normally finds it difficult to account for racial oppression when economic variables are not crystal clear. At the same time, his adherence to a version of Marxist methodology which he deems "scientific" often leads into what would appear a too uncritical notion of the successive stadia in human history, causing him at times to invoke what sounds like an absolute chronology which all nations must presumably follow (Mir 1981: I, 67). Thus he says, for instance, that: "Unfortunately, Capitalism had arrived too late to its appointment with our country" (Mir 1983: III, 696). From a Caribbean perspective, this reads as a rather mechanistic application of a Marxist chronology of human development. This form of Marxist thought (a version that had calcified in the Soviet Union), though arguably more constructive than any other Western discourse for addressing the political needs of the peoples of the Third World, does not escape the limitations of eurocentrism and, therefore, must be nativized if its liberatory potential is to be salvaged.

But in his very detailed study of the Dominican past, Mir succeeds, despite the apriority of the method he embraces, in tracing the trajectory of the Dominican people and thereby highlighting its centrality to the Caribbean experience. He effectively demonstrates the role of the communal lands, a system lasting for approximately 300 years in which usage alone determined the ownership of the land, as a "historical motor" of Dominican nationality (Mir 1983: III, 769, 793). No other element, Mir argues, so meaningfully provides a key to the understanding of the historical experience of this people than their relationship with the land. "Of course," says Mir, "it is not the land that makes history but people. Let it be clear that what this history deals with is not the religious cult of the land, but the processes of struggle it has given birth to since the first dawnings of the eighteenth century" (1983: III, 767). In many respects, that view of the land is at the core of Mir's literary works as will become clear in our discussion of the poetry and the fiction.

Just as the great conflagration of 1605 symbolized for Mir the resilience of feudalist economic tendencies, the official division of the communal lands into private lots during the 1920 land reform known as the "Sistema Torrens" marks the absolute triumph – albeit belated – of capitalism in the Dominican Republic (Mir 1983: III, 794). The arrival of capitalism under the aegis of the U.S. military government that ruled the Dominican Republic from 1916 through 1924 also marks the beginning, as Mir undertakes to show in *Historia del hambre* (1987), of a new set of calamities for the Dominican people. In this text, Mir, proceeding *ab ovo*, surveys the country's past in search for the roots of the present misery, the outright "hunger" (hambre), which caused so many Dominicans to emigrate, sometimes joining the ranks of the criminals and prostitutes abroad (Mir 1987: 125, 226, 234-35). Interestingly, he finds that hunger, far from being connatural with the historical trajectory of Dominicans, is really a "producto moderno", as modern as the automobile and the airplane and can be traced precisely to the abolition of the communal lands and the establishment of capitalism in the country (Mir 1987: 204-06). With the implementation of the "Sistema Torrens" by the U.S. occupying forces in 1920, the country was placed on the rails of capitalist development, but as land reform opened the way to economic progress, it also opened "los caminos del hambre" (the roads of hunger) since in the unequal distribution sponsored by capitalism the destitution of the poor increased as much as did the wealth of the rich (Mir 1987: 252).

Historia del hambre closes with a forward-looking vision, as is characteristic of Mir, suggesting that things will not always be the way they are now. "Everything moves, my friend," he says, quoting from Brecht (Mir 1987: 252). With *Historia del hambre* Mir completed over forty years of continuous engagement with "the muse of history". As the following pages will show, the foremost thread uniting the various facets of his literary production – from the first poems published in Santo Domingo prior to his exile in 1947, to the better known of his texts in verse (epic as well as lyrical poems), to the pieces on art and on individual poets, to his prose fiction, to his more formal historiographical pieces – is the exploration of the region's past. Mir's involvement with the past was continuous and progressive, starting with his early verse and becoming more pronounced with every successive publication. His dependence on the historical imagination accentuates Mir's socio-aesthetic kinship with other prominent writers of the Antillean world such as Juan Bosch, René Depestre, and V.S. Reid. Like them he finds it hard to dispense with historical phenomena, the events which have shaped the lives of people in the Caribbean. "These things that happen", as Sylvia Wynter would say.

Discovering the Social

Mir began writing poetry in the 1930s when he was a secondary school student. According to his own testimony, at first his poetry lacked a sense of connection with the immediate socio-cultural milieu surrounding him. The legacy of Rubén Darío's taste for the distant, geographical and chronological, as well as the recurrence of characters and motifs drawn from Greek mythology, and strange, exotic lands, was pronounced. His awakening came when a friend took some of his poems to the fiction writer Juan Bosch, then editor of the weekly literary section which appeared in the newspaper *El Listín Diario*. Bosch rejected the poems with the comment that their author had poetic talent but needed to direct his eyes to his land. Then a second submission from Mir came, showing a more autochthonous rendition of the poet's reality, and Bosch was quick to publish them on December 19, 1937 with a note welcoming Mir as perhaps the "social poet" that the country needed (Schmidt-Rodríguez; Bosch 1989: 150).

When Mir discovered a definite socio-aesthetic direction in which to guide his literary efforts, he immediately undertook to study and refine his capacity for expression within the social mode. He achieved considerable visibility in the 1930s and is reputed to have earned the praise of Fabio Fiallo (1866-1942), then the elder statesman of Dominican letters, who greeted the young poet as a maker of "auténtica poesía" (authentic poetry), saying of himself that he could now step aside to make way for the innovations of Mir. Similarly, poems of his appeared in the canonical *Antología poética dominicana* (1943), edited by Pedro René Contín y Aybar, one of the key figures of the Dominican intellectual establishment at the time. Significantly, Contín y Aybar's brief remarks of introduction to Mir's poems imply a slight condemnation of Mir's predilection for social themes. The editor reminisced nostalgically for an earlier time when the young poet had been viewed as "the Benjamin of Dominican poets", for his lyrical tone, the intimate, confessional quality of his poems. Contín y Aybar expressed his regret at Mir's "drastic shift" to "social problems", seeing in it a mental attitude of snobbery which he thought the poet would outgrow, especially since, in his view, Mir had recently begun to write "with the same lyrical intensity of his beginnings" (Contín y Aybar 1943: 265).

Like Contín y Aybar, Franklin Mieses Burgos, the principal figure in the aestheticist, Western-oriented movement known as "La Poesía Sorprendida" which dominated literary activity in the 1940s, spoke of what he saw as an unproductive tension in Mir's poetry. The representatives of "Poesía Sorprendida" dissociated themselves from the "essences of national life" and committed themselves to the poetic expression of "cosmic sentiments and the spiritual meanderings that characterize the contemporary soul," says literary historian Joaquín Balaguer (1970: 316). Informed by such aesthetics, Mieses Burgos regretted the "tension" stemming from the opposition between what he termed Mir's "authentically lyrical nature" and the poet's obstinacy in pursuing an epic tone, with damaging consequences for the "authenticity" of his work and for the possibilities of an otherwise great poet (cited in Baeza Flores 1977: 153). The perception of a dual vein, social and personal, coexisting in this period of Mir's early verse attracted the attention of other commentators who did not, on the whole, view it as disabling. For the Cuban scholar Otto Olivera the "despondency" reflected in Mir's exploration of the personal and the social "concern" apparent in his evocation of the national ambiance arise from the same delicate and persistent grief that permeates his vision (Olivera 1957: 153-54).

Both Contín y Aybar and Mieses Burgos in their rejection of the "epic" or "social" accent of Mir's early poetry were adhering to the unwritten rules that governed artistic production under the regime of dictator Rafael Leonidas Trujillo, who had come to power in 1930 and would remain there until his death thirty years later. The Trujillo regime succeeded in dominating all intellectual and artistic endeavours in the country through a combination of intimidation and "generous" support. No government before Trujillo had invested comparable levels of resources in fostering intellectual activity and constructing an image of national identity and an official definition of Dominican culture as the iron-fisted dictatorship did. Literary and cultural journals emerged with the support of the government, which had its own vigorous publishing house. Historiography boomed with researchers working under the auspices of the State. Whole breeds of poets, such as the poetic generation of 1948, came into view as a result of the publication opportunities made available by the regime (Torres-Saillant 1994: 55). The understanding, of course, was that no one would strike a discordant note. Members of the intelligentsia, of which Contín y Aybar and Mieses Burgos were prominent literary representatives, contributed to advancing the nationalist myth that construed the "Era of Trujillo" as the reign of a "patria nueva" (new fatherland) that broke with the ignominies of the past and brought everlasting happiness and peace to the Dominican family (Mateo 1993: 16). Mir's early poems contained a measure of social discontent that the literary establishment, while not willing to censor it at first, could not let pass without some expression of disapproval.

Mir's early poems, then, placed him in a delicate position with respect to the aesthetics favoured by the Trujillo regime. The poems published in Contín y Aybar's anthology illustrate both of the currents identified by commentators on the early Mir. The short poem "Pour toi" combines a classical metrical arrangement with images drawn from a register characteristic of Federico García Lorca to produce a love poem in a personal tone not unlike that of the courtly tradition: "Menudo lino de amores/abona mis noches tuyas/y me florecen de sueños/como los cielos de luna" – Slight love clothes/cultivate my nights and yours/and they blossom in dreams/like the moon-filled skies (Mir 1943: 272). Another poem significantly entitled "Abulía" presents us with a speaker who sings his lack of direction, his impotence, and loss of will power. It evokes the spiritual bankruptcy of the speaker, whose life has "forgotten the way" and has only the contours of a "yawn" to travel in: "Después de todo, yo soy mío./Mi vida es un navío/que ha cabido en el charco de un bostezo" – After all, I am mine./My life is a ship/ that's stranded in the pool of a yawn (p. 266). These texts evoke aspects of an intimate mode in that the speaker appears to relate to the world as an individual engaged above all in the business of articulating the experience of his subjectivity.

On the other hand, Mir's concern with the experience of the collective occupies him in the poem "Grito para enterrar a un maestro", which dramatizes the speaker's mourning for the death of a beloved teacher. A teacher by the very nature of his or her social function is someone who is valued primarily in relation to a collective, which is why, in voicing the farewell, the speaker assumes the first person plural: "No te decimos adiós" – We do not say good-bye to you" (p. 269). The figure of the teacher acquires significance also in so far as it is associated with a message of light that can perpetuate itself in generations to come. Thus, we hear: "Tu mano sembrada/eternamente enflorará el cultivo./Siempre tu voz palpitará en el aula/como un millón de corazones vivos" – Your planted hand/will forever nourish the crops./Your voice will always flutter in the classroom/like a million palpitating hearts (p. 269). The image of the sower appropriately articulates the poet's view of the teacher whose job is to scatter over his pupils, and consequently his pupils' pupils, the seeds of learning.

A poem entitled "Bolero son", also in Contín y Aybar's anthology, goes farther into the realm of social commentary. The poem is rich in sonority as well as in visual motifs drawn from the local environment. The "son" referred to in the title alludes to the number being played by the six musicians whose drama constitutes the subject of the poem. The speaker construes them as six workers whose backs are bent by the weight of their labour ("seis espaldas que dobla el trabajo" (p. 267)). Their job is to forge someone else's joy, and we are made to see their plight by contrast to the luxury of those whom they entertain, people who are sufficiently well off to hail "the sweat" of the musicians' performance with the bubbles of "blond champagne". The poem's rhythm reproduces the tempo of the musical number being played by the workers/musicians and suggests the enthusiasm of the players, which derives not from the frivolous dance they are currently brightening with their music but from their knowledge that because of their present work, tomorrow they will be able to feed their families. In other words: "el sexteto se anima pues sabe,/que el tizón de esta noche, mañana/bailará crepitante en su anafe,/y un calor de higüeyanos burenes/caldeará feculentos casabes" – the band is encouraged by knowing/ that tonight's fire tomorrow/will dance crackling in their stove,/and the heat from Higüey's famous pots/will cook feculent cassavas (p. 268). The poverty of players "supliciados del ritmo y del hambre" – tortured by rhythm and hunger – contrasts with the opulence of those at the dance, making the social inequality of the local environment plainly clear. At the same time, the culturally native scenario envisioned by the hungry musicians, the firebrand being kindled under the "anafe" (portable stove used locally in rural areas) to warm the "burenes" (earthen cooking pots used by local peasants) in which to cook the "casabes" (foodstuff known as cassava bread dating back to pre-Columbian times in the area) contrasts decidedly with the European associations elicited by the "rubios champanes" (blond champagnes). The implication of the contrast is simple: the upper classes, who live the most privileged lives, are spiritually and culturally distant from the local milieu.

The majority of Mir's poems that appeared in Contín y Aybar's anthology recall the poetic diction of García Lorca. The one entitled "Alegría de la mañana blanca" would fit perfectly in García Lorca's *Romancero gitano* (1928) or *Canciones* (1936). Mir has disclaimed the direct influence of the poet from Granada during his formative years, affirming that his knowledge of García Lorca's poetry, as well as that of Pablo Neruda, came rather late since he had consciously tried to "protect" himself from their influence (Schmidt-Rodríguez 1983: 39). But the Chilean poet and critic Alberto Baeza Flores, who has written an extended commentary on the early Mir, has shown a considerable correspondence between him and the Spanish poet (Baeza Flores 1977: 241-65). Mariano Lebrón Saviñón (1982: 46) and Marcio Veloz Maggiolo (cited in Rosario Candelier 1977: 256-57), to cite only two names of well-known Dominican men of letters, have similarly highlighted the presence of García Lorca in the early Mir. Assuming, then, that Mir's dismissal of any direct influence from García Lorca is worthy of credence and not merely a chronic case of authorial conceit, one could understand the resemblance in terms of Mir making a parallel discovery of rural cultural resources as García Lorca had made in his popular poetry. In García Lorca, Baeza Flores estimates, Mir came upon the rich source of "la poesía popular" (1977: 248). García Lorca had explored the directness, gracefulness, and simplicity of popular communication, and Mir undertook a comparable exploration using the local milieu and drawing from the resources of the Dominican folk (Baeza Flores 1977: 249). It could very well be that the Lorquian model made a harmonious fit with the socioculturally conscious aesthetic quest to which Mir had committed himself.

Mir's "Poema del llanto trigueño" caused the newspaper *La Opinión* to hail him as the first "socialist poet" in his country (Lebrón Saviñón 1982: 46; Contín y Aybar 1943: 265). The poem dramatizes the plight of female shirt-makers who, coming to the capital from the interior must endure multiple forms of oppression. The poem, as published in Contín y Aybar's anthology, begins with a speaker describing in the present tense an everyday scene at "la calle del Conde", one of the oldest and traditionally most commercially active streets in the city of Santo Domingo. The attention focuses on the shirts shown in the display windows of stores. The suggestion immediately voiced is that though a shirt may look pretty to a window shopper, its attractive appearance conceals a bitter drama of underpaid and overworked women peddling at the sewing machine and cutting endlessly with their scissors: "La tragedia! /El monorrítmico son de los pedales sonámbulos;/el secreto fatídico y tenaz de las tijeras" – The tragedy!/The monorythmic song of somnambulant pedals/the ominous, tenacious secret of the scissors (Mir 1943: 240). The speaker evokes the general situation of working class women, their exploitation and dehumanization, and suggests that the "history" of the shirt-makers parallels the plight of the whole land which is currently being "exprimida como una fruta" (squeezed like a fruit) and "ordeñada como una vaca" (milked like a cow) by unfeeling predators. The second part of the poem particularizes the drama by narrating the story of a young woman coming from rural Monte Plata to the capital hoping to forge for herself a decent future. Weakened doubly by the alien urban environment and by the innocence of her years, she easily falls prey to the lecherous mendacity of Niño Rivera. Now a single mother, having been abandoned with his child, she has no alternative but to accept her excessive work and meagre salary. She can barely make ends meet: "y un ogro le está pagando/con un pan veinte docenas!" – and an ogre is paying her/for twenty bundles a loaf of bread (p. 242). In part three, the history of pain dramatized in the plight of the young woman from Monte Plata symbolizes the larger suffering of the country, a history written with the blood of the Dominican people: "y dondequiera, un dolor rojo de sangre en mi tierra" – and everywhere, a blood-red pain in my homeland (p. 243).

"Poema del llanto trigueño" draws abundantly on contrasts. The articles of clothing on display at "la calle de Conde" are divided into contrasting colours: some white here and some black there. Likewise, framed within traditional colour symbolism, the young woman comes to Santo Domingo with "ensueños blancos" (white illusions) but must meet a bitter set of "verdades negras" (black truths). Her rural background contrasts with the industrial urban setting she must confront. The colour symbolism is used to strengthen the contrasts which are more social than ethnic, but it is clear that the young woman is a "trigueña," which in Dominican usage suggests a mulatto woman (Caamaño de Fernández 1989: 133-34; Candelier 1977: 294). The racial features of Niño Rivera and the factory owners who exploit her are not given, but one assumes them to be white or light-skinned since in the Dominican Republic the upper classes are generally lighter than the masses of the people. And it is clear that the young woman is culturally and spiritually closer to the land than her exploiters – who exploit the land the same way they do her.

Baeza Flores has correctly observed that "Poema del llanto trigueño" prefigures many of the preoccupations that would characterize the Mir of the long poems that have earned him a central place in contemporary Dominican literature, pointing to a number of recurring images and motifs that reappear in fuller expression later in *Hay un país en el mundo* (1949), the best known of Mir's poetic works both in his country and abroad. The association of the exploitation of the female labourers and the exploitation of the native land, both depleted by the depredation of the ruling class, becomes a central motif in Mir's longer poems, as Baeza Flores notes. As in his later work in various genres, in the early poetry of Mir: "The land is not just the image of Dominicanness, but it is, in addition, the land itself, the actual soil, that symbolizes the country" (Baeza Flores 1977: 262).

Dissidence and Exile

The firmness with which Mir seems to have determined his socio-aesthetic course by the time his poems appeared in Contín y Aybar's anthology made him suspect in the eyes of the establishment. His anthologist, Contín y Aybar, who thought it "snobbish" for poets to be meddling with social issues, was evidently so disapproving of a large part of Mir's poetic production that when, eight years later, he published a second edition of his celebrated anthology, he conveniently excised Mir's poems and omitted any mention of his name. Trujillo's regime had achieved a perfect synchrony between the intellectual establishment and the political power structure. By 1951, when the second edition of the anthology appeared, Mir had already begun his long exile. Though he had endured only relatively mild harassment from the regime's intelligence agents, his link with anti-Trujillo circles had become quite visible. The tone of his poetry which was aggressive to the *status quo*, and the nature of his acquaintances, the closest of whom had ended up in prison or in the grave, amounted to a "provocation" which could only bring him harm (Piña Contreras 1980: 46). In 1941 he had obtained his law degree from the state university in the capital, after which he served as a secondary school teacher until 1947, when, using illness as a pretext, he obtained permission to travel abroad, and began an absence that would last fifteen years (Piña Contreras 1980: 46; "Mir, Pedro" 1988: 336).

During his exile Mir underwent what he himself described as "a very profound anonymity" (Piña Contreras 1980: 47). Living abroad came without glamour for him. He did not enjoy the visibility of prestigious political expatriates such as Bosch, who befriended Pedro Henríquez Ureña, Nicolás Guillén, Rómulo Gallegos, and Miguel Otero Silva, among other major literary figures of Latin America. Nor did he form part of famous intellectual circles. Rather, settled in Cuba, where he earned a quiet living doing menial jobs, he continued to write, publishing there his first volume *Hay un país en el mundo* in 1949, eliciting no fanfare (Torres-Saillant 1993: viii). The fortune which befell *Hay un país en el mundo* vividly illustrates Mir's invisibility in the Caribbean and Latin-American literary scene after he left his native land. Suffice it to mention that though the book had appeared in Cuba in 1949, neither the Dominican poet Antonio Fernández Spencer, writing in Madrid in 1953, nor the Cuban scholar Otto Olivera, writing in Syracuse in 1957, had heard about it since both referred to the author as having published "no books" (Fernández Spencer 1953: 66; Olivera 1957: 154). Dominican readers remained oblivious to the existence of the book until the early 1960s when, the dictator dead and the regime presumably finished, Mir went back home.

Fernández Spencer included poems by Mir in his anthology *Nueva poesía dominicana* (1953), choosing from texts published in Dominican newspapers, magazines, and in Contín y Aybar's anthology before the poet's departure (Fernández Spencer 1953: 63). The ten poems selected by Fernández Spencer further illustrate the dominant themes, tone, and motifs that characterized Mir's early production. Among them, "Plática del pozo" is a text whose lyrical vein has earned the enthusiastic praise of critics who represent different generations and presumably different ways of reading in Dominican literature (Lebrón Saviñón 1982: 49; Veloz Maggiolo 1972: 165). One could also read in the poem a perfect marriage between the lyrical and the social. The poet here creates the character of a well, personified, which reflects upon what it sees in the surroundings. Uttering its thoughts from the perspective of the personal "I", the well tells of how it has for long witnessed the life of the island: "Since then the island ends in my lips" (p. 244). But the larger part of the well's words take the form of a plaint motivated by human penury. It grieves over the death of a young woman who throws herself in its water, a hurricane that shakes the stability of the landscape, and, above all, the plight of the people, whose silence and "broken smiles" betray their deep sorrow: "Veo los brazos marcados y el silencio/de rostros retorcidos y la risa tronchada" – I see the arms branded and the silence/of contorted visages and the broken smile (Mir 1953: 246). The social statement of the poem, the indictment of the prevailing order is unequivocal. The well's solidarity with those who are suffering has very clear political implications, particularly if seen against the background of the Trujillo dictatorship.

For Fernández Spencer the merit of "Plática del pozo" lies in the fact that the poem's conspicuous "social content" does not express itself in "harsh verses", and he insists that the virtue of Mir's handling of political matter in poetry is precisely his injecting it with lyrical beauty (p. 64). But also significant for the present study is the evocation of the physical surroundings of the native land. The well, the hurricane, and other indicators of the regional landscape visually place the scenery in the Caribbean. "Material de mi aldea", also selected by Fernández Spencer, features a speaker who reminisces about his ancestors and the birth of his village, recalling a past which included "negros importados" (imported black slaves) like the past of most other old Caribbean villages (p. 235). "Evocación del ruido" recalls an earlier, happier time and records the moment when the present malaise became established. The violence of the present forced itself upon the land as a "gran ruido" (loud noise) which, oddly enough, manages to institute a reign of silence: "it silenced every mouth" (p. 238). Silence in this and other poems by Mir has the connotation of submission, decay, and destruction, much in the way it does in Brathwaite.

The telluric drive, the sensibility bound to the earth that constantly reflects upon the physical space of the native land becomes more clearly evident in "La vida manda que pueble estos caminos", in which the speaker considers his mission, dictated by life itself, to populate "these roads", which are variously called "gory", "old" and "dark." A possible reading of this plea to have the land inhabited anew may be the desire to replenish or renovate the spirit of resistance. This desire would appear more overtly expressed in the poet's *Hay un país en el mundo*: "Men are needed/for so much land" (Mir 1993: 11). The concern with the land reflected in the direct reference to roads reappears in the poem significantly entitled "Terruño", also anthologized by Fernández Spencer. The very title, which rendered into English suggests "clod of earth" or "native soil", carries the sense of an affective disposition toward the homeland. The speaker looks at his dear land from the various cardinal points and sees everywhere the sight of constant bewailing and the shedding of infinite tears: "Esta tierra de llanto, del hondo llanto de infinitas lágrimas" – This land of sorrow, of the deep sorrow of infinite tears (Mir 1953: 237). In singing his lament for the sorrowful state of the land the speaker presents us with a threnodic song for the plight of his people. Mir's poems frequently contain a correspondence between the soil and the human beings who live on the soil and whose livelihood depends on the soil. In his clod of earth, not only the land but also the sun begins with the people, represented by the worker, who always appears as an indomitable repository of hope. Thus: "diré que el sol empieza con la breve sien del herrero,/que siempre es mediodía en sus pupilas" – I will say that the sun begins with the minute temple of the smith/ that it is always noon in his eyelids (p. 236).

The texts selected by Contín y Aybar and by Fernández Spencer illustrate Mir's poetic dedication to the soil and the people of his native land, his tendency to scrutinize social reality, to search for the origin of the prevailing conditions, and to explore and celebrate the possible sources of strength. His early poetry shows him engaged with the historical imagination, with his analysis of present conditions usually entailing a look at the past. In Mir, as in Brathwaite and Depestre, a retrospective look prepares the poet for articulating his hope for the future. As argued before, history in the region is inseparable from the political. Thus, reflection on prevailing conditions in the Dominican Republic and elsewhere in the region frequently refer the speaker to a search for origins to gain the understanding required for any proposed remedy. The position one assumes with regard to the past in the Antilles presuppose a political posture since that position will inform how one views the future. One can say confidently of Mir, as has been said of Césaire, that for him "the political consciousness of the individual is and must necessarily be a historical consciousness (Owusu-Sarpong 1986: 244).

Epic and History

In the long poems which begin with *Hay un país en el mundo*, Mir's work acquires an ever-increasing historical sense. This poem is a chant of protest, featuring a speaker who, assuming a panoptic vantage point, looks at his native land and is appalled. The obvious reference is to the Trujillo dictatorship, whose ruthless regime had wiped out all political opposition in the country and succeeded in instituting a system of control of the minds and bodies of individuals that closely resembled the tyrannical efficiency of Orwell's Big Brother. Yet one can find no anti-Trujillo slogan or any sort of personalized recrimination in the poem. Instead, the speaker undertakes to reveal the socio-historical context in which such a grievous reality exists. In the opening of the poem, as translated by Donald D. Walsh, the speaker begins his analysis by placing the country geographically: "There is a country in the world/situated/right in the sun's path./A native of night./Situated/in an improbable archipelago/ of sugar and alcohol" (Mir 1193: 3). The association of sugar and alcohol with the Caribbean region, as well as the unpleasant images that follow, such as the simile "abused and kicked/like a young girl's hips" (p. 5) put a heavy socio-historical weight on the very geography of the place. The geography is thus linked with a legacy of suffering in the region, not unlike the way in which Césaire's *Cahier d'un retour au pays natal* connects the geography with the bitter human experience evoked by "the hungry Antilles, the Antilles pitted with smallpox, the Antilles dynamited by alcohol, stranded in the mud of this bay, in the dust of this town sinisterly stranded" (Césaire 1983: 35).

As the poem continues and the dissecting glance of the speaker spans over the native soil, his attention rests on the unbelievable fact that in this country ("país inverosímil"), which abounds in land, the peasants have no land: "where birds swim or fly but in between/there is only land:/the peasants have no land" (Mir 1993: 15). This observation leads immediately to the need for explaining who possesses the land. This he does by invoking the song of the sugar plantation, "a song" which consists of single lines naming component parts of the country, including mountains, the water, and the grass, followed by the refrain "they belong to the company" ("son del ingenio"), which ascribes the ownership of all the landscape to the sugar plantations. The landscape includes the people, who are called upon to invest their human capital either as workers for, or as salaried defenders of the sugar plantations: "and the limbs of the simplest man/belong to the company/and his youthful veins/belong to the company/and the guards with rifles for voices/belong to the company" (p. 17).

The link between the sugar plantation and Trujillo's dreadful regime, as the poem implies, accords with the analysis of most historians irrespective of their ideological persuasion. The sugar industry flourished in the Dominican Republic following the American military occupation of 1916 and the subsequent implementation of land reforms that favoured that industry. When the Americans released the rule of the nation to a Dominican administration in 1924, sugar plantations, which were controlled by and served the interests of foreign capital, were at their peak. Moreover, the young Trujillo, who had received his training by the occupying forces, was already chief of the national guard, a body which the American military government had instituted (Moya Pons 1995: 323). The sugar plantations (and that includes the reference to "alcohol" since Dominican rum was one of the country's main exports) account for the peasants' lack of land and support the social order responsible for the reign of terror. As a result we have a country which is hardly worthy of the name: "This is a country unworthy of being called a country./Call it rather tomb, coffin, hole, or sepulchre" (Mir 1993: 21). We have also a country in which silence has conquered the hearts of the lawyers, the poets, and the judges: "lawyers/who are no more than tablets and silence, with poets/who are no more than mist and silence, and the silent/judges" (p. 21).

Once the appalled onlooker has articulated his country's present calamity via a historical analysis, his projection of the future seems to follow naturally. As the poem draws to a close, he envisions the arrival from the mountains of an "enlightened rumour", a sort of liberatory trumpet-call that will not only put an end to the monopoly of silence but will also revive the spirit of resistance that lies dormant in the people's past. The messianic vision is not clear on the precise form the resistance will take, but it leaves no doubt about the impending violence and bloodshed: "there will again be blood in the country./There will again be blood in the country" (p. 25).

The Dominican Republic did see instances of bloodshed in the years following the publication of Mir's poem. Two anti-Trujillo armed incursions came from abroad, organized by Dominican exiles, in 1949 and 1959. Although both were unsuccessful, the latter shook the stability of the regime by inspiring conspiracy from within, eliciting increased repression by the dictatorship, and unleashing a chain of repercussions that would result in the death of the tyrant on May 30, 1961 (Moya Pons 1995: 373). Dominican readers of *Hay un país en el mundo* have tended to see a prophetic element in the poem in light of the aforementioned violent events. Mir's explanation of this supposed prophetic element is significant for what it tells of his understanding of the relationship between the past and the future. He believes there is no magic or miracle in the augury ascribed to his poetry but merely a historical dynamic: "Thus, I see nothing prodigious nor miraculous in foretelling the outcome of a situation that historically would of necessity reach a given end" (Piña Contreras 1980: 53).

The grand conception, the large regional scope of *Hay un país en el mundo* displays an unmistakable "epic breath" (aliento épico), to use the phrase a critic applies to Mir's poetry (Pérez-Montaner 1974: 55). This characteristic of the poem has been amply examined by Victor Fernández-Fragoso whose doctoral dissertation studied four major poems by Mir, viewing them together as a "national epic" (Fernández-Spencer 1978: 51-65). The text has national and regional dimensions in that its relevancy pertains to the historical condition of both the Dominican Republic and the rest of the Caribbean, as has been observed by the Cuban scholar Mercedes Santos Moray, who argues that Mir's poem provides images not only "of his people" but "of all the Antilles" (Santos Moray 1973: 142). Similarly like most other epic chants, the core of its subject matter is history. The Dominican poet Héctor Incháustegui perhaps put it most succinctly when he described *Hay un país en el mundo* as "our history, history of our sorrow and of our defencelessness" (Incháustegui 1977: 174).

The historiographical texture increases and the epical tenor is heightened in *Contracanto a Walt Whitman: canto a nosotros mismos* (1952), the next long poem by Mir. Published in Guatemala, where the poet had travelled to participate in some poetry recitals, the text is truly an epopeia of the relationship between the United States and the rest of the Americas (De Jesús 1982: 83). Consisting of seventeen sections, the poem is conceived as a "counter-song" to Walt Whitman, with particular allusion to the American poet's *Song of Myself*. It tells of "the growth of the United States and American democracy on the basis of an exalted notion of self" which is then "swallowed and imprisoned by the growth of selfishness, expressed in the growth of Banks, Trusts, and Monopolies", culminating in the need to advance toward and exploit the other Americas, as summarized by Didier Tisdel Jaen, the author of an English translation of part of the poem (Tisdel Jaen 1969: 83). The poem's narrative voice delves into an analysis of the American past to recreate the context within which it once seemed feasible to assert one's individuality, since even people of lowly station could hope to gain access to the material possessions which guaranteed independence. But now the vast American territory has been so fully absorbed by the reproductive needs of capital that the individual has no space within which to achieve realization.

The historical evocation begins by looking far back into the American past. The speaker tells of a time long ago when the land was "pure", when vegetation and the soil had neither "names" nor "fences". We get thus a picture of pre-European times in America. Then came the colonial moment, which evolved into the early democracy. This development came about not without violence, chiefly against native Americans and slaves. But on the whole, there prevailed the sense, at least among the settlers, that there were limitless possibilities for personal growth. As growth demanded a mindset of self-confidence and faith, the atmosphere of development gave rise to the gospel of individualism and the celebration of the "I". "Self-confidence/was essential/Faith was essential./And ever so gently was forged the song:/I the cowboy and I the adventurer/and I the pioneer and I the gold panner...," the speaker goes on to recall (Mir 1993: 63). As the celebration of the "I" gains currency in all spheres of life, it does so in poetry as well, hence the self-referentiality of the great American poet: "and I/Walt Whitman,/a kosmos,/of Manhattan the son...!" (p. 63).

In the view of the speaker in *Contracanto a Walt Whitman*, Whitman's emphasis on individuality was legitimate and appropriate in that it really captured the sentiment of the collective. Whitman's "I" arose in the context of a democracy that enabled the people to feel they had control over their individual life, liberty, and pursuit of happiness. Paradoxically, then, the poet's "I" was not individualistic in an estranging or alienating sense. It derived from a feeling of equality, and in that respect it was a popular, collective, democratic "I". For the people saw themselves collectively in that "I", or as the poem says: "And all the people saw themselves/when they heard the world/I/.../and I was Democracy, the people's family name" (p. 69).

One might contest the historical accuracy of the picture drawn by Mir's speaker regarding the presumed equality enjoyed in early America by the people, even if we restrict the term to encompass solely the white community. Historians of the colonial period and the early Republic in the United States could easily adduce evidence to show that the people, as referred to in "We the people", normally included only persons with certain assets, thus making the claim of a generalized equality, even among whites, difficult to sustain. But this does not detract from the significance of the picture, whereby the poet renders his perception of the evolution of the concept of individuality. At the metaphorical level, one might value Mir's account of what in the poem he perceives as the changes undergone by a people in the stages of its historical development. Perhaps most importantly, his vision shows the understanding that a people's historical experience not only shapes its character but also its artistic expression.

Whitman in the *Contracanto* appears as the direct product of the historical experience of a given people. His greatness, the poem seems to say, lies precisely in how gloriously he succeeded in assuming the voice of his people. The following lines provide a reflection on the nature of Whitman's achievement and illustrate Mir's view of the relationship between poet and community. The speaker rhetorically asks: "For/what has a great, undeniable poet been/but a crystal-clear pool/where a people discover their perfect likeness?/What has he been/but a deep garden/where all men recognize themselves/through language?/And what but the chord of a boundless guitar/where the fingers of the people play/their simple, their own, their, strong and/true, innumerable song?" (Mir 1993: 67).

In this celebration of Whitman's greatness, the speaker legitimizes the American bard and his self-assertiveness. But the historical context changed in the course of time. Soon the old individualism lost its original humanity. As the dynamics of capital reproduction and capitalist accumulation progressed in the North American territory, the ethos of individual self-realization gave way to the ambition of the multimillionaires whose economic rule, as manifested in monopolies and trusts, tended to crush the individual possibilities of the common man. With their financial *locus* in Wall Street, the paladins of capital, symbolized in the figure of Mr. Babbitt (an obvious allusion to the character in Sinclair Lewis's 1922 novel *Babbitt*), stretched their greedy hands into the rest of the New World. Whitman did not lead expansionistic projects, but those who do, using both financial and military means, employ a language that resembles his: "'I, Babbitt, a kosmos,/of Manhattan the son./He'll only tell you:/Bring me the Antilles/on several rapid-fire calibers, on machine-gun/belts,/on the caterpillar treads of tanks/bring me the Antilles" (p. 77). After the Antilles fall, the rest of the Americas with their natural resources must be engulfed by Mr. Babbitt's voracity: "Bring me all those nations in sugar, in nitrate,/in tin, in oil, in bananas,/in syrup/bring me all those nations'" (p. 79).

Since monopoly and expansionism imply for the speaker in *Contracanto* a loss of individuality, the many being dispossessed by the very few, Mr. Babbitt's brandishing of Whitman's "I" is seen as a desecration. Therefore, he, the "son of the Caribbean,/ Antillean to be exact", as he calls himself in the proemium, must declare the word "I" void and useless. It no longer serves as "the accomplished word,/the password to begin the world" as it once did for good old Whitman (p. 89). Now the time has come for the word "We" (nosotros) to put on its show. And that is precisely what the "counter-song" is about: the people, the wretched of the earth, conjured by the Antillean voice, coming to update Whitman's song by affirming their collective identity with the same vigour with which the old poet had affirmed the individual. The counter-song thus seeks to rescue the "democratic Walt Whitman" from any association with the likes of Babbitt, who use the poet's "tongue" in expansionistic projects and deprive whole nations of their humanity. The speaker, assuming a collective voice, speaking from the Caribbean, "full of pupils/dilated throughout the islands" (p. 47), rises to "justify" Whitman, as the American bard had implored in the 1867 short poem entitled "Poets to Come".

Contracanto a Walt Whitman manifests great admiration for the author of *Leaves of Grass*. At the same time it shows a passionate interest in the historical development of the United States in so far as that development has had significant repercussions on the Caribbean experience. Informed by Mir's notion that humankind "has a past and that past explains us" and that history and poetry are very closely linked, the poem is one of the most telling examples of the Caribbean writer's "servitude" to the muse of history (Schmidt-Rodríguez 1983: 40). The poem also goes a long way to illustrate Mir's insistence on his Antillean identity. While it intends to cover the drama of all the countries of the Americas, the speaker always expresses himself from a Caribbean perspective and the focal point of the "counter-song" remains in the region. It is interesting in this respect that Fernández Fragoso, who reads this poem as an "épica americana", also sees in it the "true Caribbeanness" of Mir (Fernández Fragoso 1978: 66).

Hope as Weapon of the Lowly

The year after *Contracanto*, Mir's small collection *Seis momentos de esperanza* (1953) appeared in Guatemala (Alcántara Almánzar 1979: 242). The volume consists of six texts, hence the title, which translates into English as "Six moments of hope". Here the concept of hope as a necessary outlook for the oppressed peoples of the Americas reaches the fervour of a gospel. We are presented with a lyrical voice that speaks a distinct regional creed with an indomitable faith in the future. This collection inaugurates Mir's undaunted commitment to celebrating the pre-eminence of hope in an overt and assertive manner, an element that would later be recognized as a trademark of his work. In connection with a subsequent book, the Puerto Rican writer Manuel Maldonado Denis would associate Mir's wielding of the weapon of hope with the characteristic diction of the Antillean world. He says: "Like every great poet whose vital orbit is the Caribbean, Mir brings to his poetic cosmos the profound concern of someone who has understood the causes of the despair and the hope that animate our region" (Maldonado Denis 1973: 22).

The central poem in the collection is entitled "Si alguien quiere saber cúal es mi patria". The poem speaks of the unity of the Americas. One should not ask him, the speaker says, where his homeland is or whether it has natural beauties and natural resources which belong to foreign interests: "Do not try to know if there are forests, trails/a multitude of far-off peninsulas,/or if there are four mountain chains,/all upright,/or if there are several destinies of bays/and all foreign" (Mir 1993: 29). The common plight of the whole hemisphere makes the question of who comes from where in the region meaningless: "And so, we the peoples of America go about/so numerous, so one. Let nobody/ask/about anybody's country" (p. 35). All the national units in the area share one common sorrow: "Twenty countries for a single anguish" (p. 35). The text does not call for the elimination of national barriers, as has been suggested by Doris Sommer, who faults Mir's "poetic ideology" for not taking the internationalist ideal all the way (Sommer 1983: 252-53). The poem rather grieves over the fact that in the region no one can boast of having a homeland because all the homelands are controlled by foreign capitalist centres. The text does not proclaim the unity of the hemisphere as a desideratum. It merely describes the unity such as it exists, which is very limited. It recognizes their "unité dans la misère," their general dependence, and their collective being in the interests of another.

"Si alguien quiere saber cual es mi patria" ends with a hopeful vision, as most of Mir's work does. We have argued that Mir's hopeful vision is a constant with many other Caribbean writers. The speaker in the poem envisions a day when all miracles will be possible and the life the people desire in the region will not be as unlikely as a miracle: "When every miracle is possible/and/the miracle of life is no longer a miracle" (p. 39). It will then make sense to speak of the homeland, and the people will rejoice in making multicoloured shirts for their own use and will take their freedom around all the Antilles: "They will bear them on the wind through the valleys/of all the Antilles" (p. 41). Then it will be appropriate to boast of "a great, immense, steadfast country for all" and there will be no place for tears (p. 45). We note that though the speaker describes the global plight of the Americas, his glance stays in the Caribbean. Similarly, the descriptive images through which he suggests the homelands, which he would rather leave unnamed, (sugarcane, machete, batey, etc.) all tend to evoke the region.

The other texts in *Seis momentos de esperanza* include "La vida manda que pueble estos caminos" and "Terruño" which we have discussed as part of the selection by Fernández Spencer. The rest celebrate the worker and the land and express, with urgent expectation, the belief in a better world soon to come. In "Moneda de mi patria" the speaker-poet looks at the plantation where he sees that "como al buey,/al carretero lo desangra el día" – the work-day bleeds the cartwright/as it does the bull (Mir 1962: 55). He sees blood in the hills (colinas) and in the sugar factory (batey), reflecting the inhumane treatment endured by the workers. Yet he recognizes the present moment as "the eve of nearing joy", as he feels his own poetry being fuelled by the people's inevitable liberation (pp. 55-56). Here the certainty that the oppressed will rise is the principal cause of the optimistic outlook. In "Sonetillo final de la esperanza", the shortest of the poems in the collection, the growing seed of discontent among the farmers in the field (los labradores) and among the workers in the factory (los trabajadores) leads in the last line to a recognition of hope: "Y esta es la esperanza" – And this is our hope (p. 59).

Finally, in "Dominí", in which the speaker addresses a character who represents the local working class, he assures the workers of solidarity on their behalf. Against physical surroundings evoked through Caribbean images, we hear of Dominí's exploitation by the plantation: "En tu girón de archipiélago/de ron y cañaveral,/chupado por el murciélago/numeroso del central" – In your bit of archipelago/of canebrake and rum/emaciated by the plantation's/thirsty bat (Mir 1982: 29). Exploitation and oppression can lead to a feeling of powerlessness and, consequently, despondency. The speaker questions Dominí's passivity: "Hay un mundo de quehaceres/y tú duermes o algo así" – There is a world of things to do/and you seem as if asleep (p. 30). To awaken him, to give him strength, he reminds him of the millions of people all over the world, "del ecuador hasta el polo" – from the equator to the pole, who share his agony and therefore his struggle. The poem emphasizes the hope contained in the awareness of solidarity when in the closing lines what had been the refrain is uttered as an exclamation: "Dominí, no estás tan solo,/no estás tan solo, Dominí!" – Dominí, you're not alone,/you're not alone, Dominí! (p. 32).

The years following the publication of *Seis momentos de esperanza* constitute a hiatus in Mir's poetic production. He himself has said that the difficulties he encountered in exile at that time were of such a magnitude that he could not write another poem until he returned to Santo Domingo in 1962 (De Jesús 1982: 83). Yet, upon his arrival, he immediately became known as a faithful interpreter of the collective sentiment of the Dominican people. Critics soon began speaking favourably of his melodic lyricism and his social commitment. Established Dominican writers saluted the marriage in his work of the personal and the social (M. Henríquez Ureña 1966: 451-52; Incháustegui Cabral 1968: 108). A poet from a younger generation, Ramón Francisco, placed Mir among a few Dominican bards in whose texts we see the native landscape and the local folk "moving forward" for the first time (Francisco 1969: 112). The still younger Pedro Conde proclaimed him as an illustrious ancestor with Federico Bermúdez (1884-1921) of social poetry in Santo Domingo and of the outburst of "poesía joven" (youthful poetry) that began in the country around 1965 (Conde 1970: 10). Different generations of Dominican critics highlighted the fact that the moral urgency of Mir's message did not lessen the aesthetic altitude of his poetry, and that the political content of his subject matter never descends to the level of the polemical pamphlet (Balaguer 1970: 318; Alcántara Almánzar 1979: 55).

The Cuban critic Santos Moray's reference to Mir as "poeta nacional" as early as 1973, nine years before the official conferral of that title upon him, suggests the extent to which the communication between his poetry and the people whose dreams and aspirations it purported to interpret was apparent from an early date (Santos Moray 1973: 141). Like Carter, in the case of Guyana, he became the indisputable poet of the people. In addition to the relevancy of the subject matter, the communicative success of Mir's poetry had a stylistic basis. Mir succeeded in combining traditional metrics and other formal resources with nationally relevant themes, such as a focus on the indigenous plantation (Veloz Maggiolo 1972: 46). The poet Manuel Rueda characterized Mir's aesthetic uniqueness as "the rare symbiosis" of elements often considered dichotomous. He stressed the combination in Mir's verse "of realism and subjectivism, social themes and formal preciosity, verbalism and conceptualism" which the poet manages to blend into a coherent poetic cosmos (Rueda and Hernández Rueda 1972: 12). The rhythms of Mir's poetry caters to the people, but the *preciocismo* of his language does not, says another critic, who speaks of Mir's successful utilization of popular elements as derived from the autochthonous Dominican environment (Rosario Candelier 1977: 10, 256). From these various yet complementary readings of the characteristic style of the poetry of Mir, it would seem reasonable to explain his popularity with the general public in terms of his success in handling themes and forms that his native audience found appealing. His poetry spoke to them at a cultural level in the sort of utterance his people found "eloquent", to borrow a term used by one of the critics (Rosario Candelier 1980: 40; 1982: 159-63).

The great popularity enjoyed by the poetry Mir had already written before he returned home perhaps compensates for his poetic inactivity since *Seis momentos de esperanza*. Mir wrote as someone who assigned great value to what words can do once uttered. The historical sensibility that informed his production also caused him to restrict his creation to literary exercises that he believed could contribute positively to the historical moment of which he was a part. He allowed no space to frivolity. Nor would he espouse the commonplace notion so often repeated by successful authors during interviews that one writes because one cannot control the compulsion to write. Mir wrote out of a need and a desire to shed light on events that wanted clarification. His conviction that one writes not to satisfy some interior yearning for individual expression but to foster the betterment of one's people in society led to Mir's self-imposed silence at times when he felt his sense of hope faltering (Personal communication). At any rate, Mir had a second absence from his native land in 1963 presumably for health-related reasons (Fernández Fragoso 1978: 15). The political turmoil generated by the overthrow of President Juan Bosch, the first head of state that Dominicans had been able to elect in a truly democratic election in the twentieth century, may also lurk behind his decision to endure a second exile.

History and Heroines

Mir published poetry again in 1969, the same year when his essays *Tres leyendas de colores* and *El gran incendio* appeared. Of the two slim volumes of verse that he committed to print in that year, only one, *Amén de Mariposas*, has gained recognition. The other, *Poemas de buen amor ... y a veces de fantasía*, has gone unnoticed by critics and anthologists, who have omitted it from compilations, including the collected poems published by Siglo XXI Editores in 1994. *Amén de mariposas*, a long poem in the epic mode, deals with an event that shook Dominican society during the last months of the Trujillo dictatorship. It evokes the death of Patria, Minerva, and María Teresa Mirabal, three sisters from a middle-class, respectable family who were murdered by the agents of Trujillo on November 25, 1960. The assassination of the Mirabal sisters, who along with their husbands had been imprisoned on account of their participation in left-wing political organizing, intensified the atmosphere of anti-Trujillo feeling in the country (Moya Pons 1995: 372). The poem features a speaker who bewails thus: "When I learned that the three Mirabal sisters had/fallen/I said to myself:/ established society is dead" (Mir 1993: 117). He grieves over the brutal murder of "three of society's mirrors/three refinements of the arm and the pride of men/three and at the same time mothers" (p. 119). For many, the speaker in the poem included, the deaths of those "butterflies" (mariposas), who were mothers as well as wives, marked the beginning of the end of the dictatorship.

The poem is divided into two parts. The first begins with an elegiac reflection on the implications of the murder, suggesting that having overstepped the limits of the conceivable, nothing now has sanctity, and civil society has reached its end. The murders, like everything, had a history, which went back a year, when rebels, coming from abroad, marched against Trujillo's militia. The insurgents gave their lives "at Maimón/and Estero Hondo/at a few shots from Constanza/in the very heart of 1959" (p. 123). The rebels failed in their attempt to free their country from the dictatorship, but their patriotic example had internal repercussions. The opposition movement "14 de Junio", named to commemorate the day when the insurgents arrived in 1959, organized clandestinely to work toward an insurrection from within (Raful 1983: 24-26). As the historian Frank Moya Pons notes, "New conspiracies arose even among Trujillo's close associates. One of these conspiracies had the support of the U.S. government, whose leaders thought that the time had come to put an end to his long tyranny" (Moya Pons 1995: 372).

The speaker in *Amén de mariposas* is not content to retrace the historical steps that explain the murder of the three butterflies back to the anti-Trujillo insurrection the year before. He suggests more distant origins which take us back through sequential layers of the country's past from the conquest that began in 1492 through United States domination in the twentieth century. The following lines, from the English version rendered by Roberto Márquez, which was published in the United States prior to the translation by Donald D. Walsh that I have used in the previous quotes, illustrate succinctly the retrospective examination offered by the poem: "It did not happen once because I cannot tell the story/of this ancient country from which Latin America was/born/for everybody knows it came forth from her vertebrae/in a metallic night called/silence/from a vertebra called Slavery/from another vertebra called Encomienda/from another called plantation/and that from a great spinal column there came down/intact/the Monroe Doctrine" (Mir 1974: 217).

The assassination of the Mirabal sisters which occurred in November suggests to the speaker the assassination of John F. Kennedy, who was also killed in November and has now become "a small inflammation of the earth/ in Arlington Cemetery" (1974: 221). The poem develops the parallel in the second part, and thus, in stressing the difference yet sameness of the two deaths, speaks of the uncontrollability of murder. When it reached the three Dominican sisters, the speaker laments, it marked the end of our time: "at the/end end end/of the Christian Era" (1974: 227). But the speaker is not disheartened. There is hope to be gained even from disaster since "the necessarily weak is the necessarily strong" and especially when one has the certainty that the greatest empires on the planet cannot withstand "the death/ of certain certain/weaknesses amen/to butterflies" (1993: 139). In lamenting the three victims of cruelty, Mir both places the deaths of the Mirabal sisters in the crux of Dominican history and shows the despicable act as an affront to the most elementary values of human decency in established society. By comparison with other literary texts inspired by the same event, written by female authors, Mir's poem lacks a true elegiac evocation of the three murdered sisters as historical beings, as women who of their own accord confronted the challenge posed to them by their history. Mir's speaker mourns the loss not of three protagonists of action but "three refinements of the arm and the pride of men/and at the same time mothers."

As has often been the case with male Caribbean writers, Mir imagines Dominican history as a series of exploits performed by men, with women by their side providing inspiration to spur them on. Yet, a gender-conscious look at the Dominican past would challenge the notion that restricts the arena of action to male actors. The Dominican Republic came into being in 1844, and already by 1849 the folk poet and political activist Manuela Aybar Rodríguez had committed to print a pamphlet entitled *Historia de una mujer* (A Woman's Story), in which she chronicled her direct involvement in the movement that brought down the government of Manuel Jiménes, the second head of the incipient state. In the text she speaks nonchalantly about her barely escaping death at the hands of armed henchmen from the political faction she opposed and of her efforts to elevate the figure of General Pedro Santana to a heroic stature. Her poems, which she printed in her own house, and went about the streets distributing by herself, secured for Santana the title of "Liberator", which the Dominican Congress conferred upon him in 1848 (Rodríguez Demorizi 1938: 84-85).

Dominican literature features a woman, Salomé Ureña de Henríquez (1850-1894), among the two or three nineteenth-century founders acknowledged by the scholars. A champion of the education of women and of their active participation in public life, Ureña scorned the intellectual superficiality that male-centred society traditionally associated with the sphere of women. She began publishing poems under the pen name of Herminia but, characteristically, she immediately abandoned the pseudonym when she discovered that "another 'Herminia' published a somewhat frivolous article on French fashions in a local newspaper" (Paravisini-Gebert 1990: 523). Another champion of the education of women, Evangelina Rodríguez (1879-1947), an author and activist for women's rights, the first woman physician in the history of the Dominican Republic, lived in San Pedro de Macorís, Mir's hometown, from her childhood until her death, which look place in precisely the year when Mir went into exile. She took a firm stand in public affairs. She opposed the Trujillo dictatorship and suffered the consequences. Her opposition resulted in professional ostracism: exclusion from medical associations and scientific congresses. She suffered in her own flesh the brutality of the regime. The bailiffs of the tyranny "beat her up ruthlessly and imprisoned her in the fortress of San Pedro", leaving her unconscious on a deserted road after several days "of interrogation and torture" (Zaglul 1980: 120). She died a mad woman. Her biographer, the Dominican psychiatrist Antonio Zaglul, was convinced that her mental illness had resulted from a "sociogenic" process (1980: 115). The social forces against her as a woman physician in a professional space traditionally reserved for men, a black person of lowly origins before a negrophobic elitist establishment, and a dissident voice in a cold-hearted dictatorship, literally drove her out of her mind.

The historical Mirabal sisters, then, inherited a long legacy of political activism, cultural leadership, and social resistance initiated by women. They had historical models to urge them on to the path of dissidence. Thus, in evoking them, Aída Cartagena Portalatín construes them as active agents of action: "The Mirabal sisters were there/Each breast burning with/the pain – the cross/[...]/The three loved their Nation/the drum-freedom/The three were murdered – each one/was a banner/A huge banner/that wrapped their bodies/together with their torn flesh" (Cartagena Portalatín 1995: 153-55). Moreover, in contrast to Mir's speaker, who assigns to Minerva, Patria, and María Teresa an identity by reference to them as "the pride of men", Cartagena Portalatín's speaker identifies them by association with their immediate female ancestor: "'How beautiful on the flagpole' they are/ The daughters of Doña Chea/Mother of the Mirabal sisters" (1995: 155). Cartagena Portalatín had ample reason to assert the active role of the Mirabal sisters as women assuming their rightful place in history. For she herself, as a woman writer who gained distinction in the literary establishment during Trujillo's dictatorship, had had to demand a space as a woman. Her 1955 poetry book *Una mujer está sola* contains poems that read as manifestos of women's rights. The title poem opens with these lines: "A woman is alone. Alone with herself./With open eyes and open arms./With a heart opened by a wide silence./She awaits in the desperate and despairing night,/without losing hope./She believes herself to be in the leading vessel/lit by creation's saddest light" (1988: 72). The opening stanza from "Estación en la tierra", another poem in the volume, speaks forcefully of the need for women to assert their ontological independence: "I don't believe I am here for nothing./ A woman is wanting here, and I am that woman./I am not weeping. I don't want to reconcile myself/to someone else's deeds" (1988: 76).

The feminist scholar, Daisy Cocco de Filippis, has described Cartagena Portalatín's career, beginning in the 1940s as "a young woman, born and raised in the small coffee-plantation town of Moca", as a feat that combatted "the deafening silence" to which Dominican literary and cultural histories relegated women (Cocco de Filippis 1988: 11). Cocco de Filippis gives the esteemed writer a decisive leadership role in charting the path of contemporary female authors in the Dominican Republic: "Following on the footsteps of Aída Cartagena Portalatín, the spiritual mother of twentieth-century Dominican poetry written by women, Dominican women have finally broken the silence traditionally ascribed to their condition of women to express their own reality with their own words" (Cocco de Filippis 1988b: 14).

In *Tres leyendas de colores* Mir describes the novelist Galván's glorification of Enriquillo calling Galván "a modern-day Enriquillo". Similarly, one could explain Cartagena Portalatín's affirmation of the Mirabal sisters as active makers of history by a comparable equation. She is to Dominican literature as they are to Dominican politics. But perhaps the characterization of the murdered sisters that most sharply contrasts with the secondary identity attributed to them in *Amén de mariposas* is that of the Dominican-descended U.S. writer Julia Alvarez, whose novel *In the Times of the Butterflies* (1994) echoes Mir's poem in the title and may even be read as a countersong to it. Alvarez' novel dramatizes the existential plight of creative and independent-minded women and the tension stemming from their necessary clash with the restrictions placed on a woman's place in a male-centred society. *In the Time of the Butterflies* stages a compelling confrontation between four ordinary and heroic women in the Dominican Republic during Trujillo's rule and the phallocentric social order that upheld the ruthless dictatorship.

Alvarez remains generally faithful to the historical material that fuels her text: the political subversion, persecution, incarceration, and martyrdom of the Mirabal sisters – a chapter that has inspired many Dominican poems and popular songs. What was new to Dominicans at home and captivated readers elsewhere was the depiction of the Mirabal sisters in the full extent of their courageous yet fragile humanity. By staying clear of any impulse to deify, the kind of impulse that "created our tyrant", the novelist has rescued the Mirabal sisters from the realm of myth to place them in the arena of ordinary human existence. As a result they now can serve "as models for women fighting against injustices of all kinds" (Alvarez 1994: 324). The character of Dedé, the surviving sister who inherited the burden of telling the world about "the girls", provides the novelist with an ideal passageway to the characters' early years, permitting us not only to glance at each young woman's personality, talents and yearnings, but also to comprehend that surviving to tell the tragedy is a no less tragic end.

Through the sharp scalpel of her fiction, Alvarez shapes the characters of the Mirabal sisters as agents of subversion who pay no heed to the pretence of social harmony in a harshly oppressive society. Minerva, Patria, María Teresa, and Dedé all step outside the boundaries prescribed for them by an essentially misogynistic political structure with ramifications in the family, school, church, and the workplace. They join an underground movement against a tyranny that punished implacably even the mildest forms of dissent. The dissidence of these women offends the regime even more than that of the men. Indeed, when the scheme to slay them is planned, the high command of the secret service becomes directly involved in engineering an ambush. Their husbands have conspired against the government too, but there is less haste to kill them. Perhaps the reason is that in a phallocracy, female insubordination threatens the very core of the power structure. Thus their subjugation must include not only their public will as citizens but also the private sovereignty of their bodies. Captain Peña Rivera, for instance, uses his power and influence to possess the gentle Patria. Minerva, for her part, must struggle to resist the carnal advances of the chief Trujillo himself (p.110). We have here a system engaged in the cult of manhood, with Trujillo leading the country both as absolute ruler and as preeminent dominator of women. It is not incidental that opposition to the regime is deemed unmanly and offenders earn sexually demeaning epithets. The official press, for instance, can think of no greater insult for the underground opposition than to call them "A party for homosexuals and criminals" (p. 77).

In many respects, the Mirabal sisters, as evoked by Alvarez, are composite parts of a complex, archetypical dissident woman disentangling herself from the throes of man-made definitions of womanhood. *In the Time of the Butterflies* deconstructs the misogynistic dimension of the Trujillo dictatorship with subtlety and beauty. The book shows us the pernicious replication of political oppression in all social spheres, public and private, with the sort of turbulent quiescence that Alvarez's flair for understatement can capture. The fact that a writer as committed to empowering his people as Mir should fail to give women their due as agents of action in history should warn us of the difficulty of articulating a fully humanistic vision of liberation. It should also alert us to the mental barriers that Caribbean women writers encounter when treading intellectual ground that tradition has defined as the sphere of males.

On the Utility of Love

As *Amén de mariposas* creates a historical framework within which to understand a singular murder, Mir's other volume of poetry in 1969, *Poemas de buen amor… y a veces de fantasía*, may be said to historicize the idea of love. In this book Mir seeks to achieve a love poetry that accords with his vision of reality. He portrays love as a condition which takes place within parameters dictated by concrete human imperatives. As he presents it, love occurs in time and space, that is, in the historical experience. The poet avoids the abstractness and otherworldliness that usually shrouds the idea of love in the European literary tradition. Catullus sang to Lesbia. Petrarch sang to Laura. Ronsard sang to Cassandre. Yet in every instance the beloved lady rarely comes anywhere near the materiality of a real woman made of flesh and bone. Her adoring lover invariably paints her as an idealized suprahuman entity.

Until *Poemas de buen amor* Mir had intentionally stayed away from love poetry. "The topic of love, which I take to be an issue involving two individuals, was forbidden in my poetic project," he said once in an interview, adding that he reserved love matters to the realm of his private life (Ornes 1971: 16A). But since he recognized that love was an universal theme that concerned all of humanity, he tried to pursue that "universality" in *Poemas de buen amor* by tackling "a way of articulating the issue of love that would not be in conflict with my poetic project" (Ornes 1971: 16A). Mir complained that modern poetry, even that of poets as innovative as Neruda, differs from the old tradition only in the form, but on the whole, it has failed to recreate the tangible reality of the beloved (Piña Contreras 1980: 52). He, on the other hand, retains the traditional forms. Many of the texts in *Poemas de buen amor* are cast in the sonnet form. In a conversation with young Dominican writers shortly after the publication of this book, Mir discarded the dichotomy of the old and the new: "the old becomes inserted in the new at a higher level of development, as new, with a new content; in other words, a sonnet or a madrigal written in the twentieth century, with the same metrical requirements as in days of old, has a different sense if it captures the drama of our time" (Mir et al. 1972: 3). This logic explains the overall musicality and various metrical devices coming from traditional Spanish poetry that figure substantially in *Poemas de buen amor*. However, as the male speaker sings to the beloved, we see reality in all its crude beauty. Mir has said that "the ultimate aim of love is not poetry but the reproduction of the human species" (Piña Contreras 1980: 52), and this materialistic view appears clearly displayed in the book, which depicts the scent of human flesh and the presence of carnal appetite through its pages.

In keeping with Mir's desire to concretize love, the texts in the volume often evoke the immediacy of sex as a biological mandate to which the lovers succumb. These lines from the second poem in the collection show the lovers obeying the erotic command felt in their veins that makes them roll in the sand and engage in sexual intercourse: "Algo como un naufragio oportuno/se estremeció en nuestras venas/y apagando los ojos y arrastrándonos/conjugamos el verbo arena" – Something like an opportune shipwreck/was stirred up in our veins/and clouding our eyes and crawling/ we conjugated the verb sand (Mir 1969: II). In another poem, the physical exchange of the consummation begins with the beloved's loss of her maidenhead. After the act, the speaker says: "Cargando mi mochila pasajera,/ me dije en el umbral de su cadera:/ – por aquí no ha pasado un solo amor…" – With my travelling knapsack on my shoulders/I thought at the threshold of her hips./ – No other love has passed through here… (IV). Since in the real world intercourse has biological consequences, here the speaker becomes aware after abundant lovemaking that his seed has begun to gestate within the woman: "le descubrí en la vuelta del aliento/un niño breve/con mis ojos pardos" – I discovered at the turn of her breath/a little boy/with my brown eyes (V). On one occasion, he speaks of his desire to impregnate his beloved: "abre tus dos maneras/de caminar/sobre una tangente del planeta/y enséñame a poblar" – Open your two ways/of walking/over one of the planet's tangents/ and teach me to populate (XI).

Sex appears throughout *Poemas de buen amor* as a dynamic force that follows the dictates of the cycles of nature and is inextricably tied to the procreation of the human population. In the poem entitled "Muchedumbre" the relationship between love, sex, and the reproduction of the species acquires the value of an equation. Literally, from the erotic joining of "Ella" (woman) with "El Hombre" (man) there has resulted what we call "la Humanidad" (humanity), says the poem (XV). In this book, then, Mir places love within the concrete parameters of the historical experience. He endeavours to have us see the love that unites man and woman in the poems in terms of the role love plays in human society, hence the emphasis on sex, pregnancy, and reproduction which are perhaps the most tangible expressions of the materiality of that role. It is in this attempt to render love touchable, to historicize it, that the volume is intended, as Mir himself once declared, to supplement his social poetry (Piña Contreras 1980: 53). In placing sexual communication in a materialistic framework, Mir succeeds in articulating a historical vision of the erotic, a theory of love that may strike some readers as a bit puritanical in that it evinces a teleological understanding of carnal desire. Many would prefer views that stress human sexuality as a source of joy that has value and significance in and of itself. But Mir's placement of all human meaning within the contours of historical time disposes him toward a focus on a biological mandate that has social consequences. Views that privilege the pleasure to be derived from sex without attention to the sociology and biology behind it may seem more appealing at a purely lyrical level but they are not necessarily truer. A significant virtue of Mir's conceptualization of sex and love in *Poemas de buen amor* is that the compulsion to historicize, to explicate human action according to forces that transcend individual volition, precludes the idea of a dominant subject who feasts upon the body of a dominated object. Mir's eroticism stays clear of the representation that reduces females to mere objects of male desire or fantasy. *Poemas de buen amor* grants to women, with their clothes off, the dignity and humanity that *Amén de mariposas* denies them, with their clothes on. For us, reading and writing a generation after the Stonewall riots, one wishes Mir had stayed clear of the heteronormative assumptions connoted by his linking sexuality inextricably to reproduction, which by implication assigns rigid roles to males and females.

The Individual and the Collective

The two volumes of verse published by Mir in 1969 construct larger frames within which to explain singular events. Historical and cosmic parameters shed light on a brutal murder and on the contact of two naked bodies. Both volumes exhibit a consistent stylistic and thematic flow. Organized more loosely in form as well as content, *Viaje a la muchedumbre* (1971), his next volume of poetry, consists of thirteen poems that in various ways reflect on the relationship between the individual and the collective. The opening text, "Autorretrato", suggests for the Cuban poet Rafael Catalá the inexorability of the connection between person and community since both the socially committed and the non-committed partake of the plurality (Catalá 1976: 105). The self may be individually named but that does not preclude its containing multitudes. Thus, the speaker draws a parallel between his name and the name of his native land: "Y tengo un sólo nombre en estos versos,/me llamo Pedro Mir, señores./Pero mi pueblo tiene un solo nombre/natal/y por las calles nocturnas/le circulan numerosos nombres" – And I have only one name in these verses/my name is Pedro Mir, my friends./But my country has only one name/native/and on its nocturnal streets/walk numerous names – (Mir 1971: 7). Even the whole world has one name only, yet it encompasses vast pluralities.

The part is always linked to a vaster totality: "igual que nuestra isla en el mar de las Antillas/como un poeta o como un ciudadano único" – Just as our island in the sea of the Antilles/a poet or a citizen alone (p. 7). Mir's conceptual project in "Autorretrato" attempts to overcome the dichotomy of the one and the many, the individual and the community. The speaker in the poem annuls the dichotomy by declaring the inevitable harmony of both, a declaration that one finds echoed in the work of René Depestre, Brathwaite, and many other Caribbean writers. In the same vein, "Viaje a la muchedumbre", the title poem of the collection, tackles the self's recognition and embrace of the multitude and the poetic presentation of the community. The image evoked is that of the speaker's joyous surrender, a sort of healthy bath in their bold, energizing waters. Likewise, in the expressiveness of a dance in "Tarantela", the speaker perceives not only a symbol of the unity and interdependence of the people but also the power of the local setting to keep the seed of survival alive and to perpetuate the love and the dreams of the people despite their present pain: "para un pueblo dolor, una isla sueño,/toda en trance de amor y de rodillas" – for a people in pain,/an island of dream,/fully in trance and on its knees (p. 15).

A number of the poems in *Viaje a la muchedumbre*, such as "Aniversario" (p. 16), "Kyrsis" (pp. 19-21), "Crónica de la metrópoli" (pp. 23-25), and "Flores al sumo pontífice" (pp. 36-30), contain indications of how individual happenings or apparently isolated agonies occur in relation to global historical forces. The weight of the large historical forces becomes more pressing in the latter part of the volume, as illustrated in the poem "Al portaviones 'intrépido'" whose wrathful speaker addresses the aircraft carrier USS *Intrepid* that deployed 1500 marines in Santo Domingo in

February 1962 (Mir 1971: 27). The speaker, whose voice and tone remain passionately irate throughout, blasts the renowned *Intrepid* for having dared to blemish the "dulce bahía" (sweet bay) of Santo Domingo with the inherently violent presence of its military might. If such a mighty power as the USA, which is capable of obliterating the Antilles with one blow, felt the need to bring its menace to the Dominican people, the speaker concludes it must be because of fear, fear of the imperishable power of resistance inscribed in the historical legacy of Dominicans: "other forces terrify you/wider than the empire" (Mir 1993: 105). The poem ends with the speaker enjoining the *Intrepid* to leave lest it be crushed by the wrathful indignation of the people of the Caribbean, as well as by the region's hurricanes: "leave with the help of the diluted wind,/for there are passions of dark hurricanes/throughout the Antillean archipelago,/and do not come back, [lest] the consuming passion/of all women and all men/of all peoples/ achieve what is achieved throughout the world by them, out of boundless rage/and you, [only] out of fear" (p. 109).

Viaje a la muchedumbre features poems that respond directly to recognizable moments in the Dominican past and in the author's biography. The poem entitled "Elegía del 14 de junio" dated 1959, offers a statement of solidarity with the anti-Trujillo expedition that arrived on Dominican shores in that year (Mir 1971: 33-35). Likewise "Balada del exiliado" evokes the doleful exile of the speaker. His involuntary distance keeps him apart from the ashes of his mother buried in the native land. Consistent with Mir's own trauma of exile, the poem endeavours to articulate a vision that fuses the expatriate's individual grief with the historical plight of his country which, in its dependence upon foreign economic interests, seems to endure a comparable exile. He and his homeland are equally depatriated. "Yo cantando baladas por tierras del exilio/ella en cristales de azúcar por playas extranjeras" – I singing ballads through foreign lands/She spreading sugar crystals through alien shores (Mir 1971: 43).

A poem, entitled "Ni un paso atrás", dated 1965, constitutes a compelling chant of solidarity with the armed defenders of the nation against the "snakes" (reptiles), the enemies of the nation. The "snakes,/from our own wretches to vile foreigners" (Mir 1993: 111). The text alludes to the historical episode Dominicans recognize as the Revolution of 1965. Following the overthrow of the constitutional government of Juan Bosch by an alliance of business leaders, the heads of the Catholic Church, and the remnants of Trujillo's military chiefs in September 1963, a succession of provisional governments proved to be more committed to favouring the entrenched oligarchy than to fostering democratic agendas. The military forces supporting these conservative regimes were ruthless in crushing opposition to their rule, as was the case with the insurgent movement headed by Manuel A. Tavarez Justo (Manolo), the husband of Trujillo's victim Minerva Mirabal, who died at the hands of government forces in a mountainous section of the province of San José de las Matas called Las Manaclas in December 1963. In reaction to the government's repressive rule, an uprising occurred on April 24, 1965, headed by a liberal faction of the military that demanded the immediate restoration of the constitutional government. The rebellion gained support among the popular masses, and the "constitutionalistas" had virtually triumphed when four days later the urgent landing of US marines came to side with the right-wing oligarchy and to destroy the people's hope for liberation (Moreno 1970: 34-35; Gómez-Wangüermert 1974: 82-83).

Finally "Meditación a orillas de la tarde" (Meditation at the edge of the afternoon), the last of the poems that make up *Viaje a la muchedumbre* (Voyage to the multitudes) synthesizes the concerns raised throughout the collection: the issues of the individual and the collective, person and society, country and region, against the immediacy of a concrete history. The historical consciousness takes the contemporary reality of the region, struggling to remain free from the tentacles of empire, as an indication of the indomitability of Caribbean people. The sameness of the plight of the peoples of the region, in origin, suffering, dreams, and achievements, leads to a declaration of their indissoluble unity: "we are all knots of a single stem/ and our hungers and our dreams/sense each other through the same gestures and the same/works" (Mir 1993: 169). Their common experience and the awareness of their collective survival through centuries of depredation ("ever since/these flowering caravels") serve as the ground upon which to proclaim a common future: "We shall be happy, we peoples of the Caribbean" (p. 171). The future, of course, is conceived in a good light, and it is interesting to see that the certainty with which the promising future is foreseen rests upon the notion that in view of the region's peculiar legacy of suffering and being for powerful others, the time for a new beginning can simply wait no longer: "Our emancipated, mestizo name is victorious./Yes, of course! We have suffered much and our blood/has enriched many. It was time! Let us greet/the hour" (p. 171). In other words, the moment of the redress has come. The collective voice of the poem derives its positive vision of the future from the sense that a scrutiny of the past guarantees that view of things to come.

The title of *Viaje a la muchedumbre* was used by Jaime Labastida for a selection of Mir's poems published by Mexico's Siglo XXI Editores in 1972. The Mexican edition of Mir's selected poems largely accounts for the readership he has accrued outside of his country since then. Suffice it to say that, with very few exceptions, the critical appreciations of Mir's poetry that we have found outside of the Dominican Republic were written after publication of the Mexican anthology by individuals who had read Labastida's selection. As with any selection, however, the volume prepared by Labastida offers an incomplete picture of Mir's verse production, with a marked emphasis on the longer and more overtly political poems. None of the poems written prior to Mir's exile, nor the love poems, or those exploring telluric motifs appears here. Also, Labastida called the collection *Viaje a la muchedumbre* (1972) without indicating that he had borrowed the title from one of Mir's published books. He does not even include the sonnet "Viaje a la muchedumbre" that gave the original volume its title. But despite these shortcomings, the Mexican anthology is valuable not only for helping to make Mir's poetry better known beyond Dominican shores but also for including the sequence *Concierto de esperanza para la mano izquierda* which had not been published elsewhere before.

Hope versus History

The *Concierto*, as the words "concerto of hope" in the title suggest, recalls the inveterate celebration of hope that we discussed before in connection with *Seis momentos de esperanza*. Indeed, this sequence epitomizes Mir's long devotion to the concept of hope that is perceptible all through his verse production, but here the intensity and the formality acquire the texture of a manifesto. The sequence not only voices a hopeful outlook but it also articulates what sounds like a theory of hope. In the poem entitled "A capriccio", the obdurate speaker reveals that his song has a concrete historical framework which serves as its catalyst: "This concerto/ responds to its own/concrete situation/because in essence/all has been reduced to dust. Dust! (Mir 1993: 147). The realization that "all has been reduced to dust" impresses upon the speaker the need for a clarion call to hope as the ultimate guarantee of the people's survival and their perseverance in the struggle: "And we must order/a flourish of hope/ from the first bugler/and from the last drummer/in the battalion of/the morning" (1993: 149). Our hope exists *per forza*, the speaker seems to say. As we read later in the sequence, only hope can kill death and promise to renew the people's youthfulness: "Hope is the death of death./Hope is the hope/of renewing the people's youth" (p. 157).

Donald Walsh, who translated *Concierto* into English, gave its date of composition as 1971 (1978: 106). That detail can give a sense of the immediate situation alluded to by the speaker in the sequence. In 1971 Joaquín Balaguer was in the second of his three consecutive four-year terms as president of the Dominican Republic. While Balaguer's government was nominally a representative democracy, it met most expressions of popular opposition with ruthless violence. Murders and incarceration of left-wing spokespersons became trademarks of his administration. All the leaders who had gained distinction as representing voices of change were systematically wiped out. For Mir, who had celebrated the spirit of resistance of the Dominican people, the government of Balaguer was a challenge to the vision of hope. In “Una carta de Pedro Mir a Balaguer”, an open letter from the poet to the President published in *El Listín Diario* on 23 January 1971, Mir distanced himself radically from any association with the government by publicly rejecting a presidential appointment to serve in a newly formed Culture Institute. Mir declared that Balaguer's other appointees included ‘the most retrograde forces of our country, sectors that are responsible for the survival of the most negative traditions.”

A protégé of Trujillo, Balaguer had come to power following the popular revolutionary war of 1965 in which the people's desire to save their only constitutionally elected government in half a century had been crushed by the military might of the United States and their Dominican partners. The brief liberatory ambiance that had prevailed in the country following Trujillo's demise, the joyful enthusiasm and general exaltation of freedom that had permeated the air in those hopeful years, seemed to have come “to dust”. The first poem in the *Concierto* evokes with pathos the atmosphere of defeat: “The rollers fell on the cobblestones. And/dawn as she danced became a cloud of dust./Oh, everything was left reduced to dust: Dust!” (Mir 1993: 141). “That is what this country has been reduced to,” says the poem, which closes thus: “And from the island/of Santo Domingo situated in the Caribbean Sea/where murder through fear and through terror/ announces its lasting dominion over the world” (1993: 145). But, as the speaker insists in “Andante”, in the face of present misery hope strives to inscribe itself in the hearts of the people: “the laws of history vibrate beneath the feet/of the double basses while the cellos/of the human heart resound and erupt/deafeningly throughout all the confines/in a rousing solo of hope” (1993: 153).

The *Concierto* has the intensity of a gospel of hope, and in that respect it prefigures *El huracán Neruda* (1975), the last of Mir's published poems. Executed in the grand epic manner of his long poems, *El huracán Neruda* appeared after a rumour had circulated that Mir had given up on writing poetry (Labastida 1975: xiv; Sommer 1979: 219). Mir had had occasion to deny the rumour in a 1974 interview, explaining that he had not written poetry since *Viaje a la muchedumbre* (1971) merely because, with other endeavours keeping him physically and intellectually occupied, he had not felt the compulsion to do so, but that he would be glad to undertake the writing of verse if he found “appropriate conditions” (Piña Contreras 1980: 56-57). Predictably, the compulsion would come from a historical conjuncture affecting the peoples of the Americas. In other words, he had to wait until “the muse of history” fuelled his inspiration. In an interview Mir recalled that, amid the insistence of those around him that he should write poetry again, some Mexican friends asked him specifically to write something about Chile, and that led to his composition of *El huracán Neruda* (Santana 1978: 13). The Chile in question was the Chile of the first year of the military junta, when the dictatorship of Augusto Pinochet had already shown its claws.

General Pinochet had become the chief of the Chilean state after heading a military coup on September 11, 1973 against Salvador Allende, the first socialist president ever to come to power through constitutional elections in the Americas. Allende died in the Presidential palace, allegedly by his own hand, as the troops of the conspirators reported. His death dealt a grievous blow to the idea that the will of the people, who had voted for an agent of change and social equality, could really carry any weight in the eyes of the Chilean guardians of capitalism and their international overseers. Only twelve days later, on September 23, 1973, the Chilean poet Neruda, who had sung against empire, also died. These two Chilean deaths form the thematic axes on which *El huracán Neruda* rotates. These two deaths seemed to cast dark shadows on the future since both poet and political leader symbolized bright horizons and new human possibilities. Yet, we soon see that for Mir those deaths, far from marking an end of hope, represent the birth of a new dawn.

Divided in thirteen parts, the poem features a speaker who addresses Neruda calling him "Padre", echoing the Chilean poet's own form of address in invoking the liberator Simón Bolívar in the poem "Un canto para Bolívar" (Neruda 1973: 302-03). Likewise, Neruda's lines: "el estaño bolívar tiene un fulgor bolívar,/el pájaro bolívar sobre el volcán bolívar" – the bolivar tin has a bolivar glow,/the bolivar bird over the volcano bolivar – are echoed throughout Mir's poem. The text begins thus: "Han pasado las horas sobre el volcán neruda/y el delirio y la fiebre sobre el temblor neruda" – The hours have passed over the volcano neruda/and the raving and the fever over the neruda tremor (Mir 1994: 187). Reminiscent of Odysseus or Aeneas descending to the kingdom of Hades to gain insight from the foreknowledge of the honoured dead, the speaker in *El huracán Neruda* asks the Chilean poet to shed light on the confusion of present horror. "What has happened, Father? suddenly everything harms us./ Everything, even the water itself has become unbearable," he asks, as rendered in a partial English translation (Finke 1986: 233). The question, of course, serves merely as pretext for delving into the historical implications of the death of Allende. For Allende, we read, "had all of his blood committed" (tenía toda su sangre comprometida,) and in his blood "se hallaba comprometida la humanidad/ entera" – the whole of humanity was committed (Mir 1994: 193). His demise, therefore, constitutes a serious loss for all humanity. Thus: "La sangre universal de Salvador Allende inundó a todo Chile/y siguió creciendo en el recuerdo humano y en la estirpe/vegetal y en el instinto de todos los seres inanimados" – The universal blood of Salvador Allende flooded all of Chile/ and it kept growing in the memory of human kind and in nature's lineage/and in the drive of all inanimate creatures (p. 198).

To combat the agony of defeat, the speaker in *El huracán Neruda* appeals to the visionary insight of poetry, personified in Neruda and conceived as the clearest sound coming from the collective: "de la garganta del pueblo sale su más limpia nota" – from the throat/of the people the clearest note springs forth (p. 199). Here again we come upon Mir's idea of the poet as a vehicle for articulating the multitudinous voice of the people. The people, Mir has claimed, lack an effective voice because it consists of millions of individual voices, but the poet – and the artist in general – has the ability to gather all those voices into one coherent voice that expresses the hopes, aspirations, and struggles of the collective (De Jesús 1982: 84). But the poet can also claim the gift of prophecy. The speaker addresses Neruda, acknowledging the Chilean poet's prophetic lines: "La poesía,/tu poesía, anunció que el capitán/Bolívar capitán del pueblo, volvería" – Poetry,/your poetry, foretold that captain/ Bolívar captain of the people, would return (Mir 1994: 199). He then asserts that in the present ambiance of death one can read a birth of hope. Assuming a prophetic stance, he undertakes to announce a new dawn: "Entonces podemos anunciar que hemos entrado estrepitosamente/en ese gran sistema de estupor y sacrificio que denominamos/una aurora" – Then we can announce that we have boisterously arrived/at that great system of amazement and sacrifice that we call/a dawn (p. 202). The beneficial effects of the new age announced by the "indómita aurora" (indomitable dawn) will not only touch all of humanity and traverse all layers of historical time, but it will involve "todo el sistema planetario" (our whole galaxy) and the minutest clefts of the cosmic universe (p. 207).

In the affirmation that "La vida misma se nutre de la misma muerte" – Life itself feeds even upon death (p. 209) is the epitome of the speaker's undying faith in the inexorability of a better world. Nothing is lost. From Allende's death will come new heroes more robust and less alone in Chile and elsewhere. From Neruda's legacy will come new poetry, yielding poems that will materialize in hope, in action, in struggle, in the expected dawn. The following lines from *El huracán Neruda* succinctly illustrate this vision of the role of poetry: "Vendrán otros poemas de amor y de alegría/de un ruego inesperado y esperanza absoluta/que tejerán las manos y serán muchas manos/que la alzarán al pueblo y serán muchos pueblos/Y el idioma del mundo serán esos poemas/que las doncellas bravas llevarán al mercado/para comprar con ellos metales inauditos/y goces increíbles y pájaros de fuego" – Other love poems will come and poems of joy/of an unexpected plea and an absolute glee/that hands shall weave and will become many hands/which they shall raise for the people and will become many peoples./And the language of the world will be those poems/which the courageous maidens will take to the market place/ to buy with/them unheard of metals/and unbelievable joys and firebirds (p. 210). These closing lines show a dynamic whereby the poet, armed with a gospel of hope and the weapon of poetry finds in the passage of history a vision of utopia. In many respects, the passage epitomizes the dominant current of Mir's poetic output from his first published verses to *El huracán Neruda*. A perceptive reader of Mir has spoken of his poetry as directed toward "the search for the logic of history", claiming that in moving from the past to the future, from narration to prophesy, the poet Mir reveals a given "historical understanding" as well as a "desire to transform history" (Matos Moquete 1988: 202).

As Fernández-Fragoso observed in his study of Mir, *El huracán Neruda* articulates a vision of change in history in which the darkness of night is always followed by a bright dawn which cancels it, and, by association, human pain becomes reduced because "the certainty of change is the raw material of hope", and it is precisely this "hope" (esperanza) that moves us forward and keeps us in constant expectation of the "arrival of dawn" (Fernández-Fragoso 1978: 170, 178). The observation applies equally well to Mir's entire verse production. Similarly, Matos Moquete's panoramic look at Mir's poetic *oeuvre* identifies the prophetic tenor, with all the various uses of narrating the stormy history of the people, the prediction of a glistening future, the utopian embracing of hope, and the announcement of punishment for oppressors, as primary components of "the political action contained in Mir's poetry, his political poetics" (Matos Moquete 1988: 211). Mir's vision, informed by the sense of history, soars to international and even universal heights but always "starting from his native land" (García Lorenzo 1984: 19); the fulcrum which enables the vision to attain celestial altitude is always the legacy of the human experience in his Antillean homeland. In this respect Mir remains essentially Caribbean. Roberto Fernández Retamar no doubt wished to highlight the regional significance of Mir's work by grouping his poetry together with that of the Haitian Roumain (1907-1944) and the Haitian-Dominican Jacques Viau Renaud (1942-1965) in an anthology that, as Santos Moray has said, underscores "the currency of Antillean unity" (Fernández Retamar 1974; Santos Moray 1975: 138).

A Discrepant Aesthetics

The foregoing discussion shows clear parallels between Mir's historiographical essays and his poetry. The pages that follow will evince a correspondence among all the genres and disciplines he has tackled. One could argue that the various texts that make up his *oeuvre* complement one another in terms of consistency of intent, thematic configuration, and socio-aesthetic orientation, forming a unified literary project. In this respect, his pronouncements on art theory and criticism and aesthetics, might appear to be the least congruent with the rest of his production. Mir's first formal consideration of the field of aesthetics appeared in his *Apertura a la estética* (1974), a book meant to satisfy a practical need in the classroom at the Autonomous University of Santo Domingo where he served as Professor of Aesthetics.

With an instructional purpose, *Apertura a la estética* undertakes to trace and elucidate the history of aesthetics. Mir conceives of aesthetics as a science whose origins date back to the foundational work of Alexander Gottlieb Baumgarten (Mir 1974b: 42). While for pedagogical reasons he explains the positions of the various schools of thought that have been prominent in the study of aesthetics, Mir declares his allegiance to Marxist dialectics as the most reliable method to reveal the "mystery" of the aesthetic experience (1974b: 13). Since he views art as sensual experience, he believes the concerns of aesthetics belong in the realm of the discernable. Thus of Hegel, "a giant in the field of aesthetics", Mir states that the German philosopher suffered from a problem typical of giants: his head was often too far from his feet (p. 50). For Mir, art evolved historically as human beings in their social development felt the need to communicate in order to survive, and it is therefore connected with the idea of work. Indeed art and language, those two axes of human communication, are in effect "two work tools" (p. 113).

The Dominican critic Diógenes Céspedes, who studied at the Université de Paris at Vincennes under Henri Meschonnic, has challenged Mir's view of aesthetics as a "science". He argues that Mir falls in the trap of a search that cannot but be idealistic in nature: a search for the essence of the work of art (Céspedes 1976: 286). Céspedes upholds the idea sustained by his teacher Meschonnic that "aesthetics can be nothing else but idealistic" (Meschonnic 1973: 175). Mir presumably subscribes to a scheme of thought that from a Marxist perspective retakes positions already superseded by linguistics, semiotics, and Lacanian psychoanalysis, which, interestingly, Céspedes refers to as "ciencias" (Céspedes 1976: 289). Another critic contends that *Apertura a la estética* shows a self-proclaimed Marxist advancing unmistakably "rationalist" and even "metaphysical" elements in his pedagogical discourse (Arvelo 1984: 55). In discarding Mir's discourse as a metaphysics, Céspedes has denied it originality and reduced its theorizing to a mere repetition of old postulates that go back to Plato and Aristotle (Céspedes 1985: 215, 222). A young university professor echoes Céspedes' negative assessment of Mir's discourse on aesthetics and art, finding it wanting in "critical and methodological rigour" (Berroa 1988: 29).

Whatever the merits of the recriminations against Mir as historian of aesthetics hurled by Céspedes and others, they have skipped his most significant fault: the failure to contextualize artistic phenomena within clearly delineated socio-cultural parameters. In *Apertura a la estética* and in another textbook on the subject of art, *Fundamentos de teoría y crítica de arte*, Mir seems to have no quarrel with the notion that equates the development of humankind with the history of the West. Jacob Bronowski, the Western

Renaissance man *par excellence*, upholds this ethnocentric view in his famous televised survey of human achievement that appeared subsequently in book form. The possibility that in the future the "ascent of man" might be embodied by a civilization other than the West fills Bronowski with a sense of sad foreboding (Bronowski 1973: 437). Mir does not challenge Western ethnocentrism even though renditions of art history conceived under its influence tend to leave the contributions of his people out of the story. In introducing the Western theories of art examined in his book, Mir affirms that these show a "process of development of humanity which reveals the victory of mankind over the surrounding environment" (Mir 1979: 29-30). One could say of both texts, then, that in presenting overviews of aesthetic judgment in history, they remain chronically Eurocentric and lack the sense of a cultural perspective. The Marxist approach does not aid Mir in providing a view of artistic phenomena that can suit the indigenous artistic expression of the Caribbean or other parts of the Third World. One can criticize the work of Mir here by saying, as Brathwaite says of a book by Walter Rodney, that it needs some dialect to go along with its dialectics (Brathwaite 1973: 99). In other words, he ought to have nativized his rendition of aesthetic phenomena at least so as to make it consistent with his own historiography and his own poetry.

Two recent monographic essays by Mir seem to have been motivated by the need to respond to Céspedes and other critics concerning his privileging the field of aesthetics to explain artistic phenomena. In *La estética del soldadito* (1991) he assesses classical, romantic, and modern theories of art to identify the challenges that the discipline created by Baumgarten has survived through the ages. After surveying the central tenets in the pertinent works of a host of thinkers, including Benedetto Croce, Ferdinand de Saussure, Georg Lukacs, Claude Lévi-Strauss, Roman Jakobson and Roland Barthes, he argues that aesthetics as a field of inquiry, far from being dead, is sure to survive the "prestige" of linguistics and the advent of semiotics (Mir 1991: 358-59). The other volume, *El lapicida de los ojos morados* (1993), in a similar vein, sets out to tackle what the author construes as a virtual conspiracy: "they want to kill Aesthetics to put in its place Linguistics (the 'structural' kind, of course) or to kill Art to put Language in its place and, consciously or unconsciously, to kill man and put in its place animal" (Mir 1993b: 20). Hundreds of pages later, after travelling through centuries of debate on the relationship between art, language, and communication, Mir assures his reader that "Aesthetics has today, and will have always, a good reason to exist" (Mir 1993b: 309).

Mir does an admirable job in meeting the intellectual challenge posed by his critics. He defends his views on aesthetics vigorously and updates the scholarly tools with which to justify his adherence to that discipline. But his two recent books remain as hopelessly Eurocentric as the earlier ones. For some reason, Caribbean literature and art, the experience of creolization that he so convincingly narrates in *Tres leyendas de colores*, or the region's cultural and historical specificity that his poetry captures so passionately, never enter into his discussion of artistic communication or aesthetic phenomena. Clearly his reflection on the nature of art deviates sharply from the cultural orientation of the rest of his works. However, the books in question retain important linkages with Mir's poetry and history, particularly in the emphasis on the relationship between the artist and society.

Apertura a la estética, like his subsequent books on aesthetics, upholds Mir's undaunted belief in the power of the word as an efficacious tool not only to make art but to achieve "the transformation of the world" (1974: 156). He rejects the inveterate tendency among aesthetes to view the artist as belonging to a special breed. Instead he posits that one must understand artists not in that which separates them from the community of human beings but in that which through their creativity explains the rest of humanity (Mir 1974: 180). In keeping with his proverbial optimism, Mir sees "una gran perspectiva" (a very bright future) for the artists of tomorrow (p. 242). Likewise, in *Fundamentos de teoría y crítica de arte* he maintains that, since the work of art exists above all as a means of human communication in this rugged and brambly world of ours, which craves to expand the limits of communication among the members of the species, we have arrived at the eve of a new development in the New World, and can state that: "For art in our region, we are living a great moment" (Mir 1979: 126). Concerning the role of the critic, Mir appeals to a model that locates the aesthetic object historically in terms of culture and class. The critic, he says, has the duty to tell us the meaning of a work of art within a discrete system of signification, its meaning, that is: "for a given society, for a given sector or social class, with which one identifies and in favour of which, consciously or unconsciously, one takes sides" (Mir 1979: 194-95). These pronouncements certainly accord with the poetics informing his verse production.

Mir has also written critical texts that celebrate or evoke the legacy of specific artists, chiefly writers, and these are not discrepant with his own writing. A propos of the Puerto Rican poet Julia de Burgos, he writes nostalgically of the effect her poetry had on the "soul" of the members of his generation, or as he puts it, "in our tiny Antillean soul" (Mir 1973b: 42). Similarly, when we read his essay on Neruda, following the Chilean poet's death, we can see distinctly the ideas and images (even the vocabulary) that later germinate in verse in *El huracán Neruda*. The death of Neruda, he says, led to the realization that the people of even a great poet are always above the poet, and the whole of humanity above the given people, anticipating the internationalism and universalism expressed in the long poem (Mir 1974c: 9). Neruda, Mir states, came to Latin-American poetry as part of a history, following in the footsteps of Rubén Darío, Juana de Ibarbourou,

Alfonsina Storni, and Gabriela Mistral, and when he arrived his poetry gave voice to a history, the history of the struggles of the peoples of Latin America and, by association, of the whole of humanity, for whom the Chilean poet's death marked a rebirth of hope (Mir 1974c: 12-13).

But perhaps most significant for what it reveals about Mir's own poetics is his evocation of the revered José Martí, the late nineteenth-century Cuban writer and ideologue. Mir maintains that if one limits the search for "the poetry of Martí" to his verse production one would sacrifice the bulk of his poetry, suggesting that Martí's *Diarios* contain perhaps the Cuban writer's "dearest poetry" (Mir 1981a: 10-11). Martí's *Diarios*, consisting of campaign memoirs and travel writings, are prose texts, and Mir's characterization of them as poetry implies a view of poetic activity that defies the boundaries of conventional genre. Whatever validity this judgment may have in illuminating the nature of Martí's writings, one may apply it to Mir's own practice of overstepping generic boundaries. Mir advances the idea that Martí made his poetry out of "the intimate breath of the people" and in the hearts of the people, which, Mir insists, is the ultimate lodging of true poetry (Mir 1981a: 13, 15).

The vision attributed to Martí parallels the radical humanism of Mir's own writings. For him, humanity and the good of humanity alone can legitimize the work of the artist. That is how he explains, at the end of his notes on Marti, his speaking without discriminating between Marti's poetry and political activism. Mir's view of the poet parallels Marti's conception of the hero. In "Tres heroes", a text from Martí's *La edad de oro*, which Mir refers to admiringly, the Cuban thinker calls "heroes" those who fight to make their people free or those who would endure poverty and misfortune for the sake of a "great truth" (Martí 1971: 67). For Martí, as for Mir, the people are always above the individual, though the individual may succeed in being one step ahead by articulating effectively the needs of the collective, as Bolívar did according to Martí or as Neruda did according to Mir (Martí 1971: 63; Mir 1974b: 12). In both, the human experience, the events of their historical condition, nourishes and justifies their poetry. When Bosch writes in the prologue to Mir's text (1981: 3) on Martí that the Dominican writer "lives his poetry on a daily basis", he could not have chosen a more apt form of praise, for such is precisely the virtue that Mir finds in the work of Martí: the unity of artist and political being in history.

Fiction as the History of Memory

Mir's prose writings, in addition to the historiographical essays, the monographs on aesthetics, and the critical pieces, include a substantial body of journalistic chronicles (crónicas) and three volumes of fiction. His column "Ayer menos cuarto" appeared regularly in the newspaper *El Nacional* from late 1970 through to the beginning of 1971. He then published "El dominicano de las nieves: Crónicas de un pez soluble" in the latter half of 1972 for the weekly magazine *Ahora!*, where his column "Crónicas de un sí y un no" also appeared throughout 1973. These chronicles concern themselves generally with current events nationally and internationally as well as with diverse subjects that range from historical reflections, to socio-political commentary, to childhood recollections, to thoughts on the nature of poetry and art. Mir had also written for Dominican newspapers in the 1940s before he left for exile. Between January and February 1979, he published a series of six articles collectively entitled "Serie Dades" which capture his impressions of an eventful trip to France that he made in the company of several Dominican writers, intellectuals, and artists. The articles appeared in *El Nacional*, the daily that for the remainder of 1979 would also publish "Serie Star (ser i estar)," a series of "crónicas" along the lines of his earlier columns. Throughout the hundreds of pages that make up the corpus of Mir's "crónicas", two things remain consistently apparent: the author's awareness of human action as explainable in historical time and his clear sense of the interconnection between the Dominican Republic and the rest of the world. A gathering of Mir's columns and other journalistic writings over three decades now exists as the book entitled *Ayer menos cuarto y otras crónicas: 1945–1980*, published by the Dominican Republic's Biblioteca Nacional in 2000 and compiled by Francisco Rodríquez de Léon, an educator and author whom the CUNY Dominican Studies Institute of the City University of New York commissioned to prepare this important volume.

To complete this inquiry into Mir's dedication to the historical imagination in the scrutiny of the Caribbean experience, I now consider his three volumes of prose fiction. Mir first tried his hand at writing fiction in *La gran hazaña de Límber y después otoño* (1977), a collection of three animal fables linked by the story of a non-committal man wooing an evasive young woman by the sea. The book presents us with a Caribbean cosmos wherein the lives of a dog, a monkey, and a horse are intertwined with the experience of humans within historical circumstances that determine their destinies. In the first story, "La gran hazaña de Límber", the main character is a dog by the name of Límber, a derivation of "Lindbergh", that got its name from the enthusiasm elicited in San Pedro de Macorís by the historic transatlantic exploit of the American aviator in May 1927 (Mir 1977: 13-14). In a feat comparable to that of Lindbergh, the dog, in pursuit of its owners who have to move from the cosmopolitan city of San Pedro de Macorís to the small village of Yaguate, runs the intervening 120 kilometres nonstop, twice in a row. Límber's journey, which culminates in his death, occurs also in connection with a historical event that shook the foundations of the then opulent city of San Pedro de Macorís, the hometown of the family that owns the dog. They have to move to distant and humble Yaguate because of the economic crisis that affects the better-off people in the city beginning on "Black Friday", that is, the day after "Black Thursday", which refers to the date of the stock market crash of October 1929 in the United States and the start of the economic slump known in the West as the Great Depression. Had this event not happened, and had the Dominican sugar industry on which the prosperity of the family depended not been connected to the U.S. economy, chances are that they would not have had to move and the confusion that led to Límber's travail would not have taken place. Límber, then, appears as the pawn of larger historical circumstances in the Caribbean region and beyond.

The regional specificity of the dramas narrated in the book is made explicit in "Gos", whose title alludes to the main character, a monkey whom the narrator refers to as "deeply Antillean" (Mir 1977: 51). Gos was born in Saint Kitts, one of the smaller English-speaking Caribbean islands, and grew up and met its death in San Pedro de Macorís. The story itself is very moving, particularly because of the anthropomorphic depiction of the character of Gos. The monkey comes to the southern Dominican city through the agency of one of the immigrants from the Windward Islands (Mir 1977: 63). Subsequently, from the house of Mr. Porf, its Dominican home, the monkey gets to establish contact, copulate with, and impregnate a female mate brought from another Caribbean island (p. 70). The whole scenario created for Gos's story corresponds fittingly to the ambiance of inter-Caribbean migration associated with the sugar industry. The events surrounding the monkey's life and death make sense above all in the historical experience of the Dominican plantation that has relied on inter-Caribbean migrant farmhands, Haitians in other cities, but in San Pedro de Macorís mostly labourers from the Anglophone Antilles.

The third animal fable in *La gran hazaña de Límber y después otoño* (The Rise and Fall of Limber) occurs against a more familiar historical background: the dictatorship of Trujillo. With a grey colt as the main character, hence the title "El potro gris", the story relates intertextually to the fable "El potro salvaje" written by the Uruguayan master of short fiction Horacio Quiroga (1878-1937). The narrator insists on drawing a parallel between the gray colt and Quiroga's young horse in order to highlight their differences. Quiroga's horse comes from the desert to the city to live on the pageant of its formidable speed, runs desperately to impress managers and turfites, and through long and passionate perseverance manages to gain recognition at the racetrack and achieve a position of comfort and respect. The narrator in Quiroga's story tells us that, having aged and being no longer menaced by hunger, the prosperous horse loses its authentic vigour and settles into non-committal performance strategies that are still calculated to please the race-goers and managers. Youth and hunger, the narrator suggests, provide the sort of motivation and compulsion that make the performance authentic because: "Youth and hunger are the most precious gift that life can grant to a strong heart" (Quiroga 1978: 86).

Quiroga's fable invites an allegorical reading as the drama of the artist who must juggle with seemingly conflicting loyalties: personal well-being, relationship with consumers, and commitment to the craft. The horse in Mir's story, on the other hand, must confront a dilemma with a larger social and political content. Since the horse comes to a country with an oppressive government that has instituted a reign of silence, it must face a historical conjuncture where one can hardly avoid taking sides politically. Thus when the grey colt starts winning at the track, the popular masses interpret its victorious races as expressive of their own wishes of liberation. The mood of celebration and the irrepressible joy its feats elicit in the people causes the horse to be "seen ever more closely as an enemy of the government" (Mir 1977: 105). Therefore, the machinery of the government must seek to deprive the horse of its prestige and social significance (p. 115). The government sends for the best possible horse on the international market to run against and defeat the grey colt. The racetrack becomes an arena for a fierce combat between a horse that represents the people and one that represents the repressive regime, and to avoid endangering his life the owner of the grey colt opts to appease the government by deliberately keeping the popular contender from winning (pp. 124-25). As a result, the people and their horse are eclipsed for the time being, but the legacy of the horse's exploits remains, and when eventually the regime falls the people erect a monument to perpetuate the memory of the grey colt that consumed its heart "in the obstinate struggle against silence" (p. 128).

The story of the grey colt, like the others in the volume, exemplifies Mir's tendency to historicize individual and even private experience. The lives, the passions, and the deaths of Límber, Gos, and the grey colt and those of the humans with whom they coincide at given historical conjunctures show the susceptibility of the characters to political events and social conditions in general. The romance of the young sweethearts the narrator describes in "Post scriptum", the last part of *La gran hazaña de Límber y después otoño*, evolves in the euphoria produced by the popular horse in "El potro gris". Similarly, the dynamics of their "private life" occurs within and is shaped by the restrictions imposed by the ruling order (p. 141). Their drama and those of other characters in the book happens in a regional milieu that one recognizes as particular to the Caribbean. The historical phenomena we witness accord fittingly with the peculiarities of the human experience in the region. Horse-racing is also immensely popular in parts of the Anglophone Caribbean, and two authors, the Guyanese Cyril Dabydeen in his novel, *The Wizard Swami* (1989) and the Trinidadian Wayne Brown in his story, "Bring on the Trumpeters" (*The Scent of the Past:*

Stories and Remembrances, [c1970] 2011), quite independently explore the same kind of conflict between the people's choice of the Creole horse and the metropolitan horse backed by the business elite.

A sense of interconnectedness pervades the book. Not only do people and animals share common conjunctures but the various separate stories of the volume become interlaced. The characters and their physical surroundings seem to blend in rather meaningful ways as exemplified by the way the narrator in the last part of the volume interweaves the fortuitous meeting of the young sweethearts with a pertinent description of the landscape as they walk along the streets of the Dominican capital swathed by winds blowing from the Caribbean sea (pp. 117-18). The interweaving of all the experiences narrated in the book gets accentuated stylistically by the uninterrupted flow of the prose. The book lacks formal separations between sentences or other forms of punctuation, making the various stories in the book (those of the three animals, the frame, and the young sweethearts) read as one continuous text.

As Mir continued to produce fiction, he had ampler grounds for essaying the same continuous, flowing narrative prose style. His novel *Cuando amaban las tierras comuneras* (1978), appeared one year after the above collection under the prestigious imprint of Siglo XXI Editores in Mexico. Also uninterrupted by punctuation, the novel exhibits a compelling narrative mode. It chronicles the experiences of various individuals whose lives are indelibly marked by events occurring in modern Dominican history, chiefly the two United States occupations of the country in 1916-1924 and 1965. The destinies of the characters also flow almost as if emulating the fluidity of the prose. Silvestre, the principal figure, awakens to adult life in the political shockwave caused by the 1916 invasion, beginning on the day when, on the way to school, he hears Old Villamán, his teacher's father, shout from his speeding horse to the school children a warning about the imminent danger the country faces: "boys, get back home, the country is in danger" (Mir 1978: 45). Fifty years later, in the wave of another military intervention, he hears the same phrase again, this time pronounced by a woman named Urbana, who later reveals herself to be the daughter he did not know he had procreated (p. 291).

Within hearing of Urbana's warning is a boy named Bonifacio Lindero. The boy's father, a wealthy landowner, belongs to a family that amassed its fortune as a consequence of land reforms implemented by the American military government that ruled the country during the 1916-1924 occupation. The boy's mother, Romanita, dies moments after giving birth to him of an illness that had been provoked by the shocking news of the death of a dear friend, murdered by the repressive regime of a tyrant who has come to power through the channels established by the occupying forces beginning in 1916 and whose demise would subsequently unleash the chain of events leading again to the occupation of 1965. As the novel draws to a close we encounter the boy Bonifacio riding in a car together with Silvestre and Urbana towards the capital, the scene of the 1965 armed resistance championed by the *comandos* of the people called "constitucionalistas" against the invaders and their local agents (p. 328). And just as three generations of people who awaken to self-knowledge in connection with the foreign invasion of their land coincide in that car, so do several periods and layers of Dominican history come into play to add significance to the fifty years chronicled in the novel.

Caribbean Context and the Critics

Cuando amaban las tierras comuneras has aroused considerable critical attention both nationally and internationally, and critics have naturally focused on the historical framework of the novel. They have hailed the author's masterful recreation of events in Dominican history and his skilful portrayal of characters whose destinies are shaped by events taking place in their homeland (Sanz 1980: 52; Muciño 1978: 64-65; 1979: 167). The Dominican Rosario Candelier, in a taxonomy of the Dominican novel, has classified *Cuando amaban las tierras comuneras* under the current he calls "neo-historicismo", a mode that he traces back to the tradition of the historical novel that flourished in European Romanticism with such practitioners as Sir Walter Scott (Candelier 1988: 255-56). A more regionally informed critical perspective would have found antecedents in the Caribbean itself, with such novelists as Edgar Mittelholzer and V.S. Reid. The most important criticism of *Cuando amaban* has come from the United States. An early reviewer ascribed to it as many "flaws" (fallas) as it has "accomplishments" (logros), concluding that the text, despite its "conventional" rhetoric sustains and saves itself as a work of art (Barradas 1978: 96). Another scholar has authored a long essay on *Cuando amaban* which focuses on the presence of "historical time" in the works of Mir and on the writer's role as "chronicler of the memorable", that is, as chronicler of the past human experience which the collective must continue to remember in order to live in the present (Berroa 1988: 38). But the critic who has most closely scrutinized *Cuando amaban* is the scholar Doris Sommer, the author of two long essays on it.

Sommer's first critique appeared one year after the publication of Mir's novel. There she set out to show that although Mir espouses a "nominally Marxist" politics, his "metaphoric transformation of reality into art" seems to owe "more to Romantic preciosity than to dialectical materialism" and that, consequently, "form and content remain disjointed throughout the novel" (Sommer 1979: 220). Sommer debates the "mystical function" assigned to the land in the novel since such depiction "is generally associated with Romantic ideology" (p. 232), as well as the sexist implications she perceives in Mir's "concept of patriotism" (p. 237), and the "economic reasoning" exhibited in the novel which she finds "questionable" (p. 242), among other things.

In attacking Mir's ideology in the novel, Sommer claims to be launching "an implicit criticism of the mystification in literature that purports to be Marxist", so that she merely intends to offer "an illustration of the pitfalls of popular-front art" (p. 234). But in reading the novel exclusively in terms of the assumed ideology of the author, with particular reference to Western intellectual constructs such as Marxism, Romanticism, and historical materialism, she fails to recognize the work as the product of a given culture. Likewise, she overlooks the fact that what the author draws from to fill the pages of the novel and to produce the magic of his mythopoesis is not "History" in the abstract Hegelian sense, but Dominican history, that is, the concrete human experience of a discrete portion of humankind in a given time and a given place. An awareness of this fact would radically change one's assessment of details, apparently minor, such as the symbolism of Silvestre's and Urbana's names. For Sommer, Urbana's name, understood as suggestive of an opposition to her rural background, accentuated by the name of her father Silvestre, remains meaningful only until they both meet in the big city: "afterwards her name is superfluous" (p. 248). But the character's name means more than the purely etymological derivation from the Latin *urbs*. The name Urbana also symbolizes the legacy of resistance of the Dominican people since it alludes to the name of Gregorio Urbano Gilbert (1899-1970), a real-life Dominican who, a teenager in 1916, was among the first to fight the troops of the occupying forces. Like Silvestre, Urbano Gilbert may be said to have awakened to maturity in the political turmoil unleashed by the American invasion. And just as we learn of Silvestre in the novel, when in actuality the resistance of the "gavilleros" proved ineffective against the military might of the U.S., Urbano Gilbert went on to another arena to continue the war on behalf of national sovereignty. He went to the mountains of Nicaragua and, as we learn from his memoirs, joined the revolutionary troops of Augusto César Sandino (Urbano Gilbert 1975; 1979). In *Cuando amaban* Urbana hears from Silvestre that he went to Nicaragua and there met Urbano Gilbert: "I met Gilbert... and through him I learned about Sandino... and we fought together in the Segovias mountains" (Mir 1978: 308). The parallel between Mir's Silvestre, Urbana's father, and the real-life Urbano Gilbert make the association between Urbana and Urbano hard to miss if one has Dominican history in mind at the time of reading.

In reading Mir's novel Sommer does not transcend the limitations of the Eurocentric perspective. In her subsequent discussion of two other Dominican writers, René del Risco Bermúdez and Marcio Veloz Maggiolo, she utters this incidental but telling comment: "If del Risco is a Lord Byron,

Veloz Maggiolo is a Dorian Gray" (Sommer 1980: 224). The remark suggests the attitude of a Eurocentric critic for whom meaning is always enunciated in terms of Western references. The significance of a non-Western text is not articulated by educing values that are intrinsic to the world of the text but rather those that are intrinsic to the Western world of the critic. We can see that mindset at work in Sommer's reproachful discussion of the conspicuous celebration of the Dominican soil in *Cuando amaban*. It is the words that Silvestre addresses to some youths in the capital, succinctly expressing a vision of the soil, that earns her rebuke. Silvestre says: "all there is in God's world is the land because that is what people live on, and everything else also lives on the land and we ourselves are made of the land and we are plants except that we have no roots but that's only because we cannot see them for in fact all people have roots and they have them deeply buried in their land" (Mir 1978: 286). For Sommer this "passionately anti-modern insistence on the need for the People's soul to be rooted in the Land is reminiscent of a 'Volkish' Romanticism that resisted industrialization by reasserting tradition"(Sommer 1983: 256).

Mir's novel does celebrate the soil. Indeed, "los terrenos comuneros", the communal lands which ceased to be communal when the U.S. government imposed land reforms that required the effective privatization of all the land for which a deed of ownership did not exist, occupy a central position as a character in the novel (Mir 1983: 766-67). The land has been at the core of Mir's work from the very beginning of his literary career, as Baeza Flores aptly noted in relation to his poetry in the late 1930s and the early 1940s. But Sommer finds "reactionary implications" in the celebration of the soil since such "mystification of man's bond to the soil was fundamental to Nazism and to fascism in general" (Sommer 1983: 265). Though she excuses Mir of any "intentional" fascism, she finds that his "kinship with the ideology of the far right is unmistakably indicated in the major themes of the novel", and she illustrates her claim by reference to the passage quoted above in which Silvestre affirms that "everyone is firmly rooted 'en su tierra' rather than 'en la tierra'" (p.266). This suggests to her that for Mir "one's soul is bound through birth and culture" to one particular plot of land, a notion which, she maintains, exhibits clear affinities with Romantic and, consequently, with fascist thought. In Germany, she argues, the legacy of Romanticism evolved into "the twentieth century *Volkish* cult of irrationality, pantheistic spiritualism and nationalism", and Mir's novel enters into what she considers a "disturbing" kinship with that tradition (Sommer 1983: 266).

Sommer's equation between celebration of the soil and fascism does not seem tenable in the discrete historical context recreated by the novel. Whatever value the equation may have in terms of the intellectual history of Germany, it simply lacks applicability to explain events in the Dominican Republic. Sommer fails to consider the role of the land in the development of the Dominican nation. One need only delve into the pages of the country's historical experience to find that the land in the Dominican Republic has historically suffered the impending threat of occupation, annexation, or mortgaging by foreign imperial forces. The country has also endured the opportunism of the native ruling classes whose lack of attachment to the soil has at various times led them to seek to sell, rent, or annex the country in whole or in part to foreign imperial bidders. Most Dominicans remember these as turncoats, individuals whose personal and class interests caused them to betray their country. On the other hand, most Dominicans remember as revered heroes and heroines those individuals who, like Juan Pablo Duarte, María Trinidad Sánchez, and Gregorio Luperón, sacrificed their personal well-being in the struggle to preserve the sovereignty of their nation.

The Dominican experience does not differ drastically from the experience of other nations in the Caribbean region and even in mainland Latin America. Sommer's disparaging interpretation of Mir's concept of the soil merely imposes upon her Caribbean subject matter an analytical model imported from a discretely European historical conjuncture. In other words, since European fascists celebrated the soil, Mir's celebration of the soil must perforce be inherently fascist, she reasons. She makes no concession to the socio-cultural and political uniqueness of the idea of "land" in the Caribbean, where the preservation of particular plots of land from the onslaught of Western imperialism has been among the most crucial tests the people of the region have had to pass through the centuries.

Other critics of Mir's *Cuando amaban* have recognised the socio-cultural matrix and the unique history that inform the novel. Laguna-Díaz argues that while Mir's "socio-historical thought" is eclectic and does not subscribe in every respect to a particular school, the thinking is coherent and stays within a materialist perspective of history (Laguna-Díaz 1982: 27). The novel, in other words, highlights the kind of approach Mir brought to all his historical research, his reliance on the people as the most direct "source" of their own history (Laguna-Díaz 1982: 28). The novel suggests that when official historians omit the history of the people, one must look for it in the genesis of the society's institutions, customs, and beliefs, and that for Mir the Dominican people with all its constituent elements came into being in connection with the communal lands and the type of society they generated (ibid. p. 28). Another critic claims that the novel delves in the historical experience of the Dominican people, who, in the ample sense suggested by the "terrenos comuneros" have in the past lived communally, to predict that the Dominican Republic will have a socialist future (Davis 1979: 180). She interprets the novel's open-ended conclusion (the scene of Silvestre, Urbana, and the young Bonifacio riding towards the insurgents in the capital) as a journey into the future that symbolizes the region's collective protest against the Caribbean's age-old wrongs: "sugarcane…, dependence, poverty, and foreign intervention" (Davis 1979: 183).

The best reading of Mir's novel to date, in so far as it contextualizes it culturally and historically, has been that of Fernanda Steele, who has compared *Cuando amaban* with *The Dragon Can't Dance* (1979), the novel by Trinidadian author Earl W. Lovelace. Considering the shared Caribbean historical background against which the events of both novels develop, Steele observes that both texts owe much to myth, given the often archetypal form in which the characters are cast (Steele 1982: 182-83). One can recognize a mythical quality in Mir's Silvestre, Urbana, and Bonifacio just as in Lovelace's Sylvia, Aldrick, and Fisheye. But their mythical dimension does not negate the imminence of their historical relevancy for the people of the contemporary Caribbean. Steele reasons that perhaps elsewhere, in a different context where the situations encountered by the characters do not so closely resemble those faced by the real-life people of the region, or perhaps even here but "in a distant future", they might belong solely in the realm of myth and myth-making but not here, or for the time being (p. 200). The implication, of course, is that even a mythical approach to literature ought to refrain from imposing its paradigms on Caribbean writing without a careful consideration of the historical immediacy of even the archetypal forms in the region. Mir's "gavilleros" and Lovelace's "bad Johns" may be said to partake simultaneously of the mythical and the historical in the Caribbean imagination. Thus Silvestre, for instance, "is both man, rooted in a particular time, and symbol of time's limitlessness; both rebel, 'gavillero', taking part in a movement which defended a particular time's way of perceiving one's way of life, and symbol of a people's right to the freedom of perceiving and shaping their way of life" (p. 196). Silvestre, one might say, embodies the symbiosis of history and myth.

Steele observes that *Cuando amaban* concentrates not on the "powerful figures who generally people the history textbooks" but rather on "the ordinary people, those people who make history because of the resistance they oppose to decisions made by others and which affect their lives so deeply" (p. 195). She affirms also that though the events of the novel are rooted in the past, they project into the future (pp. 199-200). Contrary to Sommer, Steele examines the way the novel exemplifies the convergence of the personal and the social in the shaping of character. In this respect, she notes that the moment Silvestre joins the insurgent "gavilleros", the narrative stops tracing his steps "as an individual", and upon the mention of his disappearance and possible death, we read about the insurgent movement "as a whole", with the probable implication that it is not "in the achievements of one individual, but in the combined achievements of many" that one ought to look for the heroism of the people's resistance (pp.

198-199). In short, by reading the novel in its own Caribbean context, as is witnessed in the comparison with the novel of another West Indian author, Steele succeeds in educing much of the socio-aesthetic and cultural significance of Mir's text that escapes Sommer.

History, Self, and the Caribbean

Mir's last prose fiction text, *(Buen viaje, Pancho Valentín!* (1981), draws on the form of the memoir to enact the personal drama of a man returning to his country after a long absence and the tension deriving from the historical situation of his homeland at the time of his arrival. Pancho Valentín is the first-person narrator who arrives in Santo Domingo in 1963, attracted by the "breathable atmosphere" prevailing there after 30 years of uneasiness (Mir 1981c: 29). This places his return in the midst of a very crucial historical moment for the Dominican Republic. The speaker alludes obviously to the end of the ruthless dictatorship of Trujillo and the subsequent democratic election of Juan Bosch as president of the Republic. For many it was the first time in the twentieth century that Dominicans had been allowed to breathe democratic air. At the same time, when subsequently Pancho Valentín, in conversation with his generous friend D., reveals his loss of enthusiasm, he expresses his gloom in terms of the drastic turn in the political ambiance of the nation. He says he can only see "shadows" (sombras) as he refers to these events: "Overthrow of the democratic government, blood in the mountain, the liberal element displaced from power, persecution in the cities, deportations, imprisonments, and the divine goblet" (Mir 1981c: 46). Obviously, the speaker has in mind the fall of Bosch only seven months after he had occupied the presidency (from February 27 to September 25) by a military coup, the death in the mountains (sangre en las montañas) of Manolo Távarez Justo and the many other civilians who took up arms to protest the aggression against the popular will, and all the oppression that followed. The "divine goblet" probably refers to the militant role of Catholic leaders in the anti-Bosch campaign that preceded the overthrow. The Revolution of 1965 that figures so significantly in *Cuando amaban* follows soon after.

It should suffice to say here that *Buen viaje, Pancho Valentín!*, though presented as an account of a private life, the personal travail of an exile trying to survive in a country that has changed as much as he in the many years of his absence, achieves dramatic tension in the larger movement of public history. Mir draws considerably on autobiographical material, and an examination of the parallels between Pancho Valentín's "return to the native land" and that of Mir himself, whose complete name is Pedro Julio Mir Valentín ("Pancho" being a byname of "Pedro"), would make an interesting exercise. Consistent with the style of memoirs, the first-person narrative's sentences, often short and separated by ellipses, resemble the discontinuous progression of a diary. It is not unlikely, given Mir's admiration for the great Antillean thinker and patriot, that he may have chosen as his model the *Diarios* of Martí, particularly the one entitled *De Cabo Haitiano a Dos Ríos* (1895), which ends with these words: "and Valentín brings me a jug of boiled sweetened water with fig leaves" (Martí 1964: 243). On the whole, the text lacks the fluidity and the linguistic virtuosity that makes *La gran hazaña de Límber* and *Cuando amaban* entrancing texts. But the compulsion to historicize private experience is as visible here as in the rest of Mir's production.

Mir's fiction has many connections in form and content with his poetry. A reviewer has said of his first novel, and we would extend it to all his prose fiction, that it "compares with the epic" (Arisa Averasturi 1980: 26). It could very well be that Mir's work, including the historiographical essays, has harmonized lyrical subjectivity with epic intent, much as the same kind of harmony appears in the work of Brathwaite, another major poet-historian of the Caribbean. "Where Brathwaite focuses on the ethnocultural evolution of the islands, Mir addresses himself to the socio-economic evolution of Caribbean peoples," says a scholar who draws a parallel between the two Antillean writers (Irish 1990: 26). Mir and Brathwaite exhibit a similar concern with the way conventional historiography has configured the Caribbean past, and both feel compelled to articulate renditions of the past that illuminate the road to a promissory future. Similarly, both have produced *oeuvres* that accentuate the cultural and historical commonality of the peoples of the region. When Mir published his first volume of verse, *Hay un país en el mundo*, the Havana newspaper *Hoy* published on 12 June 1949 a review by the Cuban critic Angel Augier that saluted the text for its evocation of "this harmonious Antillean universe" (Augier 1977: 499). Forty-three years later, when Mir travelled to New York in connection with a major day-long conference devoted to his literary work, the Puerto Rican fiction writer Ed Vega saluted him thus: "Given the visionary spirit of such men as Pedro Mir, our children and the generations they raise may live to see a Caribbean Economic Federation of free countries that extends like the tail of a magnificent marine comet to the shores of South America" (Vega 1992: 108).

The principal element that has caused Mir's readers, through many decades, to recognize in his texts a wholistic vision of the Caribbean region is the constant search for the origins of present conditions in the past experience of the peoples of the Antillean world. It is the worship of the muse of history, his possession by the historical imagination that makes Mir's works distinctively Caribbean. It is in his particular engagement with history that one most readily recognizes the imprint of Caribbean literature. To be sure, Western literature too has incorporated historical phenomena. Despite Aristotle's understanding, European literary discourse has concerned itself with "what actually happened" at least as much as with "what could and would happen either probably or inevitably" (Aristotle 1973: 35). As Lionel Gossman has shown, Voltaire seems to have "preferred his epics to be true and his histories to be epic" (Gossman 1978: 11). Voltaire boasted that *La Henriade* (1728) was a poem "based on a known history" in which "the truth" was respected, whereas in his *Siècle de Louis XV*, a straight history, he aimed "to make a great picture of events that are worthy of being painted, and to keep the reader's eyes trained on the leading characters", for, as he adds, "History, like tragedy, requires an exposition, a central action, and a dénouement" (Gossman 1978: 11, 13).

In such authors as Voltaire the writing of history is governed by a given poetics just as much as literature is. Structurally, literature and history may very well have more in common than we would like to think. Louis O. Mink says that "narrative form in history, as in fiction, is an artifice, the product of an individual imagination" (Mink 1978: 145). Hayden White, whose well-known study of nineteenth-century historiography focuses on "linguistic protocols", "modes of poetic discourse", "tropes", and "modes of emplotment" that are normally associated with literary composition, exhorts historians to draw historiography "back once more to an intimate connection with its literary basis" (White 1973: 426; 1978: 62). Certainly, the literary artists in the Western tradition have constantly had recourse to the documentary past to produce their work. *La chanson de Roland*, William Shakespeare's *Julius Caesar*, and Peter Weiss's *Marat/Sade* are some obvious examples.

What makes the historical sense in Caribbean literature unique is the urgency resulting from the need to correct earlier renditions of the region's past. The Caribbean literary writer must confront the many misconceptions, misconstructions, or even plain factual errors contained in the versions of the Caribbean past bequeathed by the colonial chroniclers of the New World. Even today, years after the quincentenary of the Columbian era, it seems necessary, for instance, to clarify with Mir that Columbus only "discovered" the region for the eyes of the West: "But not for the aborigines who had lived there since time immemorial" (Mir 1987: 7). An outsider cannot discover lands that are inhabited by other humans. Jan Carew, the Guyanese fiction writer who has also become a practising historian, revises the conventional Western rendition of the "discovery" in this bitingly ironic sentence: "On the morning of October 12, 1492, a gathering of Arawakian Lucayos discovered Christopher Columbus and his sailors on the eastern shore of their homeland of Guanahani" (Carew 1988: 3). Like Mir, Carew felt it was time that the records be set straight.

When the historians of the colonial enterprise first chronicled events in the Caribbean they wrote for Europe. The lives of aborigines, blacks, and even creolized whites mattered only in so far as they affected Europe. In time, though, the people of the region became aware of themselves as authentic cultural beings and asserted their position as speaking subjects with the right to chronicle their own human drama. Their chronicle, however, could not be innocent. It had a prior rendition to contend with. It had to answer. The colonial scribes had said much and omitted much. Much of what they said cried out for correction. And much of what they omitted cried for inclusion. Like that of Africa, where history until recently "was considered as synonymous with the activities of the Europeans in Africa", as Saburi Biobaku has said, the history of the Caribbean was seldom narrated from a focus on the experience of the indigenous, creolized people (Biobaku 1959: 98). Thus, as in Africa, so in the Caribbean, giving "the truthful image of history" has political implications. In the region historians often serve, in the words of Modilim Achufusi, as "guide and political advisors of their people" (Achufusi 1959: 6).

The foregoing context largely explains the corrective impulse in the historical imagination that pervades Caribbean literature. In the Caribbean, as Glissant has pointed out, history is not the province of the historians alone. The passion with which novelists, dramatists, and essayists have approached the events surrounding the Haitian revolution (from Chauvet to Carpentier, to Walcott, to Césaire, to C.L.R. James) reveals their compelling dedication to reconstruct, recreate, or even remember the human legacy of the region: the *little culture* for Brathwaite or *el pueblo* for Mir. The memory of the past, perhaps because the past remains unresolved since the region has not yet attained its effective sovereignty in economic and political terms, surfaces constantly in Caribbean texts. "History, unreconciled and pressing, is their natural element; memory is their metier, the *primum mobile* of their re-evaluative posture, the source of all prophecy," says Roberto Márquez of Caribbean writers (Márquez 1989: 295). The critic illustrates Antillean literature's grappling with history in these words from Glissant's *La Lézarde*: "On the day when I finally fasten my hands upon its wrinkled stem and pull with irresistible power… when my memories are quiet and strong, and I finally translate them into words, then I shall perceive the unique and essential qualities of this place. The innumerable petty miseries, the manifold beauties eclipsed by the painful necessity of combat and birth" (ibid. p. 295). Mir concentrated nearly six decades of artistic and intellectual effort on the task of recording the past to explain the present and illuminate the future. He succeeded in translating into words the human legacy of the region and, like few others, perceived "the essential qualities" of his homeland in the very heart of the Caribbean.

CHAPTER 6

CONCLUSION: TOWARD A DECENTRALIZED LITERARY ORDER

> Political changes will depend on political action. But cultural politics demand that all of us who are at the centre by racial privilege or education or both become *marginals* and learn to view ourselves, if only at moments of ironic consciousness, from an ethnopoetic point of view.
>
> Michel Benamou (1977: 159)

The foregoing chapters sought to demonstrate the unity of the literary production of the people of the Antillean world irrespective of their different languages and national origins. I attempted to show Caribbean literature as a distinct corpus whose socio-aesthetic identity, intrinsic to the region, has developed along a path that differs from those of the literatures of the Western tradition and the mainland Latin American tradition. I have used the term Caribbean poetics to isolate the socio-aesthetic paradigms that illustrate the cohesiveness of the literary act as it has taken place in the area at least over the last eight decades. The works of the Barbadian Kamau Brathwaite, the Haitian René Depestre, and the Dominican Pedro Mir provided the basis for highlighting the involvement with language, religion, and history as some of the most important distinguishing features of Caribbean poetics. Now some connections are called for.

Caribbean Points of Contacts

Nothing connects the works of Brathwaite, Depestre and Mir more evidently than the shared sense of urgency in their approach to and treatment of the Caribbean experience. Mir's devotion to the historical imagination, Depestre's response to the spiritual imperative, and Brathwaite's exploration of the nativization of language rise to a similar degree of militant passion. The fervour and immediacy they exhibit accord with the crucial place of history, the sacred, and language in construing a conceptual rendition of the Caribbean as a culture area. These are concepts one would normally need to deal with in any attempt to fathom Caribbean life: the people, the region, and the people's experience in the region. Our three authors resemble each other, in other words, in that they appear committed with equal zeal to the mission of rewriting the Caribbean and, in so doing, providing a truer picture of the people of the region as cultural beings.

Caribbean literature is informed by a historic need of expression. One might call it a need for a *prise de parole*. In an interview with Depestre, Césaire once described the impetus of his literary beginnings, which occurred in the context of his Afro-Antillean awakening, with these words: "There was, to wit, this fact: I had things to say to the world" (cited in Depestre 1974: 168-69). This need is, in fact, a trademark of contemporary Caribbean literature. The expressive drive to communicate the regional experience weighs more heavily in the imagination of the writers from the region than any individual need to voice the drama of a given writer's interior universe. In this respect, Caribbean writers who achieve prominence in the region tend not to be individual talents who create in isolation but rather talented translators of the collective experience. The texts of the literary artists we have looked at in this study derive their significance primarily from what they say about their regional reality. Mir's *Hay un país en el mundo*, Depestre's *Un arc-en-ciel pour l'Occident chrétien*, and Brathwaite's *Mother Poem*, for instance, achieve their aesthetic end in the evocation of circumstances and conditions which are explicative of the Caribbean world.

Caribbean literature deals largely with the cultural and political problems of the region. The characters that populate the pages of this literature stand generally as regional types and symbols rather than as singular individuals. The figures of Prospero, Ariel and Caliban recur so frequently because of their suggestive potential to represent social paradigms that symbolize whole segments of the Caribbean population. The drama of a Hamlet, a Segismundo, a Raskolnikoff, or a Leopold Bloom, attached as they are to the private confines or the personal labyrinths of an individual mind, seem to enter the Caribbean imagination less frequently. The Silvestre of Mir's *Cuando amaban las tierras comuneras*, the Henri Postel of Depestre's *Le mât de cocagne*, and the first person singular in Brathwaite's *Sun Poem* or *X/Self*, intensely personal as they may be, evoke whole sections of what could be called the human fauna in the region. They transcend the role of individual actors to connote, archetypically, major components of the collective in the Caribbean experience.

Our reading of the works of Mir, Depestre and Brathwaite shows, too, that the Antillean writer's practically inescapable dedication to the analysis of Caribbean life does not preclude a constant preoccupation with the rest of the world. Each of our three authors evinces a recognition of the inexorable interdependence of all nations in the modern era. Depestre's frequent allusion to the horrors of the nuclear age and the emphasis on world peace expresses a shared awareness that all the peoples of the globe confront a common danger and, therefore, must share a collective commitment to salvation. Their internationalist vision becomes evident in particular in their pronouncements on behalf of all "the wretched of the earth".

A significant point of contact between the three writers, which also has to do with their shared sense of urgency, is the multigeneric nature of their work. They resort to different genres often simultaneously to treat the same material and to voice similar concerns. Mir's *Raíces dominicanas de la Doctrina de Monroe*, for instance, may be said to develop in essay form some thematic implications arising from the verse of his *Contracanto a Walt Whitman*. Witness also Mir's employment of literary elements in his historiographical essays. In the same way, in *Le mât de cocagne*, the novel by Depestre, we come upon a dramatization of some of the negative consequences of the concept of Negritude when manipulated by reactionary forces, and we immediately recognize his concern since he has taken it up at length in various expository texts, such as *Bonjour et adieu à la négritude*. Some of the short fiction of *Alleluia pour une femme-jardin* may read as a prosed recasting of some of the issues covered by the poem *Un arc-en-ciel pour l'Occident chrétien*. Brathwaite's application of the Caliban-Prospero motif in the analysis of Sam Sharpe in one of his historiographical essays parallels his treatment of Caliban in the verse of *Islands*. Similarly, the re-evaluative presentation of the character of Uncle Tom in the poetry of *The Arrivants* seems to echo the re-evaluation of slave culture that we gather from the monographic essay *The Development of Creole Society in Jamaica: 1770-1820*.

How representative the multigeneric tendency among Caribbean writers can perhaps be suggested by merely listing, for instance, a sampling of those who have written both fiction and poetry; this includes McKay, Lamming, Harris, Salkey, Carew, Neville Dawes, and more recently Cyril Dabydeen, David Dabydeen, Fred D'Aguiar, Kwame Dawes, among numerous others. In addition to practising different genres, Brathwaite, Depestre and Mir probe the boundaries of the genres they practice so as to expand them. Their poems, for instance, manifest a confluence of modes. In Mir we find the stern diction of epic interwoven with prosaic elements, the structural relaxation of song, and the melodic musicality of traditional lyric poetry. A similar generic hybridization occurs in the work of Depestre, whose *Un arc-en-ciel pour l'Occident chrétien*, for example, incorporates stylistic resources from lyric and narrative poetry as well as from drama and prose composition. Brathwaite, particularly in his second poetic trilogy, draws from a variety of registers, going from the often confessional tone of *Mother Poem* to passages in *X/Self* that appear to emulate the lofty prose diction of Medieval chronicles.

The three authors' rapport with the linguistic possibilities available to them can be seen to be linked with their hybridization of form. In Mir's fiction, the standard and formal Spanish of the narrative voice often lapses into the autochthonous peasant forms and linguistic mannerisms of the characters. In Depestre, the juxtaposition of the "français littéraire" and the local colour of Haitian usage produces the linguistic atmosphere of what the author has referred to as "l'usage maternel du français", regardless of whether or not morphologically recognizable Creole forms are actually used. In Brathwaite's works, standard British English and West Indian dialect forms are combined throughout. The peculiar morphological formations resulting from splitting and slashing words so typical of his poetry also find their way into his essays, many of which have appeared in the book *Roots* (Brathwaite 1986, 1993). The three writers, at any rate, draw from the various shades and ranges of what Figueroa has called "the language continuum" in the Caribbean region.

Mir, Depestre and Brathwaite share also a common attitude towards the performative or stylistic aspects of language. They show a preference for abundant usage rather than laconic utterings. They rejoice in the word. They celebrate and express faith in the word. The deep crisis which has beset Western intellectuals in the twentieth century, which has led to so many tomes devoted to language as an object of agonised reflection, of loss of faith in its referential accuracy, its "purity" and communicative capacity, has hardly disturbed these Caribbean writers. They exude a fervent belief in the power of language not only to make art but also to change the world. Their faith in language translates into a belief in the crucial role literature can play in bringing about or welcoming the better world that we must all struggle to achieve. The announcement of a new dawn is expressed by the arrival in Mir of a "nueva poesía", in Depestre of a certain "état de poésie", and in Brathwaite of the kingdom of Caribbeanized "Nommos".

Our three writers reconcile the vision of the literary artist with that of the thinker. Mir explains the role of the poet in society by adducing the process whereby a community chooses or produces leaders. The prominence given in Brathwaite's poetic texts to the alternative voices of the folk in such characters as Tom corresponds fittingly to his own scholarly dedication to unearthing the "little culture", the unwritten achievements of the folk. His bibliographical investigations and his cultural activism on behalf of such figures as Nanny and Sam Sharpe parallel the thematic concerns of his poetry. His critical work, such as *Contradictory Omens* (1974), engages both with works of the literary imagination and fundamental socio-political issues of cultural ethnocentricity. In Depestre, the ideas prevalent in the artistic texts accord with the writer's political and cultural views as expressed in the essays in a strikingly harmonious manner, so much so that his presentation of vodou, for instance, has become less politicized in keeping with the less radical view of the world he now espouses.

Their thematic preoccupations and topical concerns constitute another major area that shows the commonality between the three Caribbean writers. We have sketched the focus on history, the sacred, and language in their works, but such concepts are woven into a canvas whose overall texture corresponds in every respect to aspects of the Antillean experience. In their texts one comes upon a human legacy that has in one way or another been connected with the residual products of slavery, the plantation economy, racial oppression and racial mixture, the ensuing social gradations of skin colour, the contingency and sometimes hostility of the tropical environment, the legacies of the relationship between master and slave that persist in contemporary societies as well as the various resulting human types, such as the maroon figure, the docile servant or the ambivalent Ariel. Other components of that human legacy include local music and dance as well as popular festive forms such as carnival, the human flux of emigration and immigration, the clash and convergence of cultural models and traditions such as the European, African, Indian (Hindu and Muslim), and Native American in formations of an Antillean ontology, and the various occurrences of armed rebellions in the region as a means for Antilleans to assert their humanity.

The texts of Brathwaite, Depestre and Mir refer to a socio-historical reality that is endemically Caribbean. They share the almost universal preoccupation of Caribbean literary artists with the overall Caribbean situation. Cultural reflection is crucial to a Caribbean poetics that is rooted in the ontological self-consciousness of people in the region. Historical events have made people here aware of themselves as objects of reflection. In view of that reflection, one can say that the fundamental *topos* of Caribbean poetics is the Caribbean itself. Since such a reflection entails an exploration of cultural identity, Caribbean texts in speaking about people in the region almost inevitably seek to contribute to delineating the contours of a regional identity. Caribbean poetics is informed by the human experience in the region which both provides its fundamental raw material and, ultimately, yields its system of significance. This system of significance is marked by the struggle for cultural authenticity discussed below.

The centrality of cultural identity in Caribbean poetics clearly directs our attention to the colonial transaction. Caribbean discourse in general may be said to have its genesis in the Antillean's confrontation with the colonial past in the area. The culturally self-conscious diction of Caribbean poetics has to do with the affirmation of difference elicited by the need to appropriate one's own identity by disassociating it from the ontology upheld by the dominant order inherited from colonial times. Mir's corrective rendition of the area's history, Depestre's assertive localization of the sacred, and Brathwaite's celebration of a nativized rendition of the word clearly share a tone that one might call *contestataire* and a distinctly contingent attitude vis-à-vis preexisting images of the Caribbean. These writers enter into decisive conversations with a colonial legacy and its neo-colonial manifestations beyond formal independence. Whether they correct or affirm, revise or deny adapt or update, recycle or subvert, they are dealing directly or indirectly with colonial intertexts. The similarity between the Dominican, the Haitian, and the Barbadian author, indeed, the resemblance among Caribbean writers in general, has to do in large measure with their shared colonial context.

Western colonialism not only invented the Caribbean but it has also provided the context in relation to which the region and its people become one. The transaction began with the fortuitous arrival of the Spanish on the island which they thenceforward called Hispaniola, setting in motion the historical collisions of peoples out of which the invention of the Caribbean would come. The Dutch, the English, and the French soon followed attracted by the fertility of the tropical soil, the potential productivity of the aboriginal work force, the enticing flora and fauna, the coveted precious metals and stones and, eventually, the economic viability of African slavery and the success of the plantation. The commonality of the factors that attracted them considerably outweighs any distinct national flavour each of the aforementioned European powers may have imprinted upon the particular sections of the Caribbean region over which each of them reigned. European colonialism in the area shared this essential aim: capital accumulation and expansion of the sphere of influence of the metropolis.

Whether the individual imperial nations spoke Dutch, French, English or Spanish or professed this or that form of Christian dogma, the kinds of social relations that developed in the region remained virtually uniform. The colonial powers pursued essentially similar economic options throughout the region: slavery, sugar plantation and other forms tropical agriculture, and mineral exploitation among the most prominent. From the shared economic model derived a common set of social dynamics marked by the interaction of social polarities: master and slave, white and non-white (black, East Indian, Native American, etc.), European and non-European, metropolitan and creole. The common backdrop of European colonialism, then, has led to a strikingly homogeneous cultural formation in the Caribbean among the various nations that, despite their different languages and their historical links with different colonial powers, have cohered into one pan-Caribbean culture. Caribbean poetics, embedded in the homogeneity between cultural and artistic expressions in the region, is best understood against this common colonial background of the Antillean region. Nor does the homogeneity preclude the region's cultural diversity – a creative paradox that Brathwaite has captured in the formulation "unity is submarine", unconsciously echoing the words of the Dominican poet Osvaldo Bazil, who in 1918 situated "the ties that link" the lands in the region "underneath the waters of the sea and in their History."

Marginality, Dependence, and Human Culture

The condition of marginality, which provides a major unifying principle in Caribbean poetics, is about a relationship to Western colonialism. Succinctly put, Antillean literature is marginal in so far as it is the product of marginal societies. Though most Caribbean nations have attained their juridical independence, they remain for the most part economically and politically dependent upon the highly industrialized Western capitalist centres, which puts them in a peripheral position in regards to the metropolitan societies with which they have been historically linked – V.S. Naipaul's the Third World's third world (Naipaul 1973: 250). The concept of marginality has thus far been used mostly with reference to the lack of participation of individuals or groups in spheres considered decisive and desirable to those without such access, as Gino Germani explains (1973: 21, 66). The dynamic that stems from the interaction between the "inclusive" and the "exclusive", to borrow the language of Edmond Cros, may perhaps also be applied to the rapport among nations (Cros 1981: 23). Marginality generally names a "spatial situation" to describe a condition of social subordination and relegation of individuals or groups in relation to a dominant sector within the same society (Alonso Hernández 1980: 113). But if one assumes the "spatial situation" to occur not only within a single society but also in the wider sphere of a global economic system, the dynamic becomes identical with the condition of dependence suffered by many nations today. We could thus apply the concept of marginality not just to the relationship between groups in a given society but also to the relationship between societies in a given international order.

The close relationship between marginality and dependence as proposed here is borne out by Theotonio Dos Santos's classic definition of dependence: "a situation in which a certain group of countries have their economy conditioned by the development and expansion of the economies of countries to which they are subordinated" (1982: 305). André Gunder Frank, applying the concept to Latin America, puts it in a historical context: "This dependence is the result of the historical development and contemporary structure of world capitalism, to which Latin America is subordinated, and the economic, political, social, and cultural policies generated by the resulting class structure, especially by the class interests of the dominant bourgeoisie" (Frank 1972: 19).

Dependent nations, understood in the sense suggested by Dos Santos and Frank, may, we would propose, be considered marginal in relation to the nations dominating the core of the given economic order. For what stands out in the dynamic of such an international economic order is the secondary position of certain nations in the making of global decisions even if such decisions affect them most profoundly. Marginality or dependence thus bespeaks a condition of *being-for-another* for the countries in question. In the sphere of cultural products the same conditions operate as in economic relationships. In most cases, cultural and artistic artifacts from marginal nations must contend with the fact that the principles of legitimation that are thought to confer or deny validity in the global order are dictated in the core nations.

Human culture has no centre. The Earth does have a physical core, which may well encompass the source of the planet's geomagnetic field, but that geological core has no cultural counterpart. The complex, unending web of achievement that, through recorded and unrecorded time, has enabled our species to meet the challenge of survival did not emanate exclusively from a discrete point of the globe. No individual geography or society may profess to hold the key to ingenuity and resourcefulness. Nor do we owe the vast legacy of knowledge and wisdom available to men and women today to a single branch of the human family. The world is not the handiwork of a debased deity intent on distributing mental endowments unfairly among the nations of the earth. Whether we reason religiously or secularly, we must concede that intelligence and creativity is indeed the shared patrimony of all humanity. We can satisfy ourselves that beauty, talent, and strength are the monopoly of no particular country, people, or race.

We live in a world characterized by unequal development and unbalanced relations of force. Only a few countries direct or partake of the benefits of the economic and political power that largely dictates the lives or deaths of people everywhere. In the current world system some countries inhabit the centre and many reside on the margins. The much acclaimed global economy notwithstanding, the dynamic of director and directed societies continues to reign supreme. Even in this age of contested borders and territorial changes ushered in by the disintegration of the Soviet Union, there is still an international composite of social formations brought to their present state by either conquest or defeat. Certain nations at given moments of their history undertook successful ventures of encroachment that helped them rise above and dominate others. Their present pre-eminence derives from specific historical conditions that once did not exist and will cease to exist at some foreseeable point in the future.

But the most important of all caveats for our present purpose is that human culture does not follow the logic of power and domination. The political and economic presence of today's central nations should not blind us as to the plurality of accomplishments bequeathed to us by the collective genius of the species. When we assess the cultural and intellectual products of humankind, we ought to remain militantly aware that people everywhere, since time immemorial, have mastered the necessary skills to discern and dissect their world, to imagine and describe the configuration of reality, as well as to half-perceive and half-create the contours of experience. We must beware of surrendering to the pernicious schemes of thought that would have us view a particular society's limitless ability to destroy, conquer or control as evidence of its superior culture and intellectual attainment. We should, in other words, avoid ideological quicksands lest we end up all swallowed by it.

We should resist falling under the seductive spell of the imperial imagination (McGann 1988: 230). For one thing, imperial minds wrongly and dangerously equate might with greatness. Such minds can muster no respect for those who lose, which means they are fated to disrespect large portions of the earth's population, which consists mostly of losers. Eduardo Galeano starts his renowned *Open Veins of Latin America* with this bitter declaration: "The division of labour among nations is that some specialize in winning and others in losing. Our part of the world, known today as Latin America, was precocious: it has specialized in losing ever since the remote times when Renaissance Europeans ventured across the ocean and buried their teeth in the throats of the Indian civilizations" (Galeano 1974: 11). This major Uruguayan author's threnodic meditation on the Latin American predicament could be extended to most countries of Africa, the Caribbean, and some of Asia. The inhabitants of those spaces, billions of people who can hardly claim any ability to control the affairs of the world, do not do well in the regard of imperial thinkers. Too often the descendants of the winners, blinded by their life of inherited privilege, become arrogant and self-complacent to the point of vaunting, vociferously at times, the superior value of their particular ways. Impervious to the historical contingency of the centrality they enjoy in world affairs, they assume that theirs constitutes the culture of the universal. When Max Weber, without trepidation, restricted "universal value" to cultural phenomena taking place in the West he did not base his affirmation on a careful and exhaustive scrutiny of cultural phenomena throughout the globe (Weber 1963: 13). He probably thought that all he needed to see was perceptible from where he stood. As it often happens, he mistook his centre of power for a centre of human culture.

Humanists and the Logic of Power: A Plea

The perception that the West holds the key to human value and the creative genius of the species permeates most global renditions of art and literature available in the United States. H. W. Janson's now classic *History of Art*, an erudite and voluminous "Survey of the Major Visual Arts from the Dawn of History to the Present Day", as the subtitle of its second edition reads, provides a case in point. The current edition, which starts with the Venus of Willendorf about 25,000 years ago and brings the chronicle of the artistic production of humanity to twentieth-century photography, retains its original reflection on "primitive art", meaning the artifacts produced by "the so-called primitive societies of tropical Africa, the islands of the South Pacific, and the Americas" (Janson 1986:35). While granting that the term "primitive" is a "somewhat unfortunate word", since it tends to suggest "quite wrongly – that these societies represent the original condition of mankind", the author adopts it anyway "as a convenient label for a way of life that has passed through the Neolithic Revolution but shows no sign of evolving in the direction of the 'historic' civilizations" (Janson 1986: 35).

A somewhat less timid reservation with respect to the term "primitive" would object to its too linear notion of human development and its subjecting the very concept of humanity to specific milestones in a rigid chronology. If we accept that today's "primitive" societies in tropical Africa, the South Pacific, and the Americas correspond to an earlier stage of the species, to "the original condition of mankind", we are virtually bound to place the people in those societies on a pre-human step of the evolutionary ladder, the rank of humanity referring exclusively to the so-called "historic civilizations". Janson cites some of the defining characteristics of "primitive" societies: their essentially rural and self-sufficient nature, their social and political organization in villages and tribes rather than in cities or states, their lack of written records, and their dependence on orality for preservation of their own history (Janson 1986: 35-36). Stasis rather than dynamism, the art historian tells us, typifies life in "primitive" societies, which lack "the inner drive for expansion that we take for granted in ours", and he insists that they "tend to be strongly isolationist and defensive toward outsiders; they represent a stable but precarious balance of man and his environment, ill-equipped to survive contact with urban civilizations. Most of them have proved tragically helpless against encroachment by the West" (p. 36).

But Janson's definition of primitive societies harbours a moral problem. On the one hand, it privileges the drive to expand over the equally human desire to stay the same, to be left in peace, unconquered and unharmed. If anything, the drive for expansion has too often led nations to commit genocide, to perpetrate slavery, and to steal territories to the fatal detriment of whole human masses. If we give value to the desire for expansion as part of the dynamism of the west, can we honestly deny that the likes of Adolf Hitler and Benito Mussolini had an any less legitimate "inner drive for expansion"? Rightly, neither the Nazi nor Fascist expansionist policies would elicit praise from any humanist scholars today. But don't we make ourselves vulnerable to a charge of hypocrisy if we denounce Nazi and Fascist aggression toward other nations and ethnic groups as "crimes against humanity" while simultaneously upholding the drive to expand as a supreme virtue of civilized people?

Furthermore, Janson's assessment of the social and political norms of "primitive" societies suffers from a curious inconsistency. On the one hand it construes as a weakness their isolationism and defensiveness toward outsiders, but at the same time it admits that the incursion of Western outsiders has often led to their tragic demise. In truth, a reader with the ability to empathize with the vanquished, would probably see a neglected strength in that "weakness". This is the burden, indeed, of Wilson Harris's fiction, most explicitly in *The Sleepers of Roraima* (1970) and *The Age of the Rainmakers* (1971). In other words, one would wish the vanquished of the colonised world had been more firmly isolationist and defensive toward the Western intruder, that the Arawaks had been less cordial, less open, less hospitable when they discovered strangers on their shore on Friday, October 12, 1492. In his diary, Columbus wrote that upon seeing him and his men, the Indians, who "were well built, with handsome bodies and fine features", appeared "very pleased and became so friendly that it was a wonder to see. Afterwards they swam out to the ships' boats where we were and brought parrots and balls of cotton thread and spears and many other things" (Columbus 1990:29). One cannot help musing nostalgically that perhaps the Arawaks might be around in much larger numbers had they been less friendly to the Admiral and his entourage. However, not all will feel nostalgia for the decimated Arawaks. For not all have learned to identify with the loser. Thus, Janson does not appear more than slightly touched by the tragedy of "primitive" societies that have suffered the cruel "encroachment of the West" and he hastens to describe the lethal influx of unfriendly hordes in purely environmental terms and ones that lay the responsibility on the "helplessness" of the defeated. . Devoid of indignation, he tells the tragedy of their devastation and utter defeat at the hands of a fierce and mighty foe simply as an unfitness "to survive contact with urban civilizations."

I insist on this conversation with Janson's view of history, human development and culture primarily because he speaks as an art historian and humanist, which matters tremendously to the concern of the present work, which posits that one's regard for the various segments of the human family largely determines one's appreciation of their artistic and cultural products. A scholar who can recount the elimination of a given society using innocuous terms will most likely not deem the people in that society capable of the spiritual elevation associated with great artistic creation. That explains perhaps Janson's assessment of a nineteenth-century plastered skull from New Guinea's Sepik River. He speaks of its "unrelieved savagery of expression" that "makes it hard for us to think of these heads as works of art" (Janson 1986: 36). At the same time, he grants artistic qualities to a comparable artifact, a 7000 B.C. sculptured head from a group found in Jericho, Jordan (p. 30). His preference appears particularly striking in that to the lay observer the Jericho head will probably look plainer, less elaborate, and ultimately less imaginative than the Sepik River one. We can have little doubt that for Janson the Jericho of 9000 years ago comes closer to his vision of humanity than the New Guinea of the nineteenth-century due to his viewing Jericho as more intimately connected with the West, which constitutes the actual focus of his narrative. It, therefore, comes as no surprise that Anthony F. Janson, who prepared the third expanded edition of Janson's *History of Art*, feels no sense of conflict at his decision to delete a section on the meeting of East and West carried by the previous edition. He explains his editorial choice thus: "The entire study of Third World art is presently being transformed so dramatically that a new synthesis will not be possible for at least another decade" (Janson 1986: 8). His conscious editorial decision to leave out vast geographies, myriad culture areas, and numerous segments of the human family from his panoramic survey does not lead to a reconsideration of the title, which, as it stands, purports to tell about the artistic productions of the entire species. His reason is simple: in the book at hand humanity means the West.

Imperial thinking, which normally relies on metaphors of military conquest and territorial expansion, breeds a kind of judgment on cultural forms, intellectual production and aesthetic objects that succumbs to the logic of power. I would venture to argue that unless one can manage to put aside that habit of thought when weighing aesthetic objects and cultural artifacts one cannot really call oneself a humanist, a rank that art historians and literary scholars are too ready to claim for themselves. Either we transcend the logic of power, which causes us to relish our centrality and boast our superiority over those who have lost, or we acknowledge our partnership with the generals whose job is to lead armies against nationalist resistance and revolutionary movements overseas. We normally assume that the likes of Douglas McArthur and George S. Patton, to speak of highly regarded American military chiefs, differ in their ideals from literary scholars and art historians. We grant that it behooves soldiers to wish to defeat and dominate their foe so as better to spread their country's domain over the nations of the earth. But the compulsions of the learned men and women who devote their lives to exploring aesthetic objects presumably correspond to a less coercive understanding of the relationship between nations.

The plea to scholars in core countries to abandon the logic which has reared them intellectually may be futile to say the least. Obviously, Western thinkers will not find it easy to conceive of a world in which they do not control the centre. Even for Jacob Bronowski, one of the most sensitive twentieth-century humanists the West has produced, picturing a scenario in which his civilization might not dominate the movement of humanity evokes a sense of gloom: "Humanity has the right to change its colour. And yet, wedded as I am in the civilization that nurtured me, I should feel it to be infinitely sad" (Bronowski 1973: 437). How, then, can we ask the children of empire voluntarily to let go of their sense of centrality? The imperial mind needs a centre, at which it sees itself and from which the other constituents of the world derive their relative value, that centre alone having the power to give or take away meaning, like the Lord invoked by Ecclesiasticus. Perhaps the only thing that may serve to justify this plea is that literary scholars, in so far as they fancy themselves humanists, presumably aspire to identify with values that speak to humanity in its largest possible sense. Here they have a chance to test the level of their commitment to that aspiration, not least because they deal mostly with abstractions, and in that respect they seem less bound by the concrete imperatives that regulate the actions of soldiers, legislators, investors, priests and functionaries. Charged with the task of arranging, assessing, decoding and tabulating literary texts, they work in a somewhat autonomous field. Though their judgement can seldom escape biases of class, gender, culture, ideology and race, one must assume that they have a better chance of venturing outside the prevailing schemes of thought than those whose job deals directly with the management of power.

A Multicultural Theory of Literature: On Modern Poetics

The effort to talk about literary phenomena from a perspective that does not derive its logic from a cultural or political hegemony requires a bold leap of the imagination. Without that leap, even scholars who show awareness of and sensitivity to multicultural concerns may helplessly yield to hierarchical arrangements that raise one sole master culture to the uttermost pinnacle of value and meaning. The current, enlarged edition of the *Princeton Encyclopedia of Poetry and Poetics* (Preminger 1974), which remains unchallenged as an authoritative reference source for literary scholars and students, is remarkably inclusive of literatures from various cultures and ethnic groups. The book dedicates competent entries to literary traditions as disparate as the Mongolian, Yoruba, Araucanian, Puerto Rican, Armenian, Chinese, Indian, Albanian, Japanese, African, Haitian and African-American, to name only a few. Yet, the major entry entitled "Modern Poetics", which surveys aesthetic trends and currents in poetic expression from 1750 to the second part of the present century, confines the discussion to developments taking place in England, France, Germany, Italy, the United States, Russia and Spain (Preminger 1974: 503-26). The non-Western literary traditions acknowledged elsewhere in the *Princeton Encyclopedia* do not find even the slightest place in the discussion. The exclusion becomes serious when we recall that poetics, as a field of inquiry, teaches us about the "categories that allow us to grasp simultaneously the unity and variety of literary work", as Ducrot and Todorov have indicated (1979: 78-79). Poetics, as an area of study, purports to reveal to us the "internal theory of literature", thereby promising to give us a conceptual understanding of that which makes literature literary, the essence of the art, in other words. The editors of the *Princeton Encyclopedia*, who could harbour enough respect for the artistic writings of non-Western peoples as to accord them scholarly space in the compilation, did not seem to find them sufficiently meaningful to aid in the understanding of the literary act as it has manifested itself internationally since the second half of the eighteenth century. It appears that, once again, we have come upon the notion that implicitly denies the capability of speaking meaningfully about the various branches of the human family to those cultures that are marginal with respect to the West. Apparently, only the West has the authority to achieve such transnational and transcultural communication.

Michel Benamou urges thinkers in the core countries to engage in a bit of mental acrobatics to avoid doing injustice to the cultural genius of the less empowered nations and cultures: to "become *marginal* and learn to view ourselves, if only at moments of ironic consciousness, from an ethnopoetic point of view" (Benamou 1977: 159). The Argentinian writer Jorge Luis Borges, with his customary insight, simply suggests that we remember how large and unfathomable humanity is. When it comes to weighing the literary productions of humankind, we will only manage to apprehend a portion, but our ignorance in no way negates their greatness. In an essay about "the classics", he says: "my ignorance of Malay or Hungarian letters is total, but I am sure that if time granted me the occasion to study them, I would find in them all the nourishment required by the soul. In addition to linguistic barriers, political and geographical ones also interfere" (Borges 1974: 773).

Borges did not think that a book becomes a classic on account of a fixed set of aesthetic merits but due to an act of faith. In that respect every culture has its own legitimate canonical texts: "A classic is a book that a nation, a group of nations, or the passage of time have chosen to read as if all the contents of its pages were deliberate, fatal, as profound as the cosmos, and capable of endless interpretations .. a book that, generations upon generations, urged by diverse motives, have read with anticipated fervour and a mysterious loyalty" (Borges 1974: 773). Those thoughts suggest to me that any body of artistic texts from any culture, no matter how alien or how unfamiliar to us, can equally serve as the legitimate basis for a meaningful discussion of the art of literature. If we feel enough sympathy as to try to delve into its system of significance, any literary tradition, either of the core or the periphery, will speak eloquently to the universal, among other things, because universality is relative and no single culture has a monopoly over it. Since the first edition of this study, it is worth noting the appearance of Pascale Casanova's *The World Republic of Letters* (2004) which examines the shifts in the centres of literary power and the choices available to writers at the literary margins.

Marginality and Caribbean Newness

The concept of marginality as it relates to interaction among nations with unequal claims to predominance in the current world order, proves useful in the study of literatures from subaltern cultures. There are obviously many kinds of regional marginality that may result in situations resembling that of Caribbean writers vis-à-vis the Western tradition. Perhaps the emergence of African literature most resembles the state of Caribbean writing with respect to the dominant cultural centre. They are both artistic products of Third World cultures mediated by the dynamics of Western colonialism. Both bodies of writings may be said to localize manifestations of the poetics of the marginal within given socio-historical and regional confines.

What makes Caribbean poetics different from other occurrences of the poetics of the marginal, even those in the Third World that have been mediated by colonialism, is the uniqueness of the Caribbean as a culture area. Unlike other parts of the world, in the Caribbean all the elements of cultural definition and even the people themselves have come from abroad in the course of the post-Columbian era. Ancient Africa, the seat of great indigenous civilizations, survived the plundering of the European invaders to a sufficient degree. The survival of cultural forms and cultural artifacts has allowed modern scholars such as Leo Frobenius, Cheik Anta Diop and Walter Rodney to reconstruct the past and to show that the notion "of the 'barbaric Negro' is a European invention" (Diop 1974: 160). The fact that there are extant cultural products that proclaim a living legacy from ancient and traditional Africa has made possible an African revival in the twentieth century. Such a legacy has not only fuelled the imagination of contemporary poets such as Léopold Sédar Senghor, but also it has given writers such as Ngugi Wa Thiong'o the option to write in precolonial African languages. Likewise, in India Rabindranath Tagore, writing mostly in Bengali, or Raja Rao, writing mostly in English, could draw from the ancient, precolonial cultural legacy to kindle their imagination and bring their aesthetic visions to fruition.

Caribbean writers have had no such option. The cultural and human legacy of the native inhabitants of the region suffered decimation by the invading forces in the first few decades of the original European colonization of the region. The aboriginal inhabitants who survived have not, on the whole, as yet regained meaningful political empowerment and have not, as a result, exerted significant pressure in the process of cultural self-definition that has been activated in the area. (However, in Guyana where there is a significant and growing minority Amerindian population, just emerging from a position of extreme marginality, there is evidence of increasingly visible acts of cultural self-definition.) Nor do Caribbean writers have ancient, indigenous vernaculars to which they can resort as an alternative to the European tongue, though some creative literature in Suriname has been written in Sarnami Hindi (Bhojpuri) and devotional literature has been published in Hindi in Trinidad and Guyana. Even the Caribbean Creoles known to us have derived essentially from the fusion of imported elements. A Caribbean culture does exist, and it is autochthonous, vibrant, and original.

But that originality comes essentially from two forces: syncretism and creolization. Syncretism describes the process whereby all incoming elements have experienced fusion. Creolization, in its turn, speaks of the effective nativization of all tributary traditions that have come into the Antillean world and have shaped the Caribbean experience since 1492. In that respect, Caribbean culture is drastically new, which puts the genesis too close in time to permit literary artists to forget it. This probably explains what we would call the hypermnesic element of Caribbean poetics, that is, the uncommon compulsion to remember, to look for meaning in the exploration of past experience. Caribbean poetics, at any rate, is the artistic rendition of the need of Antilleans to articulate and understand their cultural identity, an identity which includes a vision of the past and a vision of the future.

The Caribbean and the Canon

The articulation of Caribbean poetics has implications for the field of comparative poetics and for a multicultural approach to the study of world literature. The act of differentiating a Caribbean poetics, placed in a cultural tradition and informed by a system of signification that separates it from Western poetics, and existing alongside various other culture-specific poetic systems, may perhaps suggest the need to form an independent canon that can accommodate many literary traditions. But the formation of a new canon, as Cornel West warns, should not proceed without a previous examination of the pitfalls of the old ones (West 1987: 197). Comparatists in particular ought to concern themselves with culturally expanding the range and value system of their discipline more than with just transforming the existing canon or courteously making room for selected texts from hitherto excluded literatures. (And such selected texts tend to fit the Western-centred paradigm rather than challenge it.) Earl Miner closes an essay on the theoretical and methodological implications of comparative poetics with this enunciation: "the aims of our study are too important to be left to the definitions of any single one of us or to the methods devised in any single literary tradition. Such individual or chauvinistic pride would defeat the aims of comparative study of literature" (Miner 1986: 30-31). Miner's warning arises from the realization that "much of what passes for literary theory in the West", or even *comparative* literature as presently practised, "is seldom comparative in any radical way" (Miner 1986: 1).

To try to correct the unfortunate situation pointed out by Miner, we would have to be guided by what Anne Paolucci calls "a self-perfecting, scholarly diplomacy for our global multinational literary community" (Paolucci 1980: 28). Paolucci believes that such "scholarly diplomacy" requires a new brand of comparatist, one who has the ability to recognize differences between cultural models and the different literatures they consequently produce. She posits that: "The comparatist who does not recognize the distinct characteristics of Greek, Chinese, Bengali, French, Turkish, Nigerian, Macedonian, Croatian, Australian, American, Malaysian, Canadian and other literatures and peoples can hardly be a competent representative of his literary area. And the specialist in 'other' non-Western emergent or neglected literatures cannot expect to be taken seriously if he dismisses automatically the experience of comparative literary study in the West" (Paolucci 1980: 27-28).

Miner and Paolucci concur that literary systems are linked to specific cultures and distinct human experiences. Literary traditions are historically determined entities that exist within the parameters of place and time. The proposal contained in Miner's demand for a genuinely comparative approach to literary studies and Paolucci's advocacy of a multinational literary diplomacy, should not be taken lightly. It is tantamount to an outright revision of how we view literature and literary achievement. It entails the consideration of a truly global literary order, which would presuppose a decentralized view of human culture. This, in its turn, would necessitate the total removal of the idea of power as a definitive measure of human achievement.

Power, the Canon, the Rise of the West

The Western literary canon has made too many concessions to the celebration of power. Too many of the great works that have earned a place in the canonical repertoire hail the courageous exploits of one people prevailing upon another. Too often the great books of the West induce the beginning reader of literature to identify with conquerors and to feast upon the defeat of the vanquished. European epic, for instance, follows the Virgilian model in *The Aeneid*, which celebrates conquest, militaristic valour, and the building of empire. The Virgilian model kindled the European imagination probably because of the demands of the political moment that started in the Middle Ages, when the West began to become aware of itself as a project with a given direction and was engaged in the necessary process of socio-cultural self-definition. By the early eleventh century the process of Western self-differentiation was apparently well under way to judge from the ethnic and religious self-consciousness of *La chanson de Roland*. The heroes gain moral ascendancy in the universe of the anonymous poem in proportion to their efficacy in the killing of Saracens, who appear portrayed as essentially different beings. The poet involves the divine order in his position. When a Frenchman dies his soul normally goes to heaven, but when a Saracen warrior bites the dust, we hear things like: "Then Satan comes and hales his soul away" (Anon 1973:100). The dichotomy is clearly of Christian versus non-Christian, but it sets the stage for the more encompassing differentiations that would follow in time.

As the dichotomy becomes denser with ethnic, racial and cultural implications over the centuries, it incorporates the opposition of civilization versus barbarism Thus in Tasso's sixteenth-century poem *Gerusalemme liberata*, Godfrey, the leader of the Crusaders who first marched on Jerusalem, achieves a climactic triumph for Christendom when he slays Emiren, the remaining leader of the pagan host. But in freeing "the holy house of Christ", the blood he draws from the enemy also "spoils their barbaric ornaments and their pomps" (Tasso 1983: 493-494; 1987: 468). Godfrey's defeat of the pagan forces entails, then, a victory of the Christian West over barbaric peoples and their culture.

We find the same attitude of differentiation in Alonso de Ercilla's *La araucana*, the late sixteenth century epic glorifying the exploits of the Spanish in South America. Diego de Almagro, the narrator tells us, "a Chile caminó determinado/de extender y ensanchar la fe de Cristo" – to Chile committed he trekked/to spread and expand the Christian faith, and it would subsequently fall upon Valdivia to continue the pacification of "los bárbaros" (the barbarians) by "los nuestros" (our own), as the Spanish and the aborigenes are dichotomously characterized in the poem (Ercilla 1979: 162). Likewise, in Luis de Camoês's *Os Lusíadas*, which sings the heroic deeds of the Portuguese in the "terras viciosas" (vicious lands) of Africa and Asia, including Vasco da Gama's encounter with the "malina/Gente que segue o torpe Mahamede" – evil people who follow the foolish Muhammed, a socio-cultural line is clearly drawn to divide the occidental from the non-occidental, with the latter normally being depicted as of lesser human value (Camoês 1980: 71, 96). In both of these epics of overseas colonial conquests, the non-European, non-Christian is portrayed as less civilized and, consequently, deserving of the havoc wrought upon them by the invading Christian host.

By the sixteenth century, the West had already achieved a distinct socio-cultural identity, and the Roman imperial model was central to that identity. The West had come of age. Edith Hamilton's *The Roman Way to Western Civilization* declared the West – which includes the United States – as the progeny of the Roman empire. She speaks of the time "when Carthage had been twice defeated and the foundations were solidly laid of the Roman civilization to which our own goes directly back" (Hamilton 1957: 11). She traces the West back to the consolidation of Roman might through the military crushing of overseas peoples. But one could probably show that it was really in the Middle Ages, when the Roman imperial model was adopted, that the tendency to adduce such a genealogy was born. The Punic Wars alluded to by Hamilton actually yielded a wealth of symbolism, given their locality in North Africa, to those concerned with highlighting elements of ethnological difference between the conqueror and the conquered.

Petrarch, who is commonly recognized as one of the very first Western humanists, was also among the first to exploit the ethnically differentiating potential of the Punic Wars. In his epic poem celebrating the glorious exploits of Scipio in Africa, he speaks of "barbarian lands" and legitimizes the political yoking of the Carthaginians. The defeat of the Carthaginians and the ensuing annexation of their territory to imperial Rome is what the closing of the poem celebrates in these boastful lines: "With Carthage overthrown,/no nation henceforth will deem it a shame/to wear the yoke and call the men of Rome/Quirinus' sons, invincible in war,/the rightful lords and rulers of the world" (Petrarca: 1926: 275; 1977: 236-37). Petrarch's poem clearly subscribes to the Virgilian model that celebrates the crushing of one people by another for the benefit of empire.

One might argue that much in the system of signification and the scale of values within which Western epic literature speaks to Western readers is intertwined with the adoration of imperial might and the glorification of power. Nor is it only the epic poets who partake of this adoration. Suffice it to mention two giants of nineteenth century lyric poetry: Victor Hugo and Alfred Lord Tennyson. The former apotheosized the imperial mission of Napoleon Bonaparte in the East. These lines from the poem "Lui" in *Les Orientales* give the measure of Hugo's fervent admiration for Napoleon's imperial greatness: "L'Egypte resplendit des feux de son aurore;/Son astre impérial se lève à l'orient./Vainqueur, enthousiaste, éclatant de prestiges,/ Prodige, il étonna la terre des prodiges – Egypt glittered in the flares of its dawn;/Its imperial star rises pointing East./Vanquisher, enthusiast, breaker of charms,/A prodigy himself, he astonished a/prodigious land (cited in Said 1979: 82-83). Tennyson, for his part, sang admiringly to "ever broadening England and her throne/ In our vast Orient", and included himself among those "who love/Our ocean empire with her boundless homes" (cited in Brantlinger 1988: 3). In lines like these Tennyson exalted the pride of Victorian England in what was then called "the genius of the race", a genius which, put crudely, manifested itself in the effective domination of overseas peoples and lands (Brantlinger 1988: 7). We would venture to say that Tennyson's commitment to the celebration of empire is typical of Western colonialism in its classical form. A meticulous survey of Western texts during the period in question could substantiate this assertion, even if we ought to recognise the existence of a distinct counter-discourse in the work of some of the Romantics: Blake, Shelley, Byron, early Wordsworth.

The many concessions made to the celebration of power in Western literature may trace their origin to the socio-political forces that initially cohered into the Western project. The West derives its socio-cultural identity from the marriage of the Roman imperial model with the ancient Hebrew religious tradition that later metamorphosed into Christianity. Samir Amin's argument about the formation of the West differs from mine in that he traces it to the Renaissance whereas I believe one must start with the Crusades. Yet Amin's account of the adoption of Christianity is enlightening: "But in order for Christianity to become the foundation of European identity, a sweeping totalizing and historical interpretation had to be developed, stressing its alleged timeless characteristics and opposing it to other religions and philosophies, such as Islam and Hinduism" (Amin 1989: 98). Amin adds that "the uniqueness of Christianity had to be magnified and adorned with particular and exclusive virtues that, by simple teleology, account for the superiority of the West and its conquest of other peoples" (Amin 98-99). While, again, his tracing of the process differs from mine chronologically, Amin is convincing when he points to a systematic religious and ethnic differentiation that resulted in the cultural phenomenon which he calls Eurocentrism.

Eurocentrism came about as the West, having constituted itself as a project with a given direction, had recourse to the Roman imperial model in the construction of a socio-cultural self-image. Rome's formidable legacy of conquest of overseas peoples and territorial expansionism proved worthy of emulation. In addition, the Judeo-Christian tradition, whose religious teleology allows for the subjection of one people by another, provided a complementary discourse of legitimation. *The Old Testament*, for instance, presents us with a godhead that has very clear ethnic affiliations. Though creator of the whole human species, he makes his covenant with one particular people, the children of Israel, to whom he promises power over all the nations of the earth. The people of Israel become thus a special people with a divinely ordained historic mission. In *The Aeneid*, the Romans too appear portrayed as a chosen people who enjoy the favour of the divine order in their quest to build the empire. Whether prompted by the apparent commonalities between the two traditions or purely by dint of chance and historical circumstance, the Romans and the Judeo-Christians came to merge into one socio-cultural model with one political destiny. Perhaps one should credit Constantine the Great (280-337) and Theodosius the Great (347-395) with having laid an early foundation for this historic connection. The union of the two legacies, out of which the Christian West gradually evolved, explains the subsequent partnership of *The Bible* and the sword in the conquest and pacification of overseas peoples in Africa, Asia, and the Americas during the enterprise of colonialism, which solidified the West politically and economically and gave the project its final socio-cultural cohesion.

Beyond Power as a Vehicle of Legitimation

An appraisal of the achievements of Western literature cannot escape reference to the rise to power of the West in the international sphere. When one looks at world literature and sees the West at the centre, one is invariably informed by the centrality of the West in the distribution of power among the nations of the earth. Arnold Toynbee, reflecting on how "the great non-Western majority of mankind" would perceive the West in light of the interaction between "the West and the world" for the past five centuries, offered over four decades ago this succinct impression: "Different though the non-Western peoples of the world may be from one another in race, language, civilization, and religion, if any Western inquirer asks them their opinion of the West, he will hear them all giving the same answer: ...The West, they will tell him, has been the arch-aggressor of modern times, and each will have their own experience of Western aggression to bring up against him. ...the peoples of Africa and Asia will remind him that Western missionaries, traders, and soldiers from across the sea have been pushing into their countries from the coasts since the fifteenth century. The Asians will remind him that, within the same period the Westerners have occupied the lion's share of the world's last vacant lands in the Americas, Australia, New Zealand, and South and East Africa. The Africans will remind him that they were enslaved and deported across the Atlantic in order to serve the European colonizers of the Americas as living tools to minister to their Western masters' greed for wealth. The descendants of the aboriginal population of North America will remind him that their ancestors were swept aside to make room for the West European intruders and for their African slaves" (Toynbee 1953: 2-3).

That background persuades us that the hegemony of the West has resulted from the success of the imperial model and the crushing of peoples and territorial possessions in what is now known as the Third World. One cannot extricate the globalization of Western aesthetic objects and cultural forms from the establishment of Western capitalism as a dominant economic and political force in world affairs. The West reached its hegemony at the expense of other peoples and cultures of the globe. The literary hegemony of the West derives directly from that relation of power between nations.

Perhaps nothing sheds so much light on the role of power in literary relations as the rise of Third World literatures after World War II. The literatures of those formerly subject peoples have come into view precisely to the extent to which they have challenged the validity of Western hegemony. As the Western tradition spread its claim to universality with the consolidation of Western colonialism, so Third World literatures have enhanced their visibility internationally with the rise of anti-colonialist consciousness. The proliferation of Third World texts, particularly those written in European languages, marks an artistic response from these marginal peoples and cultures to the intellectual hegemony of the West. "Critics have come to interpret the works of contemporary Third-World authors writing in European languages as an act of subversion directed against the whole ideological system embodied in the literary codes they have inherited from the colonizing powers," says the comparative literature scholar Claus Clüver (Clüver 1986). The texts of these writers constitute, in effect, a counter-discourse to the dominant discourse of the Western canon, even though many texts came into being as "exotic" adjuncts to metropolitan writing – whatever their writers' intentions.

Once one recognizes the close relationship between power and literary hegemony, that lascivious marriage between the gun and the pen, one should hope comparatists would feel it their duty to seek to break that unholy alliance. This is, of course, a moral issue, which assumes that comparatists should aspire to become humanists who decry oppression and who concern themselves with humanity rather than with the mightiest component of it. Certainly we cannot change the past. The colonial transaction, for instance, did put the pen at the service of the gun. Many writers did step forward to justify, glorify, immortalize the predominance of power. We cannot erase the writing on their pages. Nor can we deny that what we are today inescapably refers in some way to the movement of empire. But one should hope that we all, even the beneficiaries of the movement of empire, can recognize genocide when we see it. A holocaust perpetrated against human beings, no matter what their colour or race, is not rendered less deplorable by the mere fact that it led to a great epic poem from the ranks of the perpetrators.

We may still read past celebrations of power and the movement of empire. But we need not celebrate them ourselves. Nor should we allow power to determine our literary judgment. Today we are sufficiently well versed in irony to be able to deconstruct even the discourses that have reared us and that have trained us to see power as the ultimate dispenser of value. Current Western inquiry into the nature of language and the critique of received ideas implicit in most critical theory have made considerable contributions in this area. But historical circumstances too have helped. For one thing, Asia, Africa and the Caribbean seem a lot less distant from the Western metropoles than they used to. International migration, spurred by the labour demands of late capitalism, has reterritorialized great portions of mankind in the twentieth century. As a result, Westerners now easily and frequently come upon Asians, Africans or West Indians walking the streets of Paris, New York, or London. Depending on their class status, Westerners and these formerly distant peoples may even live in the same neighbourhood, share the same apartment building, and attend the same school.

Today, at any rate, we are better equipped to see through the great edifices: the great pyramids of Giza, the Chinese Wall, the Parthenon, the Coliseum, the Machupicchu monuments in Cuzco, and possibly grieve for the victims whose blood was spilt in their construction. We are now cognizant with Walter Benjamin that "There is no document of civilization which is not at the same time a document of barbarism", and that, in the words of Maynard Solomon, "The cultural possessions of mankind, the highest achievements of the spirit, were born *intra feces et urinas* of class oppression" (Benjamin 1979: 560; Solomon 1979: 547). We now realize that to celebrate the exploits of Alexander in the East, the glory of the pioneers who "won" the West in the United States, the deeds of Vasco da Gama in Africa and India, the courage of Cortez and Pizarro in South America, and the like, is to be enamoured of the conqueror. It is also to side with the winner against the vanquished, to celebrate holocaust, to subscribe to the notion that might is right. It is, in short, to pave the road to Auschwitz-Birkenau.

Literary judgment must disassociate itself from power lest it should find itself sponsoring holocaust. It must not be informed by a vision that occupies itself merely with the march of Alexander upon the peoples of the East without regard for the latter's sorrowful defeat. It must recognize the depatriation and dehumanization endured by Native Americans when the pioneers undertook to win the West. It must not ignore the tragedy that befell the native inhabitants of Africa, Asia and the Americas when European warriors went overseas to achieve their epic deeds. No account of the human experience may deem itself complete if it omits the knowledge gained through the suffering of the vanquished. To be indifferent to the genocides and ethnic oppressions of the past is to invite their repetition in the future. The vision of the vanquished must form part of any reflection that purports to speak globally about the nature of literature. In literature, we need to pay close attention to the texts of the multitudinous "unrepresented selves" (Quasha and Rothenberg 1973: xxxii). Poetry, Jerome Rothenberg reassures us in the exploration of what he calls *ethnopoetics*, "like language itself, [exists] everywhere: as powerful, even complex, in its presumed beginnings as in many of its later works" (Rothenberg 1985: xvii). A comparatist, therefore, ought not to fall into the trap of associating poetry only with the intellectual and artistic legacy of the conquerors or of a cultural tradition that through historical circumstance happened to end up at the centre of power in the international order. Literature is as large as humanity itself. The scope of the comparatist must open as wide as possible to encompass the greatest possible portion of the large literary legacy of humanity.

Toward A Decentralized Theory of World Literature

Our current sense of irony, if nothing else, should make it possible for us to conceive of a world literary order that is not based on the political hegemony of one socio-cultural construct over the productions of marginalized peoples and cultures. We are now in a position to approach literature from a more fully humanist perspective. We can seek to disrobe ourselves of the limiting garment of ethnocentrism. With Rothenberg, we can perhaps embrace "a modernism" that aims to change "ways of speaking/thinking/doing that have too long robbed us of the freedom to be human to the full extent of our powers and yearnings" (Rothenberg 1983: xiv). We can now aspire to assume "a proper sphere of totalization – one that is horizontally international and vertically transcultural and transhistorical," as Jerome J. McGann has advocated (McGann 1988: 224). McGann insightfully indicates, however, that for "a proper sphere of totalization" to come about one must emancipate oneself from the imperial imagination. "To relinquish an empire is no easy task," he says, and he ends with this sharp pronouncement: "To relinquish an imperial imagination is also difficult, and a no less urgent task. Empires are maintained by imperial intellects. Cultural studies, and literary work in particular, function either to build or to unbuild such minds" (McGann 1988: 230).

To emancipate oneself from what McGann calls the imperial imagination is to adopt a scheme of thought that does not privilege the predominance of power as the ultimate dispenser of value. It is difficult, indeed, especially since we have been trained to worship power. But, if we can muster enough irony to proclaim that might is not necessarily right, we will abandon the ways of the "imperial intellect". A clue as to the mental attitude that we might wish to emulate appears in a passage from Book XXIV in *The Iliad* of Homer, that very ancient sage who wrote his hexameters centuries before the West came into being. When Priam comes, a suppliant, to the ships of the Achaeans to ransom the body of his dead son Hector, the fearsome Achilleus shows enough wisdom not to rejoice in the gore of his victory. Instead, "He took the old man's hand and pushed him/gently away, and the two remembered, as Priam sat huddled/at the feet of Achilleus and wept close for manslaughtering Hector/and Achilleus wept now for his own father, now again/for Patroklos. The sound of their mourning moved in the house" (Homer 1983: 488). In this passage, Achilleus, who has slain not only Hector but also many other of Priam's children, tries to console the suffering old man by placing the war between the Trojans and their Achaean invaders in a large tragic frame: "Such is the way the gods spun life for unfortunate mortals,/that we live in unhappiness, but the gods themselves have no sorrows" (Homer 1983: 489). As he continues speaking with the intention of assuaging the Trojan elder's lamentation, Achilleus intimates that he knows he has brought the old man grief but not without enduring a share himself. He bewails the misfortune of Peleus, his own father:

> a single all-untimely child he had, and I give him
> no care as he grows old, since far from the land of my fathers
> I sit here in Troy, and bring nothing but sorrow to you and your children.
> And you, old sir, we are told you prospered once; for as much

as Lesbos, Makar's hold, confines to the north above it
and Phrygia from the north confines, and enormous Hellespont,
of these, old sir, you were lord once in your wealth and your children.
But now the Uranian gods brought us, an affliction upon you,
forever there is fighting about your city, and men killed (Homer 489).

In the above passage the poet averts the illusion that might is right. Certainly the Achaeans marched on Ilion in order to defeat the Trojans, and we learn in the poem that they achieved their end. But in the lines above, Achilleus, the best of the Achaeans, knows full well the pain he has brought upon the enemy, the Trojans, whose humanity he never denies. Homer does not attempt to portray the winner as inherently good nor the loser as inherently bad. The words of Achilleus suggest that in their clash he perceives the dismal condition of human existence, a human tragedy that befalls the victor as well as the vanquished. The way he articulates the gravity of human suffering evokes *pathos* for one *ethnos* as well as for the other. This humanistic vision allows no room for ethnocentrism. Achilleus exhibits the knowledge that power is contingent, not permanent, and that in and of itself it cannot define human worth. Their encounter reveals both Achilleus and Priam as pawns of historical circumstance and the insanity of war.

If we, like Homer, manage to step outside the imperial imagination, having put an end to our subservience to power as a vehicle of legitimation, we may perhaps arrive at the conception of a truly global literary tradition, one that has no centre. A centre implies a hegemony, which, in its turn, comes about through the preponderance of power. It insinuates a model of human achievement which induces one to wish to become the perpetrator so as to dominate the core. A centre implies a cultural hierarchy among the peoples of the earth, which insinuates, in turn, that the experience and the products of certain human groups have more intrinsic value than those of others. It suggests that we cannot imagine an international order in which equality prevails. For equality abhors a centre. Even if generals, tycoons, and other empire builders prove unable to imagine the world without their grip on the centre of power, we must hope that the literary scholar who is informed by a humanistic and not an ethnocentric view of the world will be able to conceive a decentralized view of human culture and, consequently, a decentralized literary order. A world literary tradition, conceived without a centre, will mark the divorce of power and literary judgment. Only in the context of a decentralized literary order, with the inherent admission that every component of human culture is equally central to the culture of the universal, can comparative literature and poetics become truly multicultural and claim moral validity as fields of humanistic intellectual inquiry.

AFTERWORD: CARIBBEAN POETICS IN A NEW CENTURY

I. Preamble

The momentum of Antillean writing in the twenty-first century, when few of the major builders of twentieth-century Caribbean letters remain living or still productive, reveals the ascendancy of the diaspora as a largely transformative presence. We witness a scenario wherein Caribbean-descended writers appear to compete effectively for the attention of readers on the literary markets of the Christian West. The works of Bea Vianen, Astrid Roemer and Denis Henriquez seem to fare well in The Netherlands. Fiction writer Gisèle Pineau and poet Jocelyn Valverde suffer no want of audiences in France. Caryl Phillips and Pauline Melville enjoy prestige in the United Kingdom. Similarly, Paule Marshall, Julia Alvarez, Cristina Garcia, Edwidge Danticat, and Esmeralda Santiago have often entered the best-selling charts in the United States. Elsewhere, I have contended that to grasp the Caribbean experience "one has to train one's eyes on three primary spaces: the insular, the continental, and the diasporic", adding that no "serious attempt to understand holistically the cluster of societies involved" can dispense with any of the three (Torres-Saillant 2006: 21). While often dealing with writers in exile (who do not belong in the collective we call *the diaspora*), the core of *Caribbean Poetics* has focused primarily on literary artists and thinkers from the region (irrespective of how long they may have lived abroad). The study has concerned itself first and foremost with authors connected directly through birth, socialization, and identification to the tellurian geography of the islands and the continental rim-lands that make up the physical space of the Antillean world. The pages that follow in this "Afterword" retain the focus on the tellurian geography but duly pay pertinent attention to the region's rapport with "the cultural and existential geography created" in Europe, Canada and the United States by "generations of emigrants" (Torres-Saillant 2006: 250).

The "Epilogue" to my *An Intellectual History of the Caribbean* meditates on the implications of the rise to visibility of intellectual and artistic voices of the Caribbean diaspora on the global market (Torres-Saillant 2006: 243-

253). I argued that the international prominence of Western-educated, Caribbean-descended writers and thinkers might have the unintended effect of supplanting the voices of their counterparts in the tellurian geography of the Antillean world. Men and women of letters from the region generally lack the backing of a viable book industry that can propel their words outside of their native lands. As a result, Caribbean diasporic voices from the West may monopolize the ability to speak influentially about the Antillean world. The story of the Caribbean, told by writers rooted culturally and socially in centres of the intellectual industry of the West, could perhaps reach remote corners of the planet, going farther than it could possibly have gone when writers from the region (located either at home or in exile) led the effort of telling. This could suggest the possibility that Caribbean bodies of knowledge will overcome their former marginality. The scenario points to a mixed blessing. Having the telling of the Caribbean story in the hands of diasporic voices without civic or political rootedness in the countries of the region could increase its reach, culminating perhaps in its finding its proper place within the narrative of humanity. But it could also mean that, socialized as they are by the formative institutions of the Western metropolis, diaspora writers may have little access to the story of the Antillean world other than through the typically exoticized rendition found in Western versions of the Caribbean, or that it is those kinds of renditions that find favour in metropolitan corporate publishing. Diasporic voices could thus end up resorting to the deployment of "borrowed eyes" when looking at or imagining the ancestral homelands of their parents. Whether Caribbean-descended writers of Canada, the United States and Europe will collaborate in epistemic solidarity with their counterparts in the region or operate as discursive and ideological competitors against them will depend on the political location and ethnic identification of individual writers. But there seems to be little reason to doubt that the cultural geography inhabited by the diaspora now intersects profoundly with the texture of life in the region. I contend that the intersection has largely reconfigured the texture of the literary production connected to the Caribbean experience, urging the student of this corpus to confront conceptual difficulties that have now gained prominence, even if they may have already existed within the corpus in less pronounced ways.

The difficult location of Zadie Smith's first novel, *White Teeth* (2000), in relation to the corpus of writings we think of as Caribbean literature, offers a useful starting point to attempt to prefigure the emphases, texture, and dominant direction of this corpus in the twenty-first century. Based on the intellectual and artistic trends we have witnessed over the last two decades, and given the close ties between the literary act and the history of thought in the region, I would like to suggest at the outset that Caribbean writers will for the most part continue to distance themselves exponentially from the features that typified their predecessors. The homogenizing affirmation of Caribbean identity that typified the foundational documents of twentieth-century creole nationalist thought from the region has morphed into a growing tendency to challenge identitarian fixities, a tendency which began to surface in the 1960s, but had not become dominant. Similarly, evocations of the uniqueness of the Caribbean person, as a peculiar product of a distinct homogenizing historical experience, has tended to give way to the habit of investigating the creases within Caribbean personhood by stressing the diverse tensions borne out by internal differences of class, language, race, sexuality, gender and ethnic ancestry. The popular in music, social practices, dance and non-literate figurations has risen in prominence, at times competing with the power of the intellectual to promote the upliftment of the less empowered and to shed light on the intricacies of Caribbean life. This seems to be occurring in a more widespread manner than it did when select members of the *litterati* found inspiration in the popular arts at least as far back as the 1970s. By the same token, along with a widespread critique of nationalism, texts that engage the past, the present, and the future of Caribbean communities have increasingly stressed the long history of transnational exchange that has shaped the lives of the populations in question. They have tended to foreground diasporic locations as integral to the Caribbean experience from the very start of the colonial transaction. They thus show the extent to which the very geography within which Caribbean writing may be said to exist can hardly correspond to the national contours of given nation-states. This is hardly new in Caribbean literary history, as the binational locations of Saint-John Perse and Jean Rhys would indicate, but today the translocal spread of the Caribbean experience in literary practice and representation has attained a formerly unseen centredness.

II. Inhabiting a Diverse World

The spectacular success of Zadie Smith's *White Teeth*, a novel that became a sensation the instant it appeared in print in the last year of the twentieth century, further increasing its popularity through an adaptation as a BBC-TV mini-series, brought Jamaican characters to the average British household. Clara Bowden, a beautiful black Jamaican woman with false teeth arrives in England in 1972, at the age of seventeen, in the company of her mother Hortense, a vociferously fanatic Jehovah's Witness whose husband, Darcus Bowden, already in London, has failed to save enough money to bring his family to join him. Darcus, debilitated by a mysterious illness, is confined to an armchair from which he never removes himself, silently watching television except for the occasional utterance of "Hmph" (Smith 2001:31). Clara marries Archibald Jones, a lower-middle-class white Englishman, and they have a daughter, Irie, a bright but impressionable young woman who, in the words of a reviewer, holds "the novel together" (Lowe 2001:179). Clarence and Denzel, two old Creole-speaking Jamaicans, regulars at O'Donnell's Café, a site to which the scene of the action recurringly returns throughout the novel, complete the Caribbean *dramatis personae*.

One might hasten to classify *White Teeth* as a Caribbean text given the prominence of characters, situations, and historical memories linking London institutions to the Caribbean. Glenard Oak, the school the young characters attend, is named after a benefactor who had made his wealth in the malefaction of colonial exploitation on the islands (Smith 2001:303-307). However, such a classification does not exhaust the book's identity. The characters in the novel inhabit urban northwest London in the last three decades of the twentieth century, and they share their time and space with members of other branches of the human family. Archibald and Clara live in intimate proximity with Bangladeshi Muslim immigrant Samad Miah Iqbal, his self assertive wife Alsana, and their two sons Magid and Millat. The two families, in turn, interact intensively with Jewish-descended, Oxford University scientist Marcus Chalfen, his devoted Irish wife Joyce, and their wilful son Joshua. In the collage of ethnic heritages that the novel interweaves, *White Teeth* "jumps across walls of race and class in a manner typical of late twentieth-century multicultural youth culture in London", making it, in the words of Jan Lowe, unwise to attempt "to fit it neatly and entirely into any past or present literary tradition." Nonetheless, she recognizes the way "Caribbean culture and its legacy" emerge in the text as the primary source of resistance in "the melting pot of Britain's multicultural youth culture" (Lowe 175,171). Smith herself seems to stress the currency of the Caribbean in the London that her characters inhabit. At one point the narrator comments, when describing an exchange between Samad's two boys: "'*Cha*, man! Believe, I don't want to tax dat crap,' said Millat with the Jamaican accent that all kids, whatever their nationality, used to express scorn" (Smith 2001:167).

Though left unglossed, the title of Jan Lowe's review of *White Teeth*, "No More Lonely Londoners", alludes to the title of the 1956 novel by Samuel Selvon to suggest that the Caribbean immigrants and their children who populate Smith's novel are no longer "lonely". Unlike the characters in *The Lonely Londoners*, who inhabit a West Indian enclave, in isolation from other ethnically differentiated segments of the city population, Smith's characters regularly interact, influence, are influenced by, and intermarry with people of Asian, Jewish, Irish, Arab and white English descent. They, in other words, form part of the fabric of which London society is made. Smith probably had this in mind when she replied to the question, "How were you trying to approach multiracial London?" by saying, "I was just trying to approach London. I don't think of it as a theme, or even as a significant thing about the city. This is what modern life is like. If I were to write a book about London in which there were only white people, I think that would be kind of bizarre" (Smith 2006). We might be justified in deducing from this pithy remark that the literary instinct to do justice to the interracial and multicultural tapestry of modern London carries more weight in the novel than the desire to tell the story of Caribbean people. Her Jamaicans represent only one of the colours that give London its polychromatic hue.

Ironically, many of the features that render *White Teeth* problematic as a member of the Caribbean family of literary texts correspond dynamically to the emphases that set the most recent literary developments in the Caribbean apart from the works of earlier generations. Indeed, the novel consistently invites reflection on the most recurring issues surfacing in the body of utterances that one might generically describe as the "new" Caribbean thought, namely the formulations interpretive of the region's past, present and future voiced by the generation of writers, scholars, and thinkers that began their publishing careers in the 1980s. Brian Meeks places the emergence of new paradigms for the study of the Caribbean in the context of the deleterious consequences of three decades of economic decline, structural adjustment, and the failure of development projects in the region that signalled "the demise of an entire notion of sovereignty and non-alignment" (Meeks 2001: ix). The economic and political futility ushered in by the 1980s brought about "the debilitating retreat of the intellectual both from politics and the project of serious inquiry" (xiv). Concomitantly, a new generation of Caribbean academics, made up of younger scholars formed in Canada, the United States and Europe who, by virtue of their emigration had escaped the "corrosive effect of economic decline" in the region, engaged in an eclectic interdisciplinary search for fitting approaches to understanding the human drama of their homelands (xv). Despite the elements of retreat from engagement with the radical decolonising project, Meeks described their development as "a renaissance" in Caribbean social, economic, and political thought (xiii). Salient emphases among the representatives of these new voices on the horizon of Caribbean thought include critiques of nationalism, post-Marxist formulations, deployment of postmodernist and postcolonial axes of analysis, and problematizations of previously established ways of imagining the Caribbean community.

In a study that approaches the Caribbean as a site within the larger global geography of postcolonialism, anthropologist David Scott deploys a sensitive critique of Afrocentric interpretations of Caribbean culture as represented by the work of Kamau Brathwaite (Scott 1999:107). Scott thus allies himself conceptually, though not uncritically, with Paul Gilroy's adamant rebuke of cultural nationalists and racial essentialists, crediting Gilroy with breaking with rationalist historiography and cultural nationalism in black diaspora criticism (110-111, 118). Scott's nonchalant advice, however, that we read Frantz Fanon "with" Michel Foucault reveals a willingness to relinquish from the outset the ambition to assert the Caribbean as a self-sustaining site of intellectual production (195). As it relates to the overall movement of society, he envisions a political scenario in which "Jamaica would no longer be about political parties, periodic elections, or even Parliament", but would be refashioned so as to "multiply the relational identities that can be enacted or practised, the subjectivities that can appear as constituent members of a pluralizable, public sphere" (218). In thinking the Caribbean, Scott decentres and departiculiarizes so as to arrive at a new conceptualization of "postcolonial politics" (224). Anthropologist Charles V. Carnegie, a Caribbeanist of the same generation, shares the impetus to decentre but retains the commitment to particularize the Caribbean experience as an instance with the capability to contribute meaningful knowledge to the rest of the human family. Convinced that the nation-state neither assures well-being nor is amenable to reform, Carnegie represents the Caribbean as a region that, expressly formed on the orbit of the nation state, has continuously breached its "ideological and political claims and reach", thus assigning to the region an exemplary position in world affairs (Carnegie 2002: 83). The Caribbean, in his view, leads other parts of the world in the practice of "transnational modes of dwelling", making available potential models for "new modes of belonging" (65).

In keeping with the complex manner of figuration reflected in the interventions of Scott and Carnegie, the evocations of Caribbean life penned by the literary artists since the 1980s have leaned toward the decentring of national belonging, ethnicity, and identity as a whole. The Jamaican poet, fiction writer, and cultural historian Olive Senior has asserted her hybrid ancestry by taking a decentred view of identity. She has said, "I represent many races and I'm not rejecting any of them to please anybody" (Tanna 2004). The title story in her second collection of short fiction, *Arrival of the Snake-Woman* (1989), creates the character of an Indian woman as the protagonist who confronts and subverts the structure of patriarchal abuse by exerting herself in her ethnic difference and sexual subjectivity. Senior's foregrounding of an Indian woman to enact a stance of Caribbean womanhood undeniably contributes to inscribing the memory of rural India "on the Caribbean landscape", evincing "the Indian indentured experience as an integral part of a larger historical experience, sharing a common language of both disinheritance and self-determination with the Afro-Caribbean majority and other ethnic and mixed-race minorities" (Mehta 2004: 228). Caribbean writers who themselves trace their ancestry back to India have compellingly voiced the urgency of moving beyond "conventionally defined paradigms of Caribbean-ness" that have relegated the Indo-Caribbean heritage to a rank of invisibility.

One can see the urgency to assert a presence in characteristic lines from David Dabydeen's *Coolie Odyssey* (1984): "We mark our memory in songs/ Fleshed in the emptiness of folk,/Poems that scrape bowls and bone/In English basements far from home" (Dabydeen 2005: 302-303). Having left Guyana for England at the age of twelve, Dabydeen's voice is complex. It contains Indo-Guyanese memory; it deals with the Indo-Caribbean experience in Britain – a mongrel identity amongst "real" Asians (*The Intended* 1991); it re-engages with the ethnic conflicts that persist in Guyana; it imagines a history that goes back to India (*The Counting House* 1996). Literary efforts to mark the Indian presence in the countries of the region go back at least to the Guyanese compilation *Anthology of Local Indian Verse*, edited by C. E. J. Ramcharitar-Lalla (British Guiana, 1934). None of the poets included seems to have achieved enough distinction to be remembered today, but in recent decades few could ignore the talent of the late Mahadai Das, in her earlier work committed to bearing witness to the endurance of her Indian Guyanese heritage. Her first collection of poems, *I Want to be a Poetess of My People* (1977), traces the roots of her community from indentureship to independence. Included in that volume, the memorable poem "They Came in Ships" contains lines that effectively weave her gender and ethnic self-affirmation: "I stand 'twixt posterity's horizon/And her history./I, alone today, am alive,/Seeing beyond, looking ahead" (Das 2010: 25-27). Das's work builds on that of Rajkumari Singh and its elements of gender protest, and her later poems, collected along with previously published volumes in *A Leaf in His Ear* (2010), explore a sensibility that regards the "heritage" suggested by "They Came in Ships" as altogether more problematic in terms of issues of gender and ethnocentricity.

That the compulsion to bear witness is hardly circumscribable to English-speaking writers is clear from the estimable work of the Surinamese Jit Narain, whose verse, in Dutch as well as in Sarnami, memorializes the Hindustani immigrant experience in Surinam. "Why he left India, that I can fathom;/that India never left him, is the burden I bear," says a poem of his that meditates on the parental origins of his ethnic awareness (Narain 2005: 240). On the whole, Indo-Caribbean writers, and particularly the women, have demonstrated ideological sophistication in exalting their Indian roots while simultaneously "exposing the perniciousness of Hindu racial, class and gender prejudice" (Mehta 2004: 228). Though each in her own distinctive voice, such authors as Mahadai Das, Ramabai Espinet, Jan Shinebourne, Rosanne Kanhai, Shani Mootoo, Lakshmi Persaud, Lelawattee Manoo-Rahming, Rajandaye Ramkisoon-Chen, Oonya Kempadoo, Narmala Shewcharan and Ryhaan Shah seem jointly to aspire to a capacious understanding of Caribbean identity that facilitates the natural recognition of ethno-racial difference, the equitable partnership of males and females in the public and private domains, and the necessarily transnational space of belonging (229). That the overwhelming majority of these Indo-Caribbean women writers have taken up residence elsewhere makes the separation of their identitarian space and the discrete geography of their ancestral homeland particularly relevant. Whilst Indo-Caribbean women authors have attracted most recent academic and publishing attention, it should be noted that the post Naipaul, Ismith Khan and Sam Selvon generation of male writers have also focused on previously unexpressed dimensions of Indo-Caribbean experience. Roopall Monar's fiction (1986, 1989) has explored the lives of the Indian working class on the sugar estates of Guyana; Harischandra Khemraj's *Cosmic Dance* (1994) offers a powerfully insightful investigation of Indian racial and gender attitudes; whilst the writing of Raymond Ramcharitar in *The Island Quintet* (2009) examines deep fissures within Indo-Trinidadian cultural identities, including in matters of sexual orientation. Other significant male Indo-Caribbean authors to emerge during the past twenty years include Kevin Baldeosingh, Cyril Dabydeen, Arnold Itwaru, Rabindranath Maharaj and Sasenarine Persaud.

III. Multiple Origins, Destinations, Visions

Invested in disrupting conventional fixities regarding ancestry and geography as determinants of identity, the Guyanese-born short fiction writer, novelist and actress Pauline Melville seems to relish the difficulty that her own origins present to those requiring homogeneity. She reminds us that reggae legend Bob Marley chose to identify with his black roots inherited from his mother, but he could have conceivably leaned toward his father's Anglo-Scottish ancestry (Melville 1992:742). Melville stresses an exploration of complexity of ancestry that earlier works such as *The Guyana Quartet* by Wilson Harris (hugely admired by Melville), *The Obeah Man* by Ismith Khan, Jan Carew's *The Wild Coast*, and *Other Leopards* by Denis Williams had memorably undertaken. The title story in Melville's collection of short fiction *The Migration of Ghosts* features a couple made up of Guyanese landowner Vincent Dawes and his Amerindian wife Loretta, as they, five years into their marriage, travel to London and Prague prior to returning to Brazil, where Victor has a smallholding. Walking across a bridge in Prague they come upon a band of six young musicians playing traditional Slovakian songs on fiddles and a drum. When Loretta looks at the drummer's face she catches her breath in astonishment: "He was unmistakably a native Indian like her: the same jet-black straight hair, the same brown face and flat features and fat brown eyelids over black pebble eyes" (Melville 1999: 186). Sharing his wife's impression of the drummer as "an Amerindian boy", Vincent approaches the young man in search of confirmation. After an exchange in which the speakers tried to overcome their language barriers, Vincent comes back with a negative finding. Apparently, a native of Mongolia in the former USSR, the young man migrated to Prague with his parents only a few years before. Vincent, an educated man, the child of communist parents, who "always went somewhere in the Eastern bloc for our summer holidays" during his childhood, knows enough history to offer a plausible explanation of the intriguing resemblance: "your people are supposed to have come over from Mongolia originally, across the Bering Strait" (187). The daughter of a Macusi Indian from the Guyanese side of the Brazilian border, Loretta comes face to face with a distant relative in Prague, a world away from home. The scene closes as the young man slings the drum across his shoulder, eyeing Loretta with curiosity, nodding acknowledgement, and giving a little bow, while she smiles back at him: "They faced each other across tens of thousands of years" (187).

Melville has described her own ancestry in a way that perhaps explains her interest in investigating the elasticity and complexity of roots as they extend over vast expanses of space and time. "I look completely English. My mother is English, second of ten children from a London family, a tribe of Anglo-Saxons if ever there was one, blonde and blue-eyed. The photographs show St. Augustine's angels in hand-me-down clothes. My father was born in Guyana (or British Guiana as it was then), also the second of ten children. The photographs show a genetic bouquet of African, Amerindian and European features, a family gazing out from dark, watchful eyes – all except one, who turned out with the looks of a Dutchman. But then, Berbice, their birthplace, was a Dutch colony in the eighteenth century. I am the whitey in the woodpile" (Melville 1992: 740). A document kept safely in a drawer at home, her great-great grandmother's baptism certificate, dated 13 June 1832, which identifies her ancestress as "Slave of D. Melville", enables her to remain mindful of her loaded identity: "White present, black past, a good position for… shifting boundaries and unfixing fixities"(740). "I think of my Amerindian forbears," she says, recalling their presumed arrival "originally from Mongolia", to ask rhetorically: "Do I have a Mongolian herdsman galloping along the spidery pathways of my DNA?" (742). Melville, of course, did not expect an answer when she wrote those words in 1991. But her own literary insight, as captured in the encounter of Loretta with her distant relative in Prague, would seem to venture an answer: that the Mongolian herdsman will have by now been transformed, appearing not as a horseman but as a displaced worker who has ended up in the land of the Czechs, whose culture (beginning with traditional Slovakian songs) he has begun to internalize in order to eke out a living.

Another aspect of Melville's fiction relevant to the present discussion is her characters' often unproblematic location in more than one national geography as they smoothly straddle disparate polities and class locations. The scene of the action in the story "English Table Wuk", for instance, takes places in Georgetown, Guyana, but Auntie May, the owner of the house, is on her way to take a flight to Miami that afternoon, and she, thus, cannot afford the time to mind the guests her niece Adriana has brought to the house. Home "from studying sociology at university in England", where her radical classmates disapproved of her upbringing, namely her coming from a middle-class family which employed servants, Adriana must negotiate different social sensibilities, leading at times to awkward moments (Melville 1998:198). Her aunt gone to the airport, Adriana mistakes as a theft what is a loan of china, antique silver knives and forks to Gita, one of the maids. Her initial distrust gradually turns into curiosity and she learns about the annual ceremony (of cross-cultural and inter-class displacement) near the burial ground, where the descendants of slaves set an elegant and abundant banquet ("the wealth of the display" in sharp contrast "to the appearance of the people") for the purpose of appeasing "the spirits of the English dead who bury across de road right here," as Gita explains (206, 208).

With her tendency to foreground the varied and hybrid texture of life for Caribbean people in terms of the ethno-racial, geographical, social, and cultural location of her characters, Melville belongs to a generation of writers that abhors homogeneity in the dissection of their societies of origin. Among the most provocative manifestations of that outlook is afforded by Robert Antoni, whose novels explore the multilocality of Caribbean life that he himself embodies. Born in Detroit, Michigan, to Trinidadian parents, Antoni spent many of his formative years in the Bahamas and studied creative writing in US universities. A biographical sketch attached to one of his widely circulated stories highlights the fact that he "carries three passports: US, Trinidad and Tobago, and the Bahamas" (Antoni 2000). His award-winning first novel *Divina Trace* (1991) introduced readers to the fictional island of Corpus Christi, the ground on which his characters congregate across several books. Stylistically the novel enacts a festival of multiplicity as all eight characters – the unifying narrator Johnny Domingo, Jr. and seven additional speakers – contribute to assemble the assorted account of Magdalena Divina. Consistent with their diverse origins, experiences, perspectives and desires, their testimonies are conveyed through a variety of genres, narrative techniques, and expressive forms to suit the distinct voice of each individual speaker. Antoni's second novel, *Blessed is the Fruit* (1997), turns on the initially distant and ultimately tender relationship between a white mistress, Lilla, and her longtime black servant, Vel. The race and class divide that sets them socially apart crumbles under the weight of the tenderness brought about by the gender solidarity that the latter's pregnancy triggers.

Carnival (2005), the author's third novel, adds complexity of outlook to the Caribbean's difficult interweavings of class, race and gender. The white Trinidadian narrator, William Fletcher, an economically well-off expatriate, reunites by chance at a bar in New York City with his childhood friends Lawrence and Rachel, and his boyhood love for the latter is quickly rekindled. They resolve to return to their country together during carnival time to reconnect with their homeland. Rather than experiencing their country's amiable embrace, the three expatriates endure the frenzy of dance, music, drunkenness and uninhibited sensuality, followed by an eventful foray deep into the island's mountainous interior, in a manner that further exacerbates their disconnection from Trinidad. The tensions borne of the interplay of race, sex and violence prove too conspicuous for the equalizing masks of carnival to mitigate them. David Dabydeen, whose review of *Carnival* stresses the novel's intertextual rapport with Ernest Hemingway's *The Sun Also Rises* (1926), finds that Antoni weaves into the story a "desperately tender and hopeful" outlook communicated through "a beauty" that is "always within human reach, however slowly we move towards it, hobbled by the self-inflicted wounds of race, class, and gender" (Dabydeen 2006). It remains true, however, that the novel refrains from endorsing a view of Caribbean self-affirmation insofar as the Trinidadian expatriates end the novel by flying back to their deracinated lives in Europe and the United States.

The ending of *Carnival*, though perhaps "hopeful" at some generically human level, may be said to represent the ambivalence of the latest generation of Caribbean writers to commit themselves to a specifically Caribbean vision of the future. It will perhaps not be deemed an excessive extrapolation to discern a despondent outlook in the Heather Royes' poem whose speaker sees no point in continuing to read poetry: "Mesmerised by the present,/forsaking the past, my mind/a jealous lover holds each moment/much longer than it lasts./Time slips away and with it/dreams./I no longer read poetry" (Royes 2005: 197). On the whole, present-day formulations of Caribbean prospects will at best convey a sense of ambivalence about the possibility of any positive outcome. At one level the ambivalence may reflect the pervasiveness of a Western postmodern sensibility that has influenced writers and intellectuals in the Caribbean, particularly in the context of the perceived failure of autochthonous projects. A critical observer of this phenomenon has noted that postmodernism developed in the industrialized, consumer-driven societies where thinkers have rendered class an antiquated concept and that it is mostly through an act of intellectual mimicry that the postmodern sensibility has found echo in non-industrialized Caribbean societies (Cline 2002:499). More acerbically, Norman Girvan has charged a generation of Caribbean intellectuals with having abandoned the tradition of "indigenous thought" and fallen under the sway of the "spurious assertions of the universal validity of the neo-liberal globalist paradigm" (Girvan 2010). But irrespective of the influence of postmodernism, especially as it relates to its reticence to conceive of any notion of history that might hearken to the certainties espoused by Enlightenment thinkers about the future of the species, the new cohorts of writers and thinkers chronicling the Caribbean experience and conceptualizing the structure of life there have reasons of their own to flaunt their distance from the formulations of their elders regarding the representation and the prospects of the Caribbean community.

From the perspective of the present, and the tendency for Caribbean literary criticism to fissure into a variety of identity positions (of ethnicity, gender, sexuality and location) figurations of the Caribbean person in the literature and thought of the nationalist past often appeared to take a monolithic form. Evincing an alleged homogeneity that today is regarded as primarily denoting a record of exclusion, an earlier generation of authors has been charged with envisioning the Caribbean person through the recurring image of a black male of humble extraction endowed with a revolutionary vision or a state of mind conducive to liberatory missions. One thinks of Jacques Roumain's Manuel in *Gouverneurs de la rosée* (1944), the archetypal Caliban conceptualized by George Lamming in *The Pleasures of Exile* (1960), the generic Maroon in Anton de Kom's *We, Slaves of Surinam* (1934), or the ex-slave turned independence warrior in the character of Esteban Montejo from Miguel Barnet's *Autobiografia de un cimarron* (1968), to name only a few of the most prominent texts. By contrast, the menu of race, class, gender, and ideological options currently available to writers to epitomize the human drama in the Caribbean has considerably expanded. The cast of characters who at present serve literary artists as archetypes to evoke or remember their region's past need not follow the moral or political prescriptions discernible in the texts of their predecessors. A widely circulated heralding of Cuba's future possibilities may come via the sex-driven Cuca Martinez whose life in Havana follows the call of the wild as she holds on to her obsessive and unrequited love for the unreliable and hardly corrigible Juan Perez in Zoé Valdés' *Te di la vida entera* (1998). With greater frequency and self-assurance than in the texts of earlier generations, now the protagonist may take the form of a cross-dresser such as Lowe, the Chinese woman who for decades has passed as a male shopkeeper in rural Jamaica, from Patricia Powell's novel *Pagoda* (1998). Similarly, writers now display a greater inclination than did their predecessors to draw on historical imagination to portray what it may have felt like for a white heiress of her father's Caribbean plantation to travel from the safety of England to take stock of her property of business, land, and slaves, as does Emily in Caryl Phillips' novel *Cambridge* (1991), or for a free black, slave-owning businesswoman in eighteenth-century Surinam to compete successfully in the white male-controlled plantation economy as does Elisabeth Samson in *De vrije negerin Elisabeth: Gevangene van Kleur* (2000) by Cynthia McLeod.

Besides a greater flexibility of sexual mores, an ampler recognition of the multiplicity of ethnic and cultural roots of the population, a quicker willingness to acknowledge class differences, and a wider recognition of ideological diversity informing the sensibility of people in the region, the texts of the newer generation of Caribbean writers also seem to reflect a keener observation of the mobility of the Caribbean person, not only from the region to elsewhere in the globe, but also within societies in the region itself. For instance, the site of the clash between the clairvoyant Zule and her murderous foe Simila in Mayra Montero's *Del rojo de su sombra* (1996) is the Dominican Republic, but the characters are mostly Haitian as a result of decades of labour migration that resulted in the spreading of bateyes and immigrant settlements along the border that divides the two countries. A Cuban who, born in Havana in 1952, has lived in Puerto Rico since settling there in 1972, Montero has first-hand knowledge of intra-Caribbean mobility.

In Mayra Santos Febres' *Sirena Selena vestida de pena* (2000), Leocadio, the Dominican main character begins his career in San Juan, Puerto Rico, where at the age of fifteen he has dim prospects given his drug habit and social destitution. But enchanted by his beauty and alluring singing voice, Martha Divine, the transsexual owner of the cabaret the Blue Danube, rescues him from the streets and turns him into a transvestite diva. After Leocadio's success in Puerto Rico, Martha then engineers his foray into the entertainment circles of the Dominican Republic, where the young man's beauty, voice, and magnetism gain him the adoration of an affluent businessman. That Martha should think of Santo Domingo as a destination for Leocadio (despite the young man's Dominican origins), might seem odd given the "otherness" that things Dominican often occupy in Puerto Rican society. The migratory flow of unskilled workers from the Dominican Republic tends to locate these immigrants as socially marginal in Puerto Rico. Perhaps the author's destabilizing of the notion of marginality connects to her exploration of transvestism and transsexuality as well as to her resignification of the Dominican space. Explaining her attraction to the subject of her novel, Santos Febres has said: "I do not believe in fixed marginalities, perhaps because several apply to me. I am a woman, black, Caribbean, and who knows which other things that relegate me to a margin. But I have seen that this margin is always mobile. Sometimes I find myself at the centre (by reason of education, perhaps of class), and sometimes I am despised (by reason of skin colour, or for coming from a country colonized by the United States). Precisely because of that mobility I allow myself to travel through various worlds, various margins, and sometimes even through the centre. I thus get connected with the people who, like me, walk around the place transgressing social boundaries" (Morgado 2000).

This intra-Caribbean mobility of people that has featured in recent representations of the region has also been noted by George Lamming who argues for "a concept of Nation that is not defined by specific territorial boundaries", precisely because of his awareness of the historical scattering of Caribbean peoples across various latitudes within and beyond the region (Lamming 2000: 32). Lamming points to the advent of "the transnational family", a phenomenon "which does not allow a funeral in Barbados to take place for over a week after the death" to allow time for relatives to arrive "from Jamaica, Trinidad, Guyana, Toronto, Birmingham, Brooklyn" (32). Lamming contends that the rise of "the transnational household" results from two factors, "the political and cultural consequences of sexual intercourse" and "the economic compulsion to migrate" (33). He recalls his first sojourn in Trinidad in 1946 when he took up residence in Belmont: "I discovered that in every family I got to know, the only Trinidadians by birth were the children. Mothers, fathers, aunts, uncles had originated elsewhere" (33). Regarding labour mobility, he notes that "from the middle of the nineteenth century to the second decade of the twentieth, Barbados provided over fifty thousand workers to Guyana and Trinidad", and that the population of Trinidad and Tobago doubled from 1844 to 1881 owing to "this movement of our peoples from St. Vincent, Grenada, and as far as St. Martin in the northeast" (Lamming 33). The gradual intermingling of people in the region, which in Lamming's view gives credence to the contention by his friend George Beckford that it is only the governments that remain aloof to the already existing integration, continues a process that began over one hundred years ago (33). Scholars looking at the border crossing of slaves from one colonial domain to another, or between territories, in order to enhance their chances of freedom, would extend Lamming's chronology to some two centuries earlier. Until 1790, slaves from Danish, French, English, and other colonies could escape to Spanish colonial domains and generally count on receiving succour and winning their freedom. By the same token, runaways fled from St. Croix and St. Thomas to Puerto Rico and the smaller island of Vieques, from St. Domingue across to the mountainous Santo Domingo border, from Jamaica's northern coast to Cuba, and from eastern Caribbean islands to Trinidad, creating a long pattern of "transfrontier marronage throughout the region" (Carnegie 2002:118-119).

IV. Diaspora as Locus of Identity

The history of transnational life may actually be coterminous with the chronology of colonialism and its aftermath in the Caribbean, which has been a cradle of cross-cultural marriages, the widening and intertwining of intraregional family networks, and the multiplicity of identities that ensue from such relations. The mobility of Caribbean slaves also involved overseas relocations. We may gather this from the fact that up to 1700 "all slaves in South Carolina came from the Caribbean and Barbados in particular", and that throughout the eighteenth century from fifteen to twenty percent of all enslaved workers came from the same origin (James 2001:396). Early in the seventeenth century slaves from Barbados made up a substantial portion of Virginia's black population, and as late as 1860 one in five black Bostonians had come from Barbados or elsewhere in the Caribbean (James 396-97). The heavy flow of intra-Caribbean and centrifugal migration normally followed the fluctuations of the plantation economy. For instance, between 1924 and 1940, workers from Grenada, Barbados, Antigua, and St. Kitts gravitated to employment opportunities available to them in the oil refineries of Aruba and Curaçao, whereas in the period roughly from 1945 to 1965 the European metropolises and the United States emerged as predominant destinations for mass Caribbean emigration (Conway 2003:340-341). During the mid 1960s, with the removal of racially discriminatory biases in immigration legislation, Canada began to rival the other major destinations for migrants from the Anglophone Caribbean, leading to today's substantial immigrant settlements in Toronto, Montreal, and Quebec (344, 348).

Consistent with the momentum bequeathed by the long history of mobility, intra-regional migration and emigration from the region has continued to grow, with nearly 5.5 million people leaving the Caribbean between 1950 and 1989, an exodus that has turned the émigré population into "an important source of household income" in many Caribbean societies as well as a major aspect of "people-based integration within the social life of the region" (Girvan 2001: 14-15). Since the conquest and colonization that started in 1492 mobilized large masses of people from Europe, Africa and Asia, and since the colonial transaction itself promoted the regular flow of humans between Western metropolises and their overseas territories, the historical experience of the Caribbean may be said to have revolved around the constant rapport between "here and elsewhere". Glancing at the past five hundred years, demographer Aaron Segal has argued that "the Caribbean region has borne the deepest and most continuous impact from international migration of any region in the world" (Cited in Carnegie 2002: 99). "Everybody in the Caribbean comes from somewhere else," says Stuart Hall, a thought which, compounded by the awareness of the historical forces that have caused people from the region to go elsewhere, probably explains his understanding of the Caribbean as "the first, the original, and the purest diaspora" (Hall 2001: 27-28). By the same token, relying on his literary insight, sociologist and novelist Orlando Patterson decades ago encouraged a view of the Anansi legend as a representation of migrancy: "The spider is a migrant. It can live anywhere, in trees or houses or caves or nowhere in particular, for the spider carries its home, its only real home, buried in its belly" (Patterson 1978: 134).

A meaningful consequence of the intense involvement of Caribbean people in migratory movements is the creation of a literary tradition with tributaries spreading across different polities, geographies, languages, and cultural heritages. Increasingly, the makers of the corpus of Caribbean letters seem to live and work elsewhere. To illustrate this point, let it suffice to observe that in the volume of interviews of fourteen Anglophone Caribbean poets put together by Kwame Dawes only three – St. Lucians John Robert Lee, Jane King and Kendel Hippolyte – reside in the region. The remainder make their home elsewhere: Trinidadian Claire Harris in Calgary, Jamaican Olive Senior mostly in Toronto, Guyanese Cyril Dabydeen in Ottawa, Jamaican Lorna Goodison in Michigan, Trinidadian Ramabai Espinet in Canada, Guyanese Grace Nichols in Britain, Jamaican Lillian Allen in Canada, Jamaican Opal Palmer Adisa in Oakland, California, Guyanese David Dabydeen in the United Kingdom, Jamaican Afua Cooper in Toronto, and Guyanese-descendant, English-born Fred D'Aguiar then in Florida (Dawes 2001). Consistent with the foregoing, one notes a tendency among literary scholars and compilers of anthologies to erase the boundary between literature produced in the region and the writings crafted by the emigres and their children, even when, as a result of an education and a literary training gained elsewhere, language differences have emerged. Seeking to conceptualize their grouping of poets from the region and the diaspora in their anthology of Caribbean verse, editors Stewart Brown and Mark McWatt have posited that, not only does migration exist as "the defining experience of Caribbean 'being'", but that, unlike those of earlier generations, migrations today no longer entail "a breaking of ties" with the original homelands, making it hard to draw a rigid line between here and there. They propose that: "The twenty-first century Caribbean aesthetic depends less on a lived geography than on a distinctive perspective on history, a perspective that reflects the creole nature of Caribbean societies" (Brown and McWatt 2005: xxii).

The merging of here and there that Brown and McWatt articulate seems to be assumed as self evident in the literary compendia of others. In a recent compilation, Haitian-American fiction writer Edwidge Danticat, who was raised in the United States and writes in English, and Myriam Chancy, who grew up in Canada, appear considered in the same breath with authors based in Haiti such as Yanick Lahens and Jan J. Dominique, who write in French, and the Creolophone poet and novelist Franketiénne, without any apparent compulsion on the part of the editors to draw distinctions (Sourieau and Balutansky 2004). Similarly, a study of the poetry of "contemporary Caribbean women", focusing on poets from the Anglophone region, makes no distinction between poets based in the native land, such as the late Mahadai Das, who began and ended her life in Guyana, those based in Canada, such as M. Nourbese Phillip, and longtime residents of Britain such as Amryl Johnson, Valerie Bloom, and Grace Nichols (Narain 2002). Showing further that the tendency to fuse the diasporic with the homeland space as one seamless literary terrain applies across the various language origins of Caribbean writers, a recent study focuses on the work of Michele Cliff, Jamaica Kincaid, Edwidge Danticat, Jan J. Dominique, Julia Alvarez, and Rosario Ferre for an examination of questions related to body, nation, and empire. This study of "Modern Caribbean Literature by Women" displays a predominance of diaspora voices in representing the Caribbean experience to the world (Adjarin 2004). Perhaps as a result of the increasing transnationality of the corpus of Caribbean writing, its straddling of geographies and nations, the tension between "exile and return" that many scholars once recognized as a motif in the region's seminal texts has begun to lose currency (Dash 1994:451). However, the fact that many of the anthologies and studies referred to above were written or edited by writers or scholars based in the USA, Canada or Britain, and published for predominantly metropolitan readerships, raises the question of how far metropolitan institutional and publishing power has distorted our perceptions. It may well be that we do not adequately know what writers based in the Caribbean (and not necessarily known to metropolitan editors) may be doing.

While writers in the diaspora today may still echo the yearnings of migrant voices stretching back at least to Mary Prince, the West Indian slave who escaped to London and there published her *History* in 1831, the relative ease with which contemporary writers have owned to their binationality as inhabitants of a diasporic space would seem to suggest an overcoming, for some at least, of "the anxiety and polemics" that formerly "marked the issue of a Caribbean writer's physical location" (Meehan and Miller 2003: 329). Whether or not we might agree with Louis James' claim that the deterritorializing of Caribbean writing grants it "global significance", placing it "in a central position within world literature", one must recognize the value of his observation concerning the "shadowy borders between Caribbean writing in English, and Black British, Black United States and Black Canadian writing" (James 1999: 212-214). Indeed, one can discern among diasporic voices of the current generation a propinquity to occupy an identitarian location that transcends or displaces the contours of

Caribbeanness. The collection *Empire Windrush*, whose title evokes a distinct moment in the history of West Indian mobility to the British Isles, groups Caribbean-descended writers like Beryl Gilroy, Meiling Jin, Andrea Levy, Victor Headley and Merle Collins with authors originating from Africa and other parts of the "Commonwealth", the organizing principle of the volume centring around "writing about Black Britain" (Wambu 1998). Another collection brings the texts of six Caribbean authors together with similar numbers of Asians and African writers, focusing on "the impact of Britain" on them as the overreaching theme (Dennis and Khan 2000). These collections for the most part choose to rely on reactive identity formulations by stressing the blackness of the writers in contradistinction to the whiteness of the mainstream, in one case, and the cultural otherness of the writers included, in contradistinction to the Englishness that defines the centre, in the other. Since writers from an Anglophone Caribbean heritage share with writers from other corners of the "Commonwealth" a difficult rapport with whiteness and the cultural values of Englishness, they have generally come to share the embrace of the new geopolitics of identity. In particular, this has involved renaming the domain of the British Commonwealth (and including territories dominated by the other imperial powers as well) with the rubric of the "postcolonial world". Blackness, cultural otherness with respect to a Western mainstream, and now postcoloniality have become available to Caribbean heritage writers as large identitarian spaces that subsume their region-specific Caribbeanness.

V. Change of the Gender Guard

With the rise of women as a predominant presence among the makers of Caribbean literature in the 1980s, significant new paradigms have entered the conversation regarding the nature and texture of Caribbean people and their relationship with other branches of the human family (James 1999: 199; Meehan and Miller 2003: 328). Often the notion of travel, the existential gliding over large expanses of culturally or politically marked soil, has provided the thematic basis for reading the works of contemporary Caribbean women authors (Hoving 2001). Trinidadian literary scholar Rhonda Cobham and Grenadian fiction writer and poet Merle Collins chose the intersection of gender, race, and cultural otherness – namely the markers afforded by the category "Black women in Britain" – as the identitarian space within which to place the works of six Anglophone Caribbean women writers in their anthology *Watchers and Seekers* (Cobham and Collins 1988). Similarly, in her exploration of the "migratory subject" in the works of Afro-Caribbean women authors (along with the texts of African American, Black British, and African women writers), Carole Boyce Davies expresses her understanding of the literature produced by black female authors as "not as a fixed, geographical, ethnically or nationally bound category of writing", but as one whose study requires "cross-cultural, transnational, diasporic perspectives" (Davies 1994:4). Haitian-Canadian fiction writer and scholar Myriam J. A. Chancy also draws on a combination of blackness and migration to organize an understanding of the works of Afro-Caribbean women writers based in Britain (Joan Riley and Beryl Gilroy), Canada (M. Nourbese Phillip, Dionne Brand, Makeda Silvera and Afua Cooper), and the United States (Audre Lorde, Rosa Guy, Michelle Cliff, and Marie Chauvet). Chancy's study, however, retains the commitment to organizing a Caribbean-focused literary knowledge, and when she expands her inquiry into the African-American literary terrain of the United States, she finds conceptual justification in the strong cross-cultural ties that have historically linked the US black and Afro-Caribbean communities (Chancy 1997: xviii). She strengthens this point by stressing the African American women writers who traced their origins back to the Caribbean and wrote about it, such as Audre Lorde, Paule Marshall and June Jordan, as well as by arguing that Afro-Caribbean women writers generally adopt the tenets of US-based black feminism as being pertinent to their own particular geopolitical situation (Chancy xviii: 17). The inclusion of Francophone Haitian novelist Marie Chauvet in a study that focuses primarily on the writings of Anglophone Afro-Caribbean women is explained by the time Chauvet spent in exile in the United States, since exile, along with blackness, provides the key axis of analysis in Chancy's monograph (168). The experience of exile actualizes what Chancy refers to as "the paradox of home", namely the existential scenario whereby the ancestral homeland can alternate, concurrently occur, or offer a choice between "the site of self-discovery and the point of no return" in the writer's imagination (xi).

As the foregoing would suggest, Caribbean women follow diverse routes to chart their identitarian path in representing the world to which they belong. They do not collectively adhere to any one single metadiscourse to evoke their human experience in the Caribbean and its diaspora. Womanist and Third World perspectives, along with Postcolonialism and Afrocentrism, appear in their formulations in varying degrees of emphasis, making for a variegated figuration of the structure of Caribbean life. Even the renunciation of the idea of homeland as a stable dwelling space may find expression in their texts, as we gather from the exiled Cuban poet Belkis Cuza Male's poem, "My Mother's Homeland", which, among other things, says: "My mother always said/your homeland is any place,/preferably the place where you die" (Cuza Male 2005: 191). This matters a great deal in the light of the predominant role of women among the literary figures who have achieved distinction since the 1980s (Baugh 2001: 264).

Few documents of feminist dissidence have articulated women's sense of protest against the traps of patriarchy's deference toward the disempowered feminine more cogently than these lines from "Woman Descendant" by Cynthia James: "this is your daughter/.../my womb is eternity/my back-bone is history/.../to be free from fixations/that commend me and degrade me,/disrespect me in respect" (James 2005: 233). The literary emergence of women was manifested in a series of compilations such as *Jamaica Woman* (1980), edited by Mervyn Morris and Pamela Mordecai, to *Creation Fire* (1990), edited by Ramabai Espinet. As the "demography" of West Indian poetry shifted, with diaspora and region-based authors contending for predominance in the continued construction of the Caribbean corpus, women again seemed to lead the way. The names of Jean "Binta" Breeze, Mahadai Das, Opal Palmer Adisa, Claudia Rankine, Claire Harris, Dionne Brand, M. Nourbese Phillip, Merle Collins, Christine Craig, Gloria Escoffery, Lorna Goodison, Judith Hamilton, Jane King, Meiling Jin, Jennifer Rahim, Beverly Brown, and Cynthia James, among others, achieved considerable distinction (Baugh 2001: 270-272). And to the extent to which diaspora voices, particularly in the United States, increased in number and significance, the centrality of women was further accentuated. Indeed, the overwhelming majority of the truly successful US Caribbean diaspora writers are indisputably women: Paule Marshall, Edwidge Danticat, Julia Alvarez, Cristina Garcia, Esmeralda Santiago, Rhina P. Espaillat, to name only the most highly regarded, best-selling, and award-winning literary figures who have conquered the American book market in recent decades. Given the efflorescence of women in the region and in the vast geography of the diaspora, one must concede that at present they play a major role in the maintenance and advancement of the literary tradition. With that change of gender guard has come necessarily a greater degree of aesthetic, social, ideological, thematic, and formal diversity than the Caribbean corpus seemed to show in earlier decades.

VI. Enduring Visions of the Popular

Contemporaneous with the rise of women writers, Caribbean literature has seen a foregrounding of formerly devalued expressive forms from the realm of popular culture. To be sure, Caribbean writing was never wholly remote from popular and folk expressive forms. This was documented in, among other things, Kamau Brathwaite's early effort to formulate the emergence of the "jazz novel" in the Caribbean, giving *Brother Man* by Roger Mais and *A Quality of Violence* by Andrew Salkey as illustrations (Brathwaite 1968: 124-125). Similarly, the momentous cultural study *Beyond a Boundary* (1963) by the Trinidadian C. L. R.

James, which offers a sociocultural meditation on cricket, Gordon Rohlehr's *Calypso and Society in Pre-Independence Trinidad* (1990), which provides an engaging cultural history of a highly esteemed musical form, and more recently Carolyn Cooper's writing on dancehall in *Noises in the Blood: Orality, Gender and the 'Vulgar' Body of Jamaican Popular Culture* (1993) give a clear sense of the proximity that learned discourse has maintained to the expressions and social practices of the popular masses. Three of the central novels in the literary histories of Cuba, Puerto Rico and the Dominican Republic – respectively *Tres tristes tigres* (1968) by Guillermo Cabrera Infante, *La guaracha del macho Camacho* (1976) by Luis Rafael Sanchez and *Solo cenizas hallaras* (1980) by Pedro Verges –are steeped in the evocation of each society's habits of musical consumption and popular speech patterns. By the same token, in the national corpus of Haitian literature, the work of Rene Depestre, Jacques Stephen Alexis, Marie Vieau Chauvet and Franketiénne displays an invariable engagement with, discussion of, or position on vodou, the religion of the Haitian masses. The chapter on Kamau Brathwaite in this study shows how long an engagement with the creole language of the masses has pervaded Caribbean writing. Indeed, one could dismiss the relatively recent importation of "cultural studies" – with its enhanced attention to the expressive arts and social practices of the lower strata of society – as a paradigm that really contributes nothing much new to the Caribbean other than the naming of a practice that had existed all along.

Nevertheless, the last couple of decades have witnessed something new in the rise of the popular, particularly in performative aspects of literature, or the coinage "orature". Louise Bennett's pioneering work as a performance artist and poet writing exclusively in Jamaican dialect from the 1930s onward had to wait several decades to gain acceptance as a form offering anything other than carefree merriment. Kamau Brathwaite's poetic praxis, beginning with *Rights of Passage* (1967), which conceptualized the Creole language as fundamental to the Caribbean's worldview, lent weight to Bennett's precedent. Since the 1970s, we have seen the striking development of oral or "dub" poetry as a major expressive art form with great public appeal, their performances, especially in Europe, often gaining them a popularity similar to that of reggae musicians. The performance poets in this form differ from earlier generations of reciters and storytellers in that generally their language follows the rhythms of reggae music. Although concentrating on composing their words strictly for the ear and for sound recordings, several among them have successfully made the passage into print. These include the island-based Jamaican poets Oku Onuora, Mutabaruka, Jean "Binta" Breeze, and the late Michael Smith; the Canadian-based Lillian Allen, and Linton Kwesi Johnson, who lives and works in London (Senior 2003: 289). Edward Baugh has also highlighted the accomplishments of Paul Keens-Douglas, whose *Tim Tim* (1976), and many succeeding volumes, displayed a storyteller's folk art in poetry, as well as John Agard, who made a mark with his *Man to Pan* (1982) [Baugh 2001: 269-270]. Significantly, *Wheel and Come Again* (1998), an anthology of "reggae poetry" compiled by the Ghanaian-Jamaican poet Kwame Dawes, features many of the best known West Indian scribal poets comfortably side by side with some of the most verbally accomplished dub poets. That the turn to dialect has occurred in prose no less than in poetry is shown in Merle Collins' novel *Angel* (1987), which is written almost entirely in Grenadian Creole.

One popular art form, calypso, has continued to express the vision of regional integration, from Mighty Sparrow's 1958, "We All Is One" and "Federation", and Louise Bennett's "Dear Departed Federation" sang its demise when it floundered in 1962 (Rohlehr 2001: 276). Calypsonians sang to applaud the formation of CARICOM in the song of that name by Chalkdust and "Caribbean Unity" by Stalin, both in 1979, and as late as the 1990s, calypsonian David Rudder's "One Caribbean" still invoked an undaunted vision of regional unity: "One Caribbean, One Caribbean/One heart together in a changing world/One Caribbean, One Caribbean/One love, one heart, one soul/Reaching for a common goal" (Rohlehr 2001: 276, 290, 304). Rohlehr, a Guyanese who is based in Trinidad, attests to the survival of the dream of Caribbean unity and regional integration among calypsonians, whose unitarian hope is not deterred by the grimness that surrounds them.

VII. The Micro-Spatial Gaze

Concomitant with the survival of the dream of Caribbean integration, contemporary Caribbean discourse reveals also the contrasting compulsion to assert the specificity of discrete nations and societies in the region. Perhaps consistent with the precedent established by the works of Luis Rafael Sánchez, Puerto Rican fiction, as illustrated by such salient younger practitioners as Mayra Santos Febres, displays a distinct micro-spatial quality, its action concentrated on minute localities even while the texts aspire to evoking a representative Caribbean milieu. Edgardo Rodríguez Julía's *San Juan, ciudad soñada* (2005), a moving autobiographical evocation of the Puerto Rican capital, the author's native city, reflects the microscopic gaze of much recent writing from the region. The affirmation of the differentiated space of the author's cultural experience often supposes an attitude of refusal to embrace a reactive identity, a derivative ontology such as anti-colonialist formulations often seemed to espouse. Amongst the generation of Anglophone writers who arrived in London in the 1950s, there were those among them – Lamming, Naipaul and John Hearne – who took their sense of West Indianness to the extent of inventing composite, imaginary Caribbean islands – San Cristobal, St Isabella and Cuyuna – as the sites of their novels. Many young writers today proceed as if unencumbered by the urgency to define themselves in contradistinction to a Western subject or to "write back" to a metropolitan mainstream. The erotic novels and short fiction of Dominican writer Ligia Minaya, such as *Cuando me asalta el recuerdo de ti* (2003), deal with the marital or romantic conflicts of couples specifically in the city of Santo Domingo. *La isla del Cundeamor* by Sweden-based Cuban writer René Vázquez Díaz evokes the very specific cosmos of Cuban exiles in Miami to shed light on some of the homeland's historical avatars, and the short story by Senel Paz "Strawberries and Chocolate", later turned into a successful film, circumscribes to discrete spaces within the city of Havana the exploration of the problem of diverse sexual orientations against the backdrop of traditional Cuban mores. There is perhaps a degree of paradox here. In Anglophone Caribbean writing it is possible to argue that the more national it has become – the more Trinidadian, Guyanese or Jamaican – the more it has become distinctively Caribbean in its cultural reference and language. The paradox is the challenge to persuade Caribbean readers that writing from outside their own island speaks to them.

Consistent with the emphasis to write small – geographically speaking – one notes a tendency to unearth, highlight, or mythicize very particular historical moments from the writers' countries of origin. Olga Nolla's *El castillo de la memoria* (1996) thus chronicles the arrival of Juan Ponce de Leon in sixteenth-century Puerto Rico as the explorer, seen through the eyes of Lope Lopez de Villalba, engages in a quest for the fountain of youth. The novel *De langste maand* (The longest month) by Diana Lebacs examines urban violence in Curacao during the 1980s, and Edwidge Danticat's *The Farming of Bones* (1998) memorializes the massacre of Haitian immigrants and Haitian-Dominican residents of the border regions in October 1937. The horrendous murder of the Mirabal sisters in 1960 by the Trujillo dictatorship gave Julia Alvarez the material to weave the plot of her novel *In the Time of the Butterflies* (1994), and post-blitz London gave Andrea Levy the place of convergence for her Jamaican and English characters to negotiate the racial and social divide they inherit from their colonial past in her award-winning novel, *A Small Island* (2005). Another dimension of that tendency to represent the Caribbean experience by targeting a slice of history in a differentiated site is expressed by the unabashed affirmation of one's locality that Daniel Maximin voices in extolling his native Guadeloupe: "You dare to write that your love for your island is not a reflection of the foreigner's gaze. And if you dare to write it and describe it yourself in the present, without guilt and without recourse to courts of the past nor to juries of the future, ...then you will dare to let your writing body lovingly mold its wayward path to the future, as its uprooted sap nourishes your store of spirit" (Maximin 1998: 19). Ironically, that sense of comfort in the validity of one's locality harmonizes beautifully with the complementary vision of one's place as merely a point within a larger spectrum to which one remains inexorably connected. At the end of *Caraibe sur Seine*, a novel for young readers by Gisele Pineau, Lindy, the girl whose immigrant experience in Paris the novel recounts, derives consolation for the separation from her best friends with a conviction of her profound connectedness to the rest of the globe: "though very far from one another, we are not dispersed. We are on the same earth, and our dreams have no limit, because the earth is an island" (Pineau 2003: 171).

VIII. Queering the Literary Space

We have already made reference to the novel by Santos Febres *Sirena Selena*, which explores the reality of homoerotic desire, cross-dressing, and transsexuality in both Puerto Rico and the Dominican Republic. These, along with the story by Senel Paz, which daringly investigates same-sex love in the proverbially hetero-normative context of socialist Cuba, point to pioneering instances of what we might call the queering of the literary space in the Caribbean. This is clearly another meaningful emphasis we find in various writers of newer generations, a feature that Zadie Smith captures memorably by highlighting in the plot the lesbian character of Neena, whom her aunt Alsana addresses via the epithet "Niece-of-Shame" (79). These interventions, however, still tread the arena of the eccentric and the socially exceptional, and that probably has to do with the marginal location that non-heterosexual individuals continue to occupy in Caribbean societies. Suffice it to say that in the Dominican Republic a public gathering of gays and lesbians did not occur until 1 July 2001, and this after the coordinators received several rejections to their application for preferred city locations where they could hold their assembly, the authorities presumably justifying their denial on the grounds of protecting public morality. Five years later, one can still read the news of discotheques, bars, and other entertainment establishments in Santo Domingo's "Zona Colonial" being closed down by local authorities, and their patrons arrested, for serving as meeting points for a homosexual clientele (Redaccíon 2006). During the April 2001 Santo Domingo Book Fair, the Minister of Culture, a politician and literary figure named Tony Raful, barged into the kiosk sponsored by a Dominican gay and lesbian advocacy group known as Gaylesdom.

He showed up in the company of several police officers to forcibly remove all display or publicity items that he judged offensive to the rabidly homophobic sensibility of Nicolás de Jesús Cardinal López Rodríguez, who had days before imprecated vociferously against the Ministry of Culture for granting space in the Book Fair to a gay and lesbian kiosk, urging that the Gaylesdom exhibit be burned instead of displayed. The embodiment of bigotry, Cardinal López Rodríguez habitually uses the power of his pulpit to cast aspersions on gays and lesbians, with an occasional barrage of scorn launched against single mothers and peasants fighting against abusive landlords in the rural areas. The tolerance that Dominican society shows toward the ideological obscurantism of this prelate suggests that it has not yet made much progress towards the goal of recognizing diversity as a fundamental democratic value and ensuring the protection of the entire population's civil rights.

That adverse reality notwithstanding, the yearly parade of the LGBTQ community has continued, with an increasing number of self-identified heterosexuals advocating respect for people with different sexual orientations. The launching in 2004 of the collection *Desde la Orilla: hacia una nacionalidad sin desalojos* (Torres-Saillant, Hernández, and Jiménez 2004), a compilation of conference addresses on various aspects of Dominican diversity which devoted three chapters to sexual orientation, challenged the scholarly community to take the matter seriously. Later the same year the fiction writer Mélida García and the Santo Domingo publisher Miguel de Camps teamed up as co-editors of the first ever Dominican anthology that brings together "gay writings" from the country's literature (García and De Camps 2004). At the 2006 International Congress of the Latin American Studies Association, which took place in San Juan, Puerto Rico, sociologist Ginetta Candelario, cultural studies scholar Carlos Decena and literary critic Maja Horn successfully introduced the topic of Dominican sexuality in a panel entitled "Queering Quisqueya". Apart from examining the extent to which a gay man living under the auspices of a traditional middle-class household can find himself implicated in the maintenance of patriarchal paradigms as they pertain to the construction of masculinity, the panel ventured a re-examination of the legacies of early Dominican feminist thinkers, activists, and writers such as Evangelina Rodriguez Perozo, Petronila Gómez and Hilma Contreras with an eye to identifying the foundational elements of a discourse that more than half a century ago had the courage to challenge hetero-normative assumptions in Dominican society. Different Caribbean societies will reveal different scenarios regarding the struggle against entrenched homophobia, but, as with the Dominican case, the queering of the literary space will most likely come about as a result of both the emergence of a new sexual ideology made current by writers and thinkers of the newer generations as well as through a concentrated effort to unearth the submerged legacies of dissidence owed to earlier generations and which we can only now boast the sensibility to appreciate. The collection *Our Caribbean: A Gathering of Lesbian and Gay Writing from the Antilles*, edited by Thomas Glave, a Jamaican writer based in the USA, expands the coverage by including authors from various linguistic blocs of the region, perhaps suggesting another site of regional unity in the revolt against heteronormative assumptions. Glave himself has published several collections of short stories and essays, and is part of a generation that is bringing new energies to Caribbean writing, which includes Jamaican Kei Miller and Trinidadian Anton Nimblett, who join an earlier generation of mainly Canadian-based LGBT writers such as Dionne Brand, Silvera Makeda and Nigel Thomas.

IX. Expanding the Internal Geography

Perhaps the one area in which the newer generations of Caribbean writers and thinkers have done the least to distinguish themselves from their predecessors has been the continued configuration of a geographically, culturally and linguistically narrow image of the region. The new voices continue to deploy the term "islands" to invoke the region despite the indisputable geographical fact that countries located smack dab in the middle of the Caribbean experience such as Belize, French Guiana, Guyana and Surinam lie firmly on the South American continent. To these we should add the Atlantic portions of such Latin American republics as Colombia, Costa Rica, Panama and Venezuela, whose ecological and cultural traits resemble the core Caribbean societies as much as they differ from the overall texture of life in the non-coastal areas of the republics in question. The word "archipelago" recurs frequently in the language with which Edouard Glissant conceptualizes the region, just as it does in the formulations of the late Antonio Benitez Rojo, who conceived of the region figuratively as a "repeating island." But any terminology that homogenizes the geographical visage of the region on the basis of its insular facet not only diminishes its magnitude but it enfeebles its cultural vastness. The Atlantic rimland regions of continental Latin America and the mainland Caribbean societies have contributed greatly to the overall literary corpus. The mention of Belize's Zee Edgell, Guyanas's Wilson Harris, and Surinam's Albert Helman should suffice to illustrate this point. We can see the limits of the insular vision in a recent volume of scholarly essays on the "cultures of the Hispanic Caribbean" that focuses almost exclusively on Cuba, the Dominican Republic, and Puerto Rico (James and Perivolaris 2000). In only three chapters out of seventeen, the volume makes gestures to Colombia and Venezuela: Jorge Marban's look at representations of the African heritage in four Venezuelan novels published between 1931 and 1950, Lancelot Cowie's survey of the recurrence of the cult of Reina María Lionza in Venezuelan fiction of various periods, and Gilberto Gómez Ocampo's comparative reading of Colombian novelist Hector Rojas Herazo and Cuban writer Virgilio Pinera as they both confront the problematic of modernity. Yet, while both the general editor of the series and the compilers of the volume refer to the "*circum*-Caribbean", their project remains overwhelmingly insular. They concern themselves primarily with the problem of reconciling the presumably disparate literary and intellectual products of societies marked by differing sociopolitical systems, namely a "revolutionary dictatorship in Cuba, democratic authoritarianism in the Dominican Republic, and the continued colonization of Puerto Rico by the United States" (James 2000: 2).

Much gets lost in any conceptual configuration of the Caribbean that reduces the region to its insular parts, particularly as it relates to the literary corpus. The insular prism truncates the region's literary history, killing the hope that we might get closer to chronicling it in its entirety, an enterprise that we have only just begun and which cries for satisfactory execution. The map of Caribbean writing will change significantly once we learn to factor in the literary activity taking place on the coastal regions of South America; Veracruz, and the Yucatan Peninsula of Mexico in the North; and the riverine zones of Central America. I would contend that the tabulation of literary texts will become more difficult, almost unwieldy, and therefore truer since simplification of reality always involves a falsification. I would envision a map of Caribbean writing that recognizes the remarkable literary career of Oscar Collazos, the author of numerous works of fiction and expository prose, including *Los días de la paciencia* (1976), *Todo por nada* (1980), and *Jóvenes pobres amantes* (1983); the accomplished poetry of Rómulo Bustos Aguirre, whose collected verse entitled *Oración del impuro: Obra reunida* (2004) appeared under the university press of Colombia's Universidad Nacional; the outstanding contributions of short fiction writer and novelist Roberto Burgos Cantor, author of compelling texts such as *Lo amador* (1981) and *Quiero es cantar* (1998); and the equally distinguished legacy of novelist and playwright Fanny Buitrago, whose novel *Los pañamanes* (1979) occupied Benítez Rojo's attention for a chapter of *The Repeating Island*. This is only a minute sampling of the literary artists who would have to come to the fore if we consider merely the most salient figures from the Caribbean region of Colombia, where cities such as Santa Marta, Cartagena, and Barranquilla have for generations been vibrant sites of artistic and intellectual production. Imagine if we looked into the Caribbean coasts of the other Latin American republics that qualify! For one thing, an exploration of the "Hispanic Caribbean" literature that chooses to limit its search to the islands of the Greater Antilles would at best seem bizarre.

A native of Barranquilla, Buitrago drew her plot for *Los panamanes* from the colonial history of the archipelago made up of San Andres, Santa Catalina, and Providencia, a cluster of islands that from 1822 have formed part of Colombia, having previously been claimed by English colonists. The Colombian government in 1868 placed the archipelago under the administrative control of Bogota as "territories", but the islands continued to suffer isolation not only from the rest of the Hispanic Caribbean but also from mainland Colombia itself. Situated over 480 km off the Caribbean coast of Colombia and only some 180 km from the Nicaraguan coast, the islands do not show up in most general maps of the Caribbean. Because of an original colonization by English Puritans and their economic linkage to the plantation system that spread throughout what later became the British West Indies, before and after emancipation the islands for a long time had greater commercial and cultural contact with Cayman Islands and Jamaica than with mainland Colombia. The conflict between Britain and Spain over the colonial control of the islands lasted from 1632 to 1822, but the estrangement of the archipelago from Colombia survived the era of conflict (Sandner 2003: 36, 267). In fact, Colombia waited until well into the twentieth century to attempt the integration of the archipelago culturally and socially through a campaign of "Colombianization". This was presumably not an easy feat if we consider that until the beginning of the twentieth century only the government personnel in the archipelago spoke Spanish, the majority of the population speaking primarily English and the Creole that served as the common language of the uneducated folk (Ratter 2001: 56). Today the Colombian State recognizes both Spanish and English as official languages of the archipelago.

The body of utterances produced by the residents of San Andres, Providencia, and Santa Catalina, an archipelago that necessarily ought to fit within an inclusive understanding of the "Hispanic Caribbean," will ideally figure among the tributaries that make up the large corpus we end up acknowledging as Caribbean literature. The San Andres native Hazel Robinson Abraham, interested in recovering the submerged history of the formation of Creole societies on the islands, has dedicated two novels toward that end. *No Give Up, Maan* (2002) tells the story of the islands prior to Colombia's attempt to incorporate them into the nation, and *Sail Ahoy*!!! (!Vela a la vista!) (2004) evokes the process whereby the islanders developed a mastery of the sea and turned it into their principal source of sustenance. Beginning to facilitate the availability of the words of the islanders to the overall region, the Caribbean Studies Institute at the San Andres Campus of the Universidad Nacional de Colombia has devoted several issues of its *Cuadernos del Caribe* to capturing the ideas, life stories, voices, and yearnings of the residents of the archipelago. Issue No. 4 consists of 36 first-person texts composed by the editors on the basis of long interviews conducted with "people who have a visible role in the life of the islands and who, in various ways, have contributed and continue to contribute to shaping their future", representing the voices of ordinary people, differing from an earlier cohort of local government and community leaders convened by the Institute to hear their perception of the condition of life on the archipelago and the most pressing needs of the local population (Ramirez and Restrepo 2002: 13). Coming from different walks of life, levels of schooling, professional training, and ways of participating in community advancement, the speakers in the collection bear predominantly English names, the majority being "raizales" (natives), those residents who trace their origins back to the enslaved workers brought in the eighteenth century from Belize, Cayman Islands, and Jamaica by settlers under authorization by the Spanish colonial authorities.

In sum, a vision of the Caribbean that views the region through an insular prism will be less ready to perceive the human experience – hence the works and the words – of continental Caribbean societies as well as of the numerous Caribbean communities inhabiting the rimland areas. Furthermore, since the idea of "islands" or "archipelago" that informs the learned discourse on the Caribbean is really not geographical but political, island clusters that exist within a differentiated polity will tend to stay out of consideration by proponents of panoptic visions of the Caribbean, and island nation-states such as Jamaica or Cuba or the non-independent insular territories that answer juridically to a colonial metropolis overseas will monopolize the name. The Colombian archipelago is hardly the only one that could enter this discussion, but it suffices to show that insular visions of the Caribbean do injustice to the region's numerous continental sites as well as to those islands that by virtue of their small size and their inconvenient location have trouble attracting the attention of the cartographers who design the Caribbean region's general maps.

X. Present Aboriginals and Future Cross-Linguals

A more attentive focus on the continental Caribbean will bring into clearer view those spaces within the region's geography whose populations have a significant aboriginal, indigenous component, who can trace their origins directly to the communities that inhabited the Americas prior to the conquest and colonization over five centuries ago. Despite insightful evocations found in the works of Wilson Harris, Pauline Melville and in Kevin Baldeosingh's remarkable transhistorical novel *The Ten Incarnations of Adam Avatar* (2005), literary representations of the Caribbean generally seem to reflect the enduring legacy of the myth of "the absent aboriginal" that the contributors to *Indigenous Resurgence in the Contemporary Caribbean* aim to interrupt (Forte 2006). With the work of sociopolitical organizing and the cultural self-affirmation launched in the last two decades by Amerindian advocates in Belize, French Guiana, Guyana and Surinam, new figurations of the Caribbean will necessarily have to account for the aborigines, with their culture, their works and their words, as an inescapable presence within the region's pan-ethnic human family. The work of Amerindian visual artists such as the Guyanese George Simon will undoubtedly be followed by the work of Amerindian writers. Similarly, mixed ancestry Afro-Amerindian groups like the Black Caribs of Belize, St. Vincent, and the Grenadines, as well as the Garifuna of Honduras, Guatemala and Nicaragua will enter the sphere of utterances in a truly holistic vision of Caribbean literature and thought.

The new Caribbean poetics, in other words, is called upon to make a greater attempt than has been made thus far to circumvent the region's historic fragmentation as reflected in the combined geographical and political complications that impinge on the lesser visibility of isolated territories such as those of San Andres, Providencia, and Santa Catalina. But it has to make an even greater attempt to circumvent the truly debilitating linguistic balkanization that has historically impeded appropriate intraregional exchanges of words, knowledge and thought. Some twenty indigenous languages, as many as fifty Creoles, the four major European tongues that the colonial powers brought with them, and the Asian languages that came with the indentured workers after the 1838 emancipation render the Caribbean region a virtual Tower of Babel. The linguistic barriers to those aspiring to apprehend the region holistically sometimes seem practically insurmountable, discouraging intra-Caribbean literary and intellectual conversation. The sense of that insurmountability perhaps explains the tendency of many in the learned community to cultivate their monolingual garden, each in their distinct subsection in isolation from the rest of the polyglot region. That tendency shows up in the otherwise impressive collection *New Caribbean Thought: A Reader* (Meeks and Lindahl 2001) and the compelling monograph *The Caribbean: An Intellectual History 1774-2003* (Benn 2004) whose use of the holistic term "Caribbean" in the titles raise cross-lingual hopes which the Anglophone-centric nature of their contents immediately frustrates.

Elsewhere I have noted the damaging intellectual self-sufficiency of the view of creolity as a quintessence of Caribbean identity posited by the celebrated Martinican authors Jean Bernabé, Patrick Chamoiseau, and Raphäel Confiant as a function of the exclusively Francophone origin of the sources used by those authors (Torres-Saillant 1997: 29-30). That linguistic isolationism creates a scenario in which, for instance, the major contributions of Anton de Kom, Boeli van Leeuwen, and Astrid Roemer, coming from the Dutch-speaking side, will seldom succeed at crossing the linguistic border to Anglophone, Francophone, or Spanish-speaking literary conversations, just as the seminal essay *Tres leyendas de colores* by Pedro Mir will fail to join the company of the better-known books of essential Caribbean thought, such as *The Black Jacobins* by C. L. R. James and *Peau noire, masques blancs* by Frantz Fanon. Such is the scenario in which one finds the venerable George Lamming lamenting the possibility "that a generation of graduates from the University of the West Indies, including the History Department, would have left that institution knowing little or nothing about Marti, perhaps the most creative thinker the region has produced" (Lamming 2000: 46). Interestingly, the essay in which Lamming conveys this sorrow has become available in Spanish and French in addition to the English original thanks to the visionary initiative of Lasana M. Sekou, a publisher and poet from St. Martin, whose House of Nehesi Publishers seems to have taken on, at a much more modest scale, the unprecedented cross-lingual project that Cuba's Casa de las Americas kept alive from the start of the socialist government to the 1980s.

During the golden years when the Cuban Revolution enjoyed economic stability, Casa de las Americas encouraged literary creativity in the region by opening the prestigious Casa Award to participants writing in any of the languages of the Americas while sponsoring Spanish translations of numerous literary texts from across the language spectrum. For instance, the existing Spanish versions of Lamming's novels *In the Castle of my Skin* and *Natives of my Person* came out in 1979 as part of the Casa initiative. Similarly, the literary and intellectual productions of Anton de Kom, Aimé Césaire, Kamau Brathwaite, Rene Depestre, and Jacques Roumain, to name only a few, first entered the sphere of the Hispanophone world through Casa's invaluable enterprise. Today the socialist government that supported that initiative no longer enjoys its former prosperity and the neoliberal states that abound in the rest of the region have not exhibited a comparable commitment to ameliorating the bane of Caribbean fragmentation by forging bridges of artistic and intellectual communication across the various divides of language and geography. Therefore, it may have to fall upon enlightened private advocates like Sekou to endeavour to create structures, their magnitude notwithstanding, that may contribute to bringing the multilingual voices of the Caribbean to speak within hearing range of one another, thereby affording us a fuller, larger, more complex – hence truer – view of the body of utterances we call Caribbean literature. One could envision here an inclusive corpus of texts brought together by the force of a chaos as beautiful and real as that which colours the polychromatic texture of the variegated cosmos inhabited by Zadie Smith's characters in *White Teeth*.

BIBLIOGRAPHY

Abrams, M.H., et al., Eds. *The Norton Anthology of English Literature*, 3rd. ed. (New York: W.W. Norton, 1974).

Achufusi, Modilim. "Devoirs et responsabilités des historiens Africains", *Présence Africaine* 27/28 (1959): 81-95.

Acosta-Belén, Edna. "Notes on the Evolution of the Puerto Rican Novel", *Latin American Literary Review* 8.16 (1980): 183-195.

Addo. S. "Introduction", Edward K. Brathwaite. *Four Plays for Primary Schools* (London and Accra: Longmans Green and Co., 1964).

Adjarian, M.M. *Allegories of Desire: Body, Nation, and Empire in Modern Caribbean Literature by Women* (Westport, Conn, and London: Praeger, 2004).

Adonis (Ali Ahmad Said Esber). *An Introduction to Arab Poetics* (University of Texas Press, 1990).

Aidoo, Ama Ata. "Akan and English", *West Africa* (21 September 1968): 1099.

Aiyejina, Funso. "The Death and Rebirth of African Deities in Edward Brathwaite's *Islands*", *World Literature Written in English* 23.2 (1984): 397-404.

Alcántara Almánzar, José, Ed. *Antología de la literatura dominicana* (Santo Domingo: Editora Cultural Dominicana, 1972).

——. *Estudios de poesía dominicana* (Santo Domingo: Alfa y Omega, 1979).

Alexandre, Guy. "La relación francés/créole en Haití: Trato, función, evolución y perspectivas", *Francophonie et Caraïbe/Francofonía y Caribe*. Ed. Jacques Leylavergne (Santo Domingo: Casa de Francia, 1993), 185-192.

Alexis, Jacques Stéphen. "Du réalisme merveilleux des haïtiens", *Présence Africaine* 8-9-10 (1956): 245-271.

——. *Romancero aux étoiles* (Paris: Gallimard, Collection "L'Imaginaire", 1960).

Alleyne, Mervyn C. "A Linguistic Perspective on the Caribbean", *Caribbean Contours*. Ed. Sidney W. Mintz and Sally Price (Baltimore and London: Johns Hopkins University Press, 1985), 155-179.

Allis, Jeanette B. *West Indian Literature: An Index to Criticism* (Boston: G.K. Hall & Co., 1981).

——. "West Indian Literature: A Case for Regional Criticism". In Smilowitz & Quarles, 7-18.

Allsopp, Richard. "La influencia africana sobre el idioma del Caribe [1971]". In Moreno Fraginals, 129-151.

Alonso Hernández, José Luis. "Didácticas de los marginalismos", *Imprévue* 1 (1980): 113-128.

"Altamira, Rafael". *Enciclopedia Universal Ilustrada*. Vol. 4 (Madrid: Espasa-Calpe, 1958): 957.

Althusser, Louis. *For Marx*. Trans. Ben Brewster (London: Verso-NLB, 1979).

Amin, Samir. *La déconnexion: Pour sortir du système mondial* (Paris: La Découverte, 1986).

——. *Delinking: Towards a Polycentric World*. Trans. Michael Wolfers (London: Zed Books Ltd., 1990).
——. *Eurocentrism*. Trans. Russell Moore (New York: Monthly Review Press, 1989).
Anderson Imbert, Enrique. *Historia de la literatura hispanoamericana*, 2 vols. (México: Fondo de Cultura Económica, 1961).
——. *Spanish American Literature: A History*. Trans. John W. Falconieri (Detroit: Wayne State University Press, 1963).
Anderson Imbert, Enrique and Eugenio Florit, Eds. *Literatura hispanoamericana: Antología e introducción histórica* (New York: Holt, Rinehart and Winston, 1960).
André, Jacques. *Caraïbales: Etudes sur la littérature antillaise* (Paris: Editions Caribéennes, 1981).
Anon (Cynric Williams). *Hamel, the Obeah Man* (London: Hunt and Clarke, 1827).
Anthony, Michael. *The Year in San Fernando* (London: Andre Deutch, 1965).
Antoine, Regis. "La reception française des oeuvres antillaises francophones", *Francophonie et Caraïbe/Francofonía y Caribe*. Ed. Jacques Leylavergne (Santo Domingo: Casa de Francia, 1993), 84-93.
Antoni, Robert. *Divina Trace* (New York: Overlook Press, 1991).
——. *Blessed Is the Fruit* (New York: Henry Holt and Co., 1997)
——. "The Tale of How Iguana Got Her Wrinkles or the True Tale of El Dorado", *Barcelona Review* 20 (2000). www.barcelonareview.com/20.
——. *Carnival* (New York: Black Cat, 2005)
Aragon, Louis. Préface. *Trente et un sonnets*, by Eugène Guillevic (Paris: Editions Gallimard, 1954).
Arcinegas, German. *Biografía del Caribe* (Buenos Aires: Editorial Sudamericana, 1945).
Arias-Larreta, Abraham. *From Columbus to Bolívar*. (Kansas City: The New World Library, 1965).
Arisa Averasturi, Miguel. Review of *Cuando amaban las tierras comuneras* by Pedro Mir. *Signos* I.I (1980): 25-26.
Aristotle. *Aristotle's Theory of Poetry and Fine Art*. Ed. and trans. S.H. Butcher. (New York: Dover Publications, 1951).
——. *The Poetics*. Trans. W. Hamilton Fyfe. The Loeb Classical Library (Cambridge, Mass.: Harvard University Press, 1973).
——. *The Politics*. Trans. T.A. Sinclair (Harmondsworth: Penguin Books, 1962).
Arnold, A James. *Modernism and Negritude: The Poetry and Poetics of Aimé Césaire* (Cambridge, Mass.: Harvard University Press, 1981).
——. Introduction. *Lyric and Dramatic Poetry: 1946-1982*, by Aimé Césaire. Trans. Clayton Eshleman and Annette Smith (Charlottesville: The University Press of Virginia, CARAF Books, 1990), xi-xli.
——. "The Novelist as Critic", *World Literature Today* 67.4 (1993): 711-716.
——. [1994a] Ed. *A History of Literature in the Caribbean*. Vol. 1 (Amsterdam and Philadelphia: John Benjamins Publishing Company, 1994).
——. [1994b] "The Erotics of Colonialism in Contemporary French West Indian Literary Culture", *New West Indian Guide* 68.1-2 (1994): 1-23.

——. "Caribbean Literary Theory: Modernist and Postmodern", *New West Indian Guide* 69.1-2 (1995): 103-109.

Arroyo, Anita. *América en su literatura* (San Juan: Editorial Universitaria, 1977).

Arvelo, Alejandro. "Marxismo versus racionalismo en el capítulo sobre Hegel del libro *Apertura a la estética* de Pedro Mir", *Cuaderno de Poética* 1.2 (1984): 53-59.

Asein, Samuel Omo. "The Concept of Form: A Study of Some Ancestral Elements in Brathwaite's Trilogy", *ASAWI Bulletin* 4 (1971): 19-34.

Asante, Molefi Kete. *Afrocentricity: The Theory of Social Change* (Buffalo: Amulefi Publishing Company, 1980).

Auerbach, Erich, *Mimesis: The Representation of Reality in Western Literature.* Trans. Willard. R. Trask (Princeton, N. J.: Princeton University Press, 1953).

Augier, Angel. *De la sangre en la letra* (La Habana: Unión de Escritores y Artistas de Cuba, 1977).

Avelino, Andrés. "Manifiesto postumista", *Meridiano 70: poesía social dominicana siglo xx*. Ed. Mercédez Santos Moray. Colección La Honda (La Habana: Casa de las Américas, 1978): 275-77.

Averroes. *Averroes' Middle Commentary on Aristotle's 'Poetics'.* Trans. Charles E. Butterworth (Princeton: Princeton University Press, 1986).

Avicenna. *Avicenna's Commentary on 'The Poetics' of Aristotle: A Critical Study and an Annotated Translation of the Text*. Trans. and ed. Ismael M. Dahiyat (Leiden: E.J. Brill, 1974).

Axline, W. Andrew. *Caribbean Integration: The Politics of Regionalism* (London: Frances Pinter Ltd., 1979).

Baciu, Stefan, Ed. *Antología de la poesía latinoamericana*, 2 vols. (Albany: State University of New York Press, 1974).

Baeza Flores, Alberto. *La poesía dominicana en el siglo XX: 1943-1947* (Santiago: Universidad Católica Madre y Maestra, 1977).

Bahadur Singh, I.J., Ed. *Indians in the Caribbean* (New Delhi: Sterling Publishers, 1987).

Bailey, B.L. *Jamaican Creole Syntax: A Transformational Approach* (London: Cambridge University Press, 1965).

Baker, Jr., Houston A. *Afro-American Poetics: Revisions of Harlem and the Black Aesthetics* (Madison: University of Wisconsin Press, 1988).

Bajeux, Jean-Claude. *Antilia retrouvée* (Paris: Editions Caribéenes, 1983).

Bakhtin, Mikhail. *Rabelais and his World*. Trans. Helene Iswolsky [1968]. (Bloomington: Indiana University Press, 1984).

Balaquer, Joaquín. *Historia de la literatura dominicana*, 5ta ed. (Santo Domingo: Julio D. Póstigo & Hijos, 1970).

Baridon, Silvio F. and Raymond Philoctète, Eds. *Poésie vivante d'Haïti* (Paris: Maurice Nadeau, 1978).

Barnet, Miguel. *Autobiografía de un cimarrón* (Barcelona: Ariel, 1968).

——. *Canción de Rachel* (Buenos Aires: Editorial Galema, 1969).

Barradas, Efraín. Rev. of *Cuando amaban las tierras comuneras*, by Pedro Mir. *Sin Nombre* 9.2 (1978): 95-96.

Barthold, Bonnie J. *Black Time: Fiction of Africa, The Caribbean, and the United States* (New Haven: Yale University Press, 1981).

Bascom, William. "The Focus of Cuban Santeria". In Horowitz 522-527.
Bathersfield, Joan P. "The Treatment of Black Religion in the Caribbean Novel", Diss. Howard University, 1977.
Baudot, Paul *Oeuvres créoles* 2e ed. Trans. and ed. M. Maurice Martin (Basse-Terre: Imprimerie Officielle, 1935).
Baugh, Edward. Rev. of *Rights of Passage* by E.K.Brathwaite, *Bim* 12.45 (1967): 66-68.
——. Rev. of *Masks* by E.K.Brathwaite, *Bim* 12.47 (1968): 209-211.
——. *Critics on Caribbean Literature* (New York: St. Martin's Press, 1978).
——. "A History of Poetry", *A History of Literature in the Caribbean.* Vol. 2: English- and Dutch-Speaking Regions. Ed. A. James Arnold (Amsterdam and Philadelphia: John Benjamins Publishing Company, 2001), 227-282.
Bazil, Osvaldo. *Parnaso antillano: compilación de lo mejores poetas de Cuba, Puerto Rico y Santo Domingo* (Barcelona: Editorial Maucci, 1918).
Benamou, Michel. "The Concept of Marginality in Ethnopoetics", *Minority Language and Literature: Retrospective and Perspective*. Ed. Dexter Fisher (New York: The Modern Language Association of America, 1977), 150-159.
Benítez Rojo, Antonio. *La isla que se repite: El Caribe y la perspectiva posmoderna* (Hanover, NH: Ediciones del Norte, 1989).
——. *The Repeating Island: The Caribbean and the Postmodern Perspective*. Trans. James Maraniss (Durham: Duke University Press, 1992).
Benjamin, Walter. "Three Theses on the Philosophy of History", *Marxism and Art*. Ed. Maynard Solomon [1973]. (Detroit: Wayne State University Press, 1979), 559-561.
Benn, Denis. *The Caribbean: An Intellectual History 1774-2003* (Kingston: Ian Randle Publishers, 2004).
Bennett, Louise. *Selected Poems* (Kingston: Sangsters Book Stores, 1982).
Benoist, Jean. Ed. *L'archipel inachevé* (Montréal: Les Presses de l'Université de Montréal, 1972).
Bensen, Robert, Ed. *One People's Grief: Recent Writing from the Caribbean* (Hamilton, New Zealand: Outriggers Publishers, 1983).
Bernabé, Jean, Patrick Chamoiseau and Raphaël Confiant. *Eloge de la créolité* (Paris: Gallimard, 1989).
——. "In Praise of Creoleness", Trans. Mohamed B. Taleb Kyar. *Callaloo* 13.4 (1990): 886-909.
Berrian, Brenda and Aart Broek. *Bibliography of Women Writers from the Caribbean* (Washington: Three Continents Press, 1989).
Berroa, Rei. "Recordar para vivir: Historia, alegoría y dialéctica en la crónica de Pedro Mir", *Revista Iberoamericana* 54.142 (1988): 28-51.
Berrou, Raphaël and Pradel Pompilus, Eds. *Histoire de la littérature haïtienne illustrée par les textes*. 3 vols. (Port-au-Prince: Editions Caraïbes, 1975-77).
Berry, James, Ed. *News for Babylon: The Chatto Book of West Indian British Poetry* (London: Chatto & Windus, 1984).
Betances, Ramón Emeterio. *Betances*. Ed. Luis Bonafoux [1901] (San Juan: Instituto de Cultura Puertorriqueña, 1970).
Bilby, Kenneth M. "The Caribbean as a Musical Region", *Caribbean Contours*. Ed. Sidney Mintz and Sally Price (Baltimore and London: Johns Hopkins University Press, 1985).

Biobaku, Saburi. "Les responsabilités de l' historien africain en ce qui concerne l'histoire et l'Afrique", *Présence Africaine* 27/28 (1959): 96-99.

Birbalsingh, Frank. *Indenture and Exile: The Indo-Caribbean Experience* (Toronto: Tsar Publications, 1989).

Blair, Dorothy S. *African Literature in French* (Cambridge: Cambridge University Press, 1976).

Bloom, Harold. *The Western Canon. The Books and Schools of the Ages* (New York: Harcourt, Brace and Company, 1994).

Bosch, Juan. *De Cristóbal Colón a Fidel Castro: El Caribe, frontera imperial* (Madrid: Ediciones Alfaguara, 1970).

Brahimi-Chapuis, Denise and Gabriel Belloc, Eds. *Anthologie du roman maghrébin, négro-africain, antillais et réunionnais d'expression française* (Paris: CILF-Delagrave, 1986).

Bran, J. "Spirits, Mediums, and Believers in Contemporary Puerto Rico", *Transactions*. Series 2.20 (1957): 340-347.

Brantlinger, Patrick. *Rule of Darkness: British Literature and Imperialism 1830-1914* (Ithaca: Cornell University Press, 1988).

Brathwaite, Doris Monica. Review of V. S. Naipaul's *Middle Passage*. In *Iounaloa: Recent Writing from St. Lucia*. Edward Brathwaite, Ed. (Castries, St. Lucia. University of the West Indies. 1963) 72-73.

——. *E.K.B.: his publ. prose & poetry ; 1948-1986; a checklist* (Mona, Jamaica: Savacou Co-op., 1986).

——. *A descriptive and chronological bibliography (1950-1982) of the work of Edward Kamau Brathwaite* (London: New Beacon Books, 1988).

Brathwaite, Edward K. "The Black Angel", *Bim* 6.22 (1955): 79-87.

——. "Law and Order", *Bim* 6.23 (1955): 193-200.

——. "Sir Galahad and The Islands", *Bim* 7.25 (1957): 8-16.

——. "The Controversial Tree of Time", *Bim* 8.30 (1960): 104-114.

——. Rev. of *Voices of Ghana* by H. Swanzy. *Bim* 8.30 (1960): 131-134.

——. "The New West Indian Novelists, Part I", *Bim* 8.31 (1960): 199-210.

——. Rev. of *A Quality of Violence* by A. Salkey. *Bim* 8.31 (1960): 219-220.

——. "The New West Indian Novelists, Part II", *Bim* 8.32 (1961): 271-280.

——. "Christine." *Bim* 8.32 (1961): 246-250.

——. "Roots." *Bim* 10.37 (1963): 10-21.

——. *Four Plays for Primary Schools* (London and Accra: Longmans Green and Co., 1964).

——. Rev. of *The Scholar-Man* by O.R. Dathorne. *Bim* 10.41 (1965): 68-69.

——. Rev. of *The Castaway* by D. Walcott. *Bim* 11.42 (1966): 139-141.

——. Rev. of two Caribbean anthologies. *Bim* 11.43 (1966): 222-23.

——. "*Kyk-over-al* and the Radicals", *New World Quarterly*. Guyana Independence Issue (1966): 55-57.

——. "Cricket" [1967], *Caribbean Prose*. Ed. Andrew Salkey (London: Evans Brothers Limited, 1973), 60-67.

——. "Jazz and the West Indian Novel", Part I. *Bim* 11.44 (1967): 275-284.

——. "Jazz and the West Indian Novel", Part II. *Bim* 12.45 (1967): 39-51.

——. *Odale's Choice* (London: Evans Brothers Limited, 1967).

——. *Rights of Passage* (London: Oxford University Press, 1967).
——. "West Indian Prose Fiction in the Sixties: A Survey", *Bim* 12.47 (1968): 157-165.
——. "Jazz and the West Indian Novel", Part III. *Bim* 12.46 (1968): 115-126.
——. *Masks* (London: Oxford University Press, 1968).
——. *Islands* (London: Oxford University Press, 1969).
——. "Caribbean Critics", *Critical Quarterly* 11.3 (1969): 268-276.
——. "Creative Literature of the British West Indies During the Period of Slavery", *Savacou* 1 (1970): 46-73.
——. Rev. of Faustin Charles' *The Expatriate*. *Caribbean Quarterly* 16.2 (1970): 65-69.
——. "Rehabilitations", *Bim* 13.51 (1970): 174-184.
——. "Timehri", *Savacou* 2 (1970): 35-44.
——. "Forward", *Savacou* 3-4 (1970): 5-9.
——. *The Development of Creole Society in Jamaica: 1770-1820* (Oxford: Clarendon Press, 1971).
——. "Presencia de Africa en la literatura del Caribe" [1971], *Africa en América Latina*. In Moreno Fraginals 152-184.
——. "The Contribution of M.J. Herskovitz to Afro-American Studies", *ASAWI Bulletin* 5 (1972): 85-94.
——. "*Rap on Race*: Race and the Divided Self", *Black World* 21.9 (1972): 54-68.
——. *The Arrivants: A New World Trilogy* (London: Oxford University Press, 1973).
——. "Dialect and Dialectic", *ASAWI Bulletin* 6 (1973): 89-99.
——. "The African Presence in Caribbean Literature", *Daedalus* 103.2 (1974): 73-109.
——. *Contradictory Omens* [1974] (Mona: Savacou Publications, 1985).
——. Introduction. *Brother Man*, by Roger Mais (London: Heinemann, 1974), v-xxi.
——. *Other Exiles* (London: Oxford University Press, 1975).
——. *Days & Nights* (Mona: Caldwell Press, 1975).
——. "Caribbean Man in Space and Time", *Savacou* 11-12 (1975): 1-11.
——. *Black & Blues* (La Habana: Casa de las Américas, 1976).
——. *Black & Blues* (Benin City: Ethiope Publishing Corporation, 1976).
——. *Mother Poem* (Oxford: Oxford University Press, 1977).
——. "Caliban, Ariel and Unprospero in the Conflict of Creolization: A Study of the Slave Revolt in Jamaica in 1831-1832", *Comparative Perpectives on Slavery in the New World*. Ed. Vera Rubin and Arthur Tuden. Annals of the New York Academy of Sciences. Vol. 292. (New York: New York Academy of Sciences, 1977), 41-62.
——. *Wars of Respect: Nanny and Sam Sharpe (Nanny, Sam Sharpe and the Struggle for People's Liberation)* (Kingston: Agency for Public Information, 1977).
——. *Our Ancestral Heritage: A Bibliography of the English Speaking Caribbean* (Kingston: Savacou, 1977).
——. "The Love Axe/L: (Developing a Caribbean Aesthetic 1962-1974)", Part I. *Bim* 16.61 (1977): 53-65.

——. "The Love Axe/L: (Developing a Caribbean Aesthetic 1962-1974)", Part II. *Bim* 16.62 (1977): 101-106.

——. "The Love Axe/L: (Developing a Caribbean Aesthetic 1962-1974)", Part III. *Bim* 16.63 (1978):181-192.

——. "*Kumina*: The Spirit of African Survival in Jamaica", *Jamaica Journal* 42 (1978): 45-63.

——. "Roger Mais' *Brother Man* as Jazz Novel" [1978]. In Baugh, 103-112.

——. *Soweto* (Mona: Savacou Publications, 1979).

——. *Word-Making Man: Poem for Nicolás Guillén in Xaymayca* (Mona: Savacou Publications, 1979).

——. *Barbados Poetry ?1661-1979: A Checklist* (Kingston: Savacou, 1979).

——. *Jamaica Poetry: A Checklist* (Kingston: The Jamaica Library Service, 1979).

——. Ed. *New Poets from Jamaica* (Kingston: Savacou Publications, 1979).

——. "English in the Caribbean: Notes on Nation Language and Poetry", *English Literature: Opening Up the Canon*. Ed. Leslie A. Fiedler and Houston A. Baker (Baltimore: John Hopkins University Press, 1981), 15-53.

——. *Folk Culture of the Slaves in Jamaica*. Rev. ed. (London: New Beacon Books, 1981).

——. *Sun Poem* (Oxford University Press, 1982).

——. *Afternoon of the Status Crow* (Mona, Kingston: Savacou Cooperative, 1982).

——. "Gods of the Middle Passage: A Tennament", *Caribbean Review* 11.4 (1982): 18-19, 42-44.

——. "Caribbean Culture: Two Paradigms". *Missile and Capsule*. Ed. Jürgen Martini (Bremen: University of Bremen, 1983), 9-54.

——. *Third World Poems* (London: Longman Group Limited, 1983).

———. "Helen and the Tempest-Nègre: René Depestre's *A Rainbow for the Christian West*", *Caribbean Quarterly* 30.1 (1984): 33-47.

———. *The Colonial Encounter: Languages* (Mysore: The Centre for Commonwealth Literature and Research – University of Mysore, 1984).

——. *The History of the Voice* (London: New Beacon Books, 1984).

——. Rev. of Dionne Brand's *Winter Epigrams*, *Canadian Literature* 105 (1985):18-30.

——. "Metaphors of Underdevelopment: A Proem for Hernan Cortez", *New England Review and Breadloaf Quarterly* 7.4 (1985): 453-476.

——. "World Order Models – A Caribbean Perspective", *Caribbean Quarterly* 30.1 (1985): 53-63.

——. *Roots: Essays* (La Habana: Casas de las Américas, 1986).

——. *Jah Music* (Mona, Kingston: Savacou Cooperative, 1986).

——. *Le détonateur de visibilité/The Visibility Trigger*. Ed. and trans. Maria Francesca Mollica and Christine Pagnoulle (Belgium: Cahiers de Louvain, 1986).

——. *X/Self* (Oxford: Oxford University Press, 1987).

——. "The 4th Traveller", *Callaloo* 12.1 (1989): 184-191.

——. "The Crossing", *Native Landscapes: An Anthology of Caribbean Short Stories*. Ed. Velta J. Clarke (New York: Caribbean Research Center – Medgar Evers College, CUNY, 1989), 33-41.

——. *Sappho Sakyi's Meditations* (Mona: Savacou Press, 1990).

——. *Shar/ Hurricane Poem* (Mona: Savacou Press, 1990).

——. *Middle Passages* (Newcastle. Bloodaxe Books, 1992).
——. [1992b] "Words by Kamau Brathwaite". Presentation at the North-South Counterpoint Conference "Kamau Brathwaite and the Caribbean Word". Bronx, N.Y. Hostos Community College, CUNY. 24 October 1992.
——. [1992c] "The Search for a Caribbean Aesthetic", *Sunday Express*, 8 November 1992, 29-36.
——. [1992d] "The Search for a Caribbean Aesthetic", *Sunday Express*, 15 November 1992, 33-40.
——. *DreamStories* (London: Longman, 1994).
——. *The Zea Mexican Diary* (Madison: University of Wisconsin Press, 1994).
——. *Trench Town Rock* (USA: Lost Roads Publishers, 1994).
——. *Barabajan Poems* (Kingston, New York: Savacou North, 1994).
Breiner, Laurence. "Tradition, Society, the Figure of the Poet", *Caribbean Quarterly* 26.1-2 (1980): 1-12.
——. "Edward Kamau Brathwaite". *Dictionary of Literary Biography*. Vol. 135. *Twentieth-Century Caribbean and Black African Writers*. Second Series. Ed. Bernth Lindfors and Reinhard Sander (Detroit and London: Bruccoli Clark Layman, 1993), 8-28.
——. "The Other West Indian Poet". *Partisan Review* 56.2 (1989): 316-320.
Brennan, Paul, Ed. *You Better Believe It: Black Verse in English* (Harmondsworth: Penguin Books, 1973).
Breton, André. Préface. *Cahier d'un retour au pays natal*, by Aimé Césaire (Paris: Présence Africaine, 1983), 77-87.
Brown, Lloyd W. *West Indian Poetry*. 2nd ed. (London: Heinemann, 1984).
——. "Introduction: Regional Writers, Regional Critics". In Smilowitz and Quarles, 1-6.
Brown, Stewart, Ed. *Caribbean Poetry Now* (London: Hodder and Stoughton, 1986).
Brown, Stewart, and Mark MacWatt, Eds. *The Oxford Book of Caribbean Verse* (Oxford University Press, 2005).
Brown, Stewart, Gordon Rohlehr and Mervyn Morris, Eds. *Voiceprint: An Anthology of Oral and Related Poetry from the Caribbean* (Essex: Longman, 1989).
Bronowski, Jacob. *The Ascent of Man* (Boston: Little, Brown and Co., 1973).
Burnett, Paula, Ed. *The Penguin Book of Caribbean Verse* (Middlesex: Penguin Books, 1986).
Bush, Andrew. "Literature, History, and Literary History: A Cuban Family Romance", *Latin American Literary Review* 8.16 (1980): 161-172.
Bustos Aguirre, Romulo. *Oración del impuro: Obra reunida* (Bogotá, Colombia: Universidad Nacional de Colombia, 2004).
Caamaño de Fernández, Vicenta. *El negro en la poesía dominicana* (Santo Domingo: Centro de Estudios Avanzados de Puerto Rico y del Caribe, 1989).
Cabral, Manuel del. *Obra poética completa*. 2da ed. (Santo Domingo: Editora Alfa y Omega, 1987).
Cabrera Infante, Guillermo. *Tres tristes tigres* (Barcelona: Seix Barral, 1967).
Cailler, Bernadette. "L'efficacité poetique du Vaudou dans *Un arc-en-ciel pour l'Occident chrétien* de René Depestre", *The French Review* 53.1 (1979): 47-59.

Cameron, N.E. *Guianese Poetry Covering the Hundred Year Period, 1831-1931* (Author. Georgetown: 1931).

Camoês, Luis de. *Os Lusíadas*. Ed. Emanuel Paulo Ramos. 4a ed. (Lisboa: Porto Editora, 1986).

Campbell, George. *First Poems* (Author. Kingston: 1945. Republished Leeds: Peepal Tree Press, 2012).

Camus, Albert. *L'homme révolté* (Paris: Gallimard, 1951).

Canary, Robert H. and Henri Kozicki, Eds. *The Writing of History: Literary Form and Historical Understanding* (Madison: University of Wisconsin Press, 1978).

Cardenal, Ernesto. *Santidad de la Revolución*. 2da. ed. (Salamanca: Ediciones Sígueme, 1978).

Carnegie, Charles V. *Postnationalism Prefigured: Caribbean Borderlands* (New Brunswick, New Jersey, and London: Rutgers University Press, 2002).

Carew, Joy Gleason. "Language and Survival: Can Sranan Tongo, Suriname's Lingua Franca, Become the Official Language?" *Bim* 17.68 (1984): 103-113.

Carew, Jan. *Fulcrums of Change* (Trenton, N.J.: Africa Press, Inc., 1988).

Carpentier, Alejo. *Ecue-yamba-ó* (Madrid: Editorial España, 1933).

——. *El reino de este mundo* (México, D. F.: E.D.I.A.P.S.A. [Edición y Distribución de Publicaciones], 1949).

——. *El acoso* (Buenos Aires: Editorial Losada, 1956).

——. *The Kingdom of this World*. Trans. Harriet de Onís (New York: Alfred A. Knopf, 1957).

——. *Ensayos* (La Habana: Editorial Letras Cubanas, 1984).

Carruth, Hayden. 1974. "Poetry Chronicle", *Hudson Review*, 27:2 (1974): 318-320.

Cartagena Portalin, Aida. *Una mujer está sola* (Santo Domingo: Isla Necesaria, 1955).

——. *Del desconsuelo al compromiso/From Desolation to Compromise: Bilingual Anthology of the Poetry of Aida Cartagena Portalatín*. Ed. Daisy Cocco de Filippis. Trans. Emma Jane Robinett and Daisy Cocco de Filippis (Santo Domingo: Editora Taller, 1988).

——. *Vispera del Sueño* (Santo Domingo: Feria del Libro José Martí, 1995).

——. *Yania Tierra: Poema documento – Document Poem*. Trans. M. J. Fenwick and Rosabelle White (Washington, D.C.: Azul Editions, Caribfest Series, 1995).

Carter, Martin. *Poems of Resistance from British Guiana* (London: Lawrence and Wishart, 1954).

Casanova, Pascale, *The World Republic of Letters* (Cambridge, Mass.: Harvard University Press, 2004).

Castro, Nils. "El Istmo entre los Caribes", *Casa* 20-118 (1980): 80-84.

Catalá, Rafael. "Una lectura de 'Autorretrato' de Pedro Mir", *Caribe* 12 (1976): 95-108.

Cervantes Saavedra, Miguel de. *The Adventures of Don Quijote*. Trans. J.M. Cohen (Harmondsworth: Penguin Books, 1976).

Césaire, Aimé. *Cahier d'un retour au pays natal* [1939] (Paris: Présence Africaine, 1983).

——. *Discours sur le colonialisme* [1950] (Paris: Présence Africaine, 1955).
——. "Préface", *Végétations de clarté* by René Depestre (Paris: Pierre Seghers, 1951), 9-12.
——. "Réponse à Depestre Poète haïtien (Eléments d'un art poétique)", *Présence Africaine* 1-2 (1955): 114-116.
——. *Lettre à Maurice Thorez*. 2d. ed. (Paris: Présence Africaine, 1956).
——. *Ferrements: poèmes* (Paris: Editions du Seuil, 1960).
——. *La tragédie du roi Christophe* (Paris: Présence Africaine, 1963).
Céspedes, Diógenes. *Escritos criticos* (Santo Domingo: Editora Cultural Dominicana, 1976).
——. *Lenguaje y poesía en Santo Domingo en el siglo XX* (Santo Domingo: Editora Universitaria UASD, 1985).
Chamberlin, J. Edward. *Come Back to Me My Language: Poetry and the West Indies* (Illinois: University of Illinois Press, 1993).
Chamoiseau, Patrick. *Eloge de la créolité* [with Bernabé and Confiant] (Paris: Gallimard, 1989).
Chamoiseau, Patrick and Raphäel Confiant. *Lettres créoles. Tracées antillaises et continentales de la littérature 1635-1975* (Paris: Hatier, 1991).
——. "Reflections on Maryse Condé's *Traversée de la mangrove*", *Callaloo* 14.2 (1991): 389-395.
——. *Texaco* (Paris: Gallimard, 1992).
Chancy, Myriam J. A. *Searching for Safe Spaces: Afro-Caribbean Women Writers in Exile* (Philadelphia: Temple University Press, 1997).
Chang, Victor L. "The Historical Novels of H.G. De Lisser". In McWatt, 12-17.
Chapman, Charles E. *History of Spain* (New York: The Free Press, 1965).
Charles, Christophe. *La poésie feminine haïtienne: histoire et anthologie de Virginie Sampeur à nos jours* (Port-au-Prince, Haiti: Editions Choucoune, 1980).
Chauvet, Marie Vieux. *Fille d'Haïti* (Paris: Fasquelle, 1954).
——. *Le danse sur le volcan* (Paris: Plon, 1957).
——. *Fonds de Nègres* (Port-au-Prince: Henri Deschamps, 1960).
——. *Amour, colère et folie* (Paris: Gallimard, 1968).
Chee, Tham Seong, Ed. *Essays on Literature and Society in Southwest Asia* (Singapore: Singapore University Press, 1981).
Chevrier, Jacques. *Littérature négre: Afrique, Antilles, Madagascar*. 2nd. ed. (Paris: Armand Colin, 1974).
Cicero, Marcus Tullius. *Cicero XX: De senectute, de amicitia, de divinatione*. Trans. William Armistead Falconer. The Loeb Classical Library. (Cambridge, Mass.: Harvard University Press, 1979).
The Cloud of Unknowing. Trans. Ira Progroff (New York: The Julian Press, 1957).
Clark, Vèvè A. "I Have Made Peace with My Island: An Interview with Maryse Condé", *Callaloo* 12.1 (1989): 86-133.
Cline, Thomas. "On Reconstructing A Political Economy of the Caribbean". In Meeks and Lindahl, 498-520.
Clüver, Claus. "Third-World Literatures in the Canon of Undergraduate Curricula", *ACLA Newsletter* 17.2 (1986): n.p.

Coates, Carrol F. "Introduction", *The Festival of the Greasy Pole*, by René Depestre. Trans. Carrol F. Coates (Charlottesville and London: University of Virginia Press, 1990), xv-li.

Cobham, Rhonda, and Merle Collins, Eds. *Watchers and Seekers: Creative Writing by Black Women* (New York: Peter Bedrick Books, 1988).

Cocco de Filippis, Daisy. "Introduction", *Del desconsuelo al compromiso/From Desolation to Compromise: Bilingual Anthology of the Poetry of Aida Cartagena Portalatín*. Ed. Daisy Cocco de Filippis. Trans. Emma Jane Robinett and Daisy Cocco de Filippis (Santo Domingo: Editora Taller, 1988). 9-17.

——. Ed. *Sin otro profeta que su canto: Antología de poesía escrita por dominicanas* (Santo Domingo: Editora Taller, 1988).

Coin, Jeannette Bercovici. "Social Aspects of Black Poetry in Luis Palés Matos, Nicolás Guillén, and Manuel del Cabral". Diss. New York University, 1976.

Cobb, Martha. *Harlem, Haiti, and Havana* (Washington: Three Continents Press, 1979).

——. "Redefining the Definitions in Afro-Hispanic Literature", *CLA Journal* 27.2 (1972): 147-159.

Collins, Merle. *Angel* (Seattle: The Seal Press, 1988; new and revised edition Leeds: Peepal Tree Press, 2010).

Colón Zayas, Eliseo, Ed. *Literatura del Caribe* (Madrid: Editorial Playor, 1984).

Comitas, Lambros. *The Complete Caribbeana 1900-1975*. 4 vols. (New York: KTO Press, 1977).

Concatti, Rolando. "Valeurs Chrétiennes et Révolution", *Christianisme et révolution*. Ed. J. Neffa and J. Costa (Paris: Lettre, 1968), 63-69.

Condé, Maryse. "Literature of the French Caribbean", *Latin America and the Caribbean Handbook*. Ed. Claudio Veliz (New York: Praeger, 1968). 786-788.

——. "Autour d'une littérature antillaise", *Présence Africaine* 81 (1972): 170-176.

——. Ed. *Le roman antillais*. 2 vols. (Paris: Fernand Nathan Editeur, 1977).

——. Ed. *La poésie antillaise* (Paris: Fernand Nathan Editeur, 1977).

——. *La parole des femmes: Essai sur des romancières des Antilles de langue française* (Paris: Editions L'Harmattan, 1979).

——. *Traversée de la mangrove*. (Paris: Mercure de France, 1989).

——. *I Tituba, Black Witch of Salem*. Trans. Richard Philcox. Foreword by Angela Davis. Afterword by Ann Armstrong Scarboro (Charlottesville and London: University Press of Virginia, CARAF Books, 1992).

——. "Order, Disorder, Freedom, and the West Indian Writer", *Yale French Studies* 83 (1993): 121-135.

——. Condé, Maryse and Francoise Pfaff. *Entretiens avec Maryse Condé: suivis d'une bibliographie complete* (Paris: Editions Karthala, 1993).

Conde, Pedro, Ed. *Antología informal* (Santo Domingo: Editora Nacional, 1970).

——. "Dos décadas de poesía dominicana (1965-1985)", *Impacto Socialista* 2da. Etapa. 1.2 (1985): 47-53.

Confiant, Raphäel. *Eloge de la créolité* [with Chamoiseau and Bernabé] (Paris. Gallimard, 1989).

Confiant, Raphäel and Patrick Chamoiseau. *Lettres créoles. Tracées antillaises et continentales de la littérature 1635-1975* (Paris: Hatier, 1991).

Contín y Aybar, Pedro René, Ed. *Antología poética dominicana* (Santiago: Editorial El Diario, 1943).

——. Ed. *Antología poética dominicana* (Ciudad Trujillo: Librería Dominicana, 1951).

Conway, Dennis. "The Caribbean Diaspora". In Hillman and D'Agostino, 333-353.

Cortanze, Gérard de. "La solitude du poète de fond", *Le Nouvel Observateur* 12-18 Jan. 1981: n.p.

Corzani, Jack. *La littérature des Antilles-Guyane Françaises*. 6 vols. (Fort-de-France: Editions Emile Desormeaux, 1978).

——. "Guadaloupe et Martinique: La difficile voie de la Négritude et de l' Antillanité", *Présence Africaine* 76 (1970): 16-42.

Couffon, Claude. *René Depestre* (Paris: Editions Seghers, 1986).

Coulthard, G.R. *Raza y color en la literatura antillana* (Sevilla: Escuela de Estudios Hispanoamericanos de Sevilla, 1958).

——. *Race and Colour in Caribbean Literature* (New York: Oxford University Press, 1962).

——. Ed. *Caribbean Literature: An Anthology* (London: University of London Press, 1966).

——. "Edward Brathwaite y el neo-africanismo antillano", *Cuadernos Americanos* 184.5 (1972): 170-177.

Crassweller, Robert D. *The Caribbean Community: Changing Societies and U.S. Policy* (New York: Council on Foreign Relations/Praeger Publishers, 1972).

Creighton, Al. "Commoner and King: Contrasting Linguistic Performances in the Dialogue of the Dispossessed". In McWatt, 55-68.

Cros, Edmond. "Effets sur la génétique textuelle de la situation marginalisée du sujet: Eléments pour une synthèse", *Imprévue* 1 (1980/1): 23-30.

Cruickshank, John. *Albert Camus and the Literature of Revolt* (London: Oxford University Press, 1960).

Cruz-Malavé, Arnaldo. "La historia y el bolero en *Sólo cenizas hallarás (Bolero)*", *Revista Iberoamericana* 54. 142 (1988): 63-72.

Cudjoe, Selwyn. *Resistance and Caribbean Literature* (Athens: Ohio University Press, 1980).

——. *Caribbean women writers : essays from the first international conference* (Wellesley: Calaloux Publications, 1990).

Cuesta, José Enamorado. *El imperialismo y la revolución en el Caribe*. 3rd. ed. (Río Piedras: Ediciones Puerto, 1974).

Culler, Jonathan. *On Deconstruction* (Ithaca: Cornell University Press, 1982).

Cumberland, Richard. *The West Indian. Eighteenth Century Plays*. Ed. John Hampden (London: Everyman Library, 1928,1964).

Cuza Male, Belkis. "My Mother's Homeland". In Brown and McWatt, 191.

Dabydeen, Cyril. *The Wizard Swami* (Leeds: Peepal Tree Press,1989).

——. Review of *Middle Passages* by Kamau Brathwaite, *World Literature Today* 67.2 (1993): 425-26.

Dabydeen, David. "Carnival by Robert Antoni: Dances with Bulbs and Turtles", *The Independent* Online, 19 May 2006.

——. *Coolie Odyssey*. Excerpt in Brown and McWatt, 299-303.

Dalton, Roque et al. [1969]. *El intelectual y la sociedad*. 4th ed. Colección Mínima 28 (México, D. F.: Siglo XXI Editores, 1985).

Darío, Rubén. *Poesía* (Caracas: Biblioteca Ayacucho, 1977).

Darwin, Charles. *The Descent of Man*. Rev. ed. (New York: Merrill and Baker, 1874).

Das, Mahadai. "They Came in Ships", *A Leaf in His Ear: Collected Poems* (Leeds: Peepal Tree Press, 2010), 25-27.

Dash, J. Michael. "Marvelous Realism – The Way Out of Négritude", *Black Images* 3.1 (1974): 81-95.

——. "Towards a West Indian Literary Aesthetics – The Example of Aimé Césaire", *Black Images* 3.1 (1974): 21-28.

——. "Edward Brathwaite", *West Indian Literature*. Ed. Bruce King (Hamden, Connecticut: Archon Books, 1979), 210-227.

——. *Literature and Ideology in Haiti: 1915-1961* (Totowa, New Jersey: Barnes & Noble Books, 1981).

——. "The French Connection", *Bim* 17.66/67 (1983): 110-115.

——. Rev. of *The Visibility Trigger* and *Jah Music* by Edward Kamau Brathwaite, *Journal of West Indian Literature* 1.2 (1987): 87-90.

——. "The World and the Word: French Caribbean Writing in the Twentieth Century", *Callaloo* 11.1 (1988): 112-130.

——. *Haiti and the United States: National Stereotypes and the Literary Imagination* (New York: St. Martin's Press, 1988).

——. "Exile and Recent Literature", *A History of Literature in the Caribbean*. Volume I. Hispanic and Francophone Regions. Ed. A James Arnold (Amsterdam and Philadelphia: John Benjamins Publishing Company, 1994), 451-461.

Dathorne, O.R., Ed. *Caribbean Narrative* (London: Heinemann, 1966).

——. Ed. *Caribbean Verse* (London: Heinemann, 1967).

——. *Dark Ancestor: The Literature of the Black Man in the Caribbean* (Baton Rouge: Louisiana University Press, 1981).

Davies, Carole Boyce and Fido, Elaine. Eds. *Out of the Kumbla: Caribbean Women and Literature* (Trenton, N.J.: Africa World Press, 1990).

——. *Black Women, Writing, and Identity: Migrations of the Subject* (London and New York: Routledge, 1994).

Davis, Lisa. "Revolución socialista en las antillas: *Cuando amaban las tierras comuneras* del dominicano Pedro Mir", *Latin American Fiction Today*. Ed. Rose S. Minc (Montclair: Hispamérica/Montclair State College, 1979), 179-184.

Davis, Martha Ellen. *La otra ciencia: el vodú dominicano como religión y medicina populares* (Santo Domingo: Editora de La UASD, 1987).

Dawes, Kwame. "Liminal". In Brown and McWatt, 332-333.

——. Ed. *Wheel and Come Again: An Anthology of Reggae Poetry* (Leeds: Peepal Tree Press, 1998).

——. *Natural Mysticism: Towards A New Reggae Aesthetic in Caribbean Literature* (Leeds: Peepal Tree Press, 1999).

——. Ed. *Talk Yuh Talk: Interviews with Anglophone Caribbean Poets* (Charlottesville and London: University Press of Virginia, 2001).

Dawes, Neville. *Prolegomena to Caribbean Literature* (Kingston: Institute of Jamaica, 1977).
——. *The Last Enchantment* (London: MacGibbon and Kee, 1960. Reprinted Leeds: Peepal Tree Press, 2009).
——. *Fugue and Other Writing* (Leeds: Peepal Tree Press, 2012).
Dayan, Joan. Introduction. *A Rainbow for the Christian West*, by René Depestre. Trans. Joan Dayan (Amherst: University of Massachusetts, 1977), 1-106.
——. "René Depestre and the Symbiosis of Poetry and Revolution", *Modern Language Studies*. 10.1 (1979/80): 75-81.
——. "The Figure of Negation: Some Thoughts on a Landscape by Césaire", *The French Review* 56.3 (1983): 411-23.
——. "*Halleluyah for a Garden Woman*: The Caribbean Adam and His Pretext", *The French Review* 59.4 (1986): 581-95.
——. "Writers and the Gods: Vodoun in the Haitian Imigination", MLA Convention. New Orleans, Louisiana. Dec. 29, 1988.
——. "The Beat and the Bawdy", *The Nation*, 9 Apr. 1988: 504-07.
——. "Caribbean Cannibals and Whores", *Raritan* 9.2 (1989): 45-67.
——. "Vodou, or the Voice of the Gods", *Raritan* 10.3 (1991): 32-57.
——. "Reading Women in the Caribbean: Marie Chauvet's *Love, Anger, and Madness*", *Displacements: Women, Tradition, Literatures in French*. Ed. Joan DeJean and Nancy K. Miller (Baltimore and London: Johns Hopkins University Press, 1991), 228-253.
——. "Playing Caliban: Césaire's *Tempest*", *Arizona Quarterly* 48.4 (1992): 125-45
——. "France Reads Haiti: An Interview with René Depestre", *Yale French Studies* 83 (1993): 136-153.
——. "France Reads Haiti: René Depestre's *Hadriana dans tous me rêves*", *Yale French Studies* 83 (1993): 154-175.
D'Costa, Jean. "The Poetry of Edward Brathwaite", *Jamaica Journal* 2.3. (1968): 24-26.
Debrot, Cola. "Literature of the Netherlands Antilles", *Panorama das literaturas das Americas*. Ed. Joaquin Montezuma Carvalho. Vol. 4 (Angola: Ediçâo do Municipio de Nova Lisboa, 1963), 1897-1935.
Degras, Priska. "Le bestiaire fabuleux dans *Un arc-en-ciel pour l'Occident chrétien* de René Depestre", *Littératures insulaires: Caraïbes et Mascareignes* (Paris: Editions L'Harmattan, 1983), 67-81.
Deive, Carlos Esteban. *El indio, el negro y la vida tradicional dominicana* (Santo Domingo: Museo del Hombre Dominicano, 1978).
——. *Vodú y magia en Santo Domingo*. 2da. ed. (Santo Domingo: Museo del Hombre Dominicano, 1979).
De Jesús, Dionisio. "Entrevista a Pedro Mir", *Extensión* 4 (1982): 83-85.
De Lisser, H.G. *Revenge: A Tale of Old Jamaica* (Kingston: Gleaner Co., 1919).
Deleuze, Gilles and Félix Guatari. *Kafka: Pour une littérature mineure* (Paris: Minuit, 1975).
Dennis, Ferdinand, and Naseem Khan, Eds. *Voices of the Crossing: The Impact of Britain on Writers from Asia, the Caribbean and Africa* (London: Serpent's Tail, 2000).
Depestre, René. *Etincelles* (Port-au-Prince: Imprimerie de l'Etat, 1945).

——. *Gerbe de sang* (Port-au-Prince: Imprimerie de l'Etat, 1946).
——. *Végétation de clarté* (Paris: Pierre Séghers, 1951).
——. *Traduit du grand large* (Paris: Pierre Séghers, 1952).
——. "Lettre à Charles Dobzynski", *Optique* 18 (1955): 46-50.
——. "Réponse à Aimé Césaire: Introduction à un art poétique haïtien", *Présence Africaine* 4 (1955): 42-62.
——. "Une lettre à *Optique*", *Optique* 24 (1956): 5-6.
——. "Une Rose de vents noirs", *Présence Africaine*. 11 (1956/57): 110-115.
——. *Minerai noir* (Paris: Présence Africaine, 1957).
——. *Journal d'un animal marin* (Paris: Pierre Seghers, 1964).
——. *Un arc-en-ciel pour l'Occident chrétien* (Paris: Présence Africaine, 1966).
——. "Langston Hughes or The Hand on the Plough of Poetry", *Présence Africaine*. In English. 30.58 (1966): 184-186.
——. "El que no tiene congo", *Présence Africaine* 61 (1967): 121-132.
——. *Cantate d'Octobre à la vie et à la mort du Commandant Ernesto Che Guevara* (La Habana: Instituto del Libro, 1968).
——. *Por la revolución, por le poesía* (La Habana: Instituto del Libro, 1969).
——. "Breve historia de la literatura haitiana", *Panorama actual de la literatura latinoamericana* (Caracas: Editorial Fundamentos, 1971).
——. "Literatura antillana de expresión francesa: Guadalupe y Martinica", *Panorama actual de la literatura latinoamericana* (Caracas: Editoral Fundamentos, 1971), 348-368.
——. "Problemas de la identidad del hombre negro en las literaturas antillanas", *Influencia del Africa en las literaturas antillanas*, by Henri Bangou, René Depestre, and George Lamming (Montevideo: ILAC, 1972), 23-39.
——. *A Rainbow for the Christian West*. Trans. Jack Hirschman (Fairfax, California: The Red Hill Press, 1972).
——. *Alléluia pour une femme-jardin* (Ottawa: Leméac, Collection Francophonie Vivante, 1973).
——. *Pour la révolution, pour la poésie* (Québec: Lémeac, Collection Francophonie Vivante, 1974).
——. "El asalto al Moncada: revés victorioso de la Revolución Latinoamericana", *El asalto al Moncada y la Revolución Latinoamericana*, by René Depestre, et al. (Mexico: Editorial Nuestro Tiempo, S.A., 1975), 9-101.
——. *El palo ensebado*. Trans. Pedro de Arce (Santo Domingo: Editora Taller, 1977). Reprint of La Habana: Editorial Arte y Literatura, 1975.
——. *Poète à Cuba* (Paris: Editions Pierre Jean Oswald, 1976).
——. "Homo Papadocus", *Europe* 54.569 (1976): 56-64.
——. *A Rainbow for the Christian West*. Trans. Joan Dayan (Amherst: University of Massachusetts Press, 1977).
——. *Le mât de cocagne* (Paris: Editions Gallimard, 1979).
——. "The Bewitched Reality of Haïtian Art", *UNESCO Courier* Feb. 1979: 28-33.
——. *En état de poésie* (Paris: Les Editeurs Français Reunis, 1980).
——. "Mito e identidad en la historia del Caribe", *Casa de las Américas* 118 (1980): 38-41.
——. "Saludo y despedida a la negritud". In Moreno Fraginals, 337-62.

——. *Bonjour et adieu à la négritude* (Paris: Editions Robert Laffont, 1981).
——. "Castles in the Air: Haiti's Painters of High Spirits", *UNESCO Courier* July 1984: 36.
——. "Adresse inaugurale", *The Voice of the Writer 1984*, 23-25.
——. "Les échanges littéraires", *The Voice of the Writer 1984*. Papers from 47th International P.E.N. Congress (Tokyo: The Japan P.E.N. Club, 1986), 137-140.
——. Interview. *Le pouvoir des mots, les maux du pouvoir (Des romanciers haïtiens de l'exile),* by Jean Jonassaint (Paris: Editions de l'Arcantère, 1986), 186-211.
——. *Hadriana dans tous mes rêves* (Paris: Editions Gallimard, 1988).
——. *The Festival of the Greasy Pole*. Trans. Carrol Coates (Charlottesville: University Press of Virginia, CARAF Books, 1990).
——. *Journal d'un animal marin: Choix de poèmes 1956-1990* (Paris: Gallimard, 1990).
——. *Eros dans un train chinois* (Paris: Gallimard, 1990).
——. *Anthologie personnelle* (Paris: Actes Sud/Hubert Nyssen Editeur, 1993).
Desnoes, Edmundo. *Memories del subdesarrolo* (La Habana: Ediciones Unión, 1965).
Dévèze, Michel. *Antilles, Guyanes, La mer des Caraïbes de 1492 à 1789* (Paris: Societé d'Edition d'Enseignement Supérieur, 1977).
Diccionario Enciclopédico Dominicano (Santo Domingo: Sociedad Editorial Dominicana, 1988).
Dictionary of Comparative Religion. Ed. S. G. F. Brandon (New York: Charles Scribner's Sons, 1970).
Diop, Cheik Anta. *The African Origin of Civilization*. Trans. and ed. Mercer Cook (Chicago: Laurence Hill Books, 1974).
Dircks, Richard I. *Richard Cumberland* (Boston: Twayne Publishers, 1976).
Dolezel, Lubomire. *Occidental Poetics: Tradition and Progress* (Lincoln: University of Nebraska Press, 1990).
"The Dominican Republic", *Encyclopedia Britannica*. Micropedia. 15th ed., 1979.
Dore Cabral, Carlos. "Reflexiones sobre la identidad cultural del Caribe: El caso dominicano", *Casa de las Américas* 20.118 (1980): 75-79.
Dos Santos, Theotonio. *Imperialismo y dependencia*. 3rd. ed. (México: Ediciones Era, 1982).
Ducrot, Oswald and Tzvetan Todorov, *Encyclopedic Dictionary of the Sciences of Language*. Trans. Catherine Porter (Baltimore: Johns Hopkins University Press, 1979).
Durkheim, Emile. *The Elementary Forms of Religious Life*. Trans. Joseph Ward Swain (New York: The Free Press, 1915).
Eagleton, Terry. *Literary Theory: An Introduction* (Minneapolis: University of Minnesota Press, 1983).
Edwards, John. *Language, Society, and Identity* (Oxford: Basil Blackwell, 1985).
Eliade, Mircea. *Patterns in Comparative Religion*. Trans. Rosemary Sheed (New York: Meridian-NAL, 1963).
——. *The Quest: History and Meaning in Religion* (Chicago: University of Chicago Press, 1969).
Eliot, T.S. *Selected Essays* New Edition (New York: Harcourt, Brace & World, 1950).

——. *The Complete Poems and Plays: 1909-1950* (New York: Harcourt, Brace & World, 1971).

Elizabeth, Hector and Jean-Jacques Seymour. *Les caraïbes, des brûlots sur la mer: ABC géopolitique du bassin caribéen* (Paris, Editions Caribéennes, 1981).

Engber, Marjorie. *The Caribbean: Fiction and Poetry* (New York: Center for Inter-American Studies, 1970).

Ercilla, Alonso de. *La Araucana*. 5ta. ed. (México: Editorial Porrúa, 1979).

Esteves, Carmen and Paravasini-Gebert, Lizabeth. *Green Cane and Juicy Flotsam: Short Stories by Caribbean Women* (Rutgers University Press, 1991).

Fanon, Frantz. *Peau noire, masques blancs* (Paris: Editions du Seuil, 1952).

——. "Antillais et Africains", *Esprit* (1955): 263-268.

Ferdinand, Joseph. "The New Political Statement in Haitian Fiction", in Luis, *Voices from Under*, 1984, 127-146.

Fernández Fragoso, Victor. "De la noche a la muchedumbre: Los cantos épicos de Pedro Mir", Diss. University of Connecticut, 1978.

Fernández-Marcané, Leonardo, Ed. *Cuentos del Caribe* (Madrid: Editorial Playor, 1978).

Fernández Moreno, César, Ed. *América Latina en su literatura* (México-Paris: Siglo XXI-UNESCO, 1972).

Fernández Olmos, Margarita. "La narrativa dominicana contemporánea", *Revista Iberoamericana* 54.142 (1988): 73-87.

Fernández Olmos, Margarite, and Lizabeth Paravisini-Gebert, Eds. *Remaking a Lost Harmony: Stories from the Hispanic Caribbean* (Fredonia, N.Y.: White Pine Press, 1995).

Fernández Retamar, Roberto, Ed. *Poemas de una isla y dos pueblos: Jacques Roumain, Pedro Mir y Jacques Viau* (La Habana: Casa de las Américas, Colección La Honda, 1974).

——. *Para una teoría de la literatura hispanoamericana*. 4ta. ed. (La Habana: Editorial Pueblo y Educación, 1984).

Fernández Spencer, Antonio, Ed. *Nueva poesía dominicana* (Madrid: Ediciones Cultura Hispánica, 1953).

Ferreira, Manuel, Ed. *No reino de Caliban: Antologia panorâmica da poesía africana de expressâo portuguesa*. Vol. 1. (Lisboa: Seara Nova, 1975. 3 vols.).

Ferrer Gutiérrez, Virgilio. *Luperón: brida y espuela* (La Habana: Carasa y Ca., 1940).

Fido, Elaine Savory. "Spectrum and Prism", *Bim* 18.69 (1985): 73-78.

Figueroa, John, Ed. *Caribbean Voices*. 2 vols. [1971] (New York: Robert B. Luce Co., 1973).

——. "Derek Walcott's 'Poopa, Da' Was a Fête!' and Evan Jones's 'Lament of the Banana Man'". In Baugh 149-152.

Finke, Wayne H., Trans. "The Hurricane Neruda", by Pedro Mir. *Anthology of Contemporary Latin American Literature 1960-1984*. Ed. Barry J. Luby and Wayne H. Finke (Cranbury, New Jersey: Associated University Press, 1986), 233-235.

Finn, Julio. *Voices of Négritude* (London: Quartet Books, 1988).

Fitz, Earl E. *Rediscovering The New World: Inter-American Literature in a Comparative Context* (University of Iowa Press, 1991).

Fleischmann, Ulrich. "The Formation and Evolution of a Literary Discourse: One, Two or Three Literatures". In Arnold 1994, 317-338.

Forlong, J.G. R. *Faiths of Man: Encyclopedia of Religions* [1906] (New York: University Books, 1964).

Forte, Maximilian Christian, Ed. *Indigenous Resurgence in the Contemporary Caribbean: Amerindian Survival and Revival* (New York: Peter Lang, 2006).

Francisco, Ramón. *Literatura dominicana 60* (Santiago: Universidad Católica Madre y Maestra, 1969).

Franco, Jean, *An Introduction to Spanish American Literature* (Cambridge: Cambridge University Press, 1969).

Frank, André Gunder. "Economic Dependence, Class Structure, and Underdevelopment Policy", *Dependence and Underdevelopment: Latin America's Political Economy*, with James D. Cockroft et al. (Garden City, New York: Anchor Books, 1972), 19-45.

Freire, Paulo. *Cultural Action for Freedom* (Cambridge, Mass.: Harvard Educational Review, 1970).

——. *Pedagogy of the Oppressed* [1970] (New York: Continuum, 1986).

Freud, Sigmund. *The Complete Psychological Works of Sigmund Freud*. Trans. James Strachey. Vol. 6. (London: The Hogarth Press, 1960).

Galeano, Eduardo. *Open Veins of Latin America: Five Centuries of the Pillage of a Continent*. Trans. Cedric Belfrage (New York and London: Monthly Review Press, 1974).

Galván, Manuel de Jesús, *Enriquillo: leyenda histórica Dominicana* (Imprenta de Garcia Hermanos, 1882).

García Lorenzo, Orlando. "Historia y poesía en Pedro Mir", *Bohemia* 76.5 (1984): 16-19.

Garcia, Mélida, and Miguel de Camps Jimenez, Ed. *Antologia de la literatura gay en la Republica Dominicana* (Santo Domingo: Editora Manati, 2004).

Garret, Naomi. *The Renaissance of Haitian Poetry* (Paris: Présence Africaine, 1963).

Gastmann, Albert. *Historical Dictionary of the French and Netherlands Antilles* (Lanham, MD.: Scarecrow Press, 1978).

Gates, Henry Louis, Jr., Ed. *Race, Writing, and Difference* (Chicago: University of Chicago Press, 1986).

——. *The Signifying Monkey: A Theory of African American Literary Criticism* (New York: Oxford University Press, 1988).

Germani, Gino. *El concepto de la marginalidad* (Buenos Aires: Ediciones Nueva Visión, 1973).

Gibbs, James, Ed. *A Handbook for African Writers* (Oxford: Hans Zell Publishers, 1986).

Giddens, Anthony. "Jürgen Habermas". In Skinner, 121-139.

Gikandi, Simon. *Writing in Limbo: Modernism and Caribbean Literature* (Ithaca: Cornell University Press, 1992).

Gilbert, Sandra M. and Susan Gubar. *The Madwoman in the Attic: The Woman Writer and the Nineteenth Century Literary Imagination* (New Haven: Yale University Press, 1979).

Gilkes, Michael. *Racial Identity and Individual Consciousness in the Caribbean Novel* (Georgetown, Guyana: Ministry of Information and Culture, 1975).

——. *The West Indian Novel* (Boston: Twayne, 1981).
Girvan, Norman. "Reinterpreting the Caribbean". In Meeks and Lindahl, 3-23.
——. "New World's Song for Freedom", *Trinidad and Tobago Review* online. <http://www.normangirvan.info/wp-content/uploads/2020/new-world-book-launch2.pdf>
Glazier, Stephen. "The Religious Mosaic: Playful Celebration in Trinidadian Shango", *Play and Culture* (Champaign, IL: Human Kinetics Press, 1988).
——. *Caribbean Ethnicity Revisited* (New York: Gordon and Breach Science Publishers, 1985).
Glissant, Edouard. *Monsieur Toussaint* (Paris: Seuil, 1961).
——. *Le Quatrieme Siecle* (Paris: Seuil, 1964).
——. *Le discours antillais* (Paris: Editions Gallimard, 1981).
——. *Caribbean Discourse*. Trans. J. Michael Dash (Charlottesville: University Press of Virginia, CARAF Books, 1989).
Goic, Cedomil, Ed. *Historia y crítica de la literatura hispanoamericana*. 3 vols. (Barcelona: Editorial Crítica, 1988).
Gómez Gil, Orlando. *Historia crítica de la literatura hispanoamericana* (New York: Holt, Rinehart and Winston, 1968).
Gómez-Wangüermert. "La crisis dominicana", *La revolución dominicana de abril vista por Cuba*, by Antonio Riccardi, et al. [1965]. (Santo Domingo: Editora de la UASD, 1974), 75-150.
González, José Luis. *El país de cuatro pisos y otros ensayos*. 4ta. ed. (Río Piedras: Ediciones Huracán, 1984).
——. *Nueva visita al cuarto piso* (Madrid: Flamboyán, 1986).
González, José Luis and Mónica Mansour, Eds. *Poesía negra de América* (México: Ediciones Era, 1976).
González Echeverría, Roberto. "Literature of the Hispanic Caribbean", *Latin American Literary Review* 8.16 (1980): 1-20.
——. *The Voice of The Masters* (Austin: University of Texas Press, 1985).
Goodwin, K.L. "Incentive and Obliqueness in Political Poetry: Kasaipwaloa, Brathwaite, and Soyinka", *Awakened Conscience: Studies in Commonwealth Literature*. Ed. C.D. Narasimhaiah (New Delhi: Sterling Publishers, 1978). 251-260.
——. *Understanding African Poetry: A Study of Ten Poets* (London: Heinemann, 1982).
Gorky, Maxim. *Collected Works in Ten Volumes*. Vol. 10 (Moscow: Progress Publishers, 1982).
Gossman, Lionel. "History and Literature: Reproduction or Significative". In Canary and Kozicki, 3-39.
Grant, Damian. "Emerging Image: The Poetry of Edward Brathwaite", *Critical Quarterly* 12.2 (1970): 186-192.
Gratiant, Gilbert. "Place du 'créole' dans l'expression antillaise", *Présence Africaine* 14/15 (1957): 252-255.
Griffiths, Gareth. *Double Exile: African and West Indian Writing Between Cultures* (London: Marion Boyars, 1978).
"Guevara, 'Che'". Macropaedia. *Encyclopedia Britannica*. 15th ed.

Guevara, Ernesto Che *Obras escogidas: 1957-1967*. Vol. 2 (La Habana: Editorial de Ciencias Sociales, 1985).

Guérin, Daniel. *Les Antilles décolonisées* (Paris: Présence Africaine, 1956).

Guillén, Nicolás. "Nación y mestizaje", *Casa de las Américas* 6.36/7 (1966): 70-74.

——. *Antología mayor*. 2da. ed. (México: Editorial Diógenes, S.A., 1974).

——. *Obra poética*. Vol. 1. Ed. Angel Augier (La Habana: Editorial Letras Cubanas, 1980).

Guiness, Gerald. *Here and Elsewhere: Essay on Caribbean Literature* (Rio Pedras: University of Puerto Rico, 1993).

Gumperz, John J., Ed. *Language and Social Identity* (New York: Cambridge University Press, 1982).

Habekost, Christian. "Dub Poetry – Culture of Resistance", *Alternative Cultures in the Caribbean*. Ed. Thomas Bremer and Ulrich Fleischmann (Frankfurt: Vervuert Verlag, Bibliotheca Iberoamericana, 1993), 205-216.

Hall, Stuart. "Negotiating Caribbean Identities". In Meeks and Lindahl, 24-39.

Hamilton, Edith. *The Roman Way to Western Civilization* [1932] (New York: Mentor Books, 1957).

Harris, Rodney E., Norman R. Shapiro, and Micheline F. Harris Eds. *Palabres: contes et poèmes de l'Afrique noire et des Antilles* (Glenview, Illinois: Scott, Foresman and Co., 1973).

Hartwig, Robert J., "Depestre, René, *Eros dans un train chinois*", *French Review* vol 65 no. 6 (May 1992) 1077-1078.

Hastings, James, Ed. *Encyclopedia of Religion and Ethics*. Vol 12 (New York: Charles Scribner's Sons, 1908-1937). 13 vols.

Hegel, G.W. Friedrich. *The Philosophy of History*. Trans. J. Sibrie (New York: Dover Publications, 1956).

——. *Hegel on Tragedy*. Ed. Anne and Henry Paolucci (New York: Harper Torchbooks, 1962).

Henderson, Bill, Ed. *Rotten Reviews: A Literary Companion* (Harmondsworth: Penguin Books, 1987).

Henríquez Ureña, Max. *Panorama histórico de la literatura dominicana* (Rio de Janeiro: Universidad del Brasil, 1945).

——. *Panorama histórico de la literatura dominicana*. 2da. ed. Vol. 2 (Santo Domingo: Editorial Dominicana, 1966).

Henríquez Ureña, Pedro. *Seis ensayos en busca de nuestra expresión* (Buenos Aires: B.A.B.E.L./Biblioteca Argentina de Buenas Ediciones Literarias, 1928).

——. *Obra crítica*. Ed. Susana Speratti Piñero (México: Fondo de Cultura Economica, 1960).

——. *La utopía de América*. Ed. Angel Rama and Rafael Gutiérrez Girardot (Caracas: Biblioteca Ayacucho, 1978).

——. *El español en Santo Domingo*. 4ta. ed. (Santo Domingo: Editora Taller, 1982).

Herdeck, Donald E. *Caribbean Writers: Bio-Bibliographical-Critical Encyclopedia* (Washington: Three Continents Press, 1979).

Hernández de Norman, Isabel. *La novela criolla en las Antillas* (New York: Plus Ultra Educational Publishers, 1977).

Hernández Franco, Tomás. *Yelidá: Poema* (El Salvador: Sargazo, 1942).

Hernández Torres, Ruth. "Image de l'antillais dans un texte importé", *Universidades* Oct.-Dec. (1985): 99-120.

Hill, Errol. "The Emergence of a Caribbean Aesthetic", *Bim* 17.66-67 (1983): 101-109.

Hillman, Richard S. and Thomas J. D. D'Agostino, Eds. *Understanding the Contemporary Caribbean* (Boulder, London, and Kingston: Lynne Rienner Publishers and Ian Randle Publishers, 2003).

Hirschman, Jack. "Introduction", *A Rainbow for the Christian West*, by René Depestre. Trans. Jack Hirschman (Fairfax, CA: The Red Hill Press, 1972), 3-8.

Hoetink, Harry. "Race and Colour in the Caribbean", in *Caribbean Contours*, Ed. Mintz, Sidney and Price, Sally (Baltimore: Johns Hopkins University Press, 1985).

Hoffmann, Léon François. Introduction. *Georges*, by Alexandre Dumas (Paris: Editions Gallimard, 1974), 7-23.

——. *Le roman haïtien: idéologie et structure* (Québec: Editions Naamans, 1982).

——. *Haiti: Couleurs, croyances, creole* (Port au Prince: Editions H. Deschamps/ CIDHCA, 1990).

Hoffmansthal, Hugo von. *Selected Prose*. Trans. Mary Hottinger and Tania and James Stern (New York: Pantheon Books, 1952).

Hollingshead, L. "The Puerto Rican Spiritualist as Psychiatrist", *American Journal of Psychiatry*. 67 (1961): 17-22.

Holly, Marcia. "Consciousness and Authenticity: Toward a Feminist Aesthetic", *Feminist Literary Criticism*. Ed. Josephine Donovan (Lexington: University Press of Kentucky, 1975), 38-47.

Holm, John. *Pidgins and Creoles*. 2 Vols. (Cambridge: Cambridge University Press, 1989).

Homar, Susan. "La memoria del mundo en el fondo del lenguage: lengua e identidad en tres novelas del Caribe". Diss. New York University, 1982.

Homer. *The Iliad of Homer*. Trans. Richmond Lattimore [1951] (Chicago: University of Chicago Press, 1961).

Horowitz, Michael M., Ed. *Peoples and Cultures of the Caribbean: An Anthropological Reader* (New York: The Natural History Press, 1971).

Hostos, Eugenio María de. *Hostos en Santo Domingo*. Ed. Emilio Rodríguez Demorizi. Vol. 2. (Santo Domingo: J.R. vda. García, 1942).

Hoving, Isabel. *In Praise of New Travellers: Reading Caribbean Migrant Women Writers* (Stanford: Stanford University Press, 2001).

Howes, Barbara, Ed. *From the Green Antilles: Writings of the Caribbean* (New York: McMillan, 1966).

Hoy, David. "Jacques Derrida". In Skinner, 41-64.

Hughes, Langston and Arna Bontemps, Eds. *The Poetry of the Negro 1746-1949* (New York: Doubleday, 1949).

Hughes, Langston. "The Negro Artist and the Racial Mountain", *The Black Aesthetic*. Ed. Addison Gayle, Jr. (Garden City, New York: Doubleday & Company, 1971), 175-181.

Hugo, Victor. *Les Contemplations*. Nouvelle Edition. Ed. Joseph Vianey (Paris: Librairie Hachette, 1922).

Hulme, Peter. *Colonial Encounters: Europe and Native Caribbean* (London: Methuen, 1986).

Incháustegui Cabral, Héctor. *Escritores y artistas dominicanos* (Santiago: Universidad Católica Madre y Maestra, 1977).

——. *De literatura dominicana siglo XX* (Santiago: Universidad Católica Madre y Maestra, 1968).

Irele, Abiola. *The African Experience in Literature and Ideology* (London: Heinemann, 1981).

Irish, James. "A Cuban Criollo and the Afro-Haitian World", *Savacou* 1 (1970): 98-107.

Ismond, Patricia. "Walcott versus Brathwaite", *Caribbean Quarterly* 17.3-4 (1971): 54-71.

Jabra, Jabra Ibrahim. "Modern Arabic Literature and the West", *Critical Perspectives on Modern Arabic Literature*. Ed. Issa J. Boullata (Washington: Three Continents Press, 1980), 7-22.

Jahn, Janheinz. "The Contribution of the West Indies to Poetry", *Bim* 6.21 (1954): 16-22.

——. *Muntu: An Outline of the New African Culture*. Trans. Marjorie Greene (New York: Grove Press, 1961).

James, C.L.R. *The Black Jacobins*. 2nd ed. (New York: Vintage Books, 1963).

James, Conrad. "Introduction". In James and Perivolaris, 1-8.

James, Conrad, and John Perivolaris, Eds. *The Cultures of the Hispanic Caribbean* (London and Oxford: Macmillan Caribbean, Warwick University Caribbean Studies, 2000).

James, Cynthia. "Woman Descendant". In Brown and McWatt, 233-234.

James, Louis. Rev. of *Rights of Passage*, by Edward Kamau Brathwaite, *Caribbean Quarterly* 13.1 (1967): 38-41.

——. Ed. *The Islands in Between* (London: Oxford University Press, 1968).

——. "Caribbean Poetry in English – Some Problems", *Savacou* 2 (1970): 78-99.

——. *Caribbean Literature in English* (London and New York: Longman, Longman Literature in English Series, 1999).

James, Winston. "New Light on Afro-Caribbean Social Mobility in New York City: A Critique of the Sowell Thesis". In Meeks and Lindhal, 395-427.

Jameson, Fredric. *The Prison-House of Language* (Princeton: Princeton University Press, 1974).

Jonassaint, Jean. Interview with René Depestre. In *Le pouvoir des mots, les maux du pouvoir* [*Des romanciers haïtiens de l'exil*]. (Paris: Editions de L'Arcantère, 1986), 186-211.

Jones, Bridget. "Comrade Eros: The Erotic Vein in the Writing of René Depestre", *Caribbean Quarterly* 27.4 (1981): 21-30.

Jones, Edward A. *Voices of Negritude* (Valley Forge: Judson Press, 1971).

Josef, Bella. *Historia da literatura hispanoamericana*. 2a. ed. (Rio de Janeiro: Francisco Alvez, 1982).

Juminer, Bertène. *Les bâtards* (Paris: Présence Africaine, 1961).

Kelly, Joan. *Women, History & Theory: The Essays of Joan Kelly* (Chicago and London: The University of Chicago Press, 1984).

Kennedy, Ellen Conroy. Trans. and ed. *The Negritude Poets* (New York: Thunder's Mouth Press, 1989).
Kesteloot, Lilyan. *Les écrivains noirs de langue française: Naissance d'une littérature*. 4th ed. (Brussels: Université Libre de Bruxelles, 1963).
——. Ed. *Anthologie négro-Africaine: Panorama critique des prosateurs, poètes et dramaturgues noirs du xxe siècle* (Verviers: Marabout Université, 1967).
Khan, Ismith. "Image and Self-Image In West Indian Writing". In Bahadur Singh, 45-62.
——. *The Obeah Man* (London: Hutchinson, 1964).
Khemraj, Harischandra. *Cosmic Dance* (Leeds: Peepal Tree Press, 1994).
Kincaid, Jamaica. *A Small Place* (New York: Plume, 1989).
King, Cameron and Louis James. "In Solitude for Company: The Poetry of Derek Walcott". In James 1968, 86-99.
King, Bruce. *The New English Literatures* (New York: St. Martin's Press, 1980).
Kirk, G.S. and J.E. Raven. *The Presocratic Philosophers* [1959] (Cambridge: Cambridge University Press, 1969).
Knight, Franklin. *The Caribbean: Genesis of a Fragmented Nationalism* (New York: Oxford University Press, 1978).
Knight, Franklin W. and Colin A. Palmer, Eds. *The Modern Caribbean* (Chapel Hill: University of North Carolina Press, 1979).
Knight, Vere. "Edouard Glissant: the Novel as History Rewritten", *Black Images* 3.1 (1974): 64-79.
——. "French-Caribbean Literature: A Literature of Commitment", *Revista Interamericana* 5.1 (1975): 67-92.
Kootry, Maria K. "Three West Indian Poets", *Pan-Africanist* (June 1977): 25-27.
Kundera, Milan. "The Umbrella, the Night World, and the Lonely Moon", *The New York Review of Books*, 19 December 1991: 46-50.
Kurlansky, Mark. *A Continent of Islands: Searching for a Caribbean Destiny* (Reading: Addison Wesley, 1992).
Labastida, Jaime, Ed. *Viaje a la muchedumbre*. 2da. ed., by Pedro Mir (México: Siglo XXI Editores, 1975).
Lacan, Jacques. "The Insistence of the Letter in the Unconscious", *The Structuralists: From Marx to Lévi-Strauss*. Ed. Richard and Fernande De George (New York: Anchor Books, 1972), 287-323.
Larcrosil, Michèle. *Demain Jab-Herma* (Paris: Gallimard, 1967).
Laguna-Díaz, Elpidio. "*Cuando amaban las tierras comuneras*: Visión mitopoética de una historia", *Hispamérica* 31 (1987): 15-32.
Laleau, Léon. "Trahison". In *Berrou and Pompilus*, Vol. II: 504.
Lambert, Calvin S. *Selected Poems of a West Indian* (London: The Fortune Press, 1940).
Lamming, George. *In the Castle of My Skin* (London: Michael Joseph, 1953).
——. *The Emigrants* (London: Michael Joseph, 1954).
——. "The Negro Writer and his World", *Présence Africaine* 8/9/10 (1956): 318-325.
——. *Of Age and Innocence* (London: Michael Joseph, 1958).
——. *Season of Adventure* (London: Michael Joseph, 1960).

——. *The Pleasures of Exile* (London: Michael Joseph, 1960).
——. *Natives of My Person* (London: Longman, 1972).
——. "The Peasant Roots of the West Indian Novel". In Baugh, 24-26.
——. *Coming, Coming Home: Conversations II* (Philipsburg, St. Martin: House of Nehesi Publishers, 2000).
Laranjeira, Pires. *Literatura calibanesca* (Porto: Ediçôes Afrontamento, 1985).
Lawton, David. "The Question of Creolization in Puerto Rico", *Pidginization and Creolization of Languages*. Ed. Dell Hymes (Cambridge: Cambridge University Press, 1971), 193-94.
Lawrence, Kemlin. "Trinidad English", *Caribbean Quarterly* 17.2 (1977): 36-39.
Lebrón Saviñon, Mariano. *Historia de la cultura dominicana*. Vol. 4. (Santo Domingo: Universidad Nacional Pedro Henríquez Ureña, 1982).
Leiner, Jacqueline. "René Depestre ou du surréalisme comme moyen d'accès à l`identité haïtienne dans *Un arc-en-ciel-pour l'Occident chrétien*", *Romanische Forschungen* 89.1 (1977): 37-50.
——. *Imaginaire-Language Identité culturelle Négritude* (Tubingen: Günter Narr Verlag, 1980).
Lenin, Vladimir Ilich. *Lenin on Language* (Moscow: Raduga Publishers, 1983).
——. *La literatura y el arte* (Moscú: Editorial Progreso, 1979).
Le Page, R.B. "Dialect in West Indian Literature". In Baugh, 123-129.
Levilain, Guy Viêt. "The Francophone Antilles and The Caribbean Struggle for Liberation". In Rodríguez and Zimmerman, 157-168.
——. *Cultural Identity, Négritude and Decolonization: The Haitian Situation in Light of the Socialist Humanism of Jacques Roumain and René Depestre*. Occasional Paper No. 29 (New York: American Institute for Marxist Studies, 1978).
Lévi-Strauss, Claude. *The Way of the Masks*. Trans. Sylvia Modeski (Seattle: University of Washington Press, 1982).
Lewis, Gordon K. *Main Currents in Caribbean Thought: The Historical Evolution of Caribbean Society in Its Ideological Aspects*, 1492-1900 (Lincoln: University of Nebraska Press, 1983).
Lieberman, Laurence. "A Confluence of Poets", *Poetry* 114.1 (1969): 40-58.
Lima, Wilson. "Recherche de l'Antillanité", *Présence Africaine* 76 (1970): 43-62.
Linkhorn, Renée. "Depestre, René: *Journal d'un animal marin*", *French Review*, vol. 65, no. 5 (April 1992): 852-853.
Lionnet, Françoise. *Autobiographical Voices: Race, Gender, Self-Portraiture* (Ithaca: Cornell University Press, 1989).
Livingston, James T., Ed. *Caribbean Rhythms: The Emerging English Literatures of the West Indies* (New York: Washington Square Press, 1974).
Lloréns Torres, Luis. *Obras completas*. Vol. 1. (San Juan: Instituto de Cultura Puertorriqueña, 1967).
Lloyd, David. *Nationalism and Minor Literature: James Clarence Mangan and the Emergence of Irish Cultural Nationalism* (Berkeley: University of California Press, 1987).
Lomax, Alan and Raoul Abdul, Eds. *3000 Years of Black Poetry* (New York: Dodd, Mead & Co., 1970).
López-Morales, Humberto. "The History of Literary Language". In Arnold 1994. 9-23.

Losada, Alejandro. *La literatura en la sociedad de América Latina: Perú y el Río de la Plata* (Frankfurt: Verlag Klaus Dieter Vervuert, 1983).

Lovejoy, Arthur O. *The Great Chain of Being: A Study of the History of an Idea* (Cambridge, Massachusetts: Harvard University Press, 1936).

Lowe, Jan. "No More Lonely Londoners", *Small Axe* 9 (March 2001): 166-180.

Lucie-Smith, Edward. "West Indian Writing", *The London Magazine* July 1968: 96-102.

Luis, William, Ed. *Voices from Under: Black Narrative in Latin America and the Caribbean* (Westport, Conn.: Greenwood Press, 1984).

Macaulay, Thomas Babington. *Macaulay: Prose and Poetry*. Ed. G. M. Young (Cambridge, Massachusetts: Harvard University Press, 1952).

Mahabir, Noor Kumar. *The Still Cry* (Tacarigua, Trinidad: Calaloux Publications, 1985).

Mahabir, Winston. "Our Diaspora: Sowers and Seed". In Bahadur Singh, 63-84.

Malcolm X. *Malcolm X Speaks*. Ed. George Breitman (New York: Grove Press, 1966).

Maldonado-Denis, Manuel. Rev. of *Viaje a la muchedumbre*, by Pedro Mir. *Claridad* 8 July 1973: 22.

Mañach, Jorge. "Literary Homogeneity in the Caribbean". In Wilgus, 213-215.

Mansour, Mónica. *La poesía negrista* (México: Ediciones Era, 1973).

Manzor-Coats, Lillian. "Of Witches and Other Things: Maryse Condé's Challenges to Feminist Discourse", *World Literature Today,* Vol. 67, No. 4, (Autumn, 1993): 737-744.

Maran, René. *Batouala* [1922]. Trans. Barbara Beck and Alexandre Mboukou (London: Heinemann, 1987).

Marco, Joaquín. *Literatura hispanoamericana: Del modernismo a nuestros días* (Madrid: Espasa-Calpe, 1987).

Marcuse, Herbert. "Marxism and the New Humanism: An Unfinished Revolution", *Marxism and Radical Religion*. Ed. John C. Raines and Thomas Dean (Philadelphia: Temple University Press, 1970), 5-10.

Márquez, Robert and David Arthur McMurray. Trans. and eds. *Man-Making Words: Selected Poems of Nicolás Guillén* [1972] (La Habana: Editorial Arte y Literatura, 1975).

Márquez, Robert. Introduction. *Patria o Muerte! The Great Zoo and Other Poems*, by Nicolás Guillén. Trans. Robert Márquez (New York: Monthly Review Press, 1972), 13-29.

——. Ed. *Latin American Revolutionary Poetry: A Bilingual Anthology* (New York: Monthly Review Press, 1974).

——. "Towards a Theory of Caribbean Culture and a Holistic View of the Antilles", *Process of Unity in Caribbean Society: Ideologies and Literature*. Ed. Iliana Rodriguez and Marc Zimmerman (Minneapolis: Institute for the Study of Ideologies and Literature, 1983), 96-107.

——. "Nationalism, Nation, and Ideology: Trends in the Emergence of a Caribbean Literature", *The Modern Caribbean*. Ed. Franklin W. Knight and Colin A. Palmer (Chapel Hill: University of North Carolina Press, 1989). 293-340.

——. *A World among These Islands: Essays on Literature, Race, and National Identity in Antillean America* (Amherst and Boston: University of Massachusetts Press, 2010).

Martí, José. *Obras completas*. Vol.4. (La Habana: Editorial Nacional, 1963).

——. *Páginas escogidas*. Vol.2. Ed. Roberto Fernández Retamar (La Habana: Instituto del Libro, 1971).

——. *Obras completas*. Vol. 19. (La Habana: Editorial Nacional de Cuba, 1964).

Marshall, Harold. Rev. of *Four Plays* by E.K.Brathwaite. *Bim* 10.41 (1965): 71-72.

Martinez Furé, Rogelio, Ed. and trans. *Diwán africano: Poetas de expresión francesa* (La Habana: Editorial Arte y Cultura, 1988).

Martini, Jürgen. "Literary Criticism and Aesthetics in the Caribbean I: E.K. Brathwaite", *World Literature Written in English* 24.2 (1984): 373-383.

Martz, Louis L. *The Poetry of Meditation*. 2d. ed. (New Haven: Yale University Press, 1962).

Marx, Karl. *A Contribution to the Critique of Political Economy* (New York: International Publishers, 1986). [Vol. 28 of *The Collected Works*, by Karl Marx and Frederick Engels. 50 vols.]

—— and Friedrich Engels. *On Religion* (New York: Schocken Books, 1964).

Mateo, Andrés L. *Mito y cultura en la Era de Trujillo* (Santo Domingo: Libreria La Trinitaria/Instituto del Libro, 1993).

Mateo Palmer, Margarita. *Narrativa Caribeña: Reflexiones y pronósticos* (La Habana: Editorial Pueblo y Educación, 1990).

Mathurin, Lucille. "Creole Authenticity", *Savacou* 5 (1971): 115-120.

Matos Moquete, Manuel. "Poética política en la poesía de Pedro Mir", *Revista Iberoamericana* 54.142 (1988): 199-211.

Maximin, Daniel. *L'isolé soleil* (Paris: Editions du Seuil, 1981).

——. *Lone Sun*. Trans. Clarisse Zimra (Charlottesville: University Press of Virginia, CARAF Books, 1989).

——. "Antillean Journey", *Caribbean Creolization: Reflections on the Cultural Dynamics of Language, Literature, and Identity*. Ed. Kathleen Balutansky and Marie-Agnes Sourieau (Gainesville: University Press of Florida, 1998), 13-19.

Maxwell, Marina. "Towards a Revolution in the Arts", *Savacou* 2 (1970): 19-32.

McFarlane, J.E.C. Ed. *Voices from the Summerland: An Anthology of Jamaican Poetry* (London: Fowler Wright, 1929).

——. *A Treasury of Jamaican Poetry* (London: University of London Press, 1949).

——. *A Literature in the Making* (Kingston: Pioneer Press, 1956).

McGann, Jerome. *Social Value and Poetic Acts* (Cambridge, Mass.: Harvard University Press, 1988).

McWatt, Marc A., Ed. *West Indian Literature and Its Social Context* (Cave Hill, Barbados: University of the West Indies, 1985).

——. "Edward Kamau Brathwaite", *Fifty Caribbean Writers*. Ed. Daryl Cumber Dance (New York: Greenwood Press, 1986), 58-70.

——. "The Two Faces of El Dorado: Contrasting Attitudes Towards History and Identity in West Indian Literature". In McWatt 1985, 33-47.

Meehan, Kevin, and Paul B. Miller. "Literature and Popular Culture". In Hillman and D'Agostino, 305-332.

Meeks, Brian. "On the Bump of a Revival". In Meeks and Lindahl, viii-xx.
Meeks, Brian, and Folke Lindahl, Eds. *New Caribbean Thought: A Reader* (Kingston, Jamaica: The University of West Indies Press, 2001).
Mehta, Brenda. *Diasporic (Dis) locations: Indo-Caribbean Women Writers Negotiate the 'Kala Pani'* (Kingston: University of the West Indies Press, 2004).
Melone, Thomas. *Collier de cauris (poèmes): Suivi d'une étude de Thomas Melone* (Paris: Présence Africaine, 1970).
——. "La critique littéraire et les problèmes du langage: point de vue d'un Africain", *Présence Africaine* 73 (1970): 3-19.
Melville, Pauline. "Beyond the Pale", *Daughters of Africa: An International Anthology of Words and Writings by Women of African Descent from the Ancient Egyptian to the Present*. Ed. Margaret Busby (New York: Ballantine Books, 1992). 739-743.
——. *The Migration of Ghosts* (London: Bloomsbury, 1999).
Menéndez y Pelayo, Marcelino. *Historia de la poesía hispanoamericana*. Vol. 1 (Madrid: Librería General de Victoriano Suarez, 1911).
Ménil, René. *Tracées: identité, négritude, esthétique aux Antilles* (Paris: Editions Robert Laffont, 1981).
Menneson-Rigaud, Odette. "Le role du Vaudou dans l'indépendance d'Haïti", *Présence Africaine* 17/18 (1958): 43-67.
Mercier, Roger. "La póesie des Antilles Françaises: facteurs et caractères de sa transformation", *Etudes Littéraires* 7.2 (1974): 299-306.
Merrim, Stephanie. "A Secret Idiom: The Grammar and Role of Language in *Tres Tristes Tigres*", *Latin American Literary Review* 8.16 (1980): 96-117.
Meschonnic, Henri. *Pour la poétique*. Vol. 2 (Paris: Editions Gallimard, 1973).
Métellus, Jean. *Anacoana* (Paris: Editions Hatier, 1986).
——. "La négritude et le Vaudou", *La Quinzaine Littéraire* 311 (1979): 12.
Métraux, Alfred. "Histoire du Vodou depuis la querre d'indépendance jusqu'à nos jours", *Présence Africaine* 1 (1957): 135-150.
——. *Le Vaudou Haïtien* (Paris: Editions Gallimard, 1958).
——. "Orígenes e historia de los cultos del vodú", *Casa de las Américas* 36-37 (1966): 42-62.
——. *Voodoo in Haiti*. Trans. Hugo Charteris (New York: Schocken Books, 1972).
Michel, Jean-Claude. *Les écrivains noirs et le surréalisme* (Québec: Editions Naaman, 1982).
Michener, James. *Caribbean: A Novel* (New York: Random House, 1989).
Midiohouan, Guy Ossito. *Idéologie dans la littérature négro-africaine d'expression française* (Paris: L'Harmattan, 1986).
Midgett, Douglas. "West Indian Version: Literature, History, and Identity", *Old Roots in New Lands: Historical and Anthropological Perspectives on Black Experiences in the Americas*. Ed. Anne Pescatello (Westport, Conn.: Greenwood Press, 1977), 209-242.
Miner, Earl. "Comparative Poetics: Some Theoretical and Methodological Topics for Comparative Literature". Unpublished essay, 1986. 1-31.
——. *Comparative Poetics: An Intercultural Essay on Theories of Literature* (Princeton University Press, 1990).
Mink, Louis O. "Narrative Form as a Cognitive Instrument". In Canary and Kozicki, 129-149.

Mintz, Sidney W. *Caribbean Transformations* (Chicago: Aldine Publishing Company, 1974).
——. "The Caribbean as a Socio-Cultural Area". In Horowitz, 17-46.
"Mir, Pedro." *Diccionario Enciclopédico Dominicano* (Santo Domingo: Sociedad Editorial Dominicana, 1988), 336.
Mir, Pedro. "Poemas", *Antología poética dominicana*. Ed. Pedro René Contín Aybar (Santiago: Editorial El Diario, 1943), 265-272.
——. "Poemas", *Nueva poesía dominicana*. Ed. Antonio Fernández Spencer (Madrid: Ediciones Cultura Hispánica, 1953), 231-247.
——. *Hay un país en el mundo y Seis momentos de esperanza* (Santo Domingo: Ediciones Claridad, 1962).
——. *Poemas de buen amor y a veces de fantasía* (Santo Domingo: Imprenta Nuevo Mundo, 1969).
——. "Countersong to Walt Whitman" (fragments). Trans. Didier Tisdel Jáen.
——. *Homage to Walt Whitman*. Trans. Didier Tisdel Jáen (Tuscaloosa: University of Alabama Press, 1969), 30-41.
——. *Viaje a la muchedumbre* (Santo Domingo: Ediciones Lucerna, 1971).
——. "Julia del agua." *Revista del Instituto de Cultura Puertorriqueña* 16.59 (1973):42-43.
——. "Acerca de las tentativas de unificación de la isla de Santo Domingo", *Problemas dominico-haitianos y del Caribe*, by Gérard Pierre-Charles, et al. (México: Universidad Nacional Autónoma de México, 1973), 145-178.
——. "Lo rubendariano conceptual en la muerte de Neruda", *La Palabra y el Hombre* 9 (1974): 9-13.
——. *Apertura a la estética* (Santo Domingo: Editora de la UASD, 1974).
——. *El gran incendio: los balbuceos americanos del capitalismo mundial*. 2da. ed. (Santo Domingo: Ediciones de Taller, 1974).
——. "Amen de Mariposas/Amen to Butterflies". Trans. Roberto Marquez. *Latin American Revolutionary Poetry: A Bilingual Anthology*. Ed. Roberto Marquez (New York: Monthly Review Press, 1974), 210-231.
——. *Viaje a la muchedumbre*. 2da. ed. Ed. Jaime Labastida (México: Siglo XXI Editores, 1975).
——. *El huracán Neruda: Elegía con una canción desesperada* (Santo Domingo: Ediciones de Taller, 1975).
——. *Las dos patrias de Santo Domingo: Tesis acerca de la historia de la división política de la isla en dos naciones* (Santo Domingo: Editora Cultural, S.A, 1975).
——. *La gran hazaña de Límber y después otoño* (Santo Domingo: Ediciones Sargazo, 1977).
——. *Cuando amaban las tierras comuneras* (México: Siglo XXI Editores, 1978).
——. *Tres leyendas de colores: Ensayo de interpretación de las tres primeras revoluciones del Nuevo Mundo*. 2da. ed. (Santo Domingo: Editora Taller, 1978).
——. "Selected Poems from *Concierto de esperanza para la mano izquierda*". Trans. Donald Walsh. *Latin American Literary Review* 6.12 (1978): 106-117.
——. *Fundamentos de teoría y crítica de arte* (Santo Domingo: Editora de la UASD, 1979).
——. *José Martí para la poesía y el eco para los pueblos* (Santo Domingo: n.pub., 1981).

——. *Buen viaje, Pancho Valentín! (memorias de un marinero)* (Santo Domingo: Ediciones de Taller, 1981).
——. *La noción de período en la historia dominicana*. 3 vols. (Santo Domingo: Editora de la UASD, 1981-1983).
——. *Hay un país en el mundo y otros poems* (Santo Domingo: Ediciones de Taller, 1982).
——. *Las raíces dominicanas de la Doctrina de Monroe*. 2da. ed. (Santo Domingo: Ediciones de Taller, 1984).
——. "The Hurricane Neruda". Trans. Wayne H. Finke. *Anthology of Contemporary Latin American Literature 1960-1984*. Ed. Barry J. Luby and Wayne H. Finke (Cranbury, N. J.: Associated University Press, 1986), 233-235.
——. *Historia del hambre: Sus orígenes en la historia dominicana* (Santo Domingo: Editora Corripio, 1987).
——. *La estética del soldadito* (Santo Domingo: Editora Universitaria-UASD, 1991).
——. *Countersong to Walt Whitman and Other Poems*. Trans. Jonathan Cohen and Donald D. Walsh (Washington, D. C.: Azul Editions, 1993).
——. *El lapicida de los ojos morados* (Santo Domingo: Biblioteca Taller, 1993).
——. *Primeros versos* (Santo Domingo: Biblioteca Taller, 1993).
Mir, Pedro, et al. "Conversan los poetas..." *La Gaceta Literaria de Auditorio* 17 (10 January 1972): 1-3.
Moeller, Charles. *Littérature du XX siècle et christianisme*. 5 vols. (Paris: Editions Casterman, 1953-75).
——. *Literatura del siglo XX y cristianismo*. 5 vols. Trans. Valentín García Yebra. (Madrid: Editorial Gredos, 1955-75).
Mollica, Maria-Francesca. "Introduction" to Edward Kamau Brathwaite, *Le detonateur de visibilite / The Visibility Trigger* (Belgium. Cahiers de Louvain, 1986), 5-22.
Monar, Rooplall. *Backdam People* (Leeds: Peepal Tree Press, 1986).
——. *Janjhat* (Leeds: Peepal Tree Press, 1989).
Montas, Lucien. "René Depestre et les problèmes de la poésie nationale", *Optique* 18 (1955): 44-52.
Moore, Gerald. "Mots anglais, vies africaines", *Présence Africaine* 2 (1965): 116-126.
——. *The Chosen Tongue: English Writing in the Tropical World* [1969] (New York: J. & J. Harper, 1970).
——. Rev. of *Islands* by E.K.Brathwaite, *Bim* 13.51 (1970): 186-189.
——. "The Language of West Indian Poetry". In Baugh, 130-136.
Morales, Jorge Luis, Ed. *La poesía afroantillana y negrista*. 2da. ed. (Río Piedras: Editorial Universitaria, 1981).
Moran, Ronal. *Louis Simpson* (New York: Twayne Publishers, 1972).
Mordecai, P. and Wilson, B. *Her True True Name* (London: Heinemann Caribbean Writers Series, 1989).
Moreno Fraginals, Manuel, Ed. *Africa en América Latina* (México: UNESCO-Siglo XXI, 1971).

—. *El Ingenio: Complejo economico-social Cubano del azucar* 3 vols. (La Habana: Editorial de Ciencias Sociales, 1978).

——. "En torno a la identidad cultural en el Caribe insular", *Casa* 20.118 (1980): 42-47.

Moreno, José A. *Barrios in Arms: Revolution in Santo Domingo* (Pittsburgh: University of Pittsburgh Press, 1970).

Morgado, Marcia. "Literatura para curar el asma: Una entrevista con Mayra Santos Febres", *Barcelona Review* 17 (Marzo-abril 2000): www.barcelonareview.com.

Morgan, Mary. *A Gathering of Threads* (Mona, Kingston: author, 1991).

——. "The Sea and Home in the Work of Kamau Brathwaite", Paper presented at Conference North-South Counterpoint: Kamau Brathwaite and the Caribbean Word. Bronx, New York: Hostos Community College, City University of New York, 24 October 1992.

——. "Highway to Vision: This Sea our Nexus", *World Literature Today* 68.4 (1994): 663-68.

Morris, Mervyn. "To a West Indian Definer", *Caribbean Literature: An Anthology*. Ed. G. R. Coulthard (London: University of London Press, 1966), 86-87.

——. "The Dialect Poetry of Louise Bennett". In Baugh, 137-148.

——. "Niggers Everywhere", *New World Quarterly* 3.4 (1967): 61-65.

——. "This Broken Ground: Edward Brathwaite's Trilogy of Poems", *New World Quarterly* 5.3 (1970): 14-26.

——. "Introduction". *Selected Poems* by Louise Bennett (Kingston: Sangster Book Stores, 1982), iii-xix.

——. "The Poetry of Mikey Smith". In McWatt, 48-54.

Morris, William. *The Collected Works of William Morris*. Vol. 23. Ed. May Morris (London: Longman's Green, 1910-1915).

Mouralis, Bernard. "L'insularité: espace exotique ou théâtre de l'histoire?" *Littératures insulaires: Caraïbe et Mascareignes* (Paris: Editions L'Harmattan, 1983), 13-27.

Moya Pons, Frank. *Manual de historia dominicana*. 4ta. ed. (Santiago: Universidad Católica Madre y Maestra, 1978).

——. *The Dominican Republic: A National History* (New Rochelle: Hispaniola Books, 1995).

Muciño, Carlos. Rev. of *Cuando amaban las tierras comuneras,* by Pedro Mir, *Plural* 7.80 (1978): 64-5.

Mudimbe, Valentin Y. "Un goût de la parole: Le *Journal d'un animal marin* de Réne Depestre", *Présence Africaine* 79 (1971): 85-95.

Muricy, Andrade. "Atualidade de Cruz e Sousa", *Obra completa*, by Joâo da Cruz e Sousa (Rio de Janeiro: Editôra José Aguilar, 1961), 17-58.

Murphy, Rosalie. Ed. *Contemporary Poets of the English Language* (London: St. James Press, 1970).

Naipaul, V.S. *A House for Mr Biswas* (London. Deutch, 1957).

——. *The Middle Passage* (London: Deutch, 1962; New York: Vintage Books, 1981).

——. *The Loss of Eldorado* (London. Deutch, 1969).

Nantet, Jacques. *Panorama de la littérature noire d'expression française* (Paris: Libraire Arthème Fayard, 1972).

Narain, Jit. "Working all day, dreaming all night". In Brown and McWatt, 240.
Narain, Denise de Caires. *Contemporary Caribbean Women's Poetry: Making Style* (London and New York: Routledge, 2002).
Nasta, Susheila. "Samuel Selvon: *The Lonely Londoners*", *A Handbook for Teaching Caribbean Literature*. Ed. David Dabydeen (London: Heinemann, 1988), 25-34.
Neck-Yoder, Hilda Van, Ed. "Caribbean Literature from Suriname, the Netherlands Antilles, Aruba and the Netherlands", *Callaloo*, 21.3, (Summer 1998).
Nepaulsingh, Colbert I. Review of *Myth and History in Caribbean Fiction: Alejo Carpentier, Wilson Harris, and Edouard Glissant*, by Barbara J. Webb, *Caribbean Studies* 26.1-2 (1993): 196-206.
Neruda, Pablo. *Obras completas*. Vol. 5 (Buenos Aires: Artes Gráficas Bartolomé U. Chiesinos, S.A., 1973).
New, W.H. "New Language, New World", *Awakened Conscience: Studies in Commonwealth Literature*. Ed. C.D. Narasimhaiah (New Delhi: Sterling Publishers, 1978), 360-377.
Ngugi Wa Thiong'o. *Homecoming: Essays on African and Caribbean Literature* (New York: Lawrence Hill and Co., 1973).
——. *Decolonizing the Mind: The Politics of Language in African Literature* (London: James Currey, 1986).
Nichols, Grace. "Blackout". In Brown and McWatt, 258-259.
Ntonfo, André. *L'homme et l'identité dans le roman des Antilles et Guyane Françaises* (Québec: Editions Naaman, 1982).
Nuñez, Benjamin. *Dictionary of Afro-Latin American Civilization* (Westport, Conn.: Greenwood Press, 1980).
Nuñez-Harrell, Elizabeth. "Transcending Silence: The Limitations of the Theme of Betrayal in the Novels of George Lamming", *Community Review* 7.1 (1986): 24-33.
Obenga, Théophile. *Sur le chemin des hommes: Essai sur la poésie négro-africaine* (Paris: Présence Africaine, 1984).
O'Callaghan, Evelyn. "Selected Creole Sociolinguistic Patterns in the West Indian Novel". In Smilowitz and Quarles, 125-136.
Olivera, Otto. *Breve historia de la literatura antillana* (México: Ediciones Andrea, 1957).
Onis, Harriet de. "The Short Story in the Caribbean", *The Caribbean: Peoples, Problems, and Prospects*. Ed. A. Curtis Wilgus (Gainesville: University of Florida Press, 1952), 123-134.
Ormerod, Beverly. *An Introduction to the French Caribbean Novel* (London: Heinemann, 1985).
Ornes, Antonio Emilio. "Pedro Mir considera el arte es angustia expresada", *El Caribe*, 9 octubre 1971: 16A.
Ortega, Julio, Ed. *Antología de la poesía hispanoamericana actual* (México: Siglo XXI Editores, 1987).
Otheguey, Ricardo. "The Spanish Caribbean: A Creole Perspective", *New Ways of Analyzing Variation in English*. Ed. C.J. Bailey and R. Shuy (Washington, D.C.: Georgetown University Press, 1973), 323-339.

Owusu-Sarpong, Albert. *Le temps historique dans l'oeuvre théâtrale d'Aimé Césaire* (Québec: Editions Naaman, 1986).

The Oxford Annotated Bible. Ed. Herbert G. May and Bruce M. Metzger (New York: Oxford University Press, 1962).

Palés Matos, Luis. *Poesía completa y prosa selecta*. Ed. Margot Arce de Vázquez (Caracas: Biblioteca Ayacucho, 1978).

——. *Obras 1914-1959: Tomo I Poesía*. Ed. Margot Arce de Vázquez (Río Piedras: Editorial de la Universidad de Puerto Rico, 1984).

Paolucci, Anne. "Beyond 'Comparative Literature': Multinational Literary Perspectives", *Problems in National Literary Identity and the Writer as Social Critic*. Ed. Anne Paolucci (Whitestone, New York: Griffon House Publications, 1980), 17-28.

Paquet, Sandra Pouchet. "Foreword" to *The Zea Mexican Diary: 7 Sept 1926 - 7 Sept 1986*, by Kamau Brathwaite (Madison: University of Wisconsin Press, 1993), v-xi.

Paravisini-Gebert, L. (with Carmen C. Esteves), Eds. *Green Cane and Juicy Flotsam: Short Stories by Caribbean Women* (Rutgers University Press, 1991).

——, and Olga Torres Seda. *Caribbean Women Novelists: An Annotated Critical Bibliography* (Westport, Conn.: Greenwood Press, 1993).

——. "Salomé Ureña de Henríquez", *Spanish-American Women Writers: A Bio-Bibliographical Source Book*. Ed. Diane E. Marting (Westport, Conn.: Greenwood Press, 1990), 522-31.

——. "Marie Vieux Chauvet: An Introduction", *The Women of Hispaniola: Moving Toward Tomorrow*. Ed. Daisy Cocco de Filippis (New York: York College, CUNY, 1993), 74-79.

Parker, Michael. "His Island's Voice: Kamau Brathwaite's *Middle Passages*", *Times Literary Supplement*, 27 November, 1992, 27.

Patterson, Orlando. *Children of Siyphus* (London: Hutchinson New Authors, 1964). Reissued by Peepal Tree Press, Caribbean Modern Classics, 2012.

——. *An Absence of Ruins* (London: Hutchinson, 1967). Reissued by Peepal Tree Press, Caribbean Modern Classics, 2012

——. "Migration in Caribbean Societies: Socioeconomic and Symbolic Resource", *Human Migration: Patterns and Policies*. Ed. William H.. McNeill and Ruth S. Adams (Bloomington, Indiana: Indiana University Press, 1978), 106-145.

Pedrosa Izarra, Ciriaco. *Religión y religiones* (Madrid: Ediciones Fax, 1973).

Peix, Pedro, Ed. *La narrativa yugulada* (Santo Domingo: Editorial Alfa y Omega, 1981).

Pereira, Teresinka. *Literatura antillana* (San José, Costa Rica: Editorial Universitaria Centroamericana, 1985).

Pérez-Firmat, Gustavo. *Do the Americas Have a Common Literature?* (Durham: Duke University Press, 1990).

Pérez-Montaner, Jaime. "Walt Whitman en mangas de camisa", *Chasqui* 3.3 (1974): 49-55.

Perkins, Dexter. *A History of the Monroe Doctrine*. Revised Edition (Boston: Little, Brown and Co., 1955).

Petrarca, Francesco. *L'Africa*. Ed. Nicola Festa (Firenze: G.C. Sansoni Editore, 1926).

——. *Petrach's Africa*. Trans. and annotated Thomas G. Bergen and Alice S. Wilson (New Haven: Yale University Press, 1977).

Phaf, Ineke. "Identidad afrocaribeña versus consciencia nacional en la poesía del Caribe español", *Homines* 8.2 (1984-85): 295-302.

——. "A la búsqueda de una metrópolis nacional del Caribe". Unpublished essay, 1986.

——. "Caribbean Imagination and Nation-Building in Antillean and Surinamese Literature", *Callaloo* 11.1 (1988): 148-171.

——. "Women Writers in the Dutch-Speaking Caribbean: *Life Long Poem* in the Tradition of the Surinamese *Granmourgu* (New Dawn)". In Cudjoe 1990, 357-64.

Pierre-Charles, Gérard. "Towards a Definition of Social Thought in the Caribbean", *Cultural Identity in Latin America*. Ed. UNESCO (Paris: UNESCO, 1986), 149-156.

Pike, E. Royston, Ed. *Encyclopedia of Religion and Religions* (London: George Allen and Unwin Ltd., 1951).

Piña Contreras, Guillermo. "Entrevista a Pedro Mir", *Eme Eme: Estudios Dominicanos* 8.47 (1980): 41-59.

Pizarro, Ana, Ed. *Hacia una historia de la literatura hispanoamericana* (México: El Colegio de México, 1987).

——. "Reflections on the Historiography of Caribbean Literature", *Callaloo* 11.1 (1988): 173-185.

"Platt Amendment". *Encyclopedia Britannica*. 15th ed. Micropaedia. 1979.

Pollard, Velma. "'The Dust' – A Tribute to the Folk", *Caribbean Quarterly* 2.1-2 (1980): 41-48.

Portuondo, José Antonio. "Caribbean Literary Themes in the Last Fifty Years". In Wilgus, 256-269.

Powell, Patricia. *Pagoda* (New York, Alfred Knopf, 1998).

Preminger, Alex, Frank J. Warnke, and O. B. Hardison, Jr., Eds. *Princeton Encyclopedia of Poetry and Poetics*. Enlarged Edition (Princeton: Princeton University Press, 1974).

——. and T. V. F. Brogan, Eds. *The New Princeton Encyclopedia of Poetry and Poetics* (Princeton: Princeton University Press, 1993).

Prestol Castillo, Freddy. *El Masacre se pasa a pie* (Santo Domingo: Editora Taller, 1973).

Price-Mars, Jean. *Ainsi parla l'oncle*. Nouvelle Edition. (Ottawa: Leméac, Collection Caraïbes, 1973).

Prudent, Lambert-Félix. "Les problèmes d'émergence d'une littérature créole antillaise", *Littératures insulaires* (Paris: Editions L'Harmattan, 1983), 29-54.

Puri, Shalini. *The Caribbean Post Colonial: Social Equality, Post-Nationalism and Cultural Hybridity* (New York: Palgrave MacMillan, 2004).

Qasha, George and Jerome Rothenberg, Eds. *America: A Prophesy* (New York: Random House, 1973).

Quiroga, Horacio. *Cuentos*. Ed. Edmundo Lazo (México: Editorial Porrúa, 1978).

Racine, Daniel. “La poésie des Antilles françaises face au problème de l’identité”, *Présence Francophone* 9 (1974): 72-75.
——. “French West Indian Poetry from 1900 to 1970”, *Black Images* 2.3-4 (1973): 37-38.
Raful, Tony. *Movimiento 14 de Junio: Historia y documentos* (Santo Domingo: Editora Alfa y Omega, 1983).
Rama, Carlos M., Ed. *Las Antillas para los antillanos* (San Juan: Instituto de Cultura Puertorriqueña, 1975).
Ramchand, Kenneth, Ed. *West Indian Narrative: An Introductory Anthology* (London: Thomas Nelson and Sons, 1966).
——. *The West Indian Novel and its Background* (London: Faber and Faber, 1970).
——. “The Negro and the English Language in the West Indies”, *Savacou* 1 (1970): 33-44.
——. “Concern for Criticism”, *Caribbean Quarterly* 16.2 (1970): 51-60.
——. “History and the Novel: A Literary Critic’s Approach”, *Savacou* 5 (1971): 103-113.
——. “The West Indies”, *Literatures of the World in English*. Ed. Bruce King (London: Routledge and Kegan Paul, 1974), 193-211.
——. *An Introduction to the Study of West Indian Literature* (Sunbury on-Thames: Nelson Caribbean, 1976).
——. “West Indian Literary History: Literariness, Orality, and Periodization”, *Callaloo* 11.1 (1988): 95-110.
Ramcharitar-Lalla, C.E.J. *Anthology of Local Indian Verse* (Georgetown, 1934).
Ramirez, Socorro, and Luis Alberto Restrepo. “Por que leer estas entrevistas”, *Cuadernos del Caribe: Textos y testimonios del archipielago*. No. 4. Ed. Socorro Ramirez and Luis Alberto Restrepo (San Andres: Universidad Nacional de Colombia, 2002), 13-15.
Ramraj, Victor J. “Trapdoors into a Bottomless Past”. In Bahadur Singh 85-102.
Rao, Raja. *Kanthapura* [1938] (New York: New Directions, 1976).
Ratter, Beate M. W. *Redes Caribes San Andres y Providencia y las Islas Cayman: Entre la integracion economica mundial y la autonomia cultural regional*. Trans. Jaime Polania (San Andres: Universidad Nacional de Colombia, 2001).
Real Academia Española. *Diccionario de la lengua española*. 20th ed. 2 vols. (Madrid: Real Academia Española, 1984).
Redaccion. “Batida contra los sitios gays: Cierran discoteca Arena, bar Punto y Colmadon Omar en la Zona Colonial”, *Clave Digital* 19 June 2006. *www.clavedigital.com/Portada/*
Reed, John and Clive Wake, Eds. and trans. *French African Verse* (London: Heinemann, 1972).
Register, Cheri. “American Feminist Literary Criticism: A Bibliographical Introduction”, *Feminist Literary Criticism*. Ed. Josephine Donovan (Lexington: University Press of Kentucky, 1975), 1-28.
Reid, V.S. *New Day* (New York: Knopf, 1949). Reprinted Leeds: Peepal Tree Press, 2013.
Rippy, J. Fred. *The Caribbean Danger Zone* (New York: Putnam, 1940).
Risden, Winnefred. Rev. of *Masks* by E.K.Brathwaite, *Caribbean Quarterly* 14.1-2 (1968): 145-147.

Rivera de Alvarez, Josefina. *Diccionario de literatura puertorriqueña*. 2nd ed. 2 vols. (San Juan: Instituto de Cultura Puertorriqueña, 1974).

——. *Literatura puertorriqueña: su proceso en el tiempo* (Madrid: Ediciones Panteón, 1983).

Roberts, Peter. *West Indians and their Language* (Cambridge: Cambridge University Press, 1988).

Roberts, Walter Adolphe. *The Caribbean: The Story of our Sea of Destiny* (New York: Bobbs Merrill, 1940).

Rodó, José Enrique. *Ariel* (Montevideo: Domaleche y Reyes, 1900).

Rodríquez, Emilio Jorge. "An Overview of Caribbean Literary Magazine: Its Liberating Function", *Bim* 17.66-67 (1983): 121-128.

——. *Literatura Caribeña; bojeo y cuaderno de bitácora* (Cuba: Letras Cubana, 1989).

Rodríquez, Ileana. "En busca de una expresión antillana: lo real maravilloso en Carpentier y Alexis", *Ideologies and Literature* 2.10 (1979): 56-68.

——. "La literatura del Caribe: una perspectiva unitaria", *Ideologies and Literature* 3.12 (1980): 3-15.

——. *House/Garden/Nation. Space, Gender, and Ethnicity in Post-Colonial Latin American Literature by Women* (Durham: Duke University Press, 1994).

Rodríquez, Ileana and Marc Zimmerman, Eds. *Process of Unity in Caribbean Society: Ideologies and Literature* (Mineapolis: Institute for the Study of Ideologies and Literature, 1983).

Rodríguez Demorizi, Emilio. *Santana y los poetas de su tiempo* (Santo Domingo: Editora del Caribe, 1969).

——. *Poesía popular dominicana*. 3ra. ed. (Santiago: Universidad Católica Madre y Maestra, 1938. 1979).

Rodríguez Iturbide, José. *El Caribe: Elementos para una reflexión política* (Caracas: Ediciones Centauro, 1987).

Rodríguez-Luis, Julio. "Literary Production in the Hispanic Caribbean", *Callaloo* 11.1 (1988): 132-146.

Rogler, L. and A. Hollingshead. "The Puerto Rican Spiritualist as Psychiatrist", *American Journal of Sociology* 67 (1961): 17-21.

Rohlehr, Gordon. "Samuel Selvon and the Language of the People". In Baugh, 153-161.

——. "Sparrow and the Language of Calypso", *Savacou* 2 (1970): 87-99.

——. "Islands", *Caribbean Studies* 10.4 (1971): 173-202.

——. "Blues and Rebellion: Edward Brathwaite's *Rights of Passage*." [Rohlehr 1978]. In Baugh, 63-74.

——. [1980a] "Bridges of Sound", *Caribbean Quarterly* 26.1-2 (1980): 13-31.

——. [1980b] "Background Music to *Rights of Passage*", *Caribbean Quarterly* 26.1-2 (1980): 32-40.

——. *Pathfinder: Black Awakening in 'The Arrivants' of Edward Kamau Brathwaite* (Tunapuna, Trinidad: G. Rohlehr, 1981).

——. "A Scuffling of Islands: The Dream and Reality of Caribbean Unity in Poetry and Song". In Meeks and Lindahl, 265-305.

——. "Brathwaite with a dash of Brown: Crit, the Writer and the Written Life". Mimeographed pamphlet (St. Augustine, Trinidad: University of the West Indies, 1988). Included in the author's collection *The Shape of That Hurt and Other Essays* (Trinidad: Longman Trinidad, 1992), 209-247.

——. *Voiceprint* Ed. (with Brown, Stewart and Morris, Mervyn) (London: Longman, 1989).

——. "The Rehumanization of History: Regeneration of Spirit; Apocalypse and Revolution in Brathwaite's *The Arrivants* and *X/Self*", Mimeographed pamphlet. (St. Augustine, Trinidad: University of the West Indies, 1989).

——. "Dream Journeys", Introduction to *Dreamstories* by Kamau Brathwaite (London: Longman, 1994), iii-xvi.

Rombaut, Marc. *La poésie négroafricaine d'expression française* (Paris: Editions Seghers, 1976).

Rosario Candelier, Bruno. *Lo popular y lo culto en la poesía dominicana* (Santiago: Universidad Católica Madre y Maestra, 1977).

——. "*Hay un país en el mundo* (Evocación de Pedro Mir)", *Eme Eme: Estudios Dominicanos* 8.47 (1980): 37-40.

——. *Ensayos críticos: Análisis de textos dominicanos contemporáneos* (Santiago: Universidad Católica Madre y Maestra, 1982).

——. *Tendencias de la novela dominicana* (Santiago: Universidad Católica Madre y Maestra, 1988).

Rosenberg, June. *El Gagá: religión y sociedad de un culto dominicano* (Santo Domingo: Editora de la UASD, 1979).

Ross, Alan. "Poetry", *The London Magazine* (March 1967): 96-97.

Rothenberg, Jerome, Ed. *Technicians of the Sacred*. 2nd. ed. (Berkeley: University of California Press, 1985).

——. and Diane Rothenberg, Eds. *Symposium of the Whole: A Range of Discourse Toward an Ethnopoetics* (Berkeley: University of California Press, 1983).

Royes, Heather. "I No Longer Read Poetry". In Brown and McWatt, 197.

Rueda, Manuel and Lupo Hernández Rueda, Eds. *Antología panorámica de la poesía dominicana contemporánea* (Santiago: Universidad Católica Madre y Maestra, 1972).

Ruiz del Viso, Hortensia. *Black Poetry of the Americas* (Miami: Ediciones Universal, 1972).

Saakana, Amon Saba. *The Colonial Legacy in Caribbean Literature* (London: Karnak House, 1987).

Said, Edward W. *Orientalism* (New York: Vintage Books, 1979).

Sainville, Leonard, Ed. *Romanciers et conteurs négro-africains: Anthologie*. 2 vols. (Paris: Présence Africaine, 1963-1968).

Salkey, Andrew, Ed. *Island Voices* [1965] (New York: Liveright, 1970).

——. *Breaklight: The Poetry of the Caribbean* [1971] (New York: Anchor Books, 1973).

Sánchez, Luis Rafael. *La guaracha del Macho Camacho* (Madrid: Ediciones Catedra S.A. 1976).

——. "Voyage to Caribbean Identity". Review: *Latin American Literature and Arts* 47 (1993): 20-22.

Sanderlin, George. Ed. and trans. *Bartolomé de Las Casas: A Selection of his Writings* (New York: Alfred A. Knopf, 1971).

Sandner, Gerhard. *Centroamerica y el Caribe occidental: coyunturas, crisis y conflictos 1503-1984*. Trans. Jaime Polania (San Andres: Universidad Nacional de Colombia, 2003).

Santana, Joaquín G. "Pedro Mir: (Mi poesía es hija del exilio!" *OCLAE: Organización Continental Latinoamericana de Estudiantes* 4 (1978): 12-14.

Santos Moray, Mercédez. "Mir en primera plana", *Casa de las Américas* 13.76 (1973): 139-144.

——. "Tres poetas de una isla", *Casa de las Américas* 15.90 (1975): 138-141.

——. *Meridiano 70: Poesía social dominicana siglo XX* (La Habana: Casa de las Américas, 1978).

Sanz, Julio. Rev. of *Cuando amaban las tierras comuneras*, by Pedro Mir. *AHORA*! 18.852 (1980): 52.

Saraiva, Arnaldo. *Literatura marginal izada: novos ensaios* (Porto: Ediçôes Arvore, 1980).

Sarduy, Severo. *Gestos* (Barcelona: Editorial Seix Barral, 1963).

Sarma, Gobinda Prasad. *Nationalism in Indo-Anglian Fiction* (New Delhi: Sterling Publishers, 1978).

Saunders, Catherine E. *Writing the Margin: Edith Wharton and Ellen Glasgow, and the Literary Tradition of the Ruined Woman* (Cambridge, Mass.: Harvard University Press, 1987).

Savory [Fido], Elaine. "Spectrum and Prism", *Bim* 18.69 (1985): 73-78.

——. "Returning to Sycorax/Prospero's Response: Edward Kamau Brathwaite's Word Journey". Mimeographed pamphlet, 1993. 1-37.

Scarboro, Anne Armstrong. "Womb of Shadow", *American Book Review* 9.6 (1988): 11.

——. "The Caribbean: Why Now?" *American Book Review* 9.6. (1988): 1-11.

Schmidt-Rodríguez, Aileen. "Tras el secreto de la creación literaria: Entrevista a Pedro Mir", *Areito* 10.38 (1983): 39-40.

Scott, David. *Refashioning Futures: Criticism after Postcoloniality* (Princeton: Princeton University Press, 1999).

Segal, Aaron. "The Caribbean Exodus in a Global Context: Comparative Migration Experiences", *The Caribbean Exodus*. Ed. B. Levine (New York: Praeger, 1987), 44-64.

Selden, Roman. *A Reader's Guide to Comtemporary Literary Theory* (Lexington: University Press of Kentucky, 1985).

Selvon, Samuel. "Three Into One Can't Go – East Indian, Trinidadian, West Indian". In Bahadur Singh, 31-44.

——. "Turning Christian", *Foreday Morning*. Ed. Kenneth Ramchand and Susheila Nasta (London: Longman, 1989), 202-10.

Sencíon, Viriato, *Los que falsificaron la firma de Dios* (Santo Domingo: Taller, 1992).

Senghor, Léopold Sédar, Ed. *Anthologie de la nouvelle poésie nègre et malgache* (Paris: Presses Universitaires de France, 1948).

Senior, Olive. *Arrival of the Snake-Woman and Other Stories* (Burnt Mill, Harlow, Essex: Longman, 1989).

——. *Encyclopedia of Jamaican Heritage* (St. Andrew, Jamaica: Twin Guinep Publishers, 2003).

Seymour, A.J., Ed. *New Writing in the Caribbean* (Guyana: Guyana Lithographic Co., 1972).

Shapiro, Norman, Ed. and trans. *Négritude: Black Poetry from Africa and the Caribbean* (New York: October House, 1970).

Shelton, Marie-Denise. "Women Writers of the French-Speaking Caribbean: An Overview". In Cudjoe, 1990: 346-56.

Showalter, Elaine. Ed. *The New Feminist Criticism* (New York: Pantheon Books, 1985).

Silenieks, Juris. "The Maroon Figure in Caribbean Francophone Prose". In Luis, *Voices from Under: Black Narrative in Latin America and the Caribbean*, 115-125.

Silkin, Jon. "Polarities", *Poetry* 130.4 (1977): 230-239.

Simms, Norman. *Silence and Invisibility: A Study of the Literature of the Pacific, Australia, and New Zealand* (Washington: Three Continents Press, 1986).

Simpson, George E. *Religious Cults of the Caribbean* (San Juan: Ediciones Juan Ponce de León, 1970).

Simpson, Louis. *Collected Poems* (New York: Paragon House, 1988).

Singer, Milton. "The Concept of Culture", *International Encyclopedia of the Social Sciences*. Ed. David L. Sills. Vol. 3. (New York: The McMillan Company/ The Free Press, 1968), 527-543.

Skinner, Quentin, Ed. *The Return of Grand Theory in the Human Sciences* (Cambridge: Cambridge University Press, 1985).

Slochower, Harry. "The Use of Myth in Kafka and Mann", *Spiritual Problems in Contemporary Literature*. Ed. Stanley Romaine Hopper (New York: Harper and Brothers, 1952), 117-126.

——. *Mythopoesis: Mythic Patterns in Literary Classics* (Detroit: Wayne State University Press, 1970).

Smart, Ian. "Nicolas Guillen's *Son* Poem: An African Contribution to Contemporary Caribbean Poetics", *CLA Journal* (June 1980), 358. 39.

——. "Discovering the Caribbean: Two Important Research Tools", *Caribbean Review* 10.3 (1981): 32-34.

——. *Central American Writers of West Indian Origin: A New Hispanic Literature* (Washington: Three Continents Press, 1984).

Smilowitz, Erika Sollish and Roberta Quarles, Eds. *Critical Issues in West Indian Literature* (Parkersburg, IA: Caribbean Books, 1984).

Smith, Zadie. 2000. *White Teeth* (London: Penguin Books, 2001).

Smith, Zadie. "An Interview". www.pbs.org/wgbh/masterpiece/teeth/ei_smith_int.html. Accessed 7 June 2006.

Solé, Carlos A. and María Ysabel Abreu, Eds. *Latin American Writers*. 3 vols. (New York: Charles Scribner's Sons, 1989).

Solomon, Maynard. "Walter Benjamin" [1973], *Marxism and Art*. Ed. Maynard Solomon (Detroit: Wayne State University Press, 1979), 541-547.

Sommer, Doris. "History and Romanticism in Mir's *Cuando amaban las tierras comuneras*", *Revista de Estudios Hispánicos* 6 (1979): 219-248.

——. "Good-Bye to Revolution and the Rest: Aspects of Dominican Narrative Since 1965", *Latin American Literary Review* 8.16 (1980): 223-28.

——. *One Master for Another: Populism as Patriarchal Rhetoric in Dominican Novels* (Lanham: University Press of America, 1983).

The Song of Roland. Trans. Dorothy L. Sayers (Harmondsworth: Penguin Books, 1937).

Souffrant, Claude. *Une négritude socialiste* (Paris: Librairie-Editions L'Harmattan, 1978).

Sourieau, Marie-Agnes, and Kathleen M. Balutansky, Eds. *Ecrire en pays assiege: Haiti/Writing Under Siege* (Amsterdam and New York: Editions Rodopi, 2004).

St-Victor, Roger. "La crise du français en Haïti", *Optique* 22 (1955): 71-73.

Steele, Fernanda. "Mito o no? – Myth or no Myth? ('Bad Johns' and 'Gavilleros' in Earl Lovelace's *The Dragon Can't Dance* and Pedro Mir's *Cuando amaban las tierras comuneras)*", *Myth and Superstition in Spanish Caribbean Literature*. Fifth Conference of Hispanists. Mona: University of the West Indies, 1982. 179-201.

Steward, Julian H., et al. *The People of Puerto Rico: A Study in Social Anthropology* (Urbana: University of Illinois Press, 1956).

Storni, Alfonsina. *Poesías*. 4ta. ed. (México: Editores Mexicanos Unidos, 1987).

Stow, Harriet Beecher. *Uncle Tom's Cabin* (Boston: John P. Jewitt, 1852).

Swarz-Bart, Andre and Simone. *Plat de porc aux bananes vertes* (Paris: Seuil, 1967).

Symons, Julian. Review of Edward Brathwaite's *Rights of Passage*. *Times Literary Supplement*, 16 February 1967, 125.

Tanna, Laura. "One-on-One with Olive Senior", Interview. (Part 3). *The Gleaner*, 7 November 2004.

Tasso, Torquato. *Gerusalemme Liberata*. Ed. Lanfranco Caretti (Milano: Arnaldo Mandadori Editore, 1983).

——. *Jerusalem Delivered*. Trans. and ed. Ralph Nash (Detroit: Wayne State University Press, 1987).

Taylor, Douglas. "New Languages for Old in the West Indies". In Horowitz, 77-91.

Taylor, Patrick. *The Narrative of Liberation: Perspectives on Afro-Caribbean Literature, Popular Culture, and Politics* (Ithaca: Cornell University Press, 1989).

Théobalds, Tom. "La littérature engagée et l'écrivain antillais", *Présence Africaine* 27/28 (1959): 27-36.

Thomas, David Y. *One Hundred Years of the Monroe Doctrine* (New York: The Macmillan Company, 1923).

Tirolien, Guy. *Balles d'or* (Paris: Presence Africaine, 1961).

Tisdel Jaen, Didier, Ed. and trans. *Homage to Walt Whitman: A Collection of Poems from the Spanish* (Alabama: University of Alabama Press, 1969).

Toczek, Nick, Philip Nanton, and Yan Lovelock, Eds. *Melanthika: An Anthology of Pan-Caribbean Writing* (West Yorkshire: L.W.M. Publications, 1977).

Todorov, Tzvetan. *La conquête de l'Amérique: la question de l'autre* (Paris: Editions du Seuil, 1982).

——. *The Conquest of America: The Question of the Other*. Trans. Richard Howard (New York: Harper and Row, 1984).

Torres-Ríoseco, Arturo. *The Epic of Latin American Literature* (New York: Oxford University Press, 1942).

Torres-Saillant, Silvio. "La cuentísta boschiana: Nexo dominicano con la poética caribeña", *Aproximaciones a la narrativa de Juan Bosch*. Ed. Franklin Gutiérrez (New York: Ediciones Alcance, 1989), 81-107.

——. "Caribbean Literature and Latin Americanists", *Caribbean Studies* 23.3-4 (1990): 131-138.

——. "A Poet of His People, A Poet of the World", Introduction to *Countersong to Walt Whitman and Other Poems* by Pedro Mir. Trans. Jonathan Cohen and Donald D. Walsh (Washington, D.C.: Azul editions, 1993), vii-xii.

——. "Dominican Literature and Its Criticism: Anatomy of a Troubled Identity". In Arnold 1994, 49-64.

——. "The Trials of Authenticity in Kamau Brathwaite", *World Literature Today* 68.4 (1994): 697-707.

——. "Marcio Veloz Maggiolo", *Dictionary of Literary Biography*. Vol 145. Modern Latin American Fiction Writers (Detroit: Bruccoli Clark Layman, 1994), 321-334.

——. *Caribbean Poetics: Toward an Aesthetic of West Indian Literature* (Cambridge: Cambridge University Press, 1997).

——. *An Intellectual History of the Caribbean* (Basingstoke and New York: Palgrave Macmillan, 2006).

Torres-Saillant, Silvio, Ramona Hernandez, and Blas R. Jimenez, Eds. *Desde la Orilla: hacia una nacionalidad sin desalojos* (Santo Domingo: Editora Manati and Ediciones Libreria La Trinitaria, 2004).

Toumson, Roger. *Le nègre inconsolé* (Paris, Editions Syros, 1993).

——. "Problematisation de la création culturelle aux Antilles: La question des langues", *Francophonie et Caraïbe/Francofonía y Caribe*. Ed. Jacques Leylavergne (Santo Domingo: Casa de Francia, 1993), 77-83.

Toynbee, Arnold. *The World and the West* (New York and London: Oxford University Press, 1953).

Trudgill, Peter. *Sociolinguistics: An Introduction* (Harmondsworth: Penguin Books, 1974).

Turco, Lewis. "Of Laureates and Lovers", *Saturday Review*, 14 October 1967.

Urbano Gilbert, Gregorio. *Mi lucha contra el invasor yanqui de 1916* (Santo Domingo: Editora de la UASD, 1975).

——. *Junto a Sandino* (Santo Domingo: Editora de la UASD, 1979).

Valbuena Briones, Angel. *Literatura hispanoamericana*. 2da. ed. (Barcelona: Editorial Gustavo Gili, 1965).

Van Sertima, Ivan. *Caribbean Writers: Critical Essays* (London & Port of Spain: New Beacon, 1968).

Vega, Ed. "The Dominican Republic's National Treasure", *New York Newsday* 12 March 1992. 106, 108.

Veloz Maggiolo, Marcio. *Cultura, teatro y relatos en Santo Domingo* (Santiago: Universidad Católica Madre y Maestra, 1972).

——. *La vida no tiene nombre* (Santo Domingo: Colección Testimonio, 1965).

——. *Los ángeles de hueso* (Santo Domingo: Editora Arte y Cine, 1967).

——. *De abril en adelante* (Santo Domingo: Editora Taller, 1975).

Verges, Pedro. *Sólo cenizas hallarás (Bolero)* (Valencia: Prometeo, 1980).

Viatte, Auguste. "La littérature des Antilles françaises", *Panorama das literaturas das Americas*. Ed. Joaquim de Montezuma Carvalho. Vol. 4. (Angola: Ediçâo do Municipio de Nova Lisboa, 1963), 1355-1369.

——. *Anthologie de l'Amérique francophone* (Québec: CELEF, 1971).

Vinson, James, Ed. *Contemporary Poets*. 3rd. ed. (New York: St. Martin's Press, 1980).

Village Voice Literary Supplement. "Review of Kamau Brathwaite's *Zea Mexican Diary*: *7 Sept 1926-7 Sept 1986*, *Village Voice*, 7 December 1993. 11.

Voorhoeve, Jan and Ursy M. Lichtveld, Eds. *Creole Drum: An Anthology of Creole Literature in Surinam* (New Haven: Yale University Press, 1975).

Walcott, Derek. *Henri Christophe* (Barbados: Advocate, 1950).

——. "Meanings", *Savacou* 2 (1970): 45-51.

——. "What the Twilight Says: An Overture", *Dream on Monkey Mountain and Other Plays* (New York: Farrar, Straus & Giroux, 1970), 1-40.

——. "The Muse of History". In Baugh, 38-43.

——. *Collected Poems: 1948-1984* (New York: Farrar, Straus & Giroux, 1986).

——. *The Antilles: Fragments of Epic Memory* (New York: Farrar, Straus and Giroux, 1993).

Walmsley, Anne. "The Dimensions of Song", *Bim* 13.51 (1970): 152-167.

Walsh, William. *Commonwealth Literature* (London: Oxford University Press, 1973).

Walsh, Donald, Trans. "Selected Poems from 'Concierto de esperanza para la mano izquierda' by Pedro Mir", *Latin American Literary Review* 6.12 (1978): 106-117.

Wambu, Onyekachi, Ed. *Empire Windrush: Fifty Years of Writing about Black Britain* (London: Phoenix, 1998).

Warner, Keith Q. "René Depestre the not so terrible 'enfant terrible'", *Black Images* 3.1 (1974): 46-54.

Warner-Lewis, Maureen. "Odomankoma Kyerema Se", *Caribbean Quarterly* 19.2 (1973): 51-99.

——. *Notes to 'Masks'* (Benin City: Ethiope Publishing Corporation, 1977).

——. "Trinidad Yoruba", *Caribbean Quarterly* 17.2 (1977): 40-49.

——. "The African Impact on Language and Literature in the English-Speaking Caribbean", *Africa and the Caribbean: The Legacies of a Link*. Ed. Margaret Crahan and Franklin W. Knight (Baltimore and London: Johns Hopkins University Press, 1979), 101-123.

——. "Image and Idiom in Nationalist Literature: Achebe, Ngãgi-, and Brathwaite", *Studies in Commonwealth Literature*. Ed. Eckhart Breitinger and Reinhard Sander (Bayreuth: Günter Narr Verlag Tubingen, 1985), 105-114.

Watson, Jack B. *The West Indian Heritage: A History of the West Indies* (London: John Murray, 1979).

Watts, David. *The West Indies: Patterns of Development, Culture and Environmental Change since 1492* (Cambridge: Cambridge University Press, 1990).

Webb, Barbara. *Myth and History in the Caribbean* (Amherst: University of Massachusetts Press, 1992).

Weber, Max. *The Protestant Ethic and the Spirit of Capitalism*. Trans. Talcott Parsons (New York: Charles Scribner's Sons, 1958).

Wellek, René and Austin Warren. *Theory of Literature*. 3rd. ed. (San Diego: Harcourt Brace Jovanovich, 1977).

West, Cornell. "Minority Discourse and the Pitfalls of Canon Formation", *The Yale Journal of Criticism* 1.1 (1987): 193-201.

Wheatley, Phillis. *The Collected Works of Phillis Wheatley*. Ed. John C. Shields (New York: Oxford University Press, 1988).

Wheelwright, Philip. "Religion and Poetry", *The Princeton Encyclopedia of Poetry and Poetics*. Enlarged Edition. Ed. Alex Preminger (Princeton: Princeton University Press, 1974), 688-690.

White, Hayden. *Metahistory: The Historical Imagination in Nineteenth-Century Europe* (Baltimore: The Johns Hopkins University Press, 1973).

——. "The Historical Text as Literary Artifact". In Canary and Kozicki 41-62.

Whitman, Walt. *Leaves of Grass* (Garden City: New York: International Collectors Library, n.d).

Wilgus, A. Curtis, Ed. *The Caribbean at Mid Century* (Gainesville: University of Florida Press, 1951).

Willeford, Mary Jo. "Negro New World Religions and Witchcraft", *Bim* 12.48 (1969): 216-222.

Williams, Aubrey. "The Artist in the Caribbean", *Savacou* 2 (1970): 16-32.

Williams, Denis. *Other Leopards* (London: New Authors Ltd., 1963); reissued Leeds: Peepal Tree Press in Caribbean Classics series, 2009.

——. *Image and Idea in the Arts of Guyana* (Georgetown: National History and Arts Council, Mittelholzer lecture series, 1970).

Williams, Eric. "Four Poets of the Greater Antilles", *Caribbean Quarterly* 2.4 (1952): 8-15.

——. *From Columbus to Castro: The History of the Caribbean 1492-1969* (New York: Harper & Row Publishers, 1970).

Williams, Stanley Thomas. *Richard Cumberland: His Life and Dramatic Works* (New Haven: Yale University Press, 1917).

Wilson, Edmund. Introduction. *All Men are Mad*, by Philippe Thoby-Marcelin and Pierre Marcelin (New York: Farrar, Straus & Giroux, 1970), vii-xii.

Wilson, Leslie. *Poesía afroantillana* (Miami: Ediciones Universal, 1979).

Wynter, Sylvia. "The Necessary Background". In Baugh 19-23.

——. "We Must Learn to Sit Together and Talk about a Little Culture: Reflections on West Indian Writing and Criticism, Part 1", *Jamaica Journal* 2 (Dec 1968), 23-32.

——. "We Must Learn to Sit Together and Talk about a Little Culture: Reflections on West Indian Writing and Criticism Part 2", *Jamaica Journal* 3 (March 1969), 27-42

——. "Novel and History, Plot and Plantation", *Savacou* 5 (1971): 95-102.

Yoder, Lauren W. "A Caribcentric View of the World: The Novels of Edouard Glissant", *Caribbean Review* 10.3 (1981): 24-27.

Yoyo, Emile. *Saint-John Perse et le conteur* (Paris: Bordas, Collection Etudes, 1971).

Zabus, Chantal. "A Calibanic Tempest in Anglophone and Francophone New World Writing", *Canadian Literature* 104 (1985): 35-50.

Zaglul, Antonio. *Despreciada en la vida y olvidada en la muerte biografia de Evangelina Rodriguez, la primera medica dominicana* (Santo Domingo: Taller, 1980).

Zavala, Silvio. "Bibliografía americanista de Rafael Altamira", *Boletín de la Academia Nacional de la Historia* 20/21 (1947-8): 233-274.

Zenón Cruz, Isabelo. *Narciso descubre su trasero: El negro en la cultura puertorriqueña*. 2 vols. 2da. ed. (Humacao, Puerto Rico: Editorial Fundi, 1975).

Zimmerman, Marc. "The Unity of the Caribbean and Its Literatures". In Rodríquez and Zimmerman, 28-56.

Zimra, Clarisse. "Retrieving the Prophetic Past", *American Book Review* 9.6. (1988): 7-11.

INDEX

ABOUT THE AUTHOR

Silvio Torres-Saillant is Professor of English and Director of the Humanities Council at Syracuse University, where he completed a two-year appointment as William P. Tolley Distinguished Teaching Professor in the Humanities and two terms as Director of the Latino-Latin American Studies Program. Until 2000 he was the founding director of the CUNY Dominican Studies Institute, a prestigious interdisciplinary research unit located in the campus of The City College of New York, CUNY, which has successfully promoted the burgeoning field of Dominican studies in the US academy. His publications include *An Intellectual History of the Caribbean* (Palgrave Macmillan 2006); *Caribbean Poetics: Toward an Aesthetic of West Indian Literature* (Cambridge University Press, 1997); as well as *El Tigueraje Intelectual* (2d ed. Mediabyte 2011); *An Introduction to Dominican Blackness* (CUNY Dominican Studies Institute, City College of New York, 1999; 2d. 2012); and *El Retorno de las Yolas: Ensayos Sobre Diaspora, Democracia y Dominicanidad* (Ediciones Libreria La Trinitaria, 1999). With sociologist Ramona Hernandez he co-authored *The Dominican-Americans* (Greenwood Press, 1998). He is the co-editor of *Recovering the US Hispanic Literary Heritage*, Vol. IV (Houston: Arte Publico Press, 2002); *The Challenges of Public Higher Education in the Hispanic Caribbean* (Markus Wiener Publishers, 2004); and *Desde La Orilla: Hacia Una Nacionalidad Sin Desalojos* (Ediciones Librería La Trinitaria and Editora Manati, 2004), among other volumes. He serves as Associate Editor of the journal *Latino Studies* since its inception and was one of the Senior Editors of *The Oxford Encyclopedia of Latinos and Latinas in the United States*. A frequent speaker at universities in the United States and abroad, Professor Torres-Saillant has served in doctoral seminars at Roskilde University in Copenhagen, University of Cartagena in Cartagena de Indias, and Universidad Javeriana in Bogota. He has held a Visiting Professor post at Amherst College in Massachusetts as was the 2005-2006 Wilbur Marvin Visiting Scholar in the David Rockefeller Center for Latin American Studies at Harvard University.

RECENT ACADEMIC TITLES

Jean Antoine-Dunne
Interlocking Basins of a Globe: Essays on Derek Walçott
ISBN: 9781845232207; pp. 224; pub. 2013; Price: £17.99

An essential addition to the understanding and appreciation of Walcott's work, these essays range from discussion of Walcott's earliest poetry in *Twenty-Five Poems* (1948) to his most recent collections that explore encroaching old age, *The Prodigal* (2004) and *White Egrets* (2010).

The contributors to this collection are predominantly, but not wholly, Caribbean-based, which ensures that, whilst his position as poet of the world is celebrated, the Caribbean, and more specifically St Lucia, is seen as the source to which Derek Walcott's writing constantly returns. Gordon Rohlehr offers a powerfully contextualised political and aesthetic reading of the whole range of Walcott's poetry; Harold McDermott surveys the "mulatto" aesthetics of Walcott's critical writing; Rachel Friedman, a Homer scholar, notes how Walcott's work in *Omeros and The Odyssey: A Stage Version* challenges a rereading of the original epics; Edward Baugh, perhaps the most distinguished of all Walcott critics, explores how Walcott's poetry crosses local and international spaces; Rhonda Cobham-Sander revisits the old story of the alleged competitive relationship between Walcott and Kamau Brathwaite and finds a flow of influence from the latter to the former; Louis Regis documents Walcott's writing on calypso as part of Walcott's ambivalent relationship to the popular; Jean Antoine-Dunne explores the visual/filmic imagination in Walcott's work; Edward Chamberlin, and Jennifer Toews write about the Walcott archive at the Thomas Fisher Rare Book Library, University of Toronto and make available eighteen reproductions of Derek Walcott's theatre sketches, most in full colour; Kenneth Ramchand looks closely at Walcott's approach to the Indo-Caribbean Ramlila in his Nobel speech, "The Antilles: Fragments of Epic Memory"; Antonia MacDonald, who grew up in St Lucia, confronts the problems of how to teach the real complexity of Walcott's work to young people in St Lucia; George B. Handley uses an ecocritical focus on Walcott's poems of nature to chart a persistent element of spirituality in his work; and finally, there is Patrick Anthony's essay on the ambivalent religious impulse in Walcott's later work and his focus on death and after death.